A NEW GUIDE TO ARTIFICIAL INTELLIGENCE

ABLEX SERIES IN COMPUTATIONAL SCIENCE

Derek Partridge, University of Exeter
Series Editor

A NEW GUIDE TO ARTIFICIAL INTELLIGENCE

Derek Partridge

University of Exeter

ABLEX PUBLISHING CORPORATION
NORWOOD, NEW JERSEY

Library of Congress Cataloging-in-Publication Data

Partridge, D. (Derek), 1945–
   A new guide to artificial intelligence / authored by Derek
Partridge.
      p.   cm. — (Ablex series in computational science)
   Includes bibliographical references.
   ISBN 0-89391-607-2. — ISBN 0-89391-608-0 (pbk.)
   1. Artificial intelligence. I. Title. II. Series.
Q335.P3545   1990
006.3—dc20   90-34179
                                      CIP

Ablex Publishing Corporation
355 Chestnut Street
Norwood, New Jersey 07648

To Azzie whose tireless work behind the scenes made this book possible.

Contents

List of Figures

Preface

"Not another AI book," you have every reason to utter wearily on hauling this tome into focus. A brief glance at the index will confirm that ELIZA, SHRDLU, MYCIN, TEIRESIAS, AM, etc. — all your old favorites — are here. But if I'm lucky, your tired eye will also notice that this book is saturated with discussions of "connectionist" theory and systems — the laval forms of a new species of AI, perhaps. All other AI texts take the Symbolic Search Space Paradigm as the single model for all AI — I question the desirability as well as the validity of this monolithic approach to the design and development of intelligent artifacts. In addition, oddities like AI methodology, competing AI paradigms, foundations of AI, and many other rarely discussed aspects of AI are referenced. Not only are they indexed, they are also discussed at length and with reference to the popular AI programs. That, in a few sentences (if not exactly a nutshell), is the basis for my claim that this is not just yet another AI book.

In this unslim volume I have endeavored to cover the large and growing field of AI in some detail (although gruesome details are clearly marked as such by parenthetical curly brackets and can be omitted by the busy reader who does not wish to be burdened by them but is nevertheless comforted by the knowledge that they are there). Thus this book is not one of the many so-called introductions to AI that skip across a few possibilities and leave it at that.

At the other end of the spectrum we have the genuine AI texts: Winston was the force to be reckoned with here (and Rich's text to a lesser extent), but Charniak and McDermott now looks like it might carry all before it (although Tanimoto's new text may snatch a significant share of the spoils). And these are detailed texts; in fact, it is their mass of detail which sets them apart from my offering. All the gruesome detail is there. They all revel in it. They focus on the successful programs and popular (although often unimplemented) mechanisms of the present. They exclude much of the global context and peripheral work (in, say, cognitive science); they are blinkered by R1, MYCIN, ATNs, and, at a more general level, by the predicate calculus, the Symbolic Search Space Paradigm, LISP, and PROLOG. Last year's birds may not be in this year's nests, but the same cannot be casually asserted about old AI programs (many are no more than abandoned Ph.D. thesis projects) and current expositions of the field. The moribund AI programs of yesteryear are all too frequently still used as the examples of AI today. And that is virtually all. The known inadequacies and the general problems are largely ignored or just mentioned in passing. AI is, or should be, much more than currently fashionable programs, tools, and paradigms. Especially in view of the fact that AI as a whole has not been a raging success (the expert systems subfield notwithstanding), an examination of its foundations and customary presuppositions is, one would think, quite well motivated. We do need these detailed compendiums of the current wisdom, and Charniak and McDermott, and Tanimoto, supply this need. But we also need something else. We need a broader perspective, especially in AI, a field that has always suffered from a myopic satisfaction and delight in the antics of a few performing programs. Elaine Rich's book is the only one that comes close.

There are books that examine and discuss global perspectives on AI — Boden's and Hofstadter's, for example. But these books make no attempt to cover the diversity of theories and programs that is AI. The book you are reading attempts to provide a global perspective but in conjunction with an exhaustive survey of the field. It attempts to cover all of the recognized AI work in sufficient detail to allow a critique from general concerns to be anchored whenever possible in the structure of specific AI programs. So I view this book as one that covers AI in some detail but needs to be supplemented by examinations of current projects published in the voluminous literature. It is in some sense a companion to the major AI texts, providing a broader perspective on the wealth of details that such texts contain. But it is perhaps better considered as a companion to the current AI literature, for it is only in conference proceedings and journals that something like the up-to-date details will be found, not in textbooks.

Taking vision work as an example: Tanimoto provides an exhaustive survey of AI vision work, but in 75 pages we get all of the details on the early processing operators but virtually nothing on perception as a process that intimately involves contextual information — a rich and varied fund of information whose application must be central to intelligent seeing. Horn expands the coverage of vision to 500 pages but with no significant change of emphasis (except more pure mathematics, in exchange for Tanimoto's LISP code). But there are virtually no implementations involving context, a crucial source of information for intelligent vision systems. Both Tanimoto and Horn practically ignore it (as do Charniak and McDermott) — despite the fact that Horn's book has a C3PO-ish robot playing the piano on the cover. Presumably it is thus controlled by an array of supercomputers (not shown) which are number crunching at full speed to generate the necessary image features and subsequent hand trajectories in good time for the next note. Alternatively, it might be playing a very slow tune. (I am assuming that it is not totally preprogrammed to play a certain piece of music when it and the piano are in exactly the correct relative positions, for that would be cheating, the sort of thing any elaborate toy can now do.) What it cannot be illustrating is a humanlike skill acquired and refined by constant practice, for Horn makes absolutely no mention of these developmental and cognitive aspects of vision and motor control. Industrial robots are often impressively lizard-swift, but only when they are working blindly in a very precisely configured environment.

If you want Ramer's recursive algorithm for approximating a polygon from a set of vertices, then look in Tanimoto's book; if it's the details of a relaxation algorithm for finding intrinsic images that you're after, then Charniak and McDermott's book has them; but if you want to know something about what will be necessary in an intelligent vision system — the problems of, and approaches to solutions for, applying and integrating top-down and bottom-up information — then you have almost no other choice within the set of broad AI texts but to look in this book.

To my way of thinking, the other panoramic AI texts focus too closely on particular programs and mechanisms that can be cheerfully viewed as the first steps towards truly intelligent systems. They examine, explore, and exhibit the wealth of work wherein the ultimate goals of AI have not been (and cannot be) achieved. They dissect the body of work in great detail, which is necessary but not sufficient on its own to advance the frontiers of current AI towards something more like real AI. It's like attempting to understand the neuroanatomical basis for intelligence by microscopically examining a hand. Some neurons are clearly there in the hand and the head is too difficult to tackle, even though we are well aware that the brain will be found in the head. It's as though, if we look hard enough at some failed and demonstrably inadequate attempts to reproduce intelligent behavior and ignore the hints in the larger picture, then general answers will nevertheless be forthcoming eventually — I doubt it. We must explore the larger picture with all its flaws, holes, and general lack of specificity, as well as dissect the current projects and explore inadequate formalisms. I have attempted to pursue both of these goals within a broad-based view of AI. A treatise that purports to be about forestry cannot concentrate solely on the details of a few popular species of tree, for then you won't be able to see the forest for the wood, as it were.

I do labor the details when I'm dealing with work within the Connectionist Paradigm (CP), because they are not collectively available elsewhere. Thus the CP may be getting more exposure than it deserves. If the CP gets knocked on the head shortly by some latter-day duo like Minsky and Papert (or, if this pair bestir themselves again and can do a demolition job in the spirit of Perceptrons), then this book may well go down in history as different but largely misguided. It's a chance I'm prepared to take, but not much of a chance, I believe. To begin with, the CP is built on firmer foundations than the Perceptron work ever was — it may not be totally earthquake proof, but it will be able able to withstand most tremors, even those with an epicenter in the Boston area.

In the second place, I am by no means a wholehearted advocate of the CP. For my purposes the CP is not necessarily the way of truth, but it is a significant alternative to the traditional symbolic paradigm that has dominated (not to say stagnated) most AI work for many years. The importance of the CP derives from the healthy competition that it has engendered for the symbolic paradigm. It offers another viewpoint on many AI issues, and the new perspective serves to generate questions about the significance of "fundamental" AI problems as well as about the validity of basic assumptions. As Jordan Pollack has put it (taking the very words right out of my mouth):

"The road to AI is shrewn with potholes; connectionism may be a less-travelled route, but it is not any better maintained" (Pollack, 1987a, p. 108). But it does give us a new way to approach, and thus evaluate, fundamental problems and outcomes of current AI work.

Thus search strategies, which are a fundamental problem if all AI is viewed in terms of symbolic search spaces, become inconsequential if the generic representation is a subsymbolic network. Similarly, the important AI subfields of knowledge representation and of machine learning undergo a metamorphosis in the switch from the symbolic to the connectionist paradigm as the overarching conception of AI. Within the expert systems work, important little subproblems like conflict resolution just disappear in the CP, and so on.

As for the validity of basic assumptions: Knowledge bases (as I've said) become transmuted in form, and thus the basis of validity for logical inference as the mechanism to apply has vanished (the role of logical inference may be challengeable within the symbolic paradigm, but in the CP it has hardly a role to challenge). The list goes on and on (which is also one of my failings), but, in order to get off to good start, I'll resist my proclivity for prolixity and forgo the opportunity to precis the book in this preface.

It sometimes worries me that my view of AI could perhaps be described as jaundiced. But I don't lose too much sleep over it. For, if I have replaced the rose tint of the customary AI perspective with a definitely yellowish one, then it will serve, on the whole, to redress the balance. At times I display little more than a torpid enthusiasm for many much-vaunted AI techniques and demonstration programs. I prefer to harp on the problems. Again, I think that this attitude may add a measure of balance when set against the current climate of overexuberance which surrounds the term *AI*.

Finally, the style of this book may seem too frivolous for a serious textbook. I make no apologies for that. Nonsense has a useful role to play in explanations of the scientific. High seriousness is the last refuge of, not a scoundrel exactly, but certainly someone who should be treated with a modicum of suspicion at least. A dry, ossified exposition of matters scientific has an unhealthy tendency to encourage the further dissemination of the information as proven facts, and therefore not open to question. This transmutation of status is a threat to progress in any science; it is a particularly serious one in a field as young and rapidly developing as is AI. Information is made more memorable by humour and commentary bordering on the outrageous. I hope to provoke disagreement. Work in AI is only just beginning to uncover the serious problems, so disagreement and debate are both in order. It is not clear to me that a lighthearted approach to the so-called facts and accomplishments of AI is necessarily any more misinformative than dry, hard statements of the "truth." In fact my approach makes it quite clear that what I say is not meant to be interpreted as gospel truth. I make claims in a manner that invites you to disagree — feel free to do so. This is not a treatise brimming with alembicated ideas. It is more a collection of somewhat crudely articulated alternatives and options. The merit, I believe, resides in the completeness and cohesiveness of the selection presented rather than in the highly refined state of any one line of argument.

And let me remind you of the variant of Gödel's famous theorem which asserts that every survey of sufficient complexity is doomed to incompleteness, and is most likely inconsistent as well. This book will be no exception — you can't buck theorems.

Finally, a whole heap of acknowledgments are in order. The writing of this book was split across the Atlantic: half in Las Cruces, New Mexico, and half in Exeter, Devon. I thus thank the guys (of both sexes) in the Department of Computer Science and in the Computing Research Laboratory, both part of New Mexico State University, and my new colleagues in the Department of Computer Science at the University of Exeter. In particular, Dan Fass, Dave Farwell, Paul Jeremaes, Antony Galton, and Colin Beardon gave me detailed, written reports on many of my mistakes. I was also the lucky recipient of the artistic skills of Morgan, and Figure 7.8, in particular, is all the better as a result. Ellis Horwood deserve special mention for their permission granted to me for the reuse of chunks of my earlier book. But then I have to say that the remaining blunders are mine, just in case you think that any of the foregoing ought to be held responsible.

1

AI: What Is It?

"this painted veil which those who live [and know no better] call" AI
Janczyk & Karnicki (recon.) after Shelley

Artificial Intelligence (AI) is a terrible name for any subject to have to live with. The perjorative sense of 'artificial' almost ensures that success in AI will be viewed as the production of some inferior substitute for the real thing. John McCarthy is generally credited with the blame for the name. He, so the legend goes, casually used the term to label a meeting of persons interested in the possibilities for the use of computers beyond simply number crunching. That was in the mid-1950s, and the name has resisted all attempts to displace it despite widespread agreement that it is a poor one. *Machine Intelligence* and *Computational Intelligence* are just two of the labels that various pressure groups have championed to replace AI, but all such attempted coups have failed miserably. AI is a name whose stability and resistence to change is the envy of all South American dictators, I would think.

DEFINITIONS: WHAT WOULD IT LOOK LIKE IF I SAW ONE?

So the introduction's over: now, what sorts of activities does this label actually cover? I should like at this point to trot out a definition that is neat, succinct, and, above all, definitional. With such a definition in hand, or at hand but in mind, you the reader would no longer be plagued with worries about AI or not AI when confronted with an intriguing demonstration or a new software product. But alas, although such definitions do indeed exist, they typically serve little useful purpose except to give the reader the comfortable feeling that now he or she knows what AI is; the resultant warm feeling may be very real, but it is, nevertheless, quite unwarranted. Defining AI is an exercise rather like nailing jello to a tree: with forethought, planning, and enough nails it ought to be doable, but it isn't.

Let me run by you a few of the popular definitions, or potted descriptions, for our further consideration.

1

(1) For Schank (1990, p. 13) AI is a distributed phenomenon: "potentially . . . the algorithmic study of processes in every field of enquiry"— a broad description but one that is narrowed by a list of 10 features which he considers to be characteristic of AI. The features are:

a. Representation — how do we represent what we know in a machine?
b. Decoding — translation from the real world into the representation selected;
c. Inference — the process of figuring out the significance and full meaning of a collection of knowledge represented explicitly, or sensed directly;
d. Control of Combinatorial Explosion — finding ways to limit the potentially limitless inference process;
e. Indexing — organization and labeling of memory such that relevant items can be located quickly;
f. Prediction and Recovery — ability to predict from current knowledge and recover from inevitable mistakes;
g. Dynamic Modification — "the quintessential AI issue," learning: knowledge structures must change over time;
h. Generalization — the process of drawing conclusions from disparate data, the basis of creativity;
i. Curiosity — a process of probing beyond the known and understood, of constructing both questions and explanations;
j. Creativity — the process of generating new information, often viewed as generating useful relationships between known items that were previously thought to be unrelated.

Schank admits that AI is a shifting phenomenon: What was AI yesterday may not be AI today. The field of AI is prescientific. "We all agree that we would like to endow machines with an attribute that we can't define." Hence he presents the list of features, which I have given above, as one way to attack this definitional problem. None of the features defines intelligence, but each one is an integral part of intelligence in its way, so Schank claims.

(2) Mention of the shiftingness of AI raises the oft-tendered, supposedly absurd definition: AI is the field of ill-defined problems — whenever a reasonably concrete realization of some problem is developed, it ceases to be an AI problem.

The seeming fact that AI is not a well-anchored phenomenon whose limits are known and accepted is often used as a defense against the charge that some program, or well-defined mechanism, X, is not a component of AI. Typically, the X in question (it might be, for example, a specific knowledge-based expert system) is based on a problem area that was formerly considered to be part of AI, but, now that it's been 'solved' in some sense, the mystery is gone and we remove it from the field of AI. So, the defense of X goes, "Whenever we learn how to master some AI problem, you no longer call it AI. AI is thus a residual category: It is all the unprogrammed or unformalized problems. This is silly; therefore, program X is AI." In my view this argument is also silly, and false to boot. Many of these Xs are not AI. There are problems which initially appeared to be AI problems but turn out not to be. There are also AI problems whose more readily realizable simplifications (and program X usually addresses one of these) are not AI. But that doesn't mean that all programmed problems are not AI by definition. The preponderance of not-AI charges leveled against many of the programs produced so far can be explained by the youth of this field. No one, even in AI, which is not famed for the modesty of its practitioners, would claim that we have done more that scratch the surface of the problems. Superficial scratches, which leave the bulk of the problem untouched, often do not merit the label AI, but this does not mean that no programmed system will ever deserve this label.

Nevertheless, just what is necessary in a program before it is 'really' an AI system, I don't know — I'll leave it as a problem for the reader (hint: Schank's list of features may be a good starting point, and the seventh feature may be particularly useful). P.G. Wodehouse once observed that the difference between a Scotsman with a grievance and a ray of sunshine is not hard to spot; sadly, the difference between AI and non-AI systems is nothing like as easily discernible to the naked eye.

(3) The anonymous, but widely used, definition is: AI is the study of computers doing tasks that would be considered to require intelligence if a human did them. So AI tasks are playing chess, proving theorems, diagnosing diseases, and so on. But what about conversing in English, cleaning a house, and going shopping? These appear to be much harder computational problems, but they are not ones that we typically associate with human intelligence. And what about vast mental calculations? Complex mental arithmetic is certainly a scarce skill and one that is likely to be associated with human intelligence. Yet nothing could be easier computationally. Clearly, some of this mess can be tidied up by separating out the various meanings of that slippery word *intelligence*. But, having done that, I still would not expect this definition to come out sharp and shiny.

(4) A famous and much-debated "definition" of AI, a variant of the you'll-know-it-when-you-see-it type, is due to Turing (1950, and reprinted many times). His proposal for the decision, AI or not-AI, is commonly called the Imitation Game or the Turing Test. In a nutshell: If, in a totally unlimited conversational setting (unlimited conversation but no peeking

and no requirement of vocal communication), people are generally unable to distinguish between a person and a machine, then that machine embodies AI. This ancient attempt to tie down the meaning of AI has been subjected to endless criticism, but it still carries considerable weight in the AI milieu of today. Halpern (1987) is an example of a recent demolition job on Turing's argument; this paper also contains extensive references to the many previous attempts to undermine the validity of the Imitation Game. We can consider briefly just a couple of rather different lines of attack. Consider the Rock Game: When people put their toes through a hole in a screen, either someone stamps on them (the toes, that is) or else they drop a rock on them (still the toes). Now, if these brutalized people cannot generally distinguish between the impact of a rock and that of a person on their pedal appendages, then are we going to have to admit that the rock embodies intelligence? Halpern takes the stance that the Turing Test is riddled with flaws. Thus, Turing fails to consider any outcome other than the one that ends up crediting the machine with AI. Suppose the arbiters invariably claim that the hidden person is a machine; what would that imply? Is there any way for this test to fail? Supposing, as is perhaps very likely, the arbiters fail to consistently mistake the machine for a person, what do we conclude? Is the thesis that the machine is thinking if it is consistently misidentified disproved? Most likely we will be assured that there is another bug in the program which will be fixed, and then we'll see. The crucial underlying thesis, viz., that surprise occasioned by humanlike behavior on the part of a machine is *proof* that the machine is thinking, enjoys wide, although largely tacit, support in AI. This thesis is open to the possibility of corroboration, of course, but it does not enjoy similar access to possible refutation (this foundational issue of asymmetric hypotheses in AI is revived in Chapter 3, when we consider the major paradigm of AI; it also resurfaces for a more leisurely examination in the appropriate chapter, viz., Chapter 10).

(5) A somewhat anti-intellectualist definition is given by Minsky: Intelligence is a collection of kludges (i.e., tricks that are used simply because they work, and different tricks are needed for different occasions). The most recent exposition of this line of argument is in his book, *The Society of Mind* (Minsky, 1986). So AI becomes the process of identifying these tricks and how they fit together. A similar view is offered by Chandrasekaran (1990), whose views get a considerable airing below: Intelligence is not one thing, it is really a collection of strategies — generic functional strategies, to be more precise (see below for an explication of these ponderous objects). "The task of AI as the science of intelligence is to identify these strategies concretely, and understand how they integrate into coherent wholes."

(6) Modesty almost forbids me to tender a much-loved personal defini-

tion of AI, but the interests of science must win out over my personal diffidence, so here it is: AI is a collection of algorithms that are computationally tractable, adequate approximations of intractably specified problems. The business of AI is to find useful approximate implementations of the specifications of very hard problems (i.e., workable HOWs for impossible WHATs; read on to Chapter 2, and all will become transparent, I hope). On sober reflection, it looks a bit like Minsky's description, and in addition I've failed to limit the scope of the problems that constitute AI. Thus, 'constructing a robot that is invisible to everyone but me' would seem to be a very hard problem, but not an AI problem, more like one from the realm of magic. That's enough self-criticism; it may be healthy, but I find it irksome. I'll leave the framing of further destructive observations as an exercise for the reader.

The emphasis of this description is on AI as an enterprise for finding good-enough mechanisms for impossible problems. Is this the stuff upon which a science can be built? The computer science establishment thinks not, and this line of argument is the subject of the next chapter.

(7) One popular AI text (Rich, 1983) offers the following definition: "AI is the study of how to make computers do things at which, at the moment, people are better." Another moving definition, but not in any emotional sense, I think. It is also one that exhibits the customary nebulousness, both of which points Rich draws to our attention. She admits that it is ephemeral because of reference to current state of the art in computer science, but in actuality, she claims, it is surprisingly stable, and it avoids the philosophical issues that plague attempts to define the meaning of either *Artificial* or *Intelligence*. And she has a point there. But, of course, it also has its weaknesses. Thus, there are many things that humans do much better than computers, such as walking and swimming, but attempts to build machines with similar capabilities would only be peripheral AI work. Just in case you want to take issue with me here, let me clarify my position. Sure a swimming and walking robot would be a major AI breakthrough, I suspect (and DARPA would lap it up), but the central problems of swimming and walking are not similarly central AI problems. They are problems of balance, motor coordination, and timing; these are primarily engineering problems, although a satisfactory level of solution may draw heavily on AI, and it may not. A stronger, faster, tireless walking machine could well make little use of AI techniques, but a problem-solving walking machine is another story. A machine which is capable of displacing the office boy, i.e., a goferCoke, gofersandwich, etc. machine, will need all that AI currently aspires to deliver and much more, I suspect.

(8) Winograd (in Bobrow & Hayes, 1985, p. 380) draws our attention to a rift in AI. "There are two quite different starting points to define

AI — the dream and the technology. As a dream, there is a unified (if ill-defined) goal of duplicating human intelligence in its entirety. As a technology, there is a fairly coherent body of techniques (such as heuristic search and the use of propositional representations) that distinguish the field from others in computer science. In the end, this technological base will continue to be a unified area of study (like numerical analysis, or operations research) with its special methodology. We will recognize that it is not coextensive with the dream, but is only one (possibly small) piece."

Winograd wants to argue for two, rather different, sorts of AI, and this is not an uncommon viewpoint. As we shall see, the term AI does not really label a single unified field of endeavor. And furthermore, there are quite a number of different ways in which the basic divisions can be drawn. Winograd offers us one possibility one that is in accord with my labeling of certain types of AI work as "bad paradigms" in Chapter 3 — in my view, the technology (to use Winograd's term) is also the domain of bad paradigms precisely because of the misconception that this is the core area of AI, and yet, as Winograd says, it "is only one (possibly small) piece" of the AI dream.

Further ways in which it it is useful to carve up the domain of AI are presented later in this chapter. Incidently, the Bobrow and Hayes paper from which Winograd's comments were drawn is an interesting collection of off-the-cuff (and off-the-wall) general comments on AI from long-time practitioners in, or observers of, the field. This compendium of casual comments was solicited to celebrate the publication of the 25th volume of the *Artificial Intelligence Journal.*

So back to the problem of what is AI: AI is a farrago of subfields, philosophical and methodological principles, activities pertaining to computation with logics, etc. — a bubbling cauldron in which the strongest ingredients, the ones that dominate the overall flavor, vary from major conference to major conference. Connectionism, as you shall see, is one of the flavors of the moment.

What pornography and literary style have in common, if eminent members of the judiciary and of the literati are all to be believed, is that certain persons can recognize it when they see it, despite the absence of a definition. I should very much like to be able to throw AI into the same pot alongside literary style and pornography, but sadly I can't — AI is actually worse than pornography. For although AI is similarly undefinable in any useful sense, in addition, there are, unfortunately no seers who know it when they see it. In fact, the problem is even worse than this: An observer can easily be persuaded that he has seen it, when he has not (and that goes for shes too); hence, the lamentable "look ma, no hands" approach which has been the subject of unfavorable commentary in several reviews of the field (e.g., McCarthy, 1990).

Few demonstrations are more persuasive than those with computers communicating in a human tongue. The (subconscious) reasoning seems to be along the lines of: If it understands English, then it's probably intelligent, and if it solves problems as well, then it's certainly AI. The ELIZA program is the classic example here (Weizenbaum, 1965) — hence, the ELIZA syndrome: programs demonstrating snippets of conversational dialogue or of problem-solving ability provoke an almost irresistable urge to credit the performing system with AI. Weizenbaum, ELIZA's creator, was sufficiently disturbed by the overgenerous public reaction to ELIZA that he wrote a book in order to disseminate his views on the societal dangers of AI. The book, *Computer Power and Human Reason* (Weizenbaum, 1976), argues that certain AI projects should not be pursued because they are "obscene" (his term which drew no end of flack from his detractors) or because of the societal problems that they are likely to generate.

This is the place to break up the narrative with our first True AI Story, and this one (quite contrary to most that follow) is actually true — well, I didn't make it up.

TRUE AI STORY: 1.1

ELIZA meets PARRY: the syntax is willing but the semantics is weak

It has been recorded that once, as a fortuitous result of crossed telephone connections, a computer running the ELIZA program had a conversation with one running the PARRY program (a study of paranoia); according to Cerf (1973), the conversation went something like this:

ELIZA: Good evening. Tell me your problems.
PARRY: People get on my nerves sometimes.
E: I am not sure I understand you fully.
P: You should pay more attention.
E: Suppose you should pay more attention.
P: You're entitled to your own opinion.
E: What makes you think I am entitled to my own opinion?
P: It bothers me just to be around people in general.
E: Please go on.
P: I went to the track at Bay Meadows a while back.
E: What does that suggest to you?
P: I went to the races.
E: What else would you like to discuss?
P: Horseracing interests me.
E: Why do you say that just now?

P: There's a lot of crooked gambling going on there.
E: I am not sure I understand you fully.
P: It's clear to me if not to you.
E: Do you think it's likely that not to I?
P: I went to the races.
E: Please go on.
P: I gamble on horses.
E: What does that suggest to you?
P: I went to the races.

It's all steadily down hill from here; we'll go off before ELIZA says "Please go on" again and PARRY takes the opportunity to tell us where he went for his day out again, just in case we've forgotten. A memorable description of Ava Gardner fits ELIZA and PARRY perfectly to wit, that, deep down, they're superficial.

END OF TRUE AI STORY

The above story might indeed be true (it's certainly boring enough to be true; pure fiction would be much better), but nevertheless I felt that it was unlikely enough to include it in my interleaved anthology of TRUE AI STORIES.

The modern ELIZA is the NETtalk system (Sejnowski & Rosenberg, 1986; details in Chapter 9), a system that learns how to pronounce English. The tape recording of the random babbling changing to quite understandable English is now standard equipment for introduction-to-AI talks. As a grand finale to the argument that AI is alive and with us, it is unanswerable. It is also not AI. Well, it is no more than a minor step at the beginning of what is at best a long road to AI (and at worst it is a step into a short cul de sac with AI nowhere in sight). Certainly, when NETtalk is examined, we shall see that it is an interesting demonstration but no more than that.

A HISTORY OF SCALING DOWN

The solid and respectable (I think that *hard* is the popular adjective) sciences, like chemistry and physics, progress by means of a steady accumulation of abstract results founded on repeatable experiments, with each new insight building on earlier ones. The occasional scientific revolution may shake the simplicity of this progression, but the emergent paradigm typically unifies and explains more than the one(s) it replaces, so the accumulation-of-knowledge description still holds. Newton, with commendable modesty, summed it up when he talked of being able to see so far because he was standing on the shoulders of others.

Apart from the fact that AI persons are madly trampling all over each other much of the time (standing on heads as it were, rather than on shoulders), AI is not like physics, and many have offered reasons why. With computers, logic, and well-defined programming languages playing lead roles, we have good reason to expect that AI is, or should be, a hard science. In general, it is not. What it is and what it should be are hotly debated issues which we shall consider in Chapter 10.

AI is a young whatever-it-is discipline, let us say; it is a very young discipline when compared to chemistry or physics. This is despite the fact that, through the ages, various savants have left us bits and pieces of speculation on the possibilities for the mechanization of thought. Modern AI dates from about 1950, when Alan Turing published his musings on "can machines think?". By setting the clock for modern AI to start at 1950, I have probably condemned a few worthies to the dark ages before AI, but, provided the reader realizes that there is nothing hard and fast about my timeline, no real damage is done. The golden age of cybernetics, for example, is now pre-AI, but that strikes me as not inappropriate, although feedback loops are enjoying a new lease of life within the new connectionism (but this must wait for its proper time, which is Chapter 3). It is thus too early to expect to have any meaningful long-term perspective on AI. Currently, AI is perhaps prescientific, as we've seen Schank (1990) argue.

Nevertheless, trudging in where historians of science fear to tread, I shall offer the reader some generalizations on the history of AI. First, the history of AI presents a clear pattern of scaling down rather than the more customary up. Many early projects were aimed at creating something much closer to a full-blown AI system than anyone would contemplate today: There were plans and heavily funded projects for mobile, seeing, problem-solving robots (Stanford Research Institute's Shakey; see Raphael, 1976) and the University of Edinburgh's Freddy (see Michie, 1986) are two leading examples, although as a point of accuracy I might note that Freddy wasn't designed to move but part of his environment was); there were similarly well-financed and not very long-term projects to translate text in one language into text in another which were given a rousing send-off down the wrong road by Weaver's misconception, born from the overselling of Information Theory — "When I look at an article in Russian, I say, 'This is really written in English, but has been coded in some strange symbols. I will now proceed to decode.'" (You'll find the error that launched a thousand machine translation projects in Locke & Booth, 1955, which is also a useful source of the early machine translation work.) Dreyfus (1979) delights in the resurrection and ridicule of the classic, over-optimistic predictions of the founding fathers of AI. (The pessimistic, and possibly antagonistic, reader will find much to support his or her views in Drefus's early critique, but, before you get to carried away with his sweeping, dismissive arguments, I should like you to read Pylyshyn's 1975 critique of the Dreyfus book — it's a critique of the first edition, 1972, in case you're worrying about the chronology here. While we're here in this excursus, I'll take the further liberty of recommending the more modern, secret history of AI by McCorduck, 1979, wherein she records the results of personal interviews with the stars of AI — for, quite remarkably, they are nearly all still very much alive and programming. To an unbiased reader like myself, McCorduck seems overzealous in her attempts to exonerate some of the more reckless predictors from the follies of their younger days.) The problems proved to be far more difficult than was foreseen; the projects did not succeed, and the predictions failed to come true. Nevertheless, much useful knowledge was gained in the years of pursuit of these impossible (within the prevailing constraints) goals. But the general observation was that people in AI spent a lot of the early years just learning how incredibly difficult the problem and all of the component subproblems really are. Currently, more money, just as much time, and more-knowledgeable people are concentrating on relatively minor features of the original AI problems, and they're still not outrageously successful.

Following Chandrasekaran (1990) we can view the cybernetic years, roughly the decade pre-modern-AI, as focused on adaptation driven by feedback of information on system performance. Correct performance yielded positive feedback to reinforce the correct behavior (or do nothing as the behavior was correct anyway), and more importantly incorrect behavior gave rise to negative feedback, which was used to undermine the basis for the wrong results. As I said above, we shall see strong echoes of the work of the cyberneticians when we come to examine connectionism (Chapter 3). Similarly, we shall also become aware of a resurgence of hope in brain modeling as an approach to AI, another historical thread that grew to importance in the cybernetic years. It has never died (see Arbib, 1964, 1972) but it had some very lean years until connectionism hit the headlines (examples of significant early brain modeling work are McCulloch & Pitts, 1943; Rosenblatt's formal neurons, 1962; and Hebb's cell assemblies, 1949). Chandrasekaran characterizes this era in AI as the one of pre- and quasirepresentational theories, and he sees their demise, not as a result of Minsky and Papert's(1969) formal demonstration of the inadequacies of the formal-neuron networks (as I suggest in Chapter 3), but because "powerful representational and representation manipulation tools were missing."

Hence the rise of the era of symbolic representations in AI, an era that stretches to the current time and through into the forseeable future, unless subsymbolic connectionism (Chapter 3) outperforms all expectations. I apologize for continually advertising Chapter 3, but it is there that we come to grips with the notions of symbolic and subsymbolic representations, and Chapter 6 is where many of the popular representational schemes are paraded before you.

Chandrasekaran presents AI work of the 1970s and the 1980s as divisable (without mutual exclusivity) into three classes of theorizing:

I. Architectural theories. — "the solution to the problem of intelligence is to provide a computational architecture which is intrinsically seen as the source of intelligence." Below the distinguished level lie matters of implementation, and above it are specific particulars of agents, domains, and so on. Production systems are the classic example in this class (and, yet again, we'll get to them later). This particular architectural theory views intelligence as a rule processor. The component parts of this theory of intelligence concern the strategy for processing the rules, chaining schemes and conflict resolution, for example. The actual content of any set of rules (e.g., medical diagnosis or computer system configuration) is not part of the subject matter of the science of intelligence. "The point is that the theories propose a *unitary* architecture as a priviliged level to capture intelligence."

This style of theorizing has its problems, of course. Casting a specific problem domain into the form of the chosen unitary architecture all too often starts to resemble the problem of fitting a giraffe into an elephant's skin — not impossible but decidedly awkward. Then there is the inevitable need to employ a mechanism that is not within the scope of the architecture but also clearly not domain-specific either. The use of metacontrol rules is an example of this problem within the production system architecture. Chandrasekaran also makes the point that unitary architectural theories are typically no help in distinguishing between tractable and intractable solutions in specific domains. They tend to omit higher level information-processing distinctions that are needed to give an adequate functional description of intelligence *and which may require architectural support of their own.* As an example, a well-known proponent of rule-based architectures once said: common sense is just millions and millions of rules. And the response is: Yes, and *War and Peace* is just thousands and thousands of sentences. Clearly, some higher level organizational structure is being neglected in this exchange — theoretically important architectural features exist above the level at which the chosen architecture is moored.

There is a term, which it is appropriate to introduce here, that you will see tossed around between AI folk when they're relaxing and talking about the problems in their research. Certain AI techniques are classed as *weak methods*, which refers to techniques that can be described independent of any particular task or even problem domain. Such methods, which sound like God's gift to AI, unfortunately suffer from chronic inefficiency. As Rich (1983) so vividly puts it: They get clobbered by the combinatorial explosion (note Schank feature (d) given earlier). The relevance here is that certain unitary architectures are specific realizations of a weak method. Thus the GPS architecture is a realization of the more general weak method called *means-ends analysis*. Finally, let me also indicate that a further implicit cross-link is imminent: Compare the notion of weak methods with that of the epistemic–heuristic distinction, coming shortly.

II. Logical abstraction theories. — "some version of logic [i.e., a variant of the first-order predicate calculus (Chapter 10), or at least a system where the notion of truth-based semantics is central and inference-making is characterized by truth-preserving transformations — gruesome but true] is . . . the proper language of characterizing all computation, and by extension, intelligence." Within this category of AI theories we note two, rather different subcategories:

1. Logic for abstractly characterizing and analyzing what an agent knows; and
2. Logic as a representation for knowledge, and logical deduction as the basic information processing activity in intelligence.

Theories of type II.1 were launched by McCarthy and Hayes (1969) in the famous and still much-referenced paper in which they proposed the epistemic–heuristic decomposition of intelligence. The epistemic component, the logic-based one, covers the essential details of what types of knowing is necessary for intelligent behavior, while the heuristic component takes care of how the necessary knowledge is to be represented and used with the requisite efficiency. The heuristic part is thus little more than mere implementation detail; it is clearly the epistemic component that is the focus of interest for hard scientists, and the epistemic–heuristic distinction provides reassurance that the logic-based theorizing is safe from attack on grounds of efficiency, computational tractability, representational realization, etc. — all such concerns are mere implementation detail and will be taken care of within the heuristic component once the real science has solved the crux of the problem. As Chandrasekaran points out, this does not really work. There is, for example, no way to decide in a theory-neutral fashion exactly what is epistemic and what is merely heuristic. History indicates that, in reality, the components of a theory tend to migrate from the heuristic to the epistemic side. A need for some phenomenon is vaguely recognized; experimentation and exploration begin to circumscribe it; it becomes a contribution to the heuristic component; further theoretical work on the now fairly well-identified phenomenon yields a formalization of the phenomenon; it becomes promoted to the epistemic component. As an example: default slots {to model the automatic assumption of information that is usually true in the absence of specific information to the contrary, e.g., if reasoning about cats, then assume four legs unless otherwise instructed} in Minsky's (1975) frames proposal was a piecemeal, ad hoc approach to the problem of efficient reasoning based on plausible inferences; it was clearly part of the heuristic component. Subsequent research has led to proposals for "default reasoning" and and "nonmonotonic logics," and under such labels an account of much the same phenomenon is clearly work within the epistemic component. In sum, "It is almost as if the lowly 'heuristic' component component is in fact what the action in AI is often about, while the epistemic part appropriates the nuggets of organizational wisdom that research in the heuristic component identifies."

Moving on to type II.2 theories, logic as the language of representation in AI: "Logic as knowledge representation makes a serious commitment to knowledge as propositions, and to True/False judgements as the basic *use* of knowledge. It is also closely connected to the belief that the aim of intelligence is to draw *correct* conclusions" (Chandrasekaran, 1990, p. 36, author's emphasis). Is this appropriate? One can argue that the notion of truth, viewed as the end product of a sequence of logically correct reasoning, is not fundamental to intelligence. Notions of what is relevant, of plausible inference and of adequate guesses, are more like the fundamental stuff of intelligence, not correctness in some absolute sense. If this is true, then logic is not obviously the best basis for theories of intelligence; some good reasons for using logic must be on hand. And, of course, they are: Logic is precise, logics have a well- defined semantics, etc. But "logic is neither a unique nor a priviliged way to be precise," and the semantics are not obviously at an appropriate level for the problems of intelligence.

As with all worthwhile issues there are at least two sides to the question of the desirability of logic as the representation language of AI. Unfortunately, the term *logic* when used in scientific circles seems almost instantly to suck up all of the respectable possibilities, thereby eviscerating any potential competition. My point is that logic is not irrefutably, nor even obviously, the correct or even best way to approach theorizing in AI. This is I believe a very important issue in AI, and we shall return to it for brief skirmishes here and there throughout this book; the denouement arrives in Chapter 10.

A subsequent portion of this chapter is concerned with the classification of AI work, and this is a good point to introduce one such scheme, as it maps very nicely onto the epistemic – heuristic distinction which we have just explored a little. AI work is often divided between two mutually exclusive categories: *scruffy* and *neat,* to use the technical terms. And these labels, which are not well defined (a fact that probably causes no great surprise at this point well into Chapter 1), fit quite comfortably with the epistemic–heuristic distinction, not respectively. The neats of AI pursue their goals within the constraints of hard science, and the scruffies do whatever is necessary to obtain accounts of interesting AI phenomena. The two groups tend not to see eye to eye on many issues.

III. Generic Functional theories. — such a theory is a "domain-independent, information processing strategy and . . . a functional unit of intelligence [conceived] as a process" (Chandrasekaran, 1990 p. 38). Each such theory identifies a generic functional property of intelligence which is used to solve a 'natural kind' of cognitive problem. Examples in this category are: the GPS means-ends analysis theory of problem solving (Newell & Simon, 1972; this could also be classed as a type I theory, I believe — it is introduced in Chapter 3); Schank's (1973) conceptual dependency notation and scripts (examined in the chapter on natural language processing); and the generic information processing strategies for diagnostic reasoning developed by Chandrasekaran (1987). They all typically emphasize some organizational aspect and facilitate some particular kind of inference or construction in a computationally efficient way. A major distinguishing feature from category II theories is that computational feasibility is an integral part of the theorizing — form and function, representation and control — are both important aspects of the theorizing. The primacy of representational issues in AI has, I believe, suppressed proper consideration of the essential control mechanisms to an unhealthy degree. I attempt to reinstate control alongside representation in Chapter 6.

CATEGORIZATIONS OF AI WORK

Hall and Kibler (1985) have presented a classification of AI work which is based on the methodology used; their scheme is presented and discussed in Chapter 10. There is another way to lay out a taxonomy of AI. And it has gained considerable practical importance in the light of the recent explosion and expansion of work purported to be AI. The classification scheme is based on the *use* to which the AI project is to be put. The major division employed is one that separates scientific AI from applications-oriented AI. The latter category, comprising as it does expert systems technology (Chapter 5), various manifestations of knowledge-based systems (Chapter 6 covers the realizations of knowledge bases), vision systems for industrial robots (the basis for AI vision schemes is the subject of Chapter 7), and natural language interfaces (based on a component of the work in natural language processing, which is dealt with in Chapter 8), is based on the former at least insofar as the AI is concerned. The major purpose of this book is to spread before you in an organized manner the body of work (both theory and practice) that is scientific AI. The major exception which I have granted myself leave to indulge in is expert systems technology; it has a whole chapter to itself. Why have I done this? Is it just to keep the publisher happy? It is not {but no gruesome details are available}.

The term *expert systems* covers a multitude of things, including quite possibly some sins, but that's not my concern. Mention of the term expert systems to hardcore AI hackers (and theorists) typically elicits some species of dismissive response. For many, expert systems is beyond the pale of real AI, but for me it's not; they are inextricably intertwined, I believe, and the world of so-called scientific AI can learn some useful things from a study of expert systems' technology. But by the same token AI is much much more than expert systems, quite contrary to the implications in the deluge of expert systems litrature which has been hitting the marketplace in recent years. Expert systems work has sprouted off from AI and blossomed into a viable organism on its own; it gains its independent vitality from the practical applicability (or promise of, but this is yet another issue for consideration later) of its end products, expert systems. It is precisely this large-scale practical application of systems that are at least AI-ish which is unique in AI's history and is therefore likely to provide useful feedback into the root science. This is the tack that I take in Chapter 5; it is not a parade of the famous expert systems, but an attempt to look underneath the glossy surface and expose both the sound and successful foundations as well as the stress fractures that are now becoming visible. It is particularly these latter areas of concern in expert systems' technology that are, I believe, instructive with respect to the pursuit of scientific AI.

THE GOALS OF AI RESEARCH

We can distinguish different levels of approach to the category earlier described as scientific AI. Two such levels are: one in which the theoretical primitives are the functional units of classical psychology — the cognitive science level; and one in which the primitive elements can be directly related to brain physiology — the brain modeling level.

A different approach to subdividing the class of scientific AI (one favored by, for example, Bundy, 1990) is with respect to the general aim of the research. For Bundy, work aimed at modeling human intelligence using AI techniques is cognitive science or computational psychology. And the modeling work that aims at exploring computational techniques that have the potential for simulating intelligent behavior, regardless of the nature of human intelligence, is basic or mainstream AI.

The cognitive science branch of AI seeks to throw light upon the nature of human intelligence, its scope and limitations, and how it works. Within this domain the computer is a tool for modeling theories of human intelligence. The cognitive scientist theorizes in terms of high-level concepts: long-term and short-term memory, semantic mismatch detectors, semantic networks, etc. Such components have no obvious correspondence with anatomical features of the brain; they are high-level abstractions rather closer to the behavioral characteristics that they seek to explain than to the organ from which the behavior (presumably) arises.

In mainstream AI much of the same terminology may be used, but only as convenient labels. Within this particular subcategory the results of the research are immune to any criticism based on discrepancies between the AI models and theoretical principles as well as empirical data that derive from observations of h. sapiens when he (or she) is behaving intelligently. Most AI, as the name suggests, falls into this particular subcategory, as a perusal of say, Barr and Feigenbaum (1981–1982) will confirm.

There are perhaps a number of reasons for the distance that mainstream AI puts between its theories and models, and you or I as the prime exemplars in the field. Firstly, mainstream AI does not want to be constrained by the particular solution embodied (quite literally) by the common instantiation of intelligence in the human form. If survival of the fittest is the basis of the mechanism that produced us, then our particular brand of intelligence may be less than optimal (just better than that of any of our rivals over the last n millenia). The section on "Pandering to Evolution" in a later chapter takes up this issue; it gains considerable significance when neuroanatomical constraints are employed in mainstream-like AI, i.e., when the AI project is primarily exploring the possibilities for simulating intelligence rather than attempting to further our understanding of brain functions.

Secondly, it is exceedingly difficult to justify a claim that a model is working *like* the human brain. There are many meanings of *like* in the preceding sentence, and they're all vulnerable to a concerted attack. Most AI workers have enough problems to deal with without defending their theories and models against charges like "that's not the way people do it."

By way of contrast, the brain modeling approach to AI theorizes and models in terms of units than can be related to brain structure: cell assemblies, neural networks, even individual neurons. The basic building blocks for the theory may now be directly observable, but piecing them together to explain observed behaviors represents a formidable problem. Consider explaining the details of a weather pattern in terms of intermolecular interactions rather than temperature, pressure, prevailing winds, etc. (see, for example, Arbib, 1972, and Johnston, Partridge, & Lopez, 1983; Partridge, 1985a, gives an analysis of one mechanism from a number of different levels).

So the bulk of AI research does not ostensibly seek to answer any questions at all about human intelligence — this we have called mainstream AI. "What then is the point of mainstream AI?" you might well be inclined to ask. The goal of this work is to emulate or surpass human performance of certain intelligent activities. The strongest link with human intelligence is that it represents a performance measure to strive for and then surpass.

But I would argue that, despite the almost standard disclaimer to the contrary, some degree of structural correspondence between AI modules and hypothesized mechanisms of human intelligence is both a perceivable and a necessary feature of this work, especially when a working model is to be constructed. Comprehensibility of the program is at a premium (because of the RUDE nature of AI-system development, see next chapter), and reasoning by analogy with one's own supposed thought processes is a necessary vehicle for realizing this goal. In the above-mentioned expert systems, for example, automatic explanation of the system's diagnoses (or whatever) in psychologically meaningful terms, rather than in terms of the implementation structures, is seen as an important problem. As a further and more specific example, Michie (1982) calls for a technique of "structured induction" to combat the inscrutability to man of the products of machine learning. This problem of inscrutable AI systems reaches a climax, I shall argue, in connectionistic modelling (read "THE REAL NEWS" in Chapter 3).

When we consider that cultural differences all too frequently block and distort mutual communication and understanding between instances of natural intelligence — communication difficulties are a problem within the relatively homogeneous umbrella of human intelligence — we must beware of the potential for escalation of this problem when we introduce an artificial intelligence.

The liberal use of heuristics is often given as the means of achieving, or the reason for claiming (or both), an AI system based on the notion of intelligence quite independent of any known realization such as *you* or *I*. A good heuristic is any strategy that works, and it is not explicitly linked to the mechanisms that humans apparently use. So at first glance the use of heuristics appears to deny the humanness claimed in the preceding paragraphs, but as you will see the ultimate source of heuristics is inevitably human. The result is that an AI system is bound to display a certain humanness. (But don't miss the chapter on machine learning which encompasses the potential for developing nonhuman heuristics.)

The idea of heuristics is central to most AI, so much so that what I have called mainstream AI used to be labeled "the heuristic programming approach" (see, for example, Slagle's 1971 book of that title which was *the* AI textbook of the early 1970s). This is all very convenient, as it enables me to slide imperceptibly from taxonomic chat to a consideration of these useful objects, as is entirely appropriate, if not de rigeur, in an introduction to the nature of AI.

But before we dive into the pleasures of heuristic programming, I should make it quite clear that the current use of the word *heuristic* is not quite the same as in the epistemic–heuristic distinction of McCarthy and Hayes (1969), but the similarities should be obvious. So, off into the world of the scruffies go we.

THE HEURISTIC PROGRAMMING APPROACH

"If it works, use it" is the principle behind heuristic programming. There are no awkward questions about the psychological plausibility of the heuristic under consideration. There is no demand for proof, or even need to justify its use beyond "it works; watch it and see." There can be no such awkward questions or demands, because a heuristic is a rule of thumb: a procedure that achieves a certain goal on an acceptable proportion of occasions. There are no claims of correctness for the chosen heuristic; in fact, there is more likely some assurance that it won't always work. Clearly, the domain of heuristic programming is perfect for mainstream AI. So what does one of these wonderous objects look like? Not very spectacular, I'm afraid.

The following heuristic is taught in medical school; so my doctor told me when I foolishly informed him that I had malaria. In addition, I had contracted the disease in a country from which it had supposedly been eradicted. The heuristic that he chided me with was "uncommon diseases occur infrequently." Not exactly a pearl of wisdom, you might be tempted to murmur quietly to yourself. But it enabled this doctor to dismiss my amateur diagnosis {fact: malaria is a very uncommon disease in Small Town, New Mexico, USA}, and get on with solving the problem of what was wrong with me. Unfortunately, it turned out after much testing and the elimination of all other possibilities (together with my bank balance) that I did have malaria, but that just reinforces my point about the fallability of heuristics. An alternative explanation from the diagnostician's viewpoint is that he failed to give enough weight to the heuristic which states: "don't blindly believe all that governments say about their country." This should probably have been strengthened by: "the customer is always right" (but the domain of applicability of this heuristic is department stores rather than the consulting rooms of the medical profession, so its apparent omission from the decision-making process is quite understandable). And the doubt-the-travel-brochures heuristic is just a special case of the exceedingly useful heuristic: "be skeptical about any statements issued by any government." This last piece of wisdom has been enshrined as The Second Great Lie, to wit, "I'm from the government; I'm here to help you."

Focusing back a little to somewhere closer to where we ought really to be in an AI book, a heuristic to guide machine learning might be: "a machine should learn only significant events." To incorporate a heuristic within a program, we generate an algorithm to approximate it — a heuristic algorithm, in short. So an implementation of the above heuristic must include explicit code to approximate: what makes an event significant, what aspects of a significant event will be learned, etc. So, not only do we have to come up with good heuristics, we have to make a further series of awkward, explicit decisions in order to render our heuristic machine executable.

A house-cleaning robot, for example, will require a heuristic such as: "water plants when dry." Nowadays, with rules and rule-based systems dominating the AI scene, we are more likely to frame this heuristic as: "IF the plants are dry THEN water them."

Now, that appears to be a reasonable rule that will be appropriate most of the time with some notable exceptions, for example, cacti and artificial plants. But although this statement of the heuristic would probably be sufficient if you were instructing a friend who was taking care of your house for a while, for the housecleaning robot it will need to be transformed into a precise, algorithmic rule.

Let us try for a more precise statement: Add water, in an amount appropriate for the size of the plant, to every plant whose soil has a relative moisture content less than some prespecified value.

That formulation would seem to explain what's wanted—or does it? Let me list some of the questions that would have to be answered before this heuristic attains the algorithmic specificity currently necessary in AI systems.

- What does "appropriate for" mean?—proportional to?
- If so, proportional to what?—size of plant?
- How do you measure size?—height? estimated weight? surface area of soil? volume of soil?

- "Relative moisture content" — relative to what? — size of plant? volume of soil? surface area of soil? depth of soil?
- Where do you measure the moisture content? — on soil surface? x inches below the surface? the average of several arbitrary probes?

The questions are many, reasonable answers are legion, and correct answers are exceptional. But the questions must be paired with precise answers before we obtain a machine-executable version of the original heuristic. The selection of a particular set of necessarily somewhat arbitrary answers will result in a particular algorithmic approximation to our original heuristic. There are very many such algorithmic approximations, and very few ways to choose between them.

So a heuristic implemented in an AI program is more accurately viewed as one of many possible algorithmic approximations to the heuristic — but this is an exceedingly clumsy and pedantic phrase, so I shall use instead the terms *heuristic* and *heuristic algorithm*.

The question that should be on your lips at this point is: Why do we use heuristics? Wouldn't some proven algorithm be better?

Proven algorithms would certainly be preferable, but in AI they are unfortunately either hard to find or hopelessly inefficient. The use of a heuristic represents the best known solution procedure that will succeed, if it does succeed, within reasonable time and space constraints.

The space/time tradeoffs here are not just microseconds, or even days or weeks. They may well run to centuries or the lifetime of the Universe! The search for efficient heuristics is well motivated when the only known proven algorithm will take years to terminate. People just won't wait that long.

The game of chess provides a simple example. Formal game playing is a somewhat "bad" paradigm for the presentation of AI (as I shall argue in Chapter 3), but no game, however formal, is all bad. In principle, the best move to be made from a given board configuration is easily computed. {We consider all the possible moves, all the possible replies, by the opponent, and so on until we have generated the full game tree down to all of the terminal win, lose, or draw situations. Then a mini-max algorithm is applied to specify correctly the best move to make. Unfortunately, both the space and time resources required to use this algorithm are impossible to meet.}

But the complete computation with the necessary data structures for an arbitrary board configuration in chess will in general more than overfill all existing computer memories. The time required for generating and processing the necessary information is of the order of the time that the Universe has been in existence. Clearly a heuristic is called for. In practice heuristics are used to estimate the relative goodness or badness of potential moves without generating the full game tree.

Pearl (1984) examines many heuristics in the relatively well-defined, but nevertheless rich, AI domain of games and puzzles. He states that "it is the nature of good heuristics both that they provide a simple means of indicating which among several courses of action is to be preferred, and that they are not necessarily quaranteed to identify the most effective course of action, but do so sufficiently often" (p. 4).

The guarantees, or lack of them, are one thing, but where does the heuristic come from in the first place? The sources are varied and ill-understood. Some heuristics are definitely plucked from the air (no different from many algorithms, of course). A common source of inspiration for heuristics is, naturally, oneself. Introspection is a very convenient strategy, but it must be used with caution.

To return to the chess example, I can design a first approximation to a best-move heuristic by introspection and rationalisation of the strategies that I appear to use when playing chess. Typically, the heuristic would be composed of components that compute first approximations to king threat, piece mobility, etc. But, if you are not an expert yourself, a better strategy might be to attempt to extract heuristics from an expert chess player.

Recognized experts are indeed a good source of heuristics. Unfortunately, experts are no more expert at introspection than you or I. All indications are that they are full of expertise, replete with high quality heuristics, but how to pour them out of the expert and into a program is a problem that is receiving a lot of attention. Later, in Chapter 5 and subsequently in the context of machine learning, I shall describe several approaches to this transfer of expertise problem.

Provided that the first guess for a heuristic strategy focuses upon the significant dimensions of the problem domain, then there is every chance that the heuristic can be tuned to adequacy by means of an iterative process. This tuning process may be totally automatic, in which case it is described in the section on machine learning (although the early, classic example of the checker-playing program is described below); or it may be one of a number of elaborate man-machine interaction scenarios as such it is considered in detail in the expert systems chapter (chapter 5).

The power of heuristics is such that they are much used, misused, and abused in AI. The sudden appearence of instances of the ELIZA syndrome simultaneously in large sectors of the computer-watching community can often be tracked down to a few very powerful, but totally task-specific, heuristics carefully layered into a large LISP program. Such heuristics are the "strong methods," in contrast to their weak bretheren mentioned earlier.

THE SAMUEL PHENOMENON

Samuel's (1963) checker-playing program was an early landmark study in AI. This program beat the world champion and Samuel himself; and this achievement is almost as remarkable as it appears. Samuel designed a program that played the game legally. He also included mechanisms that stored and reused successful moves; the program improved its performance with experience — it learned.

Samuel's program learned by both rote and generalization. The rote learning involved storing both expert moves as well as board configurations that it had evaluated for itself. The generalization learning was implemented as adjusting the weights associated with selected characteristics such as king advantage and piece mobility in an attempt to discover combinations that produced better play (as judged by both human experts and by direct competition against another copy of the program with different weightings).

The champion was caught off-guard in the first match, but then he analyzed the program's basic strategies and subsequently beat it easily. Although the program learned from experience, the learning was of a rudimentary and fixed nature; it did not learn new strategies of play.

The most significant achievement was that it could consistently beat its designer. Samuel has no pretensions to checker expertise; nevertheless, he did write the program and the program trounced him. Shades of the robot that refuses to obey its creator? I think so—it definitely throws doubt onto the old adage: computers can only do what you tell them to do. In a weak sense this statement is true, but it has several significant flaws when used as an assertion of the inherent limitations of AI. Samuel did not tell the computer to beat him; he told it, in a quite straightforward way, how to play legal checkers and how to improve its performance as a result of experience.

So now we also have the Samuel phenomenon in AI: With complex programs, especially if they contain learning mechanisms, it is, in practice, impossible to predict the full range of the program's possible behaviors. More succinctly, a programmer quickly loses track of exactly what he has told his program to do, or, rather, the consequences of what he has told it to do.

"Computers are literal-minded brutes and do exactly what they are told; no more and no less." Remember the Samuel phenomenon and treat such statements with caution.

2

AI And the Science of Computer Usage: The Forging of a Methodology

We have witnessed the proliferation of baroque, ill-defined and, therefore, unstable software systems. Instead of working with a formal tool, which their task requires, many programmers now live in a limbo world of folklore . . . the whole notion of a correct program — let alone a program that has been proved to be correct — becomes void a "sad remark." (Dijkstra, 1976 p. 202)

The fallacy under discussion is the widespread superstition that we can't write a computer program to do something unless one has an extremely clear, precise formulation of what is to be done, and exactly how to do it. (Minsky, 1967)

HOW TO USE THE ESSENTIAL TOOL?

AI is a tool-using enterprise (or discipline), and the tool that I have in mind is the computer. If much AI never actually gets implemented ("is currently being implemented" is AI-speak for "unimplemented"), it makes little difference. The intent to implement is there, and more importantly a working implementation is widely held to be some sort of "proof" of the theory. The exact relationship between theory and program, and the role that programs play in AI, are both serious questions for debate which we shall take up in Chapter 10. The necessary point here is much simpler: It is that programs are an important part of AI. Some AI research, it is true, is at pains to distance itself from specific styles of hardware such as the ubiquitous Turing-von Neumann architectures which have always dominated the computing landscape. Even for workers on the epistemic side of the McCarthy-Hayes distinction, potential implementability is still lurking around, a problem to be faced eventually even though it is a long way down the road and currently out of sight. Nevertheless, in principle it is there. Consideration of the heuristic component has been only postponed, not evaded entirely (if this sentence is more mysterious than usual, then you've skipped Chapter 1 or just failed to absorb at least one of the crucial bits).

23

AI is perhaps not part of computer science proper, but, because of the centrality of programs in AI, we might expect that it rests heavily on the science of computation. The current wisdom concerning the construction of programmed artifacts, which is a significant portion of what constitutes computer science, is, or should be, an important pillar supporting the edifice of AI. But is it? I think not, and in this chapter I shall explore the possible explanations for this lamentable lack of harmony between what computer science offers and what AI believes it needs. If AI makes heavy use of the computer as a tool and the science of computer usage has little to contribute to support the usage required by AI, then two possibilities present themselves: either the usage that AI requires is misguided, it is a misuse; or computer science is deficient in that it provides insufficient support for a perfectly legitimate usage of the computer as a tool. I am, of course, going to argue for this latter possibility.

This is an oddly titled chapter for a book that presents itself as an introduction to AI, and now that I've introduced the relevant subtopic the initial feeling of doubt about its appropriateness may well have given way to a firm conviction that this chapter is misplaced — not just that it should be placed elsewhere in the book, but that it should be placed in another book altogether. Let me assure you that I understand your skepticism, but it, and not this chapter, is misplaced, as you'll surely agree after I've invested a few paragraphs in justifying my strategy.

On the surface, the fact that AI and computer science are not hand in glove with each other is unfortunate but not sufficiently serious a problem to warrant the commandeering of an early chapter in an introductory AI book. But below the surface there is much friction, and hence heat, also turmoil and altercation, just because of this failure to see eye to eye. As a result AI suffers greatly, and computer science suffers as well, I maintain. Many prominent computer scientists, if they think about AI at all, dismiss it as some cheap showbiz spinoff from the real science and one for which the bubble of popular enthusiasm will soon burst — the sooner the better. As a consequence, AI-system development has not been the beneficiary of a supportive, underlying basic science. System development techniques in AI are a mess, and AI is not exactly renown for the production of robust working systems. These two assertions are related, I believe.

On the AI side, the lack of computer science support has been largely ignored, again on the surface, but the undercurrents have always been strong. At the more blasé end of the scale, AI-system developers have just hacked away merrily, cobbling together systems that can demonstrate their ideas, but with no hope, thought, or necessity for long-term system usage. The resultant fragile and feeble system can be coaxed into behaving appropriately with a few required examples of the theory, and no more is expected of it; its very existence is in some sense (what sense exactly we shall debate in Chapter 10) a vindication of the theory. Away from the happy hackers, AI persons, concerned that computer scientists ought to know what they are talking about, have kept their programming style in low profile. Unable to conform to good programming practice, they lead an unhappy existence in some limbo world of system development: not accepted computer science techniques, but not a methodology endorsed by any other reputable source either.

With AI currently in the process of coming out of the research labs and going public, not to say practical, good ideas will require good systems to carry them — systems that are robust and reliable, systems that last longer than a few well-chosen demonstrations, in a phrase: commercial-quality software systems. "But this cannot be a problem," you might feel like interjecting. "Expert systems technology is an AI-applications area, and high-quality expert systems have already been produced and are currently doing a fine job." I agree, but the reason is because expert system builders have been forging (in several of its senses, to wit, hammering out a useful tool and counterfeiting) their own system development methodology at the same time as they have been constructing the AI software. Hayes-Roth, Waterman, and Lenat (1983), for example, give a presentation of the emergent methodology of expert systems development as they see it. But this is not a methodology that expert system builders have designed to accommodate their special needs; it is the gleanings from the actual practice of building a number of successful expert systems — a post hoc rationalization of the strategies that turned out to be necessary to do the job. Similarly, on the other side of the Atlantic, Bader, Edwards, Harris-Jones, and Hannaford (1988) have developed the POLITE methodology. Again it is a spin-off from their work on building knowledge-based systems (you get to see it later in the chapter).

I'm not saying that various subareas and subinterests in AI have not and are not developing appropriate methodologies. What I'm saying is that odds and ends of good-enough methodologies exist in AI, but that there is no well-founded, satisfactory system development methodology for AI, and that this absence of an accepted and effective system development methodology is a major problem in much AI work. In addition, computer science, which is the field that legitimate computer-using disciplines ought to be able to look for guidance, does not appear to be about to provide help. And even worse, the conventional wisdom from computer science leads in totally the wrong direction for AI, and hence results in an unhelpful deflection of effort for those persons who persist in looking where guidance ought to be found.

Enough said; AI is in a methodological mess (and not just for practical applications), and it is appropriate to air the arguments at the beginning of an AI text, as all AI programs are founded on some, usually ad hoc, methodological principles. By looking at the general problem at this early stage in the book, you will, I hope, gain an understanding that will tell you why, for example, some AI projects are as they are rather than as we might like them to be. And you will also realize why, for example, many quite dramatic demonstrations of AI systems molder in successive editions of introductory AI texts rather than grow and develop, and even become manifest in practical software systems. SHRDLU, SOPHIE, SAM, SCHOLAR, TEIRESIAS, AM, EURISKO, etc., where are you now? Have no fear, most of them get a mention in this book, as is customary. I'm not a member of the Church of the Latterday Nihilists; I'll not wantonly kill off the popular legends, but I've no aversion to knocking them a bit.

FIRST SPECIFY, THEN VERIFY

The epitome of good practice in the construction of programs holds that, first, you must have a complete, precise, and formal specification of the problem to be programmed. Only then do you embark on one of the carefully constructed refinement schemes which will terminate in the existence of an executable algorithm whose correctness is verified against the specification. You must know *what* you want the program to do (the specification) before you design an algorithm for *how* to do it (the implementation); it makes obvious sense, and what's more, it can be demonstrated for small, abstract problems such as computing the greatest common divisor (GCD) of two numbers. It can also be demonstrated for a few select but quite nonsimple problems as well. Research in computer science is continually pushing the limits of this methodological ideal further and further out.

Nevertheless, it is not used (not in its pure form) on large-scale practical software. This is also within the purview of computer science, but it has so far resisted all attempts to get it under the yoke of the specify-and-verify (SAV) methodology. A complete (if not totally formal) specification can often be approximated quite closely, but formal verification of the resultant algorithm is never even close to possible. So the SAV methodology is watered down, and elaborate validation schemes have been developed to test for incorrectness in the algorithm — specify-and-test (SAT) is the methodology of practical software system construction. But computer scientists are only too well aware of this weakness and are working towards eliminating it. SAT is only a stopgap; once the science has matured, it will be SAV for everything. But is SAV appropriate for AI?

"Of course," say the computer scientists, "it is *the* correct way to construct computer programs."

"But," says the AI programmer apologetically, "I have no hope of completely specifying the correct function for diagnosing bacterial meningitis. In fact there is no agreed, correct function, there is just behavior that more or less closely accords with the best human experts. I'll be happy if my program can begin to replicate their behavior."

"Oh," [in a deep voice of authority] the computer scientist responds after some moments. Clearly, he is profoundly disturbed by this revelation. "Well, in that case, you have no business trying to write programs at all. Your problem is not appropriate for computerization. Fully specified, well-designed, and thoroughly validated software causes enough problems. The possible repercussions of the necessarily baroque and ad hoc systems that you will produce does not bear thinking about" (see Dijkstra's chapter-opening "sad remark").

"Oh," squeaks the AI person sheepishly [Do sheep squeak? Are there sheepish AI persons?],"but I have an interesting and potentially important problem here, and one of the best ways to explore it is through implementing and observing various theoretical options. In addition, there appear to be algorithms that run on meat machines [i.e., in vivo brains] that solve these problems quite effectively, so why not have algorithms running on electronic computers that do as well, or even better?"

"Sorry, but the computer is not that sort of tool. Computer science does not cater for investigative programming. It's bad enough when you know exactly what you want the thing to do; throw that touchstone away, and all hell will break loose. Why not come back when you have an appropriate problem—one that admits a nicely factored solution?"

So who is being awkward here? The overbearing and authoritarian computer scientist, or the poor AI person who just wants to make some progress on the Ph.D.? I'll leave this question open as a first exercise for the reader [hint: don't spend too long on it, it's not worth it]. A second question that you might consider is the freedom that an author gets to bias the arguments in his book. But let's move on to what may appear at first sight as special pleading for AI, but isn't. It will eventually turn out to be special pleading for all problems (excepting, perhaps, only abstract, formal ones), and that can't be called special pleading at all, can it?

THE NATURE OF AI PROBLEMS

AI problems and the problems of conventional software engineering are different. They differ in a number of crucial characteristics.

AI problems tend to be dynamic and ill-structured; they also tend to be characterized in terms of a behavioral description — i.e., rather than having, say, an abstract definition of the semantics of English, all we have is a description of how English-speaking people are likely to respond to various classes of utterance. An adequate, English-understanding AI system will respond in similar ways. The output of an algorithm to understand English (assuming that we have some agreed representation of the semantic domain) will not always (ever?) be classifiable as either correct or incorrect. It is much more likely to be more or less arguably adequate. Thus in AI system development we are, not so much implementing some well-specified problem, as exploring the adequacy of a machine-executable specification (i.e., a program) vis-á-vis a dynamic and ill-structured, performance-mode problem description.

An objection to my characterization of AI problems which should spring to the mind of every vaguely alert reader is: What about chess, checkers, etc.? What about them indeed. They are the epitome of AI problems, aren't they? Yet they are well defined in the abstract, and the behavior of a program that purports to be a chess-playing program is easily judgeable as correct or incorrect, the complications of adequacy judgments are not necessary.

To begin with, I think that I ought to come clean at this early point in the book and state one of my personal prejudices with respect to AI (and there's lots more to come they leak out implicitly, if not explicitly, throughout the book). Some problems are AI problems for no good reason other than the fact that they have been accepted as AI problems at some point or other in the short, swift course of our subject. But chess and checkers are not quite in this category, although I do believe that they fit into a fairly well-defined subarea of AI which is also called AI (I'm sad to have to report). The subarea AI stands for Artificial Intellectualism. I'm not going to fall into the attempted-definition trap again, so let me just say that this subarea is concerned with well-defined, formal, abstract problems, problems whose mastery is the preserve of something less than all of mankind, and problems whose mastery is generally taken to be indicative of superior quality little grey cells in the head of the master. Much general AI is in fact this subarea AI, and as such its usefulness has been overrated. I'll get back to this source of "bad paradigms" for AI in the next chapter. AI work outside this subarea concerns the abilities that we all possess (e.g., use of natural language for communication, and use of common sense), the harder problems of AI — dare I say, the *real* problems in AI?

But back to chess: A win, a loss, and a draw are well defined, and the legal moves are well defined, but the "best" move from an arbitrary board position is not well defined, in practice. And the relative goodness of alternative moves is similarly not well defined. We are back with the headache of judging adequacy again, and hence back in the domain of AI problems. In principle, of course, these things like "best" move are well defined. But in practice we must play chess without these comforts, and so must a computer. Chess is an AI problem (to some extent) in practice if not in principle.

While fielding the obvious objections to my assertions in this chapter, I should probably let our computer scientist, who is just bursting to bring the light of hard science into this domain of dark practices, have the opportunity to respond.

"The fundamental mistake here is to believe that, just because a problem currently eludes formal circumscription, it is in some absolute sense not a formally specifiable problem. The proper approach to this problem is not to embark on a quest for some chimerical new methodology, but to work on formal specification of these seemingly intractable problems. Perseverance will undoubtedly lead to the discovery that certain initially intractable problems can be suitably factored after all."

Let's be fair. There is some truth to this objection, but there are also some problems, important AI problems (e.g., natural language understanding), which all available evidence suggests will never be formally specifiable in a sense that is appropriate for SAV. In addition, there is a valid argument for exploring machine-executable specifications of these important but obstinate problems until such time as appropriate formal specifications are forthcoming, if they ever are. The more dubious use of exploratory programming techniques in the absence of a sound methodological basis is in the production of commercial AI software.

I can wind up this section with a brief look at the crucial question of the formal circumscribability of certain problems. The detailed technical argument as to why certain types of problem are not formally circumscribable is given by Wilks (1971). Partridge and Wilks (1987) omit all the gruesome details, and I shall follow this easier path. The reader who wishes to cast doubt on the validity of this point should obviously wade into the detailed argument with Wilks; the less skeptical can stay with me.

The natural language case is a central and relevant one. A computer that could understand and construct communications in a natural language with anything like the same facility that the average human can demonstrate would represent a major breakthrough in AI. Natural language is also an area in which a very strong case can be made that the problem is not of a type that allows complete prespecification. The set of sentences of, for example, English, is not a decidable set; That is, for any string of words there is no well-defined function that can determine if that string is a sentence of English or not. And this decision is only a small step down the road to "understanding" the strings of words. I am here only considering the notion of grammaticality: Is the string of words a sentence or not? (English teachers may claim to have staked out this ground quite clearly, but counterexamples to all 'sentence' rules are easily found. A well-defined notion of grammaticality can only be an illusion.) Schank and some others (they are given a fair hearing in Chapter 8) might claim that the question of grammaticality {i.e., syntactic issues} is not even a small step down the road to language understanding; it's a step down the wrong road. But, be that as it may, no one claims that extracting 'meaning' from strings of words {i.e., semantic issues}, the ultimate task of an AI system which understands English, is easier than deciding grammaticality. The syntactic problems appear to be far more amenable to formal treatment. Hence the overwhelming concentration of effort on grammars and parsing strategies (more of which theme you will get in Chapter 8). Yet even this subproblem appears to lack formal circumscribability.

Wilks (1990 p. 130) sums up his arguments with the statement that there is "not an intuitively acceptable bound to the set of 'meaningful sentences of English'. . . or . . . 'grammatical sentences of English.' " He claims that linguistic behavior cannot be circumscribed, and thus the view of language as a set of sentences requiring production is false.

You might feel motivated at this point to interject that the picture of AI-system development cannot be as black as I'm painting it. Practical AI-systems exist, and are successful. Practical expert systems abound, so the developers of such systems must have either solved this methodological problem or avoided it. I think that they (the expert system's builders) have done a bit of both, but largely the latter. Figure 2.2 (see below) illustrates one example of methodological development, and avoidance of the worst AI-problem features has been achieved by careful selection of the types of human expertise for practical software — this is a tricky issue, and it's given a full airing in Chapter 5.

A METHODOLOGY OF INCREMENTAL EXPLORATION

As a consequence of the peculiar nature of AI problems (as currently appears to be the case), AI systems, particularly those of mainstream and of scientific AI, tend to be developed in an incremental and exploratory manner. The methodology for AI system development is based on the run-understand-debug-edit (RUDE as it were) cycle: a program is executed; its behavioral inadequacies are analyzed, and the program is redesigned to eliminate the perceived inadequacies; the modified program is executed, etc. There is currently much debate as to how to improve this incremental development paradigm, or even whether the incremental

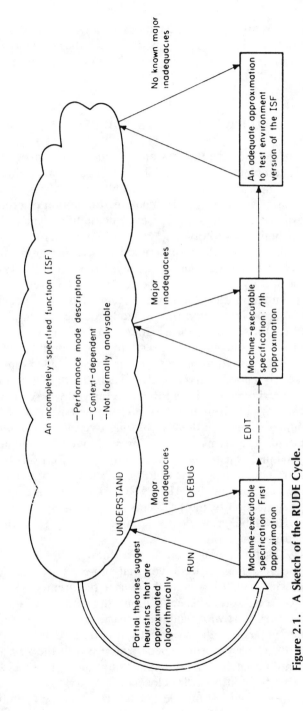

Figure 2.1. A Sketch of the RUDE Cycle.

From D. Partridge, 1986, *Artificial Intelligence Review*, 1(1), p. 29. Reprinted by permission.

phase can be prior to any implementation, if not eliminated altogether (see Kowalski, 1984; Partridge, 1986b; Mostow, 1985). Figure 2.1 is a schematic illustration of an incremental system development methodology in AI.

RAPID PROTOTYPES TO THE RESCUE?

In recognition of the fact that the task of constructing an abstract specification which is complete, correct, and describes what was wanted in the implemented system can be eased considerably by feedback of information from the observation of system behavior, the notion of prototyping was born. It was not, of course, AI or even computer science that conceived of the benefits of prototyping. I don't know where it originated, but it was certainly long before any computer scientists were devoting large portions of their waking hours to the mysteries of octal core dumps. The benefits of prototyping hinge on the fact that a concrete realization can make explicit important, hidden implications of the specification, and that a small-scale realization (i.e., a model of the system) can yield a maximum of useful feedback for a minimum of effort.

In computer science the notion of executable (or interpretable) specifications is a popular route to prototyping; it is usually called rapid prototyping, because it is a good deal quicker than actually building a model — the specification *is* the model. Thus PROLOG (as you will see in Chapter 4) is, in this respect, a gift from the gods; it is also an AI language. Hence, logic programming {gruesome details are long overdue: Logic programming is programming in terms of mechanisms derived from logic and is often, but mistakenly, equated with programming in PROLOG — all will be made clear in Chapter 4} and use of PROLOG as an executable specification language, are subfields of AI. A PROLOG program may be little more than a specification of the problem; this has its good and its bad points (at the risk of being labeled as "parenthetically repetitive": All will be revealed in Chapter 4).

Kowalski (1984), for example, presents a "new technology" for software design. He describes an iterative, trial-and-error process for "analysing the knowledge that lies behind the user requirement." But once we have the correct, formal specification, the situation is different: "Good programmers start with rigid, or at least formal, software specifications and then implement them correctly first time round — never get it wrong" (p. 10). Clearly, formal specification is still the key assumption, and the notion of a correct implementation is there also. This scheme is at least SAT, if not a lot closer to SAV.

Another "new paradigm," one designed for "software technology in the 1990s'' (Balzer, Cheatham, & Green, 1983), illustrates a second attempt to incorporate the notion of incremental development through rapid prototyping into an essentially SAV-like framework; it also introduces us to the notion of software support environments which are later to become a feature of this chapter.

In sum, an iterative component of system development, which utilizes performance data, is recognized as necessary, but it is not allowed to corrupt the beauty of the SAV philosophy. New paradigms are emerging, but they tend to hold SAV as inviolate. So, acknowledgment of the benefits of behavioral feedback for determining what you really want the system to do and not to do is not viewed as an abandonment of SAV in favor of something rather more RUDEish; it is seen as a preliminary to SAV proper, the packing of more structure at the front end in order to get the abstract specification right before launching into design and verification.

I, for one, think that these paradigms miss the crucial point for AI-systems development (and, to be fair, many of these new paradigms are not aimed explicitly at AI-systems development, although, as you will see, I don't believe that AI systems are in a world apart from conventional software). System development is still keyed to the notion of a complete, prior specification. For AI-system development the benefits of prototyping must be extended right through to feedback from the full, working system, which of course is then a prototype only in the sense that the information fed back will be used to modify it and so generate the next version of the system.

I am sure that the preoccupation with SAV is far too limiting for AI, but I'm not sure that a good system development methodology — one that regularly produces robust and reliable systems — can be developed if the major tenets of SAV are abandoned. So, if we are not to close the door on AI as practical software, if we are not content to leave it as only the substance of intriguing but totally unreliable Ph.D. project programs, then we must attempt to develop a methodology that eschews the touchstones of SAV. I can sketch out some lines of approach to this problem.

SUPPORTIVE ENVIRONMENTS

If the computer scientists refuse to help, then maybe the computer itself can be programmed to collaborate; after all, it is a good deal more controllable (that's assuming that it hasn't got any AI in it). AI programming is not, and never really has been, an activity of using a programming language, such as LISP (Chapter 4), as merely a medium for expressing a machine-executable version of an algorithm. AI languages have always been much more than that. The LISP language is in fact used in the context of a programming environment. It may be the major component of the environment, but a host of available support functions are also necessary for effective and efficient AI programming.

Programming is a task that requires an ability to master, or at least be able to hold your own with, a myriad of details. What name did I give to this quantity in the other module? Where else is this function referenced? Why did I code this function in that way last week? With respect to the goals of the programming task these details vary from utterly trivial to highly significant, but whatever their rating they all contribute to the complexity of the task.

Notice that in a properly adhered-to SAV regimen, many of these details will be introduced systematically as refinement proceeds smoothly from specification to executable algorithm. The SAV man's observation is expected to be that the height of the complexity hurdle in incremental system development is a direct result of failing to observe the strictures of SAV-think. But, if SAV is not a viable methodology for AI, then deal with this complexity barrier we must. And the general philosophy of approach has been to develop sophisticated support environments in which the computer shoulders a good deal of the burden. After all, keeping tabs on masses of details is one of the things that they do easiest and best.

FORGING A NEW METHODOLOGY

Can AI go it alone and hammer out a discipline of incremental, exploratory programming? Or will the inevitable result be a travesty of a proper system development methodology, a strategy for the proliferation of baroque systems, a recipe for escalation of the software crisis? What will we get for our efforts, a well-wrought tool, or a weak, pathetic forgery? It is an important question for the future of AI. Belief in one or other option is largely a matter of faith at the present time (should the question have been resolved adversely by the time that you, dear reader, are casting your eyes over these pages, then AI, like alchemy, will have withered, another victim of hard science).

What might this new methodology be like? It is probably environment based, and not just a system development environment but a complete-life-cycle environment. The necessary environment must be able to facilitate the introduction of modifications to change the system as a result of observation of system behavior.

How can the methodology encourage the production and continued maintenance of robust and reliable software? Even if we are not in the business of AI applications, the information gained from an exploratory demonstration program is likely to be roughly proportional to the longevity of the program. So even the pure science of AI will be well served by a methodology that allows it to avoid the customary escalating-disaster-style AI model and work on ones that perform as long-term experiments.

Components of a discipline of incremental, exploratory programming (if such a thing is possible) are anybody's guess, and so as a representative anybody I'll offer you some guesses.

> DECOMPILING—deriving consequences for the 'form' (a specification is a key, but not the only, 'form') from observations of the function;
> STEPWISE ABSTRACTION—a sequence of decompiling operations that yields succinct, conceptually transparent representations of cluttered and complex working systems;
> STRUCTURED GROWTH—(originally due to Sandewall, 1978) analogous to the successful SAV-based technique of structured programming, structured growth will comprise a set of techniques for reversing the usual entropy (i.e., degree of disorder) increase that tends to accompany incremental development;
> ADEQUACY VALIDATION—a strategy for judging a system as adequate, perhaps based on the minimization-of-misfit principle due to Alexander (1964);
> CONTROLLED MODIFICATION—a strategy of incremental change through analysis of program abstractions, subsuming both decompiling and structured growth.

I have discussed all of these potential contributions to a new AI methodology, at length, elsewhere (see Partridge, 1986a, if you just can't resist), so I'll forego the pleasure of doing it again in this book.

Several alternatives to a RUDE-based methodology have been suggested. They are called COURTEOUS (Mostow, 1985) and POLITE (Bader et al., 1988), for obvious reasons (the authors claim valid acronymic derivations, but we know better). The former was little more than a casual suggestion, but the POLITE methodology has real substance, as you can see in Figure 2.2.

The designers of POLITE have specifically addressed what they see as the glaring weaknesses of RUDE:

1. where does the initial approximation come from?;
2. lack of any control of the iterative process of system development.

There is much to discuss about an appropriate system-development methodology for AI problems, but this is not the place for it, so I shall give it a miss. This decision not to pursue the detailed methodological

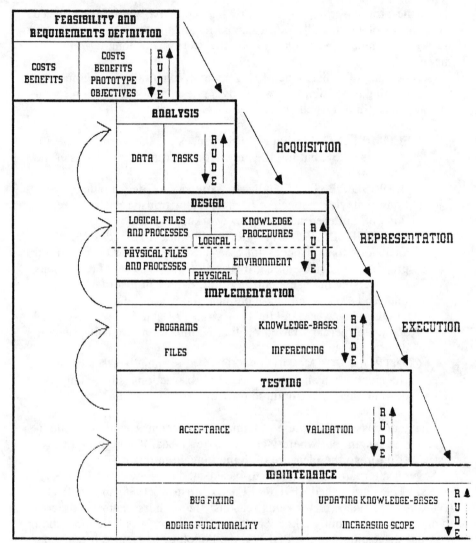

Figure 2.2.   The POLITE Methodology.

From "Practical Engineering of Knowledge-based Systems," by J. Bader, J. Edwards, C. Harris-Jones, & D. Hannaford, 1988, *Information & Software Technology, 30* (5), p. 270. Reprinted by permission.

issues further may bring a sigh of relief to the lips of those readers who are eager to get on with AI proper (i.e., a MYCIN diagnosis, a SHRDLU dialogue in the blocks world, etc.). Alternatively, if you feel cheated of essential details, I can, perhaps, console you with some references to where they may be found. Rich and Waters (1986), Agresti (1986), and Partridge (in press) are all edited collections of papers that begin to dig into the methodological issues that AI brings to software development.

IS AI SO DIFFERENT?

In this final section I want to raise the possibility that AI is not so different from conventional software engineering problems; it is the formal, abstract functions, which dominate the science-of-programming texts, that are problems apart. For years practicing software engineers have struggled with the reality of constructing adequate systems embodying ill-defined functions tailored to meet intangible user needs. I suspect that many software engineers will find themselves associating more closely with my characterization of AI-system development than with the SAV methodology. But there is a software crisis, and it is generally reckoned to be a direct consequence of failure to apply the principles of SAV. Practical software does not live up to the standards that the computer scientists say ought to be possible. Thus the software engineer is always measuring his (or her) practices up against some SAV-based model of the *right* way to do things. Current practice always proves to be inferior in one or other respect. The reaction of the software engineering community is to operate some weak travesty of SAV with apologies, or to adopt an attitude of bravado and openly scoff at academic notions of proof and verification but still use a methodology that implicitly aspires to the SAV model.

But sincere blasphemers can also be found — can't they always? Nevertheless, given the current "methodological mess" (read Bundy & Ohlsson, 1990, for this quote and their debate on this problem — it's totally different from my argument) in AI, which has become a chronic complaint, we might be well advised to listen to all the cries for understanding from the practicing software engineers. De Millo, Lipton, and Perlis (1979) launched a full broadside at the dominance of SAV-think in computer science, but the blast was absorbed without lasting damage and has now been largely forgotten. In a combative and intriguing collection of essays, Halpern (in press) attacks many aspects of the conventional wisdom of computer science. In particular, he challenges the notion that an algorithm is like a proof in mathematics, and that the development of mechanisms to prove programs correct is a useful exercise to be engaged in.

There have also been small but significant statements of dissent published in the prestigious organ of the Association for Computing Machinery (ACM), the Communications of the ACM. I allude to Swartout and Balzer (1982), who point out that specifications and implementations inevitably intertwine; and to Giddings (1984), who argues that most software, contrary to the assumptions of SAV-based models, is domain dependent, and that, thus, a new and more appropriate design methodology is required. Agresti (1986) has collected the two papers referenced above together with many others. This compendium of dissent is not as heretical as my two selected contributions might lead you to believe. It is an en masse criticism of the conventional model of software development, but it does not really challenge the basic tenets of SAV. It offers prototyping, development environments, and transformational implementation (roughly, a hope that automatic, and therefore correct, implementation of specifications will one day be possible — hence all the worries can be confined to the problem specification) as the important future directions to explore in the hope of eventually eliminating the software crisis.

My final suggestion is then that these awkward issues of methodological validity may not be a purely parochial concern of the AI community. A SAV-based methodology may be inappropriate for much of conventional software engineering as well. It may be that RUDE should be the major paradigm instead of SAV.

Your final task is to ponder the following ordered list of methodologies (from Partridge & Wilks, 1987, p. 118):

1. Only properly proved programs are OK.
2. Only programs conforming to the current standards of software engineering are OK.
3. Only programs founded on adequate logical or linguistic theories are OK.
4. Expert systems as a form of software engineering are OK.
5. AI programs that exist as practical/commercial software are OK.
6. Working AI demonstration programs are OK.

OK is a hopelessly weak term here, and readers may prefer to substitute *acceptable* or *intellectually defensible* or any term they prefer. The point of the table is its order and not the predicates attached to lines. For each level, its adherents believe that those below it are not OK! Readers may also enjoy the exercise of attaching names of individuals or companies to each line: It is easily done, and provides an easy check on the table via the transitivity-of-scorn rule. The upwards direction in the table is not simply capable of being interpreted, but a close approximation is: Anything above this line cannot be seriously performed, but might be OK if it were. By our classification, 5 and 6 are RUDE; 2, 3, and 4 are SAT; and 1 is SAV.

3

The Major Paradigms

A scientist endeavors to understand the world;
an AI person tries to simulate it.

AI has more than its fair share of paradigms. It seems that every mechanism that works on more than one specific problem is immediately elevated to the status of a paradigm. It is not such paradigms that I propose to address in this chapter. It is primarily the almost ubiquitous symbolic search space paradigm (SSSP) that I shall consider: its scope, limitations, underlying assumptions, and major components.

In addition, I shall similarly explore the parallel-networks paradigm, which I shall term the connectionist paradigm (CP), and its relationship to the SSSP. If this chapter does grow to embody a plethora of impious remarks about this popular creed, the one enshrined in the SSSP, this should not be interpreted as a lack of proper respect for a paradigm that has served AI well. It is just an automatic reaction that I have to the unquestioning obeisance accorded to this paradigm and to certain of its constituent, so-called hypotheses. So tolerate the occasional verbal kneejerk, it's nothing more than that — I'll get over it, given time.

Significant subparadigms do in fact exist. Waltz (1987), for example, lists "heuristic search; constraint propagation; blackboard systems; marker passing." In general, these subparadigms are considered later in this book in the specific contexts to which they apply, or in which they originally arose. Thus, the "constraint relaxation paradigm" is given consideration in its original context, machine vision, and subsequently mentioned in a new application area, natural-language processing, although, within Waltz's list, I single out heuristic search as distinct from his other three paradigms; heuristic search for me is a characteristic component of the SSSP, the others are not. At the more-general level of discussion that this chapter attempts to present, I do pick on some specialized paradigms, but only the bad ones. And, moreover, bad paradigms that have undue influence on the development of AI as a subject. I wish to get these unwholesome facets of AI disposed of as quickly and quietly as possible.

SYMBOLIC SEARCH SPACES

The SSSP provides the dominant model for much AI, both research and practical applications. It appears to provide an adequate characterization of many AI problems, and, in addition, this model can yield representations of the AI problems that offer the possibility of computational tractability, especially when we eschew guaranteed correctness and allow the inclusion of domain-specific heuristics. The vast majority of the successful demonstrations of AI implementations are founded, more or less directly, on the SSSP. The notion of logical inference can be neatly integrated with that of the SSSP, despite the fact that correctness in some absolute sense is not a fundamental notion with respect to human intelligence. Then logical inference and the SSSP together provide the foundation upon which current expert system technology(CEST) is built, as we shall see in a subsequent chapter.

The notion of a symbolic search space is typically associated with Newell and Simon, and, although they have no exclusive claim to it, they are largely responsible for explicit articulation of crucial aspects of, as well as important manifestations of, the general paradigm. Early statements of their view can be found both in their book *Human Problem Solving* (Newell & Simon, 1972), and in their Turing Lecture (Newell & Simon, 1976).

A symbolic search space is characterized by a set of initial states, a set of goal states, a set of intermediate states, and a set of operators which can transform one state into another. Thus, problem solving is represented as finding and applying a sequence of operators that will transform an initial state, through a sequence of intermediate states, into a goal state (see Figure 3.1).

Each state is an independently specifiable entity. Situations and events are represented at the symbolic level (this is an awkward point that we shall return to below), and intelligent decisions are forthcoming from manipulation of these symbols — symbolic representations of states of the world independent of any context or background.

In order to have some chance of solving AI problems, we must avoid exhaustive searches of the state space. Two common methods of pruning the search are:

1. Ordering the state-transformation operators such that the "best" applicable operator is always tried first;
2. Devising a state-evaluation function that can be used to rank intermediate states with respect to their "closeness" to a goal state (thus one can always choose to move to that next intermediate state which is closest to the desired goal state).

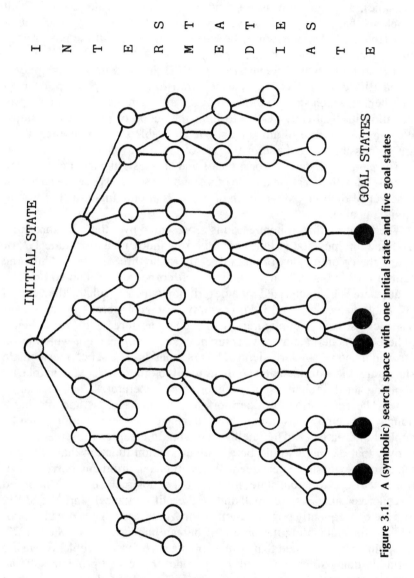

INITIAL STATE

INTERMEDIATE STATES

GOAL STATES

Figure 3.1. A (symbolic) search space with one initial state and five goal states

The above two words in scare quotes are where most of the AI must be concentrated. Finding a "best" ordering of the operators (static or dynamic), and finding a useful "closeness" function, are both difficult problems that are typically solved by the use of problem-specific heuristics. Hence, the paradigm may be widely applicable, but the power pack must be custom built for each application.

It is in these two problem areas that the decision making is concentrated (the critical decision is which transformation operator to apply and, hence, which state to move to next), although the state space representation itself already serves to limit the scope of possible decisions: We can only choose to move from one allowable state to another; there are no possibilities outside of this set of discrete, well-defined states.

The game of tic-tac-toe (or noughts and crosses), like most games, can provide us with an easy example of a symbolic search space, a space that is searched by both players each of whom is attempting to be the first to attain a goal state.

The three-by-three playing grid is represented by a three-by-three matrix, and any position is Pij, where the row index i has the value 1,2, or 3, and the column index j ranges over the same three integers. Thus, the central position is P22, and the upper-left corner is P11, and so on. The initial state is characterized by a description which stipulates that, for all allowable values of i and j, Pij is empty. The goal states (for the player using crosses) is a configuration that contains three Pij's in a "line" (where *line* is defined as row, column, or diagonal), each of which has a cross in it and no similarly defined line of noughts. The set of intermediate states are the intermediate configurations of the matrix obtainable by applying legal sequences of transformation operators from the initial state. The transformation operators are placing a cross and placing a nought in an empty position in the matrix, and the two operators must be applied alternatively. The intelligence would be supplied by method (2) above: that is, there would be a state-evaluation function that tells you which of the possible subsequent states attainable from any current position is 'closest' to a goal state. Such formal or abstract games (as opposed to concrete games like football and cricket) fit very nicely into the SSSP, and are consequently popular choices for AI research. They are also poor choices for elucidating the nature of human intelligence, as Marr (1977) has pointed out. He said that, when solving such formal problems, we are certainly doing something well, but it is not the formal problem solving; that we are very bad at (but this point will be awarded a full section of this chapter, so I shall drop it for now).

The Newell and Simon program somewhat immodestly called the General Problem Solver (GPS) is a concrete manifestation of one form of the

SSSP. It could be, and was, applied to a number of rather different problems, but the individual customization work needed to fit each problem to GPS's requirements was excessive. The problems had to be programmed in GPS! With not too much exaggeration one could claim that any FORTRAN compiler is a general problem solver. If you program your problem correctly in FORTRAN, then the compiler will "solve" it. GPS did introduce and explore the means–ends-analysis subparadigm, a general approach to well-specified problem solving that has found much useful application in AI systems.

"GPS was a dream come false," maintains Haugeland (1985, p. 183). He singles out two, crucial, unfulfilled assumptions that GPS relied on:

1. All problems are pretty much alike; and
2. *Formulating* a problem is the smaller job, compared to solving it once it's formulated.

There is little general evidence for the truth of (1), and in fact the move to expert systems can be viewed as a rejection of (1): Build special-purpose systems rather than general ones. You may recall the mention of weak methods in Chapter 1 and that means–ends analysis is one such method. Well, perhaps it's too weak to be of any real use.

The second unfulfilled assumption, so Haugeland claims, undermines, not only GPS, but heuristic search in general. The formulation of a problem, or the chosen representation if you prefer, can be the major determinant of whether we are faced with a hard or a trivial problem.

The mutilated chess board is the popular example: Remove a square from diagonally opposite corners of a chess board; can the board, which now comprises only 62 squares, be covered with exactly 31 dominoes given that each domino can cover two adjacent squares? The obvious and straightforward formulation yields a vast search space which can, in principle, be explored exhaustively: Choose a start square and generate a state for each possible placement of a domino on the chosen square and one of its neighbors; for each state place a second domino on an uncovered square, and for each of these placements generate the further set of alternative placements; and so on. In principle it is doable. You will either find a covering configuration or exhaust all possibilties. In practice, you'll exhaust yourself, wear out the computer, and run into the heat death of the Universe before the space has been thoroughly explored.

A better formulation of the problem exploits the usual two-color patterning (the two squares removed are of the same color, and each domino must cover two differently colored squares). Now the problem is trivial;

the answer is obvious — isn't it? Enough clues. This is one of the few tractable problems in this book that is left to the reader. So don't waste it.

Edward de Bono, whose "Jelly Model" of the brain gets a mention later, treats the reader to a number of such problems as part of his exposition of "lateral thinking" (de Bono, 1969). For example, in the usual style of a knockout tennis tournament, the winner of a match moves into the next round while the loser is out of the tournament. If in any round there are an odd number of players (not to be confused with a number of odd players), then one lucky person gets a bye into the next round while the rest have to slog it out in individual two-person matches. If 51 people enter a tournament, how many matches must be played to produce the tournament winner? Easy, it's just a sum of successive halvings of 51 with the minor complication of byes when the halving results in an odd number; that is, the answer is $25 + 13 + 6 + 3 + 2 + 1$. Alternatively, there must be 50 losers, hence 50 matches.

It's great fun, but sadly the point's made, so we had better move on. Much AI has focused exclusively on *solving* problems formulated within the SSSP; this approach is wide open to the criticism that the insight and imagination, indeed the bulk of the intelligent problem solving, was done by the human prior to the searching of the space formulated.

This problem has not been totally neglected in AI. Korf (1980), for example, addresses the pros and cons of changing the representation of a problem in order to make it more easily solvable, but he operates only in the domain of well-defined puzzles.

In essence, the means–ends analysis subparadigm presents problem solving as the selection of transformation operators that reduce the "distance" between a given state (initially, the starting state) and the goal state, but it typically runs into the impassable rapids (impassable with simple means–ends analysis certainly) of nonmonotonicity — that is, a solution path in which every successive step results in an intermediate state that is closer to the goal state cannot be found. This is a first example of the curse of nonmonotonicity, a general AI problem that is featured in a subsequent chapter.

Thus, if the problem is to build a car, then a system driven by means–ends analysis might observe that all cars have engines and that, if an engine is built, it will have reduced the distance between the initial no-car state and the goal state, car. Thus it tackles the subproblem of building an engine. All engines have ignition systems; hence, if it builds an ignition system, it will have reduced the distance between the no-engine and have-engine states in this subproblem. To build an ignition system, it might conclude that building spark plugs is one way to reduce the distance between the substate no-ignition-system and the subgoal state, ignition-system. Hence, it begins the car-building problem by designing a spark plug!

This fictitious example of the problems of means–ends analysis also illustrates the unfortunate repercussions that quickly compound to absurdity when the discrete-independent-states approximation to problem representation is a poor one.

Winograd and Flores (1986), whose case against the SSSP we'll see more of in Chapter 5, criticize the notion of a well-defined problem space of alternative possibilities. "It is not clear for what observer this space of alternatives exists." They describe the context-free nature of the SSSP as a failure to deal with the question of background. For real-life situations we cannot lay out a space of alternatives and assign a valuation to each. It is impossible to apply systematic decision techniques. In addition, there is always a bias inherent in formulating the situation as one of choosing between these alternatives. There is no *relevant* space of alternatives in a context-independent sense. "Relevance always comes from a pre-orientation within a background" (Winograd & Flores, 1986, p. 149). A problematic situation today may dissolve away tomorrow, or may change its apparent form drastically after living with it for a few days. The intersection of the supposed spaces of alternatives for two different people, or even for one person on one day and the next, may be empty. This is scathing criticism, especially from the creator of SHRDLU, a program which is often said to be the most-cited system in AI, and of course we'll add a few more citations to the heap before the end of this book.

A less radical account of why my car-design example fared poorly under the ministrations of means–ends analysis is also available. "Of course simple means–ends analysis generated poor solutions. You've gotta have a *plan*," the vocal reader must be itching to tell me. So let's look at the planning subfield of AI.

PLANNING INTELLIGENT SOLUTIONS

From the SSSP perspective planning is an obvious component of intelligent behavior. We don't just slavishly attempt to reduce differences or blindly follow some weak strategy; we look ahead and plan. Intelligent problem solving involves foresight and planning. An intelligent system is executing some sort of plan when trying to solve a problem. In the context of the SSSP planning becomes a process of identifying desirable future states (in particular, the goal state) and devising possible routes from the current (initially, the start) state.

The resultant plans may vary from complete (even proven correct) to decidedly skimpy, or skeletal, which means that some subplans have been elaborated while others have not. In the former case all the problem solving has been done, and it only remains for the system to actually traverse the well-marked route; whereas in the case of only a partial plan, some necessary intermediate state characteristics may have been decided upon, and these are then employed within the subsequent search to limit and to guide the selection of the next "best" state from time to time within the problem-solving traversal of the search space.

An early, significant, but only tangentially influential book on planning relevant to AI was *Plans and the Structure of Behavior* by Miller, Galanter, and Pribram (1960). The celebrity but lack of direct impact of this unlikely trio is captured in the old joke: Miller thought of it, Galanter wrote it, and Pribram believed it.

The essential contribution of this book was the notion of a TOTE (Test-Operate-Test-Exit) as illustrated in Figure 3.2.

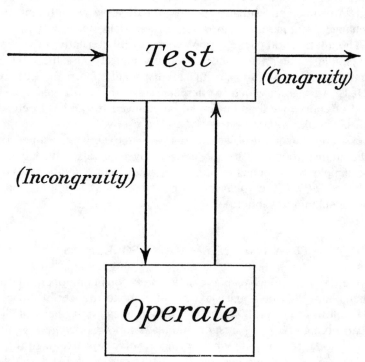

Figure 3.2.   The TOTE unit

From *Plans and Structures of Behavior* (p. 20) by G.A. Miller, E. Galanter, & K.H. Pribram, 1960. Reprinted by permission of authors.

The TOTE represents the basic pattern in terms of which plans are cast, "the test phase of the TOTE involves the specification of whatever knowledge is necessary for the comparison that is to be made, and the operation phase represents what the organism does about it" (Miller, Galanter, & Pribram, 1960, p. 31). "A plan is any hierarchical process in the organism that can control the order in which a sequence of operations is to be performed" (p. 16). The challenge for this threesome is to bridge

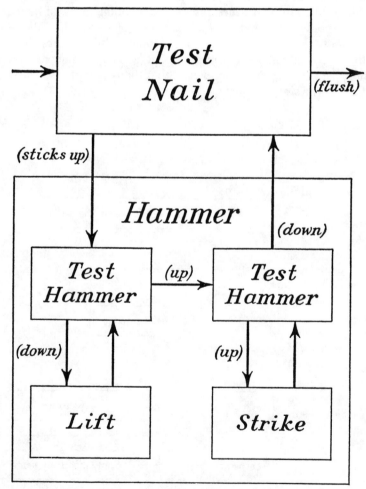

Figure 3.3.   The hierarchical plan for hammering nails

From *Plans and Structures of Behavior* (p. 36) by G.A. Miller, E. Galanter, & K.H. Pribram, 1960. Reprinted by permission of authors.

the gap between knowledge and action, and their approach is to integrate TOTEs into hierarchical structures, such as, plans. An example of one of their constructions is the plan for hammering nails illustrated in Figure 3.3.

This conception of planning was developed at the dawn of modern AI. It was clearly a "cybernetic" view, but launched in the years when this approach to explaining intelligent behavior (explanations or accounts in which feedback control loops were the dominant mechanism) was being submerged by the new AI — heuristic programming.

Miller et al. state that "the fundamental building block of the nervous system is the feedback loop," and they point out that this is the "cybernetic hypothesis" of Wiener (1948). We might also note the attempt to take the biological phenomena into account (and as our gang of three were psychologists of one sort of another, rather than computer scientists, this is not too surprising).

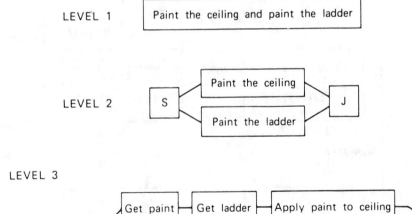

Figure 3.4. A procedural net plan for painting

From *A Structure for Plans and Behavior* (p. 10), by E.D. Sacerdoti, 1977, New York: Elsevier. Copyright 1977 by Elsevier. Reprinted by permission.

Well, it turned out that limiting plan structure to the integration of simple feedback loops was too much of a limitation. Similarly, the architecture of the human nervous system was also judged to be largely irrelevant. The computer scientists had moved in and taken over planning. They switched to logic-based planning and heuristic methods.

"So why bring up this old stuff about TOTEs?" you have every reason to demand. There is a good reason (apart from the real reason of wanting to get a famous old joke on record in hard copy). Even though planning appears to have no role in the new connectionism (the major alternative paradigm which dominates the latter half of this chapter), we shall see that feedback loops and concerns of neuroanatomy have made a comeback in recent years. Elsewhere (Partridge, 1985a) I have surveyed the modern manifestations of the feedback loop in AI. Now read on.

A number of early AI programming languages specifically addressed the issue of planning as the key to AI. The language PLANNER (Hewitt, 1972) was partly implemented by Sussman and Winograd (1970) and was used very successfully in the famous SHRDLU system (see Chapter 8). SHRDLU is regarded as the first sytem to link planning and language analysis.

The next development was to provide a mechanism for separating out the plan knowledge from the domain knowledge, the specific search space. This move gave us the language CONNIVER (McDermott & Sussman, 1972), another short-lived foray into special-purpose languages for AI programming. I review and explain the current thinking on programming languages for AI in the next chapter.

Plans then became *procedural nets*. Such a net is "a graph structure whose nodes represent actions at varying levels of detail, organized into a hierarchy of partially ordered time sequences," so Sacerdoti (1977) tells us. Sacerdoti's book, *A Structure for Plans and Behavior* (would you believe, it's as if there's a shortage of suitable words for titling books on planning) describes the NOAH system, which eschewed the "highly contrived and simplified problem domains involving [abstract representations of] toy blocks . . . [and] was designed to deal with the real and complex world of electromechanical machinery repair"(Nilsson, in the preface).

A procedural net plan is illustrated in Figure 3.4.

In this hierarchy of plans *S* stands for *split*, and *J* for *join*. This is clearly a toy plan, and it would be of little real use. Nevertheless, we can already see one awkward problem that was resolved by the Noah system in the refinement step from LEVEL 2 to LEVEL 3: The ceiling really ought to be painted before the ladder. How did NOAH figure this out? It used a hand-crafted heuristic, of course. In addition, whenever Noah was faced with selection of a plan element from a number of alternatives, it picked one, discarded the rest, and moved on; it did not 'backtrack' {i.e., when a plan failed or planning with a partial plan was thwarted, it did not return to the earlier choice points in the space and select a fresh alternative—one of the previously discarded ones; it just abandoned the project}. Later work, Tate's (1977) Nonlin system, for example, attempted to rectify this weakness. The Devisor system of Vere (1983) also developed and extended the simple Noah-style planning. Charniak and McDermott (1985) focus attention on these planning systems.

Most of the planning schemes work steadily top-down {i.e., general subplans such as 'get into room X' are successively refined until they are specified at the desired level of detail, e.g., 'go_to_doorway→open_ door→go_through_doorway' might be the next stage of refinement of my general subplan, and so on}. Alternatively, the planning system may work steadily building a complete plan at the required level of detail from beginning to end. Human planning does not appear to be constrained by either of these simple linearities, and some AI work has examined and modelled the "opportunistic" planning of humans. The Hayes-Roths (Hayes-Roth & Hayes-Roth, 1979), for example, have explored this flavor of planning. Skeletal plans are developed and elaborated in a discontinuous fashion; that is, the various subplans are developed to whatever degree is possible as and when the relevant information becomes available. They propose to use a "blackboard" architecture, which is not an edifice composed of old chalkboards, as you will find out if you read through Chapter 6. Cohen and Feigenbaum (1982), in their chapter on "Planning and Problem Solving," discuss this venture as well as the MOLGEN, a molecular genetics planning system modeled on human experiment-planning behavior.

Hurrying on and looking back, we can see that one major branch of planning can be found in the domain of natural-language processing. Sentence "understanding" and text generation both seem to require plans. Schank and Abelson (1977) attacked the former problem in their book *Scripts, Goals and Plans*, although they address the problems of plan recognition, not plan construction. Schank's scripts (which are a sort of plan for "understanding") are covered in Chapter 8. Wilensky (1983) followed up this work and presents for our consideration both PANDORA and PAM. The latter system, Plan Applier Mechanism, "has knowledge about the kinds of plans and goals people have, and uses this knowledge in accordance with the preceding [in his book, but not this one] algorithm to find explanations for the events described in a text"(p. 48). Again, we pick up the threads of this work in Chapter 8, and we look at this general category of AI work in Chapter 10 where PAM is singled out as an exemplar of "speculative" AI. Within the chapter on natural language processing (Chapter 8) we might note that the text generation scheme discussed by Appelt includes the idea of logic-based plans, and so provides a cross link between the current and the following category of planning work.

Another major branch of planning is the logic-based approach. Crudely put: The initial state is a set of axioms, the things that we know to be true; the goal state is a theorem, something that we would like to be true; and the plan is a proven path between the two, a proof of the theorem. The robot SHAKEY was an early user of such plans. If asked to go to the window, it would first prove that there was a path from where it currently was to the window. And only when it had a solid proof-plan did it change out of neutral and attempt to actually get to the window. Sadly, the real world kept intruding, gears slipped, friction failed to obey its laws, and often SHAKEY didn't make it. Raphael (1976) provides a case study of SHAKEY, and the STRIPS systems for plan generation (STRIPS, RSTRIPS, and ABSTRIPS) are described in detail by Nilsson (1980).

In this type of plan the essential unit was not a feedback loop but a triple: preconditions (the things that must be true before an operation can be applied); an action or operation; and postconditions (the things that have changed because the operation was executed). Thus, SHAKEY might have possessed, but didn't, the following ENTER_ ROOM triple:

preconditions: in_front_of_doorway & door_open
action: go_through_doorway
postconditions: through_doorway

That is, if it was in front of the doorway and the door was open, then it could go through the doorway. Thus, the only change in the state of the world as a result of executing this action was a change in its own location, but that could be critical if it was now in the room that contained the goal state window which it was planning to arrive at. Many such primitive triples can be strung together, and substantial plans can be built.

So, if SHAKEY is faced with a closed door and the necessity to get into the room, then the DOOR_OPEN triple is used in the plan immediately preceding the ENTER_ROOM triple. The DOOR_OPEN triple is:

preconditions: in_front_of_door & door_closed
action: open_door
postconditions: in_front_of_doorway & door_open

The point to notice about this trivial example is that the postconditions of DOOR_OPEN exactly match the preconditions of ENTER_ROOM; hence, the two can be linked to give a viable plan fragment (subplan), as illustrated in Figure 3.5.

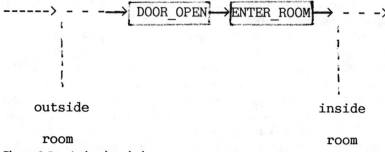

Figure 3.5. A simple subplan

I've glossed over some complications, some of which must be brought to the reader's attention even in this attempt at a cursory guide to planning in AI. Normally, the state of the planning system is defined by more than the pre- and postconditions in the triples of immediate interest. Thus our robot with the pressing need to enter the room might have had his hand raised all through our subdrama. It wasn't mentioned because it did not impact on the subplanning that was done (he can use his other hand to open the door, in case you were about to dispute this claim). To get to the point, the pre- and postconditions usually just add and delete things from the state definition of the planning system. {Hence, you should not be surprised to read of ADDLISTS and DELETELISTS in the context of planning systems.}

So what is the state of our drama after executing our two subplans, that is, at the position labeled "inside room" in Figure 3.5? Well, before executing DOOR_OPEN followed by ENTER_ROOM we know that "in_front_of_door & door_closed" was true (otherwise we couldn't have executed the DOOR_OPEN subplan. After executing the DOOR_ OPEN subplan "in_front_of_doorway & door_open" is true—the subplan tells us this. So we've added these true facts to the description of SHAKEY's current state. But, looking at the total state description, we should not be delighted to find both "door_open" and "door_closed" sitting there quietly with equal rights to the notion of truth. It may be that, in some possible world, one and the same door can be both open and closed at the same time, but this is not it. "That's easy," you might be tempted to respond, "just add '& NOT_door_closed' to the post condition of the DOOR_OPEN subplan." And, sure enough, this fixes our specific problem, but what about all the other possible effects on the world at large, or even on SHAKEY's small world, that execution of an action might cause? They cannot all be explicitly mentioned in each subplan. The problem of avoiding absurdities and yet keeping the explicit mention of subplan effects to a minimum is one manifestation of the *frame problem* in AI. A hefty section in Chapter 10 revisits this and other headaches that the logicist approach to AI brings with it. Now decide where SHAKEY really is after executing these two subplans.

Not only can such plans be built, but they can be proved correct. And this all works quite well until the door sticks during execution of the plan, or the handle comes off, or the door is locked. But, of course, these things don't happen in abstract worlds. Equally obviously, they do happen all the time in the world that we live in, which is one of the reasons why we are not constantly falling over SHAKEY's successors as we go about our business in the real world. Planning for the myriad of unforeseen eventualities that the real world exhibits is a major obstacle to progress. Elsewhere (Partridge, 1986a), I've discussed, with examples, the gulf that separates abstract AI and concrete AI. I also plug my prejudices on this issue in the final chapter. Plans for abstract problem solving and plans for a robot that must actually execute them in a real world (even a drastically simplified one) are very different classes of problem. If all this is unobvious, then I'm afraid that you'll just have to consult one of the references I've given.

Let me wind up this overly long, quick tour of planning as an SSSP subfield with a summary of current thinking. Logics are the favored formalism for much planning work, and work in planning is a driving force behind the development of new schemes of logic (see, for example, D. McDermott's, 1982, "Temporal Logic for Reasoning about Processes and Plans"). Planning research has also progressed beyond the machinations of the isolated intelligent agent with only itself and the world to worry about. Planning in multiagent environments is now of great interest (e.g., Konolige, 1982). But as a diversion you might look at Carbonell's (1983) scheme for learning plans by analogical reasoning from specific, successful solution sequences. And Eshgi's (1987) "abductive planning with event calculus" will give you some insight into the sort of thing that the logicists are up to.

Steel (1987) provides a very readable introduction to planning, uncluttered by acronymic references to the planning failures of yesteryear. But to compensate for this he appends an annotated bibliography of the AI planning literature to his article. He also discusses "interval-based planning," which I have not. Steel recommends Grant (1986) as the most comprehensive bibliography on planning that he is aware of. Charniak and McDermott (1985) devote a chapter to planning which is, as they say, a chapter about robots. This is a focus that brings us right back to the Miller et al. view of planning as a bridge between knowledge and action. On reflection, you don't really need plans for abstract problem solving, because planning *is* abstract problem solving. But much AI planning is associated with abstract problem solving, so the reader should not be nonplussed if the terminology appears disputable.

SSSP INFRASTRUCTURE

The specific problem domains considered in *Human Problem Solving* (Newell & Simon, 1972) are cryptarithmetic, logic, and chess—three classes of problems that have certain important similarities (one of which is that the discrete-independent-states approximation is not a poor one), and moreover, similarities that are significant with respect to the taxonomy of expert problem-solving domains which we consider in Chapter 5 as well as to the question of bad AI paradigms (a question that currently seems to be resisting my attempts to drop it).

Newell and Simon's approach to what I have termed the SSSP is via the *physical symbol system hypothesis*, and within this general framework they extract and classify a commonly used mechanism as the *heuristic search hypothesis*. In 1976 they stated *"The Physical Symbol System Hypothesis. A physical symbol system has the necessary and sufficient means for general intelligent action"* (Newell & Simon, 1976, p. 116, author's emphasis). (A more recent formulation is given by Newell, 1980.) This hypothesis is prefaced by a description of a physical symbol system (PSS) which is summarized as: "a machine that produces through time an evolving collection of symbol structures" (p. 116). In addition, two notions — called "designation" and "interpretation" — are presented as central to the structure of expressions (or symbol structures). "An expression designates an object if, given the expression, the system can either affect the object or behave in ways dependent on the object . . . The system can interpret an expression if the expression designates a process and if, given the expression, the system can carry out the process" (p. 116). Thus a LISP machine (not necessarily the latest AI hardware, but any computer running a LISP interpreter) is close to their idea of a PSS.

The claim is that the PSS hypothesis is an empirical one. Thus we should expect to find support and, more importantly, the possibility of contrary evidence (i.e., a basis for refutation) in empirical data. They claim that the successes of AI — the construction and demonstration of intelligent systems — is evidence for the sufficiency of the PSS hypothesis. Evidence for the necessity is claimed to lie in the successes of cognitive psychology in explaining man's intelligent behavior in terms of symbol systems. Lastly, they raise the possibility of negative evidence: specific competing alternative hypotheses as to how intelligence might be accomplished — by man or machine. They note the absence of such competing hypotheses; they mention several possible candidates for this role (such as: behaviorism or Gestalt theory), but point out that "it is not terribly difficult to give them [the potential competitors] information processing interpretations, and thereby assimilate them to the symbol system hypothesis" (Newell & Simon, 1976, p. 120). Newell and Simon attribute this ease of recruitment of potential competitors into the ranks of supporting evidence as due to the vagueness of the supposed alternatives. A more hardnosed explanation of the lack of competing alternatives is that the PSS hypothesis leaves little or no room for them, and, if this is the case, then the PSS hypothesis would seem to have added correspondingly little to the sum of our knowledge. This point is important when we come to examine connectionism as a paradigm to support AI, and when we consider the status of connectionism vis-á-vis the SSSP.

I find myself in agreement with Dietrich (1990), who, with commendable forthrightness, calls a spade a spade, and, what's more to the point, he calls these "hypotheses" AI dogma.

Within the pile of demonstrations of intelligent systems that Newell and Simon (1976) see, they also discern a fairly ubiquitous general mechanism which they frame as "the Heuristic Search Hypothesis. The solutions to problems are represented as symbol structures. A physical symbol system exercises its intelligence in problem solving by search — that is, by generating and progressively modifying symbol structures until it produces a solution structure. Physical symbol systems must use heuristic search to solve problems because such systems have [practically] limited processing resources."

A fundamental problem in explicating these ideas arises because it is never quite said what exactly a *symbol* is, or what classes of objects symbols can, and cannot, be used to represent. More precisely, what sort of things are not "symbolic"? What are the representational limits of a "symbolic" search space? The term *symbol* is a multiple warhead; it aims at different targets in different contexts. Newell and Simon originally used the word to distinguish the general use of computers as symbol processing devices from the common misconception that they were limited to number crunching applications. Thus, "symbolic" meant not-numeric. Of late the "symbolic" paradigm is more commonly distinguished from the subsymbolic paradigm of connectionism (e.g., Smolensky, 1987). In this context "symbolic" means a cognitive concept, something that we can put a conceptually meaningful label on, such as *apple, dog*, etc. It is not clear to me that, for example, the so-called subsymbolic elements of connectionist theory (to be discussed later) are not symbols, and that patterns of activation are not symbol structures. Nevertheless, there seems to be tacit agreement at least that symbols correspond roughly to unitary concepts: things for which we have simple labels ready and at hand (obviously this description, depending as it does on linguistic abilities, is fraught with problems and therefore unsatisfactory, but it captures the general idea with a minimum of fuss, I think). And unfortunately, a similar tacit belief in the converse (i.e., that simple labels designate unitary concepts) has led to no end of problems and delusions of grandeur in AI: When labels such as *intend, believe,* etc. are attached to the primitive elements of a theory, then the significance of the supposed theory cannot be taken for granted, to say the least.

Nevertheless, the elements of folk psychology are typically the symbols used in manifestations of the SSSP. As a result symbol structures, or expressions, tend to be objects such as propositions—e.g., JOHN THINKS THAT HE IS SICK. Intelligent decision making is then modeled by expressions such as: IF (THROWING-UP AND FEMALE) THEN PREGNANT 0.4. A more realistic example can be taken from the MYCIN program:

IF (GRAM-STAIN NEGATIVE) AND (SHAPE-IS ROD) AND (AEROBICITY ANAEROBIC) THEN (ORGANISM BACTEROIDES)

A set of such rules can be integrated with a logical inference mechanism, and then we have the bones of Current Expert Systems' Technology (and these we shall gnaw at in Chapter 5).

THE PIVOTAL ROLE OF SEARCHING STRATEGIES

Given that AI problems can be conceptualized in terms of discrete search spaces in which certain states are goal states — solutions to the problem — then problem solving becomes manifest as stepping through a sequence of states starting from some initial state and looking for a goal state. What makes these problems AI problems is that we do not have the wherewithal (time and/or knowledge) to look everywhere until a goal state is found. It is not usually possible to search the space exhaustively.

A second, additional or alternative, feature that characterizes AI problems is that we can't always recognize a goal state with certainty. This is the SSSP analog of the methodological issue, discussed in the previous chapter, of system output not always being clearly either correct or incorrect.

Recognizing a goal state is one thing, but first you have to locate some potential goal states. As the old saying goes (after some remodeling): A potential goal state in the hand is worth two in the search space. Thus discovering potential goal states is the first, and perhaps the major, problem. Hence, search strategies are a central concern in the SSSP.

Search spaces are usually presented as tree structures. Thus the tic-tac-toe game yields the following arboreal representation (Figure 3.6).

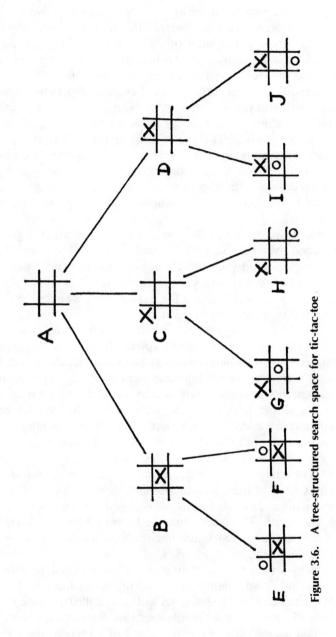

Figure 3.6. A tree-structured search space for tic-tac-toe

Now this diagram may not look much like a tree to the unbiased eye, but it is. Stand on your head, or turn the book upside down (whichever you prefer), and the arboreal character of this representation may become apparent. The single initial state (no tics, tacs, or toes, just an empty grid — state A) is the start point (called the *tree root* for reasons that elude me), and the tree branches up and out from there. Does it not?

Reestablishing once more the normal relationship between self and book: The state transformation operators are the legal moves of the game. Thus, if we add the first cross in the center of the grid, we transform state A into state B. The above illustrated chunk of the tic-tac-toe search space contains no goal states; they start to appear further on into the search space. Given an acre or two of paper and nothing better to do, one could draw out the complete search space for this game. A point to note is that, even for this exceedingly trivial game, the search space is large.

Many search spaces are really graph structures in which a given state can be reached by several alternative paths through the space, but they can still be represented, and searched, as trees (in which there is only one path from the root to any state in the tree).

There are two major strategies for exhaustively searching such trees for goal states (i.e., problem solving in the SSSP): depth-first and breadth-first searches. In a *depth-first search* you climb from the root to the tip of a branch looking for a goal state. If you don't find one, then you climb down (this is known as *backtracking*) until you reach an unexplored branch, and then you search that one right to its tip, and so on. In a depth-first search you immediately search out to the very top of the tree (although it's at the bottom of the structure in the conventional upside-down representation — hence, depth-first). Thus a depth-first search of the partial search space illustrated above would result in examining the nodes in the order: A, B, E, F, C, G, H, D, I, J.

In the major alternative strategy, *breadth-first search,* you start at the root and look at all of the states that branch directly out of the root, and then at all of the states that branch directly out of the ones you've just explored, and so on. The tree is searched level by level. A breadth-first search of the partial search space illustrated above would examine the nodes in the following order: A, B, C, D, E, F, G, H, I, J. Physically, such a strategy would be exhausting as well as exhaustive with all the necessary up and down climbing, but algorithmically there's not much to choose between them. Both strategies will search the complete tree, they just examine the states in a different order. So, if you've got some reason to believe that a gaol state is down the end of a branch, use depth-first search, and, if the rumors suggest that what you're looking for may be close to the root, then use a breadth-first search. In fact, a breadth-first search (if it terminates) is guaranteed to find the shortest path to a solution. Think about it. In most AI applications, of course, neither search is of any use on its own.

A major variant of these two basic search strategies is to work backwards from a goal state. This may appear to be rather perverse, given that it is goal states that we're looking for, but it's the existence of a path between an initial state and a goal state that confirms that the suspected goal state is indeed a goal state for that particular initial state. So, if we have some reason to suspect (e.g., a guess, or external information) that some state is the goal state that we are looking for, it may be appropriate to search backwards and confirm the suspicion by finding a path from from the initial state to this suspected goal state.

Such searching is commonly used in expert systems where it is termed *backwards reasoning* or *backwards chaining*. It will thus be dealt with in Chapter 5.

I might point out at this juncture that searching problem spaces (although not typically symbolic ones) is also characteristic of the CP. But the parallelism inherent in this paradigm results in a parallel, breadth-first search. Similarly, marker-passing mechanisms (e.g., Quillian, 1968; Fahlman, 1979; Charniak, 1983 in AI; Collins & Loftus, 1975; McClelland & Rumelhart, 1981, in the more cognitive science oriented spreading activation theories) employ a parallel, breadth-first search of a symbolic search space. But, as we shall see, the object of searches in CP-based systems is not usually the discovery of a path from some initial state to a goal state, it is the discovery of, for example, a minimum "energy" configuration of activity in the network (see the section on bath-like architectures in Chapter 6).

Exhaustive search is not usually possible, and hence, depth-first or breadth-first strategies simply form a basis upon which more complicated searches are built. In the terminology of AI: heuristics are used to prune the search space. Heuristics rules cut out large portions of the search space as areas where (according to the heuristic) goal states are unlikely to be found.

HEURISTIC PRUNING

In tic-tac-toe, for example (to persist with this example of a bad paradigm), some useful heuristics are easily devised. We can construct a heuristic state evaluation function: a function that evaluates any state in the space in terms of its 'closeness' to a goal state (for, say, the crosses player). Thus useful heuristics to incorporate into a state evaluation function might be:

- The more winning paths through any position with a cross, the better that position is (implemented as, say, the sum of the number of possible winning paths through each cross on the grid).
- The more instances of two crosses in a row with an empty third position, the better that position is.
- and so on (dream up some more for yourself).

Before you are tempted to lie back, close you eyes, and dream up some heuristics for your favorite AI problem, take note of the following example of the perils of intuitional heuristics. Consider the game un-tic-tac-toe (or three-in-a-line avoidance: the first player to get three of his symbols in a line loses). We can quite plausibly employ a heuristic that rates board states in terms of the number of ways that there is to lose for each unoccupied position on the board. The higher this heuristic value, after my move, the better is the board state rated, i.e., I should choose to place my cross (assuming that's my agreed symbol) in the lowest-rated unoccupied board position, the position through which there are the least losing paths. This plausible heuristic always leads to disaster (if one can consider a loss at un-tic-tac-toe to be disastrous).

To see this point, consider the empty board. The center position rates 4 (i.e, there are four losing paths through the center), a corner rates 3, and the middle of a side rates 2. Thus this heuristic will always direct you to place your cross in the middle of a side, but in fact the only way to avoid losing is to choose the worst-rated position, the middle of the board! (This example and numerous others are scheduled to appear in Frank Harary's forthcoming book (in preparation) on mathematical games.)

The chosen heuristic (or heuristics; you are not, of course, limited to one only) becomes part of a state evaluation function: Give the function a possible grid configuration (note: some conceivable grid configurations, like three crosses, are not possible configurations in the game), and it will give you back a number that indicates how good that state is for you (i.e., how close it is to a goal state — a winning configuration in this game playing example). A further desirable feature of the state evaluation function is that it signals the presence of an "impossible" intermediate state (i.e., a state that cannot lead to a goal state) at the earliest opportunity. The search space is pruned by examining some (or all) of the possible next states from any current state, evaluating each of them, and electing to further explore from the one that is "best". Hence, the other possible alternative states are explored no further — the branches that start with each of them are pruned out of the search space for the purposes of the current exploration. This search strategy is, you might be surprised to learn, known as a *best-first search*.

Many variants of this simplistically described mechanism are employed. Thus we may evaluate, not next states, but more distant possible future states, and then "back up" the evaluations obtained (using for example, the minimax algorithm with alpha-beta pruning) to thereby obtain indirect evaluations of the possible next states. The philosophy underlying this wheeze is that the closer a state is to the goal state, the more accurate the state evaluation function will be. This is the *"lookahead"* *strategy;* its use is somewhat paradoxical {for all the information on possible future states is in any state, so why not extract it and use it instead of actually going there? Hofstadter (1979) has an interesting discussion of this nonpressing, but curious, detail; is it just a case of implicit information being made explicit by actually generating future states?}.

A second major variant of my simplistic scheme, outlined earlier is to not discard (or prune off) all but the best state but to save the close contenders (at least) for future "backtracking" should the apparently best choice prove to be a dud. Thus in the "nicely-pruned search space" illustrated below, if nodes 12, 13, and 14 prove to be dead-ends rather than 14 being the sought-after goal state (in which case, of course, it is no longer a nicely pruned search space, for, however aesthetically pleasing it may be, the pruning cannot be classed as 'nice' if it leads to a dead end rather than a goal state), then the strategy might be to backtrack. We

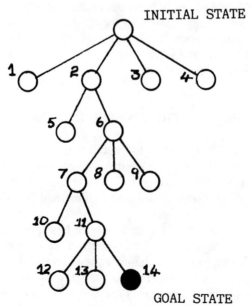

INITIAL STATE

GOAL STATE

Figure 3.7.   A nicely pruned search space

might restart the search at whichever of the pruned-off branches (i.e., the branches *rooted* — a biologically suspect, but formally correct, term — at nodes 1, 3, 4, 5, 8, 9, and 10) is heuristically rated as the best.

And so on, plausibly useful heuristics are many, ways to implement them are legion, and analytical evaluations are scarce (although quite possible in a trivial, well-defined game like tic-tac-toe — see "Bad" Paradigms, coming soon). In general, the worth of such heuristics is an empirical question: "try it and see" is the evaluation procedure.

Nilsson's (1980) introductory AI book is focused on the formal results of searching discrete, well-defined, symbolic spaces. To my way of thinking, the minimax algorithm, alpha-beta pruning, and proofs of formal "admissability" (i.e., that a given class of heuristic search algorithms will always terminate in an optimal path to a goal node whenever a path to a goal node exists), etc., which are often claimed as AI's successes (e.g., McCarthy, 1990), are all solid techniques. And, moreover, they are techniques that were significant milestones in the history of AI. But they are clearly of limited applicability (outside the 'bad' paradigms which occupy a later section of this chapter), and, as such, they are unlikely to play a major role in the future breakthroughs of AI. I thus salute them as major AI discoveries, but ones whose sell-by date has past.

Pearl (1984) provides an exhaustive treatment of heuristic-based searching of such spaces. All the details are there, which relieves me of the necessity of regurgitating them in this book, as I also happen to feel that much of this paradigm, when applied only to well-defined, abstract games and puzzles is not central to the future development of AI, as I have said. A much broader, but less directly relevant to the SSSP, view of heuristics is provided in the collection of papers edited by Groner, Groner, and Bischof (1983).

CONNECTIONISM: A POSSIBLE ALTERNATIVE?

As mentioned above, arguments to the effect that the SSSP did not apply to certain domains of human problem solving and decision making were always stymied by the retort: What then is the mechanism — magic? Something a little less insubstantial and chimerical was demanded, even in AI.

In recent years the field of connectionism has sprung up (or re-arisen Phoenix-like from the ashes of the Perceptron, as I claim in a later chapter); it appears to embody a mechanism outside the umbrella of the SSSP. It has yet to prove its real worth as a model of human decision making (i.e., the flight of the Phoenix may be short; it may leave its mark on history more in terms of initial panache than of sustained utility), but it is a concrete alternative that we can point to. Even if it does not prove to be the answer, it has at least opened up afresh the possibility that there are, or could be, significant alternatives to the SSSP. Although I might say, at this point, that it is not clear that connectionism is an alternative to the SSSP. Fields and Dietrich (1987), for example, claim that their "transition virtual machine" embodies a connectionist symbolic search space. It may be viewed more as a precisely correct mechanism for which the symbolic paradigm is an approximation. In other words, connectionism is not an independent alternative, it is just a more precise level of specification than the SSSP can lay claim to (as Smolensky, 1988, for example, argues).

The basis for the radical difference from SSSP-based mechanisms is that connectionist models are founded on networks of subsymbolic units connected by weighted links. Each unit has a current activity value. Activity is passed around the network in a parallel (or even massively parallel) manner as some function of the current activity of a unit and the weights on the links from it to other units. Thus the activity of the individual units changes over time, and the weights of the links may also be modified over time. An individual unit does not represent anything that we can put a meaningful name to, they are thus subsymbolic units. A meaningful, or symbolic, concept is represented by a pattern of activation—a group of units whose activity values all exceed some threshold. The obvious analogy between connectionist networks and neural networks, as in the brain, is both persuasive and often exploited, although arguably very tenuous (see later).

At this point, honesty compels me to interject a clarifying statement. Strictly speaking, nodes in connectionist networks can represent conceptually meaningful objects (e.g., dogs, Mary, robin, animal). The links in such symbolic connectionist networks, though, are still simply weighted arcs whose purpose is to transfer activity from node to node in a parallel fashion. But, in my estimation, it is the subsymbolic networks that hold the promise of a radical alternative paradigm to the SSSP, and so, although I shall give symbolic connectionism some space, an unqualified reference to connectionism should be taken to imply subsymbolic connectionism.

Smolensky (1987) argues for the essential differences between connectionist AI and symbolic AI, and offers reasons why the former approach is expected to be more powerful in a number of respects. For example, when a concept is represented by a pattern of activation rather than by a single unit, we appear to be freed from the need to make binary decisions — present or not present; true or false; etc. A pattern of activation may more or less approximate an ideal, and no two patterns of activation for the same concept would need to be exactly the same. These sorts of considerations sit well with many of our intuitions about human decision making.

Dreyfus and Dreyfus (1990) briefly discuss the potential of connectionist mechanisms as a realization of intuitive human expertise. It can account for why we have so much trouble extracting the symbolic rules that human experts are believed to use; they don't use such rules! A connectionist explanation of human expertise, with its distributed representations, contains no rules at the symbolic level, and it does not use logical inference either (although, as I shall argue, reasoning as if there were symbolic rules and perhaps logical inference may be necessary to support an understanding of such a connectionist system). They conclude that the "combination of phenomenology and connectionism may well be devastating to conventional AI as a *practical* endeavor. Could anything be salvaged of the cognitivist-rationalist intuition that for any domain that can be mastered, there exists a set of features and rules which explains that mastery?" (p. 408). This possibility is dealt with in its rightful place — the chapter on expert systems technology.

Lest we be carried away with the promises of connectionism, I should make it clear that very little has actually been modelled with these networks to date. And, in addition, there are already a number of difficult and unsolved problems facing the connectionist modeler (see Partridge, 1987c). The overriding concern, in my opinion, is one of comprehensibility. In order to build and use complex computer systems, we must be able to understand, at some level, how they are doing what they are observed to be doing. Distributed representations in vast networks are conceptually opaque. So how we will be able to develop, maintain, and generally manage large connectionist systems is a significant problem that has yet to be solved.

So there is a lot of promise, and, there are a lot of unsolved problems, associated with connectionism; we shall examine both aspects in general in this chapter, and in more detail in the subsequent chapters.

CONNECTIONISM: THE SECOND COMING

Recent years have seen a new upsurge of interest and experimentation with networks whose arcs are simply weighted (typically, with a real value) and whose function is to transfer activity, in parallel along each arc, according to the associated weight. The nodes accumulate incoming activity according to some specified function and pass activity on through any outgoing arcs.

I date the resurrection of connectionism from the informal conference held at La Jolla, California in June 1979. The authorized version of the details of this epochal event are recorded in hard copy in *Parallel Models of Associative Memory,* edited by Hinton and Anderson (1981). Thus for the purposes of this book, at least, 1979 is the start of the modern era of connectionism, AC1 (Anno Connectioni 1) for short. Prior to this date events in AI can be dated BC (Before Connectionism), but I'll try to resist this temptation, and occasionally I shall succeed.

Some CP-like AI research was pursued during the 10-year winter of subsymbolic discontent {i.e., from the *Perceptrons* book by Minsky & Papert, 1969, to La Jolla, 1979}. Cunningham (1972), for example, published a book detailing his research which was based on Hebb's (1949) "cell assembly" {cursory details later} model of neural architecture. He combined this CP-like architecture with Piaget's (1936) behavioral model of the learning and development of a child's sensorimotor abilities.

Much of the current wisdom and lore of connectionism is enshrined in the modern classic from the MIT Press, *Parallel Distributed Processing* (Rumelhart & McClelland, 1986). *Cognitive Science,* Vol. 9, No. 1, was devoted to "Connectionist Models and Their Applications" (see Feldman, 1985). Feldman and Ballard (1982) lay out much of the basic ideas underlying modern connectionism. But their pespective is "based explicitly on an abstraction of our current understanding of the information processing properties of neurons." Many other researchers within this general paradigm do not feel fettered by concerns of neuroanatomy. I shall argue later that these two perspectives may not be so very different in practice, because the fetters of neuroanatomy are extremely loose, so loose in fact as to be little or no real constraint on the modeling. One further useful compendium is *Neurocomputing: Foundations of Research,* edited by Anderson and Rosenfeld (1988). It is a collection of reprints, and contains many of the early papers as well as a good group of state-of-the-art expositions.

Two major categories of connectionist networks may be distinguished (as I admitted earlier): In one category, the nodes represent symbols as in conventional semantic networks (curiously, this is also the category addressed by Feldman and Ballard. What they claim is that, although is it highly unlikely that there is one neuron for each concept, the symbols are encoded in the activity of a small number of neurons; they suggest 10! Thus their symbolic nodes are not neurons, but they're close—something like Hebb's cell assemblies); in the other category, the nodes represent so-called "subsymbolic" units—it is a collection of such nodes, each with a high activity value (termed a *pattern of activation*), that represents a symbolic concept.

Examples of symbolic connectionist networks are the network for "Parallel Interpretation of Natural Language" (Pollack & Waltz, 1986, illustrated and described in Chapter 6), and those for "Visual Memory"

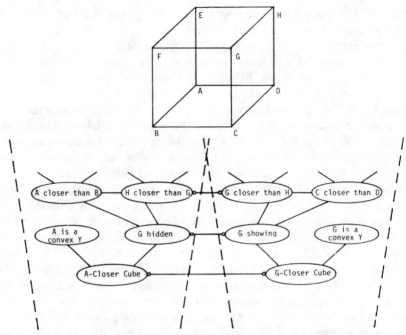

Figure 3.8.   A symbolic connectionist network that illustrates the Necker-cube phenomenon

From "A Connectionist Model of Visual Memory," by J. Feldman, in *Parallel Models of Associative Memory* (p. 65), edited by G.E. Hinton & J.A. Anderson, 1981, Hillsdale, NJ: Erlbaum. Copyright 1981 by Erlbaum. Reprinted by permission.

(Feldman, 1981). Figure 3.8 is a symbolic connectionist network of Feldman, for the two readings of the Necker cube (note the mutually inhibitory links, i.e., bidirectional arcs with negative weights, illustrated thus ∘——∘ , between nodes within the same layer):

ON NOT LOSING THEIR INHIBITIONS

Mutually inhibitory links are crucial to the success of many symbolic connectionist systems. Thus in the above example those subnets which contribute to the two mutually incompatible interpretations of the line drawing of the cube are connected by mutually inhibitory links. In this network such links ensure that only one of the two interpretations is active at any given time. In general, mutually inhibitory links ensure that activity is concentrated in only one of any number of competing nodes, thus yielding an outright winner rather than dispersing the activity among the competitors, which would give an ordered sequence of relative winners (see the Winner-Takes-All Subnets in Chapter 6). So it is important that these networks don't lose their inhibitions, except when the nodes are no longer in competition. And here is a fundamental problem that Pollack, for example, is addressing in his suggestions for dynamically reconfigurable networks. The desirability of a particular link (inhibitory or not) is often dependent upon the particular problem at hand and not a relatively static reflection of some virtually immutable feature of the world. Thus, *dog* may be in direct competition with *cat* if you're trying to classify a given four-legged, domestic carnivore. But if you're mentally amassing a collection of common household pets, then the competitive element would appear to have vanished. So it would seem that these inhibitory links (like many excitatory links) cannot be permanent structural features of a general purpose network — sometimes you need them and sometimes you don't. Reconciling the apparently transient nature of relations, which model cognitive behavior, with structurally permanent networks is a problem that we shall return to.

THE NEED FOR DECAY

A major problem with some CP-based systems is that the activity tends to become thinly spread all over the network rather than concentrated in relatively few nodes. The result is that they generate a "heat death" phenomenon instead of the desired subset of highly activated nodes (i.e., a pattern of activation). Mutually inhibitory links, as I have mentioned above, are manifestations of one strategy to combat this problem, sigmoidal activation functions (explained in Chapter 9) are another, and decay functions (the subject of this subsection) are yet another.

It appears to be desirable, perhaps necessary (although Pollack & Waltz, 1986, do not agree), to use some decay function to continually reduce the activation levels of nodes at each successive time step. Thus activity does not just "sit" in a node and gradually accumulate from more-or-less stray bits and pieces of activity that happen to arrive there from time to time. Activity levels that are not reinforced quite quickly die down due to the action of the decay function. Typically, the activity level of a node i at time t, a_{it} might be given by:

$$a_{it} = \text{DECAY } a_{it-1} + \Sigma \text{ (all incoming activity to node } i \text{ at time } t)$$

where the Σ term is a summation of activity received along incoming links — typically, a summation over all incoming links of (activity of link) *(weight of link), and DECAY is some function that reduces the activity level to which it is applied. Thus DECAY might simply be some fractional multiplier such as 0.5. This decay strategy would reduce activity levels by half at each time step, in the absence of further external excitation of a node.

As an example of a slightly more sophisticated decay function, Johnston et al. (1983) used a two-level decay function in their cell-assembly-based model of basic learning behaviors. A *cell assembly* (Hebb, 1949) is a mutually reinforcing collection of neurons that can "reverberate." That is, on achieving a certain level of activity, they can, by reinforcing each other, maintain this high activity level for a period of time in the absence of further external reinforcement. Nodes in the Johnston study were representing cell assemblies, and so the multiplicative decay factor was high for reverberating nodes (e.g., 0.9, hence, only 10% decay) and low for nonreverberating nodes (e.g., 0.1, hence, 90% decay). Thus so-called reverberating nodes maintained high activity levels for a number of time steps in the absence of further external stimulation, while the activity in nonreverberating nodes, in similar circumstances, quickly died out. Hence, a node could not achieve the reverberating state as a result of small injections of activity over an extended period, it had to receive a large dose of activity over a short period.

While on the subject of Hebb, whose ideas have for many years maintained a small but significant following, I might mention the Hebbian learning mechanism. Sharkey (1989a), for example, sketches out the neuroanatomical background to the Hebbian learning mechanism, which is based on the idea that, when two processes are active at the same time, a permanent connection is made between them. Sharkey provides examples of the Hebbian learning rule being used to associate visual pictures with words, and used in a natural-language application in which case roles are learned (case roles such as AGENT — who did it — and OBJECT — what it was done to — with respect to some ACTION — what was done; if this brief explanation doesn't clear the mists, and you desire demystification, then try Chapter 8).

SUBSYMBOLIC CONNECTIONISM: THE GOOD NEWS

Subsymbolic networks have many attractive properties that seem to support the connectionistic claim that subsymbolic networks are not just low-level implementations of semantic networks (like machine code is a low-level but essentially equivalent alternative to a high-level programming language such as FORTRAN). Thus symbolic concepts such as *apple* are not all-or-nothing entities in a subsymbolic network as they are in symbolic networks, where a node labeled *apple* is active, or it is not. In a subsymbolic network this concept is represented by a general pattern of activity; one activation of the *apple* pattern must be more or less similar to another — they need not be identical. Elimination of the necessity for all-or-nothing decisions accords well with our beliefs about intelligent reasoning, but it does raise the problem of deciding on sufficient similarity.

Apart from the possibilities for machine learning (discussed in detail in Chapter 9) and distributed representations (considered as a question of knowledge representation and thus dealt with in Chapter 6), Smolensky (1987), in his exposition of the merits of the subsymbolic paradigm in AI, discusses the benefits of both parallelism and the use of "soft constraints." Parallelism has, in all subdomains of AI, been invoked as an ultimate enhancement, and furthermore, one that will rescue the known, but intolerably slow, techniques by providing some orders of magnitude increase in processing speed. Parallelism is, like neural architectures, yet another facet of AI work with much promise and many unsolved problems. Suffice it to say that neural architectures are inherently parallel (activity values are broadcast in parallel from one set of network units to another), and thus they include the potential benefits of parallelism, which appears to be an essential component of real-time intelligence.

For Smolensky, each connection in a subsymbolic network represents a soft constraint. "The important point is that soft constraints, any one of which can be overriden by others, *have no implications singly;* they only have implications collectively. . . . The claim is that using soft constraints avoids the brittleness that hard constraints tend to produce in AI" (Smolensky, 1987, p. 103). This would certainly seem to be a significant advance on the products of the classical symbolic paradigm in AI — products that either get it absolutely right, or more often fail miserably. Intelligence is not that bimodal, and subsymbolic networks seem to avoid this pitfall.

Waltz (1987) lists six reasons for the excitement that surrounds connectionist work:

1. It's a good candidate for a major new paradigm;
2. The similarity of connectionist networks to brain architecture suggests that they may have potential in cognitive science (although I shall argue in a later section as well as in Chapter 6 that this similarity is superficial and perhaps misleading);
3. Connectionism holds promise for significant breakthroughs in machine learning (an AI subfield that constantly runs up against formidible obstacles in its SSSP manifestations — see Chapter 9);

4. Connectionist systems exhibit nontrivial fault tolerance, thereby circumventing the brittleness problem typical of SSSP systems (sometimes known as 'the china syndrome'; see the next section in this chapter);
5. Appropriate hardware is rapidly becoming available which is important for testing systems beyond the current very-small examples;
6. Connectionist systems scale-up well: "modules can be interconnected rather easily. This is because messages passed between modules are activation levels, not symbolic messages" (Waltz, 1987, p. 57).

This last claim is particularly interesting because it appears to be quite contrary to the views of Hinton (1986), who claims that one of the problems is that scaling-up of the back propagation learning algorithm (gruesome details, Chapter 9), for example, is not yet viable. The clash of these apparently contradictory claims is softened, if not avoided, when we realize that Waltz is primarily concerned with symbolic connectionist networks and Hinton with the subsymbolic ones.

WHEN IS AN AI SYSTEM LIKE A PIECE OF FINE CHINA?

There are at least two good answers to this curious question: always; and when it's an SSSP system. The brittleness of SSSP systems in AI is legendary (even if it is not universal). Occurences of the china syndrome plague most SSSP-based systems: they either get it dead right or fail miserably, there are no mediocre performances.

{The china syndrome is not to be confused with the China syndrome: the not uncommon situation in AI where we cannot reproduce the fancy results that have been published because the only person who can run the program has gone to China!}

"Brilliant" or "stupid" are the two modes of operation for far too many SSSP-based systems; one is the most easily demonstrated, and the other is the most usually presented (you figure it out).

The 'always' answer might stem from the observation that the only significant AI systems to date are SSSP systems; the connectionists may lay claim to the possibility of nonbrittle AI systems, but they have yet to deliver a substantial existence proof. Nevertheless, the CP advocates argue, as point 4 in Waltz's list and Smolensky's "soft constraints," that connnectionist systems will degrade gracefully in sharp contrast to the graceless behavior typical of SSSP systems. And there is some hardish evidence to support the claim (e.g., Smolensky, 1986).

"But," it is argued by many SSSPists, "it may be true that AI models have tended to be brittle. Nevertheless, it is not a *necessary* consequence of the SSSP approach that they should be so; see, for example, Quinlan (1987) — an implementation of nonbrittle decision trees. And see Kearns, Li, Pitt, and Valiant (1987) for a formal theory of approximate correctness. Both are SSSP-based.'' (For those readers who are tempted to have a look, but are not tempted enough to dig up the actual references, you'll be pleased to learn that both pieces of work are described in Chapter 9.)

Fodor and Pylyshyn (1988), for example, hold the view that brittleness is no more a necessary characteristic of SSSP-based systems than it is of connectionistic ones. This standpoint is in fact the key to much of their attempted demolition of the CP. They claim that the two defects in the usual arguments for preferring connectionist systems are:

1. The objections depend on properties that are not intrinsic to Classical systems — roughly the SSSP. "There can be perfectly natural Classical models that don't exhibit the objectionable features" (Fodor & Pylyshyn, 1988, p. 54).
2. "The objections are true of Classical architectures insofar as they are implemented on current computers, but need not be true of such architectures when differently (e.g., neurally) implemented. They are, in other words, directed at the implementation level rather than the cognitive level" (p. 54). {Fodor & Pylyshyn spend some time on the question of what it is to be an explanation *at the cognitive level*. The cognitive level is specified by those states of the system that encode properties of the world. The elements of most connectionistic explanations are below this level. They emphasize the way that the cognitive level states can be implemented. This is a summary, hopefully not a travesty, of their point about levels of explanation. Needless to say, the connectionists do not agree.}

Clearly, not all the news is good news. It's time to explore the dark side of the paradigm.

SUBSYMBOLIC CONNECTIONISM: THE REAL NEWS

In conventional software engineering the comprehensibility of programs is of the utmost importance to support both tracking down known errors, and alteration of the system in response to changing requirements. In fact, comprehensibility of representations is important throughout the design and implementation stages as well. In AI the necessity for readily comprehensible systems takes a huge leap in importance: most AI system development is, of necessity, exploratory, and the maintenance of dynamic (given the presence of machine learning) AI systems puts stronger demands on understandability than does the analogous task associated with static, conventional software systems (this point was argued in the previous chapter—just in case you skipped it and are now wondering what justification I can have for such assertions).

REASONING WITH AMORPHOUS COMPLEXITY

The less optimistic view of the potential of neural architectures in AI hinges on the observation that they have a disconcerting similarity to brain structure: both subsymbolic networks and brains are conceptually opaque. What the observer's eye tells the observer's brain about neuroanatomy is that it is very complicated and embodies no underlying plan, apparently (at least no plan relating to the cognitive behavior that it exhibits). The apparent chaos makes random connectivity look somewhat ordered by comparison. Subsymbolic connectionist networks of any reasonable size will present exactly the same unhelpful appearence of white noise to the curious programmer (this problem is a direct result of the knowledge representation strategy, and as such it is fully explored in Chapter 6).

The very features that make subsymbolic networks attractive — distributed representation and the simple homogeneity of activity transfer — also make them singularly incomprehensible representations to attempt to reason about. Why a certain model is doing what it is observed to be doing, and what would be needed to make it do something differently, are both extremely difficult questions to answer. They are also vitally important for the support of computational-model building as scientific research rather than as more-or-less random hacking.

Dreyfus and Dreyfus (1990) add a further twist to the knife in this understandability problem. As they point out: Not only do we face the difficulties of dispersal of our symbolic concepts within connectionistic networks, but, in addition, a self-adaptive network may learn to exhibit intelligent behavior in some domain in terms of features that are not a combination of features that people would ordinarily use. They make the point that intuitive expertise may be reliant upon distributed representations of features that are totally alien to our rational analysis of the phenomenon under study. This point is once more a mere mention of a question that is given more exposure in Chapter 6, where there is a discussion of why a belief in evolution as the mechanism responsible for intelligence is not a comforting belief, despite Simon's (1969) argument to the contrary.

So, in addition to the constituent unsolved problems such as credit assignment in machine learning and simple negation causing total reversal of meaning in natural language analysis, there is this overarching problem of understandability — more precisely, the lack of understandability. A later portion of this chapter is devoted to potential solutions to the practical problem of lack of understandability.

Despite the interest and euphoria that connectionistic research is currently generating, in reality the demonstrations of implemented networks have been limited to very small and specific problems: analysis of a specific, very simple, electronic circuit; parsing a couple of specific sentences, etc. Now, this small-scale beginning would not be so damning if it were not for the fact that these demonstration models are carefully hand crafted for the specific demonstration in mind, and fail utterly on any other task. Pollack (1986) raises this problem of static specificity in connectionist models, and he proposes a scheme for dynamic reconfiguration of these networks. Certainly something along these lines is sorely needed. Pollack's proposal of "cascaded networks" in which one network (the "context network") sets the weights in another network (the "function network") remains to be comprehensively stated.

One possible rejoinder from the CP camp might be that sophisticated learning mechanisms will obviate (or at least minimize) the need for human intervention in the development of a CP-based system. Just set up the initial network, feed it with instructive examples, and machine learning will automatically deliver the final system. This is clearly a point to be taken up in detail in the chapter on machine learning, but for the moment let me note a few points:

1. Mechanisms for machine learning are one of the particularly bright spots in the CP, but
2. Current mechanisms have limitations that fix them way below the necessary level of sophistication, and
3. Such a "black box" methodology could conceivably be an acceptable style for engineering practical systems; but could it be part of a "science"?

THE MYTH OF EMPIRICAL GUIDANCE

Another unhelpful visitation from reality comes in the form of the empirical constraints that flow from research in neuroanatomy. Figure 3.9 sketches the "sunny" view of modeling within the CP: Information about brain structure and function provides constraints on the building

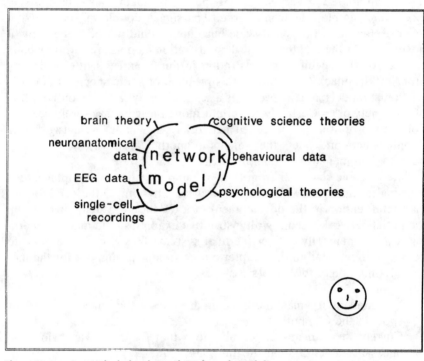

Figure 3.9. An optimistic view of CP-based modeling

blocks and the framework for interconnection, while observations of human behavior are used to reject or confirm aspects of overall system function.

In truth there is much data on the behavior of single neurons (single-cell recordings) and also on the behavior of large collections of neurons en masse (as measured by, for example, EEGs), but there is very little beyond pure speculation that relates these two classes of data either to each other or to high-level cognitive behavior (vision is something of an exception).

Inferring the behavior of a brain at the level of intelligent decision making or problem solving from the evidence of single-cell recordings (i.e., sticking a microprobe into individual neurons to record the rates at which they bleep) is like trying to shed light on the workings of a large power station by carefully recording, say, the fluctuations of a single valve whose interaction with the millions of other components is largely unknown; it's just like that, only much worse. Similarly, EEG data and the like provide some sort of "averaged" measure of the brain's electrical activity. Drawing inferences from this class of measurement is like trying to infer the internal workings of an elephant from measurements of the surface temperature at certain selected locations on its skin. It is true that the temperature measurements vary in a predictable manner and that correlations between temperatures at specific places on the body and the organism's activities can be quite good. But how can we hope to move from this type of data to predictions or even explanations of what's going on inside the beast other than in terms of heat-generating capabilities?

Consequently, there is the same paucity of firm inferences from empirical data pertaining to the behavior of moderately sized neuron networks. In addition, in most neural models the experimeters are loath to equate their network nodes with neurons (recall Feldman & Ballard's, 1982, suggestion that their symbolic nodes represent "say 10" neurons); they are usually viewed as something more like Hebb's cell assemblies — objects whose exact relationship to any observable anatomical features of the brain is never quite specified. So the reality of empirical constraints is somewhat thin for a few different reasons; the lack of empirical constraints for moderately-sized networks of neurons; inherent fundamental uncertainties about the significance and the role of neurons in our brains; and a failure to commit to any firm structural correspondences between connectionistic networks and brain anatomy. The mutually beneficial exchange of data is more of a promise of future riches when this, perhaps not awfully big, gap is bridged. It is a promise that not even the most wildly optimistic symbolic semantic network modeler is likely to see in his or her models, but it is only a promise for the future of CP-based work, nonetheless. Figure 3.10 is a realistic (or is it just pessimistic?)

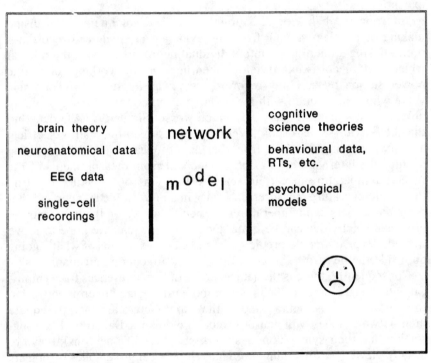

Figure 3.10.   The realistic view of CP-based modeling

view of the context of CP-based modeling. The associations with brain theory are more a promise for the future than a reality, and the small-scale of current CP-based models does not typically generate behavior that can be compared with human behavior (although there are exceptions which we shall get to).

In, for example, the Johnston et al. (1983) connectionist model of basic learning behaviors, one significant option in the mechanism for distributing activity out from a node concerned the relationship between the node's activity level and the number of outgoing links. In particular, should the amount of outgoing activity be divided between the outgoing links or duplicated for each link? Put another way: Do the recipient nodes receive an amount of activity that is dependent only upon the source node's activity level and the weight of the link, or should it also depend upon the number of recipient nodes? The empirical data contained nothing to guide this decision. And even if some relevant information on brain function were known: How does knowledge of a multimeganode network translate into constraints for a network model that is, of necessity, many orders of magnitude smaller? The strategy adopted, by default, was to explore the alternatives empirically — i.e., we used the suck-it-and-see strategy. We programmed up both alternatives and adopted the one that worked best. The finding was that the behavioral data were modeled better sometimes by one function and sometimes by the other.

WHAT'S THE STOPPING RULE?

A further problematic aspect of the CP concerns questions of timing, as it so often does when parallelism is countenanced. How do we know when a pattern of activity has emerged? Or how do we move the system on from a stable state? These are more or less opposite sides of the same problem. If the network is truly dynamic, fairly stable patterns of activation will periodically emerge and then break up again to contribute their activity to subsequent transient activation patterns. When do we attempt to "read off" some problem solution or decision or whatever?

Many current connectionist systems are one-shot constructions that are designed to head for a stable pattern of activation (a goal state in the SSSP) and stay there. Thus, it is fairly clear when a problem solution or decision or whatever has been reached, but the problem then becomes how to move the system on to subsequent decisions, etc. (see Bath-like Architectures in Chapter 6).

Another view of this problem reveals it to be the problem of sequencing. In a parallel processing system, however massively parallel it is, there also has to be a sequencing aspect: At some level, one phenomenon follows another. Nothing could be simpler in classical modeling. But the CP offers no obvious way to set up the sequencing of events.

Waltz (1987) raises this general problem as well as several others, including the problems of debugging and understanding connectionist systems. Touretzky and Hinton (1986) added some "gates" to their CP-based model of a production system in order to achieve the necessary sequential ebb and flow of activity (this project is revisited in context, in Chapter 6). Sharkey (1989b), for example, has explored several different means of producing appropriate sequences of events in his CP-based approach to natural language understanding.

Other attempts to introduce some serial ordering into CP-based models can be found in Pollack (1987b), Elman (1988), Gasser and Dyer (1988), and Jordan (1986).

SINGLE-MINDED MODELS

The emphasis in the heading of this section is very much more on the "single" rather than the "minded" aspect of connectionistic models. They are painstakingly constructed to demonstrate one task, and one task only. This is not even one sort of task (e.g., sentence parsing rather than image processing). It is one very specific task (e.g., the network will parse one sentence, or perhaps a very small set of minor variants on the chosen structure).

McCarthy (1988) provides us with just one example of this type of critique of connectionistic models. He calls it lack of *elaboration tolerance,* which is a lack of "the ability of a representation to be elaborated to take additional phenomena into account." In response, Smolensky (1988, the Author's Response section, p. 69) admits that McCarthy's charge is right on target. He continues: "At this point, connectionist models tend to be developed with the barest minimum of representational power for the target task. If the task is beefed up even a little, the model has to be scrapped." He then adds that this weakness is not inherent in CP-based models. It is just a phenomenon that we are observing at the dawn of connectionism; given time, it will, presumably, disappear.

Pollack (1989) addresses the issue of representational adequacy (see Chapter 8), and he also has something to say on the lack-of-elaboration problem. He claims that the Rumelhart and McClelland (1986) model of past-tense formation in English (e.g., kill becomes killed, but go becomes went, except for young children who erroneously say goed until it's beaten out of them) cannot be switched from, say, past to present tense without another 200,000 weighted links. And the traveling salesman network of Hopfield and Tank (1985, and coming up later in this chapter) must be entirely reconfigured if we want to add one more city to the problem.

Like so many of the imperfections of this shiny new paradigm, it remains to be seen whether intolerance to elaboration is a superficial scratch that will be polished out, or whether it is a deep gouge that the modellers will have to live with as best they can.

PHILOSOPHICAL OBJECTIONS

Fodor and Pylyshyn (1988) mount a massive and sustained attack on the CP. They maintain that the CP is not an alternative paradigm to the SSSP, or the "Classical" approach, as they term it. In their analysis there are two crucial "architectural" differences between Connectionist and Classical theories:

1. Combinatorial syntax and semantics form mental representations. Classical theories, but not Connectionist theories, take mental representations to have a *combinatorial syntax and semantics,* in which (a) there is a distinction between structurally atomic and structurally molecular representations; (b) structurally molecular representations have syntactic constituents that are themselves either structurally molecular or are structurally atomic; and (c) the semantic content of a (molecular) representation is a function of the semantic contents of its constituent parts, together with its constituent structure.

2. Structure sensitivity of processes. In Classical models, the principles by which mental states are transformed, or by which an input selects the corresponding output, are defined over structural properties of mental representations. Because Classical mental *representations* have combinatorial structure, it is possible for Classical mental *operations* to apply to them by reference to their form (Foder & Pylyshyn, 1988, p. 13, author's emphasis).

What does all this mean? We've touched on this grandslam argument already, and we'll be seeing it pop up here and there in subsequent chapters, but let me give a simple example in order to communicate the central issue.

In CP-based models representations of cognitive phenomena such as "John loves ice cream and Mary loves cats" emerge as patterns of activation and are associated with appropriate labels. Thus the pattern of activation which represents the loves of John and Mary might be labeled with JOHN LOVES ICE CREAM AND MARY LOVES CATS. The point is that this is just a single label for the phenomenon as a whole. There are no identifiable elements (e.g., subpatterns of activated nodes) of the representation that necessarily correspond to, say, the individual words in the label. Thus we cannot separate out JOHN, or ICE CREAM, or the relation LOVES within the pattern of activation that has emerged and been identified as a whole. The representation is nonmolecular; it has no internal structure (syntactic atoms) that can be combined to account for the meaning as a whole.

In a Classical model, by way of contrast, the representation of the phenomenon "John loves ice cream and Mary loves cats" will be something like the sentence JOHN LOVES ICE CREAM AND MARY LOVES CATS. The capitalized string is not longer just an indivisible label; it is structurally molecular: the meaning of the whole is based on the combination of the meaning of the constitutent elements, the individual words perhaps. The representation has combinatorial semantics. This, Fodor and Pylyshyn argue, is crucial, and this, they claim, the CP lacks.

"But if this is a problem then we'll construct CP-based models so that the necessary constituent structure is present," the connectionist might well retort. Our dynamic duo have foreseen this rejoinder. They answer it thus:

> But we are *not* claiming that you can't reconcile a Connectionist architecture . . . with a combinatorial syntax and semantics for mental representations. On the contrary, of course you can: All that's required is that you use your network to implement a Turing machine [a basic model of the modern computer], and specify a combinatorial structure for its computational language. What it appears that you can't do, however, is have both a combinatorial representation system and a Connectionist architecture *at the cognitive level.* (Fodor & Pylyshyn, 1988, p. 28, authors' emphasis)

{the cognitive level was dealt with earlier in this chapter}.

If this is all still foggy, hang on, more examples follow later in the book. If you reach the end of the book without any significant clearing of the haze, then once again I would urge you to read the original or give up on the whole thing entirely — it will then serve to provide the necessary mystery in your life. But if you do want to press on, then apart from the further examples from Fodor and Pylyshyn that pop up here and there, we look at a specific example provided by Pollack at the end of Chapter 8 — so further assistance is not too far away.

A substantial and diverse, but quite condensed, multiauthor discussion of the pros and cons of the CP can be found in the March 1988 edition of *Behavioral and Brain Sciences,* which happens to be Volume 11, Number 1.

POTENTIAL SOLUTIONS TO THE DILEMMA

Connectionist networks have many attractive qualities; however, they are also rife with basic problems. The perceptual opacity of these networks does not bode well for the prospect of solving the problems by inspection and intuitive reasoning. Three approaches that may eventually contribute to the understandability of neural architectures are outlined below.

FORMAL ANALYSIS

Formal analysis seems to be one promising route to the ready conceptualization of subsymbolic networks. One popular approach to formal analysis is to apply the tools of thermodynamics (the nodes are perhaps analogous to molecules, and the arc weights to the intermolecular energy). Thus we have the Boltzmann machine approach, in which noise is injected into the network to overcome local minima, followed by simulated annealing to discover minimum energy states of a network (see Ackley, Hinton, & Sejnowski, 1985). A closely related style of CP-based system is the "Harmony theory" models of Smolensky (1986), the formal treatment of which is based upon work in statistical mechanics. Both types of models get to show their paces in Chapter 6.

Both of these formal schemes are more than a method of analysis. They are also a methodology for problem solving with these networks. It is a general methodology that works quite nicely on a number of examples, but its advocates have yet to integrate these onetime-stabilization networks into a continuous sequence of events. Currently, we have a number of one-shot, hand-crafted, special-purpose problem-solving networks. Use of these networks to reproduce extended intelligent behavior, which involves a sequence of stabilization and destabilization to solve a connected string of subproblems, has yet to be realized.

Another, as yet largely untried, route to gaining insights through formal analysis might be to apply the power of graph theory. Hage and Harary (1983) have demonstrated how the concepts, theorems, and techniques of graph theory can be used to systematize and explain ordinary ethnographic data. It is thus reasonable to expect knowledge networks, with their fundamentally structural representations, to be even more amenable to graph theoretic analysis. One application of graph theory in this general area is provided by Nicole, Lloyd, and Ward (1988).

Graph-theoretical analyses of knowledge representation schemes appear to be scarce, if not nonexistent. Classical semantic networks, with their perceptual clarity and heterogeneous structure (see Chapter 6), would not be expected to encourage such analyses: there is both a lack of need, and an apparent difficulty associated with anything more than a superficial analysis. But connectionist networks, on the other hand, appear to offer the reverse characteristics: a pressing need for analytical insights, and a representation that invites formal analysis.

It appears that there may be two somewhat different types of graph-theoretic analyses that are suggested by current problems with connectionist networks: analyses of the scope and limitations of proposed functions (arc weight adjustment as a result of behavior; accumulation of activity in nodes; activity transfer; etc.) vis-á-vis different classes of networks (e.g., bipartite graphs or multilayer networks); and secondly, as a tool to promote understanding of the behavior of given networks and associated functions (i.e., provide insight into why a network is doing what it is observed to be doing).

The potential use of graph theoretical analysis for providing insights into the behavior of these perceptually opaque structures can be illustrated by reference to Sejnowski's NETtalk (a connectionist system that is described in detail in Chapter 9). This network successfully learned to associate the correct phonemic structure with letters (in a context of three characters either side) of English. The observed behavior clearly changes from random babbling to quite-understandable prose. This behavior is achieved by a three-layer-of-nodes network composed of 309 nodes and 18,629 weighted arcs. Some of the functions for weight manipulation have been given earlier. There are, apparently, some 300 rules for the pronunciation of English, and this network must, in some sense, have learned these rules. But the final network is totally opaque; Sejnowski and Rosenberg have found no way to interpret how the network is doing what it is clearly doing (at least, no way that provides any detailed insight). It may be possible for a graph-theoretical treatment of such networks to provide some helpful insights into network behavior, they are certainly needed.

Advocates of CP-based systems make much of the "dynamical" nature of this paradigm. Graph theory appears to be a tool for analyzing static structures, but it is not obvious to me that this apparent mismatch is a real barrier to graph-theoretic analyses. The major routes to the useful application of graph theory to connectionist network analysis, maybe via subgraph structure and homomorphism theory {the details are too gruesome to contemplate, so we'll let them pass for now, but an example is given in the section on path-like architectures in Chapter 6}. Pollack (1989), incidentally, opts for "connectionist fractal semantics" as a future boom area based on the fractal geometry of Mandelbrot (1982).

Before we depart from formal analyses of CP-based models, I really must say something about Grossberg, and this is probably the best place to do it. Grossberg and his colleagues have been publishing scholarly mathematical treatments of neural modeling starting somewhere around the first decade BC. Formal analysis has been the major and almost the only approach that has been countenanced, which is probably the reason why there is so much acrimonious disputation over priority with respect to many mechanisms within the CP. I can't understand Grossberg's publications, and I'm by no means alone (and if you're merrily skipping over the curly-bracketed trivia that I'm strewing through this book, then Grossberg's papers are not for you either). I am not rash enough to suggest where the blame for this communication breakdown should be placed, although I wouldn't be too keen to accept it. I just want to leave a pointer to an important subset of CP-based work and, at the same time, to draw your attention to the dangers of formal treatments unpadded with informal lingu'~tic verbiage — *waffle* is the technical term for the missing ingredient. See Grossberg (1987) for a key publication that will serve to take you back into the masses of relevant earlier work, if you so wish it. Alternatively, all the latest results are to be found in his book *Neural Networks and Natural Intelligence* (Grossberg, 1988).

SOFTWARE SUPPORT SYSTEMS

A rather different route to increasing the undestandability of subsymbolic networks is to build and apply software support systems: programs whose function is to interpret some aspect of the network system and present it in a more understandable form to the human user. The P3 system of Zipser and Rabin (1986) is one such system that is designed explicitly for connectionistic research.

A second possibility in this class of support systems is the "software oscilloscope" of Nieper and Boecker (1985). They describe a software equivalent of the electrical engineer's oscilloscope: a program that is "connected to" another program whose behavior we wish to explore, in order to observe certain functional characteristics of this latter program, characteristics that would otherwise be invisible to the interested observer. This idea was not developed, and has not been applied, to subsymbolic networks, but I see no reason why it should not yield useful results in this new domain.

The software oscilloscope is just one example from the newish computer science subarea called *program visualization,* which is the use of graphics to illustrate some aspect of the program or its run-time execution (see Myers, 1988, for an introduction to this realm).

APPROXIMATE TRANSLATION—THE TRUTH ABOUT
MENDACITY

This last offering is not so much another, and different, route to enhancing the understandability of network models (especially subsymbolic ones); it is more a suggestion of how we might most usefully apply both formal analytical techniques and software support systems.

One style of interpreting a mass of fine detail so that it becomes more understandable is to generate high-level approximations — i.e., to tell less than the whole truth (just as I've been doing throughout this book). There are lies, damn lies, and then approximations to the truth; it's this latter category that we want to focus on. Or as Steiner more elegantly puts it: "The shallow cascade of mendacity which attends my refusal of a boring dinner engagement is not the same thing as the un-saying of history and lives in a Stalinist encyclopedia" (Steiner, 1975, p. 221).

Thus a pattern of activation in the subsymbolic network may be approximated by a single symbolic node in a much more comprehensible, but not totally accurate, network of symbolic nodes. Smolensky (1987) makes the point that "symbol-level structures provide only approximate accounts of cognition, useful for description but not necessarily for constructing detailed formal models," and, I would add, perhaps necessary for supporting attempts to comprehend these detailed formal models in order that they may be useable (see Figure 3.11).

Michie and Johnston (1984) also suggest the need for such interpretations, but in the context of making expert systems more understandable.

The truth about the need for mendacity is that it is an essential one when faced with the complexity barriers of AI: Design, development, communication of both problems and solutions, and comprehension in general, are all issues that will benefit from the judicious use of approximations to the truth. This is not, of course, to be taken as carte blanche for flagrant lying about achievements on all fronts but a shallow cascade of medacity rather than the un-saying of fundamental truths. Something much less pernicious than blantant lying does substantial damage in presentations and publications of AI already. Nevertheless, there is, I am sure, a need for accepted, well-defined schemes of approximate representation of complex software systems; one such scheme, which I called *stepwise abstraction*, was mentioned in the previous chapter, and is detailed elsewhere (see Partridge, 1986a, for the exhaustive treatment with respect to AI software, and Partridge, 1985d, for an application to programming language definition). In addition, the blossoming new subfield of *hypertext*, addressing as it does the problem of rendering complex textual objects more comprehensible, could well contribute to the problem

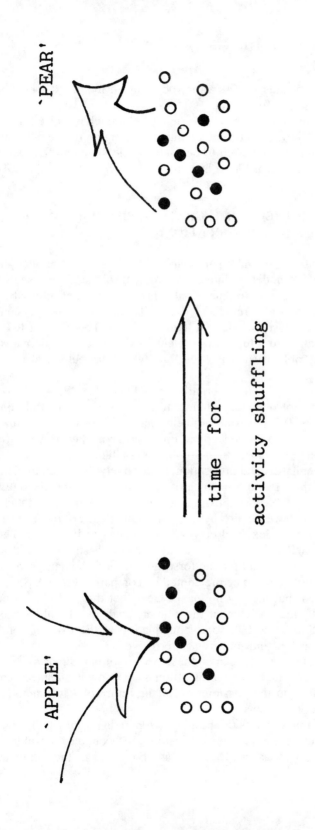

Figure 3.11. An approximate symbolic macroinference from a collection of microinferences

that we are now considering. As an introduction to hypertext, see, for example, McAleese (1989).

In sum, neural architectures of all varieties hold much promise for the realization of AI. They also present a number of difficult, unsolved problems, but above all they threaten to be useless unless we can find ways to render them comprehensible to humans.

THE SSSP AND THE CP: INTEGRATION, BIFURCATION, OR ANNILATION?

We have looked at the dominant paradigm in AI and at its scope of applicability as a basis for models of intelligent problem solving. The essential idea of problem solving as finding a path through a tree of alternative possibilities, a set of states represented as isolated entities independent of time, place, and, most importantly, human context. This appears to be a poor approximation to intelligent problem solving in certain domains: formal, abstract problems fit quite well, but everyday, real-world problems do not.

There may be a significant alternative paradigm, the CP, which, on first inspection, is not obviously subject to many of the unhelpful constraints that the SSSP imposes on problem representations. The CP may not prove viable (due to its conceptual opacity), or it may prove to be an adjunct to the SSSP rather than a competing alternative; hence, the possibilities for annilation and integration, respectively. We need to identify the scope of the CP and also to clarify the issues vis-á-vis its status with respect to the SSSP. Simplistic generalizations to the effect that, with the CP (or SSSP) we can do anything, or nothing, are not the answer. The questions are complex, and currently they need to be approached (answers are too much to expect) on a caşe-by-case basis. Suffice it to say that, at the moment (and for the forseeable future), human problem solving skills are not about to be preempted by computer systems, SSSP-based or CP-based, but it is by no means clear that this will always be the case. It is also unclear whether the ultimate goals of AI will be realized within the SSSP, the CP, some combination of the two, or some totally different, as yet undiscovered, alternative.

Most of this chapter has presented these two major paradigms as competing alternatives — the route to bifurcation in AI. Now it is appropriate to spend some time on the possibilities for the future of AI systems as integrated SSSP–CP systems.

An AI system that exploits the best of both paradigms may be the answer to some fundamental problems. Negation, for example, is problematic in the CP (as well as in PROLOG, as you'll find in the following chapter). The introduction of a simple "not" into an English sentence can generate a reversal of meaning.

For example, IT IS RAINING, and, IT IS NOT RAINING, are similar sentences with very different meanings, aren't they?

Connectionist networks are primed with activity from the meanings of the individual words and eventually cause the activation of some representation of the sentence's meaning. How can the introduction of a simple negation word initiate and sustain a radical reversal (or at least redirection) of the global patterns of activity? Perhaps negation does not need to do this. After all, the meaning of the negated sentence is in some sense quite like the meaning of the nonnegated sentence. Certainly their meanings are more similar to each other than they are to some totally different sentence like THE CAT BIT THE DOG. Could the problem of negation be tackled in terms of a symbolic component that adds some negative "bias" to the interpretation of the activity pattern generated by the nonnegated sentence?

Charniak's (1986) marker-passing theory of language comprehension is CP-like in its spreading activation technique for sentence understanding. The problem of negated sentences within this theory has not been solved. Charniak does not see his system as connectionistic (Charniak, 1987), but as a hybrid system in which he feels free to employ the useful features of both paradigms. In her talk at TINLAP3 (although not in her printed per, Lehnert, 1987), Wendy Lehnert also advocated the construction of natural-language processing systems that utilize the best from both paradigms.

Clark (1989, p. 64) presents a philosophically flavored argument that "the holy war between connectionism and classical AI may . . . have been constructed along an illusory frontier . . . the Uniformity Assumption" (i.e., that there is a single computational architecture underlying cognitive behavior — like Chandrasekaran's unitary-architecture theories of Chapter 1). Clark advocates an integrated view of the mind in which both paradigms have their place, or perhaps, more accurately, in which neither has a strong claim to be the fundamental paradigm to the exclusion of the other.

It has been suggested to me that the famous Stroop test of psychology might be a good candidate for an integrated CP-SSSP model. The basic experimental paradigm is simple: Subjects are presented with strings of colored letters (all one color in any single presentation), and their task is to name the color. Not very demanding, you might think, even for undergraduate psychology students. And you would be correct; the students get the color right time and time again with unerring accuracy. But when the string of letters is itself a color word — that is, the word RED might be printed in blue — then there is a distinct slowdown in performance.

Subjectively (if you care to subject yourself to these sorts of indignities), you will find that there is a definite urge to name the color spelled out by the word, and that you suppress this in order to comply with the instructions and name the color of the letters. On no better basis than this, I might suggest that a model of this phenomenon could employ a CP-based network to generate the meaning of the word (in this case the color named by the word) when presented with the visual stimulus of a word. And layered on top of this there might be an SSSP-based "cognitive" module whose function is to integrate the network's behavior with specific experimental instructions (i.e., in this case it would suppress the first response of the network and initiate processing to generate the letter color). It all sounds vaguely plausible (to me, at least), but perhaps no more than that. Incidently, Pollack's purely CP-based model of the Stroop phenomenon is given in Chapter 6.

Eiselt and Granger (1987) describe several versions of a model designed to mimic human behavior in a specific natural-language processing situation. They start out with a classical SSSP-based model and move to a more CP-based one; the results of both are presented and discussed.

Holland's (1986) system is presented in Chapter 9 as an example of machine learning that straddles these two paradigms. Holland himself presents it as a system that avoids the brittleness (mentioned above) traditionally associated with SSSP-based systems.

Several other aspects of cognitive behavior that suggest to me the need for an integrated system approach are:

1. The general phenomenon of (apparent?) serial processing in high-level cognitive activity — a symbolic, serial processing device layered on top of a massively (of course) parallel connectionist network.
2. The specific phenomenon of one-trial learning is readily implementable within the SSSP but problematic within the CP. Most other learning phenomena fit more comfortably in the CP (as you will see in Chapter 9).

Touretzky and Derthick (1987) define five highly desirable properties of symbol representations some of which are readily supported by the SSSP and others which seem to require CP-based mechanisms. We shall examine their proposals in the knowledge representation chapter. At this point I just wish to observe that this is another proposal that suggests an integrated-paradigm approach to AI-system building.

Chandrasekaran (1989) argues that CP-based and SSSP-based architectures are alternative implementations of information processing (IP) concepts. We will only be able to understand and thus reason about our models at the IP level. Thus it is largely a question of implementation detail (I exaggerate a little) whether the model is CP- or SSSP-based; we shall always have to be theorizing and communicating results at the IP level. He sees support for his viewpoint in the compositionality of complex, CP-based models. He uses McClelland, Rumelhart and Hinton's (1986) scheme for recognizing the word *QUEEN* as an example (although they actually use the word *TAKE* as their example). In this system, the recognition of the word is composed of the recognition of the individual letters.

> Decisions about which subnet is going to be largely responsible for Q, and which for U, etc., as well as how the feedback is going to be directed are all made by the experimenter before learning starts. The underlying IP theory is that individual characters are going to be recognized directly from pixels, but recognition of QU will be done by combining information about the presence of Q and U, as well as their joint likelihood. . . . In setting up the initial configuration the designer is actually programming the architecture to reflect the above IP theory of recognizing the word. (Chandrasekaran, 1990, pp. 26–27)

"Thus while the connectionist scheme for recognition of 'QUEEN' still makes the useful *performance* point about connectionist architectures for problems that have been assumed to require a symbolic implementation, still a significant part of the leverage comes from the IP abstractions that the scheme started out with" (p. 27). In sum: At the IP level of abstraction the distinction between the two paradigms, when applied to complex problems, becomes small relative to their commonalities.

SIMULATED EVOLUTION: GUESS AND TRY IT OUT

A minor alternative AI paradigm has been called the simulated evolution approach to AI. There is a nontrivial overlap between this paradigm and the CP and its reliance on learning mechanisms, but in a number of respects they are also quite different.

AI through simulated evolution is, of course, loosely based on Darwin's brainwave (or was it Wallace's brainwave and Darwin's data collection and management abilities?), in a word: evolution. The components of simulated evolution are:

1. A mechanism for generating new variants of a system;
2. A method for evaluating differing versions of the system and selecting the best by discarding the worst;
3. A mechanism for making copies of the remaining population of systems for input into components (1) and then (2) given above.

In addition, to the mutate–test–discard–copy cycle lots of time is also needed, some considerable number of millenia if Darwin's example is anything to go by. Again we run into the problem of the restriction to roughly Ph.D.-length projects, so something has to be done to speed up the clock.

Suffice it to say that the early, crude attempts to mechanize the basics of biological evolution and harness them in the service of AI were quite dismal failures. The projects were largely manifestations of simplistic hill climbing (the problems associated with this general mechanism are discussed in the chapter on machine learning).

The only reason for mentioning this largely abandoned and never very promising AI paradigm (apart from historical interest) is that we are beginning to see some of its features (such as learning as an automatic feedback mechanism from system performance) bobbing up in connectionist models and theories. This is quite unsurprising for several reasons: first, both simulated evolution and connectionism have learning as a major component; and second, they both have strong associations with the mechanisms of biology. Nevertheless, unsurprising as it may be, it was, I felt, worth running by you.

"BAD" PARADIGMS

One can quite easily see the appeal of games and puzzles for explicating the SSSP — even I couldn't resist it, I who am about to claim that it is a grossly misleading way to introduce AI. Game playing and puzzle solving are domains in which AI ideas can be easily demonstrated, partly, I think, because the clutter of complexity and the vagaries of ill-structure (two of the characteristic features of AI problems) are both missing. The techniques then of best-first search and of constructing admissable heuristics, for example, look to be swift and slick routes to the implementation of of intelligent problem solving, but what happens when we broaden our domain of interest to take in more ambitious AI problems? What happens when the characterization of a state is little better than an arbitrary decision, when the state transformation operators are ill-defined and hard to circumscribe, when the recognition of a goal state is a process of debate? Is the infrastructure developed for dealing with games and puzzles still useful as say, a first approximation? Or have the basic assumptions of the SSSP been so badly mauled that the useful carryover is negligible?

Is the heuristic pruning of game trees and so on that we find dominating most introductions to AI a legitimate simplification of the fundamental problems of AI, or is it more of a misleading diversion? This is the sort of question that this final part of Chapter 3 addresses. Is formal game playing a "bad" paradigm for AI. {Cautious detail: The scare quotes are being employed in an effort to ward off the outrage that some might feel when they find their much-loved and assiduously tended system unceremoniously dumped, by me, in the category of "bad" paradigms. The quotes signify that this is a special usage of "bad", and it's not, in fact, too bad — it all depends upon what you are hoping to achieve with your system.}

The rich loam of game playing (games such as chess but not football, and the underlying distinction is critical), theorem proving, and formal puzzle solving has nurtured AI from its discreet (and discrete) beginnings; they remain as major ingredients of the usual growing medium in its brash (but still discrete) present.

What makes certain games and puzzles instructive AI problems is the fact that their size or complexity (or both) puts the finding of solution paths beyond the state of the art of current, formal, analytical techniques. Again we see a characterization of AI that is liable to change. For example, if chess were to yield to formal analysis and we discover, say, that whoever goes first can always win, then chess might cease to be an AI problem (and, of course, it would not be an RI problem either) from that point in time. But currently top-class chess cannot be played using a set of well-defined rules — at least not on the basis of *only* such a set of well-defined rules. The best chess seems to be founded upon complex strategies that are subtle, situation-dependent, combinations of rules, looser guidelines, and out-and-out hunches about the psychological state of one's opponent.

The AI paradigm that is extracted from attempts to computerize chess playing and other formal problem solving is one of heuristic search, in a space of discrete, well-defined states. Thus chess playing is viewed as making choices (which one of the many possible subsequent states is the best) in a space of possibilities (the many thousands, perhaps, of possible next moves) when the choice procedure cannot be guaranteed to select the best move on all occasions. The choice procedure is primarily heuristic — i.e., the particular heuristic used has been chosen simply because it has demonstrated its worth on an acceptable proportion of occasions, as judged by the overall success of the chess-playing program.

When rated in terms of path-finding abilities, heuristic-search strategies in AI systems more closely resemble Odysseus or Moses than Davy Crockett or some other hot-shot trail follower. That is to say, the typical AI program wanders fruitlessly among the nodal landscape of its search space, not perhaps for 40 years like the Biblical desert safari, but often only because its creator will pull the plug on it long before the first decade has passed (after all, with just a few short years in which to amass a

Ph.D.-sized pile of code, a 40–year traversal of the search space is just not on).

Interestingly, Marr, in his influential discussion of AI methodology (Marr, 1977, reprinted 1990), considers problem solving with well-defined problems such as cryptarithmetic — which is not the calculations of Count Dracula, but the solving of numerical puzzles — and chess (if we just add logic, we have the three domains considered in Newell and Simon's, 1972, tome entitled *Human Problem Solving*) to be bad domains for AI research. He argued that the aim of information-processing studies is to formulate and understand the structure of the chosen problems, "not the mechanisms through which they are implemented" (Marr, 1990, p. 105). So we must find problems that we can solve well, not problems that we understand well intellectually but perform poorly on. "When we do mental arithmetic we are doing *something* well, but it is not arithmetic, and we seem far from understanding even one component of what that something is. Let us therefore concentrate on the simpler problems first, for then we have some hope of genuine advancement" (p. 105, his emphasis).

Defenders of the game-and-puzzle-solving approach to AI might claim that a desire to start out with simple problems is exactly the reason why formal games and puzzles are a popular domain for AI research. Marr's response, presumably, would be that "simpler" is not the only criterion; the simple problems should be ones that human intelligence works well on rather than the intellectually simple problems which human intelligence is rather poor at dealing with. Much of AI that has gone the route of formal problem solving mechanisms is perhaps better characterized as artificial intellectualism than artificial intelligence, and surprisingly perhaps (as Simon, 1981, for example, admits), artificial intellectualism is by far the easier of the two.

Michie (1986) claims that there is a distinction between a one-person game (i.e., a puzzle) and a two-person game and, moreover, a distinction which is "of crucial importance in the study of animal and human learning" (p. 24). He contends that a game "summarizes the essential features of most of the situations with which animals are confronted in real life, whereas most of the problems given to animals in conventional studies of learning are 'puzzles'." Hence, misleading conclusions will result "if one presents puzzles, as is the custom of experimental psychologists, to central nervous systems which have been adapted by natural selection to cope with games" (p. 25).

It is not the mismatch between an SSSP representation and reality that bothers Michie, it is the difference between the presence and absence of sentient opposition within SSSP abstractions.

Another class of "bad" paradigms for AI are those based on (usually) formal, context-free abstractions: pattern recognition, formal syntactic and formal semantic treatments of natural languages, the interpretation of images solely by means of independent, formal operators. In one sense the examples from both natural language and vision are pattern recognition problems, and as I shall deal with these two AI subfields in Chapters 8 and 7, respectively, there is no need to say more about them here.

The field of pattern recognition proper has always flirted with the possibility of being an AI subarea, but never quite made it. And I, of course, believe that this exclusion is entirely appropriate. In the last analysis (which I shall not attempt to perform), pattern recognition does intrude into many areas of AI, but, to a first approximation at least, the term *pattern recognition* typically denotes the application of formal (usually statistical) methods to extract high-level information from "images." For example, an English word might be extracted from an acoustic signal, or a tree might be recognized in a visual image. A representative example of the pattern recognition that I am discussing is that of Fu (1982).

At a general level, the paradigm whose applicability to AI I am questioning is characterized by the (almost) exclusive use of a set of independent (or context-free) operators to derive cognitive concepts from collections of data values. It is based on the assumption that all the information necessarily for interpretation of the pattern is *in* the pattern. This assumption is usually untenable in AI. And the sense in which I think that this is a bad paradigm for AI is a result of its powerful but limited utility.

Much useful and high-level information can be extracted using this paradigm, and it may be that something like the full potential of AI can be generated using it. But I don't think so. The attraction of this paradigm (AI based on a set of independent functions) together with fuzziness of its limitations has led to a concentration on it at the expense of less modular and less well-defined alternatives. A hope vested in the eventual success of context-free operators has led to a neglect of context-sensitive techniques, a failure to develop operators with some potential for sophisticated interaction. I think, that this is particularly apparent in work on computer vision, and thus I'll reiterate my concerns with the aid of specific examples in the chapter on AI vision systems. When, or if, you get there (Chapter 7), take particular note of Mayhew's (1984) categories of work in computer vision: Pattern Recognition and Image Processing versus Image Understanding.

So, my general contention here is that the pattern recognition paradigm is a "bad" one for AI because its limited successes (limited with respect to the aspirations of AI, but far from limited in a more general sense) have impeded the development of operators that are responsive to contextual guidance which may be necessary if we are ever to realize some of AI's grander goals.

A relevant aside concerns neural networks, a subspecies of connectionism, and bath-like architectures in particular (this lustral subcategory of connectionism is explained in Chapter 6). The relaxation algorithms, which can guarantee that the network settles comfortably into a solution configuration, are really just elaborate curve-fitting techniques—i.e., sophisticated enhancements of the least-squares algorithm for finding the best straight line through a set of data points. They are also very successful pattern classifiers. Both points seem to press for the expulsion of such networks from the domain of real AI. Is this just a CP manifestation of a "bad" AI paradigm? It would seem fair that the SSSP does not have a total monopoly of the class of undesirable paradigms.

I'm tempted to leave this point open for the reader to ponder, mostly because I have little idea how to sort it out (this reason must be firmly in the class of "bad reasons," no?). But before I abandon you to it, I can offer a couple of potentially useful observations.

To call a mechanism "just elaborate curve fitting" doesn't sound too good, but it may not in actuality be too damning. After all, Shakespeare's works are just words, and we are primarily just water with a few other elements mixed in. To return to the original slur: It is conceivable that human intelligence is "just elaborate curve fitting," I suppose. If the necessary degree of elaboration requires the use of heuristics and the consequent loss of the certainties that the least-squares algorithm carries with it, then I could believe that AI is just elaborate curve fitting. A last point to bear in mind is the continually recurring one of a continuum of possibilities, one end of which is patently not AI; but the other might well be. Don't be tempted into devising a simple test for differentiation, but do look at Figures 9.25 and 9.26 for another curve-fitting approach to AI.

A classic example of this type of model is to be found in the work on " 'Neural' Computation of Decisions in Optimization Problems" by Hopfield and Tank (1985). In particular, they present a curve-fitting solution to the traveling salesman problem (TSP). The TSP concerns the difficulties that a traveling salesman faces when he has to visit N cities and he wants to drive as few miles as possible — i.e., what is the minimum-length path that connects all N cities? Not a problem that puts a lot of strain on the average brain, but it is one that can absorb a lot of time, working out all the possible routes and then sorting out the shortest one. It is, in the jargon of theoretical computer scientists, *computationally intractable,* which is their way of saying that, if large numbers of cities are involved, then the simple exhaustive algorithm cannot be used because it will take too long. {For those readers who have sniffed the presence of a solid formal result here and want to know more, Gary and Johnson (1979) devote a small book to this question of computational intractability, and they include enough mathematics to satisfy everyone but the most extreme addicts. As for the TSP, with only 10 cities there are 181,440 distinct paths, and with 30 cities there are $4.4*10^{30}$ paths — that's an awful lot of paths.}

Hopfield and Tank set up their neural network such that the shortest path corresponds to the minimum of the energy function that describes the network (i.e., a bath-like architecture — see Chapter 6 for further clarification, or just suspend belief and wait till you get there). To tackle the 30-city problem, a network of 900 neurons was used. For the particular set of cities used, it was believed that the shortest path was length 4.26. The average length obtained from 100,000 paths selected at random was 12.5, with none less than 9.5. The energy-minimization style of curve-fitting used "converged to paths of less than 7 commonly, and less than 6 occasionally" (Hopfield & Tank, 1985, p. 148). Figure 3.12 illustrates three solutions to a 30–city TSP in which the length of the specific path illustrated is labeled "D". In Figure 3.12a is a path of more or less average length; Figure 3.12b illustrates the suspected minimum for this particular problem, and Figure 3.12c is a typical path obtained after the use of an "annealing" technique (see bath-like architectures in Chapter 6 for a description of the most popular "annealing" technique).

This attack on the otherwise computationally intractable TSP is "just curve fitting," but it is also quite impressive — is it AI? I am inclined not to give it the benefit of the doubt, and one reason why I think that I might be justified is that Hopfield and Tank discuss in their paper the use of heuristics which, if implemented, would replace the exhaustive search mechanism they actually used by a much reduced and therefore more "intelligent" search procedure (this is, of course, my teminology, not theirs).

A final class of "bad" paradigms are the artificial microworlds, so often the playground of the AI demos of yesteryear. The 'blocks world' is one of the most famous examples. SHRDLU (Winograd, 1972) operated there, and we'll look at that AI landmark in Chapter 8. Haugeland (1985, p. 190) lists some of the shortcomings of this approach and continues:

> To dwell on these shortcomings, however, is to miss the fundamental limitation: the micro-world itself. SHRDLU performs so glibly only because his [sic?] domain has been stripped of anything that could ever require genuine wit or understanding. In other words, far from digging down to the essential questions of AI, a microworld simply eliminates them . . . A round, frictionless wheel is a good approximation of a real wheel, because the deviations are comparatively small and theoretically localized; the blocks-world 'approximates' a playroom more as a paper plane approximates a duck.

That's clearly on the negative side, but Haugeland is, in fact, quite neutral on balance, as you will find out in Chapter 10.

The case for the microworld approach is put by Winston (1977, and toned down but not eliminated in the second edition, 1984). Originally, he wrote "limited domains of discourse are the E. coli of language research"

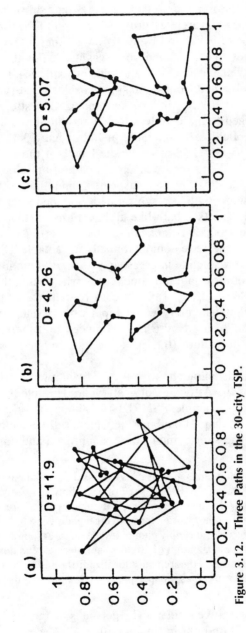

Figure 3.12. Three Paths in the 30-city TSP.

From " 'Neural' Computation of Decision in Optimization Problems," by J.J. Hopfield & D.W. Tank, 1985, *Biological Cybernetics*, 52, p. 148. Copyright 1985 by Springer-Verlag. Reprinted by permission.

(Winston, 1977, p. 157). The critical dimension along which this analogy fails concerns the the fact that E. coli is an existing, real-world system that molecular biologists must deal with as best they can, whereas limited domains of discourse are artifacts that can be created and restructured at will to facilitate the application of any particular theory. In the second edition (as I said), the explicit claim has been omitted, but still E. coli research in molecular biology is adduced in support of the use of artificial microworlds as a legitimate paradigm for AI research — the fact that one type of limited domain is a product of the imagination and the other is not, does not seem to be an important difference for Winston.

In sum, the "bad" paradigms have been a neccesary part of the maturation process for AI, but now perhaps the field has grown up and needs to look beyond these juvenile exemplars. Pattern recognition and heuristic search of a space of discrete and well-defined states may well be essential components of the ultimate AI system (if there ever is one), but they will not constitute the base paradigms of the system.

4

The Babel of AI Languages

If it's programmed in LISP, it's AI.

forgotten AI-software vendor

Along with most other computer-infested disciplines, AI has not been tardy in its efforts to invent new programming languages to solve its own particular brand of problems. An AI programming language must support flexible, dynamic systems. Minimal binding (in both its technical and non-technical senses) commitments are desirable. Both data and code should be modifiable at run time. In fact this convenient and useful division—data structure and algorithm—becomes a blurred line in AI : Data structures need to be executed, and algorithms need to be manipulated as if they are data structures.

IT'S ALL DONE BY MANIPULATING SYMBOLS

AI programming is often characterized as "symbolic" programming, and AI languages as "symbol manipulation" languages. Quite what this apparently significant use of the word *symbolic* means in this context I am not altogether sure. The reader might attempt to recall our discusssion of this popular, but blunt-edged as well as ambiguous, word in Chapter 3.

In the current context, *symbolic* appears to refer to computations that are primarily manipulating patterns of symbols (or symbol structures), as opposed to computing numeric values as a result of arithmetic operations. And this latter activity is, apparently, not viewed as symbol manipulation. You'll have to make your own decision in this demarcation dispute. (If you find it easy, then consider the status of activity level and link-weight adjustment computations which dominate in the processing of sub-symbolic AI models. Is the processing of subsymbolic networks symbolic computation? It certainly is AI.)

The major mechanism of so-called symbolic computing is pattern matching. Pattern matching may even be used to determine the execution sequence in a program: Procedures, functions, subroutines, or what you will (modules of code) may be invoked and executed, not specifically by name, but as a result of a pattern match between a stored pattern in the code module and a dynamically generated symbol structure — this is called *pattern-directed procedure invocation.*

We shall consider some manifestations of pattern matching operations within the section on PROLOG; for the moment, I shall leave this topic after a brief example of symbolic and nonsymbolic (is that numeric?) computation using the equality operator.

Consider the following expression:

$$X = Y + 1$$

which may be either true (i.e., the structures on each side of the equality operator are in some sense equal) or false (the proof of this bald assertion is left as an exercise for the reader). Furthermore, it may be either true or false as either a symbolic or nonsymbolic computation.

As a nonsymbolic computation the truth or falsity of this expression (incidentally, it looks just like a symbol structure to me) might be determined by comparing the numeric value of X with the result of adding one to the numeric value of Y. Thus, this expression as a whole would yield true as its value if, say, X has the value 3 and Y has the value 2.

As a symbolic computation, on the face of it, it is false: the pattern X is not the same as the pattern Y + 1. But if, say, X is a variable name whose value is the string Y + 1, and the right-side expression is interpreted literally as the string Y + 1, then clearly the complete expression is true.

Yet another possibility is that the variable X has the value Y1 and the right side of the equality operator is an expression in which the symbol + is interpreted as the concatenation operator when sandwiched between two literal characters such as Y and 1. Thus the right side also yields the value Y1 and thus the total expression is true. More importantly, is this a symbolic computation or not? I don't know, but presumably all of the people who blithely talk in terms of symbolic computations can tell us.

The point might be that in symbolic computing the constitutent symbols are manipulated as symbols, whereas in nonsymbolic computing we expect the numeric symbols to represent numbers, the arithmetic operators to represent arithmetic operations, and the nonnumeric symbols to be the names of variables whose values are likely to be numeric. I'm not sure, but that's my guess.

Enough of the general arguments as to why the languages commonly used in AI are different from FORTRAN, COBOL, PASCAL, and their ilk. AI does make some special demands, but the demarcation between AI and non-AI programming languages is not as well founded as many would claim. It is true that, when first exposed to the charms of LISP or PROLOG, the FORTRAN or COBOL programmer is struck by how different they are, but such a person would be similarly smitten by SNO-BOL or APL, and the're not important AI languages. To some, not insignificant extent, LISP is the dominant AI language because that's the way it turned out to be. Accident, inertia, and history as usual had substantial parts in the drama — boring but true.

So LISP is the lingua franca of AI; it is time to look at it.

LISP

LISP, one of the earliest high-level programming languages to emerge (McCarthy, 1965), is still very much the vernacular of AI, although AI aficionados actually work with the extended dialects such as MACLISP (Touretzky, 1982) or INTERLISP (Teitelman & Masinter, 1981) — dialects plus extras that constitute two of the finest program development environments available. The importance of the notion of a programming support environment rather than just a programming language derives from the incremental nature of AI system development, as discussed in Chapter 2. But, to begin with in this chapter, I'll consider the languages in isolation, and only after we have some familiarity with the individual languages will we delve into the nature of programming environments.

FLEXIBILITY

The nature of incremental system development, or exploratory programming, is such that you don't know quite where you are going to end up with your personal pile of code until you get there. An important characteristic of an AI program then is *flexibility* — keeping options open as long as possible.

LISP embodies flexibility in a number of rather different respects. Program variables have neither to be declared before usage nor to be associated with any specific "type" (e.g., integer or real, as in more conventional programming languages). No limits on data structure sizes (such as lengths of lists) need be specified. They are just grown and shrunk on demand during the running of a LISP program. Data structures can be converted to "code" and executed at any time. And as a final example, the execution sequence can be halted, backed up, and restarted at any time; i.e., a programmer typically has the flexibility to explore alternative execution paths through a given program without having to rerun the complete program. But this leads us to programming environment support facilities once again, and I'm saving them for later, am I not?

So AI programming demands a myriad of flexibilities from the programming medium, flexibilities that are neither supplied nor required in more conventional programming where the programming task is viewed more as a relatively mundane activity of coding a complete, verified, detailed design. In AI, programming is itself fundamentally a process of design (the reader should recall the notions of exploratory programming and of machine-executable specifications from Chapter 2, if this assertion seems a bit dubious). Conventional programming has its own varieties of flexibility: abstract data types, for example, are a minimum-prior-commitment device to aid the traditional process of algorithm design.

THE MAGIC OF RECURSION

You or I would program the function to compute the length of a list as a loop with a counter variable that starts at zero and is incremented by one as each iteration of the loop causes a move to the next list element. When the loop reaches the last list element, it stops, and the value of the counter variable is the length of the list. But the recursive thinker would not.

He (or she) would quickly observe that the length of a list is just the length of the list without its first element plus one (for the first element). And, of course, the length of an empty list is zero, i.e.,

$$length(L) = length(headless \ L) + 1$$

"How true," you might be prepared to concede, "but not much use." It's like observing that the largest prime number, N, won't be divisible by (N-1) as a precursor to finding N.

But you would be wrong. The analogy is false (as so many are these days). A complete, precise and readily programmable definition of the list-length function is:

length (empty list) = 0
length (LIST) = length (LIST without first element) + 1

As an example of a LISP program we can specify a function that sums a list of values, say integers, and returns that sum as its result. Consider the following pseudocode specification of such a function:

function LISTSUM,
    IF the list contains no values
        THEN return zero as the function value
        ELSE return the first list value added to
            the sum of the rest of the list values as
            the function value

The only slightly disturbing feature of this algorithm, especially to the nonrecursive programmer, is the hint of circularity in the ELSE clause. The sum of a nonempty list is obtained by adding the value of the first element to the sum of the rest of the list. There are two reasons that together save the algorithm from endless circularity:

1. The rest of the list (i.e., the list without its first element) is always shorter than the list it derives from.
2. The THEN clause returns a result for the shortest possible list (i.e., the empty list).

Thus it is true that there is a circularity within the ELSE clause: The computation of the sum of a list of values is expressed in terms of the sum of a shorter list of values. But this circular self-referencing, known as recursion, will eventually terminate when the rest of the list is empty; the function will then automatically "unwind"; it will compute the sum of the empty list, then the sum of the last list item, then the sum of the last two items, and so on, until it obtains and returns the sum of all items in the list.

In LISP the body of this function, LISTSUM would be:

```
(COND ((EMPTY LIST                    0                      )
       (     T        (PLUS(HEADOF LIST)(LISTSUM(RESTOF LIST)))))
```

if we assume appropriate definitions for the functions, EMPTY, PLUS, HEADOF, and RESTOF.

Recursion in LISP is the substitute for iteration in more conventional software engineering languages (although a conventional iteration mechanism is always also provided except in "pure" LISP — a spiritual language that is theoretically capable of being all things to all programmers, but no one dares to sully it by actual usage for practical programming. A sobering thought for the FORTRAN or COBOL person is that "pure" LISP also has no assignment statement!).

· It may be some comfort to those readers who have been dazed by this first intrusion of recursion into their computational lives that normal people do experience great difficulty in mentally executing recursion — so don't give up, you're just normal; but I hope to correct that before you reach the end of this book. This unfortunate human inability to think recursively in detail perhaps reflects a paucity of recursive structures in the natural world and a consequent absence of wetware stack structures built into the architecture of the brain. So why do AI enthusiasts persist in pushing this obviously awkward mechanism as a central feature of their art?

I shall, for a change, resist the cynical answer about the preservation of mystique. The socially acceptable answer is that the machine-executable specifications of mechanisms (i.e., algorithms, but I do have an excuse for this specific circumlocution — algorithm is a particularly inapt characterization of a PROLOG program, as you will see) for solving certain problems are most easily conceptualized and specified recursively, as opposed to iteratively with loop constructs. In fact, this ease of high-level conceptualization is one of the sources of disbelief and difficulty that the nonrecursive thinker experiences when confronted with recursive solutions to problems — that is, a recursive solution often appears to be obviously true, but little more than a restatement of the original problem and certainly not an algorithm for computing solutions.

For example, how can we compute whether some value X is a member of some list L?

```
function MEMBER(X,L)
  IF L is empty THEN return false
  ELSEIF X is the first element of L THEN return true
  ELSE return the result of applying the MEMBER function
       with X to the list L without its first element
```

There are three parts to this specification: if the list is empty, then X can't possibly be a member of it, right? — undubitably true; if X is the first list element, then X must be a member of the list — a similarly unassailable truth, I hope; finally, if X is a member of the tail of L, then X is a member of L — true, but suspicious as a major component of the member function perhaps. Nevertheless, this specification can be translated directly into LISP code and will compute the membership function correctly. A number of similar examples follow in the PROLOG section of this chapter.

CODE-DATA EQUIVALENCE

Apart from choking on recursion, all of us who were reared on FORTRAN, BASIC, or COBOL know that code and data are totally different quantities. The program code specifies what is to be done (compute a function, generate a report, and so on), and the data are a set of values with which to do it. You (and I) now need to erase from memory this aberrant notion. It doesn't sit well with LISP, and it's even worse as a cerebral companion to PROLOG.

One of the most important features of the LISP language for AI purposes is the equivalence between executable code and data. One reason for this can be found in the importance of adaptability in intelligent systems, and the consequent need to modify program statements of an AI system at run-time, i.e., to treat program statements like datastructures.

In the earlier example we have a segment of executable code; the body of the function LISTSUM. It is also a list of items (a LISP list is delimited by one pair of parentheses).

(COND((EMPTY LIST)O)(T(PLUS(HEADOF LIST)(LISTSUM(RESTOF LIST)))))

This list is somewhat complex in that it contains sublists that themselves contain sublists. As a list it is also a valid LISP data structure in which the list items, say the atom COND or the sublist ((EMPTY LIST)O), can be manipulated by other LISP functions.

Although all lists can be treated as data structures, only certain lists can be executed, namely those whose first element identifies a function and the rest of whose elements provide appropriate values for the parameters of the particular function identified by the first element.

As you can see, the syntax of LISP is simple. For both executable code and data the only structure is a list of objects delimited with parentheses. In fact the syntax of LISP is too simple; it is so uniform that the inherent structure of a LISP program tends to elude the human perceptual mechanism. What the programmer's eye tells the programmer's brain is that a LISP program is a collection of identifiers that has been liberally sprinkled with left and right parentheses with much the same apparent order as stars in the sky. Hence, the old joke that the name LISP is an acronym derived from Lost In Superfluous Parentheses (I leave the actual derivation as an exercise for the reader who is in need of a confidence booster at this point). The real source of the name is reputed to be List Processing, and it could well be true. The reader should, at this point, be able to appreciate the wisdom of the choice of lists as the fundamental datastructures for a language that uses recursion as a major control structure. Lists of lists can be used to represent trees, arrays, records, etc.—all the standard datastructures of conventional languages—and yet most chunks of any of these fancy list structures are themselves lists. A recursive approach to computation thrives on datastructures that can be successively whittled down to nothing while all the time remaining as bona fide datastructures of the original type. The simplest example is that a list without its first element is still a list (even if it had only one element to begin with).

But despite its perceptual opacity (or perhaps because of it), LISP is great for machines; that is to say, the syntactic simplicity and uniformity of program and data greatly simplifies the implementation of program and data as interchangeable structures. And in addition, implementations of LISP are easily equipped with a more user-friendly syntactic face for human usage (e.g., the COND function given above can typically be programmed in terms of an IF-THEN-ELSE structure which the system then immediately translates to LISPese).

The fact that LISP allows the manipulation of code-like lists as data-structures is not too surprising. It is perhaps a little shocking to think that the sane system designer would contemplate such a thing, but, given that this is the objective of some misconceived project, we could do much the same thing in, say, FORTRAN: An input character string could have the form of an executable statement, and characters within it could be swapped around, etc. Suppose that you ended up with the character string "GO TO 93"; how would you execute this string of characters? Well, in FORTRAN you couldn't ("and quite right, too," I can almost hear the non-AI enthusiasts murmur). But in LISP no holds are barred (you are at liberty to throttle yourself). In all LISP systems we have available, the function EVAL as its name suggests, evaluates (i.e., executes) the list that it is given. In fact, EVAL is virtually the LISP system itself. {The LISP system is just a three-function loop, READ-EVAL-PRINT. It reads in a list — which should be a reference to a function together with appropriate input values for that function — executes it, prints out the value returned by the function referenced, and then waits for another list to read, etc.} So EVAL turns a datastructure into code. To move in the other direction (i.e., from code to datastructure), the user can access the source code for a function that has been previously defined — it will be a list — and simply change it. It can then be stored away again as the definition of the function for subsequent execution.

THE SPECIAL ASSIGNMENT

Pure LISP has no assignment statement — i.e., no statement for setting a variable to some value! This fact ought to elicit at least some raising of eyebrows for the traditional programmer who probably knows that about half of the statements in a conventional program are usually assignment statements. But, as values can be computed and passed around using the parameter and function-result mechanisms, there is, in principle, no need for an assignment statement as such. In practice, however, it turns out to be a very handy thing to have available, despite the fact that it represents a blatant misuse of the functional philosophy.

In (nonpure) LISP the function SETQ is the function used. Thus, to assign the value 5 to the variable X, we type:

(SETQ X 5)

and the LISP system responds, quick as a flash, with

5

which is the value that this function returns. Functions always return a value; this is, in fact, the main function of a function: We send values to the function via the parameters, and the function computes with these values and sends the result back — a function should not change the value of any of its parameters, as this would be a hidden change (it is hidden inside the function body), a generally undesirable *side-effect*.

But notice that in the case of the assignment function, SETQ, the whole point of the function is not to compute a value, but to change the value of its first parameter. Considering the statement involving SETQ given above: Whatever the value of X was before SETQ was used, afterwards its value is 5.

Assignment is thus a bad sort of function. Hence, pure LISP has no truck with it.

LISTS OF PROPERTIES

This section is not a diversion into the records of a realtor's office, but a brief look at a second type of value that can be attached to LISP variables, and one that is particularly useful in AI. As you will find out in Chapter 6, building associations between objects, i.e., relating one object to another, is a key strategy in many knowledge representation schemes. The property list feature of LISP provides direct support for this requirement.

A *property list* is a list of *(attribute value)* pairs, such as (HEIGHT 6), (EYES BLUE), (FEET 2). Such a property list may be associated with a variable, say JACK. We might write this total structure as:

(JACK ((HEIGHT 6)(EYES BLUE)(FEET 2)))

Thus we can build complex structured objects for a program to manipulate in its efforts to display intelligent reasoning. Additionally, the property-list feature may be used to represent relationships in a network. Thus:

```
(ROBIN   ((ISA BIRD)))
(JACK    ((ISA ROBIN)))
(JOHN    ((OWNER_OF ROBIN)(LOVES MARY)))
(BIRD    ((HASPART WINGS)))
```

would be a property-list representation of the trivial semantic network that is used to introduce Chapter 6.

Property-list items are associated with variables, referenced, and changed using primitive functions supplied by the LISP system. We shall see them again later in this chapter.

LISP is an ancient language (not to be compared with Sanskrit, but on a par with FORTRAN), and consequently there are many varieties which have diverged so far from McCarthy's original vision that they are effectively different languages. In order to combat this diversification, a standard, Common LISP, has been defined (see Steele, 1984, if you're curious). Most LISP systems now contain all of Common LISP as a subset (or at least claim that they do). Hence, the programmer whose concern is portability can restrict himself or herself to just this subset of the goodies available.

North America has been the spawning ground for most new AI languages, although POP-2 (Popplestone, 1968) and PROLOG (see Clocksin & Mellish, 1981, for a readable exposition of this odd language) are notable exceptions.

Most AI languages are no longer with us; they exist only as exhibits in the museum of AI. The respective language manuals are material for the historian rather than the serious programmer. Language design in response to needs that were too specific seems to have been the root cause of the lack of longevity in AI languages.

CONNIVER and PLANNER, for example, were exploratory probes into the space of possible programming languages; they were directed at the area of AI applications. Much useful information was gained from them — information that was vital for mapping the space of AI programming languages which, of course, are part of the map of all programming languages. Although the map is by no means complete, the original vehicles will not be used again. The information received will facilitate the design, implementation, and launching of the next generation of investigative devices into the AI-programming-language space. {This is, of course, a meta search space for AI enthusiasts. But we can't specify the initial state, we don't know how to recognize a goal state — or even if one exists — and we're no better informed about the intermediate states or the legal operators — i.e., it's a typical AI problem!} Until much more information is collected and fitted together, the quest for an argot of AI is a fundamentally speculative enterprise.

The search for non-AI programming languages is only slightly more directed, because we possess more knowledge of the structure of this space due to relatively prolonged and extensive experimentation within it.

AI programming languages are the most recent descendents from the evolutionary line of man–machine communication. A characteristic trend within this evolutionary sequence is one of abstraction and thus a removal of detail that the programmer must be cognizant of (this also implies a loss of fine control, which can be a drawback); from machine code, through assembly codes and high-level languages, to AI languages we can clearly discern this trend of abstraction.

More conventional computer science has pursued a somewhat parallel course with the development of abstract data structures. Whether the abstraction capabilities implemented in, say, ADA and MODULA-2 will have any direct impact on AI language research remains to be seen.

PROLOG

The new boy on the block who has made a somewhat unexpected impact is PROLOG. It is a European language that provides a neatly defined and efficiently implemented theorem-proving capability; as an efficient inference engine it has a strong claim to be an essential ingredient in the management of knowledge bases for expert systems, as we shall see in the next chapter.

PROLOG (short for PROgramming in LOGic, its advocates claim; or PROtotype LOGic programming, as is rumored by its detractors; or even PROgramation et LOGique, as the purists claim as they note that, in the south of France where PROLOG was born, English is definitely not the language of choice) is based on the predicate calculus — gruesome but true (I don't hide the truth, however unpalatable), yet mercifully quite unmemorable. All that you need at your synaptic fingertips, so to speak, is the knowledge that, given the rule that:

IF A is true THEN B is true.

and the fact:

A is true.

you are at liberty to conclude:

B is true.

But who in his right mind could do otherwise? Nevertheless, having mastered this mechanism {a mechanism of logical inference quite unbelievably called *modus ponens*—would I lie to you about a thing like that?} you are nearly a master of PROLOG.

Consider our earlier function LISTSUM: it is composed of two rules (one's recursive, sorry I can't help that).

IF the list is empty THEN the sum of its values is zero.

IF the list is not empty THEN the sum of its values is the
value of the first element
plus the sum of the values in
the list without its first
element.

These two rules constitute a declaration of the logical relationships that hold between a list and the sum of its values. And as such they are almost a PROLOG program (all that needs to be added is the appropriate syntactic sugar). We haven't specified, in a conventional programming sense, how to compute this function; we have just declared the relationships that must hold if the computation is correctly done, but that is all that you have to do in PROLOG programming. The PROLOG system takes care of how exactly these specified relationships are to be realized computationally. It's almost the programmer's dream come true, but, as with all dreams, it can turn into something more like a nightmare all too quickly.

The terms *procedural, functional, declarative,* and *applicative,* as well as *symbolic* (one that I have already expressed my dissatisfaction with), are all commonly bandied about in descriptions of programming languages. Certainly these descriptors, which have emerged as accepted terminology in folk computer science, have some meaning, and some have some more meaning than others, but in general they are hazy terms. So treat with circumspection glib characterizations of programming languages presented in terms of these descriptors.

One of the less arguable uses of such descriptors is the categorization of PROLOG as a declarative language, or programming in PROLOG as declarative programming. The essence of this characterization is that programming in PROLOG is primarily a task of declaring the logical relationships upon which the desired computation rests. (Hence, the less defendable statement that programming in PROLOG is logic programming.)

THE INDEPENDENCE OF DECLARATION

In PROLOG the control structure and the declarative structure of a program are separated. A PROLOG program specifies only the relationships that hold between the computational objects {this statement is nearly completely true}. How these relationships will be processed (i.e., what control structure will be used) is separate and part of the implementation of the language. This state of affairs can be contrasted with traditional programming, where the programmer has to work with a tangle of both declarations and control structure.

It is time for a concrete example of a PROLOG program, but first we must look at the data structure that we shall use in our program; we must see how PROLOG deals with lists.

A list in PROLOG is a sequence of objects separated by commas and delimited by square brackets. Thus [a,A,1] is a list of length three. The first element is the constant "a" (denoted as a constant by the lower case used), the second element is a variable named "A" (a variable is denoted by upper case), which would normally but not necessarily be associated with a value, the third and last element of this list is the numeric constant, the number one.

An empty list contains no elements and looks like this [] — surprise, surprise. Finally, there is a list operator " ", which may be used to both behead and rehead lists (i.e., it can be used to remove the first list element or add a new head element to a list).

Now we are ready to translate our statements about lists and the sums of their values into PROLOG. The form of the "listsum" procedure {predicate, if you prefer technical nomenclature} that I have chosen uses two arguments — i.e., two quantities following the function name, enclosed in parentheses, and separated by commas. The first argument is a list, or the name of a list, and is the list whose sum is to be computed. The second argument is a numeric value, or a variable whose value will be numeric when the function is used properly, which will be the sum of the list elements when the listsum computation has been completed.

```
listsum([],0).
listsum([H|T], S):- listsum( T, Stail), S is Stail + H.
```

Let me read this for you in English. The first clause ("clause" is PROLOGese for "statement") is a true fact; it states that the sum of the values of an empty list is zero (no problems with that, I hope). The second clause is an inference rule (note the inference operator ":-") which states that S is the sum of the values of a list whose head is H and whose tail (i.e., the headless list) is T, if Stail is the sum of the values in the tail T, and (in PROLOG the "and" is represented by a comma) S is Stail plus the value of the first, or head, element H. This is also, if not equally, obviously true, isn't it? Contrary to the inalienable truth about all persons being born equal (which is, of course, quite blatantly false), all logical truths are not equally obviously true.

The two clauses given above constitute a useful PROLOG program. And one, moreover, that can either check that a given value is the sum of a given list, or, alternatively, compute the sum of a given list. How do we induce this program to execute? Well, we ask it questions about lists and sums. For example, we could ask:

```
listsum([2,3,5], 10)?
```

and the response would be:

YES

It has checked that 10 is the sum of the values in the list [2,3,5]. Or we could ask:

listsum([5,2,1], X)?

In effect we are asking if there is a value for the variable ''X'' which would make it the sum of the list [5,2,1]; again the response would be:

YES

and in addition it would tell us the value that makes the particular listsum relationship that we asked about true, i.e., X=8. In this usage the sum of the list elements has been computed.

LOSS OF CONTROL: BETTER OR WORSE?

So programming in PROLOG, declarative programming, requires only that the programmer states the individual logical relationships that must be true if the desired computation is correctly done. The PROLOG interpreter then takes over the task of controlling the computation. It decides which rule to use and when. The programmer is freed from the burden of setting up loops and ensuring that they begin and end appropriately, etc. This must all seem like a very good thing. And it would be if it was entirely true, and if we did not care how long our computations took.

First, let us look at the truth of this claim that the programmer need not be concerned with issues of control sequencing in PROLOG programming — after all, it is almost true. One major result of this nearly true claim is that statement sequencing in PROLOG can almost be random. Readers with some years of wrestling with computers behind them will remember the days when a program was a deck of punched cards. A recurring nightmare that I used to have when all of the solid progress toward my Ph.D. thesis was resident in two trays of such punched cards was that the computer operator would drop them on the computer room floor, which he (or she) did from time to time. Whenever my program was returned with an apologetic note saying that certain portions ought to be checked for correct sequencing, there followed a long and tedious period of checking the card sequence against a statement sequence in a recent listing (it is true that such cards could be numbered and automatically sorted into sequence, but the dynamic nature of AI programming is such that the use of this sequencing technique is not feasible in practice). In the nightmare version I could never manage to reconstruct the program exactly. Well, to finally get to the point, if my Ph.D. project had been written in PROLOG, I would have slept more peacefully. If a PROLOG program were to be punched on such cards, one clause per card, it is almost true to say that we could shuffle the cards before each run and the resultant randomized version of the program would be just as correct as the original; it might take more or less time to execute after successive shuffles, but the results would be the same.

As I've said, this no-effect-statement-shuffling story is almost true. So when is it not true? Well, consider the following PROLOG program, which is designed to find a path between any two vertices in a network (a problem which is closely akin to the fundamental problem of the SSSP — finding paths from initial states to goal states).

```
path(V,V).
path(V1,V2):-transition(V1,V3),path(V3,V2).
```

The first clause states the fact that there is always a path from a vertex V to that same vertex V. You can't argue with that, can you? The path is short, it is true, but it is also true that there is always a path nevertheless. The second clause states that there is a path from some vertex V1 to some vertex V2, if there is a transition from vertex V1 to some intermediate vertex V3 and there is a path from V3 to V2. This is also clearly true, but, as is the nature of recursive statements, it seems to be little more than a restatement of the problem, and certainly not an algorithm for computing paths. Yet it is.

Assuming that we have *transition* defined correctly (i.e., in terms of the set of possible moves between vertices for a given network), then the above program will search for a path between any two vertices in a network. Given the network in Figure 4.1, we can see in how this program works.

Not one of the more representative examples of a rich and complex search space, but one whose triviality has been marginally, but critically, reduced by linking the last vertex (numbered 4) back to vertex 1. Let me list the true facts about possible transitions in this network.

```
transition(1,2).
transition(2,3).
transition(3,4).
transition(4,1).
```

This set of all the possible transitions in the pathetic network (Figure 4.1) state, in effect, that there is a clockwise circular path all around the network. And this is, of course, a set of four PROLOG clauses, true facts

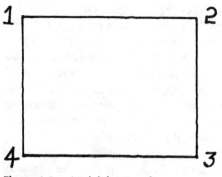

Figure 4.1.   A trivial network

which define the search space that I have illustrated. Given these four facts and the two "path" clauses, we can query this program:

path(1,2)?

Is there a path from vertex 1 to vertex 2, we might naively ask?

YES

is the firm response.

How did it do it? Well, the fact "path(V,V)." was no help, because we were concerned about the possibility of a path between two different vertices, not about a path from a vertex to itself. But the second path rule states that there is a path from 1 to 2 if there is a transition from 1 to some other vertex, and a path from that other vertex to vertex 2 (i.e., when $V1 = 1$ and $V2 = 2$). The first transition fact states that there is a transition from vertex 1 to vertex 2, so 2 is tried as an intermediate vertex (i.e., $V3$ gets the value 2).

Now the first subclause of the right side of the rule is true when $V3 = 2$, so the problem reduces to determining the truth of the second subclause (path(V3,V2)) when $V3 = 2$ and $V2 = 2$; i.e., the system must prove that path(2,2) is true. And now we can see the worth of the apparently useless fact "path(V,V).". When the variable V, is given the value 2, it states that path(2,2) is true, which is just what we wanted to know. Hence, the PROLOG system can answer 'YES' to our query.

Declarations of recursive relationships are infinitely circular, for example, path(V1,V2):-transition(V1,V3),path(V3,V2), and what gets us out of this not exactly vicious but definitely unhelpful circularity is the clause:

path(V,V). But in order for the PROLOG interpreter to cease chasing its own tail, so to speak, it must always encounter this stopping clause (i.e., there is always a path from any vertex to that same vertex) *before* it encounters the general case. PROLOG interpreters always work through the possible clauses sequentially from top to bottom. So, the upshot of all this is that, for the stopping clause to be considered before the general-case clause, the stopping clause must be higher in the list; it does not have to be directly above it, but the stopping clause does have to be somewhere above the general-case clause.

If you're not convinced, then consider a PROLOG program composed of the same set of seven clauses but with the clause path(V,V) placed at the bottom. Now we query this shuffled program:

path(1,2)?

There is no immediate answer. Some time goes by, and you tap keys randomly to determine if the computer has just died or not. Finally, you get the characteristically unenlightening message:

ENVIRONMENT STACK FULL

and the definite impression that the computer has abandoned its attempt to answer your apparently trivial query. Why? In something close to a nutshell (as close as I ever get to compressed explanation): When the problem is reduced to determining the truth of path(2,2), the system uses the general clause again (it encounters it before the stopping clause, remember) and decides that there is a path from vertex 2 to vertex 2 if there is a transition from 2 to somewhere (and there is, viz., transition(2,3)) and a path from that somewhere to 2. Hence, it "reduces" the proof of path(1,2) to a proof of path(2,3), which "reduces" to a proof of path(3,4), which "reduces" to a proof of path(4,1), which in turn reduces to a proof of path(1,2), and there is no end — at least not until the environment stack is full, whatever that means.

The other effect of shuffling the program is a purely practical one: The program may take a lot longer to execute, and, if there is more than one correct answer (i.e., more than one value for some variable that makes the question which you asked true), the correct values may be generated in a different order. The time-change feature is the one that I wish to focus on.

A change in program execution time may not seem like a problem to worry about, and certainly not something to have nightmares about in these days of cheap computer power and expensive AI-proficient persons. Gone are the bad old days of agonizing over pages of machine code in order to shave another microsecond or two off of the program's running time.

But, at the other extreme, a whole subfield of computer science is occupied with analyzing the run-time complexity of algorithms, because certain classes of algorithms are so slow that they are not practically useful. Many correct algorithms are known for a lot of awkward problems, but these algorithms are of absolutely no practical use because they take too much time to execute. As we shuffle the PROLOG deck, we may in so doing seriously undermine the practicality of our program.

An equally, or even more, serious time penalty can be generated by ignoring the sequence-control implications of alternative ways to declare the true relationships in our problem domain. A classic example is provided by sorting algorithms.

Suppose we wish to write a PROLOG program that sorts a randomly sequenced list of numbers into, say, ascending order. In the simplistic mode of PROLOG programming we need only declare the true relationships that must hold between a randomly ordered list, L, and the sorted version, S. Well, what can we say about L and S?

First, we know that, if the sorting is correct, then the list S will be ordered, but that, in addition, S must contain all the same numbers as L contains, albeit in a different order, most probably. That is to say, S must also be a permutation of L, and we've done it. Let's translate these two logical relationships into a PROLOG clause:

sort(L,S):-permuted(L,S),ordered(S).

Let me state this one for you in English. The sorted version of L is S, if S is a permutation of L, and S is ordered. Again a true statement of the relationships between S and L that must hold if S is a sorted version of L. We can now execute this PROLOG program (assuming that we add the four clauses necessary to define *permuted* and *ordered*) by querying it with, say:

sort([3,2,4], X)?

We are asking if there is a value for the variable X such that the sort relationship is true for the list [3,2,4] and that value. The answer is:

YES
X = [2,3,4]

But how was this answer computed? Compactly stated: Random permutations of L were generated, and then tested to see if they happened to be ordered. At some point one such permutation was also ordered, and that gave us the answer. This is a terribly inefficient way to sort lists of numbers. More efficient sorting programs in PROLOG can be written, but to do so demands that the programmer both understands and exploits the control structure of the PROLOG interpreter. Sterling and Shapiro (1986) explore this question in their PROLOG book on advanced programming techniques.

Thus you may begin to see why some people would argue that this separating out of control has resulted in a loss of control.

EXTRALOGICAL POLLUTANTS

Consider our earlier PROLOG "sort" clause and reverse the order of the "permuted" and "ordered" subclauses. We get:

sort(L,S):-ordered(S),permuted(L,S).

Has this switch had any effect on the correctness of this clause? As a statement in logic is it just as true as it ever was, but as a clause in a PROLOG program it will no longer function correctly. If we query this clause (again assuming appropriate definitions of *permuted* and *ordered*) with:

sort([3,2,4],X)?

we will receive only a curt error message for our trouble. Why is this? Again it is because there is more to PROLOG than pure logic and the user must be aware of this fact. The "sorted" relation (as typically written) checks that a given list of values is in order. In the previous version of "sort" a permuted version of the original list was passed to "ordered" for checking. But in the current version "ordered" has no list of numbers to check, so we get an error message. {It is conceivable that the "ordered" relation could be written to generate ordered lists of random numbers, and then "permute" could check each such ordered list to see if it happened to be a permutation of the original list. This would be a correct PROLOG program, but has little else to recommend it. Its efficiency does not bear thinking about, let alone figuring out in detail.}

What this example exposes is that the subclauses "ordered" and "permuted" are executed in left-to-right order. In logic there is no such notion; things are just true or not true. But in PROLOG some sequencing decisions had to be made, and left-to-right was the chosen order (we have already seen some repercussions of the top-to-bottom processing of complete clauses).

Another practically necessary piece of extralogical detritus in PROLOG is the "cut" operator, "!". The PROLOG interpreter is guaranteed to let you know that some input query is true, if indeed it is true with respect to the facts and rules which it has at its disposal at the time — its current database. A puzzling statement to the neophyte logician perhaps; after all, that's the least you might expect it to do. But it turns out that providing this guarantee with reasonable efficiency was the great accomplishment of the PROLOG designers.

Searching for proof of the truth of a query with respect to a given database is a classic SSSP problem (if this acronym means little or nothing to you, then you skipped Chapter 3, or else you are reading this book with insufficient care). The initial state is the initial database plus the query, intermediate states are generated by adding inferences to the database, and the goal state is attained when the query is proved true. The search space is usually portrayed as a proof tree. For example, the proof tree for the query, "sort([3,2,4],Y)?", of our earlier, correct sort program is illustrated in Figure 4.2.

In order to prove the truth of sort([3,2,4],Y) (node 1 in my proof tree, Figure 4.2), the system attempts to find a permutation of the list [3,2,4]. The clauses for "permuted" (node 3) generate and return a true permutation; it is [3,4,2]. The system then determines if it is true that this generated list is "ordered"(node 4). The clauses for "ordered" (node 5) quite promptly and correctly disillusion the system about the current path to a proof which it thinks that it is following. Node 5 returns "false" to node 4 which hands the bad news up to node 1.

So this path to a proof of the query, which looked promising with the list [3,4,2] as a true permutation of the original list, is in fact a dead end. What now? The PROLOG interpreter is not easily discouraged. It backtracks to an earlier state where there are other alternatives to try, and tries one.

In this case it tries another permutation of [3,2,4] (node 6). The code for "permuted" (node 7) returns a new true permutation, namely [2,3,4]. Hot on the trail of another potential proof path, the system determines if this particular permuted list is "ordered"(node 8), and it is (node 9). Node 9 then passes the good news up to node 8, which joyfully hands it on up with Y = [2,3,4] to node 1. Thus the proof is completed.

What's the significance of all this? Several things, I think. First, the PROLOG interpreter has no intelligence (however within reason you define it, a PROLOG system has none); it exhaustively searches the space of possible proof trees until it finds a complete proof path {a depth-first search, in case you're interested}. This means that the PROLOG inter-

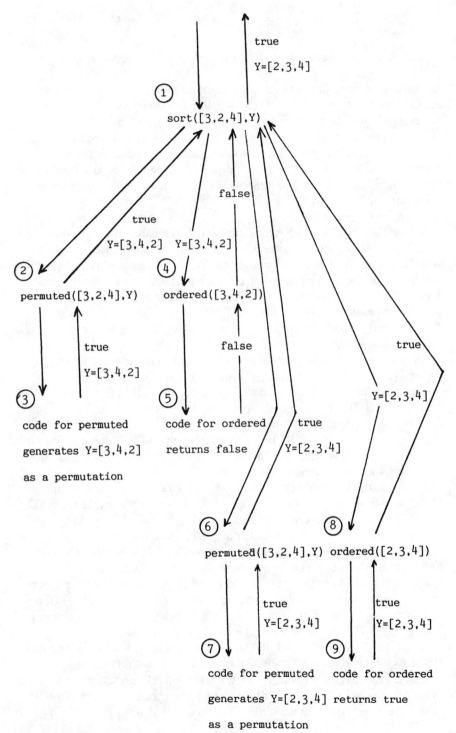

Figure 4.2. A proof tree for the query sort ([3,2,4],Y)?

preter must be able to backtrack — i.e., it must be able to go back to some earlier step in an apparent proof path, abandon all the results of the steps subsequent to the point it backs up to, and then continue forward again on the basis of a different alternative at the point it backed up to. Accurate backtracking requires complex, but well-defined, memorization and perfect recall, but after all that's what computers excel at.

Finally, we can get back to the "cut" operator. If we place a cut operator to the right of the implication operator (i.e., the ":- "), then, once the system has, in pursuit of a proof path, crossed the cut, it cannot backtrack back over it. Let me illustrate this. Suppose we insert a cut in our "sort" clause like so:

sort(L,S):-permuted(L,S),!,ordered(S).

The system will no longer be able to backtrack and try the "permuted" subclause more than once. So, if it does not generate the "ordered" permutation on the first try, the "sort" query will fail. Thus in our last example (in which "permuted" came up with an "ordered" version of the list [3,2,4] on the second attempt) the query "sort([3,2,4],Y)?" would have failed.

Our new version of "sort" is clearly not a great PROLOG program for sorting lists (we improved its efficiency, but at the cost of correctness this is not usually considered to be an improvement). So why would you want to do this? You wouldn't, at least not in the way that I have just used the cut operator. That was just a simple example. What I have not yet divulged about the PROLOG interpreter is that, not content with finding one proof of any given query, it slogs away blindly and explores all other possible proof paths!

Now you and I know that there is only one sorted version of our old friend the list [3,2,4], but the PROLOG interpreter doesn't know this (you may recall my earlier claim about absence of intelligence in these systems). If a list is large and you use my logically correct PROLOG "sort" program, you may well find yourself spending large amounts of time hanging around the keyboard waiting for the program to finish backtracking and looking for other (nonexistent) ordered versions of your original list. The cut operator can prevent this logically impeccable but quite mindless exhaustive searching.

sort(L,S):-permuted(L,S),ordered(S),!.

Having found one sorted value for S, the cut operator prevents backtracking to try alternative permutations. So the cut operator is another PROLOG feature that is present for reasons of computational efficiency but has nothing to do with logic. It is purely a pollutant whose use is frowned upon by purists (but, then, they're frowned upon by everybody else).

NEGATION AS FAILURE

A question that should be nagging at any reader who is not completely lost at this point is: What happens when a query is actually false? Logic does not encompass the idea of explicitly proving things to be false. So the PROLOG interpreter has no option but to exhaustively explore all possible proof paths, and only when every one of them fails to lead to a proof is it in a position to conclude that the current query is false. Thus, to conclude that something is false is the outcome of failing to prove that it is true. Hence, you may run across discussions of the pros and cons of negation as failure in PROLOG — not true is the result of failure to prove truth.

This strategy seems quite appropriate, but it is in fact only appropriate if the PROLOG system has all relevant rules and facts in its database {i.e., if the "closed world assumption" holds — to use more highfalutin terminology}. This is typically not the case in much AI, and we shall see some of the resultant problems surfacing in the following chapter where logical-style reasoning is the basis for expert systems.

VERIFY OR COMPUTE

Another interesting feature of PROLOG is that we can, for example, "drive" the declarative structure either backwards or forwards: either deducing the implications of our program, or checking if a given statement is true with respect to the program.

Thus the query "sort([3,2,4],Y)?" is a case of computing a value for Y which makes the "sort" relation true. In other words: is there an inference from the database such that the "sort" relation is true when L = [3,2,4]?

A query from the class of verifications with the "sort" program is "sort([3,2,4],[1,2,3])?". The system is in effect being asked to verify that the two given lists [3,2,4] and [1,2,3] are associated by the "sort" relation (in fact they're not, but that just means the result of the attempted verification will, if all goes well, be "NO" — PROLOG's way of saying that it failed to verify the truth of this relationship in this particular case).

There appear to be some interesting implications of these two modes — verify and compute — of using a PROLOG program. Analysis (Guthrie, 1985) has shown that verification of a result is never slower than computing that result, and sometimes much faster. The research investigated the possibility of increasing software reliability by using a nonprocedural (e.g., PROLOG) program to check the result of a procedural computation. These analyses may also provide insight into the optimal use of forward- and backward-chaining strategies for knowledge base inferencing in expert systems (a subject that is explored in the next chapter, but, while you're waiting for this particular link to be formed, try to associate these two modes of PROLOG processing with the general strategies for searching symbolic spaces as discussed in Chapter 3).

BIDIRECTIONALITY

In the light of the knowledge that a PROLOG program can be used to both verify specific statements and compute results, it should not be too surprising that it is called a bidirectional language. A system of logic can be used to work backwards from a potential truth (i.e., that [1,2,3] is a sorted version of [3,2,4]) and verify or not, as the case may be, that the specific, potentially true statement is a valid inference from the database of facts and rules. Alternatively, such a collection of facts and rules can be driven forwards in order to generate a set of statements that are true inferences. In the first case, the system can work back from a specific statement to determine if the database supports it. In the second case, the system works forwards from the database to determine further true inferences.

So a given PROLOG program offers the promise of being usable in two rather different ways, and the extent to which the promise is realized is dependent upon the degree to which the programmer has resisted the inclusion of extralogical pollutants.

One attempt to exploit the potential bidirectionality of PROLOG in a significant manner is described in the chapter on natural language processing. A PROLOG-based grammar for a language may be used to either analyze or generate sentences of that language.

PATTERN MATCHING

Yet one more important aspect of PROLOG that I have been glossing over in my short introduction is the role of pattern matching — an operation that is central to much computing in AI. The specific pattern matching operation employed extensively in PROLOG is called *unification*.

In my earlier descriptions of how the PROLOG interpreter deals with specific queries, I wrote, for example, that the variable Y has the value

[2,3,4]. In actuality what looks like simple assignment of a value to a variable is just a very simple case of unification. {Phrased more correctly: The variable Y unifies with the list [2,3,4], which results in the variable Y becoming instantiated with the value [2,3,4] — don't sweat over this sentence, it's not worth it.}

The pattern matching of unification is seen more easily if we revert back to the PROLOG program for, say, summing the values in a list, to wit:

```
listsum([],0).
listsum([H | T],S):-listsum(T,Stail), S is Stail + H.
```

The structure "[H | T]" in the 'listsum' rule is a pattern that will match (i.e., unify with in PROLOG jargon) certain other patterns, in particular, it will match all non-empty-list patterns. And as a result of the matching, the variables H and T may obtain values. Thus when this program is queried with say, "listsum([1,2,3],S)?", the patterns "[H | T]" and "[1,2,3]" match with the result that H = 1 and T = [2,3].

More trickily, "[H,a | T]" will match "[1,a,4]" with the result that H = 1 and T = [4], but the patterns "[H,a | T]" and "[1,2,4]" will not match. If you're beginning to grasp this, then try unifying "[H,2 | T]" with "[3,2]" — it works.

Suffice it to say that there is a powerful pattern-matching operation at the heart of PROLOG, but it is beyond the scope of this book to delve further into its intricacies.

THE PROMISES OF PROLOG

As I intimated early on in this excursion into PROLOG, it was originally conceived as the first prototype of a mechanization of a logical proof procedure. So where might it be going once the prototype has been thoroughly explored and evaluated?

PARALLELISM

One future development of PROLOG that a number of groups of researchers are working on is some manifestation of a parallel PROLOG (e.g., Concurrent PROLOG — Shapiro, 1987). Logic itself contains no concept of sequentiality — e.g., that one inference be generated before another. Current computing systems are fundamentally serial, i.e., it is critical that the order of subprocesses be specified. This mismatch between the logical basis of PROLOG and its current implementations gives rise to many problems, as we have seen in this chapter. Thus, for efficient computation the PROLOG programmer must concern himself or herself with extralogical problems, and the language must offer certain extralogical features.

With a parallel implementation of PROLOG a number of these problems would go away (a certain number would not, and some new problems would emerge, which is why parallel PROLOGs are not yet commonly available). Nevertheless, the attractions of parallel PROLOG are clear. Consider the two PROLOG clauses given below.

```
A:-B,C.
A:-D;E.
```

{Syntactic trivia: ";" is PROLOGese for "or"}

The first reads that A is true if B and C are true, and the second reads that A is true if D or E is true. In logic (but not in many PROLOG programs, e.g., the "sort" program) A is true if B and C are both true, but the truths of B and C can be determined independently and in any order, or in parallel. Similarly, the truths of D and E can be investigated independently and in parallel. Thus, in a parallel PROLOG whose goal was to determine the truth of A, four processors could be set to work simultaneously and independently on the truths of B,C,D, and E (one proof-path search per processor, of course). Then the time taken to prove the truth of A (if it is true) will be the lesser of: the maximum time for proving either B or C, or minimum time for proving D or E. {This is hard to say unambiguously in English; after all, it was not designed for saying such things, was it? A more formal statement might be:

$$ttA = min(\ max(ttB,ttC),min(ttD,ttE))$$

where ttX means "time for truth of X". In a sequential system ttA might be as bad as $(ttB + ttC + ttD + ttE)$. It is left as an exercise for the reader who must go into all this gruesome detail to justify my nonobvious claims.}

An example of the fruits of this development from PROLOG is the parallel logic language PARLOG (Conlon, 1989). It's a commercial product and can even be run on MACs and PCs (i.e., personal computers).

A SPECIFICATION LANGUAGE

There is a school of PROLOG-oriented thought which espouses the view that, even though simple declarative programming leads to dreadfully inefficient programs, it does lead quickly and easily to correct ones. Thus

PROLOG may develop into a machine- executable, problem-specification language. A specification can then be executed and checked for correctness and then compiled (i.e., automatically translated) into some more computationally efficient form.

Kowalski (1984), for example, presents this view, and Balzer, Cheatham, and Green (1983) describe a "new paradigm" for programming in which such a machine-executable specification language is necessary. But by this time, I trust that you can see that PROLOG is a far-from-perfect (or even adequate) executable specification language (hint for readers who are not seeing this problem in sharp focus: Recall the hidden sequence control in a PROLOG program, and don't forget that correctness loses a lot of its glamour if it is tied to an algorithm that is too inefficient to ever be usable).

HEURISTIC CONTROLS

Given that a PROLOG interpreter blindly explores the complete proof tree associated with a particular query and database, the AI person is naturally tempted to try and prune the search with heuristics (the classic approach described in Chapter 3). It is not at all clear exactly how to do this, but one idea is to preface rules with a heuristic "guard"(in the style of Dijkstra's, 1976, guarded commands — I hesitate to mention the AI anti-Christ, but now it's done). That is, a rule may be guarded by some prefixed expression that must evaluate to, say, true before the rule can be used. Thus the programmer then has the opportunity to employ such prefixes to constrain the search of the proof tree. The prefixed expressions do not, of course, have to be heuristic in nature (i.e., rules of thumb that seem to work) but if they are formally valid contraints then they could probably have been encoded into the rules in the first place.

As an example, recall the "sort" program one last time (I promise). There is essentially only one sorted version of any list (especially if we exclude the possibility of duplicate list elements). Thus a smart version of "sort" should quit as soon as it stumbles on a permutation that is ordered, but "sort" without a cut operator doesn't. As an alternative to the cut operator we could use a "guard" expression that was true until a solution was found and then evaluated to false, thus blocking the fruitless search for further solutions.

A major reason for the current prominence of PROLOG is the Japanese connection: The Japanese threat to dominate computer technology with "fifth generation" machines (see Feigenbaum & McCorduck, 1983) including a proposal that PROLOG might form the basis of the associated programming languages, also to be developed. It is not clear exactly how the Japanese intend to develop PROLOG, but it seems that they plan to use it as a core language on top of which they will layer the desired characteristics that PROLOG lacks. If they maintain PROLOG essentially intact and just bury it in a richer programming context, then they will have developed an integrated programming environment — which just happens to be the subject of the last major subsection of this chapter. But to ease us into the concept of such environments we can take a brief look at object-oriented programming — a significant alternative to either LISP or PROLOG, but one whose exact status as a language subclass or a complete programming paradigm or a model for man–machine interfaces is a contentious issue.

OBJECT-ORIENTED PROGRAMMING

As you can see without looking too closely, I didn't call this section Smalltalk-80 but opted for a general presentation of object-oriented programming (OOP) as a style of programming. Whether OOP is a programming paradigm in its own right, or more a style of programming that can be realized in conventional programming languages is a matter for debate, but not here.

Advocates of the programming-style viewpoint can point to the many OOP options that that exist for a wide variety of programming languages. There is, for example, a proposed extension to Common LISP known as the Common LISP Object System (CLOS). One of the two languages selected as starting points for CLOS is CommonLoops (Bobrow et al., 1986), the other, in case you're curious, is New Flavors (Moon, 1986). Kempf, Harris, D'Souza, and Snyder (1987) report on experience with CommonLoops.

But whatever the actual language selected, OOP is not like programming in FORTRAN, or COBOL, or any other traditional language. System development in the OOP style is typically tailoring a general system to specific needs by extracting particular substructures from the very general structures provided at the outset. By way of contrast, more traditional programming can be thought of in terms of building up the specific substructures required to perform the task at hand (i.e., constructing procedures and functions) from the set of primitive elements that comprise the language being used (i.e., the statements of the programming language).

Modularization is always a key strategy for managing the complexity of software system development. In traditional programming the programmer breaks the problem down into functional components and designs blocks of code to realize these modules. The particular modularization scheme chosen is dictated by consideration of the flow of control through the system as it is passed more or less explicitly from one module to the next. Subsequently, data structures are distributed through the framework of procedural modules as dictated by a strategy of localizing the data items to specific modules as much as possible. Datastructures that are used by a number of different modules may be made "global," so that a collection of modules may access a single representation of this data. In the more ancient programming languages the existence of such long-distance associations in a program was simply implicit in the the overall structuring of the set of modules that comprised the program. In more modern languages (e.g., ADA and MODULA-2) these long-distance connections must be explicitly signaled within each module, as well as restrictions on the nature of the association (e.g., information may be restricted to a one-way flow from the global datastructure into the module).

In OOP modularization is still a key strategy, and there are many parallels with the caricaturization of traditional system design that I have just presented. But there are also many differences. The basic module of OOP is an *object*. An object is an integrated collection of data and code {*instance variables* and *methods,* respectively, if you'd like a dose of jargon}. Superficially, this does not seem very different from a traditional subroutine or function (and if you want to be awkward about it, I'd find it hard to persuade you otherwise — after all, the OOP paradigm isn't extraterrestrial, it did grow out of the procedural paradigm, and its ancestry, not surprisingly, is still apparent). But there are significant differences. There are differences of modularization criteria in system design, and there are differences of module use in the solution of a problem, and these two types of difference are, of course, closely related.

The use of an object-oriented system to solve problems is typically an interactive one, whereas the traditional procedural paradigm arose in a batch processing environment — execution of the system was initiated, and the programmer was forced to take a back seat until it had worked its way through, control being passed in a more or less predetermined way from procedure to procedure, to some end point. In an interactive environment the programmer is not forced to design for a monolithic approach to sequence control. The programmer can design a system in which problems are solved by a conglomerate of autonomous subcomputations by the machine, where much of the binding that results in the specific conglomerates that solve the problem at hand is supplied "live," as it were, by the human system user. In less pretentious prose, the user of an object-oriented system has much scope to dabble in each execution of the system, and thus the system designer can, and should, take this into account during the design process. This consideration applies, of course, to any interactive environment, and is thus not a unique characteristic of OOP. It is, nevertheless, a characteristic of OOP that sets it apart from much traditional procedural programming. OOP can also claim much of the credit for what has become the standard style of interaction in modern computer systems: OOP initiated the age of WIMPs — windows, icons, mice, and pop-up menus, to be quite clear what it is that I'm referring to here.

These are all OOP contributions to the human-computer interface; the use of this technology is what makes the MACINTOSH computer, for example, a usable tool for someone who knows no programming languages. Windows provide multiple views of a computation, e.g., a listing of the program, a trace of an execution, and a diagram of the inheritance hierarchy. Icons are pictorial representations of computational objects, and the mouse is a device that senses horizontal motion and is used to point to objects on the screen. Thus we might use the mouse to point to, say, a "pencil" (i.e., an icon) on the screen in order to initiate line drawing in one of the screen windows. And pop-up menus provide a convenient "choice" mechanism for the system user. A menu is a list of options, such as run, edit, or view a program. The mouse is used to point to, and thus select, the option required. Once an option has been selected the next menu for the subsequent options, if any, pops up, and selection within its list of options becomes possible. This general style of human–computer interaction, pioneered in the OOP movement, is now widespread and commonplace in computer systems, even ones that are otherwise totally traditional in their approach to computation.

What is unique to OOP is the nature of primitive elements of sequence control. In OOP they are called *messages*. An execution of an object-oriented system is composed of a collection of messages. A message tells an object to compute something (by, say, applying one of its methods to some of its instance variable values). A message may be sent to an object and trigger a computation either directly by the system user, or indirectly as a result of a message received from another object that could not, on its own, deal with the message that it was originally sent. Objects exist in the well-defined context of more-general objects and of more-specific objects. This superclass–class–subclass hierarchy (it is, of course, not limited to three levels as the English language is, if I'm not to stretch it too much) is known as an *inheritance hierarchy,* because both data and code in an object at one level may be used by a lower-level object — the lower-level object is said to *inherit* a specific method from its superclass.

It's time for a picture to dilute the foregoing mass of words. Figure 4.3 is a three-level class hierarchy.

Wegner (1987) presents the object-oriented paradigm in the context of several alternative classification schemes for programming paradigms. Of

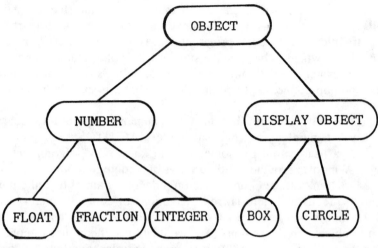

Figure 4.3.   A three-level hierarchy of classes

particular interest is his exploration of the similarities and differences between the inheritance mechanisms of OOP and biology. Further exploration of the notion of inheritance of properties and resentational schemes
to support intelligent reasoning is provided in Chapter 6, where it is considered as an issue within the general problem of knowledge representation.

   With the aid of the specific class hierarchy illustrated in Figure 4.3, I
can generate examples of the fundamental features of OOP. So, for a start
we need to be able to create objects. Let's say we want to create an
INTEGER object named X with the initial value 2. What do we do? We
send a message to the class INTEGER, telling it to use the NEW operation (*method,* if you want to be pedantic) and to associate the object that
NEW generates with the name X and the value 2. We might do it as follows:

X ← INTEGER NEW 2

so now we have an integer object named X whose value is 2. We have
sent the message "NEW 2" to the class INTEGER, and it has associated
the result (i.e., a new object whose value is 2) with the name X.
Let's add 3 to the value of this object. We type:

X + 3

and the response, not too surprisingly, is:

5

Internally, the message "+ 3" was sent to the object X, and its "+" method performed an operation that resulted in the value 5. One point to note is that the "+ 3" message gets its meaning (i.e., is associated with a specific operation) from the object that receives the message. Thus if "+ 3" were sent to a CHARACTER_STRING object, it might interpret "+" as concatenation and just add the character 3 to its current string value. Thus it is said that "+" is *overloaded* with more than one interpretation. This should not be too surprising, as the operator "+" is typically overloaded in conventional languages. Thus in FORTRAN the expression "J = I + 3" causes integer addition, while "R = F + 3.2" would cause floating_point addition. Internally, these are very different operations, and the computer system selects the appropriate one on the basis of the type (INTEGER or REAL) of the operands.

What is special about overloading in OOP is that this mechanism is generalized to all operators and is made available to the programmer (rather than a pre-defined system feature which the programmer cannot change, as in FORTRAN). But the fairly conventional language ADA, for example, offers comprehensive operator overloading facilities to the programmer as well as OOP-like class hierarchies, etc. Nevertheless, it is not classed as an OOP language.

It is time to look inside of objects. Suppose that we want to create a DISPLAY_OBJECT, a BOX, and we'll call it B1.

B1 ← BOX NEWAT:100@200

This message to the class BOX will produce a box (of default size) on the screen at location (100, 200), wherever that might be. In addition, this particular BOX object is called B1. Figure 4.4 is an illustration of the innards of the class BOX which is, of course, an object.

It might be worth noting a few features illustrated in Figure 4.4. To begin with, it contains a link-up to its superclass; this ties it into the inheritance hierarchy. Secondly, there are some *instance variables;* these are the variables needed to define and manage objects of this class, such as B1. Thus, B1 will have specific values for SIZE, TILT, and LOCATION. Thirdly, there are the *methods,* which are the legal operations on this class and objects of this class. It is these methods that will determine how messages are interpreted. Finally, you might note that the first method is somewhat different from the other two. The first method is a class

class name	BOX
superclass	DISPLAY_OBJECT
instance variable names	SIZE TILT LOCATION

methods

>   NEWAT: INITIAL_LOCATION
>
>   (code to generate a new object of default
>   SIZE and TILT, and draw it on the screen
>   at INITIAL_LOCATION; returns a pointer to
>   the new object)
>
>   SHOW:
>
>   (code to draw a particular box)
>
>   ERASE:
>
>   (code to remove a particular box from the screen)

Figure 4.4.   Some details from the class BOX

method. It is used by the class to create new objects. The second and third methods are instance methods. They are used by instances of this class (i.e., specific BOX objects like B1). Thus, SHOW would be used by B1 to display itself on the screen, and ERASE would be used for just the opposite purpose. The reader who makes it through Chapter 6 will find a striking similarity between objects in OOP and the frame data structure described therein.

There are many sources of further information on this rapidly developing paradigm, or programming style, or whatever you want to call it. A large number of books are devoted to OOP, either specific manifestations like Smalltalk (e.g., Goldberg, 1984), or the nature of OOP in general. The Association for Computing Machinery (ACM), the premier computer software "club" in the USA (despite its hardware name), has run an annual conference on OOP. It is the annual conference on OOP Systems, Languages and Applications which of course goes under the delightful acronym of OOPSLA — a designation that guaranteed success when the organizers were lucky enough to hit upon it. "What's in a name?" Don't try to tell me that the conference would smell the same whatever it was called; everything is in a name (I exaggerate, but then so did Shakespeare).

PROGRAMMING ENVIRONMENTS

The demand for dynamic capabilities in AI, run-time modification of both algorithms and data structures, quickly leads to incomprehensible programs. Dynamic systems suggest an interpreter rather than a compiler implementation. Interpreters with their closer proximity to the source code offer a more ready basis for an interactive and helpful programmer support environment than compilers do.

The scenario for AI program development is thus an arrangement of mutual benefit: Desirable language characteristics make the programmer's task more difficult, but the easiest implementation strategy can readily support the addition of modules to ameliorate the programmer's lot.

LISP ENVIRONMENTS

LISP is a terrible language to program with: Its basic structure is conceptually opaque, the flow of control through nested function calls, rather than sequentially from one statement to the next, is difficult to follow, etc. It is not the bare LISP language that is particularly useful; it is the language embedded in a support environment. This feature was one point of contrast between AI and non-AI languages: The latter were just programming languages to be judged as they stood, but the strengths of the former languages were only really evident when the language was embedded in an appropriate environment. This distinction is no longer so sharp: the thoroughly traditional language ADA, for example, has been developed together with a support environment.

Just as the neophyte LISPer is unlikely to be too impressed with bare LISP as a serious programming tool, he or she is quite likely to be equally cold about LISP within a sophisticated support environment. This is because the environment will appear to be extremely complicated to use. There will be too many options, too much to remember, and it will all seem excessive in the context of a small demonstration. And indeed it is; such environments only show their worth with large-scale problems and after a long, slow learning process. If you're going next door, then you might as well walk, but if you plan to cross the continent, then you had better learn to drive a car.

Extended dialects of LISP are one important manifestation of AI development environments, primarily because of the vast library of support subprograms that constitute an important part of these LISP extensions. The chief reason for developing AI software on a LISP machine such as the SYMBOLICS 3670 is not the fact that it directly executes LISP, but because of the support environment that comes with the machine; a major part of this environment is the 100 MIT-man-years of support functions.

Two of the important early LISP environments have already been mentioned, but at the risk of being repetitive they are MACLISP and INTERLISP. The former has developed into a number of varieties, such as ZETALISP, which is offered on the SYMBOLICS machines along with FLAVORS an OOP system. INTERLISP is still widely used as INTERLISP-D, which is in fact the basis for the LOOPS environment, a description of which follows.

The move to standardize LISP systems, through the definition of Common LISP, has also been mentioned earlier.

LOOPS

LOOPS is described as a "knowledge programming system" that "contains a number of integrated paradigms of programming" (Stefik, Bobrow, & Kahn, 1986, p. 10). It is based on a LISP environment (INTERLISP-D) with the addition of other programming paradigms: a rule-based paradigm (i.e., rule-based inferencing as demanded by expert systems technology, Chapter 5, and as provided by PROLOG), an OOP paradigm, and an *access-oriented programming* paradigm. It is this latter component that is new to us, so I'll focus in on it.

Access-oriented programming (AOP) is presented as the dual to OOP. In OOP, the sending of a message from one object to another may cause the recipient object to change its data values as well as cause other things to happen. In AOP, when a data value within an object is changed, it may cause a message to be sent.

AOP is centered on the notion of tying *annotations* to data. In LOOPS there are two manifestations of this idea:

1. *Property annotations*—the association of a property list (a LISP feature, you may recall) with data items;
2. *Active values*—the association of procedures with data items.

A program based on the AOP philosophy has two components: a traditional computation part, and a part that monitors the computations. Ideally, the monitoring part — essentially the AOP contribution — does not interfere with computational part. Thus adding and removing annotations should not cause a program to stop working, unless the program uses the annotations.

I shall focus down even further and describe active-value programming (AVP).

If a program variable is annotated with code for displaying on a screen a visual representation of the variable's value, we have a very powerful monitoring aid. Not only can we have a visual representation of the values of critical program variables, but these representations are active — that is, when the program variable is changed by means of an internal computation, say, then the visual display is automatically changed to reflect this modification of the state of the computation. It is easy to appreciate how this behavior could be achieved using AVP.

The screen display procedures are an AOP annotation to the program variable. Thus, changing the value of the variable causes a message to be sent to execute the display procedures using the new value and thus displaying the new value on the screen.

Typically, some sort of dial or gauge is used as the visual representation of a variable's value. So a change of value in the annotated variable will be seen as the movement of a needle on a dial or a column of, say, red on a vertical scale — the choice of visualization details is up to the programmer; the AVP facility just provides the underlying mechanism for tying an internal change of value to a visual display of that change.

The mechanism can also function in the opposite direction: A modifica-

tion of the visual representation (by means of, say, a mouse action) can be programmed to cause the appropriate change in the internal value of the variable being displayed.

Clearly, there are many possibilities to be explored for AOP, and perhaps for AVP in particular. It can certainly support a powerful facility for visualization of a computation, and as such can be considered as an mechanism to support the growing computer science subfield of program visualization (see Myers, 1988, for an introduction). It should also be apparent that AOP will readily support graphical simulation of processes. This notion of simulation is typically associated with OOP, and the LOOPS manifestation of AOP is based (you may recall) on the OOP paradigm.

You can recall the inheritance notion in OOP, can't you? Well, Figure 4.3 is a simple illustration of an inheritance hierarchy. Support of a multiple inheritance structure is a critical part of LOOPS. What this means is that a new object can inherit methods from several more general structures in the system. In a straightforward inheritance hierarchy, the inheritance is limited to just those structures directly above it. Let me illustrate this last point about LOOPS.

In Figure 4.3 we have a simple inheritance hierarchy, and a BOX object can inherit from the classes DISPLAY OBJECT and OBJECT but not from, say, NUMBER. Within a multiple inheritance scheme this sort of restriction is no longer in force. So in LOOPS we would be free to create, say, an INTEGER_DISPLAY OBJECT which could inherit appropriate methods and instance variables from both the INTEGER and the DISPLAY OBJECT classes. This facility clearly gives the programmer power to create exactly what is wanted wherever necessary, but there is equally clearly a cost in extra complexity of the inheritance structure with which he or she must cope with in the end.

POPLOG

PROLOG is also prominent in another AI programming languages venture: integrated multilanguage systems. POPLOG (Sloman & Hardy, 1983) is such a system and it combines POP-11 with LISP and PROLOG. The most important reason for having such a system is that different tasks in a single system can best be served by different languages. So, for example, in the implementation of an intelligent robot, the control algorithms may be best implemented in POP-II, and the knowledge base in Prolog.

Sloman (in press) summarizes POPLOG as follows:

POPLOG is a portable, integrated, environment for multiparadigm software development using a rapid-prototyping methodology to speed up development and testing. It supports a range of languages: two procedural AI languages (COMMON LISP and POP-11), a logic language (PROLOG), and a functional language Standard ML [see Wikstrom, 1987, or Harper, MacQueen, & Milner, 1986, for the details of the ML language]. It runs under VMS(tm) and UNIX(tm) on a variety of minicomputers and workstations, with a common editor (VED), window manager, and many hundreds of online teaching and help files and program library files.

To expand on this summary a little: The design of the basic POPLOG system is such that it can be tailored relatively easily to many new machines. All of the POPLOG languages have been integrated in such a way that setting up POPLOG on a new machine requires only implementation of the common high-level language {called high-level VM} on the target machine — i.e., you don't have to plough through the arduous process of implementing each of the component languages on the new machine.

The system is highly integrated in the sense that one can construct systems using just the desired features of each of the constituent languages, and the resultant system will be a coherent whole, not a loose farrago of a LISP program, and a PROLOG program, etc. What does this mean? Different languages can, for example, directly share a given data structure. And individual modules of a language can be compiled and recompiled (after modification) and are immediately automatically linked into the rest of the system. Systems that do not offer this *incremental compilation* capability will require perhaps the complete language subsystem to be recompiled and relinked back into the rest of the system whenever a module is altered — this would clearly be a serious drawback within an incremental development strategy (see the RUDE cycle in Chapter 2, if you're thinking that it is a basic mistake to be supporting this style of system development because the programmer ought not to be hacking the system in this way).

One further general feature that the closely integrated nature of the POPLOG system supports is the addition of new languages. Once a new language has been implemented in terms of POPLOG's common high-level language, it becomes an integral feature of the POPLOG system and enjoys all the benefits of the original constituent languages — i.e., full access to the editor, the development tools, all the POPLOG library facilities, and it runs on all machines that support POPLOG.

POPLOG is presented as a multiparadigm programming environment, but, whereas LOOPS offers a variety of paradigms under the umbrella of a single language, POPLOG endeavors to supply the necessary choice by integrating a variety of languages. I would not be so rash as to try to order these two strategies, but it would seem that LOOPS could offer more efficency at the cost of more difficulty in adding new paradigms.

After all the good news, there's just has to be some not-so-good news — there always is. Clearly, in a large and highly integrated system development environment such as POPLOG there are a lot of communication overheads. If the system is well designed, then the user is barely aware of all the behind-the-scenes communication (e.g., relinking a re-compiled module back into the overall system, and the checking that must be done in order to catch some of the many awkward problems that such an incremental development facility may have to face). But however well hidden these overheads are, the user will see one unfortunate effect — the system will move along rather slowly at times. Hardware advances, including exploiting parallelism, and powerful, single-user computers (such as LISP machines), will help to cancel out this time penalty, but it will probably always be noticeable, and with conventional, time-shared computers it can become a significant negative consideration. You seldom get something for nothing in this world, and it seems unlikely that you'll ever get all the flexibility and generality that systems such as PRO-LOG offer without some time cost. But, to finish on the bright side, how significant is a slightly slower system? A single high-level language may react to your commands a good deal faster than say, the POPLOG environment, but will the overall system-development time be any shorter? And what about the comparative quality of the products of each system? There are many factors, and system-response time is by no means the critical one, but it is the one that makes itself immediately apparent to the new user trying out a system for the first time.

True AI stories appear to be quite scarce in the AI-programming sub-domain, but not nonexistent. The following is a fairly faithful transcript of a short ''new research directions'' talk , the one that scooped the grand prize (Le Chapeau de Paille award) at The Expert Systems 88 Conference in Brighton, UK.

TRUE AI STORY: 4.1
DIMWIT (Do I Mean What I Tell): a PA (Programmer's Assailant) system

Some years ago Winograd (1975a) proposed that the complexity of software system design could be reduced if the human had at his or her disposal a computer system which functioned as a moderately stupid assistant. Progress has been made towards this laudable goal, and the current hopeware implementation is best described as a thoroughly stupid assistant.

But our story really begins in 1972 (or 7 BC, if you prefer), a year when

Winograd was presumably enjoying that wonderful feeling of relief that only the successful completion of an AI thesis can generate — SHRDLU had performed the requisite number of tricks and was retired to the AI Hall of Fame, nevermore to be hacked at. In that year Teitelman (1972) published his vision of a programmer's assistant; "Do what I mean" was the slogan that captured the underlying philosophy. This was the launch of the DWIM system.

This basic philosophy can be identified as the central idea that today has given us a wealth of support systems for hacking around otherwise totally impenetrable jungles of LISP code.

The DIMWIT system, which is nearly implemented, has taken this happy-hacker philosophy and pushed it just a little bit further. It not only reinterprets the user input commands to transform them into something a bit more sensible and in line with its global goals, but it also transforms the system responses such that the average idiot user will misinterpret them back to the correct meaning, but not all the time. Hence, the user is kept awake and alert through long cold nights, hunched over the keyboard by the need to constantly decide whether what appears on the screen is to be taken at face value or not.

The DIMWIT system, as befits such a fundamental advance, includes significant generalizations of the functions customarily available in state-of-the-art systems, such as INTERLISP-D, as well as embodying a strategy to combat that programming pestilence, the hacker. As an example of significant generalization, consider the UNDO function originally proposed by Teitelman, and still implemented today with barely the power that he described. Teitelman describes this operation as "perhaps the most important after-thought operation made possible by the p.a. [programmer's assistant]" (p. 9). Accidents do happen in exploratory programming, and the UNDO operation was designed to clean up after such accidents so that the system developer need never admit that anything untoward ever happened. Well, in the DIMWIT system accidents happen much more frequently — some good, some bad; you have to take the rough with the smooth. So UNDO gets a lot more use, and, moreover, not just when the programmer makes a mistake. It is also used a lot to readjust after the system's mistakes, or more commonly when you get in a real mess because several mistakes have been made and it's not clear who's to blame. But that's not the point, is it? It doesn't matter who made the mistake; what matters is that the system needs a good shuffle in the hope that something good will fall out, and several bangs on the UNDO key really shake things up.

On reflection, the previous paragraph is, I can now see, clearly open to misinterpretation. If read rather too casually, it could leave the reader with the distinct impression that hacking is condoned, encouraged even, by DIMWIT. Nothing could be further from the truth. In fact, one of the selling points behind DIMWIT is the care that must be taken when using it to develop a system. The user must think long and hard about each piece of system output. "What does it really mean?" the user has to continually ask himself or herself. This necessity for careful reflection prior to any interaction with the system effectively eradicates the hacking syndrome.

So, progress to date: A casual empirical study by the author on himself has indicated that such a philosophy can give rise to remarkably lively man–machine communication over extended periods of time. In addition, it was found that mutual misunderstanding can generate highly creative heaps of code. To date the author reports the rediscovery of semiinfinite loops (on several independent occasions); Russell's paradox (in actuality the list of all lists that are not lists of themselves started being output as a result of just a minor misunderstanding with a recursive call); similarly, it seemed that Fermat's last theorem, as well as the listings of AM and EURISKO, flashed by on the screen when a particularly creative loop structure took control for several minutes of the session. So far, we have been unable to verify that the DIMWIT-plus-author combination rediscovered the actual listings of these programs, as we have not succeeded in locating anyone who has actually seen the originals. And what's even more remarkable, all of these rediscoveries were made en route to designing a bubblesort algorithm. And there is still hope that a reasonable approximation to the bubblesort may yet be found somewhere in the 100,000 lines of code generated so far.

The pilot system has clearly proved its worth, and now work is underway on implementing stage one. The plan is to bootstrap up using the pilot system to develop the next version, and so on. Clearly there are dozens, perhaps thousands, of Ph.D.s to be had grappling with this long-term project and with very little hope of eventual success (for the project; the Ph.D.s will be smash hits, even a Computers-and-Thought lecture or two, I shouldn t be surprised). DIMWIT is without doubt a research gold-mine. I'll cease at this point, as there may be academic spies about and I've probably given away rather too much already. I left my card at the registration desk for collection by any funding agency talent scouts who know a hot topic when they see it.

(N.B. Readers, who wish to discover what the term *rediscovery* means in this context are referred to the section on computational creativity in Chapter 9.)

END OF TRUE AI STORY.

5

Current Expert Systems Technology

What's up doc?
Bugs Bunny in consultation with MYCIN, Paap (1989)

It is clear that expert systems technology is one of AI's greatest successes so far. Currently we see an ever-increasing application of expert systems, with no obvious limits to their applicability. Thus expert systems have earned a whole chapter to themselves. They are the existence proof that AI is viable outside of the carefully hand-crafted and cosseted demos wherein so much of it is to be found.

Yet there are also a number of well-recognized problems associated with this new technology. I shall argue that these problems are not the puzzles of normal science that will yield to advances within the current technology; on the contrary, they are symptoms of severe inherent limitations of this first generation technology. By reference to these problems I shall outline some important aspects of the scope and limitations of current expert systems technology. The recognition of these limitations is a prerequisite of overcoming them as well as of developing an awareness of the scope of applicability of this new technology.

I shall also take the opportunity to present a spectrum of views on the viability of logic as a mechanism to support intelligent reasoning. We have seen logic programming in the previous chapter, and in this chapter we shall see the crucial role played by logical inference in current expert systems technology (henceforth CEST).

It is now clear that CEST, which has given us the first generation of expert systems and is focused on modular knowledge bases in conjunction with efficient logical inference strategies, is one development of AI that has enormous commercial potential. The potential for the commercialization of this technology appears to be almost limitless. But there are some nagging problems: the incremental development of knowledge bases, especially as they become large; the automatic generation of meaningful explanations of unanticipated behaviors; etc.

These may be relatively self-contained problems that will, in due course, be solved or circumvented within the current technological framework. On the other hand, these problems may be the first manifestations of some fundamental limitations of CEST. It is this latter possibility that I shall put forward. Furthermore, I shall use these problems as a basis for an attempt to sketch out the scope and limitations of CEST.

Are expert systems harbingers of things to come? Yes and no. Yes, they are a first taste of the fruits of AI research as practical software, but not one that is smoothly extendible to the full potential of what AI, in a more general sense, may have to offer. In an earlier book (Partridge, 1986a) I have presented my views on what the promise and the problems of realizing the full potential of AI in practical software may be.

Other criticisms of CEST are beginning to appear, and they provide some degree of balance in an area that is prone to overstatement. Thus van de Riet (1987) deals with the question of whether the current situation around expert systems is a healthy one. He focuses largely on the R1 system (McDermott, 1981), and in particular on the maintainance problems which includes the now-acknowledged phenomenon of "unrepairable failures."

Martins (1984) supports my general claim about the inadequacies of CEST, but from the standpoint that expert system technology is composed of largely old ideas. Of course, there is nothing wrong with old ideas except that the ones that form the basis of expert systems (such as table-driven processes) have long been known to embody severe limitations. Yet these limitations are being glossed over in the rush to market this "new technology." I agree with these sentiments, and in this chapter I shall try to go further and begin to map out these limitations.

I shall consider two general problems that I feel are particularly instructive in regard to the task that I have set myself. The two problems are: the need for explanation capabilities in expert systems, and the problem of incrementally upgrading incomplete knowledge bases. But first let us review and consider the fundamental assumptions that underlie this first generation expert systems technology, and at the same time we can consider other related criticisms.

EXPERTS WITH TUNNEL VISION

The success of expert systems rests largely on the very restricted and specialized nature of the domains in which they operate as well as the exact nature of these domains. Intelligent behavior within the ill-defined empirical world (as opposed to well-defined game playing and puzzle-solving situations) is founded upon vast amounts of information. Human decision making — more precisely, expert human decision making — is the function that expert systems aspire to emulate, if not surpass.

Expert systems technology has not yet proved to be a decisive success — it appears to fare better in some areas of human expertise than others. As a result subdomains of human expertise are variously categorized, and we shall examine a few of the suggested classification schemes. A particular line of argument explored is one which maintains that certain types of human decision making (at least) are not adequately approximated by the symbolic search space paradigm of AI. Furthermore, attempts to project this inadequate model of human decision making via implementations of expert systems will be detrimental to both our image of ourselves and the future possibilities for AI software.

Finally, we shall consider the possibilities for expert systems technology within the connectionist paradigm, for CEST is, of course, a technology developed under the umbrella of the SSSP.

THE BASIC ASSUMPTIONS AND THE CRITICISMS

The basic assumptions upon which CEST rests are:

1. That the necessary knowledge can be represented as a collection of more or less independent rules; and
2. That intelligent decision making can be implemented as a logical, truth-derivation mechanism.

And both of these assumptions are true — to some extent. Remember the language PROLOG, which is an important facet of CEST: PROLOG is, of course, perfectly fitted to the implementation of CEST-based systems; it is an efficient, machine-executable implementation of just these assumptions — thus it also has limitations that parallel those of CEST.

In order to make the role of these two assumptions perfectly clear, let me offer you a very simple example. Consider an expert system for diagnosing faults in a car engine. The diagnostic knowledge might be codified as follows:

IF car_does_not_start AND battery_is_flat
THEN generator_is_faulty

IF lights_are_dim THEN battery_is_flat

etc.

These two rules are representative examples from a collection of say, 100 such rules that together represent a car mechanic's diagnostic knowledge — this is the first assumption. Now how do we use this knowledge base for diagnostic purposes?

Suppose we find that the car does not start. Looking through the knowledge base, the first rule has this fact as part of its precondition. But this particular precondition also requires that we also know that the battery is flat before we can conclude anything, and we don't know anything about the battery. Can we find anything out about this component? Again looking through the knowledge base, we see that the second rule will allow us to conclude that the battery is flat if we know that the lights are dim. We can test the lights directly. We switch on the lights, and, sure enough, they're dim alright. So, using the known fact that the lights are dim and the second rule, we conclude that the battery is flat. Now the car does not start and the battery is flat, and so we can use the first rule to conclude that the generator is faulty. And we've diagnosed the fault in the engine.

The second assumption was employed in the reasoning process. The core of the logic-based reasoning process is a mechanism that allows us to derive the truth of a conclusion to a rule once we know the truth of the precondition. In a nutshell, given the rule:

IF A is true THEN B is true (or is the diagnosis, or whatever)

and the fact that A is true, we conclude that B is also true.

The above two assumptions are particularly reliable in domains of abstract, technical expertise — domains such as mathematics, geology, chemistry, configuring computer systems, game playing and puzzle solving, domains that are, of course, the areas of success for CEST.

Examples of domains in which these assumptions are particularly weak are: natural language processing, intelligent tutoring, medical diagnosis, self-explanation of behavior, and quite menial tasks such as housecleaning.

Another assumption that is implicit in my division of domains of applicability and inapplicability of the current technology is that the knowledge is relatively static: It does not change with time to any appreciable degree, and new knowledge does not invalidate the old. The need for this assumption rests in part on the current absence of sufficiently powerful, robust, and reliable algorithms for machine learning (and as we shall see, machine learning appears to be necessary to combat the knowledge acquisition problem even in domains of relatively static knowledge). It also rests on a fundamental limitation of currently viable logics — they have trouble with things that are true at one time but not at another {the limitation is that of monotonicity; this non-user-friendly descriptor, monotonicity, may be meaningless at this point. Don't worry about it; we shall dig into it later — Chapter 10 provides full details, if you just can't wait}. Work on both machine learning and nonmonotonic logics is well underway, but until appropriate results are forthcoming the exclusion of domains of dynamic knowledge will continue.

Thus, expert systems can be constructed to analyze mass spectrograms as well as a specialist Ph.D. chemist. But the technician who runs the mass spectrometer has "expertise" that is well beyond the current technology. The Ph.D. chemist's knowledge is largely composed of (or, more accurately, can fairly successfully be approximated as) static, context-free units that, once discovered (a significant task in itself), tend to retain their validity largely irrespective of subsequent discovery, and inclusion in the knowledge base, of further such units. In addition, intelligent decisions about the interpretation of mass spectrograms can reasonably be expected to be forthcoming from a logical-proof type of process: the contruction of a relatively complete case for, or against, a hypothetical interpretation. The reasonableness of this expectation derives from the fact that mass spectrogram analysis is an abstract intellectual procedure that has been developed as a logic-like reasoning process.

The technician, on the other hand, the chap who operates the mass spectrometer, has to deal with the chemicals and their containers, the mass spectrometer itself, the power supply, the air conditioning, etc. In sum, he has to base his decisions on knowledge that is dynamic, diverse, inherently incomplete, most probably inconsistent, and not always (seldom?) subject to any logic-like reasoning procedure. The expertise of the technician is beyond the pale of CEST.

Hewitt (1990) questions the adequacy of current logic programming methods for developing the intelligent systems of the future. Of particular relevance to my current argument is his alternative to logical proof as a reasoning mechanism. He states that, "In the presence of conflicting information and contradictory beliefs, logical proof is inadequate as a reasoning mechanism. Instead we need due-process reasoning that investigates different sides of beliefs, goals, and hypotheses that arise" (p. 392).

Thus, if a mass spectrogram of compound X, which has been entirely used up, has some characteristics that do not fit well with expectations based on other knowledge of X, then it might be necessary to 'open up' the decision process. Is this really a mass spectrogram of X? Is the mass spectrometer malfunctioning, etc.? Intelligent decisions about these sorts of questions are more likely to be forthcoming from weighing and debating partial evidence for and against various hypotheses, than from attempts to construct logical proofs. The former approach to decision making is due-process reasoning and, as Hewitt says, "fundamentally different from logical proof" (p. 393). We shall return to questions of the general role of logics shortly.

Coombs and Alty (1984) suggest that CEST is misaimed: Human technical experts, they claim, are rarely required to perform the formal decision-making role that CEST is designed to fill. They claim that human experts are usually asked to assist other experts to refine and extend their understanding of a problem area — a procedure that involves educational rather than formal problem-solving skills. Thus they describe an alternative paradigm for expert systems, and one that does not have the luxury of well-defined, abstract problems.

With respect to inconsistency in knowledge bases, Hewitt offers "the Conjecture of Inconsistency: The axiomatization of the human knowledge of all physical systems are uniformly inconsistent in practice" (Hewitt, 1990, p. 390). The decision making of the mass spectrometer technician has to accommodate such inconsistency; but the Ph.D. chemist reasoning in the abstract domain of mass spectrograms and chemical structure can largely avoid the problem. We see again the limitation of CEST to abstract domains, and the exclusion of current logic-based reasoning from domains that involve the physical world to some significant degree.

In their attempt "to demonstrate that human intelligence extends far beyond factual knowledge and abstract reasoning" and hence to question much of current AI, Dreyfus and Dreyfus (1986) present an extensive critique of CEST. They discuss "structured" problem areas in which the presuppositions of mainstream AI hold. The presuppositions are that:

1. symbols represent objective, context-free features;
2. such symbols can be combined into abstract symbolic descriptions;
3. relationships can be expressed in terms of strict rules;
4. logical inference can be used to generate new states of affairs.

They contrast structured problems, which may be adequately characterized by the above four points, with "unstructured" problem areas. "Such areas contain a potentially unlimited number of possibly relevant facts and features, and the ways those elements interrelate and determine other events is unclear. Management, nursing, economic forecasting, teaching, and all social interactions fall into that very large class."

There are clear parallels between the Dreyfus and Dreyfus characterisation of CEST and my own; there are also significant differences. They are attacking current AI and attempting to demonstrate what they believe to be fundamental misconceptions in the field. I am attempting nothing so radical; my arguments are focused on CEST and, although I see nontrivial changes as necessary if certain problems are to be solved, the next generation expert systems technology could well fit comfortably within the general paradigm that Dreyfus and Dreyfus are questioning.

There is a curious disagreement about what the empirical evidence of expert system usage means. The Dreyfi (Dreyfus & Dreyfus, 1986) have looked at many of the working (or, as they might say, supposedly working) expert systems of significance, and they conclude that the viability of CEST is not proven. They are at pains to demonstrate that the practical utility of the famous expert systems is either close to zero, or that the useful versions (e.g., MACSYMA and CONGEN) are not expert systems at all.

Hayes-Roth, a veteran expert systems' practitioner and chief scientist with Teknowledge, vigorously denies the claims of the Dreyfi. He points to many dozens of systems that Teknowledge, for example, has designed and sold that are out in the world and performing quite satisfactorily.

What is the resolution of this important impasse on an issue that would seem to be a relatively simple one? Well, it is true that most of the expert systems that are used as exemplars of interesting features, such as reasoning with uncertainty and decision making in ill-defined domains, are not practical software systems. It is equally true that knowledge-based software is being developed, sold, and successfully used in many different application areas. The impasse is then caused by the lack of agreement about whether the practical software is being applied to AI problems and is constructed with significant AI constituents. Much of the available AI software is so-called primarily on the basis of a simple, rule-based component from which results are derived by means of a mechanism of logical inference. The target problem, at the level addressed by the actual software, contains few of the features that characterize AI problems: Typically, the answers generated are clearly correct or incorrect, and the domain of relevant information is quite limited and well defined. But this sort of argument for the claim that CEST is unproven as a viable AI technology would be challenged by the believers on the basis that, whenever AI succeeds, it is no longer called AI, and that this is no basis for denying the validity of CEST.

Both sides of this dispute can lay claim to some measure of validity, I believe. AI (as you must surely realize by now) is not subject to neat definition, and thus the term *AI software* serves admirably as the focus for endless debate — a course that I shall follow no longer. Instead I shall attempt to characterize the problems for which CEST does seem to be applicable.

WHAT CAN BE CESTED?

Most people will readily admit that CEST has its limitations (don't we all?). So the burning question for those members of the human race whose prime concern is the construction of practical AI software is: What can be CESTed? "How can I tell if my particular problem is one that will yield to CEST?" is a very common request from all sectors of society.

Sadly, no definitive test is known, but ad hoc guidelines abound. For example, if the skill is one that can be successfully acquired after the age of 30, then CEST is likely to be applicable. Can the problem be fully described over the telephone? If so, then CEST may be applicable, and so on.

The point of burdening you with these blunderous tests is not that one of them may prove to be an effective decision procedure for you. Their worth lies in the possibility that you may begin to see some underlying rationale in terms of the subsequent discussion concerning abstract, technological expertise, and intuitive expertise.

Waterman (1986) attempts to provide guidance on this question. He lists seven characteristics that are necessarily true of a domain within which expert systems development is possible. Here's the list: the task does not require common sense; the task requires only cognitive skills; experts can articulate their methods; genuine experts exist; experts agree on solutions; the task is not too difficult; the task is not poorly understood.

I'll leave you to ponder this list, and whether this collection of strictures necessarily rules out AI problems.

Meanwhile, I'll move on and focus down to look more closely at the "explanation" and knowledge acquisition problems.

EXPLANATIONS AND CONTEXT SENSITIVITY

Context sensitivity is a feature of AI that helps to distinguish AI that is currently viable in practical software, and AI that is not. The critical test, I argue, is how context-free or loosely coupled to its context an AI problem is. Tightly coupled context sensitivity characterizes the empty set of practical AI software.

Science thrives on context-free problems: problems that can be solved irrespective of the context in which they occur. Thus the square root of an integer is calculable in a predetermined and correct way, no matter where the integer originated nor to what use the answer will be put. Contrast the problem of understanding natural language, when, for example, the human user and expert system participate in a dialogue to determine the type of explanation required: The meaning of a sentence may depend more upon who is saying it and why they are saying it than it does upon the actual words used to construct the sentence. Truly context-free problems are, in fact, somewhat scarce; abstract scientific domains are the major preserve of these objects. The question of interest then becomes:

to what extent our context-free abstraction can adequately account for the corresponding phenomena in the empirical world. Simon (1969) has an interesting argument to support his contention that although many real-world systems, such as you and I, are not collections of context-free subsystems, they do tend to have the property of *near decomposability*. In my terminology, near decomposability is loosely coupled context sensitivity. Systems that possess this property can be treated as collections of context-free modules, to a first approximation; tightly coupled context-sensitive problems cannot.

In his exploration of the possibilities for AI, Haugeland (1985, p. 50) characterizes formal systems as "self-contained; the 'outside world' is strictly irrelevant," they are also "digital," which implies that such formal systems are independent of any particular medium — chess (a formal system) can be played with bedknobs or broomsticks, but football (not a formal system) is critically dependent on certain necessary characteristics of the ball, as well as many other things. CEST certainly exploits such formal domains and the syntactic manipulation of the representations used (commonly termed a lack of *deep knowledge*), which is all that is necessary in a formal system; semantics, as meaning, necessarily relates to the "outside world." In Haugeland's terminology: the extent to which we can successfully ignore the outside world in problem solving is a measure of the possibilities for automation in general, which, of course, includes CEST. With tightly coupled, context-sensitive problems, meaning, in his sense, cannot be ignored and CEST is not applicable because the assumption of context-free knowledge units does not hold.

Another useful dimension along which we can view context sensitivity is with respect to its tendency to change — at the crudest level, is it static or dynamic? I shall argue below that many AI problems are characterized by tightly coupled and dynamic context sensitivity. Then a need to take complex and dynamic relationships into account for decision making leads us inexorably on to a need for machine learning.

To some extent context sensitivity can be internalized in the function and we have a context-free, but larger, function. Some of the knowledge encapsulated by AI implementations is internalized context.

The most realistic approaches to intelligent computer-aided instruction (CAI), for example, include a model of the user. The most important context sensitivity in this problem is that between the machine and the human being under instruction — the system user. By generating and maintaining a model of each user, the computer system has internalized the crucial context sensitivity of the problem.

Apart from the problem of maintaining up-to-date models or knowledge of the relevant aspects of an AI program's domain (i.e., machine learning, the topic of Chapter 9), an important question for a potential expert system application is: how much context do we need to internalise?

It all depends on the scope of the proposed system and on its application domain. It is clear that a useful level of expertise can be achieved in limited domains as a result of an internalization of a severely limited collection of knowledge; expert systems exhibit some AI on the basis of a narrow, domain-specific knowledge base.

What is not clear is: How much can the AI in expert systems be upgraded and extended (e.g., to include a sophisticated explanation component) within the current framework for such systems — inflexible and highly limited context sensitivity?

If we are aiming for a more general AI system, not necessarily one with the full capabilities of you or I, but, say, an expert system that takes people into account — their aims, objectives, hopes, and fears, all with respect to the particular expertise of the AI system — then the context sensitivity must be both broadened and made dynamic.

You and I have internalized a model of the world within which models of specific subworlds are developed to differing degrees, dependent upon their relative importance in our lives. We can behave sensitively, and thus have a basis for intelligent responses, to a wide range of phenomena. It is clear that our intelligence is founded upon a lot of knowledge; it is also clear that we do not know anything approaching all that there is to know. But what we do have is the ability to learn and dynamically internalize new knowledge (develop a new or expanded context sensitivity), whenever it is in our interest to do so.

In principle the state of any given person's knowledge at a given time could be fed into a computer, and the computer system could behave just as intelligently as the original person although it has no learning capability whatever. But for how long would it remain intelligent? The answer depends upon how static or dynamic is the knowledge upon which the intelligent behavior is founded.

Expertise in, say, pure mathematics could be expected to endure for long periods of time; the basic knowledge is well established and not subject to major changes. But intelligent interaction with respect to current affairs, or with any given individual, is liable to degrade rapidly — both contexts are highly dynamic. Out-of-date knowledge will soon reduce this static system to a pathetic anachronism.

So we'll just update the system's knowledge whenever necessary — every day, or every hour, or even every minute — there is still no necessity for machine learning? I think that there is, but this is an argument for the next section.

Domain-specific knowledge may be relatively static, as in the above example of pure mathematics. The implementor of an expert system, who spends an inordinate amount of time modifying the system's knowledge base, might well want to challenge that statement. But compared to knowledge of the empirical world (who and what are where, and doing what), knowledge of chemical structure, and knowledge of geological formations, and knowledge of the associations between symptoms and diseases, are decidedly static.

The fact that, even with these static knowledge bases, the knowledge engineer is largely preoccupied with modifying the knowledge base is a danger signal for the way knowledge-engineer intervention will escalate when more dynamic contexts are attempted, if we fail to incorporate self-adaptivity.

In describing XSEL, a front end to the R1 expert system, J. McDermott (1982) singles out the context-free nature of XSEL's three main tasks. He says, "The most striking characteristic of these subtasks is that for all three the decisions to be made are relatively independent both of prior and of subsequent decisions" (p. 331). And although a significant amount of knowledge is required to achieve performance adequacy, "the fact that the component selection task can be recognition driven [i.e., context free] makes XSEL conceptually quite simple" (p. 331).

The explanation task, he continues, is quite different. In reference to the knowledge-based programs of recent years, he says, "for the most part, these programs do not treat explanation as a task that requires intelligence." As a first approximation to the user-context sensitivity necessary for good explanations, XSEL has five kinds of information from which to generate an explanation. The adequacy of this fixed, five-point, discrete approximation to the continuum of user context remains to be seen.

My argument is not that such discrete simulations cannot support the rich and continuous context sensitivity within user-and-system interaction — such would be one of the well-known Dreyfus fallacies. What I am saying is that, however sophisticated the discrete approximation becomes, it will need to be self-adaptive in order to exhibit the explanation capabilities of an average human being. Again we return to the question of: are the capabilities of an average human being necessary? Clearly, in some very practical sense, they are not, but, to achieve anything like the full potential of the promise of expert systems, a surprising amount of such capabilities will be necessary.

An analogous argument based on the reasoning capabilities of current expert systems is given by Wos, Overbeek, Lusk, and Boyle (1984). They state, in their text on automated reasoning, that current expert systems rely largely on "focused reasoning" (i.e., reasoning with known procedures that can be well controlled). They argue that "unfocused reasoning" (i.e., no well-defined procedure is known that will directly yield the answer) must be used, or else we will overlook many possible applications. In their words, "many significant applications will require unfocused reasoning" (p. 388).

Returning to the specific limitations of system rigidity, Boden (1984), for example, also discussing expert systems, states that "current systems are relatively simple and inflexible, and restricted to very narrow domains. They can be incrementally improved, but only up to a point" (p. 9). She also sees machine learning as a pressing problem for the future. "If a program cannot learn for itself, its development is limited by the time and ability of the programmer to provide it with new information and ideas" (p. 12).

Clearly, Boden's ideas are supportive of my argument, although she does not seem to view machine learning as playing quite the same unique and crucial role as I do. Nevertheless, this brings us onto the question of the need for, or necessity of, machine learning in expert systems. I will argue that it is a necessity in practice if not in principle; the alternative is a severely limited application of expert systems technology in practical software.

UPDATING KNOWLEDGE BASES AND MACHINE LEARNING

"To be blunt, an AI program that doesn't learn is no AI program at all" (Schank, 1983, p. 4). I wouldn't go that far (and neither would he at other times, I suspect), but, even neglecting the hyperbole, Schank is clearly with me in spirit. Although we agree on the importance of learning, I am happy with the term AI software as applied to adequate implementations of complex, open-ended problems, even though they make no pretensions to learn.

And although not so dramatic, my point is somewhat harder to substantiate. I would agree with Schank (1983, p. 4) that, "Learning is, after all, the quintessential AI issue." But it does not necessarily follow that expert systems must involve machine learning. The result of a learning behavior can always, in principle at least, be simulated by periodic updating of the system by some outside agency.

In practice we are already witnessing a renewal of interest in machine learning (this AI subfield is described en masse and in toto, but in English I hasten to add, in Chapter 9). Machine learning is the key to a strategy for alleviating the problems generated by the knowledge bases used in expert systems — problems of both construction and maintenance of large and complex, but relatively static, collections of information. We find this point made in the review of AI chaired by Waltz (1983), and in almost every other mention of the knowledge acquisition problem.

Michie (1982), for example, in his review of the state of the art in machine learning, sees a practical need for machine learning in terms of increasing programmer productivity. He then focuses on a semiautomated scheme for knowledge acquisition—he calls this scheme "structured induction."

Waltz's committee, in their state-of-the-art report on AI, cite "the ability to learn from experience" as one of a small number of "important characteristics that such machines would have to have before AI could be said to have succeeded" (Waltz, 1983, p. 55). They do not single out machine learning as I would, but to my mind the other characteristics that they list — such as common sense and the ability to deal appropriately with natural language input — all imply a prerequisite machine learning ability. This would seem to cast the machine learning characteristic in a more fundamental role than they appear to accord it.

From his long perspective on the AI scene, Samuel (1983) singles out natural-language communication and learning as the two basic problems of AI. He goes on to say "that the desired progress in man–machine communication will not be made until it is treated as a learning problem . . . In fact, I look on learning as the central problem of AI research" (p. 1155). So it seems that I am in good company with my extreme view.

It is clear that, in practice at least, there is general agreement on the importance of machine learning as a research problem which still needs to be solved to some reasonable degree.

The limits of nonadaptive expert systems are those problems that involve interaction with neither people nor any other aspect of the empirical world, except in a very subsidiary role. This is clearly a characterization that is closely akin to the earlier ones based on loosely coupled context sensitivity and static contexts.

The possibility of having a knowledge-based AI system that behaves intelligently without a self-adaptive capability will only be viable in the domains of relatively static knowledge. That restriction largely excludes intelligent interaction with people and the domains of everyday expertise, such as house cleaning. It is a limitation to intellectual expertise in largely theoretical domains — there's clearly lots of scope for current expert systems technology there, but it is also a domain of applicability that excludes many aspects of human endeavor, aspects that we might expect to be suitable targets for expert systems technology.

Remember that I am not arguing that CEST cannot go any further without nontrivial machine learning. There may be decades of useful and exciting expansion of the applications of nonlearning expert systems. I am making the case that, without sophisticated machine learning, our options will always be limited; large and important sections of potential application areas will be excluded, and the full potential of expert systems as practical software will not be achieved.

Even if we can agree that sophisticated adaptivity will be necessary in certain expert systems, that still leaves the question of the degree to which the system will have to be self-adaptive. A given need to assimilate information may be implemented in many ways. In particular, there is a spectrum of possibilities, from totally automated discovery to a fairly trivial ability to accept from a human tutor mentally predigested information. This latter possibility does not really qualify to be called nontrivial machine learning, but there are many strategies, intermediate between these two extremes, that do qualify (see Michalski, Carbonell, & Mitchell, 1983, 1986, for a thorough coverage of the current state of the art in machine learning).

It may be possible to implement the necessary sophisticated adaptivity in terms of a fairly simple program, and a smart and dedicated human tutor — and this is a valid approach to take when researching the problem. But for commercial AI it falls foul of all of the previous arguments for the necessity of machine learning — i.e., human beings will be doing all of the difficult work, and this onerous task will be different for every individual copy of the software.

For nontrivial machine learning a lot of knowledge concerning the program's organization and goals and objectives must be available somewhere — either in the program itself or in the human tutor. The main point underlying the necessity for machine learning is that no human being has to maintain, at his or her finger tips, all of this knowledge about the program (and remember, each copy of the program is an individual) such that he or she can accurately modify it at the drop of a new significant fact.

So, although the necessity for machine learning does mean that the machine and not the human should indeed be shouldering the burden, it is again not at all clear how far we can go with AI into dynamic contexts by sharing the load to some extent. Indeed, the real power of AI may reside in an intimate man–machine relationship — a symbiotic superintelligence. But I do not believe that this partnership will work if all of the learning and adaptation has to come through the organic partner.

It is clear that incrementally upgrading nontrivial knowledge bases presents formidible complexity problems. In the first volume of their book on machine learning, Michalski, Carbonell, and Mitchell (1983, 1986) state that one need for automated learning is that humans quickly become incapable of upgrading AI systems, because they cannot maintain an understanding of the system to the necessary logical depth. The requirement that the machine bears the burden of the learning is a specific measure to lessen the complexity that the associated humans have to manage. This is true even in the relatively static domains where expert systems currently promise to be effective. For even in these relatively static domains, the concept of a complete knowledge base is not seriously entertained. Incremental upgrading is an intrinsic feature of the use of such systems, not just of their development. Rather than a developmental nuisance that will go away as soon as we learn to specify our knowledge bases properly, incremental upgrading must be countenanced for the life of the system — it is part of what makes an AI system rather than a conventional software engineering system. I have argued elsewhere, at length in Partridge (1986a) and more succinctly in Partridge (1985c, 1986b), that incremental development of a machine-executable specification, throughout the life of a system, is a fundamental feature of the AI domain. It is not just the code-hacking syndrome that AI will divest itself of as soon as it becomes sufficiently mature. Code hacking is prevalent in AI, and it should be discouraged, but what it should give way to is a disciplined development of the Run-Understand-Debug-Edit cycle (the RUDE paradigm). AI problems are typically not amenable to complete prior specification; thus, the goal of AI system development should not be the SAV paradigm that conventional software science aspires to (this viewpoint is argued in Partridge & Wilks, 1987, and much closer at hand in Chapter 2). If we then consider possible applications in dynamic environments, such as house cleaning, domains outside of the relatively fixed, abstract domains of medical diagnosis and mass spectrogram analysis, the incremental upgrading problem leaps in difficulty by at least an order of magnitude.

In sum, I claim that the explanation problem associated with current expert system's technology is a manifestation of the fact that this technology is inherently limited to the relatively static and relatively context-free domain of abstract technical expertise. The problem of incrementally upgrading knowledge bases also partly derives from the context sensitivity typically associated with the AI domain. But it is also indicative of the incremental system development paradigm needed in AI (which to some extent is itself due to the context sensitivity feature). In addition, this necessity for continual knowledge base updating, even in these relatively static domains, suggests that some reasonable level of solution to the problem of machine learning will be required in order that these limitations on current expert system's technology may be overcome.

The point is that these two types of problem do not appear to be individual problems that will be solvable within the current expert system's technology; they are symptoms of inherent limitations within the technology. Some indication that current limitations are not generally acknowledged as fundamental challenges to the presuppositions of CEST can be found, for example, in Steels (1985). Steels offers a characterization of "Second Generation Expert Systems," "a substantial jump forward in expert systems technology" that touches on "the nature of the potential problem domains, the type of reasoning being performed, the explanation capabilities, and most importantly the way knowledge acquisition is performed" (p. 213). A grand manifesto, and one that leads us to expect either that much of my earlier anaysis is incorrect (because the explanation problem, etc., have been solved within CEST), or that my characterization of CEST is outdated (because these second generation systems employ a new technology that is not subject to the limitations of CEST). Neither of these implications is correct. In fact the assumptions of CEST are not challenged, but, in addition, we are promised "expert systems [that] can learn new rules by examining the results of deep reasoning" (p. 213).

The reality turns out to be exhaustive back-chaining search of a complete causally linked (i.e., A causes B; B causes C; etc.) set of rules; this procedure is called *deep reasoning*. The claimed causal knowledge is of exactly the type that has been exposed as simplistic in the extreme by Chandrasekaran and Mittal (1983), and the use of the term deep reasoning is a blatant overglorification of a trivial process (McDermott, 1976, exposed this pernicious trend in AI many years ago). Worse than this, the noninnovative suggestions will not work in practice, because success is predicated upon having a *complete* causal network. If the deep reasoning exhausts the network without finding a reason for the current problem, then it concludes that the reason is, for example, a faulty internal component in the physical system being diagnosed — this presupposes that no causal rule is missing, that is, that the knowledge is complete. This requirement is very surprising, because one of the features that makes expert systems AI rather than conventional software engineering is that we must abandon the luxury of completeness: One thing that we know for certain about any knowledge base is that it does not contain all potentially relevant knowledge, whatever the domain — i.e., knowledge bases are necessarily incomplete.

When the learning of new rules is explained by Steels, we see that it consists of the addition of a direct "anomaly-causes-problem" rule, where the particular anomaly and problem are those linked by the prior deep reasoning process. It is a new manifestation of the "memo function" feature explored in the language POP-2 (Michie, 1968). In effect a lookup table of previously computed results is maintained to provide a faster response than recomputing the result for subsequent accesses to the knowledge base with repetitions of earlier diagnosed problems. The many problems associated with this simple idea have been well known for a long time, and although Steels demonstrates an awareness of some of the limitations of this mechanism, he offers no solutions that might transform the memo-function idea into a machine learning mechanism that will be useful in practice. The full scope and limitations of such success-driven learning mechanisms are thoroughly reviewed in Chapter 9.

LET'S DIG DEEPER

Having mentioned the notions of deep reasoning and causal knowledge in the previous section, this might be a good time to look at the general idea of *deep knowledge*.

The heuristic rules that are typically codified in the hope of reproducing some human's expertise within a computer system are representations of only superficial knowledge — so the argument goes. And, although we have little in the way of clear ideas about what knowledge is (the next chapter should help some in this regard, but it offers no definitive answer — as usual), we can, nevertheless, take on board, without much trouble, the relativity notion that distinguishes superficial knowledge from deep knowledge.

So what's a heuristic rule that represents only superficial knowledge? Here's the common example:

IF car_does_not_start AND battery_is_flat
THEN generator_is_faulty

I hope that this typical rule holds no mystery for you, and that, even if your car-fixing expertise is exhausted after checking the oil and water, this rule looks like it could contribute to the diagnosis of car-engine problems. So why is it heuristic, and why is it superficial?

It is heuristic because it will not always work. It is quite possible for the car not to start and for the battery to be flat, and yet for the generator to be blameless. {For car fixers who also like to keep abreast of the unsolved problems: Consider the possibility that someone has stolen the starter motor and shorted out the battery in so doing.}

Furthermore, this rule codifies only superficial knowledge in the sense that it contains no information about why it might be reasonable to conclude that the generator is faulty if the car doesn't start and the battery is flat. It represents just a superficial relationship that can often be quite useful. It is not a representation that will support deep reasoning in situations where it does not solve the problem at hand. Such rules can then be blamed for a number of problems within CEST.

For example, attempts to improve the expertise of the system, and thus take into account the situations when the above heuristic fails, lead to a proliferation of variants of this rule as well as to complications with the rule itself. New rules are needed to take care of the situations when the car does start or the battery is not flat but, nevertheless, the generator is faulty {i.e., the logical relationship that is the total precondition is not true, but the conclusion is in fact true}. And the original rule itself can grow into a monster as new tests are added to filter out all of the situations when the car does not start and the battery is flat but the generator is just perfect {i.e., situations when the heuristic fails, the preconditions are true but the conclusion is not}. These two trends together constitute the deep reason (to employ the topical terminology) why knowledge bases quickly grow out of control as attempts are made to upgrade the level expertise exhibited by the system. There is one of those nasty laws of diminishing returns at work — successively smaller increases in level of expertise must be bought at the cost of successively larger increases in system complexity.

The use of such superficial heuristics is also thought to be a prime reason why the china syndrome (described in Chapter 3) is endemic in CEST. The typical expert system is blindly inferring around in its knowledge base, searching for, or attempting to justify, a solution to the particular problem that it has been posed. It has no way to know when a heuristic fails. It has no means of realizing when a solution (or the justification of a hypothesis) requires the use of some knowledge that it does not have. The certainties that come with a logical inference engine are predicated upon certain qualities of the information over which it inferences. One of the necessary qualities is completeness; in the current context, this means that the knowledge base must contain *all* of the relevant knowledge pertaining to the particular problems that the system tackles. You may recall the earlier discussion of incompleteness as a defining characteristic of AI, and of the problem of what is *relevant* knowledge, let alone *all relevant* knowledge. The next section looks at this sort of issue in more detail.

I take it that even the most steadfast believer in simple CEST will go along with the argument that the typical codification of superficial knowledge is a weak point in the technology. Hence the call for deep knowledge. "Alright, but what is it?" you ought to be saying to yourself.

Deep knowledge is information that will support reasoning about why, and therefore when, the superficial, heuristic rules will be applicable, and will not be applicable. This is sometimes called reasoning from first principles, although it would be better called reasoning from underlying principles (as there are no first ones, there are just layers of successively deeper ones). There is a wealth of alternative terminology in this particular neck (I'm tempted to say *bottleneck,* but I won't) of the knowledge-base woods. You'll find very similar ideas under the labels "qualitative process theory," or "qualitative reasoning," or "causal reasoning," or "envisionment" (see, for example, Forbus, 1984; Kuipers, 1982, 1985).

The call for deep knowledge, then, is in response to the well-recognized inadequacies of the superficial, heuristic rules that typically constitute a knowledge base. There is fairly general agreement on this point, but, apart from recognition of the need, there is no consensus on what exactly is needed (other than that it should be deep knowledge), let alone how it should be represented.

One favored approach to the codification of deep knowledge is to implement a causal model of the system of interest. Thus, the car–engine–troubleshooter expert system might contain, as a codification of deep knowledge, a causal model of an internal combustion engine. Such a model would contain the information that the battery is a storage device for electrical power, and that the car's lights use up electrical power, and that the generator produces electrical power when the engine is running, etc. With such a model a deep reasoning system should be able deduce that, if the lights are left on and the engine is not running, then the battery will go flat, etc.

Given this sort of codification of information (or deep knowledge, if you prefer), and the appropriate reasoning strategies, the system should be able to explain why the earlier heuristic rule works for much of the time. It should also be able to predict when this rule is unlikely to be correct (e.g., when the car lights have been left on overnight), and so on.

This is all quite plausible, I think, but the problem of how to represent, and how to reason efficiently and effectively, with a causal model is very much an unsolved problem. And the situation is no different with the other schemes for deep knowledge.

Before leaving this topic, I need to make a point about deep knowledge and the scope of CEST. Up until now, I have tended to describe shallow-knowledge rules as both superficial and heuristic. Deep knowledge by way of contrast appears to be both less shallow (embodying as it does some reasons why the shallow rules are mostly true) and nonheuristic. Information about a battery storing electrical power, for example, is not heuristic information. It is always true. A causal model of an internal combustion engine can be based largely on the laws of physics, you might think. So you might be led to conclude that deep knowledge is nonheuristic knowledge. Please don't, for you would be wrong.

Consider a system to diagnose faults in an organic system, say you or me. We don't know all the nonheuristic rules that would constitute a causal model of this "engine" (and if we did, many of them might be far too complicated to practically useful — we'd be likely to use heuristic approximations). So the underlying causal model is at least partially heuristic in nature.

Consider a system for financial planning for a company. Is there an underlying causal model? Certainly there are precious few first principles to reason from. Nevertheless, I suspect that there are some underlying principles, but that they are largely heuristic in nature. So deep knowledge does not necessarily mean nonheuristic.

For those readers who wish to follow up on the idea of deep knowledge, a tutorial and bibliography on the subject has been produced by Price and Lee (1988). This will give you many further references back into the relevant literature.

A last point about deep knowledge, and one that provides a cross-link with explanation-based learning in Chapter 9, concerns the possibilities for interaction between superficial and deep knowledge. This section, arguing as it does that deep knowledge systems might avoid many of the pitfalls of CEST, is not to be interpreted as a grounds for deep knowledge systems *instead* of superficial knowledge systems — both are needed. The superficial, heuristic knowledge will provide adequate and efficient behavior most of the time. Recourse to deep knowledge is more an occasional strategy to be used when the superficial heuristics are inadequate.

The deep knowledge is the foundation upon which expertise is built, and the superficial, heuristic knowledge is the derived information that allows real-time, intelligent expertise to be exhibited most of the time. Assuming that this last statement is somewhere close to the truth, the question arises: How is the superficial knowledge derived from the deep knowledge? Well, to some degree, it isn't. There is evidence to suggest that expertise may be founded on the abstraction of deep knowledge from collections of particular experiences. The scheme for inductive generalization of decision trees from a collection of specific examples (described later in this chapter) would be an example of this strategy. Nevertheless, there is also evidence to suggest that technical experts, at least, first absorb largely the deep knowledge of their chosen domain of expertise. And it is only as a result of subsequent practice that true expertise develops. One interpretation of this is that experience in the domain, working with specific example problems, enables the expert to generate a finely tuned collection of superficial, heuristic rules from the deep knowledge already possessed. Worden (1989) suggests something like this, and he further suggests that the mechanism by which specific examples are used to generate efficient, superficial heuristics from the more ponderous first principles, or deep knowledge, is explanation-based learning. This is an interesting twist on a hot topic in machine learning, and we shall return to it in Chapter 9.

So, I would maintain, the first generation of expert systems technology is still very much the CEST that I have attempted to characterize above. Can we begin to circumscribe the scope and limitations of CEST? I think that we can begin to do better than the rules of thumb given earlier. Ernst and Ojha (1986), for example, have provided an analysis of the scope of practical utility of CEST with respect to business knowledge-based systems. I make no claim to have identified the most critical inherent limitations with great accuracy. There are certainly other, largely independent and equally pressing, limitations of CEST: for example, reasoning with uncertainty, and the inability to employ spatial and isomorphic representations. Nevertheless, I am sure that efforts to define some aspects of the scope and limitations of this new technology will be beneficial. It will help to counterbalance the usual oversell. It will help to locate the problems that need to be tackled. And, in the meantime, it will serve to guide future applications into those domains where success is most likely.

I am not trying to be alarmist, and I don't see my viewpoint as defeatist. But I do believe that many of the problems that beset the expert system developer will not be solved by a few more rules in the knowledge base, or any such fix within the current expert systems technology. If this is true it does not mean that expert systems are doomed, or severely limited forever; it means that, when these problems are solved (as part of mainstream AI research), the new, or expanded, resultant expert systems technology can be applied to extend both the domain and efficacy of expert systems. But before they can be solved, they must be recognized as fundamental problems outside the scope of current expert system technology.

LOGICAL DECISION MAKING

There has long been a general belief among AI workers that some form of logic underlies human decision making. It is part of the modern embodiment of what Winograd and Flores (1986) call the "rationalistic tradition." This general tradition carries the stamp of respectability and distinguishes intelligent decision making from the behavior of the lower animals (and of course places our mental capacity on the very top of the heap). Certain human decision making does appear to be a manifestation of underlying logical mechanisms, but other human decision making behavior cannot be so clearly accounted for by known logics. This unfortunate state of affairs may be due to our failure to correctly analyze the resistent behaviors, or it may be due to a failure to formulate the necessary system of logic. In either case, time and research can be expected to induce these resistent aspects of human decision making to succumb to the charms of a logic-based mechanism.

Certainly the successful applications of CEST attest to the viability of quite simple logical inference techniques in some areas of human decision making, but what about the currently resistent areas? Can we draw any conclusions there? I think so, and I think that the most likely conclusion is that some aspects of human decision making appear to be totally immune to attack by any conceivable system of symbolic logic. But before I present evidence to support this latter view, we might consider one type of logic that is popularly believed to answer the awkward question of lack of certainty in human decision making; I am referring to fuzzy logic (Zadeh, 1975).

Fuzzy logic allows the treatment of degrees of certainty about decisions. Thus, is a six-foot man tall? This is not a yes or no decision (if it is for you, then change the height in question by small increments until it is no longer a clear-cut decision). A six-foot man is more likely to be classed as tall than a five-foot six-inch one, and so on. Fuzzy logic gives us a formalization that is intuitively appealing as a mechanism that might support this type of human decision making.

In fuzzy logic the truth value for a decision about tallness based on a man's height varies smoothly from very close to 100% true for a seven-foot man to very close to 0% true for a four-footer. Under a fuzzy logic interpretation, a six-foot man has something like an 80% right to be classed as tall; he is not just either tall or not-tall, as he would have to be in classical logic. This type of logic is clearly more appealing than classical logic as a potential model for human decision making, but it is far from an adequate solution.

Fuzzy logic, like classical logic and formalisms in general, is a context-free formalism; much human decision making is highly context sensitive. Thus an intelligent decision about the tallness of a six-foot man can often only be made once we know something about the context of the decision. Is it a six-foot pigmy, or a six-foot bastketball player that we are deciding about? The former is definitely tall; the latter is definitely not. A knowledge of contextual details allows us to make intelligent decisions. The context-free nature of fuzzy logic, as well as other logics, puts them at a severe disadvantage as potential mechanisms to support human decision making. It is, of course, true that conventional conditional statements, such as IF PIGMIES THEN TALL IS 0.6*TALL, can easily capture any well-defined and simple contextual dependency, but real-world context sensitivities are more typically dynamic, ill-defined and interdependent. Logics can in principle take care of all these problems, but in practice they tend to become unwieldy and unmanageable even in highly-simplified worlds.

Fuzzy logic as a model of approximate reasoning in expert systems (see, for example, Negoita 1985) should be treated with circumspection.

The more usual application of logic to model expert human decision making imposes not only a context-free requirement on the process, but also the necessity for monotonicity, completeness, and consistency, all with respect to the knowledge base. The monotonicity requirement means that no new knowledge can ever invalidate previous truths — clearly an awkward constraint to live with when modeling decision making in a changing world, or in a world in which earlier decisions based on the best evidence then available may need to be reassessed as new data comes to light. Again, monotonicity is no insurmountable problem in principle, but in practice it has proved to be a formidable obstacle for logic-based systems. The completeness and consistency of available knowledge for intelligent human decision making can seldom be assumed, even if we dismiss the implications of Gödel's theorem. So, it is not surprising that the CEST model of human decision making is a little closer to reality in some domains than in others. It works out fairly well in areas of human decision making where our methods are based on fairly complete, consistent, and context-free units — typically areas of abstract technical expertise, such as symbolic integration and mass spectrogram analysis. We shall now move away from criticisms of individual aspects of current modeling techniques and on to rather more wholesale criticisms of the SSSP and CEST.

HUMAN AND COMPUTER DECISION MAKING

Dreyfus and Dreyfus (1986) claim that CEST is a travesty of most expert human decision making and that the minimal success of CEST (despite popular opinion to the contrary) is a reality and a testimony to the validity of their arguments. First they present a five-level model of human expertise and contrast it with the typical model upon which CEST is based: that a human expert has acquired and internalized a set of rules, and that expert decision making is a manifestation of following (perhaps unconsciously) these rules. Furthermore, the rules can be represented as context-free symbolic expressions. Dreyfus and Dreyfus propose that such rule following is much more characteristic of novices; experts more or less abandon such rules and base their decisions on what they can intuitively 'see' needs to be done, and on their ability to discriminate thousands of special cases. They go on to distinguish domains of intuitive human expertise (such as driving a car) and domains in which there are no intuitive experts (such as configuring complex computer systems, and loading cargo vehicles). CEST may be an adequate model of human decision making in the latter domain, but not in the former. We shall return to the vexing question of what mechanisms might begin to account for human decision making in these intuitive domains, and might begin to explain awkward apparent phenomena like Gestalt perceptions of what needs to be done or is important to consider.

It is still possible to claim that, despite subjective feelings that rules are not being followed, intuitive experts are in fact making rule-based decisions although they know it not. The vast collection of finely discriminated rules that must be searched and followed almost instantaneously may be an implausible model, but it is not an impossible one. Searle (1984) takes an even stronger line with his contention that rule following by computers and apparent rule following by humans are fundamentally different phenomena. And the fundamental difference is, for Searle, a key piece of the reason why computers will never be able to make decisions in the way that humans do it. His argument, which I do not subscribe to, is, roughly, that brains cause minds whose components, mental states, have meaning (semantics). Computer programs on the other hand are formal objects and thus purely syntactic. Pure syntax is insufficient to generate semantics, thus computer programs cannot cause minds. Similarly, computer models of human decision making are just that — i.e., models. It is therefore a gross misunderstanding (and thus a potential source of societal danger) to claim a significance equivalence between any (possible) computer model of human decision making, and human decision making itself. This is a radical viewpoint, but one that has many adherents, a number of whom arrive at this opinion as a result of destroyed beliefs about particular AI software, unrealistic beliefs that are all too commonly fostered by the hype that seems to be a necessary part of marketing software in this area. Searle's argument gets its proper exposure later (see "Let's not be Searle-ish" in Chapter 10).

Winograd and Flores (1986, p. 14) write that "Current thinking about computers and their impact on society has been shaped by a rationalistic tradition that needs to be re-examined and challenged as a source of understanding." To someone trained in science and technology the correctness of the rationalistic orientation is self-evident. The only conceivable alternative is some kind of mysticism, and that is totally unpalatable. Dreyfus's (1979) book *What Computers Can't Do* was frequently attacked from just this standpoint. Some potential and scientifically acceptable alternatives are now available, and we shall examine one in the next section.

But for Winograd and Flores (1986, p. 17), the response is "to show the non-obviousness of the rationalistic orientation and to reveal the blindness that it generates." What I have called the SSSP is, for them, the dominant manifestation of the rationalistic tradition in AI. They claim that the use of rational decision making as a model of human decision making is highly restrictive.

> It does not lead us to see irrationality in a situation as manifested in wrong alternatives and wrong preferences. Although it is often helpful to use methods for evaluating and choosing among alternatives, these methods are harmful when they blind us to a larger realm of concern for human behavior. (p. 145)

They reject as utter nonsense the oft-proposed notion that computer decision-making systems may be preferable to human ones because the computer systems will be free of prejudice and bias. Quite rightly, they point out that the computer system will just embody biases that inevitably come with the decision-making information supplied, whether the programmer intended it or not. They quote from Gadamer: "Prejudices are biases of our openness to the world. They are simply conditions whereby we experience something" (Winograd & Flores, 1986, p. 157). It is with the erroneous belief that a computerized decision-making system can be free from such biases that much scope for societal problems resides — the false belief in objectivity.

The arguments are presented, not as a reason for abandoning hope of applying computer technology in certain domains, but as a prelude to describing a different approach to the design of such systems. In essence, we must abandon the idea of design as an abstract process whose outcome will be the satisfaction of some context-free need (rather like the formal specifications upon which 'good' software engineering design is predicated). A design always comes from within a context, and the need it will satisfy exists only within a context. Flexibility is of the utmost importance, as there will always be unanticipated breakdowns in the matching of the designed artifact to the real-world situation that is was designed to cope with.

These discussions are applied to many examples of real-world decision making (e.g., what to do about a major breakdown of your old car). In such domains the SSSP appears to be inapplicable. However, Winograd and Flores (1986, p. 152) believe that a computer can help explore preconstrained sets of alternatives as manifest in "decision support systems." But, "as with so-called 'expert systems' there is both an appropriate domain of activities for such tools, and a danger in seeing them as doing too much." What are the appropriate and inappropriate domains of human decision making?

CLASSES OF HUMAN DECISION MAKING

For Winograd and Flores, as well as many other commentators (e.g. Hewitt, 1989; Partridge, 1987b), the crucial distinction between the domains of human decision making for which the SSSP is, and is not, a good model concern the distinction between formal, abstract, intellectual problems and real-world, everyday problems (recall the problem domains modeled in *Human Problem Solving*). The former class yield objectively specifiable sets of well-defined, independent alternative states; the latter class do not, at least not without drastic reshaping and simplifying of the original problem.

Hewitt (1989) describes the distinction as that between "open systems [that] are always subject to communications and constraints from outside" (p. 383), and "artificial domains like chess and mathematical theorem proving" (p. 388). Problem space search and logical inference can yield reasonable models of this latter class, but open systems seem to call for exploration of possibilities and due process reasoning in which necessarily incomplete evidence for and against some decision is weighed up.

Partridge (1986a) attempts to characterize the essential difference in terms of loosely coupled and tightly coupled context sensitivity. This demarcation begins to explain why, in addition to formal puzzle solving and game playing, certain informal, concrete problems appear to be successfully subsumed under the SSSP. For example, the expert system R1 is successfully configuring VAX computer systems. It is certainly a concrete, real-world problem, but it happens to also be a problem in which expert-human-quality decisions can be generated within the scope of CEST. It is a problem that is only loosely coupled to its context; a correct configuration is specifiable in a largely context-free manner (in a way that the "correct" meaning of any sentence, for example, is not). And, moreover, it appears that internally the problem can be decomposed into a fixed set of the alternative possibilities.

But the distinction cannot be this simple. Consider chess: Certainly it is a formal, abstract problem, but it is also one in which the predicted successes for AI have not appeared. Why is this? The SSSP is certainly seems to be applicable. The states (board configurations) are well defined and independent of each other, and the set of transformations operators (the legal chess moves) are equally well defined and mutually independent, for any given state. Dreyfus and Dreyfus (1990) offer us an answer. They prefer to characterize the two domains as domains of intuitive and nonintuitive human expertise. Thus, chess and medical diagnosis, domains of intuitive human expertise, have not been attacked with great success by computer systems modeled under the SSSP, whereas configuring complex computer systems is a problem for which there are no intuitive human experts: The human experts on this problem are obliged to figure it out in a state-space search manner. It is thus not at all surprising that a computer system with its superior speed and accuracy, doing things in the same way as the human expert, can generate more accurate results. But what is the intuitive human expert doing if he is not searching a space of alternative possibilities?

An explanation of what the human decision maker may be doing if he is not explicitly searching a space of alternative possibilities can be found in the "spreading-activation" theories of psychology. Collins and Loftus (1975) review, explain, and elaborate on spreading-activation theories of semantic processing.

In this class of theories knowledge is represented as a network of concept nodes (or perhaps two networks, a lexical and a conceptual one) connected with bidirectional links and with a "criteriality" associated with each each direction of each link. Criterialities are numbers indicating how essential a link is to the meaning of a concept. Different kinds of links are typically defined. There may be superordinate links such as AN-IMAL—DOG, and modifier links such as DOG—BROWN, etc.

A search in memory involves tracing in parallel along the links from the node of each concept specified in the input words — the nodes pass "activation" along the links to all directly connected nodes. The parallel spreading activation constantly expands, and, as each node is activated, a tag (containing information about the source of the activation) is left behind. When activation reaches a tagged node, an "intersection" has been found — i.e., a relationship between two initially activated nodes. Decision rules are then used to evaluate the significance of the intersecting paths.

This model of human decision making can account for much empirical data as Collins and Loftus demonstrate, and it is not an explicit examining, selecting, and rejecting of alternative possibilities, but it is not far removed from the SSSP either. However, if we relax the requirement that nodes represent symbolic concepts and we cease to differentiate between types of links, then a more radical conception of human decision making does appear. As a result, human decision making is seen as the emergence of a decision from a dynamically interacting net of primitive elements. The symbolic constraints that select the 'best' decision in the SSSP have become activated subsymbolic patterns of elements in the network, patterns that interact and combine to yield a relatively stable pattern which can be interpreted as a symbolic decision — now we have moved the theory decisively into the realm of modern connectionism.

CONNECTIONISM: A POSSIBLE ANSWER?

As mentioned above arguments to the effect that the SSSP did not apply to certain domains of human problem solving and decision making were always stymied by the retort: What then is the mechanism — magic? In recent years the field of connectionism has sprung up; it appears to embody a mechanism outside the umbrella of the SSSP. It has yet to prove its real worth as a model of human decision making, but it is a concrete alternative that we can point to. Even if it does not prove to be the answer, it has at least opened up afresh the possibility that there are, or could be, significant alternatives to the SSSP. Although I might say, at this point, that it is not clear that connectionism is an alternative to the SSSP (as we've discussed in Chapter 3). It may be viewed more as a precisely correct mechanism for which the symbolic paradigm is an approximation. Alternatively, the CP may be little more than an implementation strategy for information-processing theories (Chapter 1).

However we decide to view the CP, there are some indications that CP-based expert systems may not be subject to many of the limitations of CEST. Smolensky (1986), for example, describes a connectionist model of knowledge about a simple electronic circuit (this model is fully described in Chapter 6), and he points out that, even though it contains no symbolic rules and no logical inference mechanism, it behaves as if it does when presented with complete and consistent questions. In addition, when it is given incomplete or inconsistent information it does not collapse, as is typical with classical CEST-based systems. Instead it responds with the best answer that can be given in the circumstances.

Dreyfus and Dreyfus (1990) briefly discuss the potential of connectionist mechanisms as a realization of intuitive human expertise. They can account for why we have so much trouble extracting the symbolic rules that human experts are believed to use; human experts don't use such rules! A connectionist explanation of human expertise, with its distributed representations, contains no rules at the symbolic level, and it does not use logical inference either. They conclude that the "combination of phenomenology and connectionism may well be devastating to conventional AI as a *practical* endeavor. Could anything be salvaged of the cognitivist-rationalist intuition that for any domain that can be mastered, there exists a set of features and rules which explains that mastery?" (p. 408).

Lest we be carried away with the promises of connectionism, I should make it clear that very little has actually been modeled with these networks to date. And, in addition, there are already a number of difficult and unsolved problems facing the connectionist modeler (see Partridge, 1987c). The overriding concern, in my opinion, is one of comprehensibility (as I'm sure you know, if you've read chapter 3). In order to build and use complex computer systems, we must be able to understand, at some level, how they are doing what they are observed to be doing. Distributed representations in vast networks are conceptually opaque. So how we will be able to develop, maintain, and generally manage large connectionist systems is a significant problem that has yet to be solved.

KNOWLEDGE ELICITATION

An important AI subarea, which has spun off the expert systems work, is that of *knowledge elicitation,* or *knowledge acquisition* (an older term which carries with it the implication that knowledge is some concrete quantity to be mined from certain human heads): How do we get the the knowledge that a human expert undoubtedly has out of the wetware and into an explicit representation — typically a set of rules? The dominant methodology, knowledge-engineer-controlled grilling of the domain expert, has itself thrown up some awkward subproblems. Hence we see several alternatives emerging, and I'll deal with them after the knowledge engineers have shown their paces.

KNOWLEDGE ENGINEERS AND THE THIRD DEGREE

We have already questioned the validity of what is perhaps the fundamental underlying assumption of this particular knowledge elicitation technique: that a domain expert's expertise is based upon a set of rules, and furthermore, a set of rules that he or she can articulate if given enough coaxing. But granted that this assumption could hold true, how do we get the domain expert to spill the beans concerning his expertise? The obvious answer is clearly; "we just ask him how he does what he is observed to do."

Unfortunately, domain experts are no more expert at introspection than you or I. They will typically tell the knowledge engineer a supposed rule. The knowledge engineer then translates it into code, executes the code, and finds that the rule doesn't work; i.e., the rule does not support the required expert behavior. So this methodology becomes one of to and fro between the domain expert and the knowledge engineer. Each testing of the rules should provide more specific questions that the domain expert will answer and thereby improve the rule set.

This is typically a lengthy process which involves the simultaneous presence of two scarce and thus expensive persons. Hence this has been dubbed the "knowledge acquisition bottleneck" or the expert-human-knowledge-in-the-bottle problem.

It is perhaps another example of a fundamental AI problem that fades in significance when we introduce a subparadigm shift. The two subsequent approaches are attempts to implement such shifts and thereby circumvent some of these problems.

AUTOMATIC LEARNING FROM EXAMPLES

A proposal championed largely by Michie (1982, 1983, 1990) is based on the observation that, although experts are not good at verbalizing their rules (assuming they have rules to verbalize), they are good at making decisions when presented with specific examples — after all, this is what their expertise is, isn't it?

So this approach to knowledge acquisition uses the techniques of machine learning (automatic induction, actually; see Chapter 9) to automatically generate a general decision mechanism from a set of specific examples. Some successes have been forthcoming, but automatic induction algorithms are not as powerful and generalized as one would like them to be.

Nevertheless, this approach holds promise: firstly because machine learning techniques will undoubtedly improve in the coming years; and secondly, because it rests on no assumptions that the expert does embody a set of verbalizable rules. See Michalski and Chilausky (1980) for an impressive example of the automatic rule-induction system at work.

This style of knowledge acquisition is sometimes compared with the way in which humans acquire expert knowledge: The apprentice observes many examples of the master's expertise, and expertise is developed in the apprentice as a result of continual observation and practice with feedback from the master. The analogy with automatic rule-induction techniques is a bit weak, but it serves to provide us with a cross-link to the AI subfield of machine learning.

Learning from observation is thought to be a particularly promising mechanism for acquiring knowledge from human experts for knowledge-based systems. De Jong and Mooney (1986) make this point, and claim that it accounts for the increasing amount of work in the machine learning subfield of *learning apprentice systems,* for example, Mitchell, Mahadevan, and Steinberg (1985) and Wilkins, Clancey, and Buchanan (1985). They make their points in the context of a discussion on explanation-based learning which is given a full airing in Chapter 9.

EMPIRICAL TECHNIQUES

This is the least explored and therefore least evaluated of the three approaches to acquiring expert knowledge. It is perhaps significant that the collection of specific techniques that constitute the empirical methods use the term *elicitation* rather than *acquisition,* which is favored in the knowledge-engineer scenario. The empirical techniques are characterized by subtlety — the domain expert is induced to part with his or her knowledge without really knowing it. The knowledge-engineer-interview technique is a good deal more direct — it's not the facts that are demanded, but just the rules.

One technique that has been employed is to generate a list of all of the concepts used within a domain. In the domain of fighter pilots, the concepts are: *barrel roll, high yoyo,* etc. (these terms are, apparently, the verbal currency of jet fighter maneuvres; it is not significant that they mean nothing to you or me). Experts within the domain, in this particular case fighter pilots, are then asked to rate each pair of terms as to how related they are. From this data a network can be constructed which embodies important aspects of the expert's knowledge of the domain. The last and still somewhat-missing link is to use this network to support intelligent decision making (see Cooke & MacDonald, 1986; Schvaneveldt et al., 1985). Interesting snippets of hardish information are being generated in these empirical studies. For example, in one such study Cooke and McDonald (1987) determined that only 10% of the ideas generated in an interview could be characterized as conveying IF-THEN information, i.e., were rule-like.

A comprehensive review, discussion, and extensive bibliography of knowledge acquisition methodologies is given by Neale (1988). He states that the survey indicates increasing emphasis on tools for knowledge acquisition that are used directly by the domain experts — i.e., the classical role of the knowledge engineer is eliminated. These direct strategies facilitate elicitation of the domain engineer's conceptualization of the domain, rather than just in list of facts and rules. Schvaneveldt (1990a) has edited a collection of studies of empirically based approaches to knowledge elicitation and representation.

CEST: WHERE IS IT AND WHERE IS IT GOING?

In an earlier chapter I presented the SSSP, the dominant paradigm in AI. In this chapter the discussions have focused on specific aspects of this paradigm that provide the basic assumptions of CEST. The scope of applicability of these assumptions as a basis for models of human decision making is a general viewpoint that has been explored. The essential idea of decision making as choosing among a set of alternative possibilities, a well-defined set of isolated entities independent of time, place, and, most importantly, human context. This appears to be a poor approximation to human decision making in certain domains: formal, abstract versus everyday, real-world, or intuitive versus nonintuitive. The diagnoses vary, and so do the inferences drawn: They range from the impossibility of achieving anything more than a superficial appearence of human abilities with computer systems, to beliefs that the solution of a few more puzzles within CEST will result in the duplication (or better) of many aspects of human expertise.

There is a need to identify the scope of CEST and thus avoid misapplying it when designing computer systems to fulfill some role in society. The societal impact of computer systems that claim to model (and therefore can substitute for) human decision making is expected to be significant. Simplistic generalizations to the effect that, with AI, we can do anything, or nothing, are not the answer. The questions are complex, and currently they need to be answered on a case-by-case basis.

A fundamental assumption of CEST, viz. that human experts follow symbolic rules, is under attack, and the appearence of CP-based models has lent weight to the assault.

Finally, where is CEST going? It is quite clear that, even if the more ambitious goals of expert systems are proving rather difficult to attain, a new generation of useful software is here to stay. Many small-scale "know-how" systems (e.g., d'Agapeyeff, 1986) based upon CEST are functioning in application environments as robust and reliable software. At the other end of the spectrum, TEKNOWLEDGE, for example, are now advocating "Integrated Knowledge Systems" — large-scale, knowledge-based programming environments.

I hesitate to recommend any collected sources of wisdom in this exploding domain as there are far too many "expert systems" texts for me to read them all. Hayes-Roth, Waterman, and Lenat (1983) is a very useful attempt to abstract usable generalities from the detailed mass of individual experiences with building specific systems, but it is becoming dated. Waterman (1986) is (obviously) more up to date. For those who wish to know that CEST is all wrong, Dreyfus and Dreyfus (1986) is the book to read. An attempt to set CEST into the general AI background (but solidly traditional AI, I might add) is *Artificial Intelligence and the Design of Expert Systems* by Luger and Stubblefield (1989).

In the following chapter I shall focus down on the notion of *knowledge;* schemes for both capturing and manipulating this quantity are examined, as well as what knowledge might be.

6

Knowledge Representation: A Problem of Both Structure And Function

"A little knowledge is a dangerous thing," especially in an AI program.

In this chapter we shall move away from the specifics of knowledge representation and usage to support current expert systems technology. We shall step back and take a broader look at the range of possibilities for storing and utilizing in computers this elusive but seemingly critical component of AI systems. At this time, with the AI world solidly in the grip of expert systems euphoria, we are blessed with the word *knowledge* in an adjectival role of wonderous ubiquity: we have knowledge bases (and hence Intelligent Knowledge-Based Systems, IKBSs), knowledge engineers, knowledge systems (usually also integrated), knowledge programming, knowledge competitions, the knowledge level, knowledge everything (well, almost). We don't know exactly what knowledge is, but the AI community, almost to a person, knows that it is a good thing to pack into AI systems — the more the better. Winograd (1990), to mention just one dissenting voice, takes issue with this feature of the accepted AI wisdom; he questions the view that knowledge is a commodity to be stashed, in large quantities, in intelligent artifacts.

In this chapter I shall limit myself to an examination of the ways that information is stored and accessed to support intelligent systems construction, in short, knowledge representation.

WHY NETWORKS?

There has been a persistent belief throughout the full three decades of AI's history that human knowledge is best represented as some kind of graph structure (i.e., a webby structure in which blobs, points, or nodes are connected by lines, arcs, edges, or links). AI persons typically use the terminology *semantic network*, but by definition a network is a graph having weights associated with the links (weights are just numbers whose roles will become apparent later). So-called semantic networks do not typically have weights associated with the links, but some do, and they form an important subclass, namely, connectionist networks. Currently there is a widespread commitment to the representation of knowledge as a collection of general rules and specific facts. Such knowledge bases are typically employed, with some success, in expert systems (as we saw in the previous chapter). Knowledge bases have the attraction of being pseudomodular — i.e., knowledge bases are composed of a more or less unordered collection of rules and facts in which any single element contributes the the whole in a way that is independent of the existence (or nonexistence) of any other constituent. Modularity facilitates incremental development, but the "flatness" and general homogeneity of these representations (i.e., the lack of structural organization, such as hierarchical structuring) renders them singularly opaque once they become large. Recall both PROLOG, whose strengths and weaknesses mirror those of knowledge bases as collections of rules, and the unmanageability of such knowledge bases as they become large. It is an attempt to discretize human knowledge, and it appears to be successful in limited, technical, nonintuitive domains. Applicability and utility in general remains to be seen; I am not optimistic, as you probably realized if you read the previous chapter.

Knowledge bases aside, the generic graph structure for representing knowledge is known as a *semantic network*. Typically, the nodes of a semantic network represent concepts such as: bird, robin, John, etc. And the arcs represent relations between these concepts, for example, isa, father_of, belongs_to. Woods (1975), in his famous critique, "What's in a link," states that "The major characteristic of semantic networks that distinguishes them from other candidates is the characteristic notion of a link or pointer [arc] which connects individual facts into a total structure." There are many problems with semantic networks (see Woods's (1975) paper), but we might note that they are conceptually transparent; in fact, they are too conceptually suggestive. This leads us into one of the (many) tar-pits of AI: in this case, the ELIZA syndrome (Partridge, 1986a); to wit, overly suggestive naming of objects in AI programs inevitably leads interested observers to make unwarranted, grandiose assumptions about the program's capabilities. Much of the AI community has bypassed this awkward problem, and at this juncture so shall we.

An example of a semantic network (see Figure 6.1) is:

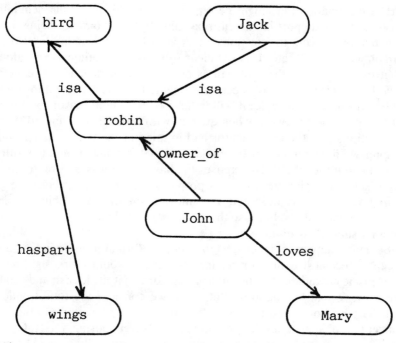

Figure 6.1.   A semantic network

Now that's an impressive bunch of knowledge, isn't it? Any system using this knowledge base will know about birds and that they have wings; it will know that robins are birds; it will know that John owns a robin and, in addition, loves Mary, etc.

Quite unfrankly, I'm impressed. And that's the root of the problem: for example, in my one-sentence survey of the knowledge captured above I slipped in the piece of knowledge that John is male. That information is not in the network; it is an implication that we draw all too readily from the name *John* and perhaps from the relationship *loves* with a node named *Mary*. Without further information about the implementation details that support reasoning with this network, the presence of the relationship "John loves Mary" tells us nothing more than that there is some binary relation between two objects; "A x B" is equivalent but far less impressive (read it as A xes B?).

So the knowledge that has really been captured by a semantic network is dependent upon the program details for reasoning with the nodes and links; it is *not* dependent upon the wealth of implications that you, or I, or anyone else brings to mind when we see the node and link labels. The sort of information that might be represented in this particular semantic network could support intelligent reasoning by, for example, being used to generate answers to questions: such as, "Is Jack a robin?", "Do all birds have wings?", etc. It is not clear from the semantic network alone what the answers to these questions ought to be; it depends on exactly how the arc properties have been implemented. Typically, the implementation will be very specific; it will behave reliably (and reasonably) only for this particular network when queried with just the very limited types of questions that the implementor had in mind at the time. Later in this chapter we'll take a look at Brachman's (1985) critique intriguingly titled "I lied about the trees." He exposes the basic weaknesses of representational schemes using *isa* links and property–inheritance strategies; e.g., if Figure 6.1 has represented the information that a "robin haspart wings," it can only be because the node *robin* has inherited this property from its superclass *bird*.

Semantic networks, lacking as they do any formal basis or indeed any accepted formal structure for manipulating them, would at first sight seem to be prime candidates for the enterprising formalist to move in and establish firm, formal foundations. But when we consider the total freedom to label both nodes and arcs with (almost) any combination of complex conceptual objects and relations, the chances of imposing a useful, general formal semantics on such structures looks decidedly slim. AI types have tried; John McCarthy, for example, has spent the last 30 years searching for a workable, formal epistemology for AI — he is still looking, hard. Similarly, Alan Robinson of resolution principle fame {any text on the language PROLOG will provide the gruesome meaning of this nonobvious phrase; I mention it in passing in Chapter 4} is persuaded that first-order logics (Chapter 10 explains these formal animals) are the way to go, because we understand so much about them. The fact that many AI problems do not appear to fit into the framework of such logical schemes (e.g., they resist useful approximation as a collection of context-free elements) may be more a reflection of our misconception of the problems than a limitation inherent in first-order logics. However, it still remains to be demonstrated that reduction machines, for example, are a viable approach to problems other than the context-free collections of constituent parts that comprise mathematical expressions. Belief that, say, natural language understanding can be treated in this manner is currently little more than a act of faith.

The highly suggestive node and arc names typically employed in semantic networks may have a firm foundational basis in a formalism such as the predicate calculus — gruesome details have been delayed until Chapter 10. The fancy names are then just labels selected from a sets of quantities which in themselves have a formal semantic basis. Thus the node names might be elements of a set of atomic symbols and the arc names elements of a set of predicates. In this case the network may well represent a formally defined object, but the formalization has been gained at the cost of a severe loss in power. So, for example, the arc labeled *isa* has a formally defined semantics, but the semantics will be limited to a simple "syntactic" relationship (such as set membership) between the primitive, structureless elements represented by the nodes. The richness of the relation *is a* in ordinary English has been utterly obliterated. The predicate calculus is widely believed to be inadequate for the description of many aspects of human knowledge, e.g., the inability to cope with the inconsistencies that are characteristic of much human knowledge (see, for example, Hewitt's 1985 criticism).

A second route to placing semantic network representations on firmer foundations is to base them on empirical data. In this case the node and arc names will be labels for quantities derived from a statistical analysis perhaps. In any event the meaning of any particular network will be founded on an interpretation of the underlying analysis and data; it may well be questionable, but it will also be explicit — that is the important thing. Schvaneveldt et al. (1985) present such a basis for their link-weighted networks. This general avenue of approach to the representation of human knowledge was examined in the previous chapter in the context of knowledge elicitation strategies, a component of expert system's technology.

Before we move on with this firm belief that networks, in some guise or other, are the way to go, let us just briefly consider Fodor's argument against this comfortable presupposition. Fodor (1990) argues that a belief in intentional realism (sorry about the philosophese here, but hang on, plainer English follows), coupled with the language of thought (LOT) hypothesis, leads to the conclusion that cognitive architecture must exhibit constituent structure in a way that is not necessarily true of networks. Thus the fundamental characteristic of cognitive architecture is that it has constituent structure at the level of semantic interpretation such as a Turing-von Neumann (TVN) architecture (i.e., a regular computer) necessarily does; the appropriate architecture may be implementable in terms of a network, but there is no necessity for a network representation.

The major steps along the route to Fodor's contention are: first, a belief in intentional realism: a belief that mental states have associated intentional objects, and that these objects have causal roles — i.e., intentional realism is the name of a scheme for accounting for how we can connect thoughts with actions. Thus, the state of having a symbol "I raise my left hand" in my intention box, causes my left hand to rise. As Fodor says: Although it is hard to see how this could be, in the absence of serious competitors intentional realism must be taken seriously. He also points out that belief in intentional realism does not entail a belief in the necessity for constituent structure of these objects. A different action, however similar to the original (e.g., I raise my left hand and left foot), may be attributed quite simply to the presence of a different intentional object in my intention box.

The second step in his argument is belief in the LOT hypothesis, which claims that mental states have constituent structure: The intentional objects are relatively complex expressions whose content is determined in some regular way by the content of their constituent parts — i.e., something like a sentence must go into the intention box. Support for this hypothesis derives from the observation that our linguistic capacities are systematic, and from a belief that the function of language is to express thoughts. Thus our cognitive capacities have constituent structure, as is reflected in our use of language. The systematicity argument is based on facts such as: If a native speaker knows what "John loves Mary" means, he or she will also, of necessity, know what "Mary loves John" means. This result does not follow by inference; it is a consequence of the constituent structure of thought: belief in the complex thought "John loves Mary" is due to an understanding of the constituent parts and their particular interrelationship. The same constituents may contribute, via different interrelationships, to other beliefs.

In sum, natural language has combinatorial semantics. Linguistic capacity has combinatorial semantics. So thought has combinatorial semantics, if we accept that the function of language is to express thought.

A TVN architecture must have such constituent structure, at the level of intentions. A network architecture can be constructed to exhibit any required systematicity relations, but systematicity (and hence, such relations) must logically follow from cognitive architecture. Thus networks may be sufficient, but they are clearly not necessary — at least, not for Fodor, nor for Pylyshyn; you may recall their joint blitz on connectionism, which I reviewed in Chapter 3.

WHY NEURONS?

Belief that the brain is primarily responsible for intelligent behavior, coupled with the observation that a prominent feature of this organ is a vast network of neurons, leads to the belief that representations of knowledge based on networks of neuron-like units may one day exhibit structural, as well as behavioral, correspondences with the workings of the brain.

Hence network representations may serve to further our understanding of the biological basis for intelligence. Additionally, advances in neurophysiology may provide guiding constraints for the network modellers — the benefits are expected to flow in both directions (but remember the cautionary section in Chapter 3 — The Myth of Empirical Guidance).

Certainly, if one's prime interest is biological, a desire to make progress in understanding how it is that the biological object homo sapiens can do what it can do, then neural architectures are probably a major route to realizing these objectives vis-á-vis man's cognitive abilities. But if the desire is an understanding and perhaps reproduction of intelligence itself, without particular regard for the specific biological manifestation that happens to be at hand, then the expediency of employing neural architectures becomes a more open question. Much of AI is in this latter category. Even that AI work which does aspire to shed light on the nature of human intelligence typically does not aim nor claim to be doing so at the neuroanatomical level. Theorizing, modeling, testing, and explaining human intelligence is typically in terms of concepts way above neuroanatomy. The constituents of such AI theories and models are long-term memory, primary drives, motivation, etc., not neurons.

Nevertheless, as I mentioned above (and especially in the light of the less-than-dramatic successes of the higher-level modeling), the temptations of neuroanatomy are compelling: use of the only proven architecture, and a further source of contraints to provide guidance in the research. But let us examine the first of my two listed "good reasons" for employing neuroarchitectures in AI: It is the architecture that supports the only known intelligent system; we have an existence proof of the sufficiency of neural networks. I purposely avoided saying that neural architecture is also necessary, for that is exactly the question which I am now raising.

The neural tangle that we all carry around in our heads is typically claimed to be the result of one of two possible mechanisms: the workings of a general omnipotent designer (GOD, to employ yet another of the acronymic reductions so beloved in the AI world), or of evolution — the details of neither of which seem to be universally agreed upon, but, as I need to go no further than superficial generalities to make this point in my argument, that is not a problem. Adherents to the former belief must perforce bet on the necessity of neural architectures, and I'll let them continue on their way at this point with no further harassment. But what about the evolutionists? The products of evolution appear to be optimal and ideal on occasion, but sometimes the absence of the guiding hand of an all-knowing being (or even, someone vaguely aware of what the future may hold) is all too painfully apparent.

PANDERING TO EVOLUTION: BEWARE OF CLASSICAL RECONDITIONING

Next time that you find yourself at a decent zoo or ambling through the dense bamboo forests high in the mountains of Western China, look out for a giant panda — it's unmistakable, a sort of oversized, black-and-white, licorice allsort with fur on it. Anyway, however it is that you manage to get to close quarters with this animal, use the opportunity to observe its hands. You will be amazed to see that it possesses the usual complement of five fingers, and then one more, making six in all. Or, as a variant of the old schoolboy joke goes: not six fingers, but four fingers and two thumbs. More precisely, it has four fingers, one true thumb, and one fake one — not a plastic prosthesis (I hasten to add) but an all-natural one ("no artificial nothing"). In point of fact this sixth digit is a reconditioned wrist bone. This fake thumb sported by the average Panda is not anatomically a finger at all. It is constructed from a wrist bone because the Panda's true thumb was committed to another role long before the Panda elected to live exclusively on bamboo leaves, which need to be stripped off the stalks efficiently (a task that is aided by the possession of an opposable thumb). The Panda's thumb is "a contraption, not a lovely contrivance. But it does the job" (Gould, 1980). In the parlance of software engineering, it's a patch job, a kludge: all the available information indicates that the required change in system behavior was not generated by a structured process of redesign and reimplementation.

The important question for us is: Which class of mechanism is our neural architecture, contraption or lovely contrivance? We can be certain that it did not initially evolve to support intelligent behavior, for all of the organisms that we patronizingly refer to as lower animals exhibit disturbingly similar interior head-work (at least before we reach rock bottom in the animal world). There is an argument that we alone have a third layer (on top of the reptilian and mammalian components), the cerebral cortex, which is exactly the chunk that accounts for our intellectual superiority over the rest of the animal kingdom (see Koestler, 1967, for a very readable, if not anatomically overprecise, exposition of this view). But even this, the "thinking-man's brain," is constructed from the same old component (with, it appears, a somewhat different, but not radically different, style of interconnection) that evolved to keep the first crustacean out of harm's way, namely the neuron. So we must view our current neural architecture as definitely a potential contraption that has fallen together, and somewhat fortuitously, is sufficient to do the job. I might add, at this point, that our current neural architecture is *necessarily* sufficient to do the job, for, if it were not, we would not be in any position to comment on its failure (assuming that the conventional wisdom is correct in locating the seat of our cognitive capacities in the brain).

In addition to these sobering thoughts, we must face the fact that, even if neural architectures are in some sense optimal for cognition, it is thoroughly unlikely that they would be optimal in a sense demanded by AI: There is no reason to expect perceptual transparency from the products of evolution (nor of an all-knowing designer, incidentally; he or she would presumably just get it right first time). Design and development in evolution does not require perspicuity of representation (for who is there to look at, and tinker with, the current version?); for success in AI, on the other hand, it is of paramount importance. An apparent counterargument was presented by Simon (1962), who was, as always, at pains to show that AI can, and will, be doing great things in the near future. He argued that the products of evolution are likely to have the property of "near decomposability": a functional modularity that, he quite rightly maintained, is a necessary prerequisite for human comprehension of complex phenomena. This apparent contradiction between what the products of evolution are likely to exhibit in terms of human comprehensibility is resolved by the observation that the existence of functional modularity does not entail physical modularity. Thus the modularity of function may not be reflected in the physical organization (quite apart from the problem of reconciling our folk theories of the functional components of intelligence with the functional components that were thrown up by evolution). But all that aside: networks of neurons are the only known sufficient architecture, so it would be silly to ignore them completely.

NEURAL ARCHITECTURES: IN THE BEGINNING

Early milestones along the road of neural architectures are the "cell assemblies" of Hebb (1949) and the "formal neurons" of Rosenblatt (1962). Rosenblatt also invented the simple neuron-like learning networks called *perceptrons*. Minsky and Papert (1969) produced a thorough formal analysis of the computational power of the perceptron networks. {Gruesome detail: I hereby absolve you from all feelings of guilt if you skip on to the next batch of chatty stuff. By definition, a bipartite graph G is a graph in which the node set V can be partitioned into 2 subsets V1 and V2 such that every edge of G joins V1 with V2 (Harary, 1969). A *layer,* in connectionist terminology, is this set of edges, except that, because they are directional, they are arcs. An important glitch in this attempted definition is due to lateral inhibitory links between nodes in the same subset. This feature gets a full subsection later in the chapter. Thus, bipartite graphs are one-layered in the terminology of connectionism. When Minsky and Papert proved that these single-layer networks were limited to learning first order predicates, further research on such simple-node networks was stifled for many years — until AC 1 you may recall.}

The basic element of perceptrons is the *threshold logic unit,* a type of formal neuron that has n inputs, each associated with a real-valued weight. The total input to the unit is the sum of the activity on each input arc multiplied by the appropriate arc weight. The unit gives an output of 1 if this sum exceeds a threshold, ϴ; otherwise it gives an output of zero. {More formally, the output is the truth value of the expression:

$$\sum_i a_i w_i > \Theta$$

where a_i is the activity on the ith input arc and w_i is its weight. Notice that this simple output function is discontinuous; i.e., the output is either 1 or zero according to whether the threshold ϴ is exceeded or not, there are no intermediate output values — it is a binary threshold unit. As you are obviously reading these petty details, you might as well make the extra effort and store them away to be retrieved when sigmoidal functions crop up later in this book — Chapter 9, as we're in high-precision mode at this point.}

Here are a couple of clarificatory pictures; they may be worth a few thousand words, or just a few dozen if they're curly bracketed ones. In any event, they will provide a beacon in the darkness for those readers who are visual rather than verbal.

A formal neuron is also a threshold logic unit, in case you were wondering.

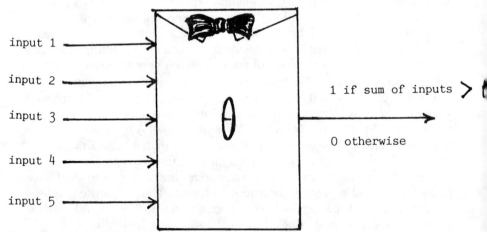

Figure 6.2. A neuron in formal dress

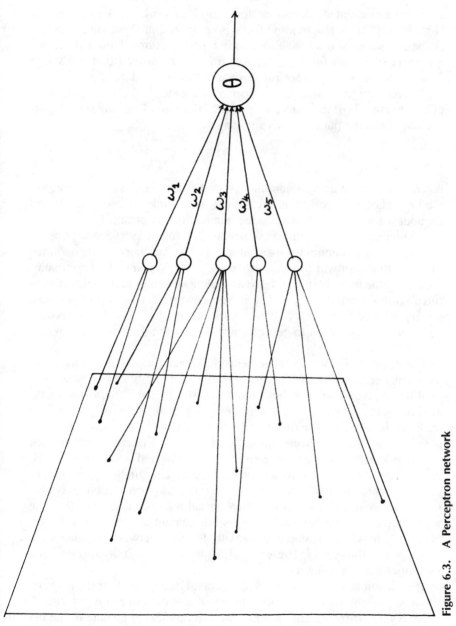

Figure 6.3. A Perceptron network

A modern point of departure for neural networks was provided by Hopfield (1982). A Hopfield network is composed of these simple on-off elements and all of the links function in both directions. Hopfield proved a number of results for his nets. In particular he proved that the stable states of these networks are the minimum "energy" states.

{Thoroughly gruesomely: The energy of a state, E is given by the sum of the thresholds of the active units minus the sum of the weights of connections between pairs of active units.

$$E = \sum_i s_i \theta_i - \sum_{i<j} s_i s_j w_{ij}$$

where s_i is the ith unit (which has a 0 or 1 value, inactive or active, are the only choices here), w_{ij} is the weight of the link between the ith and jth nodes, and $i<j$, (just to keep the summations in check).}

An important point about these networks is that they will always settle into an energy minimum from any starting state, but there is no guarantee that the minimum will the global one and not just some local minimum. Hence, all the fuss about simulated annealing and computational temperatures that you will be exposed to in subsequent descriptions of problem solving with certain types of CP-based systems (the class of bath-like architectures, if you want to get technical — they are dealt with as a whole later in this chapter).

The essential feature of these neuron-like networks that distinguishes them from semantic networks proper is their simplicity and homogeneity (and this is, paradoxically, both the major strength and the major weakness of these architectures). The nodes contain an "activity" value, and each arc is associated with a weight that controls how much activity is passed along the arcs from one node to another. Functions are defined on the nodes to specify how activity is accumulated and how it is dispersed along the arcs that lead from each node. The simplicity and homogeneity of these networks makes them perceptually opaque, but may also make them particularly amenable to formal analysis in a way that the unrestricted and perceptively suggestive semantic networks are not. Hence we have, for example, a formally founded network-learning algorithm due to Rumelhart, Hinton, and Williams (1986) (fully discussed in its proper place in Chapter 9).

Having attempted to provide some general background for the associationistic presumption, which dominates all attempts to represent knowledge to support intelligent systems, we can now explore some of the details. As usual I'll deal with the possibilities in terms of the two major paradigms, and I'll put the CP in front for a change. But first a few words (to be taken figuratively, of course) about the roles of structure and function in representation are called for.

KNOWLEDGE REPRESENTATION: STRUCTURE AND FUNCTION

The term *knowledge representation* is misleadingly suggestive of form or structure with no hint of processes to manipulate that structure. A knowledge representation is (to use computer science terminology) a data structure, but a data structure is a structure together with the allowable operations on that structure. In fact the set of allowable operations (the things that can be done with the structure) usually provide most of the specification of the data structure. Thus, a collection of objects is a *set* if one can test for membership, etc.; it is an *array* if elements can be randomly accessed by means of an index, etc.

We have seen one undesirable consequence of this aspect of knowledge representation already in terms of the seductive tendencies of semantic networks — we infer a whole host of operations from the relation names; usually some trivial subset of these suggested operations is actually implemented. This relatively simple point of structure and function can lead us into a morass of technical subtlety concerning the nature of notations and their meanings. I am of course not going to wallow in this mire. Nevertheless, a few of the most significant points should be brought out for consideration, given the centrality of the notion of knowledge representation in AI, and I can do so with ease.

McDermott's (1986) assault on the use of logic in AI, which gets its proper exposure in context in Chapter 10, claims that the logicist's goal is a "content theory" (i.e., a theory of what people know). It is a theory of knowledge {in the form of logical axioms, but this is currently immaterial, so don't agonize over it} that is independent of any specific program to operate on it. McDermott further claims (with support from Birnbaum, 1986, I gather) that "in most cases there is no way to develop a 'content theory' without a 'process model'" (i.e., an explanation of how this knowledge should be used).{For those who are dutifully reading these curly-bracketed interjections and who think that they have spotted yet another flaw in the arguments presented: Please note that logical deduction is considered and dismissed as an adequate process model — Chapter 10 reveals all.}

The content-theory style of knowledge representation is what we might term a static theory of knowledge — i.e., structure without function. The elements of the theory are given meaning by tying them to a more basic theory, e.g., set theory or number theory. The meaning of a representation is given by what it "denotes" in the underlying, basic theory, and the soundness of the underlying theory guarantees a similar soundness in the representation of knowledge built on top. Such representations are said to have a *denotational semantics* (but don't lose any sleep over it).

Much work in AI is based on an intertangled content theory and process model. You are invited to refer back to Figure 6.1 for a prime example. Typically, the emphasis is on the process-model aspect: i.e., exotic representational structures which have little meaning on their own are manipulated in interesting ways by a program. This approach is profoundly disturbing to the formalist, but his or her favored scheme of first a pure representation, denotationally grounded, and unsullied by specific processing mechanisms appears to be doomed to failure. In truth, there are some low-probability ways out for the pure representationalist; the reader is referred to McDermott's article for the gruesome details, although I touch on them in Chapter 10. It is not insignificant that the classic process-model-dominated approaches to AI are labeled "speculative" AI in Chapter 10 (not by me, I hasten to add).

Why not have a dual semantics — denotational guarantees together with procedural completeness? Why not, indeed; it is certainly possible. A pure PROLOG program is one example. It has the denotational meaning supplied via logic, and it has a procedural meaning supplied by the PROLOG interpreter — the program can be run, and by so doing we can generate new representations from old.

For anyone who has delved into AI's murky past, most of the foregoing should read as a resurrection of the old procedural–declarative controversy (see Winograd, 1975b, for a representative contribution to this issue in its heyday): roughly, should knowledge be represented as datastructures or coded into procedures? Interest in this issue waxes and wanes. It has been on the wane for a few years, so a rewaxing, in terms of an assault on logicism, is about due.

Another link back to the early days is provided by the epistemic–heuristic distinction (a Chapter 1 issue — for those readers who have the distinct feeling that this term ought to mean something to them, but doesn't). Chandrasekaran (1990) brings this out in his discussion: The epistemic theorizing is the development of a content theory; the subsequent heuristic theorizing adds a process model. McDermott is clearly challenging the validity of this widely accepted distinction as a model for the persuance of AI goals. Chandrasekaran frames his own challenge in terms of an unhelpful separation of representation and control. He prefers 'generic functional theories' within which computational theorizing is an integral part of the overall effort; i.e., the process model is included from the beginning.

But, as I mentioned earlier, this argument is not restricted to logicists. Thus "the knowledge-level" approach to AI (coming shortly) is an example of a content theory before process model, and is thus subject to much the same criticism as logicism. Similarly, Lenat, Prakesh, and Shepard (1986) CYC project is covered by McDermott's interdict. Lenat presents the CYC project in terms of the laudible goal of first constructing a rich information base (tens of thousands of pieces of knowledge, i.e., a machine-readable encylopedia), which ought to be sufficient to support common-sense reasoning, then think about designing systems to use the knowledge base. Quite justifiably, he charges the AI world with attempting to build fancy systems which have only a laughably small knowledge base at their disposal. If the current belief in the criticality of knowledge is correct, then these systems are crippled from the outset. Elaborate domain-specific heuristics can atone for some inadequacies of the available knowledge base, but they cannot provide total compensation. He plans to spend about 10 years building up this encylopedic knowledge base. But accumulation of a mass of "knowledge elements" (i.e., facts, etc.) with no associated functions for using the knowledge (i.e., no process model) is clearly an example of a pure content theory and as such falls under the same strictures as logicism. Accumulation of facts, etc., independent of any mechanism for using these facts, is an undirected and endless task. In McDermott's words, "You cannot start listing facts people know, expressed in logic or any other notation, without saying something about how you assume they will be used by a program, and hence what class of inferences you are trying to account for. . . . How will they know when they are making progress?"

"The knowledge level" approach espoused by Newell (1981) is (as I've already said) similarly flawed. But because of its importance in AI, it recurs in several subsequent places in this book and we must explore it further. Newell's discussion of the knowledge level presents the slogan equation:

REPRESENTATION = KNOWLEDGE + ACCESS

For Newell, of course, the definition of REPRESENTATION is in terms of symbol systems; the definition is:

> a symbol system that encodes a body of knowledge. It [the theory of the knowledge level] does not provide a *theory* of representation, which properly exists only at the symbol level and which tells how to create representations with particular properties, how to analyse their efficiency, etc." (1981, p. 14, author's emphasis)

In Newell's view there is a "knowledge level" immediately above the symbol level, and we must have a clear conception of knowledge before there is a chance of agreeing on adequate representations which are at the symbol level. Clearly, knowledge must be represented if we are to study it. Logic, Newell (1981, p. 12) points out, is an obvious candidate for a system to represent knowledge: "Logic is just a representation of knowledge. It is not the knowledge itself, but a structure at the symbol level." Figure 6.4 is Newell's picture of the knowledge level in the general context of computer system levels.

All levels are clearly not created equal. The knowledge level is unique. For example, it is a medium that is not realized in physical space in a passive way, but only in an active process of selection. The basic claim pictured in Figure 6.4 is made explicit in "the knowledge-level hypothesis":

There exists a distinct computer systems level, lying immediately above the symbol level, which is characterized by knowledge as the medium and the principle of rationality as the law of behavior" (Newell, 1981, p. 7) (this governing principle is given below).

Newell also points out the manifest shortcomings of logics, and suggests that logics are not privileged. They are just one possibility among many such as algebraic mathematics and chemical notations. "The development of AI is the story of constructing many other systems that are not logics but can be used as representations of knowledge" (p. 13). Questioning the divine right of logic as *the* notation for AI is renewed with a vengence in Chapter 10.

According to Newell (1981, p. 6, author's emphasis)

> The system at the knowledge level is the agent. The components at the knowledge level are *goals, actions* and *bodies*. Thus, an agent is composed of a set of actions, a set of goals and a body. The medium at the knowledge level is *knowledge* (as might be suspected). Thus, the agent processes its knowledge to determine the actions to take. Finally, the behavior law is the *principle of rationality:* Actions are selected to attain the agent's goals.

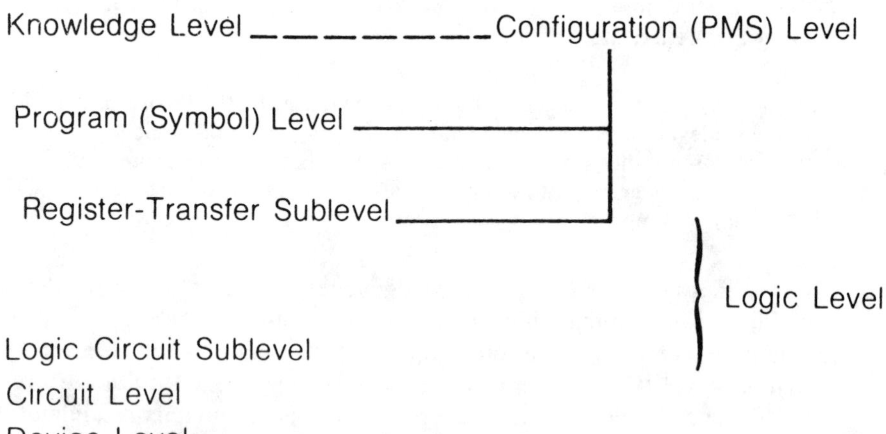

Knowledge Level _ _ _ _ _ _ _ _ Configuration (PMS) Level

Program (Symbol) Level _____

Register-Transfer Sublevel_____

Logic Level

Logic Circuit Sublevel

Circuit Level

Device Level

Figure 6.4.   The knowledge-level view of computer system levels

In order to make this quotation more meaningful, we need to know the *principle of rationality;* it is:

> If an agent has knowledge that one of its actions will lead to one of its goals, then the agent will select that action. (Newell, 1981, p. 8)

The reader who is not cruising through this narrative in a dream must now be wondering what the agent does when it does not have the knowledge that one of its actions will lead to one of its goals. Lack of obvious connection between any action in the current set and achievement of a goal, which in addition does not interfere with the possibility of also achieving other important goals, may not be an uncommon situation in real-world, intelligent problem solving. In fact, one might almost claim that it's a characteristic. The principle is woefully silent on all but the relatively straightforward situations, it seems to me. Anyway, Newell also concedes that his principle is not sufficient to determine behavior in many situations. So he adds that "some of these situations can be covered by adding auxiliary principles. Thus we can think of an *extended principle of rationality,* building out from the *central* or *main* principle, given above" (p. 8, author's emphasis). Following Newell's lead, I'll leave this peripheral problem as an exercise for the reader.

The further problems that Newell does discuss seem to assume that the architectural framework at the knowledge level is SSSP based with a strong production-system flavor. This is not surprising, given the dominance of production system schemes at Newell's home base (production systems come up for consideration towards the end of this chapter). The architecture is formulated in terms of sets of actions and of goals, and of selecting one action from a subset in which each individual action with lead to achievement of some goal. The reader should link these ideas back to the criticism of the SSSP by Winograd and Flores (1986, but closer at hand in Chapters 3 and 5) and also carry them forward to the impending discussion of production systems.

To return to the specific question of what is knowledge according the knowledge-level picture: So far, it has been described as the medium at the knowledge level. Newell elevates this into a complete definition:

> *Knowledge:* Whatever can be ascribed to an agent, such that its behavior can be computed according to the principle of rationality.

Knowledge is thus characterized entirely functionally, not structurally. At first sight this claim would seem to be at odds with my earlier charge that the theory of the knowledge level was a content theory without a process model. There is, of course, no problem. Within Newell's scheme, knowledge is characterized by its effect on the overall behavior of the system; nothing is said about *how* the knowledge is to be used to produce the appropriate system behavior. Thus there is no process model (although there are perhaps the bones of such a model in the production system skeleton alluded to earlier).

It is time to move on. We have still to consider knowledge representation within the CP.

THE SSSP AND THE CP: REPRESENTATIONAL ISSUES

The way that Fodor and Pylyshyn (1988) summarize the essential difference between "Classicists [i.e., SSSPists] and Connectionists" is that Connectionists assign semantic content (i.e., meaning) to nodes or aggregates of nodes, and Classicists assign meaning to "expressions," such as "The yellow dog" or "$10 = 5*2$". Further than this, Connectionists "acknowledge *only causal connectedness* as a primitive relation among nodes; When you know how activation and inhibition flow among them, you know everything there is to know about how the nodes in a network are related. By contrast, Classical theories acknowledge not only causal relations . . . but also a range of structural relations, of which constituency is paradigmatic." (We'll get to the importance of constituents soon, although the notion was discussed in Chapter 3.)

They then footnote the detail that meaning is determined by the total state of the network, i.e., the totality of which nodes are activated and which nodes are not. But for most purposes it's okay to say that a conceptually meaningful structure, in a CP-based system, is a pattern of activation.

For Fodor and Pylyshyn, you may recall, the CP is just a lower, and not very handy, representational level than the SSSP. So they presumably would see little of deep significance in the specific representational schemes utilized by Connectionists. But, working under the assumption that they could possibly be wrong (an assumption that would be rated anywhere from certainly true to indubitably false by different persons each with full knowledge of the facts), I'll give considerable space to a presentation of knowledge representation from a CP perspective.

But before I move on to details, we might note that Chandrasekaran (1990) advocates a somewhat similar view and briefly examine the basis of his chosen viewpoint. He argues that "connectionist (and symbolic) approaches are both *realizations* of a more abstract level of description, viz., *the information processing (IP) level*" (p. 25, author's emphasis). He claims that belief in IP theory is almost universal among workers in AI; the belief is stated as: "Significant (all?) aspects of cognition and perception are best understood/modeled as *information processing activities on representations*" (p. 14, my emphasis). So what is this IP theory? The idea, usually associated with Marr (1977), is to examine the phenomenon of interest and "first, identify an information processing function with a clear specification about what kind of information needs to be made available as output by the function. Then specify a particular IP theory for achieving this function by stating what kinds of information the theory proposes need to be represented at various stages in the processing." At this stage there is no commitment to specific algorithms for realizing the theory in a computational model. Thus there is no commitment to either the CP or the SSSP. Subsequent implementations can go either way, or both ways.

Let's now take a look at the representational strategies to be found within our two chosen paradigms; I'll take the CP first.

KNOWLEDGE REPRESENTATION IN THE CP

A key aspect of knowledge representation in the CP is the notion of *distributed representations*. This is a characteristic structural feature of the subsymbolic school; it is also a salient characteristic in the symbolic connectionism school, but the distributedness has vacated structure and settled solely in function — symbolic functions, such as logical inference, are represented to some degree of approximation by a collection of activity transfers (Smolensky's, 1988, microinferences).

FUNCTIONALLY DISTRIBUTED REPRESENTATIONS

If there is any one thing that is true of all connectionist systems, it is that they are functionally distributed — i.e., the primary mechanism for processing the network is parallel transfer of activity values, entities that as individuals typically have no semantic interpretation at the level of cognitive phenomena.

SYMBOLIC CONNECTIONIST REPRESENTATIONS

In a symbolic connectionist representation, the nodes of the network represent concepts at the level of cognitive phenomena: astronomer, star, A closer_than G, the word *red,* the color red, and so on. Such networks qualify as CP-based systems because the arcs connecting the nodes are associated with *weights* (typically real numbers, 3.12, 4.5, etc.; you can probably invent some yourself) and the principal operation on this structure is the transfer of activity values along these arcs. A more useful categorization is in terms of localized or distributed representations: Subsymbolic networks embody distributed representations of symbolic entities; symbolic networks may be either localized (each symbolic entity is represented by a node), or both localized and distributed (some symbolic entities are represented by individual nodes, and others are not, they are only manifest in patterns of activated nodes — this is typically termed a *distributed representation*).

It is debatable whether the distributed concepts are represented simply by a collection of nodes, or whether they are represented only when the collection is activated. I guess that I favor the latter possibility. Thus I would have to say that an unactivated distributed representation is a *potential* representation of the set of symbolic entities that can be represented by the set of possible patterns of activation.

In a localized connectionist network we might say that the objects are represented symbolically but that the operations are subsymbolic. These are functionally distributed representations of knowledge. Examples abound, for this form of knowledge representation, lying as it does between classical semantic networks and subsymbolic connectionism, enjoys something of the best of both worlds. Much of the conceptual clarity of semantic networks is combined with the intriguing possibilities of massively parallel activation-passing mechanisms. Of course, the dedicated subsymbolists would maintain that much of the power of microstructuring (i.e., use of a pattern of active nodes to represent say, Astronomer, and not just a single, unitary node) is not available to symbolic connectionist systems. Where the balance of truth actually lies is an open question (and as such it is clearly a suitable problem for the reader).

Consider the following sentence:

THE ASTRONOMER MARRIED A STAR.

Did you feel the change in the meaning that you associated with the word STAR — first as a celestial body and then as a celluloid one from the suburbs of L.A. (i.e., Hollywood). If you did not experience this double-take phenomenon, then find someone sympathetic to talk to. What more can I say?

It is when the constraints of marriage assert themselves (as is their tendency) that the meaning changes. Initially the mention of ASTRONO-MER suggests heavenly star, but then marriage requires human bodies, so Hollywood-star is the only meaning that fits.

The following network (Figure 6.5) was used by Pollack and Waltz (1986) to demonstrate this subjective cognitive phenomenon. Figure 6.5 illustrates the final outcome of the parse: MOVIE-STAR node has outcompeted both of its rivals and is enjoying a wealth of activation (illustrated as dark shading).

The double-take phenomenon can thus be explained in terms of the above network as an activity-flow phenomenon. The input word AS-

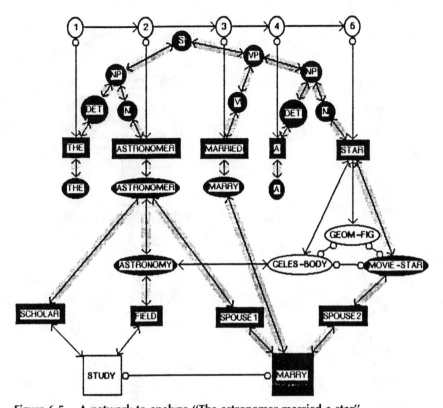

Figure 6.5.   A network to analyze "The astronomer married a star"

From *On Connectionist Models of Natural Language Processing,* by J.B. Pollack, 1987a. Reprinted by permission.

TRONOMER quickly activates the CELES-BODY meaning of STAR via the common concept ASTRONOMY; then, subsequently, the input word MARRIED activates the MOVIE-STAR meaning as the only acceptable one of the three competing meanings. And the three meanings (CELES-BODY; MOVIE-STAR; GEOM-FIG) are competing because of the mutually inhibitory links (illustrated O————O) between each pair of meanings. We shall return to the significance of this subnet shortly.

In terms of activation flow and processing steps, the CELES-BODY meaning is dominant at cycle 27; there is a balance of power between CELES-BODY and MOVIE-STAR at cycle 42; and finally MOVIE-STAR wins at cycle 85. The following graph (Figure 6.6) is a plot of the activation values of the CELES-BODY and MOVIE-STAR nodes over time.

Pollack and Waltz discuss the use of context-setting nodes to model context-directed interpretation of language (such nodes would preactivate certain concept nodes and thus bias the network to a certain interpretation) and suggest instead that concepts should be connected to thousands

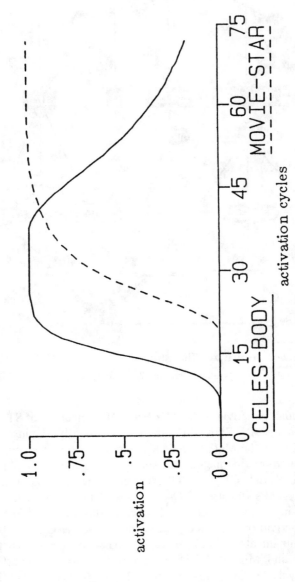

Figure 6.6. Activation levels in the network of Figure 6.5

From *On Connectionist Models of Natural Language Processing*, by J.B. Pollack, 1987a. Reprinted by permission.

of "microfeatures" (i.e., small-scale features — dubious objects which we must return to at a later place), which hold the promise of reproducing the necessary subtlety in context sensitivity. This observation threatens to catapult us into subsymbolic connectionism before we are quite ready, so I'll drop it for now.

In Chapter 3 we saw the network of Feldman which mimics the perceptual alternation induced by the Necker cube. More recently, Pollack (1987a) has designed a network to reproduce the Stroop phenomenon (Stroop, 1935), you may recall that I introduced this phenomenon in Chapter 3. Stroop showed that there is interference between perceptual systems (e.g., the color that a word is printed in and its meaning). We are quick to recognize the color words BLUE, RED, etc. when they are printed in the same neutral color, say, black. Not too surprising, you might observe. But if the word BLUE is printed in red, and the word RED in yellow, and so on, then our reaction times for recognition are significantly slower. The explanation is that the color of the word interferes with our recognition of its meaning, which is also a color. Pollack designed the following network (see Figure 6.7):

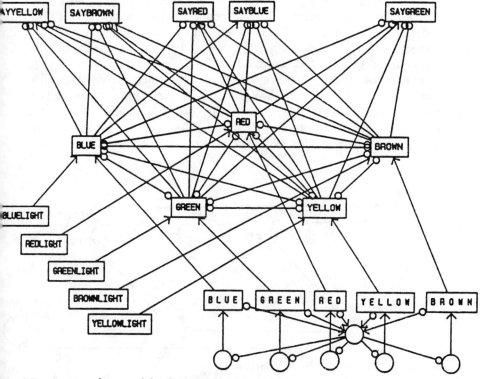

ure 6.7. A network to model color-name interference

m *On Connectionist Models of Natural Language Processing,* by J.B. Pollack, 1987a. Reprinted by permission.

Nodes in the lower left signify color perception; those on the lower right simulate the output of a word-recognition system; in the middle is a mutually inhibitory subnet; and at the top are thresholded output nodes. Again there is a subnet (in the middle) of mutually inhibitory nodes. It is time to focus down on this class of subnet.

WINNER-TAKES-ALL SUBNETS

A group of nodes that each have an inhibitory connection to all other nodes in the group is known as a *winner-takes-all subnet* (WTAS). In this structure the negative link weights (hence inhibitory connections) drain activity from the node that they are connected to. A *mutual-inhibition link* (illustrated thus: O————O) represents the case where both nodes are attempting to suck activity from the node at the other end of the link. One mutual-inhibition link is really a conflation of two inhibitory links, often called *lateral inhibitory links* (as in the neuroanatomy of the visual system; see Chapter 7). In terms of my earlier attempt to formally classify networks in terms of layers of arcs, these lateral inhibitory links (also formally arcs) are typically used to connect nodes within a subset of nodes that separates two layers of excitatory arcs. This is getting involved, perhaps a diagram will help (it will at the very least give you some respite from the relentless words).

At first sight this structure suggests a scenario where activity is continually shuttled back and forth through the mutual-inhibition link as the two nodes alternatively rob each other of the contested quantity of activity. But the amount of activity that a node sucks out of its neighbor along an inhibitory link is typically proportional to the activity value of the vam-

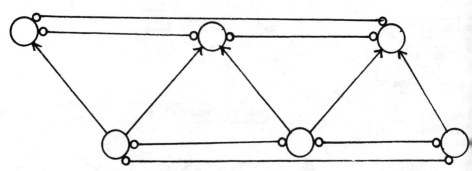

Figure 6.8.   Lateral inhibitory connections

pire node. The overall effect is to concentrate activity in that node which has the most to start with — i.e., the winner-takes-all.

This type of connectionist structure has already been mentioned in Chapter 3 as an example of the problem of the static nature of connectionist networks. Exactly which group of nodes are in direct competition depends to some extent on the particular problem at hand. Thus WTASs cannot be fixed features of a general representation of knowledge, although currently they tend to be designed and demonstrated for one specific example. Dynamically reconfigurable networks are a future event (hopefully) within the CP.

Consider also the number of links that a WTAS demands. Every node needs a bidirectional link to all other nodes. If you do the sums (an optional exercise for the reader who likes that sort of thing), it turns out that, for a WTAS of n nodes, $\frac{n(n-1)}{2}$ bidirectional inhibitory links are needed. That's a lot of links, take my word for it. But the really depressing part is that this number increases in leaps and bounds as the number of nodes, n, in the WTAS increases {the increase in necessary links is $O(n*n)$ — just plot n against $n*n$, and you'll quickly get the picture, as it were}.

Touretzky and Hinton (1986) avoid this sufeit-of-necessary-links problem by implementing an equivalent structure that requires only $2*n$ unidirectional connections (in practice, but $3*n$ in theory). The trick is to use "a special regulatory unit" which has one link in and one link out to all n nodes of the WTAS (hence $2*n$ links). The excitatory connections in determine which nodes will be inhibited and to what degree, and the inhibitory connections out are used to effect the required inhibition on each of the nodes.

Touretzky and Hinton implement their set of production rules as a WTAS, so that only one rule can be active at any time.

A last point is that the importance of WTASs may be an artifact of symbolic connnectionism (and perhaps of neuroanatomy also). Certainly, when network nodes do not represent conceptually meaningful objects, it is more difficult to visualize the role of WTASs. Inhibitory links are important, but a WTAS as such is a qualitatively different substructure.

Feldman and Ballard (1982) provide a gentle introduction to WTASs within their overall introduction to connectionist models.

HYBRID CONNECTIONISM

A number of connectionist systems involve a mix of localized and distributed representation (as I've said, there is some rough equivalence between localized and symbolic, and between distributed and subsymbolic, but the sooner we can free ourselves of this word *symbolic* the better. I'll try to wean this narrative away from it.) Sejnowski and Rosenberg's (1986) NETtalk system (already mentioned in Chapter 3, and considered in detail in Chapter 9) contains both distributed and localized structural representations of the information needed. For current purposes all that is necessary is to examine these two classes of structural representation within their system.

The system maps letters (A to Z, plus word boundaries and a couple of punctuation marks — 29 entities in all) to phonemes (each phoneme is some combination of 21 articulatory features, such as voicing, plus five additional features to encode stress and syllable boundaries — 26 features in all). A letter is thus represented locally (i.e., nondistributedly or symbolically). Thus the letter A input will activate the single node that encodes for A. But the output of a particular phoneme is manifest as some pattern of activation within the nodes representing the 26 phonemic features. Any given feature node may participate in the encoding of many different phonemes; it is thus a distributed representation of the phonemes.

The activity values of nodes could range from nearly zero to nearly one (in Chapter 9 I attempt to explain this seemingly perverse avoidance of the actual maximum and minimum activity values, and try to pass it off as a perfectly rational idea). The accepted phonemes of English were transformed into patterns of activation within the 26 phonemic-feature nodes. Hence, a set of "correct" patterns of activation was obtained. "The output was considered a 'perfect match' if the value of each articulatory feature was within a margin of 0.1 of its correct value" (Sejnowski & Rosenberg, 1986, p. 7).

So that is an example of a hybrid system, and we shall examine both the details of its activity-processing mechanism (i.e., the process model) and its performance in Chapter 9.

TOTALLY DISTRIBUTED REPRESENTATIONS

In this category, the ultimate manifestation of distributed thinking (an accolade or not, dependent upon the context), we can examine connectionist systems that come closest to escaping the all-embracing purview of the physical symbol system hypothesis.

Smolensky's (1986) tour of "harmony theory" uses a simple circuit analysis system as an example. The system "can be used to model the *intuition* that allows experts to answer, without any conscious application of 'rules', questions" about the behavior of a given circuit as certain components are varied; e.g., what happens to the current and voltage when the resistance of a specific resistor is increased?

The fundamental idea formalized in harmony theory is that a "knowledge base is a set of *knowledge atoms* that configure themselves dynamically in each context to form" a context appropriate for the specific problem which has arisen. A network appropriate for harmony theory is two-layered: there is a layer of "knowledge atoms"("fragments of representations that accumulate with experience") and a "layer of nodes that comprises a representation of the state of the . . . problem domain with which the system deals." Let's push on into Smolensky's example in order to clarify some of this.

The example system solves problems about a simple electronic circuit with two resistors, R1 and R2, in series, and a voltage across both of them, Vtotal. The circuit is illustrated in Figure 6. 9.

The necessary knowledge (in this case resistances, currents, voltages, and the three possible qualitative changes: up, down, and same) is encoded into a set of atoms, so as to obey the basic laws governing such circuits (i.e., Ohm's Law, V = I∗R, and Rtotal = R1 + R2 for resistors in series, and also Kirchoff's Law, whose gruesome details I've forgotten, but, as I'm getting along nicely without them, I expect that you can do the same). A knowledge atom was created for each combination of changes in the variables that does not violate the law. Thus, if V must equal I∗R, then, with R1 remaining the same, if I goes down, so must V1 (the voltage across R1). The resultant knowledge atom is (Idown V1down R1same). Smolensky conceives of this atom of knowledge as a memory trace that might be left behind after experiencing many problems in the domain. A knowledge atom consistent with the resistance-sum law is (R1up R2up

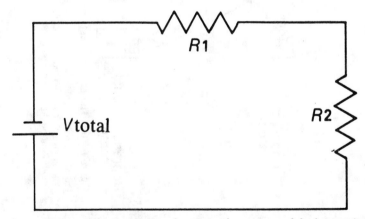

Figure 6.9.   The example circuit for a harmony-theoretic model of expertise

From "Formal Modeling of Subsymbolic Processes: An Introduction to Harmony Theory," by P. Smolensky, in *Advances in Cognitive Science,* edited by N.E. Sharkey, 1986, Chichester, England: Ellis Horwood. Copyright 1986 by Ellis Horwood. Reprinted by permission.

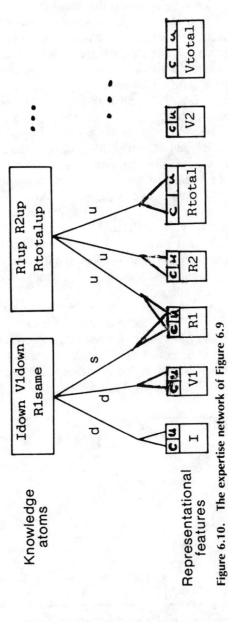

Figure 6.10. The expertise network of Figure 6.9

From "Formal Modeling of Subsymbolic Processes: An Introduction to Harmony Theory," by P. Smolensky, in *Advances in Cognitive Science*, edited by N.E. Sharkey, 1986, Chichester, England: Ellis, Horwood. Copyright 1986 by Ellis Horwood. Reprinted by permission.

Rtotalup). A total of 65 knowledge atoms were devised. A schematic diagram of part of his network is provided in Figure 6.10.

Each of the seven circuit variables was represented by a binary feature node as illustrated (thus, *"Icu"* all active means current changes up, whereas *"Ic"* active means current changes, but not up, therefore down — get the picture?). And, of course, on the links 'd' stands for *down,* and "s" for *same,* and "u" is left as an exercise for the reader (hint: don't waste too much time on it).

So how does this structure solve problems? Apparently, if the question is "What happens when R1 is increased?" this given information is encoded by fixing (*clamping* is a common connectionist term for this) the appropriate feature node coding to represent "increase R1" (i.e., R1cu). This active node then activates atoms that are consistent with this representation (e.g., the atom (R1up R2up Rtotalup)), which in turn activates features that are consistent with the active knowledge atoms (e.g., R2cu and Rtotalcu).

In reality, activity bounces around the system with nodes and atoms becoming activated and deactivated on a probabilistic basis, with the probability of a state dependent upon its "harmony." {Those readers with a craving for details might like to know what exactly this function is. Well, it's

$$\text{probability of a state proportional to } e^{H/T}$$

where H is the harmony of the state and T is some constant called the *computational temperature.* Any more-than-novice physicists might be reminded of an important relation in statistical physics; this is both appropriate and significant.} After the activity has bounced probabilistically around for some time, it will (hopefully) settle into some high-probability, and thus high-harmony, state. The resultant pattern of activation in the feature nodes is then the answer to our original query. So, for R2up, as the initial information, we should expect the finally active features to be Rtotalcu (which is read off as Rtotalup), Ic (which is Idown), and so on.

All that remains, I think, is to tell you how the "harmony" of a state is defined and then tidy up some loose ends. A state of the system is defined by a set of active atoms and a list of the values for all the representational features. The harmony of such a state is a sum of terms. One for each atom times the "strength" of the atom. This "strength" is computed from the similarity between the list of features defining the atom (e.g. atom (Idown V1down R1same) is defined by <Ic V1c R1 - - - - >, i.e., first feature Idown, second feature V1down, third feature R1same, and no connections to last four features — see earlier network diagram), and the actual list of values for all the representational features. Harmony is thus a measure of the self-consistency of the system — how well the defining features of the active knowledge atoms match with the active representational features. The theory says that the best answer to a query (a set of system constraints input by clamping appropriate representational features to certain values) is provided by a maximally self consistent state of the system. And this is obtained by letting the activity bounce around wildly at a high computational temperature (high value of T) and slowly cooling the system. This is because lower computational temperatures favor the emergence of the higher harmony states.

Several points to note: first, the harmony system is searching for a minimum "energy" state and may get locked into a high local minimum if it is not cooled slowly enough (this general problem rearises and is discussed in Chapter 9). The minimum energy, or maximum harmony, state is not necessarily a "correct" answer; it is the best compromise for the given input information. If that information is incomplete, the system will choose one of the several possible states of highest harmony (i.e., there are several partial and equally good answers to the incompletely specified problem). If the input information is inconsistent, the system's answer will be one that violates as few problem domain constraints as possible. Contrast this behavior with SSSP-based logical inference systems such as those we looked at in the previous chapter.

In a system to be described in more detail later when we have had some exposure to production systems, Touretzky and Hinton (1986) describe "coarse coded" or distributed representations of 'working memory' and of production rules. The representation is based on triples (a surprisingly popular basic structure — I know not why). They need to be able to represent any subset of three-letter triples, (F A B) and (C K R), for example. There are apparently over 15,000 such triples, but only about six need to be stored in the working memory at one time.

Their coarse-coded representation uses 2,000 binary state units. Each such unit is a partial representation of 216 specific triples (the initial assignments of representational responsibility are made randomly). A triple is stored in memory by turning on every unit that partially represents it— 28 receptors, on average. Now, as these units also partially represent other triples, turning the appropriate units on for one triple will result in partial representations of many other triples. When two triples, (F A B) and (F C D), are represented (i.e., 100% of their representative units are active), the next best represented triple, (F N B), has only 42% active, and the average activity over all other possible triples is 2.7%. This result is typical and thus a simple thresholding operation on the memory yields only (F A B) and (F C D).

The benefits of this coarse coding include robustness and "unlimited" capacity. Individual units may be erroneously turned off or on and have virtually no effect on the current state of working memory in terms of triples. This representation has no fixed capacity, but the cost is a decrease in its ability to distinguish stored items from potential but not-currently stored items as the number of stored items increases.

A clear drawback of this representational scheme is that triples stored for a long time will gradually fade away as other triples are continually deleted. This is because the deletion of a triple means turning off all the active units which represent that triple; but then these units also partially represent other triples, such as the one that we want to keep. Hence, deleting any specific triple is likely to decrease the strength of representation of all other triples currently being represented. So over time a triple that should be permanently represented just fades away. An answer to this problem is periodic refreshment of the working memory; i.e., all units are activated for each triple that is currently represented.

A now standard reference in connectionist arguments about the abilities of the CP to support analogues of high-level symbolic representational structures is the work of Rumelhart, Smolensky, McClelland, and Hinton (1986) on room schemata — these structures are collections of information about, in this case, rooms. Such integrated collections have long been hypothesized as necessary to support intelligent reasoning. These schemata typically become manifest in AI programs as "frames" (later in this chapter) or "scripts" (dealt with in the chapter on natural language processing).

In the connectionist study of room schemata 40 room features were selected — features like has-ceiling, has-window, and so on. Subjects (i.e., people, usually undergraduate psychology students) were used to describe some imagined rooms (e.g., bedroom, office) using this set of 40 features. After some statistical magic on the descriptions generated, a network was constructed with one node for each feature and links as directed by the data. The resultant network can perform inferences about rooms in much the same general way as can be done with the localized room schemata typically used in SSSP-based systems. For example, if the network is asked "what else is likely to be in a room containing a ceiling and an oven?" (i.e., has-ceiling and has-oven nodes are fixed as active — clamped, right?), the system will finally settle to a state where, say, coffeepot and coffeecup are active but not fireplace and computer — i.e., the room is a kitchen.

This is another harmony theory system in which activity ricochets around to gradually settle into a maximum harmony state as the computational temperature is cooled. The major point is that, in this representation, there are no units for kitchens, bathrooms, etc. The prototypical kitchen is a pattern of activation. The nodes are not subsymbolic, but the representation of the room types is distributed, and any one node may contribute to more than one room type.

This is a famous example of the power of connectionist systems; it can also provide us with a cautionary reminder — a brake on overexuberance. Schvaneveldt (1990b) subjects this rooms-schemata experiment to very close scrutiny. He collects exactly the same data and processes it with both totally conventional (e.g., cluster analysis) and connectionist strategies as well as applying his own "Pathfinder" treatment. He also collects a second set of data and processes it with the same spectrum of strategies. This second dataset, called co-occurrence data, is obtained by asking subjects to judge the frequency of co-occurrence of all pairs of features (thus the pair bathtub–toilet would be expected to get a high rating, while the bathtub–coffeepot pair is expected to be much lower). Schvaneveldt points out that in the Rumelhart et al. experiment subjects were told to imagine rooms when generating their results, so it is not surprising that their judgments revealed rooms. Without going into the many results that Schvaneveldt presents, let me just note that the connectionist treatment appears, in many respects, to be no better (and sometimes inferior) to the conventional approaches.

Figure 6.11 is an example of the type of diagram often used to display the state of a distributed representation. This one illustrates family relationships and is given by Hinton (1989) — the details that should constitute a full and complete explanation are given in Chapter 9. But for the moment you can note that it is a representation of a five-layer network (the input and output layers are each represented by two rows of white squares, and one row for each of the three hidden layers). The layers are illustrated in order starting with the input layer at the bottom. The white squares show the activity levels in the units, and the sizes of the squares illustrate the relative amounts of activity in each unit. The two active input units represent a person "Colin" and a relationship between persons, in this case, "has-aunt". The two highly active output units (marked with black dots) represent the two persons who are Colin's aunts. The network, as illustrated, is thus in a state of answering the question 'who are Colin's aunts?'

PATH-LIKE ARCHITECTURES IN THE CP

In certain of the connectionist systems that we have looked at so far (e.g., Sejnowski & Rosenberg's NETtalk, and Pollack's Stroop-effect model), the structure is such that activity is pushed in at one end, bounces around and through the network, to finally emerge at the other end as an output. In sum, such a network is a conduit through which activity flows. It is this type of network architecture that the back-propagation learning algorithms of Chapter 9 are designed to work on. {These path-like networks are often, in the jargon of graph theory, *homomorphic* to a path — especially if any WTASs are treated as single nodes.}

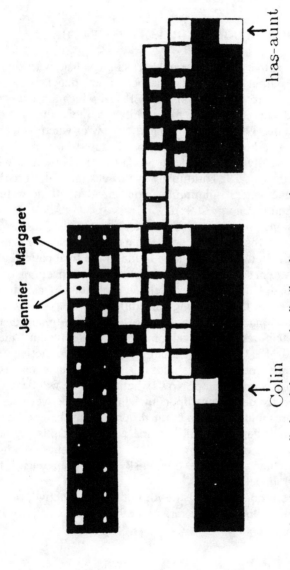

Figure 6.11. A display of the state of a distributed representation

From "Connectionist Learning Procedures," by G.E. Hinton, 1989, *Artificial Intelligence*. Copyright 1989 by Elsevier. Reprinted by permission.

This class of CP-based architectures, often called feed-forward networks, is particularly important with respect to learning by back propagation, as we shall see in Chapter 9.

BATH-LIKE ARCHITECTURES IN THE CP

The major alternative to path-like networks in which activity zips through from input to output nodes (with the occasional ricochetting around a WTAS en route) are the bath-like networks in which activity slumps to the bottom and will remain there for eternity, happily occupying the minimum energy state of the system. No matter how or where you introduce the water into a bathtub, it may slop around more or less randomly for a while, but eventually it will settle to lie flat on the bottom; it will never do anything different. The bathtub always solves the water problem with exactly the same general solution (no pun intended) — the water settles down to a minimum energy state.

Similarly, some connectionist networks resemble bathtubs. You pour some activity into the network, and the answer to whatever problem the network was devised to solve will be found in the final pattern of activation that the system settles down to. In truth, the connectionist networks may solve a small family of closely related problems (by clamping different subsets of nodes), but nothing very different.

The Boltzman machine is a popular example of a totally distributed, bath-like architecture. It is a development of the Hopfield net idea which I mentioned earlier. In a Hopfield net a node becomes active whenever its activity level exceeds its threshold. In a Boltzman machine probability is brought in to liven things up. Now, whether a node will become active is probabilistically dependent upon the difference between its activity level and its threshold — the larger the difference, the higher the probability that the particular node will become active. But this probability of becoming active is not just proportional to this difference. It's much fancier than that (and quite like Smolensky's "harmoniums," they are closely related models).

{If $p_{i,a}$ is the probability that the ith node will be active, or on, when the net is in state "a" and the difference between its activity level and threshold is $\triangle_{i,a}$, then:

$$p_{i,a} = \frac{1}{1 + e^{\frac{-\triangle_{i,a}}{T}}}$$

where T is our old friend the computational temperature. The point of all these formal frills is that now the system can be guaranteed to settle into a global energy minimum. But this guarantee is only valid if the system starts at a high temperature and is cooled infinitely slowly to a temperature close to zero. This "infinitely slowly" clause tends to throw a wrench in the works, but in practice something a little faster can usually also do the trick — the trick is called *simulated annealing*; see Kirkpatrick, Gelatt, & Vecchi, 1983.}

For those readers who wisely skip the curly-bracketed trivia, the introduction of a fancy probability function buys us the hope of the best solution to a problem rather than something less satisfactory which is all that Hopfield nets promise.

The average Boltzmann machine (e.g., Ackley, Hinton, & Sejnowski, 1985) will always eventually subside into an energy minimum (i.e., the network will always generate a minimum energy solution to the problem; see Chapter 9 for a discussion of the search for minima in CP-based networks), and that's that. It is not going to rouse itself and go off (shooting activity around with the panache that massive parallelism makes possible) and generate subsequent inferences, decisions, or problem solutions. It's like pouring rain on a mountain range: The water just rushes downhill, using all the usual paths and always ending up in the same rivers on the plains. {One snag with this metaphor is that the activity in connectionist networks sometimes can get trapped in a local minimum configuration, but that's just a hollow high up in the mountain that catches the rushing water and holds it — so no snag.}

In order to get the average mountain range to do anything radically different with the rainfall a massive (but not necessarily parallel) earth moving and rock blasting scheme will be needed; similarly, it is no easy task to reconfigure connectionist systems. Pollack (1987a) bemoans the fixity of typical connectionist systems. He provides examples from networks designed to process natural language, which are limited to analyzing sentences of a fixed maximum length (e.g., Cottrell, 1985; Selman, 1985) and which are severely limited in what structures they can represent (e.g., Rumelhart & McClelland, 1986, cannot represent words with repetitive constituents — *banana* would apparently be an unrepresentable word).

Interestingly (but just an aside), De Bono (1969) advocated, and it was quite the rage for a few years, a very similar, in style, model of the brain. He described cognitive processes in terms of liquid flow on the "memory surface" of the "Jelly Model" (which last term roughly translated for the readers in the New World is *Jello Model*).

Another bath-like class of system with a similarly homely sounding name is the harmonium system of Smolensky (1986). We toured the structure and workings of harmoniums earlier, so it should be obvious that problem solving is viewed as a "completion task" — to use Smolensky's own words. A problem statement becomes some initial constraints in the

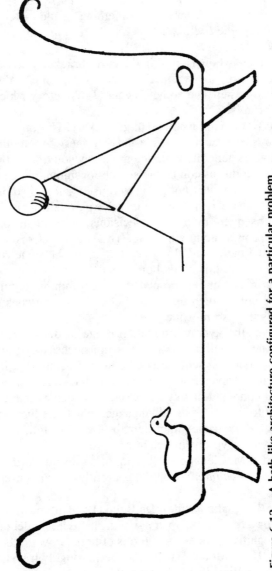

Figure 6.12. A bath-like architecture configured for a particular problem

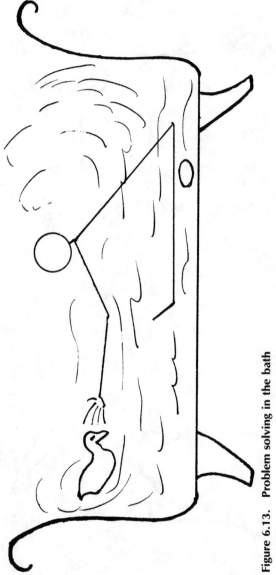

Figure 6.13. Problem solving in the bath

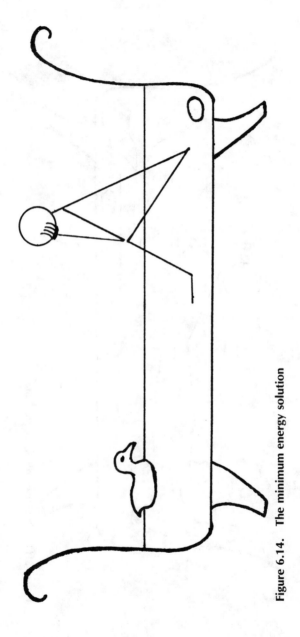

Figure 6.14.   The minimum energy solution

network (like a soap dish, a rubber duck, and a particular person in a bathtub), and problem solving is finding the minimum energy state consistent with these fixed constraints (like the water settling over the soap dish, under the rubber duck, and around the person). Smolensky does talk of "dynamic reconfiguration" in harmony models, but by this he does *not* mean that the electronic circuit we considered can be dynamically reconfigured for other problems (or even other circuits). He means that activity zips around generating patterns of activation, as demanded by the particular problem constraints — i.e., you get different answers for different questions about the circuit (it wouldn't be much good if you didn't, would it?).

A less-than-totally serious picture here might serve to at least brighten the moment for you even if it fails to throw some more enduring light on the nature of bath-like architectures (see Figures 6.12, 6.13, and 6.14).

A totally serious example of parsing in the bath (although they call it "parsing as an energy minimization problem," I admit) is described by Selman and Hirst (1987), and it is presented in Chapter 8.

So what architecture and functionality are we looking for? It's hard to say, especially as the complete system could well be some amalgam of CP-based and SSSP-based components (as suggested in Chapter 3). But if a connectionist network is to reproduce intelligent behavior, we might expect a functionality that has transient stable states such that activity settles into some configuration for a while and then moves on — a functionality that we find, for example, in Hebb's cell assemblies.

Touretzky and Hinton (1986) have begun to achieve this settle-and-flow behavior with their "Distributed Connectionist Production System." Essentially, they have to install some gates in their network in order to control the flow of activity at crucial stages of the typical rule-match-memory-update cycle of symbolic production systems.

Feldman and Ballard (1982) discuss the apparent unsuitability of connectionist models to represent sequences of events. They "present computational solutions to the problems of sequence that appear to be consistent with known structural and performance constraints. These are, again, too crude to be taken literally but do suggest that connectionist models can describe the phenomena."

KNOWLEDGE REPRESENTATION IN THE SSSP

Now we are in familiar territory for knowledge representation in AI. Units of our representation stand for clearly articulatable things, and the information that is pushed around is also comfortably symbolic.

Apart from the knowledge representation chapter in every self-respecting AI text book, there is a very useful collection of papers edited by Brachman and Levesque (1985). So there is much readily available information on this vast AI subfield. Nevertheless, in the interests of completeness and in order to bring out some cross relationships with CP-based work, I shall delve into the delights of semantic networks, production systems, frames, etc.

As a general introduction I shall use the points singled out by Brachman and Levesque. There are two issues of overall adequacy:

1. Expressive adequacy — what can be represented? They ask if every representation language should be a notational variant of full first-order logic. And they complain of the lack of precise statements about what exactly can or is being represented.
2. Reasoning efficiency — can the representation support processing that generates results at an acceptable speed?

Three more issues concerning basic questions about the limits and validity of conventional knowledge representation schemes.

1. Primitives — what are the primitive elements? For example, in Chapter 8 we shall see Schank's attempt to lay out a set of primitive elements for natural language processing.
2. Metarepresentation — there appears to be a need for knowledge about knowledge, but there is no general agreement on the relationship of metaknowledge to the basic-level knowledge.
3. Incompleteness — the problems of reasoning with knowledge that is known to be incomplete. This problem is aggravated by the customary use of logic-based reasoning, but as we have seen (e.g., in Smolenksy's, 1987, CP-based circuit analysis system), incompleteness is not the same important and difficult problem once we depart from the logic-based approach to AI.

LOGIC-BASED REPRESENTATIONS

The following simple example illustrates a popular approach to knowledge representation in a LISPese notation.

```
(F1   (HOBBIT BILBO) )
(F2   (UNCLEOF FRODO BILBO) )
(R1   (IFTHEN (UNCLEOF X Y) (NEPHEWOF Y X)) )
(R2   (IFTHEN (AND (UNCLEOF X Y)(HOBBIT Y)) (HOBBIT X) )
```

Four entries constitute this knowledge base: two facts, F1 and F2; and two rules, R1 and R2. The two facts are the given "truths" of the system, and, in combination with the rules, they allow us to infer further true statements. Thus if we take R1 and set the value of X as FRODO and Y as BILBO, the truth of the resultant condition (UNCLEOF FRODO BILBO), given by F2, enables us to infer the conclusion, to wit, (NEPH-EWOF BILBO FRODO), and so on.

Specific knowledge may be stored as facts, general knowledge may be stored as rules, and by combining the two we can infer many other facts.

The above example is an example of a logical representation of knowledge. This class of representation has the advantage that we can employ the well-defined semantics of logic. In addition the knowledge base is a fairly simple collection of readily understandable units.

But the fact that such knowledge bases are a more or less homogeneous collection of simple units results in an overall "flatness," a lack of perceptible higher-level structure, and hence a lack of comprehensibility. In addition, the well-defined nature of the basic logical operations is obtained at the cost of severe limitations on applicability in representations of the empirical world, some problematic areas are: incremental acquisition of knowledge; beliefs about truth rather than truth in some absolute sense; and the combination of general assumptions with exceptional situations that may override the normal assumption.

All of these characteristics of empirical knowledge and its use to support intelligent behavior can be reduced to the necessity to be able to add new knowledge that may then alter the truth of some current knowledge. In logical terms this leads us into a less-well-understood logical world — the domain of nonmonotonic logic (this logically unhealthy feature of our world is inspected in Chapter 10, together with an examination of the role of logic in the foundations of AI).

Thus in the above example an initial belief (as opposed to an absolute axiomatic truth) that (HOBBIT BILBO) is true might have to be abandoned in the light of subsequent evidence. In general this sort of change is likely to have repercussions throughout the knowledge base; it is this context-sensitivity that, as we know, is typical of AI problems and thus undermines the utility of these simple logical representations of knowledge.

From an early, enthusiastic commitment to logical schemes based on the observation that some reasoning is logic based, there was subsequent disenchantment and rejection due to the realization that much of the information processing necessary to support intelligent behavior did not appear to be logic based at all — at least not based on any simple and well-understood logic. In an appendix to an essay on knowledge representation Minsky (1981) explains why he thinks that "logical" approaches will not work. One of his points of argument is that logical axioms are "permissive" — i.e., "Each axiom added means more theorems: none can disappear" (p. 125). Hewitt (1985) challenges the sufficiency of current logic-based techniques for developing the intelligent systems of the future, as we've already seen.

Nevertheless, current interest has turned somewhat back to logical schemes in two ways: first, there are efforts to construct more powerful logics; and second, there is interest in hybrid schemes that partition representations of knowledge such that logic is used where it is appropriate and other schemes are used where logic does not seem to be appropriate — a high-level modularization of the knowledge representation problem.

An important problem with this logical type of scheme is that, even if a logically valid procedure, such as deduction, is possible in principle for some application, it may not be possible in practice. The practical impossibility is a result of the fact that the logical mechanisms are unguided and then the number of search paths quickly becomes the limiting factor.

For example, using the above knowledge base, we can deduce the truth of (HOBBIT FRODO). This involves using both F1 and F2 to allow us to draw the required inference from R2. However, it could have involved any other sequence of the knowledge-base elements — the algorithm just has to keep trying all possibilities until it succeeds (if it can succeed). This unguided, brute-force approach quickly becomes too time-consuming for all but the most trivial of knowledge bases.

Even worse, consider for one moment the original knowledge base with one extra rule, R3, which says that, if X is the NEPHEWOF Y, then Y is the UNCLEOF X. That would appear to be a true and an innocuous piece of information to add.

```
(F1   (HOBBIT BILBO) )
(F2   (UNCLEOF FRODO BILBO) )
(R1   (IFTHEN (UNCLEOF X Y) (NEPHEWOF Y X)) )
(R2   (IFTHEN (AND (UNCLEOF X Y)(HOBBIT Y)) (HOBBIT X) )
(R3   (IFTHEN (NEPHEWOF Y X) (UNCLEOF X Y)) )
```

If now we want to examine the truth of (HOBBIT FRODO), we can deduce from F2 and R1 that (NEPHEWOF BILBO FRODO) is true. This is not what we want, so we push on and we use, say, R3; then we know (UNCLEOF FRODO BILBO) is true, but this is not what we want either, so we use R1, etc. It is quite possible to follow around endless loops of deductions that are not at all obvious in more complex situations — there is, in general, no guarantee that attempted proofs will terminate. {Turing and his halting problem haunt us even here.}

So, even within their limited domain, automatic theorem-proving mechanisms require guidance before they become viable schemes. Two general control strategies are forwards and backwards chaining. In a forwards-chaining strategy, we start with our knowledge base and generate implications from it, hoping to chance upon the particular one that we are interested in proving.

The opposite strategy is somewhat more guided (it could hardly be less). We start with what we want to prove (e.g., (HOBBIT FRODO)) and determine what would have to be true in order to prove this goal. With the earlier knowledge base we can see that our goal will be the conclusion of R2 if we replace X by FRODO. Thus we now need to determine the truth of the condition of R2 with this replacement. We need now to prove both: (UNCLEOF FRODO Y) for some value of Y, and (HOBBIT Y) for the same value of Y.

F2 and F1 give us the proofs we need when Y is replaced by BILBO. Hence, we proved the original theorem by chaining backwards from it. All this chat about searching forwards and backwards should touch on ancient memories, ones that were installed as you read dutifully through Chapter 3.

Other somewhat directed proof strategies are available, for example the resolution principle (the key to PROLOG, you might recall), but the amount of guidance is still minimal and insufficient for many practical applications — much more guidance is required.

A solution might be to use sophisticated heuristic control strategies that can exploit both the general context of a situation and the specifics of each individual attempted proof. This possibility was briefly explored in Chapter 4; the general problem is, of course, far from solved.

Having reached this point, I shall briefly consider the two other major classes of knowledge representation schemes while at the same time also continue with some more general problems of knowledge representation and use.

Mylopoulos and Levesque (1984) provide a concise and informative overview of knowledge representation. They characterize the other two classes of schemes as procedural and network representations.

PROCEDURAL REPRESENTATIONS OF KNOWLEDGE

In a procedural scheme, knowledge is represented as a set of processes. One or more processes is activated by certain states and the execution of the activated process(es) transforms the current state into a new one, and so on.

Production systems are one type of procedural knowledge representation. You will, of course, recall one or more of the several previous mentions of production systems. The bones of a production-system architecture can be laid out as in Figure 6.15.

The major components, as you can see, are a collection of rules, each of which is composed of a condition and an action, a working memory (WM) which contains information that defines the current state of the system, and a control loop which cycles continually from rules to WM and back again.

The operation of a production system is to match the conditions of the rules against the information in the WM and to *fire* a rule that matches, i.e., a rule whose condition evaluates as true given the values in the WM. What if more than one rule matches the current WM? The typical strategy is to select just one of the rules that can be fired from the subset that could possibly be fired. This selection process is called *conflict resolution*. Conflict resolution usually involves heuristic strategies and is thus a major focus of the AI in the production system (the other such focus is the rules themselves). It is time for an example.

The earlier logical knowledge base might be represented by the following productions:

R1: (UNCLEOF X Y) → (NEPHEWOF Y X)
R2: (UNCLEOF X Y) AND (HOBBIT Y) → (HOBBIT X)

and the current state, or working memory, which is given by the facts:

F1: (HOBBIT BILBO)
F2: (UNCLEOF FRODO BILBO)

With this somewhat less than awe-inspiring example, we would find that the condition parts of both R1 and R2 will match the WM. We've run straight into a situation that requires a strategy for conflict resolution. In keeping with the general level of this example, I'll set up a similarly trivial strategy for conflict resolution; it is: Assuming that the control regime attempts to match rule conditions against the WM sequentially from top to bottom in the list of rules, fire the first rule that matches. It doesn't exactly take your breath away, but it does the job.

Thus, in the current situation, rule R1 will fire, although I've not yet told you what execution of the action part is meant to achieve. Typically,

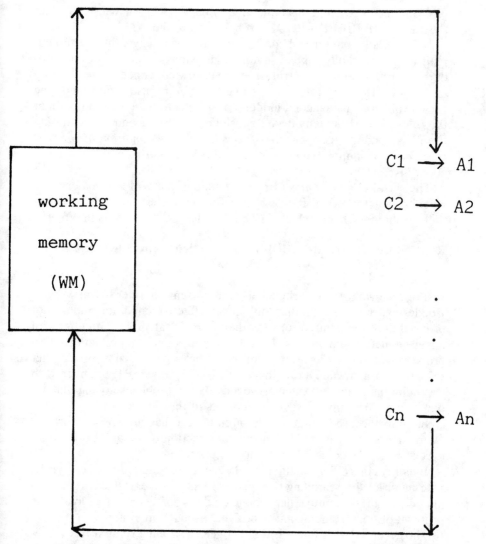

Figure 6.15. The skeleton of a production system

execution of the action part of a rule (i.e., firing the rule) will change the state of the WM by adding and/or deleting information. In addition, the action part may generate some information that is external to the production system proper. Thus an action part may output a message, for example. So, in the current example, the firing of R1 will cause the fact (NEPHEWOF BILBO FRODO) to be added to the WM.

Now, although my trivial conflict resolution strategy contains no heuristics and is painfully simple, several nonobvious features about the production system follow. Control structure is now contained in the *ordering* of the rules. Different rule orders will give different results on exactly the same problem. I have added hidden constraints to the condition parts of the rules. This is obvious if you consider that the second rule can only fire if its condition part matches the WM *and the condition of the first rule does not match*. This brings us onto a second piece of bad news about my system.

The second rule can *never* fire. Any state of the WM that matches R2 will also match R1, which will thus be fired in preference under the conflict resolution scheme which I proposed. The second rule is in effect:

R2: (UNCLEOF X Y) AND (HOBBIT Y) AND (NOT(UNCLEOF X Y))
      → (HOBBIT X)

Just in case you're wondering: This is not a sensible rule. If you weren't wondering, then take another look at the effective condition and do not proceed until the penny drops (as they say). Clearly, this condition can never be met. The point that I want to make is that the problem is not a problem with rule R2 itself, but a problem that is generated by my conflict resolution strategy and a rule that precedes R2, to wit, R1. So, even with my ludicrously simple example, we already see problems arising that are due to the interaction of several elements of the system.

In sum, the production system architecture has proven its worth in many diverse models in AI, but the construction of a major production-system-based model is not without its headaches.

Building control information into the set of production rules can eliminate much of the searching that plagues logical schemes. But the introduction of these context dependencies does, of course, aggravate the problem of understanding and modifying production systems.

The general tradeoff here is that between searching context-free representations and providing guidance at the cost of introducing context dependencies.

Anderson (1987) feels that the production system architecture has several advantages over alternative representations of knowledge. Like an astute politician, he wants to claim the vast middle ground between extremist architects of micro- or macro-schools. Production system rules are relatively well-structured, simple and homogeneous, and independent of one another. *Well-structured* is a somewhat fuzzy term, but it seems undeniable that, in contrast to connectionist networks, it is easier to understand what is learned and probably easier to predict consequences such as transfer of a learned skill from one domain to another. In being simple and homogeneous, productions contrast with the more macro symbolic representations such as schema (e.g., Schank & Abelson, 1977, and with frames later in this chapter). Thus it should be easier to implement a simple learning mechanism to construct new production rules compared with new schemata. Independence of production rules allows for incremental learning as productions are added (or deleted). It may also permit graceful degradation, which is touted as a characteristic virtue of CP-based systems.

One drawback to the production system architecture for application in CEST is the need to elicit the necessary productions from the experts. This is not always easy. Johnson (1983) found that the reasons, rules, and heuristics given by experts as descriptions of what they were doing could not, in some cases, even account for their own behavior. A knowledge engineer trying to build an expert system may elicit very few descriptions that conform to condition-action rules.

A detailed description of Anderson's ACT∗ production system model is provided in the chapter on machine learning.

One final point concerns stopping these systems. My skeletal architecture was an infinite loop. The system can be stopped by an external agent when some desired information appears in the WM — information like the answer to the specific problem that the system happens to be working on. Alternatively, it will grind to a halt whenever no rule matches information in the current WM. For, clearly, no further progress can be made without the introduction of external information.

Touretzky and Hinton (1986) describe a CP-based production-system model. On a small scale they demonstrate that it is feasible for connectionist systems to reproduce certain constituents of symbolic models (e.g., consistent variable binding, so that, if a variable X gets the value 'A' in the condition part of the rule, then any Xs in the action part also pick up this "A" value), and that such distributed models exhibit a number of interesting emergent properties (e.g., damage resistence).

SEMANTIC NETWORKS

The third type of scheme represents knowledge as a collection of "objects" and relationships between them — that is, a network representation, often called a *semantic network,* as we well know. A semantic network representation of our knowledge base might be:

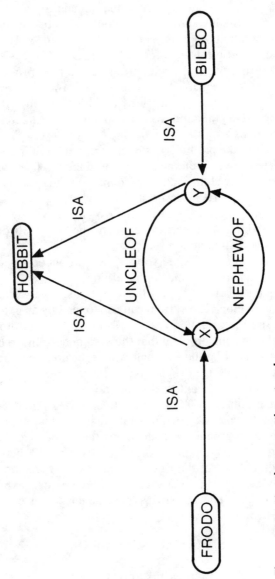

Figure 6.16. Another semantic network

I say that the above representation "might be" a reasonable interpretation of the original logical representation, because the semantic net representation does not define much (anything?). This is the major drawback of such representations; there is no well-defined formal semantics for network representations.

I think that the network that I have drawn looks like a plausible rendering of the original representation, but how to interpret it in any well-defined sense is not defined.

One difference between the logical and the network representation that I have provided is that the latter is symmetrical and the former is not. I can demonstrate this lack of symmetry about the HOBBITs in the logical scheme by substituting FRODO for BILBO in F1 of the original representation, and then trying to prove (HOBBIT BILBO) — it cannot be done. F1 appears to be redundant in the semantic network; the fact that BILBO and FRODO are both HOBBITs appears to be an implication of F2, R1, and R2 in the semantic network representation.

But in the semantic network BILBO and FRODO are symmetrical, with the exception of the complementary relations UNCLEOF and NEPHEWOF.

This introduction of symmetry is just one manifestation of the fact that the logical representation is a collection of context-free units, while the semantic network is a single unit — information must be added in order to generate a cohesive whole.

In particular the logical representation specifies that the UNCLEOF relation implies NEPHEWOF but not vice versa — the semantic network includes the complementary implication, apparently. In addition, the graphical representation is a considerable aid to understanding, in a general sense, the knowledge structure being represented.

But all three representational schemes, semantic nets in particular, have a tendency to induce the ELIZA syndrome in unsuspecting onlookers. You might, for example, be inclined to view my knowledge representations as somewhat male chauvinistic. Nothing could be further from the truth (or my mind)!

Surely the axiom that says UNCLEOF implies NEPHEWOF with no mention of NIECEOF is indicative of a bias in favor of the XY chromosome combination? And Bilbo and Frodo were male Hobbits, weren't they? No, and Yes, are the answers, in that order. The relationship UNCLEOF has no necessary connection with the status of a parent's male sibling, and Bilbo is not necesarily BILBO.

There is no mention of sex in any form in my knowledge bases — in fact, there is no mention of anything semantic (apart from the formal semantics of say logic). Each of the well-defined processes described has been a syntactic activity — formal manipulations of abstract patterns that were arbitrarily labeled. It is in the reading of everyday semantic interpretations into these labels that the ELIZA syndrome strikes.

Woods (1975) addresses the general problem of what the notations and structures used in semantic networks can mean, and with the need for an explicit understanding of the intended meaning for various types of links and arcs. He also examines the representational adequacy of semantic networks for knowledge representation and finds them lacking in a number of important respects.

The problem of the unfounded persuasiveness of semantics networks is another example of the form–content problem. The form of semantic networks constitutes a difficult-to-resist temptation to the human perceptual mechanism — we invariably assume that a rich content underlies the representation, and the richness of our assumptions is rarely warranted by the semantics actually implemented.

Elsewhere (Partridge, 1978) I have previously drawn attention to the syntax–semantics (or form–content) confusion that surrounds semantic network representations. I have argued that syntax and semantics are neither absolute nor clearly separable concepts; this mixing and lack of absolute definitions are, I claim, major reasons why semantic networks invariably infect the casual observer with the ELIZA syndrome.

Hayes (1979), in a searching examination of knowledge representation, addresses this problem in terms of the "fidelity" of a formalization.

> It is perilously easy to *think* that one's formalization has captured a concept (because one has used a convincing-sounding token to stand for it, for example), when in fact, for all the formalization knows the token might denote something altogether more elementary. (Hayes, 1979, p. 251, author's emphasis)

Brachman (1985) goes further than this: He argues that efforts to represent common-sense knowledge (e.g., that a three-legged elephant is still an elephant, despite the fact that elephants have four legs) "has led to naive mechanisms that both admit arbitrary, bizarre representations and force the ignorance of crucial, obvious facts" (p. 92). This is a serious charge, and we must explore it further.

Let's focus on one of the less-odd parts of the earlier semantic network in Figure 6.1 (see Figure 6.17).

One of the useful features that this knowledge representation should buy us is the ability to represent a specific property which is common to all individuals of a class (e.g., all individual birds have wings) just once. We do this by attaching the general property to the class node, in this case "bird", and all specific birds that we represent can *inherit* this property automatically. Such inheritance schemes are an integral part of many rep-

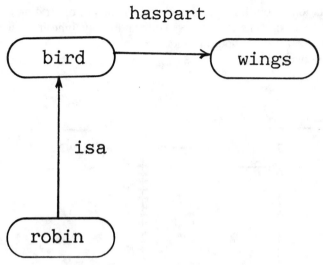

Figure 6.17.   A small semantic network

resentations of information that are designed to support AI systems. Now, these inheritance structures work fine if the property to be represented is a *defining* feature of the class. So "four-sided" works fine as an inheritable property of the class "quadrilaterals." But for natural classes, such as "bird", problems arise. {Brief aside: For the reader who is attempting to build the big picture, the root of this particular problem is to be found in the oft-recurring problem of a dearth in AI of abstract definitions, which are not travesties — from definition of the term *AI* itself through to definition of many subfield and component parts, the same problem arises with boring regularity.}

It may be true that the property of having wings is partially what defines a bird. However, a wingless robin is gruesome but nevertheless quite plausible in a way that a three-sided quadrilateral is not. The resultant problem for the inheritance strategy is that the property is sort-of defining, normally true, typically true, or to be assumed true in the absence of evidence to the contrary — the possible interpretations are many, and they're all ill defined. What do we do about this? If we are to represent information that can support intelligent reasoning, we have to be able to represent the notion that birds have wings, but that any poor robin who happens, as a result of some ghastly accident, to have been separated from its appendages for flight is still indisputably a bird. We need to represent the notion that birds *typically* have wings, but that any individual need not necessarily have them.

The standard solution is to introduce a means of overriding properties that instances of a general class wouls normally inherit — a "cancel link," in effect. So the poor grounded robin, let's call it Joe, can be fitted into the network as follows:

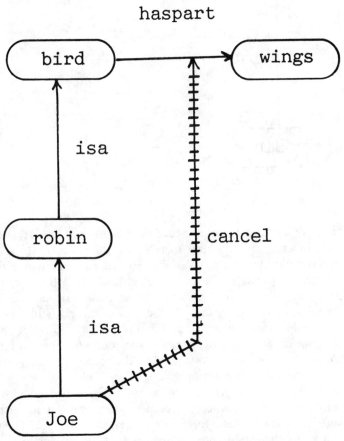

Figure 6.18. Joe the wingless robin

Thus, the casual interpretation of the "bird-wings" relationship, i.e., "every bird has wings," is not accurate. Having wings is a default property — we assume that every bird has wings unless we have direct evidence to the contrary. A better interpretation of the relationship in question is that "birds typically have wings," or "birds usually have wings." But then what is the precise meaning of *typically* or of *usually*, the meaning that the network processing algorithm will embody? There isn't one, as I said before. Once absolute definitional status is abandoned, we are catapulted into a limbo world of hazy meaning and multiple interpretations. The plausible descriptions of what the network represents is just a hedge, because *every* is clearly not correct. Thus such structures in semantic networks (and default slots in frames — coming soon) do not define *necessary* conditions and will not support reasoning based on unequivocal, universal statements, e.g., that every wosname has a whatsit. The rules are made to be broken — sometimes. And there's the crunch. We need to distinguish in our representations between relationships that are "typically" true and those that must always be true, i.e., those that are definitional — a square always has four sides, and a robin is always a bird. Such relationships are not candidates for cancellation. Thus we see the reasons for Brachman's conclusion:

> The call to arms sounded by Fahlman (1979) and Minsky (in Kolata, 1982) for the need to represent three-legged elephants and dead ducks (or those with their feet set in concrete), while crucially important if AI is ever to get a hold of "common sense", has led to naive mechanisms that both admit arbitrary, bizarre representations and force the ignorance of crucial, obvious facts. (p. 92)

The form of inheritance that I have been discussing is called *downward inheritance;* it exploits the fact that specific instances of a class share many features in common, and that, thus, these features need be represented only once, in association with the class node. In addition, the examples have been restricted to inheritance between objects. What else could we want to represent?

Well, we might want to represent actions and continue to exploit an inheritance mechanism. Thus "moving relocates an object" and "walking is a type of moving," so we might want walking to inherit the "relocation" property. Alternatively, we might want a strategy for *upward inheritance* — a basis for reasoning from the particular to the general. Returning to our feathered friend, Joe: we might know that "Joe preens his feathers" and as "Joe is a bird" a mechanism of upward inheritance might allow us to reason that "birds preen their feathers."

The possibilities for storing information in one place and transferring it through the network to support reasoning elsewhere are many and varied, and mostly fraught with danger. Thus, beware the properties of the set as distinct from the properties of elements of the set. For example, "birds are found on every continent" and "a robin is a bird" should not permit us to reason that "robins are found on every continent." "But who could confuse such things?" you might well feel motivated to interject. Not you or I, perhaps; but for most AI systems the story is very different. For the reader who feels compelled to get to the bottom of this very knotty problem, let me wish him or her luck and point toward Touretzky's (1986) treatment of the mathematical foundations of inheritance systems.

A closely related criticism of most current knowledge bases is that the knowledge represented does not embody a deep understanding of the domain; it is instead a collection of "pattern → action" rules — a representation of superficial knowledge that excludes the possibility of using such knowledge to solve hard problems. The underlying principles are absent and so cannot be used to support deep reasoning.

As we have covered the deep-knowledge issue in the previous chapter — the perceived need for it together with little idea about what it might be — I'll resist the temptation to repeat it all. Chandrasekaran and Mittal (1983) provide a lucid examination of this issue, and they stress that, despite the many calls for more deep knowledge, there is no general agreement on the form and content of these deeper structures. In particular they illustrate that the popular belief, that "causal" knowledge is deep knowledge, does not stand up to close scrutiny — in a nutshell: substituting "pattern CAUSES action" for "pattern → action" is no guarantee that deeper knowledge has been encoded.

Let us deal with one last and important question concerning representations of knowledge in general and the application of a logic-based process model. Suppose you are told that the computer in front of you contains an expert system — an expert on Middle-earth (i.e., you are given a context within which to draw semantic implications such as BILBO is Bilbo). Digging deeply into your own knowledge base (the one in your head), you retrieve something about little people named Hobbits, and a question for the expert system springs into mind — you type the query:

(HOBBIT HOLLY)?

What is the correct response, given that the expert system only has our original, ludicrously small, knowledge base to work with?

Clearly the response should be that this statement is false (Holly is a Hobbie, not a Hobbit), and the system would soon fail to deduce the truth of this query; thus it would correctly ouput:

No, Holly is not a Hobbit.

But I have glossed over an important implication here; it is that failure to prove truth implies falsity. There is nothing in the knowledge base that allows us to explicitly conclude that Holly is not a hobbit—i.e., no instance or possibility of deducing NOT (HOBBIT HOLLY).

Under the same rules the queries (WIZARD GANDALF) and (BAD-GUYS GOBLINS) would turn out to be false. And we know that they are true, at least in Middle-earth—and there is the crux of the problem. As Levesque (1984) says, "the user of the knowledge base must distinguish between what is known by the knowledge base and what is true in the intended application area." Knowledge bases tend to be incomplete: i.e., they often do not have all the information necessary to answer a query.

Incompleteness of knowledge bases is a property that we must be able to cope within the ill-defined and dynamic domains of AI. A common way to deal with this incompleteness problem is to use the so-called *closed world assumption:* The knowledge base is assumed to know everything about its world, and thus, if it doesn't know that something is true, then that something is false.

Unfortunately, this straightforward solution to the incompleteness problem is not very satisfactory in some AI applications; the system needs to know about what it doesn't know (as a guide to knowledge acquisition, for example) as distinct from knowing that certain things are false.

Here we see again a need for metaknowledge arising. As usual, special-purpose heuristics have been the route to dealing with this general problem. Collins, Warnock, Aiello, and Miller (1975) describe a selection of such strategies and illustrate their choices with SCHOLAR (Carbonell, 1970), the geography tutoring system that I used as an example earlier.

The beginnings of a generalized and formal approach to these problems of incomplete knowledge bases has been described by Levesque (1984). He is developing a formal language within which one can query a knowledge base as to what it knows and does not know. Thus in our earlier example the metalevel query:

Do you know that Holly is a Hobbit?

would be answered,

I do not know that Holly is a Hobbit.

(i.e., neither (HOBBIT HOLLY) nor NOT(HOBBIT HOLLY) can be proven within the current knowledge base).

I should emphasize that, although Levesque's work is a promising approach to the possibility for formalizing metaknowledge, it is ongoing research, and a number of important problems must be solved before it can become a practically useful technique.

ELEMENTS OF STRUCTURED KNOWLEDGE: FRAMES, SCRIPTS, AND SCHEMATA

Finally, we must focus down and look at the structured elements of knowledge in AI systems — the declarative units, if you like, which are manipulated within the processing schemes described above. In keeping with the accepted view that intelligence is based upon the associationistic properties of knowledge — i.e., that one thing always leads to another — the units of declarative knowledge tend to be, not elementary facts, but cohesive clusters of related facts. The term *frame,* due to Minsky (1975), is perhaps the most common name for such collections of knowledge. Schank's *scripts* are designed to capture the sequencing of events (such as: enter-sit-order-eat-pay-leave in the famous restaurant script) as well as collect together the related facts (the props like chairs and tables, and the actors like waitresses and managers). Scripts were designed, and have been primarily used, in the natural-language subfield of AI and are thus dealt with in Chapter 8.

The term *schema* or *schemata* (when in the plural) is the one used more by psychologists and cognitive scientists than it is by honest-to-goodness AI types. Schemata may also be more of an abstract knowledge representation unit, while frames, as is appropriate for computer hackers, tend to be more concrete, even if they are not always part of an implemented and working system. But, in general, I see no very significant differences between them; hence, I shall concentrate on frames in order to convey the general principles in as short a space as is decently possible.

A frame is a fancy record structure. It is not only a collection of data items that possess some similarity, i.e., all related to say, the concept of a chair (just to pick a concept at random). The chair record might be a collection of data items such as color, seat covering material, height of seat from floor, etc. The notion of a chair frame spiffs up this general idea considerably.

A chair frame will, in addition to be a simple collection of relevant facts, contain links to more general concepts such as furniture — i.e., a chair is a "type of" furniture. The point of this so-called superordinate link is that the chair frame can inherit properties of the furniture frame without having to repeat all of these properties within the chair frame (and in every other type-of-furniture frame). One such inherited property might be "typically found in houses", this is characteristic of all furniture and, thus, of chairs. A frame may also have links down to more specialized frames such as an arm-chair frame and a deck-chair frame.

Stored within the chair frame explicitly are various categories of data item; these items are usually associated with frame *slots* — i.e., a place for a specific piece of information which may, or may not, be filled in any particular frame. Some slots for the chair frame will be purely optional; e.g., a chair-owner slot will have a value if we happen to know the owner of the current chair; otherwise it will be empty. Some will perhaps always have to be filled, e.g., number-of-legs (for some obscure reason). In this latter case *default values* may be supplied. That is to say, if, when a particular chair frame is constructed, we have no explicit statement of how many legs this particular chair has, then a default value of "four" may be automatically filled in. This use of default values is particularly useful with data structures to support intelligent reasoning, because it is a mechanism for utilizing implicit information. If we are reasoning about a particular chair, we are likely to assume, in the absence of any information to the contrary, that it has four legs. The frame data structure offers us a mechanism with which to mimic this ability.

Despite all their admirable qualities, frames and schemata have many unsatisfactory properties when considered as the basic knowledge elements to support intelligent reasoning. Their major drawback stems perhaps from the very fact that the idea of a frame or schema encapsulates knowledge. Neat packages of knowledge (even with the odd links to other packages) are great for the management of complexity, but they jar with the (apparent) fluidity of intelligent reasoning.

In a frame-based system there are always awkward problems of situations that fall between frames or schemata, and questions of when to change frames or schemata. Similarly, there are always situations which do not fit any particular frame or schema very comfortably. Thus, if I sit on a log it becomes, to some extent, a chair (thus a friend might say, "Can I share your chair?"), but this possibility is unlikely to be in any chair frame. As another example, is a large marquee on the lawn to be reasoned about using a room schemata (rooms don't usually have grass on the floor, but they do have tables and chairs in and a ceiling overhead)?

As usual I've got a CP-based stab at this knotty AI problem. Touretzky and Geva (1987) describe frame-like concept structures in which the slot names (e.g., chair color) and the slot fillers (e.g., puce) "are diffuse patterns of activation spread over a collection of units." They claim that this representational scheme allows then to encode subtle variations on the accepted slot fillers.

Having surveyed the general background to AI, we are now ready to explore the major subdomains in detail. Vision, natural language, and learning are the subjects of the next three chapters, in that order.

7

Vision: Seeing is Perceiving

Famous last words: "all the information is there."

Computer processing of images is often claimed as one of the areas of success in AI. And, in addition, this area is characterized by the use of formal techniques. What the exact relationship between these two attributes (successful and formalized) might be is an interesting question to which we shall return shortly. The process of interpreting images is variously called *pattern recognition* (a "bad" AI paradigm, you may remember from Chapter 3), *image analysis, image interpretation, scene recognition,* or even *scene understanding.* These names reflect, to a first approximation at least, a spectrum of approaches to vision systems that are progressively more AI-ish as we move from pattern recognition to scene understanding.

At the non-AI end of this spectrum the view is taken that (virtually) all the necessary information is coded into the image. The task of the computer system is to apply image decoding algorithms (e.g., find *edges*) and thereby piece together image features to generate patterns — the 2-D representations of objects in this 3-D world. All the information is in the image, for where else could it be? Mayhew (1984, p. 28), for example, distinguishes "two parallel sometimes overlapping, but often very different areas in computer vision": *Pattern Recognition and Image Processing* (PRIP) and *Image Understanding* (IU). The main differences are:

1. The kinds of images processed;
2. The primary aims of the research/application.

In IU there is an attempt to understand the principles and processes of visual competence with little regard for immediate practical application. PRIP is more an engineering endeavor often dealing with unnatural images (e.g., satellite "pictures") and for which special purpose techniques (such as laser rangefinding) are entirely appropriate.

PRIP typically yields powerful but special-purpose vision systems that are useless outside of the specific domain and for the specific task for which they were originally designed. This is the non-AI end of the spectrum of approaches to machine vision; it is the IU work that is more AI-ish, and this is the approach that I shall follow in this chapter.

The AI-oriented approach (i.e., roughly Mayhew's IU category) takes the view that an image can only be interpreted within a context. The other, and necessary, source of information (apart from the image) is thus the context, which itself has a variety of interpretations (a variety that I shall, in due course, endeavor to organize and present as yet another spectrum of possibilities). Vision systems in AI then interpret an image in terms of both the image itself and the many information sources external to the image — i.e., its context.

Processing mechanisms that derive their information from these two rather different information sources are often termed *bottom-up* (if they are using information in the image) and *top-down* (if the information source is contextual) strategies. One of the major challenges to any intelligent vision system is flexible integration of bottom-up and top-down mechanisms.

The successes of AI vision work have leaned heavily on bottom-up image analysis techniques. And the fact that this AI subfield has been more successful than, say, natural language processing (see next chapter) may not be due to the fact that it got off to an early start so much as because seeing may be more of a cognitively impenetrable process than speaking and listening (more on the modularity of the human mind, later). What this means is that, if the human process of seeing is largely independent of other cognitive activities, we should expect to be able to construct intelligent seeing machines without the necessity of also solving the many other problems of intelligent behavior.

A second, and equally difficult to evaluate, factor is the role of mathematical formalisms in AI vision work. Are the successes due to the employment of formal techniques for, say, edge finding and pattern classification? Or is the fact that a relatively context-free application of image operators can be used to interpret images with some success just another reflection of the somewhat fortuitous modularity of human vision (and hence, the possibility of modular intelligent vision systems)?

Unfortunately, the answer to this problem is not in the back of the book (or of any other book), but let me offer a further complication to compound this issue. The claim that vision is one of the success stories in AI, when compared to, say, the natural language processing subfield, is not beyond dispute. AI vision systems can no more look at an average scene in the real world and analyze it than a natural language system can understand unconstrained sentences of English. Nevertheless, AI vision systems are out and about in the factories of the world, and they are doing a lot of useful work, but then so are natural language interface systems (see next chapter).

A final observation on the relative difficulty of AI vision work and natural language processing is that natural language input is typically generated by an uncontrollable, and notoriously unpredictable, system, to wit, a specimen of homo sapiens. Vision system input, on the other hand, is typically generated by pointing a camera at some carefully selected corner of the world. Certainly the world at large offers a rich selection of such corners to point cameras at, but preselection and the relatively static nature of the empirical world (when contrasted with natural language) suggests to me at least that successful vision systems can be founded on fundamentally less demanding input information.

Before we push on into the convolutions of Gaussian curves with second derivatives of image intensity (it's an empty threat, so don't get nervous), let me attempt to create the atmosphere within which the majority of computer vision systems operate.

Imagine that you've been asleep for a long time, a very long time. I'm not talking about the average Sunday-morning lay in; the length of time that I'm asking you to consider is something more like a million years. Now, that's a long sleep. Let's not worry about the mechanics of this scenario; it's only a thought experiment, which means that we are free to ignore the awkward glitches. Now, imagine further that you're just coming round to consciousness after this long snooze. The world that you used to inhabit has long since vanished; you are surfacing in a totally alien environment. Nothing looks at all familiar. There is nothing that you can relate to: no obvious people, no cosy cryogenic couch, no chairs, no recognizable room. At that moment, just as you are about to scream and conk out again, an array of 1,000 x 1,000 black and white squares floods your visual system, and you are asked what you can recognize in the image!

Well, that is how the average computer vision system is treated — only worse. It is not just the case that the computer system has little knowledge of the world around it from which the image is drawn; typically, it has absolutely no knowledge of the existence of a world outside itself, let alone specific features of this world. This may be good for the computer vision system's peace of mind (i.e., it has no piece of mind to not be at peace) but it is far from helpful when the task is to interpret images in terms of objects in the world that it knows little or nothing about.

The case for context-free vision is sometimes made by a speaker who pulls something from his pocket and throws it onto the surface of the overhead projector that he has been using. The resultant fuzzy image projected onto the screen might look like Figure 7.1.

"It is a key," we respond, more or less instantly and with alacrity, pleased to see something recognizable on the screen for a change, a wel-

Figure 7.1.   An image with no context

come respite from the preceding equational concoctions ("probably the key to his front door," we are thinking). So, the case is proven. We had no prior knowledge that the object to be projected next would be a key, yet we recognized it as such immediately. We had no context to work with and yet we correctly identified the image as that of a key. Thus human vision can be purely bottom-up.

"But," the committed top-downists cry out with perceptible asperity, "wait a minute. We each had a wealth of contextual information to bring to bear during recognition of the key." And they are right; even though the recognition was initiated without a smooth contextual build up, our knowledge of the world and of people provides a multitude of constraints on what that projected image might be an image of. For example, it was a hard, metallic object that clanked onto the projection surface; it was something that people carry around in their pocket, etc. I submit that the key-recognition drama could just as easily have been closely directed by a top-down strategy.

Now, if our long-time sleeper was subjected to the same recognition test, he or she would not do as well, because time will have robbed him or her of most of the plausible inferences that we are free to draw upon. Context-free recognition, to the degree practiced by most computer vision systems, is just not possible for us, in the sense that we are always operating within a plethora of contextual contraints. We cannot test the pure bottom-up recognition hypothesis with humans, which does not mean that it is false; it just means that casual attempts to demonstrate its truth are false. So beware of the glib demo. The questions aren't that simple; they seldom are.

An alternative pair of names for bottom-up and top-down processing are *early* and *late* processing, respectively. This new nomenclature is not entirely accurate as an alternative to bottom-up and top-down, but it is close enough to be useful. The terminology early and late has its origins in the human visual process. Early processing of the visual input to the eye is initiated long before the visual signals reach the brain. There is a complicated tangle of neural stuff that connects the eyeball to the brain, and it just can't resist messing about with the input signal as it passes it along to the ultimate tangle in the cranium. Thus by the time the brain gets its neurons on the visual signal, the signal is not what it originally was. The brain is late, and so is its processing of the visual signal. In computer vision, early processing uses the clean, well-defined, formal operations which are then followed by a farrago of heuristic processes that are perhaps most charitably described as better late than never (although it is not clear that all the neats in the bottom-up brigade would agree that never is too long to hold off on the heuristic ad hoc-ery). In addition, early processing is potentially a parallel process (not to say massively parallel); the basic operations (of say, intensity averaging) to be performed quite independently on large numbers of the primitive picture elements provide a nearly ideal situation for the exploitation of the promise of parallelism in AI. Hence, the existence of special-purpose parallel hardware for vision work; there are array processors, pyramid architectures, etc. Each of these are essentially computers for the early processing in a vision system. Uhr (1987) provides a useful review and commentary on the possibilities for applying the various parallel computer architectures to the problems of AI.

By way of contrast the late processing is more likely to be implemented as a sequential, top-down-based classification of the flotsam and jetsum generated by the parallel pixel crunching. The late processing picks out collections of the debris (bits of edges, vertices, planes, etc.) and associates them with some object (e.g., a cube, or a hammer). This is not to say that the later visual processing should be a sequential process. Quite the contrary; the human ability to see objects in images is more plausibly interpreted as a parallel process at all levels, as we shall see. But there is, nevertheless, a reasonable argument to be made for the degree of parallelism to be reduced as processing moves from early to late — the parallelism changes from massive to mere, perhaps. Think about the vast numbers of pixels in the raw image and the relatively small number of candidate objects to be associated with areas of the image. But putting that aside, all of the neat, formal, top-down algorithms that work outside of toy-world contexts are still waiting to be discovered. This fact reduces top-down processing strategies to collections of dubious heuristics that nevertheless seem to work, sometimes. Having mentioned pixels, I can no longer postpone exposing you to some details of bottom-up image processing.

BOTTOMING IN: OPERATORS CANNY, UNCANNY, AND CANNYLESS

At the risk of taking some of the keen edge off this expository commentary on vision processing in AI, I've decided to start at the bottom and work systematically through to the top — dull stuff, but I'll see what I can do. Alternatively stated, I'm going to begin working through the ingredients of early processing and end up with the various manifestations of late processing strategies. But I am going to reverse the usual order of emphasis; I'll refer you elsewhere for the mathematical nitty gritty of early processing operations, and I'll give the messy late stuff a fair shake for a change (so if all you really wanted from this book was the algorithm for a fast Gaussian contortion of something or other — hard luck; it may not be too late to get your money back).

At rock bottom, so to speak, there are "pixels," so here we go.

PIXEL PROCESSING

Lest we get off on the wrong foot, let me state categorically at the outset that, whatever any other purported exposé of AI may tell you, the word *pixel* is not the French for female pixie. It is the result of a contraction (and minor expansion) of the term *picture element*. Suffice it to say that the atoms of computer vision are pixels, small, discrete blobs which may be simply black or white, or may vary in intensity and color to a degree proportional to the available budget — multihued pixels are expensive; they can also carry a lot of information usable by bottom-up mechanisms. An old saw (after resharpening) expresses the general philosophy of the dyed-in-the-wool bottom-upists: Take care of the pixels and the pictures will take care of themselves.

Not only do pixels come in elaborate ranges of color and intensity but also in vast numbers, and again in general the more pixels you have available, the more opportunity the pixel-crunching operators will have to extract useful information from the image. So the task of a vision system, when the image is hot off the lens, is to reduce a vast array (and I mean it literally for a change) of pixels down to something of more manageable proportions.

Typically, the initial operations involve noise reduction (e.g., more or less random pixels that should be black and are white), often manifest as a smoothing operation (e.g., adjacent pixel intensities are brought closer together, thus yielding a smoother intensity gradient across a series of pixels), and grouping operations that can both reduce the size of the pixel array and at the same time reduce the noise in the image.

Ultimately, these initial image operators will generate the first-image *features* — perhaps edgelets (baby edges, of course, which if nurtured with compassionate operators and the right sort of context will grow up to become healthy adult edges of things like tables and chairs, or more often, blocks) and a resultant primal sketch. A *primal sketch* is an image composed of edgelets rather than pixels.

Edgelets are generated from similarly valued pixels (all black rather than white, or all the 35th shade of gray, etc.) that are side by side and adjacent to pixels of very different intensity (which sounds sort of contradictory, but all will become clear soon, I hope). The general philosophy seems to be that the features in a pixel array are to be found in abrupt changes in pixel intensity (edgy features) and also in uniformity of pixel intensity (surfaces or planes). Is there anything left? Well, of course, there are all of the pixels that are different but of similar intensity and color to their nearest and dearest neighbors.

This would be the point to wade into an ocean of mathematics (and lose all my readers who think that mathematics is for the birds if not for that perverse subset of humanity, the mathematicians), if this were that kind of book, but it's not — I keep my promises. Nevertheless, I'll give you a taste of the formal approach to dispel any illusions that you might be missing something because of my willful refusals to parade the equations in front of you.

In the best of all possible worlds, where both Newton and Leibnitz would have been forcibly restrained when they attempted to invent the differential calculus, we wouldn't have second derivatives to worry about and hence no zero crossings. But this, as I'm sure that you know full well, is not the best of all possible worlds; it's just the best we've got. So let's get on with it.

The intensity values in a line of pixels might well look like this:

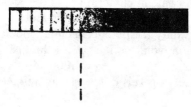

Figure 7.2.   A line of pixels

which can be represented graphically like this:

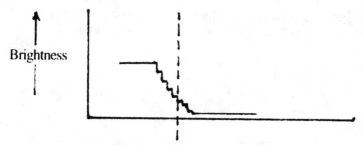

Figure 7.3.   A graph of the line of pixels illustrated in Figure 7.2

There is clearly an abrupt change in intensity in this line of pixels (it is strongly recommended that readers who are at all puzzled by this statement close their eyes, take a deep breath, calm down, and skip on to the next section — just pretend it never happened). For readers whose constitutions can take a graph or two, here's another:

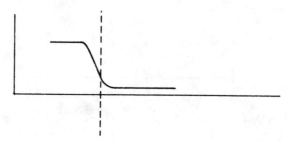

Figure 7.4.   A smoothing of the graph in Figure 7.3

No startling developments (I hope); I've just smoothed out the intensity values given earlier. This curve can now be — wait for it — differentiated (sorry, but I had to refer to horrors like that sooner or later). And if that's not bad enough, there's still the last step to come. The result of differentiating the intensity curve is another curve (the first derivative, illustrated below). This first derivative curve can also be differentiated giving us the final curve (the second derivative, illustrated below the first derivative curve).

{Gruesome detail: Skip it without penalty if you're close to satiated. Both derivatives are of intensity with respect to distance across the line of pixels. The process of differentiation tells us the rate and direction of change of slope in the curve differentiated. A horizontal line has zero slope, and any maximum (or minimum) value has a horizontal segment however small at the maximum (or minimum) position.}

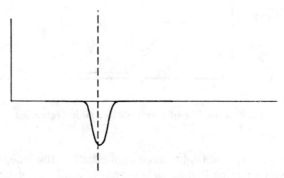

Figure 7.5.   The result of differentiating the curve in Figure 7.4

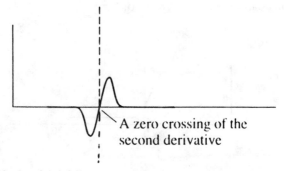

A zero crossing of the second derivative

Figure 7.6.   The result of differentiating the curve of Figure 7.5

The question that must be bursting from every right-minded reader is: "Why would you want to do such a thing?" And the answer is, in order to determine exactly where in the line of pixels the edge is to be located. The change in pixel intensity was only fairly abrupt (if I may be given leave to return to my customary level of casual description); it was a somewhat gradual change over a number of pixels, as the intensity curve above illustrates (Figure 7.4). So where do we put this edge? We put it at the point on the curve at which the intensity changes most abruptly. This is also the point on the curve at which the slope of the curve changes most abruptly, that is, the point of maximum change of slope. This point is a maximum (or minimum) value of the first derivative curve (take a look at the first derivative curve, if you doubt my word). In order to pinpoint this maximum exactly (and with the right-minded reluctance to forsake a serviceable, formal operation) we differentiate once more and get the second derivative curve, which shows at exactly what point the slope of the first derivative is at a maximum (or minimum) value — i.e., when the slope of the first derivative is both zero and changes direction on either side of this zero point, in a phrase, a zero crossing.

What all this boils down to is that a zero crossing in the second derivative curve is used to precisely locate the edge in the original line of pixels. Hence, our original line of pixels becomes interpreted as:

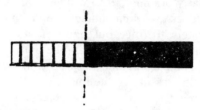

Figure 7.7.   Figure 7.2 after locating the edge point and cleaning up

Put several such lines of pixels next to each other, and we've found an edgelet at 90 degrees to the pixel lines. Replace our original pixel array by all the edgelets that we've located, and we have a primal sketch.

As Horn (1986) says, edge detection has been one of the most active fields in machine vision. Thus there are many operators designed to detect and locate edges in images. Horn lists and commentates on a veritable cornucopia of such operators. Worthy of special mention is the Canny operator (not canny, note) which is an operator developed by Canny (1983) that provides an optimal tradeoff between localization and detection. The salient point here is that this is yet another neat mathematical technique, and the suggestion of cautious shrewdness conveyed by its name is largely unwarranted — be warned. If Canny had been unfortunate enough to be named Dopey, then it would be the Dopey operator, but it would perform none the worse.

The next task is to put edgelets together and generate man-size edges, lines, and other features from whence objects might be recognizable.

EDGES AND LINES

Charniak and McDermott (1985, p. 101) classify the products of collections of edgelets as edges, bars, and blobs. "An edge is a sequence of edgelets laid end-to-end with roughly the same orientation, which separates a large light area from a dark one. A bar is a pair of edgelet sequences running along together, bounding a region lighter or darker than the surrounding region. A blob is a small group of edgelets surrounding a small patch.'' Incidentally, they also drag you through a healthy selection from the many varieties of convolutions with Gauss' masterpiece, so go there if you want a smoothing, and surprisingly soothing, presentation of formal techniques for sanding down the rough pixels, as well as most other techniques that together constitute early processing.

It doesn't take too much imagination to see that algorithms which then trundle around the primal sketch connecting up features that are close to each other (or similarly oriented, etc.) will generate large image features such as lines. What does take some imagination is to believe that lines so generated will be likely to trace out representations of objects in the world, especially ones that are supposed to be in that particular image of the world. The truth is that sometimes they do, and sometimes they don't. It all depends upon the quality of the image and how well high contrast in the image corresponds to the edges of objects in the world. And the only way to estimate the veridicality of this correspondence is to use contextual information. We find a need for late processing even at this early point in the game.

VERTICES OR JUNCTIONS

Where lines meet we have *vertices* or *junctions*. A substantial amount of early AI vision work used theories of vertices as a basic component of the vision system (see, for example, the collection of papers seductively mistitled "The Psychology of Computer Vision," Winston, 1975). Information external to the image (i.e., the constraints on physically possible vertices in an image of planar, convex blocks) can drastically reduce the range of possible junctions. Further contextual constraints can be applied as junctions are connected together thus reducing again the scope of possible macrofeatures in the image. And when some knowledge of shadows is added to the interpretation of an image of a jumble of blocks, the number of possible interpretations shrinks yet again.

Winston notes the curious fact that earlier vision workers assumed that shadows would be an annoying complication that was best eliminated by appropriate lighting, or ignored in the image. Whereas in actuality, a knowledge (even the very primitive knowledge applied) of shadows led to a simplification of the problem. Here we see another example of the principle that smaller is not necessarily simpler.

In his influential AI text Winston (1984) has a chapter entitled "Exploiting Natural Constraints," which is primarily concerned with their exploitation in computer vision work. Tanimoto (1987, p. 379) also sees the vision subfield notion of applying constraints and "the relaxation paradigm for constraint satisfaction" as general AI concepts that made their debuts in AI vision work. Zucker (1981); in his essay on "Computer Vision and Human Perception," views the study of vision as the discovery of contraints. Winston (1984) also presents the exposure of constraints as the third step in his five-step, SAV-like (see Chapter 2), "good methodology" for "safe" programming in AI. Curiously, he sees the constraints as exposed by the chosen representation rather than as an intrinsic feature of the problem.

A landmark study in this constraint exploitation approach to vision-system research was that of Waltz (1975). He worked with the notorious blocks world (see "The Case of the Missing Blocks World," next chapter), and he showed dramatic reductions in complexity that can result from the judicious introduction of top-down information to constrain the bottom-up operations. Waltz clearly demonstrated that image processing cannot proceed in a strictly level-by-level, bottom-to-top way; it must be guided, in the very lowest levels, by what makes sense at the higher levels.

This first taste of the use of top-down or contextual knowledge in image processing is leading us inexorably into the modern subdomain of model-based vision systems. But first you should glimpse a few more sources of image features. I'll lead off with a necessarily superficial feature of images — the textural quality of surfaces. One can find edges and corners and thereby enclose a surface. Alternatively (or better, additionally), one can attempt to map out surfaces which will, on ending, provide you with boundaries, if not honest to goodness edges.

TEXTURE: A TRULY SUPERFICIAL FEATURE

Another major source of clues within the image that can be exploited to assist a machine vision system is *texture*. Radical changes in texture may signal a boundary (and hence perhaps an indistinct edge), and textural distortions may provide orientation and depth information (if we assume that the texture is uniform on the object). Texture in machine vision means repeated elements; a collection of instances of some small pattern feature (such as a dot, circle, or line) is taken to represent a textured surface.

While differences in texture may signal the presence of otherwise indistinct edges (the end of one region and the beginning of another), computing useful differences requires that we develop some algorithmic measure of textural sameness — a demanding task if we require that resultant module to have general applicability. It is currently too demanding for the state of the art.

Orientation of a surface can be computed from the progressive distortion of elemental texture features, and sometimes by a neat technique of tangent direction distribution *before* the actual feature elements are extracted (Charniak & McDermott, 1985). This subdomain of AI vision work epitomizes, to my mind, much of the 'neat' results in AI. They work very nicely just as long as the underlying assumptions hold. The open question then is: How reliable are the underlying assumptions in general? The devisers of these neat techniques are, quite understandably, not at pains to publicly explore the general validity of their basic assumptions; they just demonstrate the neat technique on data for which it works, and we are left impressed but wondering. This is an all too common after-effect of AI presentations, and one in which the first component tends to diminish in intensity with time and repeated exposure. But sadly the same usually cannot be said of the wonderment; if it changes, it tends to change to bafflement.

Thus much of the texture work assumes uniform texturing and often, planar surfaces. The infamous blocks world can support these two assumptions quite easily, but in the real world outside of MIT such assumptions can look quite shakey. Consider the following two images (Figure 7.8): Which is the folded polka-dot fabric and which is the flat (plastic) lizard-skin wallet? Take your time, but it won't help.

 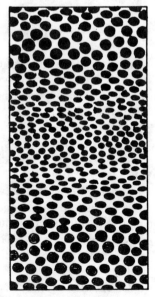

Figure 7.8.   Flat lizard-skin wallet and folded polka-dot fabric

ILLUMINATION, REFLECTANCE, AND OTHER SOURCES OF NUISANCE

So, within certain constraints that, although currently quite restrictive, are nevertheless sufficiently open to admit many useful industrial applications, the formal operators of early processing can extract from an image regions, boundaries, edges and junctions, orientations, and depth information. But there are still a few more image characteristics to be considered.

The same object from the same viewpoint can appear quite different under different lighting conditions — simple differences in illumination and, in particular, the presence of shadows can have a profound effect on the image recorded. Closely related is a characteristic of the objects themselves, and this is *reflectance:* the manner and degree to which object surfaces reflect the incident light. As mentioned earlier, these extra sources of information can be both a bane and a blessing. It doesn't help to have several more factors compounding the interpretation of an image except when these extra factors can be applied to reduce the possible interpretations. Whether an information source is a useful contraint or a compounding nuisance is largely dependent on the state of our knowledge, I believe. If we understand clearly the interactions of the various characteristics, then we can exploit the constraints that emerge in order to reduce the scope of possible interpretations of given images.

THE INTRINSIC IMAGE

Typically, this early processing is primarily aimed at finding "intrinsic images" (Barrow & Tenenbaum, 1978). Intrinsic characteristics (surface characteristics intrinsic to the scene, not dependent on idiosyncracies of the viewpoint or sensor, e.g., distance and orientation) are recovered from the image features (e.g., edges, textured regions) and represented as arrays in registration with the image array. Each such array contains values for a particular characteristic, such as surface orientation, together with explicit indication of the boundaries due to discontinuities mapped out from the original image. Such arrays are intrinsic images. Figure 7.9, whose caption could be found in any national art museum, is an illustration of intrinsic images. Thus the original image on the left might yield the two intrinsic images to its right, the first of distance, the second of orientation. {Gruesome detail: The distance image gives the range along the line of sight from the center of projection to each visible point in the image. The orientation image gives a vector representing the direction of the surface normal at every point.}

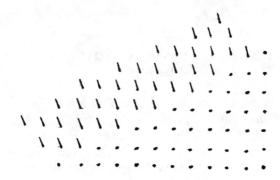

Figure 7.9. Intrinsic images and a piece of cheese

Marr (1978) coined the improbable name *2.5D sketch* for the distance and orientation intrinsic images together. As a minor, but relevant, diversion into the world of CP-based models, I can point out the work of Ballard on "parameter nets." Thus, Ballard (1987) describes the elements of a connectionist theory of low-level and intermediate-level vision. Intrinsic images, he points out, are a good class of image representation to work from, but they do not contain groupings of objects. He proposes to use "massively parallel coperative computation among intrinsic images and a set of feature networks at different levels of abstraction" to circumscribe and label parts of such images in terms of useful segments. A *segment* is a group of image parts that have the same set of parameter values in feature space. When translated, this means that we may find color segments (a group with the same hue), or edge segments (when the image parts all contribute to the same shape), etc. To broaden the scope momentarily, Ballard suggests that, for general-purpose vision systems, we shall need special-purpose parallel hardware and some innovative mathematics. But it is time to focus back down to intrinsic images.

The feature data extracted from an image by the time that we are ready to build intrinsic images is likely to be both complicated and incomplete. Thus the task of putting it all together to generate the intrinsic image is well-nigh impossible without guidance from above — ideally, divine intervention, but, failing that, we must make do with knowledge of the context.

And, assuming that all the features can be put together to yield a set of complete regions, bounded shapes, etc., there is still no guarantee that a mapping to any object description will be found let alone the correct one.

Consider the following image (Figure 7.10) in which there are seven bounded regions, four circular shapes, etc. What is it an image of?

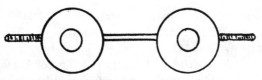

Figure 7.10.   Mystery picture number 1

Well, as a matter of fact, it's two Mexicans riding a tandem. Once you know what it is an image of, mapping the image features to objects such as bicycle wheels is easy, but there is no purely bottom-up way to make that mapping in preference to the many other possible (and more likely?) ones.

This example also illustrates the viewpoint problem. Given an explanation of this image, you had no trouble generating the rather unusual viewpoint that it entails — did you? It's a vulture's eye view, you might say, not typically available to those of us without either special powers or an airplane. Nevertheless, we can quite quickly and easily generate the necessary viewpoint on learning what the image is an image of. That sort of viewpoint flexibility, or *viewpoint independence* as it is termed, is not close to being available in AI vision systems at the moment, as you will see in the next section.

But before we press on into the endless textual stuff it's time for an exercise; let's try one more image (see Figure 7.11).

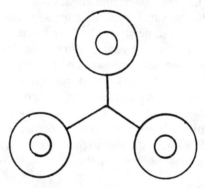

Figure 7.11.   Mystery picture number 2

So what is it? There is no necessary connection with the previous mystery picture, but there are 43 known solutions (some of them printable).

MODEL-BASED VISION SYSTEMS

There is a truism which is ruthlessly exploited in AI vision work as well as in AI more generally; it is that, if you know what you're looking for, it is easier to find it. Thus MYCIN always diagnoses some form of meningitis (and of course it performs brilliantly when confronted by patients suffering from meningitis, but if that's not your problem, then there's no point in going to MYCIN, even for a second opinion), and BACON keeps rediscovering well-known physical laws (never any new ones).

In our current context a model of what may be found in the image can be of great assistance in finding it, even deep down in the early processing. Sure we must have some model in order to recognize anything, but there is a world of difference between extracting a representation from an image using only information in the image and then matching that extracted representation with a catalogue of models of objects, and actively using the object models to guide extraction of the representation. I'll bet you a listing of AM and EURISKO (the loser gets the listing) that intelligent vision must be based on something resembling the latter strategy rather than the former.

But the latter strategy is clearly open to blatant misuse, as we shall discuss when we finally reach the nebulous strategies imputed to the human visual system. For the moment I just want to make the point that, if the system is only shown to recognize one out of a very small number of possible objects and is not shown to reject (i.e., fail to report recognition of) somewhat similar images that do not contain any of the modeled objects, then intelligent vision cannot be claimed. It may still be a very useful vision system, but is it AI? Binford (1982) surveys model-based image analysis systems. He states that, in commercial vision systems, "many special-case tricks are used that do not generally apply to worlds with many objects and many goals. However, those systems must eventually come to resemble general vision systems more than is generally acknowledged" (p. 18). The reasons for his belief in this necessity are left unstated; they are, presumably, either obvious or unknown — and they're not obvious to me.

He characterizes the "bad old days" as a time when the commonly held belief was that the development of powerful, general, operators for early processing and of generalized descriptions (i.e., bottom-up mappings from signal to symbol) was impossible. The answer (to the problem of building intelligent vision systems) was thought to lie in a combination of the available, but weak, low-level vision modules with the use of extensive world knowledge. The current reversal in what is by implication the "good new days" leaves us with the majority opinion that careful theoretical analysis and implementation of individual vision operations is essential for building vision systems, so Binford claims.

In accord with Binford's view, Brady (1981) characterizes the machine style of perception as concentrating on particular classes of visual clues such as shape from shading (e.g., Ikeuchi & Horn, 1981), shape from texture (e.g., Witkin, 1981), shape from models (e.g., Brooks, 1981). This general approach to machine perception is committed to an exhaustive exploitation of the physics of imagery (e.g., reflectance properties of objects) in an attempt to recover a maximum of the information in an image and avoid the use of ad hoc assumptions from contextual inferences. Perkins (1983) characterizes this dominant approach as "physicist's systems," which he contrasts with "pragmatist's systems," systems that are casual about benign mistakes, opportunist about whatever varied cues provide reliable paths of inference in the situation, wary of searches, sketchy unless there is a need to know, etc.

Kolers (1983) argues that computer vision systems are based upon the specification of elements of vision and rules to combine these elements. He suggests that the human visual system does not work in this way, but rather in terms of skills and dispositions. He singles out the fundamental aspect of a skill as a dependence on prior actions, "activities are carried out through transfer of components acquired in prior actions. . . . A machine's actions, however, are largely independent of what has gone before; its ability to do something is due to its design, not its past experience" (p. 266). If this point elicits the *deja vu* phenomenon, then you might be recalling my tale of the long-time sleeper; alternatively, you might not.

To some extent Kolers seems to be criticizing the absence of learning in machine vision systems, an absence which is very close to total. Ballard and Brown (1982), in their exposition of computational vision, note with disappointment the absence of learning mechanisms in this subdomain of AI. As we shall see in the next chapter, machine learning is largely absent from the subdomain of natural language processing as well (and this absence is claimed by Schank as the prime reason for denigrating his earlier work and for his move to theories of reminding). Thus machine learning has a chapter to itself, for although it should by rights be a component of all subdomains of AI, the sad reality is that it is a subdomain apart — at least for the present.

Ballard and Brown also propose that the use of domain knowledge to drive top-down perception algorithms has two bases: It's inherently interesting because human beings appear to work this way; and, as a purely practical choice, it offers the chance to accomplish visual tasks without impractical expenditure of resources, given that the parallel hardware needed to support bottom-up techniques is both expensive and not yet as generally useful as we might expect.

The model-based systems that Binford surveyed can demonstrate some success but at the cost of quite severe built-in limitations: a very small selection of recognizable objects (usually less than 10); or very sparse models of the possible 'scenes' (e.g., sky must touch upper edge of picture and road must touch lower edge); or they are inherently viewpoint dependent (i.e., the mapping from object model to image assumes a specific viewpoint of the object).

He mentions the problems of inferring surface structure and depth relations from a single image. But given more than one image (as a result of motion of either the observed or the observer, or as a result of two imaging sources, i.e., stereo vision), depth information is more easily extracted from an image. Charniak and McDermott (1985) provide an introduction to stereo techniques which will also provide a dose of formal symbolics for those readers who lapped up the second derivative and are now thirsting for more.

Depth information is also generated by direct sensing in some computer vision systems as a result of, for example, laser imaging, but this is clearly cheating, so I shall make no further mention of it. But see Besl and Jain (1985) for a review of such research, if you feel that I may be skipping over an essential AI subtopic.

Binford states that most of the systems surveyed segmented images based upon connecting points that fall into some spectral band, and then they describe the resultant shape. This approach can be contrasted with one that employs the continuity of edges to generate well-formed regions. Modesty does not seem to forbid him from repeatedly mentioning one system ACRONYM (Binford, 1982) as the sole representative from the class of vision systems that does not suffer from many of the limitations that devalue the other systems surveyed. Mayhew (1984) also singles the ACRONYM system out for special mention in his small survey of the field. For Mayhew ACRONYM is of particular interest because it contained a very powerful (and of course very specific) inference system that enabled it to correctly associate 2–D representations of shapes with stored 3–D models. If the image is one of Boeing 747s parked around gates 1 through 10 at Boston airport and taken from the left end of the public observation gallery, then ACRONYM will find those planes, but if it's not, I don't know what happens (maybe it still finds some Jumbo jets). I'm being slightly unfair again, but as long as you realize this, the point is well made.

A true story is way overdue in this chapter, but here is one at last. It is shorter than average, but no less true.

TRUE AI STORY: 7.1

There is an extremely neat and formal bunch of operators that can recognize no end of different tools — hammers, pliers, wrenches (that's with an *r* as in *spanner*), etc. This vision system that embodies these neat techniques is sometimes called the carpenter's mate (as in *assistant* rather than *spouse,* I think). Presumably, the system is being developed as either an aid for blind carpenters or for industrial robots that like to do some wood work in their spare time; it does not matter.

Well, apparently, when it sees what the homo sapiens of this world take to be a zebra, the carpenter's mate reports (presumably to the carpenter) that it sees a complete toolkit containing an overabundance of crowbars, probably a burglar's toolkit.

END OF TRUE AI STORY

So, when the assumptions underlying the early processing operators (assumptions such as that high contrast is an object edge) are not valid, neither are the features (and hence, the objects) found by the operators. And along similar lines, simple model-based image analysis works well when the image in question is indeed an image of one of the few objects in the catalogue of models. Furthermore, the viewpoint must also be the (or more rarely, one of the) anticipated viewpoint(s). But what sort of object is a formal model of a Boeing 747, or of a person, or of anything that is not a simple, regular, geometric object?

BEER CANS, BROOMSTICKS, ETC.

Beer cans and broomsticks are just examples of the 3–D shape known as a cylinder. The generalized cylinder tends towards a broomstick as the major axis is lengthened and sectional diameter is decreased (or at least not increased). In other words if you stretch out a cylinder you're likely to end up with something that resembles a broomstick. Similarly, if you squash down the same cylinder (or one rather like it), you might get a sort of beer can, provided you don't beat down on it too hard, in which case you're likely to be taking home something more like a flat dinner plate. It almost goes without saying (nevertheless, I'll say it) that a variety of cylinderish shapes (including bent ones) can be stuck together to model a large number of worldly objects: people, animals, prisms (if you cheat a bit and bash the rounded sides flat), etc.

The generalized cylinder is thus a rich source of modelling possibilities. The bashing, stretching, squeezing, etc., can all be done mathematically (which is not as much fun but makes for more accurate deformations and hence models). Thus, with one quite simple mathematical tool (a generalized cylinder generator), 3–D or volumetric models can be constructed and fitted to image features and in particular to depth information. A volumetric model can be used to predict quite accurately just what aspects of an object will be visible from a given viewpoint and what aspects will be hidden. This predicted information can be very useful as a source of interpretive data to assist both early feature extraction and subsequent intrinsic image contruction.

Most of the early processing vision operators are appropriate for smooth-surfaced, geometric objects such as those that populate the blocks world (real or just represented by abstract descriptions); even when we add generalized-cylinder people and animals, we have not extended our domain much further into the real world. The crumpled contortions of many natural objects are in a different class — e.g., mountain ranges. Pentland (1985) describes a fractal model of surface shape which appears to possess many of the properties required to generate 3–D representations of a continuum of surfaces from smooth to rough.

The mathematics of fractal modeling is much too grim to contemplate in this lighthearted book. The bottom line is that wonderfully realistic-looking models of natural objects, such as Yosemite Valley, can be constructed by fractal modeling. And the *natural look* (if I may retrieve this term from the unkind grip of the cosmetics industry) is achieved by a process of controlled randomness which, whatever it may mean, is probably the process of mountain building, etc. (see Mandelbrot, 1982, for a general introduction to the joys of fractals).

Solina and Bajcsy (1987) report from the GRASP laboratory that superquadratics (sorry, no explanation, just treat it as one of the great unknowns in your life) provide another formal approach to the recognition of natural phenomena, as Pentland (1986) once again pointed out. They use these splendidly named things as a basis for computer recognition of *mail pieces* (N.B.: that is *mail*, not *male*). Apparently, mail pieces is the technical term for parcels and packages which are typically not the perfect polyhedral objects that much computer vision work has focused on. It is not clear to me that they are natural objects either; perhaps seminatural is the most apt classification.

"In summary," Barrow and Tenenbaum (1981) say, "the description of images in terms of three-dimensional surfaces and their physical characteristics plays a vital role in human vision and appears to be a key intermediate level of representation necessary for general-purpose vision in natural scenes."

In their abstract they claim that "research is beginning to uncover fundamental computational principles underlying vision that apply equally to artificial and natural systems." The only ubiquitous vision principles that seem to be totally exposed (or even not totally covered) are of a very general nature, such as: early levels are primarily data-driven and, "at intermediate levels, some combination of data-driven (bottom-up) and goal-driven (top-down) operation is needed both to compensate for errors, and to avoid computational overload." This principle does not provide the aspiring computer vision system designer with a great deal of guidance, but it is, I suppose, a start.

In their survey of computational vision, Barrow and Tenenbaum observe that practical vision systems are heavily dependent on domain-specific constraints and techniques. They state that "There is thus a clear need for computer vision systems capable of dealing with less predictable and less structured scenes." So why is this? How are we going to design the necessary, more powerful computer vision systems?

One obvious place to begin to look for some answers is (as it always is in AI) in the only known, practical, working model of a generalized vision system — i.e., in the biological machines that have evolved on Earth. And although vultures, for example, have an optical precision that we can only guess at, it is man's visual capabilities that we typically attempt to emulate in AI. As long ago as 1982 Brady, in his survey of computational approaches to image understanding, stated that attention had shifted from restrictions on the domain of application (e.g., dealing with only regular polyhedra) to restrictions on visual abilities — i.e., topics corresponding to identifiable modules in the human visual system (e.g., binocular stereo vision).

Incidentally, Brady's schematic summary of his survey still provides a useful framework for presenting the big picture of work in computer vision systems. Figure 7.12 is a schematic summary that is largely based on Brady's earlier one; it may provide a useful overview of much of this chapter.

SEEING AS PERCEIVING

Barrow and Tenenbaum (1981) state that "a high-performance, general-purpose [vision] system must embody a great deal of knowledge in its models to accommodate the diversity of appearance found in real imagery." 'Model based' is a poor description (particularly in the light of the very restrictive systems mentioned above that characterize their approach as model based) of what looks to be an enormously complex computational task involving dynamic and subtle interaction between top-down and bottom-up processes (or "a delicate balance . . . between data-directed and goal-directed search," as Barrow & Tenenbaum put it).

To reinforce their point, they present the picture of a Dalmatian dog (i.e., that species of canine whose coat resembles dark blobs of shadow dappling a light, sunlit road) crossing a light, sunlit road which is dappled with dark blobs of shadow. You've probably got the picture (metaphorically at least, even literally, if you've got Gregory's, 1970, book, or any one of a number of other books on human vision); there is no obvious dog outline, but nevertheless a fairly obvious dog romping across the image. Alternative ways to make this point about the power of human vision is with a polar bear in a snowstorm at the North Pole, a black cat down a coalmine at midnight (this might be going too far), or even a zebra in a toolshed after a riotous night out (a precondition on the observer, not the zebra).

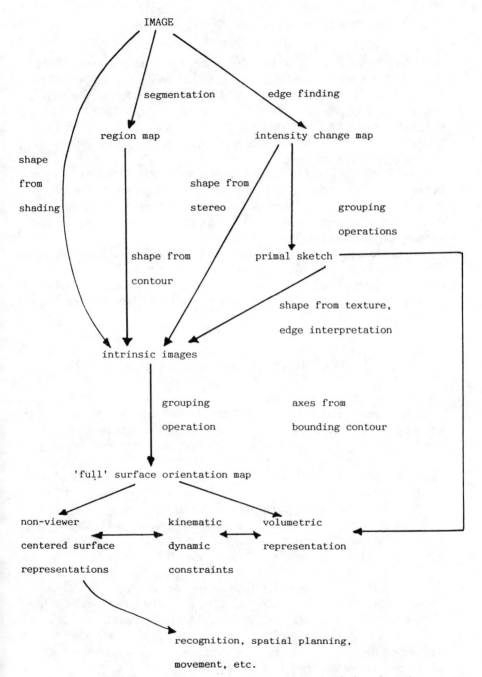

Figure 7.12. A schematic summary of computer vision work [based on Figure 1 in Brady, 1982, p. 9]

From "Computational Approaches to Image Understanding," by J.M. Brady, 1982, *Computational Surveys, 14* (1), p. 9. Copyright 1982 by Association for Computing Machinery. Reprinted by permission.

So how do we do it? Is success predicated upon the massively parallel wiring job that we all come equipped with? Or is the crucial factor that vast and unbelievably versatile database, our knowledge of the world, that presumably resides somewhere (or everywhere) within our brain-case? Or is our visual prowess largely a result of a sophisticated integration of these two rather different approaches to the processing of the masses of optical signals?

Barrow and Tenenbaum (1981) discuss very briefly some lessons from human vision that relate to attempts to construct computer vision systems. They point out that humans perceive boundaries and contours that do not depend on high contrast, nor texture change, etc., as the following images demonstrate (see Figure 7.13).

The circle and triangle that you "see" in the Figure 7.13 are illusory, aren't they? Oversight and hallucination seem to be inconvenient but unavoidable outcomes of the human approach to seeing. Let's examine why, and what the implications might be for computer vision.

OVERSIGHT AND HALLUCINATION

As good as human vision is (or as poor as it is, as a vulture might say), sometimes we fail to see things that are (or were) demonstrably there, and we "see" things that aren't there: in a word (or, more precisely, two words), oversight and hallucination. Not very nice things to say about anybody (especially the latter, which smacks of "loony" and clearly goes against the grain of the rationalist fiction about human intelligence). Nevertheless, fooling the human visual system is one of the easiest tricks to do. No self-respecting book that touches on human vision can avoid the inclusion of one or two visual illusion pictures (Gregory, 1970, and Rock, 1983, for example; the former is quite old, but the treatment is sumptuous — an old limousine and a new dune buggy).

These deficiencies of the human visual system should come as no surprise to any but the committed rationalist. For me they are necessary characteristics of intelligent behavior. They are an inevitable result of the guesswork that is necessary to make decisions and generate conclusions from masses of incomplete information within some reasonable time. Misleading this unconscious guessing mechanism just seems to be particularly easy in the visual system. Why is this?

Perkins (1983) considers the question of "Why the Human Perceiver Is a Bad Machine." He adds to the list of weaknesses: gross lapses of metric accuracy and limited abilities for error correction, backup, and top-down control. He assumes that the human weaknesses would not be

Figure 7.13. A disembodied spider and three PAC men having a chat

tolerated in a machine vision system (an example of a general question to which we shall return in the final chapter). He suggests that the reason why the human is a bad machine is that, for some reason, it doesn't matter, and that, if we explore how it is that the human perceiver can be so careless and get away with it, we might gain useful insights to assist in the development of perceiving machines.

He maintains that

the human example suggests that such physicist's care with the contributing components — shading, texture, Gestalt regularities, models, and so on — may not be the only, or even the best course. A pragmatist's perceiving machine might be designed with a more slapdash approach to some hypothetico-deductive aspects of control, but with constraint handling that incorporates the three principles outlined earlier. (Perkins, 1983, p. 360)

His three principles are:

1. *Need to know*: proceed beyond a sketchy representation only on a need-to-know basis.
2. *Reliable steps*: construct a representation of the stimulus through a series of reliable recognitions and inferences, following whatever course promises high reliability.
3. *Avoid search*: rarely explore deeply alternative representations.

Another reason for the weaknesses of human perception is that our current guessing strategy evolved in one sort of environment and is thus ill-equipped to process visual input from this new and alien environment that we all now live in (with the honorable exception of the bushmen and women of the Kalahari Desert). From this line of argument we should perhaps be quite surprised (and thankful) that oversight and hallucinations don't intrude a good deal more in our daily dealings with automobiles, office blocks, and Coke machines. Maybe less of our perceptual mechanisms are hard-wired in by evolution than I am suggesting. Perhaps we are born with significant plasticity such that detailed perceptual strategies are more shaped by the environment that we grow up in than the environment that out forebears rampaged around in. I'll leave this, like most sticky questions that I run into, as an exercise for the reader.

A further interesting feature of the ease with which the human visual system can be fooled (and one that impinges directly on AI vision work in a general sense at least) is the persistence of good visual illusions. Even when the source of the illusion is explained and the fact of the illusion is clearly demonstrated, we are still quite likely to go on seeing the original illusion.

Why is this? If the power of the human visual system is, as I've been advocating with my customary lack of subtlety, due to the integration of top-down and bottom-up processes, why doesn't the knowledge of the illusion (both that it is an illusion and how it works in some sense) step in and prevent the erroneous interpretation of the image. Why does our brain, apprised of all the relevant information, just sit back and allow us to make the same mistake time and again?

THE MODULARITY OF HUMAN VISION

There are several arguments to the effect that certain subdomains of human intelligence are modular (Fodor, 1983) or cognitively impenetrable (Pylyshyn, 1984). I run the risk of trivializing both arguments by giving you only a few-sentence summary, as each takes a whole book to present properly. But I'll chance it.

They both argue that, although perception is clearly influenced by one's beliefs in a rationally explicable way, there is a core component, the transducer, whose behavior is explainable in terms of intrinsic biological and physical properties of the system. Explanation of the behavior of such a module does not require appeal to the influence of the larger system's beliefs and goals (the cognitive processes) — it is cognitively impenetrable.

Casual observations that support the idea of the modularity or informational encapsulation of some significant component of the visual system are that we don't always see what we expect to see (sometimes we see what's really there, which may be quite different from what we expected to be there), and that visual illusions persist despite full knowledge of their illusory nature. One forceful suggestion is that some early component of our vision system, a bottom-up transducer, is impenetrable to our more general beliefs and expectations. If this is the case, and a somewhat special case under the canopy of general intelligence, then we have every reason to expect more progress and success in AI vision work than in most other subfields. This is because, to a first approximation, we should be able to build good AI vision systems while ignoring the awkward problems of both representing and bringing to bear such cognitive phenomena as beliefs and intentions.

At the same time, as it appears that human vision is to some degree and to some extent a single-minded, bottom-up process which ignores the cognitive directives of its attached brain, sometimes and in some way it is also paying attention to and obeying these orders issued from on high. As usual there is no simple and clear answer, but there is an obvious place to keep looking for guidance if not for clear answers — the human brain and its peripheral equipment.

EYEBALLS AND NERVOUS OPTICS

Perhaps more than any other subfield of AI, vision work has been tied to the nature of the corresponding human subsystem: eyeball, retina, optic tract, visual cortex, etc. are all human anatomical features that are directly involved in our ability to see, and whose functional characteristics have been exploited in computer vision work. Starting where it all begins, I think, we can look at some of the characteristics of the biological system that have had an impact on efforts to construct seeing machines.

BIOLOGICAL FEATURE DETECTORS

Hubel and Wiesel (1962), it seems, put the cat among the pigeons (or, less metaphorically, put the electrodes among the cat) when they reported the presence of quite elaborate feature detectors built into the wetware of the cat's brain.

The light receptors in the back of the eyeball (the cat's eyeball) are so connected up in the tangle of nerve cells that leads from the back of the eye into the brain (the optic tract) that groups of receptors constitute feature detectors based in individual neurons. In other words, it is not the case that the vast array of light receptors on the back of the eyeball (the retina) pick up the light, and then the neural cabling quickly runs it all into the brain for treatment. It turns out that a lot of early processing is done within the cable en route to the brain. The brain only gets a heavily censored version of the actual visual input, which is both good and bad. On the positive side the brain, which is typically very busy doing many things apart from seeing what the eyes are up to, receives a choked-down and somewhat organized version of the chaotic overabundance of stimuli that are typically raining down on the average cat's retinae (if that's the word for two retinas). But on the debit side, the brain only has the optic tract's interpretation of what is out there to work with; it has no access to the original data. And although evolution has probably done a good job in weeding out the feature detectors that would be more of a liability than an asset to the free range cat, 'unnatural' scenes can be expected to give rise to systematic perceptual errors (as is indeed the case, at least with humans if not with cats).

A commonly mentioned type of built-in feature detector is the on-off surround. We can look at this in detail, see how it contributes to higher level feature detectors, and how we end up with the grandmother cell if we're not careful. In addition, we shall see the vital role played by lateral inhibition (a firm favorite with connectionists, you may remember from Chapter 3).

Consider our old friend, the abrupt change in intensity (don't get worried, no more differentiations, I promise) and the following line of light detectors which pick up this string of intensity values (see Figure 7.14). The back-up wiring is also given (I'll spare you the nervy details; they're both quite unmemorable and liable to lead us into the sick-making biological realms of blood and guts, if we don't steer well clear from the outset).

The line of crosses represent the intensity of the light falling on the retinal receptors, as measured by a disinterested instrument — a physicist's system, quite literally. The receptor cells, highly excited by the intense light and less excited by the low-intensity light, pass their excitment back to the nerve cells behind them. But these nerve cells are connected to their nearest neighbors by lateral inhibitory connections (i.e., the more a cell is excited, the more it reduces its neighbors' excitement and thereby becomes even more excited itself). Lateral inhibition is a sharpening

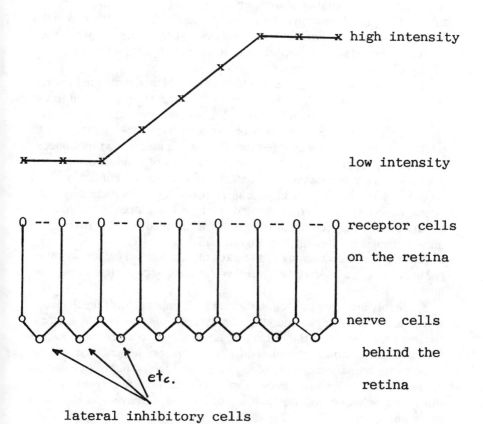

Figure 7.14.   A variation in light intensity across a slice of retina

mechanism; it enhances contrast by concentrating activity at the places where there are abrupt increases in intensity across several cells.

{A break for tedious rather than gruesome detail; feel free as usual to skip on to the next paragraph. Nerve cells or neurons do not just accumulate activity, as the connectionists would have you believe. What I refer to as increased excitation is manifest in the biological neuron as an increase in the rate at which it fires; i.e., it sends out more electrical pulses per second as it becomes more excited. The unamused neuron just sitting in the net, minding its own business, is typically idling — firing at some base rate; then inhibition can slow it down and excitation can speed it up.}

Each laterally inhibitorily connected cell takes from its neighbors a quantity of excitement proportional to its own level of excitement and thereby further increases its own excitement by something like the amount of excitement stolen. The more excited a cell is, the more it drains its neighbors of excitation. So, when all are high or all are low in excitation, nothing much happens as a result of lateral inhibition (there's just a lot of excitement trading, and all come out just as excited as when they went in). But an abrupt discontinuity in excitation level across a line of neurons becomes accentuated.

Lateral inhibition is thus a mechanism by which a stimulated neuron reduces the stimulation of other neurons to a degree proportional to the original level of stimulation. In plainer English, the more excited a neuron is, the more it reduces the level of excitement of those colleagues to which it is connected by an inhibitory link. It is a mechanism for concentrating excitement (or activity, as in the WTASs of connectionism, you may remember) and enhancing contrast. In the current context we can modify our original abrupt change in intensity levels as dictated by the lateral inhibitory connections behind the light receptors. The abrupt intensity change that fell on the retina is transformed into the even more abrupt change, as illustrated in Figure 7.15.

The result is a sharpening of the intensity change, an enhancement of contrast; an edge is perceived (Mother Nature's second derivative, you might say).

A suitably arranged collection of such edge enhancement mechanisms gives the on-off center surround mechanism. This is a more or less circular area of receptors on the retina that funnel down to a neuron in such a way that the neuron is stimulated by the transitory appearance, on the appropriate retinal receptors, of a circularish blob of light (a center-on response). There are a number of variants of this feature detector, but as this is the only one that we shall see again, I shall leave it at that, and move on.

A line of such on-center feature detectors will amount to a bar detec-

high intensity

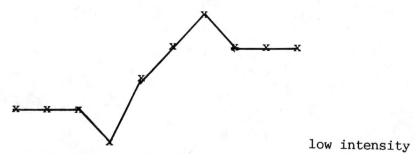

low intensity

Figure 7.15.   The brain's view of Figure 7.14

tor, and indeed Hubel and Wiesel (probing back along the optic tract) found such cells; they called them "simple" cells. Simple cells respond strongly to a bar of light at a certain orientation.

Moving right along en route to the brain, there are "complex" cells which respond to a bar of light of a particular orientation moving perpendicular to its length. There are even "hypercomplex" cells, and who knows where it will end.

So, back along the optic tract and into the brain proper, there is evidence for the combination of these more primitive feature detectors to yield ever more complex feature detector cells. But the idea that fixed detector units of ever more complex patterns are to be found as we probe deeper and deeper into the brain is a long and slippery slope down to the idea that there is a cell that uniquely responds to every pattern that we can recognize. There is even a cell that fires when you see and thus recognize your grandmother — the legendary grandmother cell. Hofstadter (1979) has the following drole illustration of the behavior of a grandmother cell (see Figure 7.16).

This seems unlikely. So somewhere along the line we must free ourselves from the wired-in pattern recognition scheme and switch to some other more versatile strategy to account for our phenomenal recognition capability. But what exactly is it? I don't know, but I can refer you back to connectionist theory (Chapters 3 and 6); it's nothing like a complete answer, but perhaps it is the best that we can do at the moment. Feldman (1981) does address the grandmother-cell issue, the notion of "pontifical cells," and claims that belief in specific functions for individual units does not entail a trip down the slippery path to the grandmother cell. "The general idea," according to Feldman (1981, p. 62), "is that each cell (or unit) carries out a computation that can be sharply defined but may only

Stimulus   Response

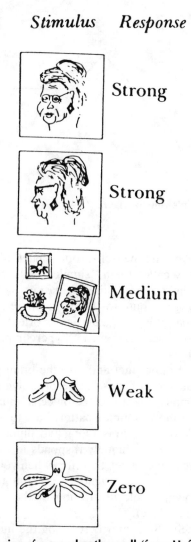

Strong

Strong

Medium

Weak

Zero

Figure 7.16.   The behavior of a grandmother cell (from Hofstadter, 1979)

From *Godel, Escher, and Bach: An Eternal Golden Braid,* by D.R. Hofstadter, 1979, New York: Basic Books. Reprinted by permission.

be meaningful as part of a larger unit. Exactly the same condition applies to individual components of an electronic circuit.''

Interestingly, Hofstadter is left floundering at this point in his weaving of the ''eternal golden braid'' (or EGB—not to be confused with EBG in Chapter 9) with a thoroughly unlikely extrapolation (i.e., the grandmother cell) but nothing to offer in its stead. This brings up a point in the sociology of AI.

Christianity did not become widespread, or even the significance of Christ generally recognized (either as a blasphemer or as a savior), until years after he was long gone. If we had had TV then, it is true, the story would have got around much faster, but still there would have been a lag time. The year A.D. 50 would still not have seen Jesus as global celebrity, even if the world had been blessed in those early days with MacNeil-Lehrer, the 9 o'clock news, and UPI. Well, the story of the coming of connectionism is somewhat similar (even though it is indeed a second coming, you may remember). Hofstadter's book was not published B.C. (i.e., Before Connectionism) but in the year A.C. 1 (i.e., Anno Connectioni 1); nevertheless, connectionism did not get a mention in 777 word-stuffed pages — this would be unthinkable now barely two digits A.C.

HUMAN PERCEPTUAL BEHAVIOR

Having looked briefly at the innards of the system, let's continue the search for clues to guide the design of computer vision systems by now observing what this mechanism does. There is a depressingly large volume of empirical data, generated by psychologists and cognitive scientists, gathered from (almost) every conceivable and highly controlled (therefore unrealistic, or not ecologically valid — this is the favored terminology, I believe) situation wherein people (usually psychology students) are perceiving things. This ocean of data is used to support or refute theories of human perception, but unfortunately most such theories are couched in terms so vague and ill-defined that they provide little or no guidance for the person who wishes to construct an AI vision system.

Meanwhile, in the AI camp there are a lot of implemented and thus well-specified models that successfully see things in certain classes of images. The contrast is in terms of precision and general validity in contexts that are perhaps ecologically invalid as against particular existence proofs of very small (and also often unreal) portions of an extensive phenomenon. So there is as yet not a great deal of direct interaction between the wealth of precise data collected by empirical psychologists and the working detailed models generated by AI types (we shall return, in Chapter 10, to this question of lack of interaction between what one would expect to be mutually supportive domains). Nevertheless, there are some attempts to bring together these two classes of approach to the understanding of human perception, and we can examine one of them, but first let me attempt to structure the phenomenon called top-down information.

BREAKING UP CONTEXT

There are really two issues that I want to deal with here: the components of contextual information, and the strategies of integration with the bottom-up information. Any scheme for dividing top-down information into separate components will of necessity be somewhat arbitrary. Nevertheless, I'll present some schemes whose merit (if any) will reside more in the convenience of having some structure to discuss than in any fundamental validity of the structural decomposition employed.

STRUCTURING TOP-DOWN INFORMATION

One approach to the partitioning of top-down information, which occurs in several models of visual perception, as you will see, is first a three-part division: world knowledge, local knowledge, and immediate knowledge. World knowledge (a commonly muted and equally commonly unimplemented idea in AI) is the more or less static knowledge of the world that we inhabit (sometimes called common-sense knowledge). In the context of a machine vision system applied to, say, countryside scenes, world knowledge includes general information that the sky will be above the ground, that trees will be growing out of the ground, that houses will be sitting on it, etc. More specific aspects of world knowledge are that houses are solid and likely to be approximately cubical with roofs on top, etc. Also we know that trees have a solid, approximately cylindrical trunk with a mass of leaves and branches on the top, and so on. The list appears to be endless, the amount of general information that we have about the world dispersed throughout our synaptic junctions appears to be depressingly large; depressing, that is, if one's goal is to represent anything like it within a computer.

Local knowledge is information that is fairly specific to the recognition task at hand (or eye). It may also involve relatively immutable facts about the world (although more task-specific facts and inferences from world knowledge); it also involves a significant component of transient information — things that happen to be true in the current specific context. Knowledge of local geography, such as the presence of poor soil, may cause some distant vegetation to be perceived as moorland rather than, say, a wheat field.

This transient knowledge may be further divided into truths that hold somewhat fortuitously and perhaps quite transitorily in the current context, and more immutable truths that are nevertheless quite specific to the current context and have thus been actively inferred from the more general world knowledge. For example, transitory information that might impact on the interpretation of a country scene is the presence of dark storm clouds in one portion of the sky. A more immutable but scene-specific source of information would be the inference that a dark strip through the distant forest is the ravine that you know exists in that forest.

Finally, we have immediate knowledge. It is characterized by extreme transitoriness; the truth of this knowledge is very short lived. This is information derived from the immediately prior perceptions, and, in the extreme, it may be information derived from one part of an image that influences interpretation of another part of the same image. For example, prior observation of a car heading off in a certain direction might allow you to infer that the moving object, gleaming in the sun in the distance, is a car, the car that you saw earlier. This inference might be further reinforced by the observation of a road in the foreground which disappears from sight but in the direction of movement of the gleaming object.

In actuality, immediate knowledge extends from clearly top-down information (i.e., information that is derived from sources external to the current image) to information that is bottom-upish (i.e., the information being used may derive from some other aspect or part of the same image).

In general terms I am trying to decompose top-down information into a spectrum that ranges from immutable universal facts to transient problem-specific facts. It is not this simple; it never is, is it? Thus, the act of perception may result in a modification to our world knowledge. For example, living in the Northern Hemisphere, you may go through life believing that the sun is always to the south, especially at about lunch time. On visiting Australia and observing that the solar collectors on the houses are all directed northwards, what may first be perceived as a fundamental blunder may subsequently serve to modify your world knowledge of the relationship between the sun and the earth.

We are straying and speculating, but this we must perforce do or else eschew most of the questions about top-down information. Most surveys of machine vision treat top-down information in an extremely limited sense, if they consider it at all. Ballard and Brown (1982, p. 346), for example, discuss "belief maintenance and goal achievement" in the context of machine vision, but they have no examples of use of such top-down information in implemented systems. Sadly, it is this vast domain of possibilities that machine vision systems have yet to penetrate; it is also the domain in which intelligent generalized vision systems all lie, so we must push on into the unknown.

On the bright side, there are groups of researchers that are concentrating on the knowledge-based side of computer vision. Thus the VISIONS group at the University of Massachusetts have, for many years, been developing "a general system for knowledge-based interpretation of natural scenes, such as house, road, and urban scenes" (Riseman & Hanson,

1987, p. 289) — well, fairly natural scenes anyway. They address the problem of attaching semantic labels, such as *window,* to portions of the image by creating tentative "islands of reliability" to which the subsequent context-directed processing can be anchored. To a large extent the initial processes are independent and thus invite parallel treatment. "The relations and expected consistencies between local interpretations form the basis for a cooperative/competitive style of processing among the possible interpretations as the system attempts to extend the islands to uninterpreted parts of the image" (Riseman & Hanson, 1987, p. 285).

The behavior in AI, when faced with a loose and general theory, is to construct programs, and to explore the implications of concrete manifestations of that theory; we shall look at one such program as well as at the VISIONS system described by Riseman and Hanson. (This methodology has its strengths and weaknesses, which we touched on in Chapter 3 and will get back to in Chapter 10.) But, prior to the examination of this exploration of the domain of top-down information in a mechanization of visual perception, let us take one example of a program that comes from the psychological side of this question—a programmed cognitive model of visual perception.

A COGNITIVE MODEL OF WORD RECOGNITION

McDonald (1981) constructed and explored the behavior of a programmed model of human word recognition behavior. As a model in cognitive science, rather than an AI system built for practical purposes, its prime goal was to "explain" all of the known empirical data derived from humans performing variously controlled versions of lexical decision tasks (roughly, word recognition). In particular, this model aimed to account for those classes of data that were considered problematic with respect to earlier models (e.g., the Logogen model, Morton, 1969).

The process of word recognition is considered by some to be prototypical in the sense that it contains many of the essential characteristics of perception in general. A commonly observed phenomenon in this domain is called *textual facilitation:* context, in the sense of immediately prior input (i.e., immediate knowledge in our earlier classification scheme), has a major effect on the speed with which we can recognize words. In particular, if two successively presented words are highly related (e.g., LION followed by TIGER), then the recognition of the second word is significantly faster than when the two words are unrelated (e.g., NURSE followed by TIGER). Similarly, frequently occurring words are recognized faster than rare words — the *frequency effect*. This latter facilitation can be accounted for by global knowledge. Our general knowledge of word occurrence frequencies biases our perception of words, but how?

In the same way that the mathematical engineers have great fun with the formal operators for early vision processing, so the psychologists revel in the behavioral intricacies elicited by controlling different combinations of variables in an experimental setup. In an uncharacteristic effort not to expose my biases, I'll treat both of these manic behaviors with the same degree of elucidation; that is, I'll gloss over the grisly details as usual.

So, in broad brush terms, the activation-verification model can account for more of the recorded data than the earlier models can. It posits a dual-process mechanism: a combination of top-down and bottom-up information which generates a list of candidate words for recognition, and a verification process that compares the candidate words with further bottom-up information. In effect the extra explanatory power of the activation-verification model can be accounted for by the verification process, which "screens" candidate perceptions and thus weeds out many top-down generated errors before recognition is reported. This behavior accords well with the data. Humans do make perceptual errors in word recognition but not as many as a purely top-down biased strategy suggests.

A further refinement of this model suggests that candidate words generated from purely top-down information (both world and local knowledge) are screened for recognition prior to any candidates generated largely from bottom-up information. And again the postulation of this structure is driven by the need to account for the data. One such piece of data is the already-mentioned speed of recognition of highly related words. Figure 7.17 is a schematic abstraction of the activation-verification model of word recognition.

As you can see, in this model bottom-up information plays two distinct roles: It contributes to the selection of secondary candidates for recognition (secondary in the sense that these candidates are considered only after all of the contextual candidates have failed to get through the verification process); it is also the prime source of information for the verification process.

A second significant feature of this model is the postulation of two separate lists of candidates for recognition, generated from different mixes of top-down information, and one list takes precedence over the other. The significance of this aspect of the model from our current perspective is that a top-down component (derived from the prior context component of immediate knowledge) generates the top-priority candidates, which are subsequently subjected to a verification check against bottom-up information. The candidates generated on the basis of bottom-up information are clearly secondary; they are only subject to verification, and thus possible recognition, if all of the top-down generated candidates fail.

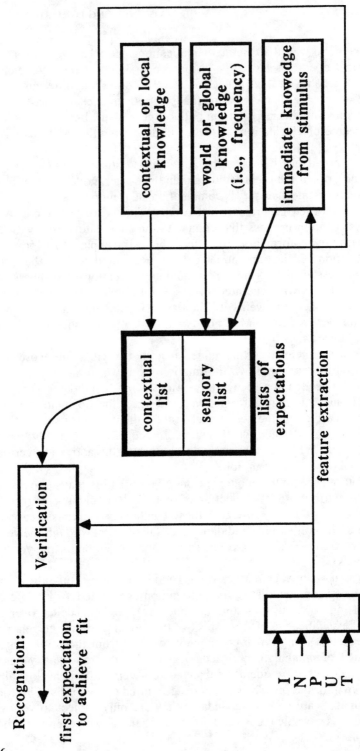

Figure 7.17. The activation-verification model of word recognition

In sum, this model suggests both a fairly specific division of top-down information, and a similarly detailed strategy of integration of top-down and bottom-up information. But the significance of the explanatory power of this model, finely tuned as it is to account for the data from tightly controlled experimental setups, is as always open to question when we consider human perception in the real, unconstrained world.

A second approach to the structuring of top-down information can be found in a more typical AI vision project.

THE EYE OF THE ROBOT

As part of a project to develop an industrial robot, but one that can function efficiently in an environment that is far less constrained than is currently the case, a module for visual perception has been implemented and tested (Partridge, Johnston, & Lopez, 1987, gives an overview of the project). The robot is termed a *cognitive industrial robot,* but, as is usual in AI, the attributed cognitiveness is more accurately descriptive of the long-term goal of the project than it is of the current implementation — the chosen name describes the hopeware rather than the hard- or software. But, to get back to the actual project, in order to function efficiently (or even function at all) in a flexibly fixtured environment (i.e., a working environment in which the customarily stringent requirements for the precise placing and orientation of known objects is relaxed), the robot attempts to discover and exploit the environmental consistencies manifest in each unique setup.

We have attempted to exploit the maxim: the unpredictability of the world makes intelligence necessary; the predictability makes it possible. In other words, the fact that significant aspects of the work environment are not prespecified means that we require an AI robot, and in order for it to function intelligently, it must detect and exploit the environmental constancies that do happen to exist.

The robotics system in question is a hand-eye robot. It is the core of the vision module, the perception algorithm, that we shall be examining. This algorithm constitutes an attempt to maximize the efficiency of recognition of important objects in an input image with respect to the robot's current task (such as, pick up a ball). The algorithm exploits top-down knowledge (general world knowledge, local knowledge, and immediate knowledge) in order to predict and check for expected objects, rather than analyze the image exhaustively and then select the closest matches. Said another way: The algorithm emphasizes top-down processes in order to minimize bottom-up or data-driven processing. It was designed on the basis of a general theory of how two parameters, *expectation* and *utility* (Partridge, Johnston, & Lopez, 1987), influence intelligent decision making, together with the fairly clear goal of producing a system that can exploit knowledge of its environment—an environment that is highly constrained by human standards, but is open and unstructured by the standards of industrial robotics.

Figure 7.18 provides an overview of the perception algorithm. The input information is an image (a 200 + 256 array of pixels generated by a video camera) and top-down information that divides approximately into three categories: a conventional "model" of the object being looked for an *expectation* as to where that object is likely to be, and a *utility* value which tells the system how important a correct identification is.

The emphasis in the vision system for the robot was practical efficiency rather than modeling human vision. Thus, although we attempted to exploit a maximum of top-down information, we also attempted to distill it down to the minimum critical information needed by the perception algorithm. Hence, the top-down information that is finally fed into the perception algorithm is little more than values for the expectedness and utility parameters (neither of which are necessarily single numbers, incidentally).

The earlier three-fold subdivision of top-down knowledge can now be superimposed on the robotics problem.

World knowledge (only an infinitesimal portion of which is actually implemented, as usual) is composed of knowledge of the manner in which objects behave in this particular world (e.g., they fall when dropped, balls roll and blocks don't), and a *catalogue* of models of the objects in the world. The first component, which is something akin to the naive physics (i.e., the 'simple,' very approximate physics of the man in the street, not the precise natural laws of the physicist) work in AI (see Hayes, 1979, 1984a, for the basic papers) is virtually absent in our current implementation. It is easy, and quite tempting, to add some isolated snippets of such knowledge (say, if dropped object is block look directly below dropping position; if ball then look around) which could then be demonstrated in highly contrived, casual-looking set pieces — true AI demo-mode. That is, we could devise situations that used just the odds and ends of world knowledge actually implemented and therefore appeared to be quite intelligent without mentioning that the system fails utterly if the demonstration task is varied at all.

General principles are available, such as those embodied in Newton's laws of motion, and a small set of closely related general rules, known as the principles of apparent motion (Ramachandran & Antis, 1986), have been incorporated in the world knowledge of the robot.

The principles of apparent motion are particularly interesting, even if I say so myself. There are three principles which seem to capture the behavior of humans when faced with a sequence of somewhat similar im-

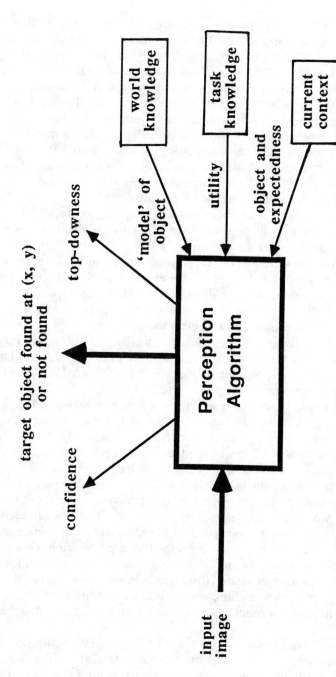

Figure 7.18. A sketch of the perception algorithm

269

ages. So, if a ball, say, is seen in one image and then recognized again in the next image in a somewhat different position, the principles mentioned will tell us whether the two ball-images will be perceived in terms of two different balls or one ball which moved in the interval between the images; it all depends on a number of fairly well-specifiable relationships between the two ball-images, relationships such as displacement, relative size and brightness, apparent direction of motion, etc. Furthermore, if the sequence of images is longer than two, these apparent motion principles can be used to generate expectations of where a goal object is likely to be in the next image. But these principles are not foolproof, not at all. It is very easy to set up the sequence of images so that the principles lead the robot to highly inefficient, and even incorrect, identification of objects in an image. They are heuristics that humans appear to use, and therefore we assume that they embody an optimal point of tradeoff between efficiency and accuracy in the long run.

So, world knowledge as far as our robotics system is currently implemented consists of a catalogue of models (about 20), and some general principles of apparent motion (three principles). That is clearly a pathetic travesty of what world knowledge should really be, but it's about par for the course. Ballard and Brown (1982) mention a visual perception program that finds tumors in chest radiographs (Ballard, 1976), but the top-down component seems to again be little more than some cursory knowledge about lung tumor location ("they are found in lungs" — is that all?) and about tumor size.

Local knowledge for the robot is primarily knowledge of the task(s) that it is to accomplish. Knowledge of a task is a plan for executing the task, which is relatively (but not totally) static knowledge. A significant dynamic component of local knowledge is comprised of the perceived environmental constancies of its current work environment (for example, that a certain target object is always found in a certain region of the image). It assimilates this component of local knowledge as a result of experience of working within a given environment. Thus this knowledge is dynamic in that it is not prespecified but gleaned from experience over time. In addition, there is no guarantee that a perceived environmental constancy is in some absolute sense a constant and not just a misperception or a temporary constancy that will disappear either gradually over time or abruptly. Hence, this component of local knowledge is inherently dynamic in that environmental constants may appear and disappear at any time.

What we have to deal with here is not only the fundamental unreliability of induction (see Chapter 9 for gruesome details) but also induction over real-world phenomena when no two repetitions are exactly the same. Induction in well-defined, abstract worlds is only a subproblem of induction in the real world.

This dynamic aspect of the robot's knowledge shades into immediate knowledge in that there are also environmental facts that are not expected to hold true beyond the task currently being executed. These highly transient constancies fall into the class of immediate knowledge under my knowledge partitioning scheme. For example, if a ball was recognized in the previous image at a certain location (and stationary, a deduction from the few previous images), and the robot did not explicitly manipulate it between images, then it will be confidently expected to appear in the same location in the next image. Thus, knowledge from immediately prior perceptions (both visual and tactile in the specific case of the hand-eye robot) can usefully be brought to bear for fast recognition of the necessary components of subsequent images.

As the last sentence implies, the vision module of the robotics system typically does not analyze complete images. The need-to-know principle of Perkins (mentioned earlier) is fundamental to our system; complete, bottom-up image analysis is only undertaken as a last resort.

The top-down information is focused by the use of our expectedness measures. To begin with, it is never the case that our system is confronted with an image and the task of identifying everything in that image. All invocations of the perception algorithm are within some context that specifies the object to be found (the target object). In addition to specifying the target object, all relevant top-down information is condensed into an expectedness measure (when, where, and how the object is expected to appear in the image).

In an effort to ensure that the inevitable errors will be benign, the system also generates a measure of the cost of a wrong perception — the utility parameter. Whereas immediate knowledge is typically the main contributor to expectedness, local knowledge is typically the major determinant of utility: The criticality of being correct about a perceived target object is, to first approximation, determined by the cost of incorrect visual information for that particular object at the current point in task execution.

World knowledge, as you may have discerned, is not contributing much to either of the main parameters (although the principles of apparent motion can have a significant effect on expectedness). This is primarily because the current implementation of world knowledge is a travesty of the general concept. More realistic implementations would have both a much larger selection of objects modeled and many other subdomains of world knowledge, such as beliefs, intentions, and goals. These latter classes of world knowledge would, for example, be expected to contribute significantly to the utility measure that is critical to our algorithm. Thus, the cost of being wrong about what you are seeing is dependent upon general goals like survival and minimizing personal discomfort, as well as upon achieving the completion of some task at hand. None of this richness is included in our current implementation of the robot's vision system, although there is clearly scope for expanding the information sources that contribute to the control of the perception algorithm. We might, for example, implement general goals in the world knowledge of the system, goals such as, avoid harming people, avoid damaging the environment, avoid self-damage, etc.

Nevertheless, when all of these limitations are taken into account, the perceptual system does behave in a way that is at least reminiscent of human behavior, and it is surprisingly comparable to the cognitive model of word recognition behavior which I described earlier. The table below summarizes the behavior of the perception algorithm.

case	1	2	3	4	5	6	7	8
expectedness	high	high	low	low	high	high	low	high
utility	low	high	high	low	high	high	high	low
correct identification of the target object	yes	yes	yes	yes	yes	yes	yes	no
correct expectation	yes	yes	yes	yes	no	no	no	no
time to identify	1.00	1.31	1.34	0.99	1.61	6.06	1.55	1.08
confidence	low	high	high	low	high	high	high	low
top-downess	high	mid	mid	high	low	low	low	high

As you can see, the algorithm exhibits fast correct recognition when the target object is correctly predicted (cases 1 to 4). {Gruesome detail: The times have all been adjusted relative to case 1. In actuality, for case 1 recognition took nearly 2 seconds, but this has no real meaning, as we were exploring only the logistics of information integration, not absolute speeds of algorithm execution — substitution of hardware components for program modules of our totally software implementation can easily produce orders of magnitude increases in speed.} Slow correct recognition is observed when the prediction is incorrect, but there is a high cost associated with being wrong (in Perkins's terminology, an error in this circumstance would not be benign — this is case 6), and fast incorrect recognition in the same situation when the error is benign (case 8).

Cases 5 and 6 appear to be very similar in the above table, except that, in case 6, recognition took five times longer than in case 5. The information missing from the table is that the incorrect expectation led the perception algorithm to a portion of the image which was empty in case 5; thus it quickly realized that the expectation was misleading and immediately brought in more bottom-up information to achieve correct recognition. In case 6, the misleading expectation focused the algorithm's attention (if I may casually impute consciousness to the algorithm) on the wrong object, but one that bore some resemblance to the target object; thus the algorithm wasted a lot of time attempting to confirm recognition of a seemingly correct (but actually incorrect) pattern in the image before it finally abandoned this part of the image and brought in more bottom-up searching to finally find the target object elsewhere.

This last feature is, we believe, crucial to any realistic perceptual strategy: dynamic flexibility in the integration of top-down and bottom-up information such that emphasis can be smoothly shifted from one to the other on the bases of both early tentative inferences from the bottom-up information and subsequent reappraisals of the reliability of the top-down information. Perception is not a case of top-down or bottom-up information; it is a problem of dynamically mixing the two so as to follow the path of maximum reliability (recall Perkins', 1983, principle of reliable steps).

GENERAL THEORIES OF VISUAL PERCEPTION

"Its all very well to ramble on about programs that can be made to behave as expected in a few (totally artificial) situations, or to wax enthusiastic about a model that accounts for some data from experimental setups that are constrained beyond belief, but what does this tell us about the magic of human perception in general?" you might want to ask (and you might succeed, provided you've taken a big enough breath to begin with). This looks very like the sort of problem that, according to the tradition established a few hundred pages earlier, should be offloaded on the reader, leaving me free to push on with something more manageable. But this time I'm not going to do that.

In fact, a general theory of visual perception was extracted from the work on these two rather different computer implementations of visual perception (see Partridge, McDonald, Johnston, & Paap, 1988, for an introduction to the strengths and weaknesses of this unlikely amalgam).

The general model of visual perception emerged as shown in Figure 7.19.

Although the top-down knowledge has once more coalesced into an indivisible lump — the knowledge base — we managed to preserve the general strategy of interaction between top-down and bottom-up information.

The commonalities between the two models described above are summarized in Figure 7.19, but a couple of aspects may bear repeating. There are clear parallel and serial aspects of the model which can be related back to the discussion early in this chapter of degrees of parallelism in human visual processing. In addition, information in the input image is used in two rather different ways: Features extracted from the image play

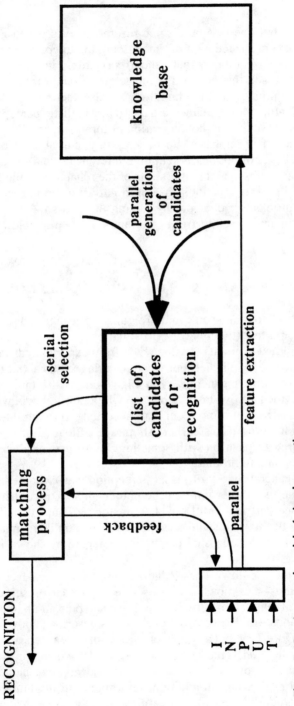

Figure 7.19. A general model of visual perception

a role in selection of the candidate objects for possible recognition, and such features also play the major role (perhaps) in the screening of the possible candidates in order to finally report recognition of one of them. Finally, we have good reasons to believe that there is some feedback of information from the screening subtask that influences the further extraction of information from the input image — neither model incorporated this aspect of the general model.

Another general, and more thoroughly explored, model is the VISIONS system for knowledge-based recognition of natural objects like houses in images. Figure 7.20 is a schematic illustration of the internal structure of the VISIONS system, as presented by Riseman and Hanson (1987).

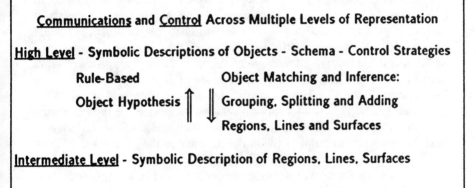

Figure 7.20.   Multiple levels of representation and processing in the VISIONS system

From "A Methodology for the Development of General Knowledge-based Vision Systems," by E.M. Riseman & A.R. Hanson, in *Vision, Brain, and Cooperative Computation* (p. 290), edited by M.A. Arbib & A.R. Hanson, 1987, Cambridge, MA: Bradford Books/MIT Press. Reprinted by permission.

The VISIONS system begins processing an image, when little is known about the scene or its contents, in a primarily bottom-up mode, and tries to generate a few reliable hypotheses about prominent image features. The resultant object hypotheses then provide the links between the image and the knowledge structures which enables control to shift to a more top-down mode. This allows the use of context and expectations in the knowledge-dependent processing which is applied to validate and extend the initial hypotheses.

A central problem is then the selection of specific subimages (Riseman and Hanson say *image events*) that are likely candidates for particular object labels. For example, the VISIONS system might choose to select a bright blue, untextured area near the top of the image as a likely candidate for the label *sky*.

The knowledge in VISIONS is represented as rules. A typical rule might map color within a specific range (say, the blues which I have called "bright blue" above) into a vote for the label *sky*. The rule which labels a collection of pixels as *grass* collects the weighted votes from rules about color, texture, location, size, and shape. Each component vote is weighted from 1 (weak) to 5 (strong or very important). An overall score for the *grass* label with respect to the specific subimage examined is computed as "a normalized weighted average of the five components" (Riseman & Hanson, 1987, p. 298). The specific function is given but is not of major importance in itself. What Riseman and Hanson do stress is that they see a need to be able to incorporate relative weightings of the individual contributions to the labeling decision, but they see also the danger of a system that leads to number twiddling in order to improve results. They finish with seven principles to guide knowledge-based research, but they make no claims for correctness or completeness of their approach. It is only a distillation of their own experiences in a problem domain that "has been so difficult that there has been little work of any generality" (p. 324).

Moving away from implemented models as the vehicle for the theory development, I can give a further example of a general scheme for human visual perception — the perceptual cycle advocated by Neisser (1976). His scheme is illustrated in Figure 7.21

For Neisser the top-down information is contained in the cognitive structures called *schemata*. They are, in his view, crucial for vision in that they prepare the perceiver to accept certain kinds of information rather than others and thus control the activity of looking. "At each moment the perceiver is constructing anticipations of certain kinds of information, that enable him to accept it as it becomes available. Often he must actively explore the optic array to make it available, by moving his eyes or his head or his body." This repeated process of anticipation, exploration, and modification constitutes the basis of the perceptual cycle illustrated above.

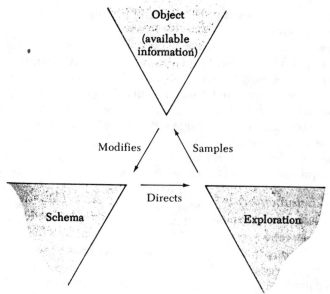

Figure 7.21.   The perceptual cycle of Neisser

From *Cognition and Reality*, (p. 21), by U. Neisser, 1976, New York: Freeman. Reprinted by permission.

According to Neisser's model there is no simple flow of information from stored knowledge (his schemata) to some central perception mechanism; it is a continuously interactive process. Even though schema direct perceptions, this does not mean that we cannot pick up unanticipated information. "Normally, however," he says, "the function of an unexpected stimulus is to initiate the cycle of perception proper."

He compares his perceptual cycle to the classical theories of perception, and does not see his proposal as a radical alternative but rather as a more generally encompassing view within which the more traditional theories can be accommodated. Thus the commonly held view that perception is the testing and confirming of hypotheses (as in Gregory, 1970, for example) is just focusing, Neisser claims, on one aspect of his perceptual cycle.

A final important aspect of a general perception mechanism concerns the ability to choose between competing models and ultimately to switch contexts in a more general sense. This selection feature is only manifest in implemented computer vision systems in the most trivial sense: there are systems that will select the most appropriate model from a very small catalogue of possibilities. All operational computer vision systems are inherently tied to a very limited domain of possibilities, so the problem of switching contexts in a radical sense does not arise. If the necessity arises, the system either crashes in ruins or merrily generates totally erroneous perceptions.

A closely related phenomenon to context switching is the recognition of unexpected information. In this latter situation attention is caught by an unexpected or novel event. This intrusion of novelty is the cue for learning (as I shall argue in Chapter 9); it is also perhaps the cue for context switching. Elsewhere I have examined the various manifesations of an input-expectation discrepancy reduction mechanism (Partridge, 1985a), its implications for context switching, and its implementation in the cognitive robotics project mentioned above. In a nutshell, the cue for context switching is a significant discrepancy between what you expected and what appears to be present (your erroneous expectations may be due to a wrong context from which they were derived), and a guide to choosing the most appropriate context may be minimization of this same discrepancy.

But, really, we currently have no idea how to organize this critical component of intelligent behavior, we just build systems that can see in one, very limited, context, and that is quite hard enough.

THE VISION OF CONNECTIONISTS

Just in case you haven't noticed, this is one chapter in which I have not been merrily thrusting CP-based alternatives into the narrative. But now is the time to see what vision systems the connectionists have been devising and building.

You have already seen a CP-based scheme for computer vision. Way back in Chapter 3 we looked at Feldman's (1981) network for reproducing the necker-cube phenomenon (see Figure 3.8 if you wish to confirm this statement). It is an example of symbolic connectionism in that the network nodes are localized (i.e., nondistributed) representations of relations such as "G hidden" or "A closer than B." It illustrates the use of lateral inhibition to simulate the alternating perception that one gets when viewing this skeletal cube. If the network is properly balanced, activity first concentrates in one of the alternative perceptions, and then, with continued exposure, to the image it should 'flip over' to the other perception, and so on.

Feldman's paper on connectionist models of visual memory (Feldman, 1981), which occurs in the "First Book of Connectionism," discusses many aspects of the CP. In particular, he makes much of the various remarkable properties of the human brain, and he argues that these properties suggest a CP-based model of human memory, especially visual memory. He states that "relaxation is the mechanism suggested here as the fundamental computational principle of neural networks'' (p. 60). Visual recognition is, for Feldman, the process of a network relaxing, or settling down, to a consistent interpretation of the sensory input.

From our introductory discussion of the massive parallelism of early image processing, we have every reason to expect that connectionistic networks of one sort or another may work very well as architectures to support image processing. In addition, certain networks, Boltzmann machines for example, would appear to offer just the right functionality for implementing the myriad of interdependent decisions (e.g., a single pixel may be noise if it is radically different from all its neighbors; otherwise, it may be part of a significant image feature) which appear to be necessary at all levels of image understanding — constraint relaxation appears to be a mechanism common to both the problem and the abstract machine.

There are a large number of successful, even practically useful, neural-network-based systems for visual recognition tasks (see, for example, the WISARD system of Aleksander, Thomas, & Bowden, 1984). In another AI book you might well find them at this point in the text, but I chose to place them (or the pointers to them) in Chapter 3. They were given some space at the end of the chapter under the rather unflattering name of bad paradigms. They are image recognition, or pattern recognition, schemes and, although they often work very well, I don't think that they have much to contribute to AI — I could be wrong. In fact, it is at this point that my grand plan (of how to lay out the domain of AI and its peripheral subjects) wears disconcertingly thin: There is a spectrum of CP-based vision systems spanning the gap between not-AI and AI systems, and there is no obvious way to slip in a firm boundary between the two classes. Aleksander (1983) discusses the emergent intelligent properties of models in precisely this subdomain of AI (or is it subdomain peripheral to AI?). For a further example, see Mesrobian and Skrzypek (1987), who describe a neural network architecture for discrimination of natural textures.

Learning is an integral part of most CP-based models. Thus, we don't tend to find CP-based models constructed for the immediate performance of some recognition task; they tend to be built to *learn* to perform the chosen task. Hence, they are models that we shall look at in the chapter on machine learning.

Hinton (1987) describes a scheme for teaching a CP-based network to recognize the same object when it is shifted sideways {translation-invariant recognition}. This may not seem like a demanding task. After all, if you can recognize a square when it's on the left side of an image, surely you can recognize exactly the same square just moved across to the right side of the next image. Of course you can, and so can a quite simple SSSP-based recognition algorithm, but consider what a problem a network faces. Parallel input of the image, en masse, down a mass of input lines will result in two quite different activation patterns being fed into the network. The problem is for the network to learn that the common subpattern in both images is to be recognized as a square, and also to generalize this knowledge so that any occurence of this subpattern will elicit output that signifies recognition of a square.

A similar project is described by Fukushima and Miyake (1982). They use a scheme of CP-based clustering — the grouping together of "similar" subsets of the input patterns {called *competitive learning* and dealt with in Chapter 9} — which is applied to the recognition of simple two-dimensional shapes in a number of different positions. After learning, the network can recognize a familiar shape in a novel position — i.e., it has generalized its recognition capability, albeit only to a very limited extent. But, according to Hinton (1989), it cheats; the learning to recognize the same shape in different positions {translation invariance again} is fudged, because there are internal layers of the network which are prewired to generalize across position.

Lehky and Sejnowski (1988) describe a CP-based system that was trained to determine surface curvatures from images of simple geometrical objects — a model of shape from shading. And again, the network was to perform this task independent of both where the curved surface occurred in the visual field, and the direction of the light source used to generate the image.

They employed a three-layer network with 122 units in the input layer, 27 in the hidden layer, and 24 in the output layer. Each unit was linked to every unit in the subsequent layer. Because they were exploring biological vision systems, the input units were constructed as either on-center or off-center units — i.e., on-center units respond with high activity when stimulated in the center and are inhibitory if simulated around the edges; off-center units have the opposite behavior. This seemingly strange functionality is found in certain real neurons (you may recall the earlier run up to the grandmother cell), which begins to explain why they chose it. But, further than this, the input layer was organized into two hexagonal arrays (with five-unit sides, which means 61 units per array, one all on-center and the other all off-center — okay?). Within each input array the receptive field centers of adjacent units overlapped. Each input image was fed into both input arrays. The 24 output units coded the system's response in terms of surface curvature magnitude and orientation. So an image of light intensities goes in (the shading information) and a description in terms of surface orientation comes out (i.e., a description of shape) — hence, shape from shading. A snapshot of the network behaving correctly, together with the input image and the output surface, is given in Figure 7.22.

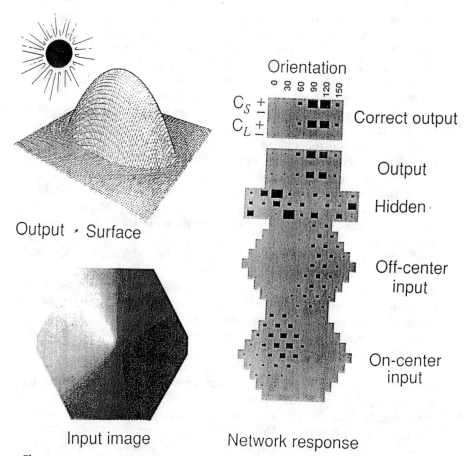

Figure 7.22.   A snapshot of the network that has learned shape from shading (from Lehky & Sejnowski, 1988)

From "Network Model of Shape-from-Shading: Neural Function Arises from both Receptive and Projective Fields," by S.R. Lehky & T.J. Sejnowski, 1988, *Nature, 333*, 452–454. Reprinted by permission.

The correct associations between the input and output units was achieved by training with the back-propagation algorithm (Chapter 9), which is a method for comparing actual output with correct output and adjusting the link weights so that it will do better next time — i.e., it is feedback error correction.

Lehky and Sejnowski (1988) report that, after starting with randomly assigned link weights, the behavior of the system leveled off when working at 88% correct after error-corrective feedback from 40,000 presentations. In addition, "the network generalized well for images not part of the training set" (p. 452). They then take some considerable space to compare the learned structure of their model with biological vision systems. From an AI-vision perspective it would have been nice to know more about the generalization properties of the trained network, but there is nothing beyond the bald statement quoted earlier.

Finally, there are many sources of further information on computer vision systems, and in most of them you'll find some AI. Horn's (1986) chunky volume on robot vision is replete with algorithmic nitty-gritty, enough to satisfy anyone who has waded through my book and come out safely on the other side overful with words but with some empty spaces where they believe algorithms ought to be. Marr's (1982) book, entitled *Vision: A Computational Investigation into the Human Representation and Processing of Visual Information,* ventures in to the intricacies of how humans might be seeing, and is well worth reading. Arbib and Hanson (1987) have edited a collection of papers entitled *Vision, Brain, and Cooperative Computation.* It is, as the title suggests, oriented towards models of biological vision systems. It contains an extensive discussion of the challenge presented by the need to devise knowledge-based computer vision systems, as well as several papers that begin to address this recognized, but largely unexplored (in terms of implemented computational models), general problem. In addition, this collection contains a final section on connectionist systems which comprises five papers. Similarly, the collection of reprinted papers on computer vision that has been edited by Fischler and Firschein (1987) contains a section composed of connectionistic contributions. It does also contain a large section entitled "Image Partitioning and Perceptual Organization," but the contents are stronger on the image partitioning than they are on the problems of perceptual organization — as you might expect. These last two hefty tomes demonstrate that the CP as now well established in the domain of computer vision, and we are sure to see its presence growing. For further perusal of CP-based vision systems you'll have to go to the journals, a number of which were mentioned as general sources of CP-based wisdom in Chapter 3.

In addition, there are some vision journals. The *IEEE Transactions on Pattern Analysis and Machine Intelligence* (*PAMI* to its friends) is not the source of AI-vision papers that its name might lead you to believe— the contents tend to concentrate on the *PA* rather than the *MI* part of the title.

8

Language Processing: what you hear is what you are

The directly informative content of natural speech is small. Information does not come naked except in the schemata of computer languages or the lexicon. It comes attenuated, flexed, coloured, alloyed by intent and the milieu in which the utterance occurs. (Steiner, 1975, p. 221)

In this chapter I shall guide the reader through the intricacies of the AI subfield optimistically misnamed *natural language processing* (NLP), which is the processing of language in all forms and at all levels; it thus includes *natural language understanding,* (NLU) as well as *computational linguistics* (CL) and a number of other neatly named subfields which will pop up when their emergence is appropriate. As this is a chapter in an AI book, I shall be taking an AI slant with respect to this subfield; thus I'll term the general area AI-NLP. As you will see, it is the use of the adjective *natural* to describe the types of languages in question that I dispute. NLP may be the ultimate goal of this branch of AI, but it it very far from descriptive of any current (or foreseeable future) achievements in the field.

In this general area of AI-NLP we find natural language interfaces (NLI), perhaps the major commercial application, with another subfield, *machine translation* (MT), also producing usable products. In the research domain, there are tutoring systems, story understanders, and a myriad of intriguing demonstrations of systems that can communicate with man. "Which man?" is the embarassing question. The answer is: any man or woman who asks the right questions and makes the right responses. Hence the root of my reluctance to ascribe to the languages implemented the quality of naturalness. In reality, we shall be considering languages that are formal (in a way that natural languages show no signs of being), or informal and unnatural, perhaps less-than-natural is more accurate, but no real improvement in description.

It has been pointed out to me that, when I attempt to communicate with a Frenchman in my half-forgotten, high-school French, the resultant dialogue will exhibit many of the features of the human–computer dialogue which I am now attacking. There will be questions that elicit no sensible response, and others that elicit no response at all (in the verbal domain). There will be many misunderstandings and misinterpretations. Am I then going to say that this is not natural-language dialogue? Of course I'm not. So why do I think that it is reasonable to dispute the naturalness of many AI-NLP systems? The answer is that I'm not demanding anything close to total flexibility and comprehension before I'm happy to award the accolade 'natural' to a language-processing system. There is a *qualitative* difference between the linguistics capabilities of current NLP systems and humans, however poorly the human has grasped the language that he or she is using. I'm quite sure that I can't draw a line to separate natural from nonnatural language usage, but I'm equally sure that no current AI-NLP systems are even close to the blurred transition zone.

It is time for an example:

Area Sales Manager:	Please tell me how many salesmen exceeded their quotas in the first 6 months of last year?
Computer:	CERTAINLY, FOUR SALESMEN EXCEEDED THEIR QUOTAS IN THE FIRST SIX MONTHS OF LAST YEAR. WOULD YOU LIKE TO KNOW ANY FURTHER DETAILS CONCERNING THESE FOUR SALESMEN?
ASM:	Yes, what was their average sales figure during this period?
Computer:	THE AVERAGE SALES FIGURE WAS 246 ITEMS. . . .

Is this an NLP system? If you're wondering about the correct answer, then consider this simpler question: Is the following picture an elephant?

Figure 8.1.   A picture of an elephant

No! It's just a picture of an elephant (or of a connectionist's mouse, as the new joke goes); it bears a number of visual similarities to an elephant, but that is all. It is lacking almost all of the properties of a real elephant. Similarly, the above dialogue bears some similarity to natural language, but as to whether such a computer is communicating in natural language is a difficult question. Just as my sketch of the large, grey animal is seriously lacking in most elephantine properties, so (to wring this analogy quite dry) any current computer system that superficially appears to be using natural language will also be found to be communicating in a medium devoid of the major linguistic properties expected of natural languages. Unfortunately, this dearth of necessary qualities is not so obvious in a snippet of dialogue that purports to be natural language communication as it is in a picture that is touted around as a real elephant. Even worse, with a little handcrafting of the computer system, the resultant dialogue is far more beguiling. For example:

Area Sales Manager: Give me the names of our two top salesmen and there sales to date.

Computer: EXCUSE ME PROFESSOR X [substitute name of person claiming to be interrogating the system] BUT I THINK THAT YOU MAY HAVE MISSPELT "THEIR" AS "THERE". ASSUMING THIS IS TRUE AS WELL AS THAT YOU WANT THE SALES TOTALS FROM JANUARY 1ST, THEN . . .

Now, that's natural language, and intelligence to boot — is it not? The trouble is that the example in the paper, report, or glossy, feature article ends there. You don't get to see how the dialogue continues — one never does, does one? It just might shed some light on the question of natural or unnatural language. Just for once we're going to see the bit that was censored; it is:

Area Sales Manager: I want those totals on the screen NOW, put them there.
Computer: EXCUSE ME PROFESSOR X, BUT I THINK THAT YOU MAY HAVE MISSPELT "THEIR" AS "THERE". ASSUMING THAT THIS IS TRUE THEN KYGV223333###22/'L;IOJ0T [the system now exhibits chronic aphasia; it is totally resistant to all subsequent coaxing and apologizing by the Area Sales Manager]

This is not a true story (they are coming later), but it might as well be; it does convey the essential reason why expressive snippets of computer dialogue abound, and computer systems that can really handle dialogue at the level of sophistication implied by the examples are nonexistent.

Enough for the moment on my contention that natural language processing by computer is an event of the future; I'm exposing my prejudices too much, too early, as usual. Let's back off and begin by taking a more global view of this AI subfield. Lots of results have been produced under the banner of AI-NLP. I'll attempt to approach the major theoretical advances as well as implemented systems from the direction of their general relevance to AI-NLP as a whole. But first let us consider the central phenomenon: natural language and, in particular, its function.

NATURAL LANGUAGE

It will come as no surprise to the reader who has read through to this point (as opposed to the browser who has dived in here by chance or by design) that I have no generally agreed upon, formal or informal, definition of the function of natural language to trot out. Inability to define our terms is one of the AI worker's major problems; unfortunately, the impracticality of the definitional approach is also one of the defining characteristics of the field.

I'll give a series of descriptions of the function of natural language, comment on them, and finally home in on the sort of definition that much AI-NLP work is based upon.

'The function of language is to express thought.' This is the type of description that Fodor (1990) uses as a step in his argument that the architecture of cognition must have constituent structure at the level of semantic interpretation. We considered his Language-Of-Thought hypothesis earlier (Chapter 3).

"The function of language is to manipulate the world, and in particular the other people in it, to one's personal advantage." In this biological determinist's view, the primary function of language is not to convey information as accurately and efficiently as possible in some absolute sense. Quite the contrary, personal survival may well necessitate the transfer of selective information as well as misinformation. This might, of course, be viewed as accurate and efficient information transfer, if we take the personal welfare of the disseminating organism (or, more accurately, its genes) as the sole consideration of importance, which is (to a crude approximation) the conviction of biological determinists.

"The function of language is to convey information from one person to another." This very general description is perhaps the accepted basis for much AI-NLP work (except that it necessarily involves two persons, hence two belief systems, etc.; most AI-NLP work involves one, if not less). The goal of *natural language generation* (NLG) is to encode the information to be transferred, and the goal of NLU is to extract the information from the encoded text. This viewpoint is also quite consistent with both of the earlier ones, although no concrete AI-NLP work begins to address issues such as that of information as deliberate misinformation.

What this example does is to highlight the scope of the term *information*, which is so vast as to effectively make it informationless in many contexts. As a brief aside, I might note that the efforts of information theory, as popularly misused, do very little to make the general term information more useful. Information theory provides a formal definition for the term information; unfortunately, the scope of the definition is totally outside of any useful meaning for most purposes (in communications engineering the story is different, but NLP has a zero overlap with normal communications engineering work).

Winograd and Flores (1986, p. 123) object to this simplistic view, which much of the AI-NLP enterprise assumes tacitly at least. They argue that "the essence of language as a human activity lies not in its ability to reflect the world, but in its characteristic of creating commitment. When we say that a person understands something, we imply that he or she has entered into the commitment implied by that understanding. But how can a computer enter into a commitment?" They continue with the point that there are useful applications of computer programs in which linguistic entities and structures (e.g., English words and syntax) are employed, but users of such systems should always recognize that the computer does not, and can never, understand the language in a human sense. Obvious, but remember the ELIZA syndrome, and that AI-NLP is the perfect breeding ground for this complaint. Clearly, Winograd and Flores see NLU as a noncomputerizable phenomenon.

Now that we have some ideas about the function of language with respect to AI-NLP work, we must also examine the typical language modes employed, and the limitations and biases that the favored mode brings with it.

WHAT MODE OF NATURAL LANGUAGE?

Spoken or written language is the major choice that I wish to address. I have said "text" above, which implies the written form, and this is the usual mode of input and output of natural language in AI-NLP systems.

The major exception was the infamous DARPA speech-understanding project of the 1970s. There was a 5-year project funded by the United States Advanced Research Projects Agency (ARPA) to demonstrate the feasibility of programming a computer "to understand" connected speech. That project terminated in 1976, having met its specifications (Medress, 1978). It employed a multilevel approach, which is typical of most approaches to reducing the complexity of NLP systems, and we shall see it again below. The various subsystems — acoustic, phonological, etc. — communicated with each other via a global data structure called a "blackboard," which the HEARSAY (Reddy, Erman, Fennell, & Neely, 1976) program made famous.

Despite the fact that the system met its goals (or maybe because the system met its goals; see Partridge, 1986a), major AI-NLP research projects using speech as the input mode ceased together with the ARPA funding. There are projects that address the problem of recognizing spoken words (e.g., Young, Russell, & Thornton, 1988; Stentiford & Steer, 1988), but they treat the problem as one of pattern recognition within a well-defined set of alternatives for speakers to whom the system has been previously tuned. Clearly, there is a long way to go before computer-based speech recognition begins to approach the human capability. And it is not obvious to me that 'more of the same' (rather than something totally different) is a strategy that will ever take us close to this ultimate goal. Thus such projects, in my view are, not AI projects and not likely to be successful except in highly limited applications (see Chapter 3 for the 'bad' AI paradigm that includes this type of pattern recognition).

We do, of course, lose a lot of useful information when the medium of communication is written words rather than spoken ones. Most of the mood, tone, and emphasis that can be so informative in spoken language is lost in the written word. There are devices like underlining, using boldface fonts, etc. that can begin to recapture this lost information, but these subtleties of the textual mode are either absent or unexploited by most (perhaps all) current models of NLP. The following three sentences illustrate this point; the words are the same in each case, but the meanings are different.

I saw you.
I *saw* you.
I saw *you.*

I could give you my interpretation of these three sentences, but I shall not; I'll leave it as an exercise that you might want to tackle when there is absolutely nothing else to do. Hirschberg (1987, p. 86) claims "that while one *may* still study **text** in silence, one *cannot* study **discourse** without taking speech into account." She gives examples: where the "tune" or "contour" a speaker employs communicates semantic or pragmatic information; where intonational contours provide information about the speaker's intentions; where accent and phrasing can help hearers disambiguate among potential syntactic parses or logical forms, etc.

But for the purposes of our current survey of work in NLP we are dealing with written, or rather keyed-in and printed-out, text — at best. Some projects don't extend to the surface form (i.e., grammatical collections of words), but start at some (supposedly) underlying representation augmented with a little hand waving to reinforce its validity. Hand waving, incidentally, tends to get a bad press. In defense of this valuable adjunct to AI presentations, I can say that, rich as it is, natural language is sometimes found to be wanting in expressive power, especially at the leading edge of a new technology. Natural language is a continuously developing phenomenon, but the response time is poor. Until it catches up with the new ideas being presented, what more can we do than wave our hands suggestively — after all, what did God give us hands for if not to wave them at awkward moments when our natural language fails us?

THE GOALS OF AI-NLP

This subfield of AI, as with AI in general, can be subdivided into roughly (very roughly) two classes of work with respect to the goals of the project. There is AI-NLP research whose primary goal is to further our understanding of human communication, and, in particular, the role that natural language plays in this communication. "Are psychological claims being made with the constituent mechanisms of the system?" would be a valid question for projects in this class. This, not surprisingly, is the more demanding approach to AI-NLP, except that the absence of any obligation to finally produce a useful, working system brings with it considerable relief.

The other class of AI-NLP work is primarily aimed at the creation of natural-language communication skills within a machine. How we arrive at them, and what the component mechanisms are, is of little concern (and certainly not something that has to be defended against charges of unhumanness). This second, engineering or applications, class of AI-NLP work is motivated by the commercial and perhaps societal need for the opening of a channel of natural language communication between the man-in-the-street (or the woman-at-the-keyboard) and computers.

NATURAL LANGUAGE: THE ESSENTIAL INGREDIENTS

As with all rational approaches to the problems of complexity, the complexity of natural language is tackled by breaking the complex problem into a collection of less-complex subproblems. In addition, we strive to identify and isolate more-or-less-independent subproblems.

A traditional division of the problem of NLU (computerized or not) has been into levels. The series of levels that we shall consider is: phonetic, phonological, lexical, syntactic, semantic, and pragmatic.

PHONETICS AND PHONOLOGY

We can deal with these two levels together. They do not enter into the scope of text processing NLU systems, and so a treatement even more cursory than usual is all that they will receive.

The phonetic level is concerned with analysis of the speech signal (the voice print) to get something like phonemes — the smallest unit of significant sound in a language. Phonology, the study of the structures that constitute a natural-language sound system, includes both phonetics and phonemics. We can single out four levels beneath that of syntax:

1. Phonetics — characteristics of speech sounds;
2. Phonemics — rules of the variations in pronounciation that occur when words are spoken together, or spoken by different people, or spoken by the same person on different occasions;
3. Morphemics — rules describing how morphemes (abstract units that consist of a predictable phoneme-unit of meaning {sememe} association — the atoms of meaning) are combined to form words;
4. Prosodics — rules describing fluctuation in stress and intonation across a sentence.

THE LEXICAL LEVEL AND ABOVE

The lexical level is concerned with the words and vocabulary of a language, while syntax refers to the allowable structures of (largely) lexical items. — i.e., grammatical issues. Semantics is a particularly tricky term, but, as we'll deal with it at length later, let's just say it concerns the meaning of structures in the language. Finally, pragmatics takes us into the nebulous world of the interactions between the language and its users. It is a topic that has received scant attention from computational linguists, and we'll continue this tradition with just one pithy subsection on pragmatics later in this chapter.

Syntax and, to a lesser extent, semantics have been the major levels of interest for AI-NLP persons, and thus these are the levels that most of the rest of this chapter addresses.

GENERATION AND ANALYSIS

Casually, we might expect that any computer system that has a significant NL processing capability would be able to both understand English (I'm going to use *English* as almost synonymous to *natural language*; this, for a change, is not a personal prejudice but a reflection of the fact that the majority of AI-NLP work has focused on the English language), and generate English in order to communicate, with roughly the same facility in both directions — although humans are invariably better recognizers than generators. Currently, this is far from true. There is little overlap between research on the recognition and understanding of natural language, on the one hand, and generation, on the other.

It is a fundamental belief that language is a two-way medium of communication, and a direct interface to thought. The fact of this observed lack of unity and equivalence between understanding and generation work in AI-NLP is not viewed as a challenge to this fundamental belief; it is a reflection of some much more mundane considerations, perhaps just a result of the way things were started somewhat fortuitously, rather like the way the Americans happen to drive on the right side of the road, and the English on the wrong one.

Of course, the NLU people have a good reason why most research is in their area: it's the harder, the real, problem. Understanding natural language is *the* fundamental problem; generation of acceptable text is a relatively much simpler problem. The generation problems of lexical choice, etc., must be based on some representation of the meaning of what is to be said; representations of meaning, such as a language understanding system must generate, are the basis for generation.

Similarly, and not surprisingly, workers on text generation hold just the opposite view, and, as they have been underrepresented to date in AI-NLP, I'll put their case first.

NATURAL LANGUAGE GENERATION (NLG)

Apart from believing that analysis is harder than text generation, there is also the belief that text analysis systems will be more useful. For example, a question–answer system must be able to analyze the productions of an uncontrollable input source (i.e., the exquisitely phrased questions put to it by you and me), and yet be able to respond in constructions of its own choice which can be more or less prefabricated, stored, and pushed out to the questioner as a whole. In other words, many responses can be *canned* (this is, I believe, the technical term). So, there is a pressing need for a bona fide analysis component in the system, but distinctly less of an urgency about providing a sophisticated generation component.

Nevertheless, NLG enthusiasts are currently predicting a flurry of activity in their domain. A number of reasons are given. First, there is a realization that any NLP system that aspires to be more than a very crude caricature of the human capability to produce informative, natural-language responses to questions must be flexible. There is a world of difference between a succession of disjoint, canned responses, which nevertheless carry the necessary information, and a sequence of sentences that exhibit textual structure as a whole. Sadly, the jump in difficulty between implementing representatives from these two classes of systems is of a comparable magnitude. The former are currently doable; the latter may be available at about the time of the next ice age (but I may be overly optimistic).

A second reason for the rise of NLG systems is the view that generation is a more illuminating task than analysis: if the basic problem is to understand natural language communication, then experimentation with NLG will be better than NLU for exposing and exploring the infrastructure of the problem. What basis is there for this somewhat radical claim?

Evaluation of NLU systems is a difficult issue, to which I shall return below; it is difficult because the product of the process is a representation of the meaning of the analyzed text, and who is to say what representation of meaning is correct, or even which of two competing representations is better? The only way to assess the relative merits of alternative representations of text meanings is to explore how well, and what ways, these representations support other cognitive activities that are to some degree directly observable (or at least inferable). The obvious example of a directly observable cognitive behavior that is also based on some representation of meaning is (you guessed it) natural language generation. Hence, generation, producing as it does (or eventually should) concrete texts whose properties can be evaluated empirically, is the more fundamental approach to understanding the phenomenon of natural language.

Furthermore, the fact that the product of NLG is directly, empirically evaluable means that researchers is this domain are forced to consider and deal with (to some extent) all of the constituent subproblems on the way to generating textual output. For significant deficiencies in the system will be patently obvious in the text generated (that's not true, but it is certainly much harder to disguise major deficiencies in generated text than in generated meaning representations).

As an example, NLG does, in effect, assay the sufficiency of the representation of meaning (or content, or semantics) upon which it is based: The representation must, of necessity, be able to support generation of structures that reflect the distinctions that the language does indeed make. An NLU system, by way of contrast, has almost total freedom to make use of any semantic representation scheme, however impoverished. The NLU task is accomplished by simply (or elaborately) mapping the input text onto the chosen representation. Upon what basis can we criticize the result? We have no access to the human analogue. We must rely on faith in some preferred representational form, scripts, schemas, frames, or what you will. It is true that, within the engineering approach, the intended use of chosen meaning representation is likely to provide constraints — but only for the specific class of usages being entertained.

A third reason that favors the NLG task is that we can eliminate the uncontrollable component of the NLU task (that's you and all the things you're free to input) without robbing the problem of any of its richness. Hence, NLG offers a major simplification of the general problem of human communication yet maintains all of the substance that makes natural language natural language.

TEXT GENERATION SYSTEMS

A text generation system can be viewed as a function mapping from representations of meanings and intentions to natural language text. However, all indications are that these are very complex functions, ones whose range is difficult to circumscribe, even in principle. Thus, high-quality text generation cannot be expected from a system that uses only some representation of the content of the proposed utterance, regardless of the complexity and completeness of the representation employed.

If the system's goal is to obtain the salt (for some peculiar reason), then how on Earth would it arrive at the following question as the text to generate?: Can you pass the salt? The only conceivable reason for this question, on the face of it, would be as a prelude (to determine if the system being interrogated is capable of the desired act) to generating the polite command: Please pass the salt. Interestingly, if the other system were, say, a robot (with genuine AI built in), then it could well accept the first question as perfectly normal, answer "Yes," and do nothing. "Is it trying to be funny?" we would have to ask ourselves; meanwhile the dinner is getting cold.

There is far more to quality text generation than capturing an abstract semantic content within a grammatically correct string of words. There is the problem of a general plan into which the present utterance must fit and do its part to convey the beliefs and intentions of the speaker, or computer system. At a somewhat less esoteric level, the generated text must mesh with the style and tone of the previously generated textual output. Stylistic considerations might to some extent be arbitrarily chosen, but once selected they must serve to constrain the possibilities for subsequently generated text.

In addition to all the influences, such as intentions, which are in some sense internal to the generating system and thus conceivably part of a "content" representation, there is the problem of assessing and incorporating a response to audience reaction — clearly external information. Thus if the human questioner is puzzled, or angered, by the computer's answer, then the computer system must have some way of sensing this and responding to it. Otherwise, high-quality natural language generation will not be possible.

Needless to say, current NLG projects are still struggling with much more basic problems. The NLG task is typically viewed as a two-part process: first, there is *strategy*, deciding what to say; second, there is *tactics*, deciding how to say it. The strategic module must combine information on the content of what is to be said with information on more global intentions, beliefs, and goals of the system. The result is a strategic specification of what is to be said. It is generally agreed that this specification should be in terms of some formal notation, but no such notations with any degree of generality or general acceptance have yet appeared.

The following schematic diagram (Figure 8.2) of the major components of an NLG system are from Appelt (1987).

Ideally, this strategic specification can be fed into the tactical subsystem that concerns only the grammatical and lexical aspects of the language to be generated. This module then chooses the appropriate grammatical constructions and, finally, the individual words needed to realize the strategic specification in text.

The advantages that accrue from such a modularization of NLG are numerous. First, the tactical component is.concerned only with grammatical aspects of the language to be generated. It need not be involved in the reasoning, etc., that goes into generating the strategic specification. And conversely, the strategic module focuses on knowledge integration and general reasoning without regard for the specific language to be generated. Clearly, such a modularization would provide a very useful portability between, say, generators of different languages.

The second advantage of this scheme is that it might contribute significantly to the realization of bidirectional systems (i.e., a combined language recognizer and generator, just like us). We shall return to this possibility after considering NLU work below.

The real snag in this encouraging story is that this proposed modularization will not succeed. According to Appelt (1985, 1987), the problem is that the strategic component is, by design, concerned only with constructing an expression (i.e., a strategic specification) because of its *meaning*, and it is likely that there will be more than one equivalent varia-

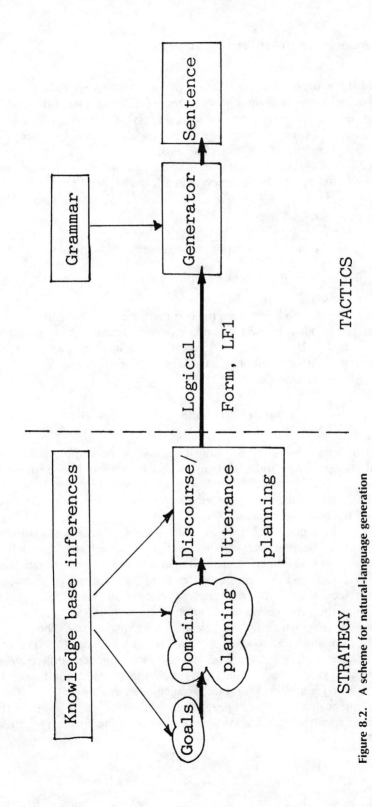

Figure 8.2. A scheme for natural-language generation

295

tions of the expression that represent the same meaning. Thus it would be possible for the strategic module to generate an expression that, while logically equivalent to the intended utterance, is quite inappropriate. And it cannot rule out the inappropriate variants without some knowledge of the surface structure of the target language.

Appelt (1987) gives the example of a strategic specification that a declarative sentence should be generated with the propositional content:

Resistance-of (R1, ohm(500))

The tactical module is then expected to generate the sentence:

"The resistence of R1 is 500 ohms."

He claims that this unlikely to be the text generated by a general grammar of English embodied in the tactical component, because its constituents bear no simple relationship to the constituents of any sentence. The preferred form of the propositional part of the strategic specification is more likely to be something like:

there exists an x, such that Resistence-of(R1,x)&(x = ohm(500)).

This form is more suitable, Appelt claims, because there is a more natural mapping from constituents of the specification to the constituents of the sentence. The equality predicate corresponds to the verb *be,* and the subject and predicate noun phrases correspond directly to the arguments of the equality predicate.

Thus, if the strategic component must have a detailed knowledge of the grammar, the practical viability of the suggested strategic/tactical modularization is seriously challenged. Yet text generation systems have been developed, and they do not suffer from this problem (e.g., Mann, 1983; McKeown, 1985). So, as Appelt says, there must be a way out. He claims that the crucial common factor in these NLG systems is that "none of the grammars employed by these systems has an explicitly represented formal semantics"(Appelt, 1987, p. 189). In Appelt's NLG system KAMP knowledge of the grammar (i.e., the intended surface structure of the text to be generated) is used by the strategic component to create a strategic specification that is logically equivalent to the propositional content of the surface speech act. Similar failure to abide by the strategic/tactical modularization convention is found in each of these other NLG systems.

EMPIRICAL GUIDANCE FOR NLG

To return to one of the major problems that is ubiquitous in AI: to wit, the problem of finding constraints on the possible mechanisms for realizing phenomena whose final outcome is all that we can directly observe — essentially, the classic black-box problem.

In this particular case, humans are the only good text generators. We can observe the text that they output, but we can not directly observe any of the pertinent aspects of the mechanism which does the generation. Possibly the only direct observation of the mechanism at work is the recording of electrical activity in the brain. At the moment, these data are of no use for making decisions about the possible mechanisms of macrophenomena such as NLG. You might remember our brief look at electrophysiological data in Chapter 3; it is too low level and too ill understood itself to provide any guidance at this time, and for the forseeable future. So, can we uncover any constraints on the mechanism that accounts for our NLG capability?

As usual we must resort to a combination of inspired guesswork and careful deduction from controlled experiments with the observable phenomenon — the methodology of empirical psychology. And even if the NLG project explicitly eschews the modeling of human behavior, controlled experiments in the style of psychology can still provide some useful guidance in an open problem in which everything is possible but almost nothing seems to work.

Kroch (1987), for example, takes the view that, if we assume that human behavior is ultimately reducable to the output of a machine, however complex, it must be the case that there are limits to the behavior we are trying to model. If we can find these limits in humans and we can characterize them theoretically, then we shall have gained some useful information to guide the modeling process. He describes experiments and presents data that suggest characteristic limitations on the human NLG ability, and thus also provide direction in developing mechanisms for realizing an artificial NLG system.

His data and subsequent analysis are consistent with a model of sentence production in which the decision on how to order the particle and direct object is unaffected by the decision on whether to use the verb-particle construction at all. It is though the production mechanism were organized into a simple decision tree in which the decision on whether to use a particle verb is made first, and then the particle object ordering decision is made independently.

Kroch (1987, p. 199) concludes: "To the extent that such a simple organization of decisions for sentence production, without complex interactions among levels, can be justified by further work, it will be possible to construct a more constrained model of the generation process."

Currently, computational theories of NLG are largely focused on the tactical component, and thus they primarily address the problems of how to control a system for syntactic and lexical choice — i.e., choosing the appropriate grammatical structures and words to express some desired meaning.

From the problem of translating communicative intent into linguistic form, we move to the hitherto more popular problem of translating linguistic form into a representation of intention and meaning — we move from NLG to NLU.

NATURAL LANGUAGE UNDERSTANDING (NLU)

NLU, sometimes called *natural language recognition,* is what springs to mind when we associate AI and NLP. The other concept that intrudes equally strongly is either *grammar,* or *syntax,* or *parsing* — all terms that pertain to the structural validity of strings of words. Thus "Colorless green ideas sleep furiously" is a well-known sentence that is clearly grammatical, or syntactically correct, but whose meaning, or semantics, is open to debate.

Even more extreme is a verse from "Jabberwockey" (not the Monty Python film, but the Lewis Carroll magnum opus):

Twas brillig, and the slithy toves
  Did gyre and gimble in the wabe:
All mimsy were the borogroves,
  And the mome raths outgrabe.

Now most of the individual words are "meaningless" (i.e., not in the O.E.D.), but it is still quite obvious that the syntax or grammar is both there and okay. Foreign readers, who may be having more trouble than their English-speaking counterparts with such minimal-semantics sentences, can find both French and German "translations" in Hofstadter (1979). Of course, if they don't understand French or German either, what can I say?

Moving on to less poetic concerns, words and sentences with the comfort of more or less obvious and accepted meanings hanging on them, we need to take a look at the dominance of syntactic concerns in NLU. Language analyzers have been able to concentrate almost exclusively on syntactic issues with comprehensive generality, whereas the language synthesizers, as we have already seen, are obliged to consider matters of content, intention, belief, etc. prior to planning the syntactic form of the text that will be generated. We shall see the repercussions of the tyranny of syntax throughout the rest of this chapter.

Now is the time to really tie down the essential ingredients of all natural languages — lexicons, syntax, semantics, etc. — and how these components can perhaps be combined to yield this amazing human capacity.

SYNTAX, GRAMMARS, AND PARSING

Now we finally have arrived at the center of interest, theory, and implementations in NLU: grammars for parsing. Is this the dominant area because it contains the fundamental issues, subproblems that must be solved before the other levels, both below and above, are tackled? Or is there some less compelling reason for the primacy of syntax and its accoutrements? After all, the word *syntactician* rolls off the tongue delightfully (just practice a bit before you take issue with me here), whereas *semantician,* or even *semanticist,* has nothing like the same lingual lubricity. Still, I'm not committed to this line of argument for the supremacy of syntax. Before we attempt either to answer such questions or to examine details of notable achievements in the field, let me first lay out a rough plan of the terrain.

Syntactic issues pertain to the matters of structure or form in a language. A *grammar* is a description or even formal specification of the allowable or legal structures in a language. *Parsing* is the process of resolving a portion of text to yield its grammatical constituents — its syntactic structure.

Thus the following is a grammar for a small chunk (more a crumb, actually) of English:

S → Np Vp (a sentence is composed of a noun phrase followed by a verb phrase)
Np → N (a noun phrase can be a noun)
Np → Det N (a noun phrase can be determiner followed by a noun)
Vp → V (a verb phrase can be a verb)
Vp → V Np (a verb phrase can be a verb followed by a noun phrase)
Det → the *or* a (a determiner is "the" or "a")
N → dog *or* cat *or* mat (a noun is "dog" or "cat" or "mat")
V → ate *or* bit (a verb is "ate" or "bit")

With this grammar I can parse the following sentence and thus determine its syntactic structure.

"the dog bit the cat"

The syntactic structure given by the above grammar is given in Figure 8.3. The parse is illustrated by means of this "tree" structure (the 'tree root' is labeled "S" and the "leaves" are words from the text parsed). We have a *parse tree,* which lays out the constituent structure of our sentence, as dictated by the particular grammar that we used. Such a grammar is typically known as a *context-free grammar* (CFG), and it is one type of grammar within the class of *phrase structure grammars* (PSG).

Before we push on to examine some alternative types of grammar and parsing strategies, spare a thought for the question of whether the above grammar is a grammar of English (remember the picture of the elephant). We shall return to this question after initiation into the rites and practices of AI-NLP.

GRAMMARS

Apparently we have the ancient Greeks to thank (if that's the word) for the essential notion of grammars — i.e., that language expressions can be

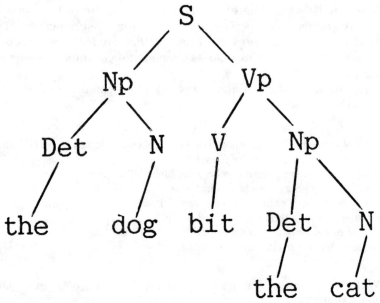

Figure 8.3.   A simple parse tree

broken down and classified in terms of "parts of speech." But, moving on to more modern times, we can start at the more or less contemporaneous emergence of a classification of grammar "types" by Chomsky in linguistics, and the design of a notation for defining the syntax of the ALGOL60 programming language, BNF notation, or Backus-Naur Form. In both domains what the AI-NLP people found was a powerful and succinct, formal notation for expressing linguistic structure — the CFG. CFGs enable us to characterize a lot of the syntactic structure of English, as well as to define a wide range of formal languages.

If, like Bishop Ussher but in a somewhat narrower context, we wish to pinpoint the start of the modern era in formal linguistics (more accurately, syntactics), then Chomsky's publication of *Syntactic Structures* in 1957 is the instant to choose (a year is a long instant, and I fully expect that a little research could shorten it considerably, but precision in the grand style of the good bishop is a lost art; it lost out to science).

Speaking formally (it won't last, so don't give up), a grammar has four components: a set of terminal symbols, e.g., words and punctuation marks; a set of nonterminal symbols, or syntactic categories, e.g., S, Np, and Vp in the CFG illustrated above; the start symbol, which is one of the nonterminals, the one that labels the sentences of the language, i.e., S in the same CFG; and a set of rewrite rules that specify how terminals may be strung together to make the legal sentences of the language being formally defined. That's quite enough formal stuff; please refer to the small formal grammar provided above for clarification. If it is less than totally obvious what the nonterminal symbols, etc., are, then perhaps you should invest some valuable time in writing out the three sets and the single symbol that comprise the four formal elements of this grammar (feel free to ignore this advice). The next time someone glibly states that a formal grammar is a four-tuple you may confidently smile and nod in full agreement, safe in your knowledge of actually having had some exposure to this unlikely sounding idea.

Chomsky delineated four types of grammar: type 0, type 1, type 2, and, yes, type 3. The formal ins and outs of this classification scheme will only slow us down (and bore us to distraction) so we'll just observe that the CFGs are type 2 and move on. Chomsky is also well known for his system of transformational grammar, and we'll look at that as soon as we've finished with the CFGs.

The use of recursive structures in a grammar enable us to define (or describe) infinite structures with finite means. (The recursion-shy reader is referred back to Chapter 4, where an exposition of the magic of recursion can be found.) Thus, English is not obviously bounded by size in many different respects: for example, a noun can be preceded by any number of adjectives. There is no point at which we are prepared to rule out a sentence as not English because there are too many adjectives.

A CFG definition of such noun phrases might be:

Np → Det Adjlist N (a noun phrase is a determiner followed by an adjective list and finally by a noun)
Adjlist → Adj (an adjective list can be a single adjective)
Adjlist → Adj Adjlist (an adjective list can be an adjective followed by an adjective list)

A spot-the-recursion quiz will be trivial to anyone who has waded through the intricacies of LISP and PROLOG in Chapter 4; the third of the above CFG rules is recursive. The second and third rules together comprise a definition of a list of adjectives which may contain any number of adjectives from one to infinity (or thereabouts). The use of recursive specifications was particularly satisfying to linguists, who saw in it some sort of answer to the old problem of human language: We appear to have infinite capacity (to recognize and generate sentences), yet we clearly have finite means (a finite brain within which to represent all of the necessary recognition and generation apparatus). Recursive rules in a grammar provide us, quite simply (the diehard antirecursionists might disagree), with a finite means for recognizing and generating infinitely many, different sentences.

Unfortunately, CFGs have severe inherent limitations as well. For example, the original small CFG would support a correct parse of:

"mat bit the dog"

which is both grammatically awkward (if not downright ungrammatical) and difficult to associate with an obvious, simple meaning.

"Okay, we can soon fix that. We'll add some more rules (who would expect such a trivial grammar to be of any real use?), partition the nouns and verbs appropriately, and soon eliminate these problematic sentences." Many have tried variants of this strategy, very fancy variants, and they simply don't work.

The next move was to augment the elements of these CFGs (or PSGs, as I've said) with tags such as singular or plural and tense information with verbs, etc. But even these augmented PSGs in which some syntactic constructs carried an awful lot of excess baggage around the parse tree fell woefully short of what was needed.

CFGs are not powerful enough to describe the structure of English (or any other natural language, I suspect). CFGs are not even powerful enough to define the syntax of programming languages. They can define a lot of it, but not all. So what must we do for natural languages? We must devise a more powerful notation.

FURIOUS TRANSFORMATIONAL GRAMMARIANS SLEEP CURIOUSLY

Chomsky developed a theory of language called *transformational grammar* (TG). He attempted to account for the human language ability in terms of a *deep structure*, a *surface structure*, and a set of *transformation rules* that provide a mapping between these two levels.

Thus, active and passive surface forms of a sentence, for example, correspond to a single deep structure and are produced from it by the application of two different sequences of transformation rules. So "John hit mary." and "Mary was hit by John." (two different sentences with something very close to but one meaning) map to a single deep structure. Central to this theory is an explication of the transformation rules and the conventions which govern their application in the derivation of natural language (see Figure 8.4).

The sequences of transformations, T1 and T2, map the deep structure (finessed in the traditional AI-NLP manner; capitalization is a generally accepted means of pretending that you have represented the meaning of a word rather than just the word itself) of some agent acting on some object to the active and the passive surface structures. The implication (and early conception) was that the meaning was solely in the deep structure; thus, transformations should be meaning preserving. But obvious problems with this concept have necessitated a revision that admits that meaning is in both levels.

So-called "standard theory" of generative grammar is given in Chomsky (1965, and summarized 1971). A CFG and a lexicon constitute the "base" of the grammar and produce the deep structures. The transformational rules then map deep structures to surface structures.

Using a TG for parsing necessarily involves first constructing from the surface string a tree to which the reverse transformations must then be applied. If our task is to construct an efficient parsing algorithm, then there are many problems with this strategy as King (1983) explains:

(a) The surface grammar produces too many spurious trees.
(b) It can be difficult to find the right sequence of transformations, e.g., the problem of transformations that are optional in the generative grammar.
(c) There are interdependencies between some transformations.
(d) Deletions in the generative mode amount to conjuring up deleted subtrees in the parser.

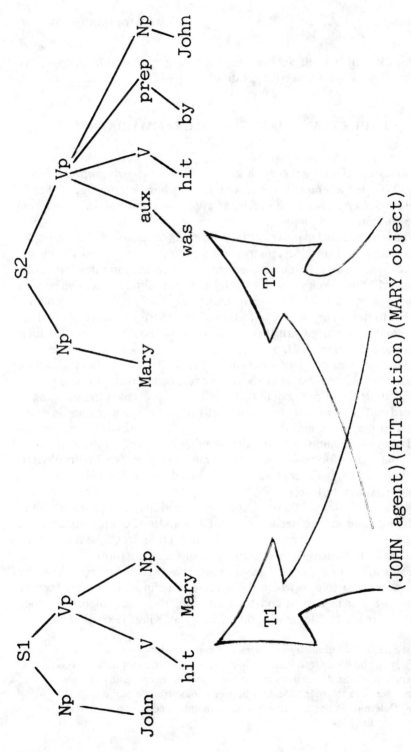

(JOHN agent)(HIT action)(MARY object)

Figure 8.4. One deep structure and two surface structures

304

(e) It is difficult to always avoid infinite cycles in a transformational sequence.

But, as King points out, despite this rather impressive list of problems, transformational parsers exist and have given quite reasonable results over a restricted (sometimes highly restricted) semantic domain.

Woods (1970) also outlines the difficulties of using TGs for parsing and uses this set of problems as a basis for extolling the virtues of transition networks, and so shall we.

TRANSITION NETWORKS: AUGMENTED AND OTHERWISE

Instead of rewrite rules we can cast a CFG in terms of a network. If we want to define a grammar for a simple sentence structure, which has four alternative structurings — "Noun Verb Noun", "Det Noun Verb Noun", "Det Noun Verb Det Noun", and "Noun Verb Det Noun" — it comes out like Figure 8.5:

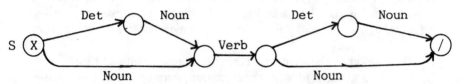

Figure 8.5.   A transition network defining a simple sentence structure

or like Figure 8.6:

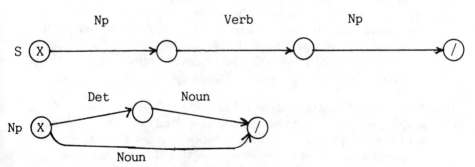

Figure 8.6.   A two-network alternative to Figure 8.5

if we separate out and name identical substructures in the first network illustrated (in case you're wondering, the "Det-Noun" substructure was removed and named "Np" — short for Noun-phrase).

Each network contains an initial node, marked "X," and a final node, marked "/." The directed arcs between nodes are labeled with the names of syntactic constructs. Each network is a syntactic specification of the syntactic construct named immediately left of the initial node.

Parsing a sentence with these networks amounts to traversing the sentence network (the one labeled "S") from the initial node to the final node by assigning successive words in the sentence to the syntactic category named on the arc being traversed at any time. The pair of graphs illustrated bring in the extra complication that some arc labels (e.g., "Np") refer, not to collections of words, but to other graphs. When the parser encounters such a label, it must jump to the named graph, traverse that in the same manner, and, when finished, jump back to the graph from where it originally jumped and continue parsing, with the remainder of the sentence not assigned to syntactic categories by the subgraph. Note also that an arc label in a network may be the name of the network itself. Yes, these networks can be recursive. Hence, the general name is *recursive transition networks* (RTN).

"Well, what has this bought us?" you might ask. "Something close to nothing," I would reply, "but it has potential." This potential is realized by augmenting the networks (hence, *augmented transition networks*, ATNs, if you've not had your ration of acronyms lately) in several ways:

1. In addition to the syntactic-construct names, tests and building actions are associated with specific arcs. Any tests must be satisfied before the arc can be traversed, and, when the arc is traversed, any specified building actions are executed.
2. A memory is added to the network set in the form of a set of registers that may be used to store syntactic constructs. Hence, a common type of building action is to change the information in some of the registers. These two sorts of augmentation facilitate the construction of grammars that come much closer (than the bare RTNs) to accepting only the more "reasonable" sentences of English — e.g., we want the parser to reject "mats bites dogs."

As an example consider the ATN in Figure 8.7.

In this somewhat contrived example (contrived to more or less duplicate a later example, so that's all to the good), the arc tests are followed by a question mark and the build actions are all "*save*"s which store information in registers. Registers are associated with each rule, and although they can only be reset by build actions in the associated rule, they can be inspected by tests in other rules. Thus the "N_number:V_number" test in the sentence rule inspects the contents of the "N_number" register associated with, and set in, the "Np" rule. This test checks

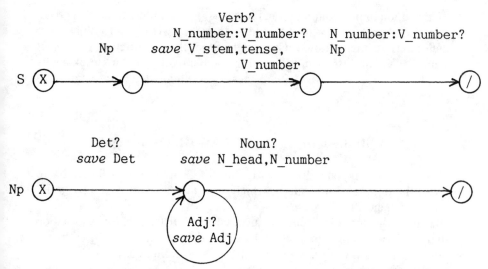

Figure 8.7. A simple ATN grammar

for agreement in number (i.e., singulars and plurals) between the subject noun and the verb. For example, we want to exclude "the dogs is barking", and who wouldn't?

We have gained much power by employing ATNs to direct parsing. We can, for example, take many context-sensitive features of syntax into account with an ATN grammar — i.e., features like subject–verb agreement. The increase in power resides largely in the building actions, which can be used to encode nonlocal syntactic interdependencies, and the tests on register contents, which ensure that the necessary interdependent restrictions are being met by later constructs in a sentence.

An important feature of ATNs from an AI-NLP standpoint was both the maximization of perceptual clarity afforded by the network notation and the not unrelated computational efficiency that could be achieved when parsing with them. Woods was the main popularizer of ATNs (see Woods, 1970), and a significant practical application can be found in the LUNAR system, built to handle natural language queries addressed to the database of geological information extracted from samples of rock brought back from the Moon (see Woods, 1973).

One major limitation of ATNs, noted by Barr and Feigenbaum (1981), is that the heavy dependence on syntax restricts the ability of ATNs to handle ungrammatical (although meaningful) sentences.

ATNs were, until recently, something of a standard for NLP work. Which leads me to the following somewhat cynical (and not my cynicism for a change), but laudably brief, statement of the history of AI-NLP:

"Once upon a time computational linguists (i.e., builders of parsers) used augmented phrase structure grammars, then they went over to ATNs, and then many of them started using augmented phrase structure grammars again."(I've forgotten who said it, but somebody did, and it struck me as apt, in a crude way.) So what are these new augmented phrase structure grammars?

UNIFICATION AND THE NEW GRAMMATISM

Casting your mind back to the early days of Chapter 4, you should try to recall the notion of unification, which is an integral part of the programming language PROLOG.

One of the spin-offs from the success of PROLOG, which is based on the development of computationally efficient algorithms for logical proof (and founded on the resolution principle and unification), has been the rise of unification grammars for NLP.

Pulman (1987, p. 40) introduces this new grammatism like this.

The prototypical unification grammar consists of a context-free skeleton, enriched with a set of feature + value specifications on the grammatical symbols in the rules and associated lexicon. These feature specifications may involve variables, and may be recursive (i.e., the values may be interpreted as referring to a whole category). Whereas parsing and generating sentences using grammars with atomical grammatical labels involves a test for equality between symbols in a rule and those in a tree, in unification grammars the test is whether two non-atomic descriptions 'unify', i.e., can be made identical by appropriate substitutions of terms. This mechanism can be used to enforce identity and cooccurrence restrictions between feature values, and to 'percolate' such values between nodes.

The following section contains an extensive example of one manifestation of unification grammars, but, before we dive into it, a few general statements are in order.

The details of the unification mechanism employed may well be system specific. Some adopt exactly the PROLOG scheme (it has advantages, if you're programming in PROLOG, which are obvious, I hope). Others accept the general idea but do not feel constrained to implement it in detail: clause for clause, or is it CAR for CAR and CDR for CDR? These free spirits are employing the general idea but tailoring it to fit the linguistic regularities that they perceive.

But for those who do go with PROLOG unification in PROLOG (a winning combination in many respects, but not a necessary one), all of the beneficences of PROLOG are automatically at their disposal — automatic backtracking, absence of control issues, etc. Alternatively, opting for the full PROLOG package, so to speak, can be viewed as a somewhat rash move in view of the restrictions that accompany it — automatic back-tracking, lack of control, etc. But we've been over this ground before, so I'll give it a miss this time, provided that you realize that a PROLOG-based unification grammar, like the moon, has a dark side which is not lit up for casual observers, such as Earthlings.

SEMANTIC DEFINITE CLAUSE GRAMMARS (SDCG)

The SDCG formalism is a development of the *definite clause grammars* (DCG) of Pereira and Warren (1980), in which predicates are added to DCGs to make them more realistic candidates for the grammatical basis of serious NLP systems. A SDCG can be used to resolve word sense ambiguities, for example, while a DCG, being a purely syntactic device, cannot.

Here is a DCG version of our earlier rewrite rule for defining a sentence:

sentence(s(Np,Vp))↦ noun_phrase(Np), verb_phrase(Vp).

I trust that this looks familiar. In the terminology of PROLOG, this clause specifies that, to prove that we have a sentence, we must prove that we have a noun_phrase followed by a verb_phrase. In the process of generating such a proof in PROLOG the subgoals on the right-side of the clause (i.e., noun_phrase(Np) and verb_phrase(Vp)) must unify with subsequences of words in the sequence of words which we are trying to prove is a sentence.

One important consequence of a successful proof is that the unification mechanism of PROLOG results in the variables Np and Vp becoming instantiated with subsequences of words from the original sentence. In plainer language, the value of Np will be the sequence of words that is the noun phrase of the sentence, and Vp likewise will have the verb phrase as its value. Finally, a successful proof will result in the structure embedded in the right-side goal or head of the clause (i.e., the (s (Np,Vp)) structure) obtaining the same variable values that were instantiated during proofs of the left-side subgoals. An example is overdue, I think.

We must first add a few more clauses to the DCG.

noun_phrase(np(Det, Noun))↦deter(Det), noun(Noun).
noun_phrase(np(Noun))↦ noun(Noun).
verb_phrase(vp(V,Np))↦ verb(V), noun_phrase(Np).

deter(det(the))↦ [the].
deter(det(a))↦ [a].
noun(n(cat))↦ [cat].
noun(n(dog))↦ [dog].
noun(n(mat))↦ [mat].
verb(v(bit))↦ [bit].
verb(v(sat))↦ [sat].

The sequence of words that we wish to prove is a sentence is: "the cat bit a dog".

It should come as no surprise to learn that this proof will go through smoothly. The final result will be 'Yes', the input sequence is indeed a sentence, and in addition we obtain the following structure:

(s(np(det(the),n(cat)),vp(v(bit),np(det(a),n(dog)))))

which is, as you may perceive, not only opaquely LISPian in structure, but, more importantly, a linearized parse tree; unlinerized, it is illustrated in see Figure 8.8.

So exploitation of the unification mechanism that is part of the PRO-LOG language results in the automatic contruction of the parse tree as a side-effect to proving the syntactic correctness of a sequence of words.

But as stated above, DCGs offer no real increase in power over CFGs. Just try "mat sat a dog," it parses beautifully. What DCGs do offer is some increase in convenience which, while nice to have, is not a major advance for NLP work. Hence, we arrive at SDCGs.

sentence(s(Subj_Np,vp(v(Verb_sense),Obj_Np))↦
                  noun_phrase(Subj_Np),
                  [word],
                  {is_verb(Word,Verb,Tense)},
                  {subject_verb_match(Subj_Np,Verb,Verb_sense)},
                  noun_phrase(Obj_Np),
                  {verb_object_match(Verb_sense,Obj_Np)}.

Very little time should be required to assure yourself that we have in-creased the complexity of our grammar. Let me explain the new classes of structure introduced. Square-brackets indicate the consuming of an in-put unit, a word or a punctuation mark. Thus in the above clause, the variable "Word" enclosed in "[]" (the second subgoal) would be instant-iated as the value of the next input unit (expected to be a word) after the first subsequence of words has unified with the first subgoal (i.e., noun_phrase).

A curly bracketed subgoal is a test that must evaluate to true for the

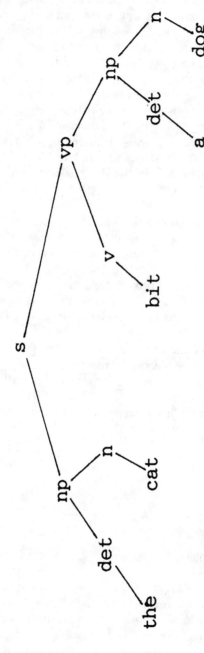

Figure 8.8. A parse tree for "the cat bit a dog"

proof to succeed you may recall (persistent amnesiacs are strongly advised to temporarily suspend reading at this point and backtrack to the PROLOG section of Chapter 4; last warning). Thus the third subgoal uses the "is_verb" predicate to test the word just instantiated, as the value of "Word" is indeed a verb (at the same time the variable "Tense" is instantiated as record of the tense of the verb for use in subsequent tests in a more ambitious grammar than ours).

The fourth subgoal (another test) checks that the subject noun phrase (i.e., the value of Subj_Np) matches the sense of the verb, the value instantiated as that of "Verb_sense". Incidentally, values for these intuitively plausible, but so far mysterious, variables "Tense", "Verb", and "Verb_sense" are obtained from the dictionary, where they are to be found associated with the words in the original sentence, as you will soon see.

The fifth subgoal instantiates the final subsequence of words as the value of "Obj_Np". And the final subgoal (also a test) checks that the earlier determined value of "Verb_sense" matches that of the object noun phrase found.

If each of these subgoals is proved (and the input sequence is totally consumed, i.e., no spare words), the input sequence is a grammatical sentence and we also have details of its syntactic and semantic structure available.

Enough of these tiresome explanations; it's time for another example. Another sentence, say "the dog bit the mat" (not exactly a random selection from the riches of the English language) can be parsed with this grammar. But first I have to give you some additional SDCG clauses, the dictionary or lexicon, and the necessary semantic codings for word senses.

```
noun_phrase(np(Det,Noun))→deter(Det),noun(Noun).
deter(the).
noun(dog,[dog1,dog2]).
noun(mat,[mat1]).
verb(bit,[bit1]).
sem(dog1,[head(animal)]).
sem(dog2,[head(man)]).
sem(mat1,[head(thing)]).
sem(bit1,[subj(animate),obj()]).
```

The lexicon of determiners, nouns, and verbs now lists and labels the different senses of each word. Thus "dog" has two senses labeled "dog1" and "dog2". The final four clauses are the semantic codings of these word senses. Thus the first semantic coding signifies that the meaning "dog1" is the usual sense of an animal. Following that the meaning "dog2" is the metaphorical sense that is applied to people. Of critical importance to the successful processing of our example sentence is the last clause, the semantic coding for the "bit1" sense of the verb "bit". This coding signifies that the "bit1" sense requires that the subject of the verb (the thing that does the biting) must be animate, but that the object (the thing that is bit) can be anything.

During parsing (if that's still the appropriate term, now that we clearly have semantic contraints built into our grammar) the first subgoal, noun_ phrase, is satisfied by "the dog", and the first sense of "dog", "dog1" is selected. The second subgoal just results in the instantiation of "Word" as "bit". The test "is_verb" checks that the value of "Word" is indeed a verb. The second test, "subject_verb_match", checks that the se- lected sense of the subject noun phrase (i.e., "dog1") is animate as the semantic coding of "bit1" demands.

The fifth subgoal is satisfied by the value "the mat", and the final test checks that the selected (and only) sense of "mat" is appropriate for the selected semantic coding of the verb (i.e., "bit1"), and it is.

Thus the sentence is proved to be correct. Similarly, the sentence "the mat bit the dog" will be unacceptable to this grammar. I leave verification of my prediction as an exercise for the reader (Hint: a helpful heuristic is that "thing"s are not "animate"; now try again).

The above grammatical scheme has been used successfully in a practi- cal machine translation system, but more on that anon. For the moment we should observe that this SDCG grammar is attempting to lead us up into the rarified atmosphere of semantics, but before we follow the guid- ance of the grammar, I need to wind up this unification grammar section and then take some parting shots at the formal syntacticians.

Unification grammars are sometimes said to be too powerful, in the sense that almost anything that one wants to specify as a linguistic mecha- nism is specifiable within the general bounds of unification grammar (al- beit somewhat clumsy specification at times). The problem is thus that unification grammars have no obvious confines. Unlike, say, CFGs, unifi- cation grammars are not falsifiable in the same sense that a theory should be potentially falsifiable if it is a useful theory. It is the falsification of theoretical proposals that is a major factor in driving science forward and on to the formulation of more powerful theories. This feature of unifica- tion grammars has caused them to be viewed more as an assembly lan- guage for NLP (convenient low-level units in terms of which higher-level theories are constructed) rather than as a theoretical contribution (in their own right) that furthers our understanding of natural language.

Nevertheless, the unification grammar idea is a neat way to cause in- formation to trickle up and down trees. As we have seen, this automatic ability to pass information around can be used to specify both context- sensitive syntactic features of language (such as subject–verb person and number agreement) and semantic contraints (such as subject–verb seman- tic category agreement).

This ability to specify a wide variety of such agreements stretches right across a grammar; i.e., the proof tree that underlies any parse may require certain types of agreement between root and leaf features (in effect) in order to constitute a successful parse rather than just another dead end which then invokes backtracking.

Such long-distance dependencies (known as a *lack of locality*) lead to combinatorial problems, one of the usual pernicious epiphenomena of AI work (recall Schank's characteristic feature (d) in Chapter 1). A closely related problem is that unification grammars can exhibit very poor performances computationally: The time/space requirements of the necessary algorithms are too demanding; the grammar becomes computationally intractable. Another common trend in AI (and, of course, not unrelated to the earlier-mentioned blight): A neat formal characterization of some aspect of intelligent behavior is impossible to apply in practice. It also appears that it is not easy to recognize lack of locality in a grammar, but it soon announces itself, if that's any consolation.

Lack of locality is particularly worrying also because it threatens to undermine the semantic aspects of NLP. As you will see from the subsequent section on semantics, a basic working assumption is that the semantics of a sentence can be composed (to some reasonable degree) from the semantics of its constituent units, independent of their contexts. Lack of locality reflects global constraints on the informational content of a sentence. As Pereira (1987, p. 36) says:

> Lack of locality means that the processor is unable to identify the exact informational contribution of an utterance element without considering the whole utterance. This is rather unsatisfactory, as one might expect that the informational contribution of an object is precisely what can be learned from an object without regard for context.

There is an oft-heard formalist's lament for loss of context-free purity, a highly desirable (perhaps essential) characteristic of systems that can be elegantly, formally described, but a largely absent characteristic of much intelligent activity, it appears. I shall briefly amplify my views on the formalists' influence on NLP, which links back to my questioning of the naturalness of the languages processed in much NLP work at the opening of this chapter and also connects forward to the semantics issues that are coming up soon.

NLP AND A FORMAL COMPLAINT

The role of a grammar can vary from prescriptive (as in a formal grammar that defines, say, a programming language) to descriptive (as in rules that describe the sentence forms which are acceptable to native speakers of a natural language). In addition, the former type of grammar must of necessity be complete, whereas the latter type never are (and some would argue that they can never be complete — see, for example, Wilks, 1971). At the formal end of the spectrum the language in question is typically defined as that set of strings generated by some grammar (a four-tuple, right?). This type of model does not work terribly well even for programming languages. The success of using formal grammars to define the syntax of programming languages is due to the fact that they define a superset of the language (i.e., the set of syntactically correct strings is a subset of the grammatically correct ones) which can be pruned down with the constraints of so-called static semantics. It is unclear whether formal languages and natural languages have anything substantive in common. Yet we persist in slipping from one to another, implying, for example, that some workable formal language tool will also work in natural language. The successes of formal, or mathematical, linguistics have been limited to either totally unnatural languages or syntactic issues in small subsets of more natural-like languages.

The difficulty with the logical approach to AI-NLP is that you have to construct a formal model with the right structural properties; i.e., the formal model must have a useful and realistic interpretation in natural language. I was very tempted to say "in the natural language domain," but use of the word *domain* implies some circumscribable phenomena which is exactly the wrong emphasis; one characteristic of natural language, which makes it a particularly unattractive target for formal approaches, is its lack of real confines. The notion of "grammaticality" is an open one, as is the "set" of meaningful strings of English words. The formalists have had very little success in building models of natural language semantics. Human language, as a product of evolution (or classical reconditioning), was not constructed on an axiomatic basis, and the chances of finding an appropriate one to retrofit the phenomenon look slim.

Once again the formal approach in an AI field has not been a unequivocable success. But the undoubted benefits of formalization may nevertheless be one day brought to bear in NLP. One word of warning before we plunge into the murky (I was going to say depths, but I'm not sure there are any) waters of theoretical, natural-language, semantics. You will become aware of a deceptively encouraging term that the formalists bandy about; it is *formal semantics*. It is not only a contradiction in terms (perhaps), but it is also a real nuisance. The existence of a formal semantics for some notation provides some assurance that the notation in question is well founded. It has little or no implications for the semantics of any language for which the well-defined notation is used to construct a grammar. When faced with a formal semantics don't draw the conclusion that the questions of semantics have thus been solved. It does not mean that the semantics (in some real sense which we shall get to below) has been formalized; it means that the symbolic constructions in the formal notation have been tied to some other formalism such as first-order logic or the lambda calculus. Well-defined abstraction (but divorced from reality) versus shakey realism is a conflict that is endemic in AI, and we shall return to it (in Chapter 10, although the eager reader is urged to read and mentally digest "McDermott's dilemma" in McDermott, 1986).

While voicing formal complaints, this might be just the right time to indulge in a final review of Chomskyan linguistics and its impact (or lack of, as we shall see) on AI-NLP. The Chomskyan tradition is a central pillar of the science of linguistics, whereas its relevance to AI-NLP is more in terms of one of the other possible worlds which is always discussed but only in order to explicitly reject it. The revolting computational linguists (described with alacrity below) were driven, in part at least, to seek semantics-based systems by what they viewed as the unhealthy preoccupation with syntax in the Chomskyan school of thought.

The shifts and changes in transformational theory over the last 30 years, coupled with Chomsky's general failure to answer his critics directly, makes any attempt to explore the intricacies of the lack of productive interaction between AI and Chomskyan linguistics far beyond the scope of both my competence and the few short paragraphs that can be spared for this topic. Wilks (1987a) is an example of a recent sally against the Chomskyan syntacticians quiet behind their formal defences — let him who is without syntax in his system cast the first aspersion.

Nevertheless, several major Chomskyan issues have not yet been raised in this book, so I shall give them a brief airing. The first of these unmentioned but hard-to-ignore proposals is the competence-performance distinction: Very roughly, *competence* is the abstract ability to recognize and generate well-formed language, and *performance* refers to overt linguistic behavior and its ungrammaticalness, etc. Controversy continues to rage around the meaning and significance of this distinction. Thus Chomsky's formal, grammaticality-based theory can be a theory of linguistic competence and as such remains aloof from the potential challenges of empirical evidence. Ungrammatical word strings, the medium of much everyday communication, floors most syntax-based NLU systems (we have already noticed this with repect to ATN-based systems), but for Chomskyans it is a question of performance and it has little bearing on their models of linguistic competence.

Wilks (1987b), on the other hand, dismisses the distinction as dust on the billiard balls: Reality (dealing as it must with the empirical world as is) never precisely matches any abstract, theoretical characterization. To take a final viewpoint: Langacker (1973) draws the analogy between a symphony and its performance. An abstract musical system that underlies the activity of musicians, but it cannot be equated with their activity. It is thus the abstract linguistic structure that we should be seeking to characterize, not actual verbal behavior. This analogy is superficially compelling, but to my mind it soon breaks down irreparably once you recognize that it is not at all clear that an abstract, well-defined specification of English exists (the written symphony) and there are quite good reasons for believing that it does not (see, for example, Wilks, 1971, discussed below).

Finally, there is a quest for the Universal Grammar — a characterization of the innate human linguistic ability, or the linguistic core that is identical in every human language. This chimerical object, for so it has proved to be, is posited by Chomsky (1973) on the basis of observations of first-language learning in children. First languages are learned with approximately equal facility, irrespective of the natural language in question or the genetic origin of the child. Additionally, despite the enormous differences in learning environments, all children from a given linguistic culture end up with much the same internalized model of the language. Hence there must be an innate human linguistic ability that is general enough to permit assimilation of any human language equally easily, and yet specific enough to yield only one grammatical model within the wide diversity of learning environments associated with each language.

Syntactic correctness, grammaticality, is the touchstone of most AI-NLP work. The semantics of natural language is variously tagged onto the syntactic structures, left to be tackled when syntactic issues have been conquered, or just ignored. Ignorance, some would have it, is bliss, but for us, with no particular theory to grind, all of the possibilities must be explored.

Before we leave the relatively closed and safe realms of syntax and venture out into the infinite space (most of it quite dull or void) of semantic issues, we might note that even the syntactic comforts are somewhat illusory in natural languages as opposed to superficially natural language-like formal languages. Wilks (1971), for example, challenges the usual assumption that grammaticality is a decidable notion with respect to a natural language. It can be decidable for a set of strings with respect to some grammar, but any given grammar is, at best, a specification of a subset of say, English. Even work that admits the possibility of syntactically ill-formed sentences (e.g., Sager, 1981; Goodman, 1984; Kwasny & Sondheimer, 1981) treats the phenomenon as one of subsequent (after a failed parse) or successive constraint relaxation. Thus the sovereignty-of-syntax principle still reigns supreme; sentences that fail to meet the test of syntactic well-formedness are then sent for remedial treatment within these schemes.

In addition, "for no sequence of words can we know of it that it cannot be included in the supposed set of meaningful sentences that make up a natural language'' (Wilks, 1990, p. 131). An appeal to meaning, it seems, is not going to provide a sound basis upon which to build our attempts to formally circumscribe natural languages. Nevertheless, appeal to meaning we must. What is the ''meaning'' of a sentence? Can we extract it? If so, what can we do with it then? All serious problems, and not ones that I can pretend to answer, but we can look at the approaches tried in AI-NLP.

SEMANTICS

Lexicalist theories of semantics — i.e., the meaning of an utterance is composed from the meanings of the lexical units, typically words — is just yet another manifestation of syntactic dominance in NLU. The other major characterization of the view that dominates semantic schemes is stated in the above sentence, but I'll bring it right out into the open. Most strategies for constructing meanings, and especially the formal ones, are compositional: The meaning of a larger unit is a function of the individual meanings of the constituent subunits. Word meanings give us sentence meanings, sentence meanings give us paragraph meanings, and so on. Like most convenient schemes in AI this one too has its good and bad moments. And given that most so-called discourse processing systems have yet to rise above the level of single-sentence processing systems, we are for the most part, and for the time being, dealing with the composition of lexical meanings to yield sentence meanings.

Winograd and Flores (1986), whose unconventional view of the human linguistic ability we have already seen, attack this compositional approach to semantics as just one manifestation of the misguided (in the context of computers and society) notion of ''the rationalistic tradition'' — explaining the operation of deterministic mechanisms whose principles can be captured in formal systems. The highest expression of this tradition, they claim, is in mathematics and logic. This tradition has given rise to formal theories of semantics in which ''the meanings of the items being composed should be fixed *without reference to the context in which they appear*'' (Winograd & Flores, 1986, p. 19, authors' emphasis). This approach is, in their view, doomed, and the rationalist orientation must be replaced if we are to design effective computer tools.

The compositional approach to semantics is the orthodoxy of the far right, and the theory that natural language has no meaning independent of context has been used to characterize the far left. But all the intermediate positions are also occupied and defended vigorously; red and blue may be the extremes (to change the metaphor slightly), but every shade of reddish-blue and of blueish-red is to be found in the world of AI-NLP.

Semantics is a slippery topic, as we can see. I've already cautioned the reader about misuse of the term formal semantics. And later, in the Foundations of AI chapter, we'll see Searle slithering gleefully down a semantic slope and trying to drag all incautious observers with him. So, perhaps we would be well advised to bat the term around a bit before we consider specific approaches.

THE MEANING OF SEMANTICS

Equally engagingly (or annoyingly, depending on your viewpoint), this section could have been titled "the semantics of meaning." The ultimate heading is, of course, "the meaning of meaning," but Ogden and Richards took out the patent on that one years ago. More precisely (if precision is the quality that we're going to adhere to for a change), this section is focused on the meaning of natural language semantics, which narrows its uncomfortably broad scope somewhat, but not a lot I suspect.

As we all know if we spare the time to think about it, there are occasions when the meaning of a sentence cannot be in the words that comprise the sentence. Some of the component words may provide a general basis for the meaning, but nothing more. In such cases the meaning may be largely in the context of the sentence. Where context can be anything from voice quality of the words uttered, preceding and succeding sentences, to goals and intentions of both the speaker and the listener. In fact, I could have terminated the last sentence at the fifth word. "And where are the confines of relevance?" asks Steiner (1975, p. 7); I understand the question, but I have no answer. The same sentence uttered at different times or in different ways will have different meanings. Similarly, a sentence may have radically different meanings for the speaker and the hearer even though neither intend it to be, or realize it is, the case.

Without getting too far out of my depth in the philosophical linguistic intricacies of where or what is discourse meaning, let us just observe that it cannot in all honesty be composed out of context-free word meanings. But this is the approach of most concrete AI-NLP projects, and it can be a useful approximation as we shall see in the later sections on machine translation and natural language interfaces. It is instructive, perhaps, to recall at this point the Fodor and Pylyshyn (1988) demolition job on the CP (Chapter 3). They attack the significance of the CP precisely because it fails to provide a molecular representation of meaning (i.e., the meaning of a sentence is an indivisible whole; it is not composed from the meaning of constituent elements). But this should not be mistaken for an argument that the meaning of a sentence can be constructed from the meaning of the constituent words only — the component words may be an important part of the meaning, but they are not the only contributors, and sometimes they are not even the major contributors.

To briefly mention a popular application of a formal compositional approach to language meaning, let us look at truth values. The truth value of a sentence is typically not a route to meaning. Different intonations, for example, on the same string of words can result in opposite truth values for that string. "That's smart," said ironically, has an opposite truth value to when it is said with normal intonation.

Theoretical studies, sometimes in conjunction with very small-scale implementations, are exploring the roles of beliefs, goals, and intentions for NLP. To the extent that work on these complexities of language meaning has not attained the level of development necessary for useful inclusion in an NLP system, the issues become more a question of knowledge representation and have been discussed in that chapter although we shall also briefly resurrect these pragmatic issues in a later section of this chapter.

So, if the meaning is not in the sentence, what is? One answer is to extract, not meaning from a sequence of words, but their "primal content," which may or may not accord closely with their meaning. The meaning of a string of words is then derived as a result of processing the extracted primal content in the appropriate context: an appealing idea, I think, but one that is still largely articulated in terms of hand waves rather than a symbolism that might be computable.

So, with respect to implemented systems that can analyze more than a couple of sentences, we typically find a meaning representation constructed from a collection of primitive units of meaning which are themselves associated with lexical items. The SDCG grammar illustrated earlier is a representative example of this common approach to the synthesis of a meaning from natural language text.

THE ATOMIC STRUCTURE OF MEANING

The compositional approach to semantics implies that there is some collection of underlying semantic primitives from which the meaning of a string of words is composed. A variety of different schemes have been advocated, differing in their advocacy for what sort of things these primitives are and how they are related to lexical items.

A Katz and Fodor (1963) proposal attached "semantic markers" to lexical items. The SDCG grammar discussed earlier is a direct descendent of this markerese proposal. Fillmore's (1968) "case grammar" gives verbs the central role and associates semantic "cases" with specific classes of verb. Construction of meaning in NLU then amounts to finding the key verbs which then direct analysis to extract from the text "fillers" for the defined cases of the verb. Thus the "give" verbs are associated with case slots for the giver, the given, and the recipient of what is given. Having found a "give" verb in a sentence, a meaning representation is built by finding information to fill these case slots (some syntactic analysis is usually necessary, but not an exhaustive parse). Schank's "conceptual dependency" notation (described below) is based on the verb case approach to meaning. Schank's scheme also illustrates a further argument that seems to tag along with the idea of semantic primitives: Is there some well-defined set of primitives that are both necessary and sufficient for representing the meanings of English?

Wilks (1977) reviews and criticizes many of the basic ideas on semantic primitives. He then presents a scheme for the construction of semantic formulae that represent word senses. He bases his system on 100 primitives and seven types of subformulae. The Wilksian "semantic preference" scheme (see for example, Wilks, 1975) contructing meaning representations from textual analysis rests on the idea of accepting that semantic representation which has maximum "semantic density." Fairly complex (tree-structured rather than elementary) word meanings are composed to yield a sentence meaning by selecting that set of the possible word meanings which fit together most comfortably (maximum "semantic overlap"). This approach tackles the problem that alternative word senses are often not simply in accord or mutually opposed. There are degrees of compatibility; preference semantics attempts to select that meaning which results from some overall maximization of word sense compatibilities. We shall review this scheme in its proper place: as an example of the work of the revolting computational linguists.

Better examples of noncompositional approaches to semantics in AI-NLP can be found, of course, in the CP-based, or CP-flavored, theories and models. Pollack and Waltz (1986), for example, attempted to build an NLU system in which the subprocesses are all interdependent (go back to Chapter 6 for further enlightenment).

Pollack (1987a) describes how concepts, such as DEER and HUNTING, are "associated with a set of 'microfeatures' that serve both (a) to define the concepts, at least partially, and (b) to associate the concept with others that share its microfeatures" (p. 35). Thus DEER is associated with HUNTING because they share the microfeatures OUTSIDE and LAKE, and the first of these microfeatures provides a much stronger association than the second one. He suggests "that microfeatures should be chosen on the basis of first principles to correspond to the major distinctions humans make about situations in the world" (p. 35) — e.g. threatening/safe, animate/inanimate.

This scheme is clearly not the same as the simple compositional approaches to meaning, but is it very different? When is a feature a microfeature? Surely not just when two concepts have a feature in common?

Finally, I can point you towards Minsky's certainly more radical, but less well-defined proposals on the nature of meaningful communications that collectively will amount to intelligent activity. He is not referring to natural language as such, but his ideas about communication between agents that collectively amount to an intelligence provide an infrastructure for the overt behavior of minds, and hence, these ideas are (in part at least) a theory a language meaning. Early on he proposes that the agents don't use a language at all, "that is, an ordered string of symbols. We will propose a parallel, spatial scheme" (Minsky, 1977, p. 1083). In the later and major exposition of this theory (Minsky, 1986), he says that words correspond to very complex mental structures. Words don't have meanings in isolation, out of context. Meaning is the way it is related to other things. "A thing with just one meaning has scarcely any meaning at all" (p. 64). The reader should be able to discern a strong undercurrent of connectionism in this theorizing.

To go deeper into Minsky's theory necessitates learning a whole new language of "K-lines," "polynemes," "isonomes," and so on. I leave it to you the reader to delve further into the world of *The Society of Mind* if your search for the meaning of language (if not the meaning of life) leads you in this direction. But be warned, Minsky's attractive model is couched in terms so far removed from the building blocks of the programmer's world that is it virtually untestable. It is thought-provoking speculation rather than scientific theory.

We shall see more of the CP-based approach towards the end of the chapter by which time I shall have disposed of the traditional perspective on AI-NLP.

THE CASE OF THE MISSING-BLOCKS WORLD

It appears to be a requirement in any discussion of NLP systems that Winograd's (1972) NLU system SHRDLU is dragged out, dusted off, and generally exposed to the wonderment of naive observers. This NLP system is typically employed to capitalize shamelessly on the ELIZA syndrome. It uses a sophisticated question-answer mode that can take account of earlier features of the dialogue (i.e., it is not simply a single-context-free-question answerer), and its understanding is deep enough for it to be instructed to manipulate objects in a blocks world. Lastly, the system was completed over a decade ago (almost an earlier era in AI terms), so just imagine what can be accomplished now.

Something closer to the truth is that it was a research project (abandoned as effectively unimprovable long ago) which could be induced, on occasion, to participate in an extended, sensible dialogue about a totally fictitious blocks world. It manipulated very sparse, abstract, representations of blocks, pyramids, etc., not a real toy world at all; and as we are all well aware, between abstract (and necessarily sparse) worlds and real worlds, there is a world of difference.

Nevertheless, SHRDLU was an important contribution to the development of NLP and it has theoretical significance in the history of this subfield, but these aspects are all too often ignored in favor of the convenient misconceptions that a simple demonstration dialogue can engender in the casual observer. This system was, for example, the first one to employ planning in the context of NLP.

The SHRDLU program was built using the theory of systemic grammar developed by Halliday (1970), which is itself an interesting concept: a theory of linguistic structure that emphasizes the features which are important for conveying meaning. Halliday was concerned with the functional demands made on language and the avoidance of conventional syntactic parsing. His work is part of the tradition that rejects the primacy of syntax view that I have been emphasizing as a central theme of much AI-NLP work. Halliday had a theory in which syntax, semantics, and pragmatics all interacted on a more-or-less independent basis, but in practice syntax drives it for the most part — it was a *heterarchical* system. (*Heterarchical* is a once-popular AI word whose heyday is over. It was used to convey a notion of noncentralized control, to contrast with the top-down control mechanisms in hierarchically organized systems. In our NLP example, syntax, semantics, and pragmatics share power in determining the direction in which the system will go — i.e., it describes a state of mild anarchy with powerful barons but no king.) We shall consider this general tradition (i.e., when syntax is dethroned) after an example of SHRDLU at work.

Rather than reiterate one of the many beguiling examples of SHRDLU and the blocks, I can offer a true AI story which I did not invent — I think that somebody else did. Certainly, Haugeland (1985) has a version with the same punch line, and I've been subjected to it in several AI talks. So even in AI, which is full of jokes but has even more books being written about it, some repetition is inevitable.

TRUE AI STORY: 8.1 SHRDLU and a "SORRY" story

Deep in the intricacies of yet another fascinating dialogue about the blocks world, it is said that the following exchange was once recorded:

Human: Put the blue pyramid on the block in the box.
SHRDLU: OK.[manipulates representation of blocks world to reflect result of executing this command.]
Human: Is there anything which is bigger than every pyramid but is not as wide as the thing that supports it?
SHRDLU: YES, THE BLUE BLOCK.
Human: Build a steeple.
SHRDLU: SORRY, I DON'T KNOW THE WORD "STEEPLE".
Human: A "steeple" is a stack which contains two green cubes and a pyramid.
SHRDLU: I UNDERSTAND.
Human: Are there any steeples now?
SHRDLU: NO.
Human: Build one.
SHRDLU: OK. [manipulates representation to reflect having built a steeple]
Human: Now build another one.
SHRDLU: SORRY, I DON'T KNOW THE WORD "NOW".
Human: "now" means immediately.
SHRDLU: SORRY, I DON'T KNOW THE WORD "MEANS".
Human: Sorry, I didn't know that you understood so little.
SHRDLU: SORRY, I DON'T KNOW THE WORD "SORRY".

END OF TRUE AI STORY

Sorry, but I just don't know quite what this sort of system performance signifies. I'll leave the drawing of a plausible moral as yet another exercise for the reader, and move to the AI-NLP subarea where the syntactician gets his or her well-overdue comeuppance.

REVOLTING COMPUTATIONAL LINGUISTS

The syntacticians may have held the field in linguistics, despite skirmishes with nontraditionalists like Halliday, but in AI-NLP, although the syntactical parsers are dominant, they have not had it all their own way. Both Ritchie (1983) and Wilks (1983), for example, have explored alternatives and assessed their merit.

Ritchie examines whether NLU can be organized around semantic constructs (rather than syntactic units), and the extent to which semantic processing can be carried out locally as a sentence is parsed. He concludes with a negative response to the first possibility, and for the second he can find little positive empirical evidence.

Ritchie suggests several ways in which the early application of semantic information (i.e., during the course of a parse rather than after generating a set of alternative parses) is expected to be useful:

1. Evaluation of the referent of a phrase, e.g., "The things on the table are . . ." If we can determine what sorts of things are being referred to, then we might have available information to eliminate ambiguities later in the sentence;
2. Application of inferences from general knowledge, e.g., "My uncle ran the London Marathon." Knowledge of "My uncle" (that he is a young athlete, or he is an old administrator for the Greater London Council) can be used to eliminate the ambiguity.

Ritchie also explored the use of a semantic rule tree, in which each node was evaluated as soon as possible; it was an ATN-based parse in which the semantic structure for each syntactic constituent was built as soon as possible.

In general, he concludes that there are no convincing examples of real benefits from these forms of early semantic processing.

Wilks (1983) discusses a range of systems that have in common a desire to avoid conventional syntactic parsing. Within this class of system he distinguishes "deep" and "superficial" parsing: Deep systems aim to parse directly from English to a semantic representation without passing through a conventional syntactic phase; superficial systems make little commitment about the nature of the representation, but view language, by way of contrast, as a flat, linear phenomenon.

Deep parsers again divide into two classes: the "micro" ones, which produce representations corresponding to clauses; and the "macro," which aim at representations that are inherently textual. For Wilks, Colby's (1975) PARRY system is an example of a superficial parser, and Weizenbaum's (1966) ELIZA is, I suppose, another. Neither system builds much (anything?) of a semantic representation, and they find no need to go through an exhaustive syntactic analysis to do so, not surprisingly. Key word (and specific pattern) recognition are used to generate responses as minor variations on a set of stored patterns.

Naturally, these systems were not major contributions to the science of AI-NLP, but like SHRDLU they are inevitably used to illustrate the more popular treatises on NLU. ELIZA is the classic example; hence, the ELIZA syndrome in AI (Partridge, 1986a): Seemingly intelligent snippets of natural-language dialogue or problem-solving ability induce in the casual observer unwarranted grandiose assumptions about the underlying abilities, and hence potential domains of application, of the host system.

In terms of Wilks's classification scheme examples of deep parsers are to be found in AI-NLP work surrounding the traditions of both Schankian conceptual-dependency and Wilks' preference semantics. We shall look at both of these approaches below.

SCRIPTED NLU AND ITS DEPENDENCIES

Another of the obligatory examples in any writings that purport to survey NLP is script-based NLU from the Schankian school whose alma mater is Yale University but, in the absence of any known cure, has spread to centers throughout the world. A *script* is a representation of knowledge that organizes the information surrounding some action (like going to eat in a restaurant) in a way that maximizes the chances of bringing the right information to bear at the right time when attempting to understand a textual description of the appropriate action. Now that sort of data structure sounds like a winner, but how do you realize it?

Well, a script is (as the name suggests) a network, not a well-defined network it's true, but a sort of network structure, nevertheless. The paths through it constitute the most likely alternative sequences of actions involved in performing the action that the particular script aspires to capture. A script is also a species of plan; one of the non-logic-based varieties (a Chapter 3 subject). A (highly simplified) restaurant script might be composed of the following "scenes."

> Customer enters restaurant.
> Customer sits at a table.
> Server brings customer a menu.
> Customer orders food.
> Server brings food.
> Customer eats food.
> Customer asks for the check.
> Server brings check.
> Customer pays cashier.
> Customer leaves restaurant.

This list of scenes is, in a useful script, expanded into a network to accommodate the major alternative sequences of the dining-out experience. One must, for example, order one's food before finding a seat in some of the less salubrious eating establishments.

A further addition to the sequences of component scenes are the extras — an essential requirement of all epic systems. Thus scripts require players, such as customer, server, manager, cashier, and chef in the restaurant script. And finally, we need props such as a restaurant, tables, chairs, etc.

The stage is now set; all we need is a story (preferably a restaurant story) to start the action. Here is such a story:

"John went into a restaurant. He ordered a hamburger. He paid the cashier and left the restaurant."

Schank's NLU system uses the script to both guide interpretation of the given text and add specific inferences suggested by the script but absent from the story. Thus the story does not say that John ate the hamburger, but from the restaurant script, the system infers that he probably did. Having processed this story the system has generated a representation of its 'meaning'. We'll get to this representation in a minute, but, as we discussed earlier, the credibility, validity, or whatever of such representations of meaning are hard to evaluate. So how does Schank support the claim that his system has understood this story? There are two ways that he does this: The system generates a paraphrase of the story, or the system answers questions about the story. The automatically generated paraphrase might be:

"John was hungry. He decided to go into a restaurant. He went into one. He sat down. The server brought him a menu. He ordered hamburger. The server brought him a hamburger. He ate the hamburger. He asked the server for his check. He paid the cashier. He left the restaurant."

Now that's not a bad paraphrase of the original story. Although it is unlikely to win a nomination for the Nobel Prize for Literature for the authoring system, it does make explicit much of the unspecified information that you and I would read into the original, perhaps over-pithy, tale. The accuracy and richness (relative to the original text) of this paraphrase does suggest that the original text was correctly mapped onto a knowledge representation that captures the essential features of eating at a restaurant. But, remember, a suggestion of AI is not necessarily AI in some more substantial sense. Now read on.

To further assess the system we might engage it in a question–answer dialogue.

Us:	What did John eat?
Computer System:	John ate a hamburger.
Us:	Why did John go into the restaurant?
CS:	John went into the restaurant because he was hungry.

Us: Why did John pay the cashier?
CS: John paid the cashier for his hamburger.

Again the temptation is fairly hard to resist — this *really* is AI. Lest we get carried away by the impact of these neat examples, I shall continue the dialogue by stealing a few lines from the John Searle Road Show (more on this trouper and his anti-AI road show in Chapter 10). Searle claims (and I see no reason to doubt him, for a change) that the above dialogue can be continued thus:

Us: Was John's hamburger more than one mile wide?
CS: !?
Us: Was the hamburger more, or less, than 3000 years old?
CS: ??

and so on. You have probably latched on to the essential point here, so I'll desist. Schank's system displays the usual brittleness associated with current AI work: It does very well in its own back yard, so to speak, which is, unfortunately, very, very small. As soon as we probe beyond its unstated but very narrow confines of competent activity, it breaks (see the china syndrome in Chapter 3).

TRUE AI STORY: 8.2 Try it again SAM

It is noised about that the Schankian NLU system, primed with the restaurant script, was once presented with the following story:

"The City Health Official went into a restaurant. He sat down. When the waitress came he asked to see the manager. He ordered most of the dishes to be processed under more hygienic conditions. As he left he paid the cashier no attention."

The paraphrase (so I've been told) ran like this:

"The City Health Official was hungry. He decided to go into a restaurant. He went into one. He sat down. The server brought him a manager. He ordered most of the dishes on the menu. The server brought him most of the dishes on the menu. He ate most of the dishes on the menu. He asked the server for his check. He paid the cashier. He left the restaurant."

END OF TRUE AI STORY

The message here is that, although a cursory syntactic analysis can be made to work on a carefully selected and small corpus of sentences by investing a lot of time, effort, expertise, and highly specific heuristics in a computer system, such a system can also be made to totally fail to understand with correspondingly little time, effort, and expertise.

The above-described style of script-based NLU can be found in the SAM system (Schank & Abelson, 1977). Hendrix and Sacerdoti (1981, p. 328) state that this approach to NLU was one of the first that attempted to deal with structured sequences of actions (i.e., discourse analysis rather than single sentence analysis). They list three limitations of the SAM system.

1. Players and props are limited to single objects. Thus, stories involving more than one customer or table, for example, are too complex. This limitation allows the tricky NLU problem of reference (i.e., which object in the world is referred to by some element of the text) to be eliminated: "the table" refers to the one and only table under consideration.
2. Scripted actions follow a strict linear sequence (and later a few strictly limited alternative sequences). This limits allowable stories to just those which follow a particular script.
3. A further limitation is one of selecting the appropriate script for a given story, a largely unaddressed problem which we have noticed before and shall notice again.

Subsequent to SAM there was PAM, which attempts to understand stories by matching the actions of the story with methods that it knows will achieve the goals of a generated goal plan. A review of the ideas underlying these systems is provided by Schank (1980). Both SAM and PAM are selected examples that feature in Figure 10.1, you might like to know.

A significant part of Schank's early achievements in NLU rested on his attempts to devise a canonical notation that was both necessary and sufficient to represent the conceptual structures underlying English text.

THE CONCEPTUAL DEPENDENCY NOTATION

In an effort to address the problem, endemic to NLU (or so it seems), of a proliferation of representations designed to capture the meaning of natural language text, Schank proposed the *conceptual dependency* (CD) notation (Schank, 1973). If everyone designs a representational scheme to suit the sorts of structures that they are extracting from their few examples of text, then the merit of their extraction process (their NLU system) will match the general utility of their representation scheme — i.e., it will be close to zero.

Contrary to the suggestion in their name, CDs (which are *not* compact discs, remember) were designed to be a notation for representing meaning independent of the specific concepts (and surface language) involved in the text. And furthermore, they were meant to be something approaching a complete notation; that is, the elements of the notation should be sufficient to represent any concept. They were not tied to limited domains like, say, restaurants (which is perhaps surprising, when you think about it). Even more surprisingly, the language-independence claim of CD theory makes it a potential interlingua (an intermediate language as used in some machine translation work).

The CD notation is composed of a small number of semantic primitives, both primitive acts and primitive states. Some examples of primitive acts are:

PTRANS The transfer of the physical location of an object. Thus the verb *put* would typically be abstracted to a PTRANS act.

MTRANS The transfer of mental information. Thus use of the verb *tell* would be likely to abstract to an MTRANS of information from one person to another.

"There exist formally defined dependency relations between given categories of concepts" (Schank, 1973, p. 194). They are listed, explained, and examplified by Schank (1973). Each such dependency has a graphical symbol — usually a sort of arrow. Then arrowy diagrams become the visual representations of meanings in CD theory. The canonical example in the canonical form is "John gave Mary a book", which is represented in Figure 8.9. Given that "p" signifies past tense, "o" objective dependency, and "R" a recipient–donor dependency, the reader is left to interpret the diagram, should he or she think that it might be a intellectually edifying experience.

The primitive states of CD theory are even more of a forgotten relic in AI. The small, well-defined number of objects in CD theory was always a laudable goal, but not very realistic. Arguments between opposing factions (reminiscent of the number-of-angels-on-pinheads disputes that graced an age before IJCAIs) blighted this field for some time without yielding much of substance. At this point in time I think that it is safe to say that the number of primitive acts is $(n + m)$, where $10 < n < 27$ and m is that positive integer which is equal to the number of extra primitives needed to accommodate the inevitable counter examples that appear whenever one specifies the n primitive acts.

In recent years Schank has moved on. A dissatisfaction with the fact that his systems keep analyzing the same texts repeatedly with nothing new and with no signs of boredom is the official reason for this move. He

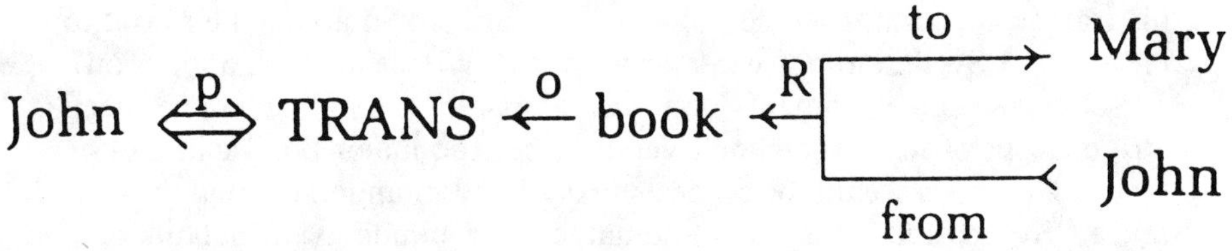

$$\text{John} \overset{p}{\Longleftrightarrow} \text{TRANS} \overset{o}{\longleftarrow} \text{book} \overset{R}{\longleftarrow} \begin{array}{c} \xrightarrow{\text{to}} \text{Mary} \\ \xleftarrow[\text{from}]{} \text{John} \end{array}$$

Figure 8.9.   A CD representation of "John gave Mary a book"

now doubts that such static systems merit classification as AI. Schank has come to believe that he has, all the time, been overlooking the central issue of AI, to wit, learning. AI systems should learn and change with time.

Schank (1982, p. 66) introduces MOPs (*memory organization packets*) and TOPs (*thematic organization packets*) and claims that "expectations are the key to understanding." Scripts are then viewed as a source of expectations, and expectation-failures drive memory development and organization. This limited view of the notion of input-expectation discrepancy reduction that Schank calls expectation failure I have criticized elsewhere (Partridge, 1985a). At the time of writing, Schank's approach to dynamic NLU is explained in terms of "reminding." Thus, understanding of a piece of text is enriched and developed as a result of some similarity between what you know of it and what you know of something else — in attempting to understand some text you are reminded of something else and your understanding of the text at hand (or in mind) is enriched. For example. . . .

A SWALE OF A TALE

By way of contrast to the syntactically rich sentences typically used as examples (or counterexamples) in linguistics and AI-NLP, Schank asks us to consider something like "Swale died." as a possible object of interest to an NLU system. Not an inspiring syntactic construct, is it? But what might be involved in understanding this sentence?

Interest in this sentence can be given a boost by the knowledge that Swale was a young, healthy, very successful racehorse about to enter a major race. On gaining this knowledge we might be reminded of the sudden, unexpected deaths of successful young pop stars (e.g., what Schank calls the Janis Joplin Memorial Reminding). Could Swale have died from a drug overdose? Let's assume that he could.

Problem: Unlike the pop stars, Swale could not have obtained and administered the drug to himself. But some human could have done it. Did his trainer give him too much of some pep drug? Did an outsider do it to ensure that Swale did not win another race? Was it murder, and so on?

Schank's embellishments and interminable remindings have been stripped out of my streamlined version, but the major point can still be made: There is a wealth of processing involved in understanding the sentence "Swale died." (and it's dominated by 'remindings,' if Schank is to be believed), but the importance of syntactic considerations is minimal.

Alternatively, Schank's Swale tale shows that, if a sentence has virtually no syntax, then you don't need sophisticated syntactic analysis in order to process it (not too surprising, you might think). Nevertheless, there may still be a lot of processing to do en route to an understanding.

The Swale Tale reminds me of the vast gap that separates a plausible description of an AI mechanism from an implementation of that mechanism which has some general applicability. Consider the processing of "Swale died." by a reminding-driven mechanism, but one that can process a somewhat richer corpus than these two words. Assume that the mechanism is embodied in a knowledge base containing some variety of knowledge, perhaps not a knowledge of so many things, of shoes — and ships — and sealing wax — of cabbages — and — kings — and why the sea is boiling hot — and whether pigs have wings. But, nevertheless, a knowledge base with some richness of alternative possibilities associated with the key remindings. Anyway, the story goes like this:

TRUE AI STORY: 8.3 Another Swale of a tale.

The two words "Swale died." become more interesting when we learn that Swale was a young, healthy, very successful racehorse. We are reminded of other successful horses that have died: Trigger, Clever Hans, and Diablo, to name but a few. But they were all performers whose fame was based on a fiction. Could it be that Swale's success was fictional too? Let's assume that it was.

Problem: Swale actually ran and won races in reality, so his success was not fictional. But the races could have been "fixed" to allow Swale to win. Did Swale work for the Mafia, who "arranged" his wins? Did Swale's owner have access to a "wonder drug" that added wings to his heels? Are we dealing with a pharmaceutical breakthrough that has unfortunate after-effects?

END OF TRUE AI STORY

What's the moral in all this? Well, to my mind, although Schank leads us through a series of remindings to uncover some fascinating meanings, he has finessed the central problem. Such remindings may well be a useful way to approach the difficult problem of NLU, but once we accept that, the real problems remain untouched. How do we select (or generate) particular remindings and ignore the very many, equally plausible, alternative remindings? How do we determine which aspects of a reminding are significant with respect to the text being understood, and which aspects can be neglected? For some the answer is "indexing," as it was earlier in this book. This is a short answer; indeed there is no more to it than this one word which makes it a very difficult answer to evaluate. It is really a statement of faith generated by general belief in the SSSP. The line of thought is that the ability to search through memory, sort out, and retrieve the important and relevant information, must be based on a smart filing system — each stored item must be indexed in some fancy way in order to efficiently find the appropriate piece(s) of information in the vast sea of possibilities. In the context of our Swale tales why is it that young–healthy–successful–died triggers the pop-star reminding rather than horse–successful–died invoking the famous-horse reminding? (And don't try to tell me that it's a maximum-number-feature-match question, or I'll bring in the brown-furry-two-eyed-sunny-day-3 p.m-in-afternoon feature list which always invokes the old-lady-with-the-mink-whatsit-in-the-tea-shop reminding.)

Yet again we see the fundamental problems of focus of attention, of the determination of significant attributes, and of similarity of complex structures almost completely unaddressed. We have a new theory of NLU, but it will shed little light on the basic issues. It's another theory in the grand AI tradition of the irrefutable and the untestable.

GIVING SEMANTICS PREFERENTIAL TREATMENT

By way of a change the section title is appropriate in both of its senses (I've resisted the temptation to find more than two, and so should you). I have already introduced Wilks's scheme of *semantic preference*, so we can just peruse a concrete example and then be on our way.

The fundamental unit of meaning representation is a *template* which corresponds to the intuitive notion of a basic agent–action–object form (i.e., the cat-bit-the-mat stuff, the cat's the agent, now work it out from there). According to Wilks (1983, p. 230, author's emphasis),"The system contained no explicitly snytactic [sic] information at all: what it knows about any English word sense is its *formula*. . . . Template structures, which actually represent sentences and their parts are built up as networks of formulas."

Figure 8.10 is a full template for "John shut the door."

Let me draw your attention to the fact that this is a nontrivial structure

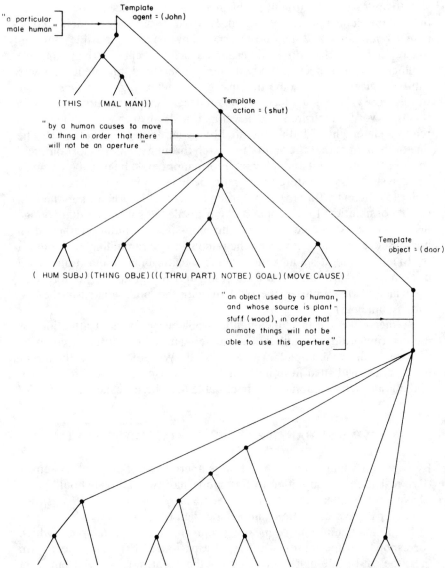

Figure 8.10. A full template for "John shut the door"

From *Computational Semantics,* by E. Charniak & Y. Wilks, 1983, Amsterdam: Elsevier. Copyright 1983 by Elsevier. Reprinted by permission.

to represent a trivial sentence. As for the templates for complex sentences, you don't want to know.

The process of building this representation starts with fragmentation
of the input sentence. This fragmentation process involves breaking the
sentence at key words like prepositions, etc. "Bare templates" are then
matched to these fragments. The parser goes from left to right through the
formula combinations (recall that, in general, there will be one formula for
each sense of a word) searching for matching fragments, but looking only
at the "head" elements of the formulae. It looks for agent, action, and
object formulae, in that order initially.

If I omit most of the gruesome details, the system arrives at the state
of having competing template matches for the text fragments. The contents of the formulae are examined, and the numbers of satisfied preferences are added up (satisfied preferences are compatible semantic features, such as 'bit' requiring an "animate" agent). Maximal satisfaction
of these preferences determines which of the competing templates becomes accepted as the structure for that fragment's template.

As Wilks points out, work in the Schankian tradition (e.g., Riesbeck,
1975) assumes that the correct interpretation fits (driven by scripted expectations or now, remindings) and that other possible interpretations do
not fit at all. The reality is that the right interpretation fits better than the
others. And preference semantics is, of course, designed to select this
best-fit meaning.

BIDIRECTIONAL NLP

As mentioned at the beginning of this chapter, the reasonable expectation
that a system which can understand natural language should also (given
some additional code) be able to generate English is not met by most NLP
work. Bidirectional systems do not seem to be that closely related to most
projects either in NLU or in NLG, but the appearance and successful
usage of unification grammars is seen as offering a new promise for the
realization of bidirectional systems.

For a grammar to function successfully as both a specification to support linguistic analysis and a specification to support text generation, that
grammar must be procedurally neutral. The grammar must be a declarative specification without procedural features which would enhance one
direction of usage but hinder the other. This is the current wisdom behind
the belief in the potential of unification grammars as a basis for bidirectional NLP systems.

Remember the two modes of executing a PROLOG program — verify
and compute? Remember the option of implementing a unification gram-

mar in PROLOG with direct importation of the specific mechanisms of PROLOG? One of the selling points of the PROLOG language is the claim (I hesitate to say fact) that programming in PROLOG involves only the construction of a statement of the logical relationships in the problem domain. A PROLOG program (so the story goes) is a declarative structure; the specification of processing control (a major headache in conventional programming) has been separated out, shunted off into the PROLOG interpreter, and can thus be ignored.

All this is true, to some extent, as we saw in Chapter 4. It can be made quite true by a competent PROLOG programmer who uses the language wisely and resists the temptation to use the convenient extralogical goodies of the language. But such goodies (for example, the "cut" operator) can transform a computationally intractable program into one that will execute within an acceptable timespan (if not sooner).

The task, then, for the implementer of a unification grammar that will effectively support a bidirectional system is to devise an efficient PROLOG implementation without employing any of the handy extralogical features offered by that language.

Huang (1986) discusses using his SDCG grammar (illustrated earlier) for a bidirectional MT system. In particular, he uses it for both parsing and generating of Chinese sentences. He singles out the "cut" operator "!" (which prevents automatic backtracking) as the major problem to be overcome when constructing an efficient bidirectional grammar. His solution is to duplicate those parts of the grammar that contain the cut operator. One set of "cut-up" grammar segments is used by the parser, and the alternative set (differently "cut-up") is used by the generator.

Huang also notes that Shapiro (1982) described a generalized ATN grammar for both analysis and generation, but to run the system two interpreters were needed, one for parsing and the other for generation. A PROLOG-implemented unification grammar holds the promise of the two in one. The major problems are: can an adequate grammar be found? and, can an efficient implementation be found? Solution of these problems requires a sophisticated analysis of PROLOG and the details of its mechanisms.

Appelt (1987) gives a schematic illustration of a bidirectional system architecture and discusses some of the problems that exist (see Figure 8.11).

PRAGMATICS?

As promised way back towards the beginning of this chapter, I shall now consider pragmatics in the context of AI-NLP. Without that specific con-

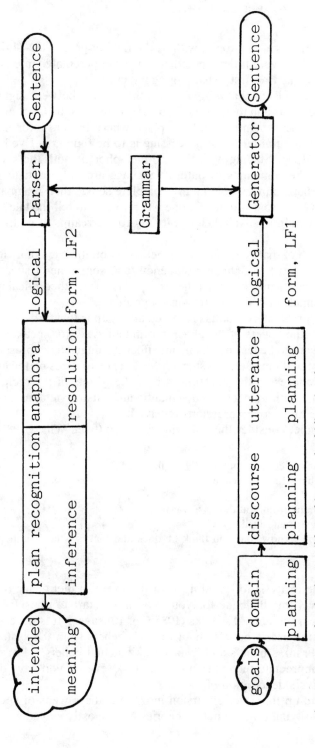

Figure 8.11. A sketch of a possible architecture for bidirectional NLP

From "Bidirectional Grammars and the Design of Natural Language Generation Systems," by D.E. Appelt, 1987, *PrePrints TINLAP3* (p. 187) Reprinted by permission.

straint, pragmatics is a vast topic; with it, the field of pragmatics shrinks to almost nothing — very little of pragmatics has yet percolated into practical AI-NLP work. But first, what is pragmatics?

The dictionary tells us that *pragmatics* is the relation between signs or linguistic expressions and their users. In other words, it is the far country, beyond syntax and semantics, and the place where the basis for many decisions about natural-language processing is to be found, as I've been suggesting all along. Staying with the geo-metaphor, if both the syntax and especially the semantics of natural language are only partially explored and perhaps unmappable in any complete sense, then pragmatics is that distant place from whence no one has returned to tell the tale, and the only information available belongs totally to the realms of myth and legend.

That's enough of that; you can get carried away on the back of a vigorous metaphor. I have to fight that tendency, and sometimes I succeed. AI-NLP work on pragmatics, what there is of it, is largely theoretical with sometimes a small-scale demonstration program.

One area of pragmatics that has received attention is that of belief systems, i.e., how the beliefs of the generator and analyzer (or speaker and hearer, if we want to be less mechanistic) effect the linguistic expressions that flow between them. Belief systems's work tends to focus on the analysis phase. It addresses the question of how the beliefs of the recipient system combine with syntactic and semantic analysis to yield an understanding of the linguistic expressions received.

As an example, consider the following dialogue (from Wilks, 1985b):

USER:	Frank is coming tomorrow I think
SYSTEM:	Perhaps I should leave
USER:	Why?
SYSTEM:	Coming from you that is a warning
USER:	Does Frank dislike you?
SYSTEM:	I don't know, but you think he does and that is what is important now.

Now, syntactic analysis followed up with the use of a dictionary is not going to unravel this dialogue for you. You must start to consider the beliefs of the participants. As Wilks (1985b, p. 10) says: "It is necessary to distinguish the user's beliefs about Frank's beliefs from the system's beliefs about Frank's beliefs and from Frank's actual beliefs." I'm sure that you can appreciate the enormity of the task, even if you have difficulty with Wilks's description of it.

Let me wind up this brief excursion into the endless webs of speech act theory, by saying that the many theories have mostly stayed as such and that relevant AI-NLP has been limited to very small-scale demonstration systems.

MACHINE TRANSLATION (MT)

Many of my informed readers will be expecting an obituarial account of the demise of MT. Not so! It is a perennial, but low-profile, subfield of NLP. As Mark Twain was supposed to have said (with a minor pronominal adjustment as the new context demands): The reports of its death are exaggerated.

A summary that's more to be recommended for its brevity than its verity would be: MT started off big, was deflated in 1966, went underground for two decades, and is just now surfacing again.

MT was one of the grand enterprises of early AI, and, as was typical of AIs formative years, they just didn't realize quite how grand a task it was. When many of the early enthusiasts realized how hard the problem really was, they downed tools and publically declared MT to be impossible (e.g., Oettinger, 1960; and Bar-Hillel, 1964). And in some extreme sense they may well be right. Steiner (1975), for example, leads the reader down into and through the subtle intricacies of language translation, which he views as a supreme achievement of the human intellect and one that can never be realized totally.

But there is surely a role for MT systems that do not aspire to such heights? Indeed there is; implemented MT systems, such as SYSTRAN (Dostert, 1957) have been functioning and providing a useful MT service throughout the dark ages of MT.

SYSTRAN is itself a particularly interesting example, for several reasons. SYSTRAN has been successfully applied to translation between several different language pairs, which is all the more surprising when we learn that it is based on a Russian–English MT system, and that much of this particular system constitutes the core of all other applications. The implication of this is either that Chomsky's unicorn, the Universal Grammar, is embodied in SYSTRAN, or more likely that the core program is not a major factor in SYSTRAN achieving the success that it undoubtedly has achieved (as suggested by Wilks, 1985a).

The further interesting feature of SYSTRAN is that we cannot readily distinguish between these two, rather different, possibilities. Much of SYSTRAN is, like many large and long-used pieces of software, a mystery and is better left as such. For a working mystery is preferable to a partially understood, inoperative system. "Leave well enough alone" is a practical maxim that unfortunately applies admirably to large-scale computer software. Thus if, by chance, the Universal Grammar was embodied by the core of SYSTRAN, we would, in all probability, be no wiser about the nature of this elusive concept than we are currently — except to say that it appears to be capable of instantiation in a well-defined class of "machine." You may remember my main reservations with regard to the connectionist paradigm in AI (Chapter 3). Well SYSTRAN, although hardly an AI program, is a clear example of the difference between having a program that solves some problem and having some theoretical insights into the structure of the problem — the two are not necessarily connected, and not easily shown to be connected if you wish to claim such a connection.

The AI-NLP work of both Schank and Wilks (described above) was applied to MT during the dark ages. Now MT looks to be about to blossom again. I have described the SDCG basis for Huang's English-Chinese translation system that is composed of approximately 5,000 PROLOG clauses (Huang, 1985). With the usual complement of rather special purpose heuristics built into the SDCG test clauses, it is close to functioning as a practical translation system.

In Europe the EUROTRA system (King & Perschke, 1984), started in 1982, is an attempt to produce a practical MT system that also adheres to the precepts of good software design and will thus also be understandable in the way that SYSTRAN is not. It seems that, while the perceptual clarity of the system is there, the performance remains to be demonstrated. Wilks (1985a) discusses many of these issues of AI and MT.

A complete issue of the journal *Future Generations Computer Systems* (vol. 2, no. 2, June 1986, to be precise) was devoted to MT. Within this special issue, Nagao (1986) gives a Japanese perspective on the current status and future trends in MT. After noting that "it is almost impossible to completely elucidate the structure of any given natural language," he lists three strategies for developing practical MT systems:

1. Limit the application to a relatively well-defined subject area such as technical papers, where even incomplete translations are of considerable value;
2. Design the application for maximum total efficiency with the possibility of human editors both pre- and posttranslation;
3. Consider the use of a so-called "restricted language (sublanguage)" as the output of a preedit stage, and therefore as the language that the MT system actually has to translate from.

He concludes by suggesting that "the focus of [MT] research is gradually shifting from syntactic parsing to semantic and context analysis" (Nagao, 1982, p. 81).

Uchida (1986) explains the two MT systems of Fujitsu: ATLAS-I, a syntax-based system that translates English into Japanese; and ATLAS-II, a semantic-based system that is aimed at high-quality, multilingual translation. He provides the following sketch (Figure 8.12) of ATLAS-II which aims to simulate human translation.

Unfortunately, but not too surprisingly, no general assessment of the capabilities of either of these two systems is given, except to say that "current technology cannot achieve perfect results" (Uchida, 1986, p. 100). Uchida concludes with a statement of belief that MT "will eventually prove superior to manual translation in terms of speed and consistency" (p. 100), and we'll leave the MT subfield with that statement of faith as yet another ponderable for the reader.

NATURAL LANGUAGE INTERFACES (NLI)

In this last section on traditional AI-NLP work (i.e., SSSP-based) we take a look at projects that constitute the major practical application of NLP systems, but products for which use of the term *natural language* probably contravenes any legislation that stipulates accuracy of description on items intended for public consumption. An NLI system is a module that is positioned between a computer that is capable of performing some useful task (e.g., an accounting task) by virtue of the existence of another piece of software also resident inside the machine, and a human being who wishes to utilize the machine's capability without having first to learn a special language. An NLI system makes the computer appear to be capable of communicating in a human language, usually English.

These systems typically recognize some very restricted subset of English and generate more-or-less prepackaged responses. So the potential user of such a system has to learn to use only a small and well-defined subset of English, and this appears to be a very acceptable substitute for many people.

Winograd and Flores (1986), as we've seen several times before, question the validity of much of the received wisdom on so-called "easy-to-learn" and "user-friendly" computer software. Communication between people, they claim, can be achieved with a minimum of words and effort because we establish domains of conversation in which there is much common preunderstanding. Much of the interaction is "transparent," by which they mean something like "subconscious." "This transparency of interaction is of utmost importance in the design of tools, including computer systems, but it is not best achieved by attempting to mimic human faculties" (p. 104). Thus a successful interface system lets a person use the core system (word processor, or whatever) without being aware of formulating and giving commands. Similarly, the user should not be dis-

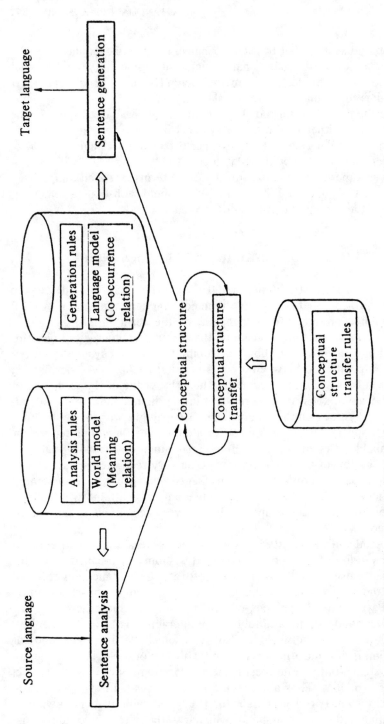

Figure 8.12.   The translation process of ATLAS-II

From "Fujitsu machine translation system: ATLAS," by H. Uchida, 1986, *Future Generations Computer Systems, 2* (2), p. 97. Copyright 1986 by Elsevier. Reprinted by permission.

342

tracted by computer responses that are outside his or her domain of interest. For example, the manipulation of words and text is the user's domain of interest if using a word processor, whereas system responses such as messages that relate to the implementation of the system are outside the user's domain.

For Winograd and Flores the central issue is the design of domains in which the actions are generated and interpreted. "A bad design forces the user to deal with complexities that belong to the wrong domain. . . . The programmer designs the language that creates the world in which the user operates" (p. 165). The point with respect to our current concerns is that natural language is by no means necessarily the best choice for an interface system. In fact, I believe that, for Winograd and Flores, natural language would never be the language of choice, because it creates in the user a belief that he or she is in the domain of human communication when the domain must in reality always be something much more restricted.

In my terminology they are arguing that NLI systems will always be problematic (especially as they become less obviously not NLP systems, i.e., not obvious travesties of NL communication) because they will inevitably induce the ELIZA syndrome in human users. I have spelled out the societal dangers of almost-AI systems elsewhere (Partridge, 1985b). I'll resist the temptation to do so again; you know where to look, if you just have to know about these things.

Nevertheless, the current reality is that many companies are developing NLI systems, and there is no shortage of prospective purchasers. It may be that the crudity of current NLI systems is such that they quickly destroy any conception that a user might have that communication can proceed in a human way. As NLI systems become more sophisticated, we may well see the problems of misinterpretation grow to challenge the simplistic view of NLI system design.

Hendrix and Sacerdoti (1981) list four potential applications of NLI systems:

1. Provide answers to questions by accessing large data bases;
2. Control complex equipment such as industrial robots, power generators, or missile systems;
3. Furnish expert advice about medical problems, mechanical repairs, how to buy stocks, or what to cook for supper;
4. Teach courses on a broad range of subjects.

Needless to say, I hope, that this is largely a wish list with notable exceptions in category (1).

Thus Woods (1973) describes an NLI system for querying the lunar rocks data base. He also describes the results of actually testing the system in a somewhat uncontrolled environment. The natural language data base query system INTELLECT, claimed as the first successful commercialization of AI technology by Artificial Intelligence Corporation, has been marketed for a number of years. Eisenberg and Hill (1984) review the state of the art for NLI systems with respect to NLI systems for personal computers.

NETWORKS FOR NLP

The traditionalists have, of course, not had it all their own way. The connectionists have been, and still are, bidding for a large share of the market. At a totally superficial level there is something quite compelling about spreading-activation models of human linguistic ability: Meanings of words and collections of words, for example, seem to just "pop out" at us. The idea that the underlying mechanism is the parallel interaction of a myriad of constraints that together produce a concentration of activity in some meaning representation is a lot more plausible than one of searching through individual alternatives looking for something that, when checked out explicitly, is found to fit the known requirements. But then again, I personally find it totally implausible that airplanes can fly, especially jumbo jets, but they definitely seem to manage it most of the time. So we must beware of plausibility arguments. Nevertheless, it is time to survey CP-based approaches to NLP.

We have already looked at a number of projects which ought to be right here, at this precise point in this book, but other demands have forced me to unveil them earlier (mostly in Chapters 3 and 6). In Chapter 6 we saw Pollack and Waltz's (1986) symbolic connectionist network for simulating the "doubletake" phenomenon that we all experience when reading garden-path sentences, such as "Jack threw a ball for charity". In the next chapter we shall get some further glimpses of vaguely NLP work. This is work that is of primary interest for the learning behavior that it exhibits (which is the case for many CP-based projects), but the application domain just happens to be that of natural language.

According to Selman (1989), the first connectionist models for NLU dealt with word sense disambiguation. The motivation was two-fold:

1. A belief in the necessity for parallel processing of multiple knowledge sources for this task;
2. The fact that spreading activation models of classical psychology can successfully simulate the data on semantic priming (e.g., humans will

recognize the word DOCTOR significantly faster if it was preceded by say, NURSE, than if it was preceded by a semantically unrelated word, such as BUTTER).

You may remember that we touched on this concept in the previous chapter when we looked at the activation-verification model of word recognition. Collins and Loftus (1975) is the basic paper to read if you want to know more about spreading activation as a theory of semantic processing. And if you've not tired of my arguments, Partridge (1987b) is the place to find this theory presented as a precursor to CP-based models of human decision making.

Selman and Hirst (1987) address the problem of parsing as an energy minimization exercise. Although this might sound like a least-effort approach which is quite appropriate for the boring task of parsing sentences, the energy minimization referred to is that of the bath-like networks and is a state that can only be attained after an extended period of activity shuffling. Indeed, the Selman and Hirst model is a species of Boltzmann machine which means that they have to subject their system to the process of simulated annealing (you had better refer back to Chapter 6 if these last two sentences have caused excessive puzzlement).

They use a symbolic or localist representation scheme for their grammar. Figure 8.13 illustrates Selman and Hirst's representation of the grammar rule, S → NP VP, which states that a sentence, S, is composed of a noun phrase, NP, followed by a verb phrase, VP. These small networks, which each represent a grammar rule, are composed of *main units* (one per syntactic category), and together they comprise a *connectionist primitive*. The output of each unit is either +1 (the unit is *active*) or −1 (the unit is *inactive*), and there are no arrows around because every link is bidirectional (or symmetric). A parsing network is constructed by link-

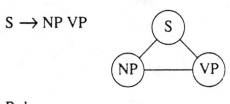

Rule

Figure 8.13.   A network representation of a grammar rule

ing these primitives together with *binder units*. So, for example, Figure 8.14 shows a parsing network for the following rules:

1. VP → VP PP
2. VP → verb
3. VP → verb NP

In Figure 8.14 the binder units are, of course, the ones that are not main units, i.e., the ones not associated with a syntactic category. Notice the use of lateral inhibition (a topic of Chapter 6); with one glance the seasoned aficionado of connectionism will appreciate that the cluster of binder units with their inhibitory links is the core of the mechanism for shunting activity into just one of the subnets representing the three grammar rules. I sincerely hope that, by this late stage in the book, most of my readers can lay reasonable claim to being similarly at home with products of the CP. I thus leave the reader to associate active binder units with specific grammar rules. But how does it parse an arbitrary input?

Well, there are, of course, some input units, and they constitute an input layer. Within this layer there are "input groups" — "each group contains a unit for each terminal symbol of the grammar" (Selman & Hirst, 1987, p. 144; as is the rest of this operational description). Successive input groups are associated with successive words of the input sentence. Initially the units of both the input and the parsing layer are inactive (−1 output, remember?). Each word of the input sentence then activates the main unit(s) representing its associated syntactic category or categories. After this initial stimulation the network begins the relaxation process, while the active input units are fixed at +1 (i.e., they are *clamped on*, to use CP jargon which should cause no one any great distress). Similarly, the input units not activated by the specific sentence

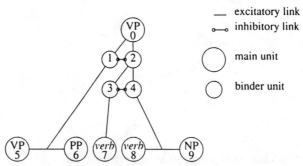

Figure 8.14.   A general parsing network

From "Connections Systems for Natural Language Understanding," by B. Selman, 1989, *Artificial Intelligence Review, 3* (1), p. 283. Copyright 1989 by Intellect, Ltd. Reprinted by permission.

being parsed are *clamped off* (if it permissable to say that). Thus the relaxation process becomes one of finding the optimal match between the specific input sentence and the internal constraints of the network which represent the grammar rules. The eventual match, a minimum energy configuration in a bath-like architecture you should recall, should then yield a correct parse of the input sentence.

If you have not been dozing as you've scanned the above narrative, you should be wondering about weights, link weights that is. They have not been mentioned with respect to this parsing scheme, and yet much of the representational load is borne by the link weights, you might say. So what are they and where do they come from for this Boltzmann-type parser?

Selman and Hirst (1987, p. 145) consider that setting the weights "is probably the most difficult problem in the design of a connectionist scheme." To begin with there is a simplification: we only need to assign relative weights; the absolute values are not important. We need to determine only that one weight should be, say, half of some other weight. Whether we then use weight values 2 and 4, or 13 and 26, and so on, makes no difference. Selman and Hirst tackle this problem by approximation and rationalization derived from parsing with the original grammar. One type of approximation is to consider only small subnets (even though the energy minimization is a global phenomenon of the network). Another type of approximation exploits the homogeneity of their networks — the network mirrors the original grammar: It is roughly a collection of discrete, alternative "connectionist primitives."

For more detail, consider Figure 8.14. This network represents three grammar rules that are equally likely (in the absence of any information to the contrary). Notice that it is the cluster of binder units that will determine whether units 5 and 6, unit 7, or units 8 and 9, are activated (i.e., whether the parse is essentially that of rule 1, 2, or 3 of the grammar, respectively). There are two links to the rule represented by units 8 and 9, and only one to unit 7, which represents rule 2. So, the reasoning goes, the weight on the link from binder unit 3 should be twice the weight on the links from 4 to 8, and from 4 to 9. And so it goes on. I'll not subject you to any more of this. In sum, the weights must be set such that states corresponding to correct parses have minimum energy. Lest you depart from this study with the view that link-weight setting is more ad hoc-ish than it really is, I should tell you that Selman (1985) has detailed a set of general rules; Selman and Hirst (1987, p. 147) present the following summary of them.

weight of excitatory link   + 1.0 in primitive with three units
                             + 2.0 in primitive with two units
weight of inhibitory link   − 3.0

They also lay out the rules for setting thresholds (i.e., the Θs).

threshold   0.0 in main unit
                      −2.0 in main unit in symmetrical environment
                      +2.0 in binder unit

So now you are fully equipped to build yourself a CP-based parsing network, should you feel the urge to do so. At least you will be when I tell you that a main unit in a symmetrical environment is a main unit linked only to pairs of binder units (that is, connected to both binders) and at most one other binder unit. You may also want to dig into the following gruesome details.

{Gruesome details are, as always, available for perusal by those readers to whom such things bring comfort. This network is basically a Boltzmann machine that uses $+1$ and -1 as output values for the units. During the simulated annealing, which is necessary to be sure of finding the energy minimum, activity is shuffled around the network in accord with the usual probability function: the output of a unit k is set to $+1$ with a probability given by:

$$\frac{1}{1 + e^{-\Delta E_k / T}}$$

where ΔE_k, the difference in energy between a state with $S_k = -1$ and $S_k = +1$ is given by:

$$\Delta E_k = 2(\sum_i W_{ki}S_i - \Theta_k)$$

and all the unmentioned terms have the usual interpretation — see Chapter 6 if you seem to be lacking a usual interpretation of any of them, and it worries you.}

If you want something to compare the above-described scheme with, Sampson (1986) presents a quite different approach to parsing using simulated annealing.

In his brief review of connectionism, past, present, and future, Pollack (1989) makes the point that all of these CP-based NLP schemes are limited to the acceptance of sentences less than or equal to some fixed, maximum length (and quite a short one). A further fundamental problem is the relatively enormous increases in network size that are required to increase the length of acceptable input sentences. Pollack claims that in Fanty's (1985) system, which automatically constructs a connectionist network that can parse a context-free grammar, the size of the network needed to parse a sentence of length n is something like $n*n*n$. Just in case you're not flabbergasted by this fact, consider the following calculations: If maximum length of a parseable sentence is 10, then the necessary network must contain 1000 units; if we wish to parse longer sentences, say two words longer, the network will require 728 *extra* units. {In technical talk: "The number of units needed for his [Fanty's] network to parse sentences of length n rises as $O(n^3)$" Pollack, 1989.}

But now it is time to move on to CP-based approaches to semantic issues, although we've already delved into some of them elsewhere (e.g., Pollack & Waltz, 1986, in Chapter 6).

Cottrell and Small (1983) use a representation scheme reminiscent of Schank's CD theory. Their model is composed of three layers of units: the lexical layer, where the input words activate word units; the word-sense layer, where units representing different senses of a word become activated; and the case-logic layer, where units that represent relationships between sentence constituent (such as a noun being the AGENT of an action). This scheme is quite similar to that of Pollack and Waltz, which we've already seen, so please thumb back to Chapter 6 for an example of this sort of CP-based NLP system. A further example that I shall do little more than refer you to is that of McClelland and Kawamoto (1986), who describe another case role assignement scheme but one that takes into account both word order and semantic constraints. As described by Selman (1989): given a sentence, the network will establish who did what to whom. The system learns from previous experience and it generalizes to unseen sentences.

This model represents a considerable departure from the others referenced above, because it uses a distributed representation of each word, and of the case roles, such as AGENT. A word is represented by a set of *microfeatures*. Any given microfeature will contribute to the representation of a number of different words — that's what makes it a microfeature.

A move into the subdomain of distributed representations (which is where we find, many would claim, the strongest case for the CP being a radically new paradigm) is also a move into a minefield of further problems. Pollack (1989), for example, raises the question of "representational adequacy" with respect to these distributed schemes. We need to be sure that a proposed model can actually represent the necessary elements of the domain being modeled. This point is closely allied to the semantic-compositionality objection of Fodor and Pylyshyn (1988) that was presented in Chapter 3 — only now it has become focused on NLP issues. Recall that the final outcome in a CP-based network is influenced by every node in the network; this is both a bane and a blessing, and currently we're interested in the former class of implication. Pollack singles out the feature-based, distributed representation of Kawamoto (1985) and notes that, if elements are represented by features distributed throughout the system, then it is difficult, if not downright impossible, to also represent larger structures involving those elements within the same system. His somewhat facetious (and therefore totally appropriate) example concerns nurses and elephants. He writes: "If all the features are needed to represent a 'Nurse', and all the features are needed to represent an 'Elephant', then the attempt to represent a 'Nurse riding an elephant' will come out either as a 'white elephant' or a rather 'large nurse with four legs' " (Pollack, 1989, p. 16). For those who are baffled by this example, consider that the concept "Nurse" will be represented by activation in a set of microfeatures which is likely to include "white", and that "large" together with "four-legged" are similarly likely to be microfeatures that contribute to the representation of "Elephant". There are no neat, isolated chunks of the network that each represent one of these two concepts; no such chunks that can be readily rearranged to yield the desired relationships between "Nurse" and "Elephant". I hope that helps.

As Pollack further says, one obvious solution to this problem is to use "separate 'pools' of units to represent elements of propositional triples," i.e., two elements of the triple will be two concepts and the third element will be the desired relationship between them. This strategy does indeed provide some measure of solution to the problem (and is thus widely used in CP-based models), but it does, of course, run into difficulties as soon as we wish to represent sentences that are not of the concept1–relationship–concept2 form, e.g., "John saw the nurse riding an elephant". In addition, the astute reader should also have made a mental note of the fact that such a triple-ish modeling strategy adds strength to the charge that the network is a mere implementation of an information processing model (I refer you right back to Chapter 3 or to Chandrasekaran, 1990, for full details).

The final problem for CP-based NLP systems is just their own special version of a general problem for CP-based systems: They are readily adaptable to new or even slightly different problems. In the current context a network may process a given sentence beautifully, but it doesn't process any other sentences nor even most rearrangements of the words in the example sentence. And furthermore, there is no way to easily modify the network to accept these further sentences. Total redesign is usually necessary. Pollack (1989), once more, notes that, in the Rumelhart and McClelland model of the learning of past tenses (a paper in Rumelhart & McClelland, 1986), "there is no obvious means to conjugate from past to present tense, without another 200,000 weights."

As a parting example, I might tell you that CP-based models are also being used for speech recognition (if this fact is of interest to you then you can follow it up by unearthing the paper by Waibel, Hanazawa, Hinton, Shikano, & Lang, 1988, if you can). But much closer at hand, you'll find a description of NETtalk in the next chapter; it is a CP-based model that learns to pronounce English.

9

Learning To Do It Right

Machine learning is a difficult, wide-open problem composed of many, interrelated, very difficult, wide-open problems

someone else

As mentioned several times earlier in this book, learning, which gives rise to adaptive behavior, ought to be an integral part of most (all?) AI subfields. Certainly, learning mechanisms have to be considered if the goal of AI is to emulate and understand human intelligence, but in addition I shall argue that learning must also be given serious consideration if the goal is, less ambitiously, just practical AI software.

The reality is, as the structure of this book reflects, that machine learning is a subfield apart. Connectionistic AI is, as we shall see, something of an exception (learning is an integral part of this approach to AI), but then connectionism itself is a subfield, if not a paradigm, apart from mainstream AI.

The separation between machine learning and other AI subfields can be justified on the grounds that we currently know very little about learning mechanisms. Thus they need to be studied in their own right, in order to upgrade our lamentably poor knowledge, before we consider integrating them with other major subfields and thereby perhaps compounding the problems. Nevertheless, there is a danger in studying machine learning divorced from the major subfields that will eventually use the learning mechanisms. The danger is that we might pursue and develop mechanisms that do not work when integrated into the broader context.

The situation is similar to the way that the formal, bottom-up operators of machine vision are not usually amenable to interruption for the injection of top-down information. Thus the development of these operators in isolation from the top-down possibilities serves to kill off attempts to explore integrated top-down and bottom-up perception algorithms — they weren't designed with eventual integration in mind and, not surprisingly, they don't integrate very well. So we must beware of machine learning algorithms developed as either formal abstractions or as manipulations of abstract, discrete, well-defined problem spaces. They may have very little utility in the ill-defined intricacies of real-world semantics or in the modification of subsymbolic perceptual schemata. But then again, they might lead to an understanding of the central issues, which can subsequently be repackaged for use in more realistic applications. It is, as usual, a matter for debate.

Before we push on to consider the significance of learning for intelligent behavior in general as well as for AI systems, we should spare a thought or two for the question: What is learning? I'm not a champion of the first-define-your-terms approach to AI, as you may have gathered by now. Nevertheless, we must have a stab at ensuring that you and I have a rough agreement, at least, on the meaning of the key terms which are bandied about.

The definitions of *learning* are many, varied and mostly not in this book. I intend to disturb the status quo as little as possible.

Hilgard and Bower (1966, p. 2), in the third edition of a classic text on learning theory, provide this definition:

> Learning is the process by which an activity originates or is changed through reacting to an encountered situation, provided that the characteristics of the change in activity cannot be explained on the basis of native response tendencies, maturation, or temporary states of the organism (e.g. fatigue, drugs, etc.).

Now, perhaps, you can see why I'm not too keen on definitions in this general area. One particularly disquieting feature of this definition (as Partridge & Paap, 1988, note) is its failure to mention the most important feature of learning in our lives, namely that learning is improvement that results from practice or profit from experience. However, additional thought will convince us that prejudices and a host of other bad habits must also be learned, and thus a definition cannot be restricted to improvements and benefits. A second notable feature of this definition is that it has little overlap with the activities of AI researchers working on machine learning. Machine learning in AI is inseparable from the idea of improvement, and moreover immediate improvement on a very restricted set of tasks. For example, in the first volume of *Machine Learning*, Simon (1983, p. 28) presented the following characterization of learning:

> Learning denotes changes in the system that are adaptive in the sense that they enable the system to do the same task or tasks drawn from the same population more effectively the next time.

I don't want to quarrel with this statement (well, not much); it captures the general idea quite nicely. But why limit the beneficial effects of learning to similar tasks? And why tie the idea of improvement to "the next time"?

As to the first question, taking a look at it from outside hard-core AI, we find that it hinges on the scope of transfer predicted by a learning theory. At the narrow end, Thorndike's (1903) identical elements theory of transfer can be taken to assume that transfer will occur only between tasks that involve the same content and that content is manifest as specific stimulus–response pairs. The widest scope is probably evident in folk lore, which in the past assumed that the study of Latin improves the mind, and also in the more contemporary belief that the same can be said about learning to program a computer. Football coaches adhere to the wide scope when they remind us that players are learning character and teamwork for the corporate boardrooms of tomorrow. If a system assimilates information while working in one domain (or population of tasks), and that information does not improve performance on that family of tasks but does yield improvements in some other domain, is that not learning in a most useful sense? This question of the scope of learning mechanisms may be an artifact of the SSSP, where changes in symbolic representations often have fairly clear and bounded applicability. It is not obvious that changing the weight of a link in a connectionist network will necessarily be limited to a change in behavior with respect to some symbolically classified "population of tasks." In fact, on changing link weights in a subsymbolic connectionist network, it is very likely to be difficult to predict the scope of the repercussions in terms of a symbolically conceived population of tasks; and this is another manifestation of the understandability problem that threatens the CP (a problem discussed in Chapter 3). In the CP (as we shall see repeatedly throughout this chapter) the conventional wisdom on machine learning looks decidedly shaky at times; for it is largely a parochial SSSP slant on the general problem of adaptive behavior.

The second point of disagreement that I have with Simon's otherwise fine definition concerns the keying of system improvement to "the next time." It precludes the possibility of things getting worse before they get better. This is the old yearning for monotonicity; see "The Curse of Non-monotonicity," a full-section-length feature coming soon in a chapter near you and preceded by several previews in upcoming local sections. Nonmonotonic improvement is, for example, quite common in the human learning of a skill. Thus, in tennis I can serve good enough, but not well. In order for me to learn to do it properly and to eventually serve much better, I shall have to practice and thereby assimilate techniques that will cause me serve much worse than I currently do for a while. Again, connectionistic learning, which is a slow, incremental buildup process (as opposed to the one-shot modification typical of learning associated with symbolic representations in the SSSP) is a direct challenge to this feature of the definition. And from within CP-based work there are numerous formal observations and experiments that demonstrate this point. For example, Rumelhart and McClelland (1986) use a technique of error-feedback correction {called *back propagation* and detailed later, you'll be pleased to know} in a CP-based model designed to simulate the standard three stages by which children acquire the past tense of verbs in English: a period within which high-frequency, but irregular past tenses are correctly produced (e.g., *came, got, gave, took, went*); followed by a period within which the regular form is acquired, but overgeneralized to the previously learned exceptions (e.g., *comed, getted, gived, taked, goed*); and the final stage, wherein both the regular forms and the exceptions are mastered. A further example is the work of Anderson (1987), which shows that a symbolic system can also mimic "the first you get worse before you get better" stage of skill acquisition. Anderson's production-system-based model {again details follow — less of them, but sooner} predicts that information assimilated when using a "perverse" EMACS text editor (i.e., a computer system that continually "misdirects" the user) carries over to improve performance with the normal EMACS, even though subjects go through one day of practice on the "perverse" EMACS, where performance success has actually decreased. Yet another example from work in the SSSP (for those readers who just can't get enough examples) will be found in the later section on explanation-based approaches to machine learning. More specifically, it will be found where the suggestion is made that efficient explanation-based learning be composed of explanation-based generalization followed by specialization to correct for overgeneralization.

A final point with respect to the improvement-the-next-time feature of the definition is that it does not preclude the possibility of a need for unlearning in the future, but only because it limits the concept of learning to the smallest time-span possible. Unlearning is an awkward topic that we shall return to at the end of this chapter.

To be fair (for a change), Simon does describe his definition as "only partially satisfactory." I would have to agree, even though Michalski (1986, p. 28), in the second volume of *Machine Learning,* quotes it with only a minor reservation about the necessity for improvement. But as I have nothing better to offer (until we get into knowledge-level learning, later in this chapter), we'll leave this excursion into definitions and get on with the questions of both the general significance of adaptive behaviors and specific manifestations (i.e., learning programs).

CAN WE HAVE INTELLIGENCE WITHOUT LEARNING?

The problem of learning can be approached at a number of different levels: from being told a new fact explicitly to deducing some hitherto unrecognized abstract relationship. In terms of the system that does the learning, it may just store a new specific fact, or it may need to integrate into its knowledge a newly discovered abstract concept. But whatever the level and style of the learning mechanism, the result of learning will be an adaptation of behavior, generally a change for the better in the long run.

Given the ill-structured nature of the empirical world and the unforeseeable perturbations that will beset any system that is attempting to behave intelligently, self-adaptation or automatic learning is highly desirable if not a necessity. Adaptive behavior, from the plant that seeks the light to the parents who raise children, is characteristic of all living organisms. The level and sophistication of adaptive behavior is a useful index of level of intelligence.

Consider the lowly bean randomly falling into the proverbial stony ground. Using this adaptability measure, the average bean seeking up and down for leaves and roots (respectively, of course), and negotiating awkwardly placed pebbles, has far more intelligence than any AI program yet constructed. Clearly, adaptive behavior is not the whole story. Equally clearly, it is one fundamental characteristic of intelligence, and one that may be critical with respect to the future development of AI.

CAN WE HAVE AI WITHOUT LEARNING?

For the AI research worker with his or her eyes on the ultimate prize — an artificial, but fully intelligent, system — the answer is, clearly, "no". But for the builder of, say, expert systems, the answer is not so unequivocal (but it's still "no," I believe, as you may remember from the earlier chapter on CEST).

Can significant AI systems that don't learn be built? The answer is "yes" (don't worry about the contradiction; I fully intend to resolve it soon). A number of nonadaptive, but interesting and instructive, AI systems are extant to buttress this answer. Nevertheless it is not clear just how far work in AI can progress and yet eschew the use of self-adaptive mechanisms. We have just scratched the surface of the possibilities for AI, and already there are awkward problems (such as expert systems explaining their behavior) that, I would argue (e.g., Partridge, 1987a, but also much closer to hand in Chapter 5), require learning mechanisms to support an adequate solution. And conversely, it is not clear how far the prime goals of practical software (i.e., robustness and reliability) can be met if self-adaptive mechanisms are utilized.

In addition there is a purely practical consideration: Michalski, Carbonell, and Mitchell (1983–1986), in the first volume of *Machine Learning*, argue that machine learning is a practical necessity. It is necessary "to ease the burden of hand-programming growing volumes of increasingly complex information'' (p. 4), they say.

As stated earlier, there are a number of varieties of machine learning, and they differ in the degree to which they are autonomous or self-contained (just one dimension of difference plucked from the many). It seems reasonable to assume that the more opportunity we have to guide and influence the learning mechanism (i.e., the less autonomous the mechanism), the easier might be the task of developing robust and appropriate mechanisms; this view captures much of the received wisdom, I believe. Thus I shall present this review of the state of the art in machine learning in terms of the degree of external guidance involved. I shall start with the mechanisms of maximum possible external interference and work through to the free and independent spirits of creativity that are purportedly imprisoned in the small but growing set of discovery (or very significantly, I shall argue, *re*discovery) algorithms.

One result of this approach to the structuring of machine learning work is that induction (generalization from a collection of specific instances), for example, which could be considered as a unified subfield of machine learning, becomes split into three separate categories: when the instances are preselected and fed to the generalization algorithm (external tutoring); when new instances are less controllably encountered by the system and must be used to incrementally modify the current generalization (learning generalities); and when all instances are known at the outset, and the task is to generate new, more-generalized information (mechanized creativity of the less dramatic variety).

Landmarks and a few particularly illustrative studies are specifically mentioned, but for an exhaustive listing of projects the reader is referred to the bibliographies on machine learning to be found in Michalski et al. (1983–1986). In addition, the categories of mechanisms given below are meant to provide some structure in a somewhat amorphous subfield of AI. They are just convenient handles that may facilitate the attainment of a cognitive grasp of this hard-to-organize subfield. They are not mutually exclusive compartments into one of which each project can be correctly stored.

A further complication is provided by the connectionistic machine learning. I have attempted to carve it up in terms of categories that are based on the SSSP. Thus, certain aspects of work in the CP may be found under headings to which an acute judgement might deny appropriateness — I admit it.

LEARNING PARADIGMS IN AI

Until quite recently, almost all work on machine learning was pursued under the aegis of the SSSP (the Symbolic Search Space Paradigm of

Chapter 3). In addition to the idea of a discrete, symbolically represented space supporting intelligent activity, machine learning added the rider that learning is manifest within the system as the addition (typically) of a symbolic structure.

An alternative view, but one that has not had significant impact in AI as yet, is given by Maturana (1980) and quoted with approval by Winograd and Flores (1986).

> Learning is not a process of accumulation of representations of the environment; it is a continuous process of transformation of behavior through continuous change in the capacity of the nervous system to synthesize it. Recall does not depend on the indefinite retention of a structural invariant that represents an entity (an idea, image, or symbol), but on the functional ability of the system to create, when certain recurrent conditions are given, a behavior that satisfies the recurrent demands or that the observer would class as a reenacting of a previous one.

"That's all very well," I can hear the SSSP person say,"but how do you begin to implement such ideas?" And that's a good point. If an approach through LISP functions or PROLOG clauses is not even vaguely suggested by the terminology used, then it's not a viable AI idea. At least that was a fairly sound standpoint in the years B.C. (Before Connectionism), but, now that the connectionists have got the bit between their teeth, the lack of an obvious LISP or PROLOG representation does not automatically condemn a theory to the limbo land of unimplementable ideas.

In the old days there was also a fairly significant body of research under the rubric *simulated evolution* (the now defunct AI paradigm that I glossed over in Chapter 3). It was driven into extinction, or at least into hiding, by a scathing review (Lindsey, 1968) of a book (Fogel, Owens, & Walsh, 1966) that contained much of the accumulated wisdom on this topic. Simulated evolution, like the real thing (if there is a real thing), is fundamentally a learning paradigm — hence, I bring it up here. To my mind modern connectionism has to some significant degree taken up the mantle that was hastily dropped in the late sixties. So, within descriptions of work in the CP, we shall see glimpses of this long-lost approach to machine learning.

Interestingly, Holland, who has been one of the few to persist with what I can describe (with my customary freedom) as evolution-based approaches to AI, describes a machine learning scheme that is symbolic rule based but in a way that is akin to both simulated evolution (with its organism that must perceptually categorize environmental stimuli, and rules that survive or not as a result of competition in terms of usefulness with other rules) and connectionism (with primitive rules that are activated in groups and incremental learning by gradually adjusting rule strengths)

(Holland, 1986). In due course, we shall look at his "bucket-brigade algorithm" for apportioning credit, as well as his "genetic algorithm" for generating better rules.

Another biologically based approach to AI that viewed learning as the fundamental behavior but is now defunct (I believe) was Cunningham's (1972) cell-assembly-based model that was introduced in an earlier chapter. This model also has affinities with modern connectionism (with its networks of activity-passing cell assemblies) and close ties with biological theory that are to be expected within the CP but are yet to emerge in strength. Cunningham implemented learning in terms of adding new network elements with appropriate connections.

I shall attempt to deal with learning in AI in the context of these two major paradigms as well as in the broad context of the general aims and aspirations of AI as a subject. First, let me summarize and illustrate the traditional view — learning as viewed through the lens of the SSSP.

LEARNING AS THE ACCRETION OF SYMBOLIC STRUCTURES

The accumulation of symbolic representations is the model for learning within the symbolic paradigm for AI. When a system learns something, it is because it has added a chunk of information to its knowledge. That is a crude characterization of learning within the symbolic paradigm. The new information is represented symbolically; thus, learning is basically a process of building up the symbolic structures that support system behavior. And this SSSP definition is very close to Michalski's (1986, p. 10) in his introductory chapter to the second volume on machine learning (although he admits the possibility of adding information, presumably beyond the pale of the SSSP, "as something else," with no further elaboration).

Typically, the learned information is manifest as added facts, added rules, added constraints that serve to refine rules, etc. Other common implementations of learning do not fit so comfortably in my simplistic characterization. Thus learning may result in parameter value adjustment, or in the incorporation of a generalized rule and the expulsion of many special cases (hence, a diminution of symbolic structure). Nevertheless, there is still an accretion of information, and it is at the symbolic (rather than subsymbolic) level.

Anderson's (1987) ACT* theory of skill acquisition is an elegantly attired model of the symbolic approach to learning, and it takes advantage of many of the concepts important to our understanding of learning and memory from the SSSP. These include heuristics as general problem-solving strategies, the distinction between declarative and procedural knowledge, compilation of procedural knowledge (i.e., packing the information down into a less transparent but more efficient representation), and rules for predicting positive transfer (i.e., information learned in association with one task enhancing the subject's ability to cope with a subsequent task). Accordingly, I shall sketch the theory in some detail so that it can be used as a prototype for symbolic learning (here I am slavishly following Partridge & Paap, 1988, yet again).

Tasks are accomplished in ACT* by the firing of productions. Productions are condition-action rules, you may remember (Chapter 6). When the specified conditions of a production are present in working memory, then the associated mental or physical action will be carried out. Anderson provides the following two "Englishified" examples of his simulation of LISP learning.

P1:   *IF* the goal is to write a solution to a problem and there is an example of a solution to a similar problem,
        THEN set a goal to map that template to the current case
P2:   *IF* the goal is to get the first element of *List1*,
        THEN write *(CAR List1)*.

The first production instantiates a general heuristic of solving problems by using structural analogy. Novices bring these general strategies to new domains. Other productions exist for trial and error search, hill-climbing (coming soon), means–ends analysis (Chapter 3), etc. (other chapters). Anderson believes that these general strategies are not learned; they are innate — part of our genetic program, the biological support software, or is it geneware?

The second production must be learned by a novice, since it is specific to LISP. It instantiates a function that gets the first element of a list (if the word *function* fails to activate a coherent pattern of neurons, then refer back to LISP functions in Chapter 4, or just push on and hope that the mists will eventually clear). The problem solved by the knowledge compilation process is how to proceed from weak, slow, highly fallible solutions based on general productions (i.e., the "weak methods" of classical AI) to strong, fast, and accurate solutions based on domain-specific productions.

I shall borrow Anderson's example of a novice LISP programmer to show how productions are combined to solve a problem and how specific productions are acquired from general productions. The learner is asked to write a LISP definition that would create a new function called FIRST, which would get the first element of a list. The theory assumes that the novice will acquire an appropriate domain-specific production by applying his or her general problem solving heuristics to the declarative knowledge that he or she has acquired about the specific domain. In this particular case the user based his or her solution on the analogy production (P1) and declarative knowledge in the form of a template for function definition and some examples.

A simulation of his or her protocol has the following characteristics. First, a hierarchical goal structure: the template was selected as an analog for building a LISP function, and subgoals were set up to map each of the major components of the template. Another characteristic of the simulation was the variable success in applying the general domain heuristics. Analogy to the template worked for mapping the function header and function name (DEFUN FIRST), but a second analogy to a specific example was needed to map the parameter (LIST1) and to map and code the arguments for the process (CAR LIST1).

The sequence of productions used to solve the first problem provides an opportunity for learning through knowledge compilation. The sequence of nine productions, involving template matching and analogy to an example, can be collapsed into a single domain-specific production that directly produces the syntax for the function definition:

P3:   *IF* the goal is to write a function of one variable,
        THEN write (DEFUN function (variable) and set as a subgoal to
        code the relation calculated by this function and then
        write).

The second sequence of six productions that accomplished the lower-level goal of coding the argument can be boiled down (i.e., compiled) to give:

P4:   *IF* the goal is to code an argument and that argument
        corresponds to a variable of the function,
        THEN write the variable name.

One feature of this knowledge compilation process, and one that is common to many specific models of symbolic learning, is that it predicts a marked improvement from a first to a second problem of the same kind. Anderson (1982, 1987) has confirmed this prediction in the domains of geometry-proof generation and of LISP programming. For example, errors in syntax for function definition (the knowledge compiled in P3) drop from 2 {a median value} in the FIRST problem described earlier to zero for a subsequent, more complex problem that requires students to define a function that will return the second element of a list. Similarly, learning times decrease dramatically. Anderson provides several other impressive one-trial learning statistics that emerge readily from his knowledge compilation process but that would be difficult for a connectionist network to mimic. Long-term gradual improvements in speedup of the skill are predicted from Anderson's additional assumption that the strength of a production increases with successful applications and that strength determines how rapidly it applies.

The ACT* system also leads to some interesting predictions with regard to transfer of competence between skills, but the details of this lead us too far astray for a basic AI book that already threatens to be too big. The interested reader is referred to Partridge and Paap (1988) for a summary of the relevant results, and to Anderson's papers for the full details.

LEARNING AS THE ADJUSTMENT OF LINK WEIGHTS

The promise of breakthroughs in machine learning is one of the major arguments for the subsymbolic paradigm in AI. And as we shall see, the customary subdivisions of machine learning, originating as they do in the symbolic paradigm, are not so appropriate for the subsymbolic approach. Nevertheless, I'll use the usual taxonomy (more or less) as it still applies to at least 90% of the machine learning projects, and I'll fit in the connectionist work wherever I can plausibly do so.

Symbolic objects and concepts in a connectionist system are represented by either a pattern of highly activated nodes (or possibly a single node of high activity, if the network is not a subsymbolic, i.e., distributed, representation). The process of learning is thus seen as adjusting link weights so that activity flows in appropriate amounts into the appropriate nodes at appropriate times. Such networks could, of course, consider learning in terms of adding nodes to the network, but typically this is not the case. Learning is link weight adjustment.

A point of contrast here between our two major AI paradigms is that the symbolic-level structures, which are the units of the SSSP conception of learning, cannot plausibly be link weight adjustment (even in symbolic connectionist systems). The elements of learning in the CP are subsymbolic. The resultant change in system behavior interpreted at the symbolic level is the combined result of many micromodifications of the system.

In fact this point of difference is sometimes used by anti subsymbolic connectionists as a crucial point of weakness in the subsymbolic paradigm. If we need to add a new relation say "owner of" to associate the entities say "John" and "Fido" in a classical semantic network or a classical rule-based representation of knowledge, (almost) nothing could be easier. We add an "owner_of" labeled arc between the nodes labeled "John" and "Fido" in the semantic network, or we add a fact

(OWNER_OF FIDO JOHN) to our knowledge base. But what can we do with the subsymbolic network? Where is, or how can we introduce this new relation? And how do we relate the pattern of activity for "John" with the pattern of activity representing "Fido"?

A trivial problem in the SSSP looks to be close to impossible (almost meaningless) in the subsymbolic CP. A subsymbolic-CP person might respond that the problem is an artifact of the SSSP and thus not applicable to the CP where learning is not a one-shot phenomenon — it is a gradual process, as in much human learning. But then humans can learn such things in one trial; for example, if I tell you (and you're paying attention because Fido has just helped himself to a chunk of flesh from your leg) that John is the owner of Fido, then I would expect you to remember that new piece of information immediately, and perhaps for ever. Clearly, we have another problem for the reader to tackle (it's too tough for me, and I shall abandon it at this point).

Interestingly, the reverse procedure, unlearning, does not seem to possess the same awkward qualities: one cannot instruct a human to forget something (i.e., unlearn it) and expect them to do so. This gives rise to the "judge's dilemma": should the jury be explicitly advised to disregard a nonrelevant piece of information and thereby have it brought to their attention, or should the bench just say nothing? In sum, this general observation accords well with CP-based systems but not with the SSSP-based ones.

Hinton (1989) provides a fine review of connectionist learning procedures, pointing out and discussing the similarities between the wide diversity of mechanisms that have been and are being explored within the CP. The paper is ram-jam full of detail — gruesome but perhaps essential for real understanding. We must bear in mind the timeless truth of the saying which points out (after some remodeling) that essentiality lies in the goals of the comprehender. But whatever the depth of understanding desired, it's a good paper. Hinton (1989, p. 189) divides connectionist learning procedures into three broad classes:

> Supervised procedures which require a teacher to specify the desired output vector, reinforcement procedures which only require a single scalar evaluation of the output, and unsupervised procedures which construct internal models that capture regularities in their input vectors without receiving any additional information.

This is a long sentence (just in case you didn't realize), and its meaning is more or less obvious or obscure depending on the particular bent of your brain, I suspect. Roughly, the three classes of CP-based learning are: external tutoring where the system is told either the correct output or just some simple difference between the correct and actual outputs (the first two classes); and the extraction of common patterns from a collection of inputs (see similarity-based generalization within the SSSP, not far ahead).

EXTERNAL TUTORING: LEARNING BY BEING TOLD

If learning is initiated and controlled by user interaction, then we have the best chance of maintaining control of the resultant beast — a pile of code that is changing all the time. This type of scheme can also be the easiest to implement, because much of the burden remains with the human tutor (although I include in this general category situations where the environment is the tutor, typically a rather disinterested one).

As this book is making a bid to be the standard compendium of the wit and wisdom of AI, I'll indulge in a trivial aside to bolster the first category of AI-related information (although the cynic may claim that the first category is no thinner than the second; they are both fleshless). It is sometimes said, with the express object of eliciting laughter, that the most important category of machine learning, the one that is never mentioned in proper texts, might be termed "learning by being old." I leave it as a problem for the reader to determine what this might mean and why it might be a joke.

But now we must move back to a consideration of information that is probably more appropriately placed in the "wisdom" category. As we have seen, the development of an AI program is necessarily an incremental process. Learning by being told, or "advice taking" as it is sometimes called, is a potentially very useful way of automating some aspects of this incremental development. It can thus play a lead role in system development rather than be just an inessential member of the supporting cast.

The original advice-taker program in AI was McCarthy's 1950s project (McCarthy, 1968), in which he outlined a predicate-calculus-based system for giving common-sense advice such as how best to get to the airport. I mention it here as a key exhibit in the history of AI; it is a fine example of AI in the days when there was little realization of how difficult the problems really are.

But a quarter of a century later the same strategy, at a less ambitious level, is of interest for tackling the problems of expert system development. An incremental process of feedback and evaluation is used to refine and extend expert system knowledge. The two essential parties are the human expert, with advice to give, and a mechanized counterpart, with advice to be woven into its current knowledge base. It is, of course, highly unlikely that these two potential communicants share a common language. So a computer expert or "knowledge engineer" is also required as a go-between; his or her humanness ensures a degree of communication with the human expert, and the actual system is his or her baby, which ensures that he or she can communicate with it, if anybody can.

The TEIRESIAS project (Davis & Lenat, 1982) was an attempt to shorten this chain of command and thereby allow direct human expert–computerized expert conferences (which incidentally releases the computer science expert, a scarce resource). Davis's system was designed to interface between a human physician and the expert medical system MYCIN.

One of the interesting aspects of TEIRESIAS is that it seizes command of the dialogue whenever possible; this all too human trait has several advantages, even for a computer. In particular it both simplifies the natural language interface by leading the human responses into situations where there are few possible responses, and tries to ensure that advice is given at the level and in the sort of chunks that it can most easily digest.

Once again we must wait for time, the great leveller, to let us know if the TEIRESIAS approach (the system itself, like MYCIN, has been long abandoned) really heralds a wave of knowledge engineers boosting the rosters of the unemployed or whether the time and effort needed to tune a TEIRESIAS for each particular expert system will instead increase their scarcity value. In principle, it is true, a generalized TEIRESIAS need only be constructed once, but such generalized solutions to AI problems have so far eluded the researchers in the field.

More recently, Haas and Hendrix (1983, p. 405) outline a system called KLAUS which can "hold a conversation with a user in English about his specific domain of interest, subsequently retrieve and display information conveyed by the user." They contrast this endeavor with the TEIRESIAS project in that KLAUS is supposed to collect and organize aggregations of individual facts for use in question-answering tasks, not in the acquisition of general rules for judgmental reasoning.

Needless to say, KLAUS is only an idea, but NANOKLAUS is implemented and functioning; in the authors' words (Haas & Hendrix, 1983, p. 405), it "is best described as a fragile, proof-of-concept system that was built to establish the feasibility of achieving the broader KLAUS goals," which, of course, it does, and work is steaming ahead on MICROKLAUS. {Interesting detail: if a nanosecond is about 1 foot, then a second is 186,000 miles. This degree of difference between the concept and the current implementation, as implied by the choice of names, speaks well for the uncharacteristic humility of these researchers.}

The significance of the KLAUS concept, which is quite like a conventional DBMS (*data base management system*), lies in its aim to manipulate concepts through interactions in English. A further differentiating goal of KLAUS is ability to represent, discuss, and reason about more complex structures than conventional DBMSs are able to do. This project gives us a cross-link with the natural-language interfaces of Chapter 8.

The KLAUS concept makes no claims for innovative language processing, except that the basic "pragmatic grammar"(Hendrix, Sacerdoti, Sagalowicz, & Slocum, 1978) , which interacts with a first-order-logic-based knowledge representation scheme (Chapter 6), is particularly rich in constructs that can be used to introduce new concepts.

Mostow (1983, p. 367) identifies "operationalization: the development of procedures to implement advice that is not directly executable by the learner" as a key problem in machine learning. We shall see some spill-over from this notion when we get to explanation-based learning. Mostow describes a system that takes high-level advice, such as "avoid taking points," transforms it into a heuristic search procedure, and thereby learns to improve its playing of the card game "hearts." Although the domain is the well-structured, abstract one of a card game, Mostow points out that it may be impossible to produce a procedure to satisfy the advice — i.e., there is no infallible way to avoid taking points. Thus the operationalization involved "differs from conventional notions of automatic programming by its heuristic nature: the procedures it produces may not always work."

The system described is rule-based classic SSSP work (as one would expect from the CMU stable), and the learning is implemented in terms of transforming the external advice into an executable procedure. The learning is implemented by means of first using the advice to instantiate a generic heuristic search procedure. This general procedure is then refined as a result of trial and error in directing strategy for playing the game. This is all accomplished with the aid of appropriate heuristics, of course. The important question then becomes: How specific are the necessary heuristics to the rediscovery of strategies for playing hearts given the advice to avoid winning points?

Mostow endeavors to demonstrate the generality of his scheme by applying it to another domain — the domain of music. He found that "many of the same rules proved applicable" (Mostow, 1983, p. 367).

Holland's (1986) system, mentioned briefly earlier, modifies itself on the basis of information from the environment, i.e., external information. This can be considered tutoring only in the loose sense of external-information-driven learning. To the extent that the external source is not an intelligent tutor (carefully selecting the information to be fed into the system), we must expect environmental-feedback learning to be more difficult than truly tutored learning.

Holland's work can be said to span both the SSSP and the CP in that he employs a symbolic-rule-based representation but manipulates it with

CP-based algorithms. We shall look at two aspects of learning in his system:

1. The generation of new rules, not from examples as in subsequent sections of this chapter, but from external feedback;
2. The modification of rule "strengths" with his "bucket-brigade algorithm" for apportioning credit.

Taking these two features in reverse order, the second type of learning is closely akin to link weight adjustment in the CP, and its major point of particular interest is in its attempt to be fair about giving credit where it is due; thus it is dealt with in the later credit section of this chapter.

This leaves us free to consider the generation of new rules for which a "genetic algorithm" is used. It is a cycle of three components:

1. Select pairs of the most successful rules (i.e., high-strength rules);
2. Apply genetic operators to create new rules (e.g., exchange randomly selected segments between the pairs);
3. Replace the least successful rules with the new ones.

The successfulness of a rule is given by its strength (compare link weight in the CP), which is modified as a result of the rule's contribution to the overall success of the system in solving the problems to which it is applied. There is considerable empirical data available (on poker playing, gas pipeline transmission problems, etc.), and there are even formal analyses of the algorithms.

You can see clearly the biological or evolutionary basis of Holland's approach to the problem of machine learning (I hope). Equally clearly, you can see a close analogue of link-weight adjustment — the fundamental learning machanism of the CP, and the one to which we shall now turn our attention.

External tutoring, in the loose sense already mentioned, also covers most of the work to date on learning in connectionist networks — Hinton's (1989) two broad classes of supervised learning. This learning is typically driven by feedback from some outside agent — the person developing the system. For each input pattern there is a correct output pattern (this is an obvious and significant limitation — i.e., the correct answers must be known).

If the output pattern is correct, no learning is called for (although the weights of the contributing links may be increased); but if the output is wrong, the weights on the links that contributed most to this wrong answer have their weights reduced. Thus the network is taught to get it right.

This scheme of connectionist learning was explored and abandoned at the dawn of AI, several decades B.C. (I am alluding to the Perceptrons affair; you may remember it from Chapter 3). Perceptrons only had one layer of weighted links connecting the input pattern to the output pattern; thus, the culprit links in any wrong results output were easily identified and punished accordingly.

Hinton (1989) details several different strategies used for link-weight adjustment in learning procedures applied to these single-layer-of-link networks (or, using less ugly terminology, networks with no hidden units). We shall look at just one of these schemes, the perceptron convergence procedure; it has the dual merit of historical significance because of its association with the Perceptron, and of avoiding the necessity to dip, once more, into the murky depths of the differential calculus.

Now the object of the learning exercise is to change the weights, the w_{ji}s, where i is an input unit and j is an output unit, so that the network eventually will produce the correct output for each input. An individual unit, or node, can be on (state value 1) or off (state value 0). The necessary change in each link weight, Δw_{ji}, is computed for each trial (i.e., put in an input pattern and observe the resultant output pattern) or case, **c,** according to the following rule:

$$\Delta w_{ji,c} = \begin{cases} 0 & \text{if the output unit behaves} \\ & \text{correctly by at least} \quad m \\[1em] +\epsilon y_{i,c} & \text{if the output unit should be} \\ & \text{on but has } x_{j,c} < m \\[1em] -\epsilon y_{i,c} & \text{if the output unit should be} \\ & \text{off but has } x_{j,c} > -m \end{cases}$$

which won't mean much to you until I tell you that $y_{i,c}$ is the state, on trial c, of the input unit associated with link weight to be changed, and that $x_{j,c}$ is the state of the output unit. The constant ϵ determines the size of weight changes (we look at the issue of "step size" later). Clearly, if ϵ is large, the Δ are also large, and the procedure takes giant steps towards its goal, but then it runs the risk of overshooting. Small steps lead to a longer process but generally increase the chances of finding the optimum configuration of weights. Finally, there is m; Hinton introduces m, the *margin,* to avoid an awkward little problem (which I shall gloss over). He tells us "that for units which should be *on* the total input is at least m and for units that should be *off* the total input is at most $-m$" (Hinton, 1989, p. 195, author's emphasis). Use of this margin, m, introduces a threshold which ensures that units whose total input falls in this margin above and below zero are unaffected by the learning procedure. Having subjected you to this margin idea, let me say that, actually, its importance is tied to more sophisticated learning procedures, and it is not really necessary in the simple perception covergence procedure; in this particular case it is a marginal point in two senses at least. Set m to zero, and it goes away.

Stated simply, but not simplistically (I hope), the three components of this learning rule can be summarized as follows: the first component (going from top to bottom, of course) does nothing to the link weights, because the network is behaving as desired; the second component increases the weight of a link associated with an output unit that is off but should be on (thus increasing its input and so improving its chances of being on next time trial c is run); and the third component decreases the weight of a link to an output unit that is on but should be off (thereby diminishing its chances of being on next time trial c is run).

I'll leave this learning procedure at this point. But I should stress that there are firm formal results concerning the convergence properties (i.e., if and when the system will learn to perform as desired) of most of these learning procedures. And this is an important strength of CP-based research. Hinton (1989) goes into the thick of it; I don't. So you know where to look if you want more information on this aspect of the learning procedures. Mention of the amenability of CP-based systems to formal analysis will lead us briefly back in time to the eclipse of the first flowering of connectionism — the age of the Perceptron itself.

At the dawn of AI, networks of primitive computing elements were doing a number or new and exciting things. Unfortunately, Minsky and Papert (1969), not content with some neat little examples, did some mathematics on these simple networks and showed that, although they could learn certain things, their repertoire was severely limited — such Perceptron networks could never learn anything more exciting than first-order predicates. First-order predicates, for those who don't know, are simple formal expressions like the one illustrated in Figure 9.1.

The two input units (X1 and X2) admit four different input vectors (i.e., [1,1],[0,0],[1,0], and [0,1]) as listed in the table in the figure. The output unit (Y1) can similarly be either on (value 1) or off (value 0), and the table shows the relationship between these possibilities that we would like the network to learn. Well, it can't; there is no way of setting the two weights and one threshold to solve this very simple task {which is a first-order predicate}.

As you can see, the limitations of the Perceptron are not very exciting, just as Minsky and Papert claimed. All this led quickly to the crucifixion of neural-net-like modeling and eventually to the second coming in 1979 at La Jolla, California, as we discussed much earlier in this book.

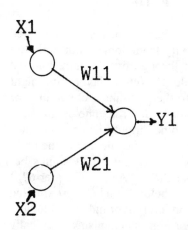

X1	X2	Y1
1	1	1
0	0	1
1	0	0
0	1	0

Figure 9.1.   A problem that defeats the Perceptron

What has changed is that, in the context of learning, the word is abroad that back propagation has slain the dragon of Perceptrons. So one particularly interesting component of this paradigm, if not of many of its current manifestations, is that the concept of learning is an intrinsic and integrated one rather than a tagged-on, somewhat separate afterthought, as it is in the SSSP.

Learning in these neuron-like networks is, as we have seen, typically implemented as functions that manipulate the arc weights on the basis of network behavior. Machine learning is a central concern in AI, and one that has proved resistant to generalized, formal approaches. These simple networks offer some hope for the discovery of formally founded, generalized learning algorithms.

When dealing with networks with no hidden layers (i.e., Perceptronish), incremental learning is easily implemented by some function that increases the strength of the weights on the arcs that contributed to a desired outcome, and that decreases the weights on the arcs that gave rise to an undesirable outcome. But in multilayered networks the credit assignment problem arises: When a desired outcome is the result of a complex process, how do we apportion credit among the constituent subprocesses? By all means give credit where it is due, but where exactly is that? Well, the answer is believed (by some people at least) to be: in just those links where "back propagation" puts it in appropriate doses. I'll try to explain this concept (i.e., back propagation) without too many gruesomely detailed parenthetical interjections, but a few such intrusions are unavoidable.

LEARNING ON THE PATH

An important subclass of connectionist networks can be approximated by a sequence of nodes that transfer activity from some input node (an approximation of the input layer), pass it through one or more internal nodes (the *hidden* layers) to an output node (the output layer, you might not be surprised to learn). I am referring to the path-like architectures or feed-forward networks described in Chapter 6. {In gruesome detail, such networks are homomorphic to a path from some "input" layer to an "output" layer — (an important class of exceptions is the one due to the presence of arcs that are adjacent because of "lateral inhibitory" links between nodes in the same subset; remember the WTASs of Chapter 6?).}

Thus the network for NETtalk, illustrated below, can be approximated by a three-node sequence: an input node, an internal or hidden node, and an output node. The back propagation learning mechanism is typically applied to such path-like networks, for it is composed of two distinct phases: first a flow of activity from input to output node, next a computation of error (correct output minus observed output) to be used as a basis for the initial "error signal," and then a second phase flow of link weight adjustment back from the output to the input nodes. At each step back through the network the required "error signals" for the current layer of links are computed from the "error signals" used in the last layer of weight adjustments. This technique of back propagation of error is viewed as one of the fundamental reasons why the CP is out of the cul-de-sac of Perceptrons and is a worthy challenger to the SSSP. So we must look at this technique in some detail.

Sejnowski and Rosenberg (1986, p. 3) state that, "until recently, learning in multilayered networks [i.e., a network with hidden units] was an unsolved problem and considered by some impossible. . . . The problem is to discover a set of weights for the hidden units given only examples of the mapping." We need a theory of back propagation. Sejnowski implemented and demonstrated a successful learning strategy for a three-layered network, constructed as in Figure 9.2.

Each of the seven input "groups" can accept a letter (or a space or one of a few punctuation marks, 29 possibilities in all and hence, 29 units per input group). Input to the network was English text, stepped across the input "groups" one character at a time. Thus if the input was "THE CAT" (seven characters, if you count the space, and you do) at one time, then it would be "HE CAT " the next time, and "E CAT S" the next time, and so on. At each time step the network attempts to pronounce the middle letter only of the seven (the three either side provide some context).

The input "groups" pass activity to units in the "hidden" layer, and

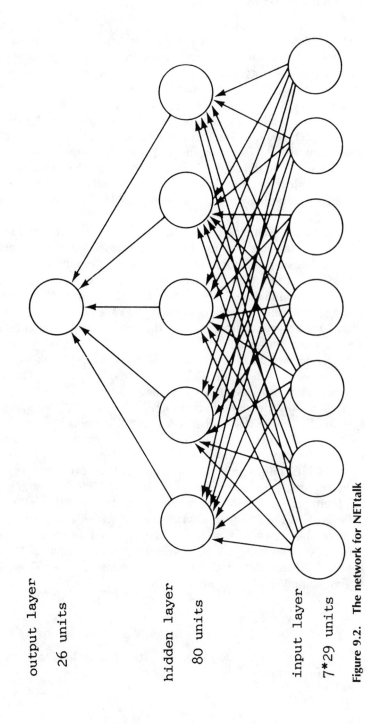

output layer

26 units

hidden layer

80 units

input layer

7*29 units

Figure 9.2. The network for NETtalk

units in the "hidden" layer (there are 80 of them) send activity to all 26 units in the output layer (these 26 output units code for the pronunciation of a letter — 21 articulatory features, such as voiced or unvoiced, plus five features for coding stress and syllable boundaries). The NETtalk network contained 309 units and 18,629 weighted links.

In sum, the input is a letter (in the context of three letters each side of it in English words), and the output is a phoneme given by the pattern of activity that results in the 26 output units. The external information that drives the learning is the difference between the phoneme generated and the correct phoneme. The general strategy is to use this discrepancy to adjust the weights in both layers of links as directed by the "back propagation" function.

The system output was classed as "perfect" when correct, and as a "best guess" when the correct phoneme was the closest one to the actual output pattern. The learning curve of the system rose rapidly at first but then flattened out in the manner typical of learning curves (read about plateaux lands in the hill-climbing country, described in a later section). The percentage of perfect pronunciation was at 55% and still rising (very slowly) after 50,000 words of learning. But the percentage of best guesses was at a much more encouraging 95%.

The tape of the pronunciation of English prose by NETtalk as it is learning is impressive, almost the ELIZA of the modern AI era. The initial random babbling quickly switches to something obviously more structured, and finally quite clear (although somewhat alien) English is spoken by the system. The implications of this successful learning system were discussed earlier (Chapter 3) as illustrative of what I believe to be the fundamental problem of the CP.

Each unit of NETtalk is linked to all units in the next layer. In the words of the authors: "the hidden units . . . form internal representations that are appropriate for solving the mapping problem of letters to phonemes. The goal of the learning algorithm is to search effectively the space of all possible weights for a set of weights that solves the problem" (p. 5). {Briefly, but nevertheless quite gruesomely, the output of the ith node — unit, in Sejnowski's and Rosenberg's terminology — P_i is obtained by first summing all of its inputs,

$$E_i = \sum_j w_{ij} P_j$$

where w_{ij} is the weight from the jth to the ith node, and then applying a sigmoidal transformation,

$$P_i = \frac{1}{1 + e^{-E_i}}$$

We can forget the niceties of the sigmoidal (not the Freudian Sigmundal, note) transformation. It's just a fancy term for some fiddling with the output activity values to ensure that they are most likely to be either high or low {and that the curve differentiates nicely — i.e., it is continuous}; we don't want nodes messing about with intermediate activity values that complicate the question of whether the recipient nodes are activated or not.

The authors graph the sigmoidal transformation as in Figure 9.3.

Normally, I would hesitate to subject you to this level of fine detail, but first, you've seen it before (remember pixel intensities? Try, because we are, I'm saddened to have to admit, going to differentiate again as well), and second, we really do need it to support our tour of back propagation.

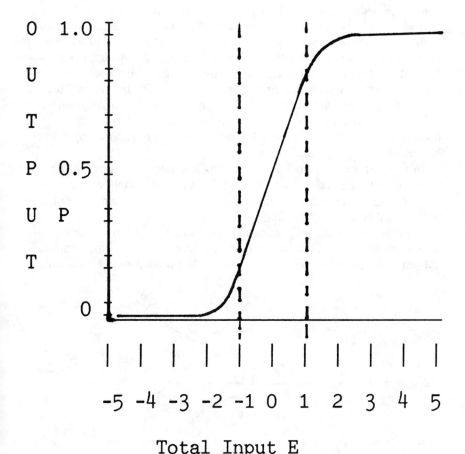

Figure 9.3.   A sigmoidal activation function

Notice first, as I said above, the output of a unit will tend to be either close to 0 or close to 1. Only if the total input is in the small range between -1 and 1 will the unit output an intermediate activity value.

Secondly, bring into consciousness (or just skip back and read) the pixilated chat about slopes of curves and differentiation. Just as with our abrupt change in pixel intensity, the above curve illustrates the behavior of a network unit and shows that it exhibits an abrupt change in output activity as input gradually increases. Where is this change of output most abrupt? Well, it's somewhere about the center of the curve — at the place where the slope of the curve is greatest, to be precise (I take the easy questions). Remind yourself that differentiation gives us the slope of the curve differentiated, and thus the derivative of the above curve will be a maximum when the unit's output is in the middle range and close to zero when the unit's output is close to either 1.0 or 0 (both are relatively horizontal, zero-slope parts of the curve). Save this knowledge for later.

Two texts were used to train the network: phonetic transcriptions from informal, continuous speech of a child; and 1,000 words chosen from a corpus of the most common words in English. The link weights were initialized to small random values uniformly distributed between -0.3 and 0.3, and then they were incrementally adjusted during training according to the discrepancy between the desired and actual phonemes generated. "For each phoneme this error was 'back propagated' from the output layer to the input layer using the learning algorithm introduced by Rumelhart et al. (1986)" (p. 6).

In order to explain the essence of this learning algorithm, let me use (see Figure 9.4) a highly simplified version of the NETtalk network: one input unit (numbered 5), one hidden unit (numbered 4), and three output units (numbered 1, 2, and 3).

Now the first phase of the learning process, the end of which is illustrated above, involves an input (the character "A") to input unit 5, a subsequent flow of activity, a_4, from 5 to the hidden unit 4, and finally

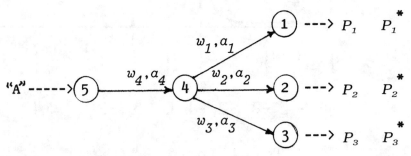

Figure 9.4. A simple path-like network

from 4 to the output units 1, 2, and 3, with activities a_1, a_2, and a_3, respectively. The outputs observed from units 1,2, and 3 are p_1, p_2, and p_3, respectively. But the phonemic representation of "A" (in its current context) is p_1^*, p_2^*, and p_3^* on units 1, 2, and 3, just as respectively.

Thus we have the initial discrepancies (p_1^* − p_1) as the basis for the error signal, D_1, to be used in adjusting the weight w_1, (p_2^* − p_2) as the basis for D_2 and adjustment of w_2, etc. The other major factor in this computation of the error signal is the derivative of the activation function (we sketched the activation function and discussed derivatives as slopes a little earlier).

In an effort to minimize the contribution of each weight to the total error in the network's observed behavior {the mean square error between desired and actual outputs}, various derivatives are computed, decomposed, and recomposed. But the upshot is that:

$$D_1 = (p_1^* − p_1)*\text{derivative of the activation function at } a_1$$

(similarly for D_2 and D_3). And that the necessary change in the weights w_1, w_2, and w_3 is Δw_1, Δw_2, and Δw_3 where:

$$\Delta w_1 = k*D_1*a_1$$
$$\Delta w_2 = k*D_2*a_2$$
$$\Delta w_3 = k*D_3*a_3$$

Where k is a constant, which controls the rate of learning (discussed later).

That's all very well, you might observe, but Perceptrons could do that; it's in the adjustment to w_4 that back propagation really has to show its paces. The error signal for w_4, D_4, is computed from D_1, D_2, and D_3 as follows:

$$D_4 = (D_1*w_1 + D_2*w_2 + D_3*w_3)* \text{ derivative of the activation function at } a_4$$

and

$$\Delta w_4 = k*D_4*a_4$$

where a_4 is the activity sent from unit 5 to unit 4, i.e., the activity sent along the link whose weight is being adjusted.

Returning to Newton's curse one final time: Notice that the change in link weight, Δw, is proportional to the value of the derivative of the activation function. This derivative is the slope of the activation function curve (illustrated above). This slope is a maximum when the activity through the link in question is about 0.5; this slope is a minimum when the activity flowing through the link is close to either 1.0 or 0. Thus this derivative component of the link-weight-adjustment algorithm caused big changes in link weight when middle-range activity was flowing, and small changes when either maximum or minimum activity was flowing. So here we have yet another feature (in addition to the sigmoidal activation function itself) that conspires to maintain activity values as either maximums or minimums — another feature that adds to network stability. In fact one might begin to wonder why (for empirical studies show that they do learn and adapt) such networks do not "freeze" into arbitrary link-weight configurations.

But better than the empirical studies, Rumelhart, Hinton, and Williams (1986) have shown that their back propagation algorithm will always follow a continuous downward path to a minimum error configuration. It is a reverse hill-climbing algorithm, and I'll deal with the problems of local and global minima (*a* minimum rather than *the* minimum) in a subsequent section, which is devoted to the techniques of scrambling across search spaces.

The above-described algorithm for back propagation has a number of limitations which don't seem to give rise to bad practical problems in the small number of quite diverse empirical studies conducted so far. Nevertheless, this algorithm is not the solution to network learning; it is a small but significant breakthrough; perhaps its significance is as a breakout of the Perceptron trap.

Before we look at another example of the back propagation algorithm in action, I should mention work on a significantly different solution to the problem of learning as a result of the feeding back of an error signal. I refer to the work on learning by the method of temporal differences (see, for example, Sutton, 1987). In this scheme the error term is not derived from the difference between the correct and the actual ouputs, but from the difference between temporally successive outputs — e.g., if on Monday a 60% chance of rain at the weekend is predicted, and on Tuesday a 70% chance is predicted, then a temporal difference system will alter memory parameters so as to increase subsequent predictions for days similar to Monday. It is claimed that,

> for most real-world prediction problems, temporal difference methods re-
> quire less memory and peak computation than conventional methods and
> produce more accurate predictions. It is argued that most problems to
> which supervised learning is currently applied are really prediction prob-
> lems of the sort to which temporal-difference methods can be applied to
> advantage. (Sutton, 1987 in abstract)

A strong statement, but one that we cannot dig into if this chapter is to remain vaguely within the bounds of a reasonable book chapter — I'll push on to the threatened example of back propagation.

Hinton (1989, p. 199) uses his own work (Hinton, 1986) to demonstrate "the ability of back-propagation to discover important underlying features of a domain." He used a multilayer network to learn the family relationships between 24 different people, as illustrated in Figure 9.5.

The information was represented as a set of triples (i.e., person1, relationship, person2), and the network was said to "know" these triples if it could produce the third term when given the first two terms as input.

Hinton used a five-layer network (see figure 9.6). The input layer was composed of 36 units: 24 for the 24 different people who could be person1 in a triple, and 12 for the 12 different family relationships represented (e.g., has-aunt). This is obviously a local, or nondistributed, representation for the input. Thus input of the first two terms in a triple amounts to activating two input units — one of the 24 for a person, and one of the 12 for a relationship. So the output layer was, as you might now guess, 24 units — one for each of the possible people who could be the third term in a triple, i.e., the person2 term. Thus, when a two-term input is put in the network, we should obtain after passage through the three hidden layers high activity in zero, one, or more of the output units, exactly the

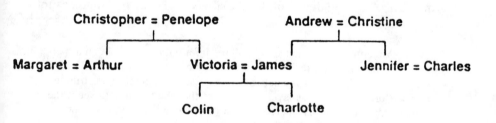

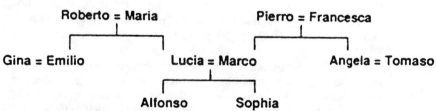

Figure 9.5.   Two family trees

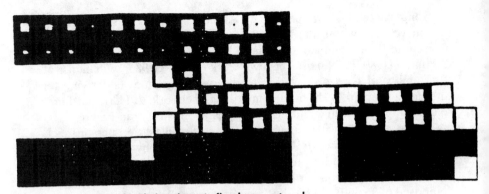

Figure 9.6.   Activity levels in Hinton's five-layer network

From "Connectionist Learning Procedures," by G.E. Hinton, 1989, *Artificial Intelligence*.
Copyright 1989 by Elsevier. Reprinted by permission.

that correspond to a correct completion of the partial triple input. This is the task that the network is to learn as a result of the back propagation procedure.

The hidden layers from input to output contained 12, 12, and 6 units, respectively, and of the 12 units in the first hidden layer, 6 are connected to the "person" input group, and 6 to the "family relationship" input group. This 'choking down' of the activity is explained by Hinton as follows:

> The architecture is designed so that all the information about an input person must be squeezed through a narrow bottleneck of 6 units in the first hidden layer. This forces the network to represent people using distributed patterns of activity in this layer. The aim of the simulation is to see if the components of these distributed patterns correspond to the important underlying features of the domain. (Hinton, 1989, pp. 200–201)

The network was subjected to prolonged training using back-propagation with 100 of the 104 possible triples. It was then tested on the remaining four. In Hinton's (1989, p. 201) words:

> It generalized correctly because during the training it learned to represent each of the people in terms of important features such as age, nationality, and the branch of the family tree that they belonged to [see Figure 9.5], even though these semantic features were not at all explicit in the input or output vectors. Using these underlying features, much of the information about family relationships can be captured by a fairly small number of 'micro-inferences' between features.

There are several rather different aspects of this study that you should notice. First, it generalized correctly. The back propagation procedure not only enabled the network to learn the 100 training examples, it also resulted in correct generalization from these training examples; i.e., the four unseen triples were completed correctly. Second, the generalization is not too surprising in that it was trained on better than 96% of the set that it generalized over.

The third point illustrates one of the great strengths of CP-based systems. Look at Figure 9.7.

Mysterious, isn't it? But a wealth of information is packed in there. It is a graphical illustration of the link weights from the 24 input units used to represent person1 in a triple to the second layer of 6 units that learned distributed representations of these people. Each block of 24 subblocks illustrates the weights to one unit in the hidden layer; thus there are six such blocks, conveniently numbered 1 through 6, okay? Within one such major block there is one subblock to represent the weight of the link from one person to the numbered hidden unit. The upper row of subblocks in each major block represent the link weight from the Anglo-named persons, as detailed in the figure; and the lower row represents the corresponding Italian-named person (i.e., corresponding with respect to the family trees illustrated earlier). White subblocks illustrate excitatory links (i.e., positive weights), and black subblocks illustrate inhibitory links (i.e., negative weights). Finally, the area of each subblock is representative of the magnitude of the link weight — the bigger the subblock, the bigger the corresponding weight; surprise, surprise. Hopefully, any mystery surrounding the interpretation of Figure 9.7 has now gone. If so, we are in a position to consider some further aspects of what this network has learned. According to Hinton, unit 1 in the hidden layer has learned to code for nationality. In major block 1, all the top row are white and the bottom row are black; this would seem to argue for a distinction in terms of the two family trees used for training, and Hinton summarizes this division as nationality. If this is a valid deduction, Christopher, for example, would seem to be more Anglo than Charles, but Roberto is far less Italian than Tomaso. Why is this? Does it mean anything significant? If not, why not? I leave these awkward questions as problems for the reader, as is customary in this book.

The major block 2, Hinton points out, appears to code for generation using three values quite consistently between the two families. Thus, the oldest generation have middling magnitude weights, the middle generation have small magnitude weights, and the babies have the large magnitude weights associated with their links to hidden-layer unit 2. The function of hidden-layer unit 3 is an enigma and as such is yet another suitable

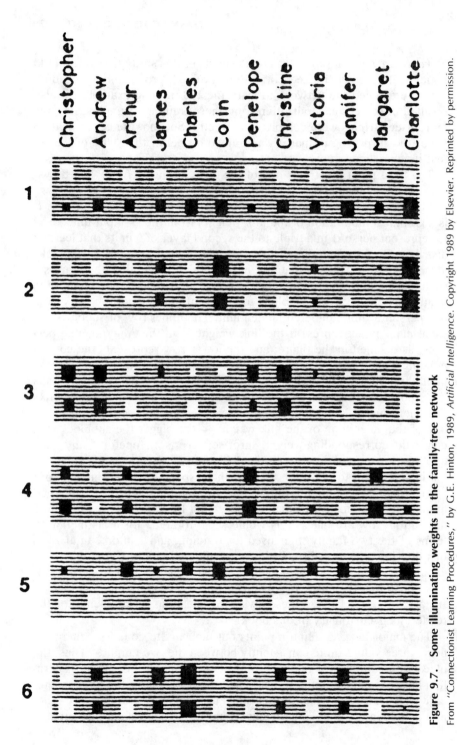

Figure 9.7. Some illuminating weights in the family-tree network

From "Connectionist Learning Procedures," by G.E. Hinton, 1989, *Artificial Intelligence.* Copyright 1989 by Elsevier. Reprinted by permission.

problem for the reader, while hidden-layer unit 4 encodes the branch of the family tree to which each person belongs.

The point here is that the system learned important features of the domain (e.g., nationality and age) without them being preselected and used to explicitly describe the training examples. This is impressive. But how impressive is it, really? A more cynical description is that a few hidden units reflect some structural characteristics of the training examples. Thus, the training examples were divided into two disjoint sets. Is it at all surprising that the network partitions the domain into two subsets (i.e., it learned the nationality feature)? Is this a further example of an IP-level theory implemented in a connectionist architecture? This last sentence is a reference back to Chapter 1 (just in case you were wondering) and can be restated as: Was the structure of the problem, the salient features, etc., coded implicitly into the input data at the outset and subsequently expressed explicitly in the internal structure of the model?

Hinton's (1989, p. 201, author's emphasis) point here is worth quoting at length:

> The learning procedure can only discover these features by searching for a set of features that make it easy to express the associations. Once these features have been discovered, the *internal* representation of each person (in the first hidden layer) is a distributed pattern of activity and similar people are represented by similar patterns. Thus the network constructs its own internal similarity metric. This is a significant advance over simulations in which good generalization is achieved because the experimenter chooses representations that already have an appropriate similarity metric.

I shall leave the reader with the question of the significance of this point as a ponderable; it is time to move on to look at the other major class of distributed CP models — the bath-like architectures.

LEARNING IN A BATH—TAKING THE PLUNGE

Within the class of bath-like connectionist architectures, the Boltzmann machine for example, learning is again link-weight adjustment, but not as a result of back propagation of error. It turns out (if you plough through all the mathematical nitty-gritty, which I'm not going to do) that individual link weights can be adjusted on the basis of local information only, and yet the local adjustment is guaranteed to be correct for global minimization of error. One of the drawbacks is that the necessary information is statistical in nature and thus must be collected from a number of "runs" of the system (i.e., problem solving, the settling down of the energy in the system, must be repeated many times both with and without clamping the network with information that it is supposed to learn about). Quite unbelievably, you have to measure small differences between large, noisy quantities — hence, the need for statistics.

Recall also that one problem-solving "run" with these architectures (try Smolensky's "harmonium model" in Chapter 6, if your memory seems to be in need of a nudge) involves many iterations, called *simulated annealing*. Hence, the learning is, as Pollack (1987a) notes, a very slow and computationally expensive process. Hinton has also pointed out that there is a slow procedure ('cooling' to achieve a true energy minimum) which has to be done many times (i.e., slowly); hence the overall process is not just slow but slow*slow {technical detail: slow^2} which is very slow indeed — it makes snails look like formula one racing cars by comparison.

Clearly, the story of Boltzmann machines cannot be all death and gloom. There is a bright side. As Hinton (1989, p. 210) puts it: "The beauty of Boltzmann machines is that the simplicity of the Boltzmann distribution [i.e., the central idea] leads to a very simple learning procedure which adjusts the weights so as to use the hidden units in an optimal way." And the reason why this should be a particularly beautiful property is that it relieves the system builder of the impossible task of setting the network up so that the hidden units represent the higher-level features of the problem domain. The simple, if time-consuming, learning procedure will sort out the optimal weights out for you.

The bones of the process can be described as follows, but first cast your mind back to Hopfield nets (Chapter 6). If your cast was accurate, you will recall that the nodes of a Hopfield net turn on when the activity level of the node exceeds its threshold. In the Boltzmann machine probability is thrown in, so that whether a unit turns on or not is dependent upon the extent to which the energy level exceeds the threshold — let's call this excess energy for node i when the net is in state a, $\Delta E_{a,i}$. {Then, for those who must know these things:

$$\Delta E_{a,i} = \sum_j w_{ij} * S_{a,j} - \Theta_i$$

where the state of the jth node when the net is in state a is $S_{a,j}$ — (which is simply "on" or "off", 1 or 0, no other choices, I'm afraid); w_{ij} is the weight of the link between nodes i and j; and Θ_i is the threshold of the ith node.}

The actual probability function is also not lacking in gruesomeness, but its general shape should be a vaguely familiar sight (if not exactly an old friend) to the reader who has being paying close attention. So here it is once more:

$$p_{a,i} = \frac{1}{1 + e^{\frac{-\Delta E_{a,i}}{T}}}$$

where $p_{a,i}$ is the probability of the ith node being "on" when the network is in state a, and T is the "computational temperature" which we discussed in the context of "harmony theory" (Chapter 6).

The actual link-weight adjustment used (i.e., the learning procedure) computes Δw_{ij} as a difference of averaged probabilities that both node i and node j are simultaneously active at thermal equilibrium when clamped and when not clamped. And again this learning procedure, bizarre as it may seem to the casual observer, is not an ad hoc strategy that seems to behave correctly on some occasions. It is a method that comes with a formal guarantee to deliver the goods — provided we live long enough to run all the necessary simulated annealings.

Although I have portrayed learning within the CP as adjustment of link weights, it can be viewed in terms of transforming one graph structure into another, and, certainly, this is the result of learning mechanisms to some extent: thus, arcs may be removed from graphs when their weights fall below a certain threshold, as in Sejnowski's NETtalk system. The question of adding arcs as a result of learning is another open and highly contentious issue. Two major camps within human learning theory, constructionists and selectionists, take opposite stands on the question of adding and deleting arcs (i.e., transforming graphs) as a result of learning. This debate is much broader than connectionism. The two schools of thought may be labeled *Darwinian learning* and *Lamarckian learning*. Darwin explained the development of species in terms of *selection* from a collection of alternatives, whereas Lamarck proposed that environmental pressures resulted in the generation of appropriate modifications. But in AI this issue is not a major one. The exception may be work within the CP, but then only that small subset which has aspirations to neuroanatomical validity. Nevertheless, when viewed in terms of graph transformation, the general problem may become both focused and formalized, hopefully, without loss of generality.

Essentially, the constructionists view learning as a process of building structure, and selectionists view it as reinforcing chosen pathways from a set of initially equal alternative possibilities. At first sight it might seem that only for constructionist implementations will learning result in graph transformations. Selectionist schemes involve only the changing of arc weights and would thus not seem to be readily applicable to graph-theoretic analysis; this is a superficial view. Selectionist-motivated networks may still be implemented (or analyzed in terms of) the addition and removal of arcs and nodes; NETtalk is one such example that I have already mentioned. Johnston et al. (1983) demonstrated that a cell-assembly model could account for a wide range of empirical data on basic human learning; they implemented an increase in arc weight strength by adding a "unit arc" between the nodes connected by the arc whose weight was to be increased. This work was also abandoned largely because of the difficulty of comprehending and hence, developing the network structures generated, which leads us back to the familiar problem of understandability of models within the CP.

CLIMBING HILLS BECAUSE THE'RE THERE

A popular subparadigm in machine learning is called *hill climbing*. In this approach, you begin with some initial structure, typically an inadequate one. This structure is modified, perhaps as the result of new information from the environment, or possibly as a result of applying some heuristic. Each modification constitutes a step in the problem space. The question then is: Is this a step up or a step down? An evaluation function rates the modified structure(s), and the one that receives the best score (i.e., is highest in the current space of structures) is retained for further modification in an attempt to reach even higher places. But, unfortunately, as with mountaineering, you sometimes have to step down in order to eventually climb to the heights, so it is with the algorithmic form: High points in the search space (i.e., solutions) are not always obtainable on a path of progressively better modifications of the function — at least, it is often impossible to find such paths although they may exist. This is another manifestation of the curse of nonmonotonicity, and it's one that hits hill-climbing strategies like an avalanche.

The initially fruitful analogy between the optimization technique called hill climbing and the physical exertions of mountaineers soon fails us dismally. The failure is not because human mountaineers are, if reports from this strange breed are to be believed, motivated by "its being there," and that this is a driving force that algorithmic optimizers seems to lack. It is because of the radical difference in behavior when, on having achieved the summit, it is given out that there may be a higher peak in the neighborhood.

The strategy, for a hill-climbing system that has reason to suspect that it is occupying only a local maximum perhaps dwarfed by some peak just across a narrow but deep canyon, is to launch itself (more or less randomly in the absence of directional information) into the search space and hope to make a landfall on the side of the bigger mountain, up which it immediately starts climbing — more a flying squirrel's then a mountaineer's strategy. Clearly, the human mountaineer would be well advised not to push the analogy any further (see Figure 9.8).

An important question for both mountaineers and hill-climbing algorithms is: How do you know when you've reached the top? (Hint: It is not the presence of a flagpole.) Just for a change, I'm going to deal with this question myself (instead of foisting it off as an exercise for the reader), and I'm going to take it on because I know the answer. At the very top, every direction will lead you down, just as at the North Pole every direction is south.

In practice, one cannot be sure that a necessarily discrete sampling of what is probably a continuum will not overlook a narrow path upward. A hill-climbing algorithm is best advised to start looking for other hills to climb as soon as the initial gains begin to level off (symbolic search spaces usually reveal themselves to be plateau lands, and connectionist networks are not obviously in topographically different country).

Mountaineers, it seems, should plant a flag, take a photo, and have a short rest before legging it back down with all haste to a hot cup of cocoa and a warm sleeping bag. For the hill-climbing algorithm every apparent end is a new beginning; for the mountaineer it's the end — until next time.

Langley, Gennari, and Iba (1987) review hill-climbing theories of learning within the SSSP. They argue that it is a more psychologically plausible search strategy than depth-first, breadth-first, etc. Psychological theories, they tell us,

> should be constrained along three dimensions:
> (1) learning must be incremental; there should be no extensive reprocessing of previously encountered instances;
> (2) the learner can entertain only one 'hypothesis' at a time; i.e., competing alternatives are not retained;
> (3) The learner has no memory of previous hypotheses that it has held; thus, there can be no direct backtracking. (p. 312)

They present and explain several projects to illustrate their ideas.

Moving to work that is intermediate between the SSSP and the CP, we can view Holland's (1986) "genetic algorithm," which was introduced in an earlier section, from an abstract fell-walker's perspective. The population of rules that comprise Holland's system are hill climbing in some "fitness" space. New rules are generated by a semirandom process that is likely to yield "fitter" rules. The least "fit" rules in the population are painlessly killed off, and the new, potentially fitter chaps are brought in to make up the numbers. The system then tackles the local terrain once more; the rules that show up fitter, by the degree to which they contribute to successful problem solving, are given a boost in fitness rating, and

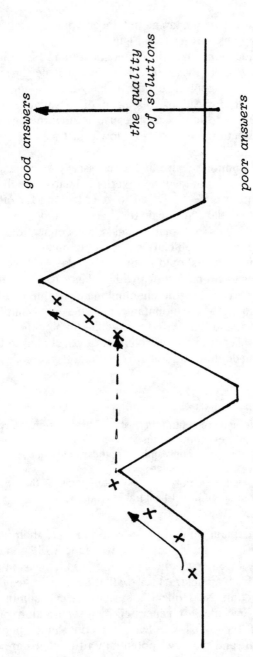

Figure 9.8. Algorithmic mountaineering

those that don't are demoted. Then the cycle of generate, adjust population, and retry is reentered, and so on.

In general the rule population is being moved up the slope of fitness, where fitness is utility in solving a class of problems. The key to whether this is hill climbing in the sense of a steady slog always upwards or only probabilistic mountaineering in which upward movement actually occurs on, say, 80% of the steps is in the nature of the new rule generation process. If the new rule generation were totally random, we might expect the system to spend roughly half its time going upward and half going downward — not a great mountaineering strategy.

Both theoretical and empirical studies lead Holland to believe that his algorithms are not random mountaineers. In addition, the fact that we are dealing with the fitness of a population of primitive rules means that random elements can be accommodated, for the occasional unfit rules can be carried for a short distance (one cycle) by the rest of the population. The attraction of randomness is closely connected with mechanized creativity, as we shall see.

The joys of roaming across the hills and dales of a search space also arises within the CP, as you may remember from our short tour of back propagation in the previous section. The goal of a back propagation algorithm is to adjust link weights and thereby minimize the error in the system. It is hill climbing in reverse: The back-propagation algorithm is attempting to get to the bottom of the deepest valley in the land of error. The peaks are maximum errors, and thus valley floors are minimum errors.

Hinton (1989, p. 199) discusses the "shape of the error surface" in his review of CP-based learning procedures. He provides all the details of how the various learning procedures scramble about in their attempts to slither efficently down the long slope to minimum error, i.e., down the error gradient.

The back-propagation algorithm is designed to always follow the error gradient down when it makes an adjustment of link weights. This is comforting; except that just as hill climbing will always take the system up to some peak, that peak may be only a foothill among some truly majestic pinnacles, so the back propagation algorithm may dump the network in the bottom of a hanging valley — just a local minimum error state.

Now there may be a way out of this valley and down again (as there is with most real hanging valleys), but there may not — abstract search spaces are not natural phenomena contoured by water and glaciers and other forces which gravity guarantees will always be moving downwards. Even if there is an outlet, say a narrow defile, that leads down to lower error minima, the algorithm has to find it — if it takes big steps in weight adjustment, the learning is rapid but a narrow downward paths may be overlooked, and small steps give more confidence in finding downward paths, but the rate of progress down may be intolerably slow. Thus, in the previous discussion of the back propagation algorithm, the step size was governed by the constant k in the equation for Δ, the link weight adjustment (see Figure 9.9).

As you can see, Achilles really did win the race but only because the tortoise fell into a manhole that Achilles did not even notice — he wasn't particularly smart, you may remember. However, although Achilles actually gets there first (to a minimum error state), the tortoise eventually descends much lower, and that is a good thing in the world of error avoidance.

Most theoretically sound hill climbing only guarantees that the system will follow the correct path if infinitely small steps are taken. So although the attainment of a maximum or minimum is guaranteed, it does take an awfully long time to get there. The sure road to Paradise loses some of its appeal if you're told that it's infinitely long. One is liable to forego the guarantees of perfection for some reasonable assurance that you'll reach the end within a reasonable time and that there's still a good chance that you'll find what you're looking for when you get there.

Rumelhart, Hinton, and Williams (1986) discuss their experiences with local minima (which have not been a problem, they report). They investigated various step sizes in the hill-descending learning algorithm, and the use of a "momentum" term to combat possible oscillation (i.e., up and down of system accuracy) with large step sizes.

Another popular connectionistic ploy, which we've glanced at before, is the Boltzmann-machine idea. It is not too inaccurate (certainly no more than usually so) to blame the Boltzmann-machine idea on the subpopulation of reconditioned physicists who have invaded connectionism. As an exercise in orienteering to find the lowest energy minimum (and hence a stable state of the system), noise (in the form of activity) is injected into the network in order to bump it out of a local minimum that it may have settled comfortably into and hopefully cause it to resettle into a more global minimum. We can also accuse these rehabilitated physicists of popularizing the term *simulated annealing* (although a desire for accuracy forces me to tell you that Kirkpatrick, Gelatt, & Vecchi, 1983, are generally blamed for this particular term, and I have no evidence that any of this trio were actually physicists in either their current or any previous incarnation). The term simulated annealing is used to describe the slow "cooling" — reduction in computational temperature, T, with successive distributions of activity throughout the network — of a system to improve the chances of it settling into a global energy minimum (as opposed to sudden quenching that may lock the system into a local minimum). Simulated annealing allows Boltzmann machines to settle into low energy

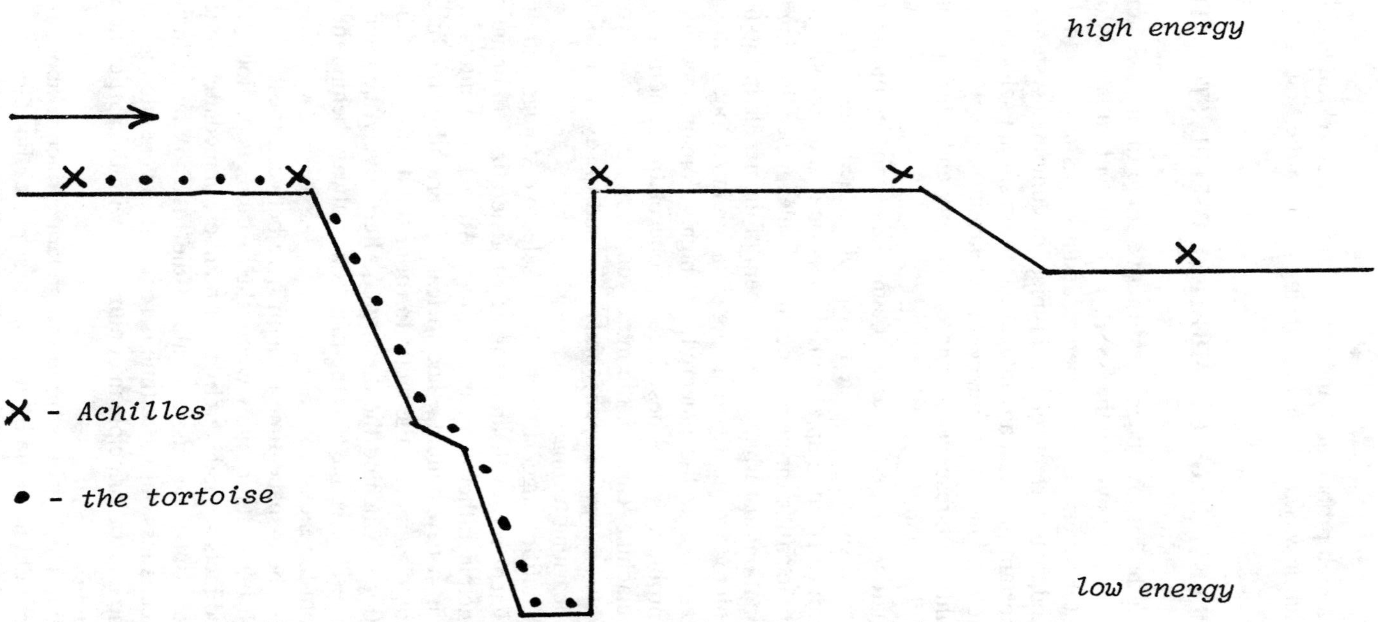

high energy

low energy

✗ – Achilles

● – the tortoise

Figure 9.9. Achilles and the tortoise in the energy landscape (the true story)

states with a high probability, and get it all done before you lose interest or forget what it was that you were trying to do in the first place.

ROTE LEARNING: IF IT MIGHT BE USEFUL, STORE IT

Rote learning has always been an attractive route to the mechanization of adaptive behaviors within the SSSP. To begin with, it is easy to implement. Just store every new experience, and it works well, given the large memories and fast, perfect retrieval typical of computer systems. It also has the important practical advantage that the resultant self-modification can be limited and localized. Hence it is a learning strategy that offers the best possibility with respect to comprehensibility and thus controllability of the overall system.

Unfortunately, the performance of a mechanism based upon blind rote learning is soon swamped by the masses of learned data that result. All available storage is eaten up at a prodigious rate, and the system spends most of its time sifting through an ocean of irrelevancies, looking for pertinent information: disturbingly reminiscent of the needle-in-the-haystack routine (an all too frequently recurring situation in AI, one that is usually overcome by a few well-engineered, but highly domain-specific, heuristics). This problem is well described by one of the famous laments of workers in machine learning: the more you know, the slower you go — an adage whose scope of applicability, I'm sad to say, is not limited to simple rote learning techniques, as we shall see.

Two possibilities suggest themselves: selective storage and organization for efficient retrieval; and storage of generalized information, one general principle rather than many facts. An expert janitor, when he started out in a new building, had to learn where all of the fuse boxes were. He could memorize the facts: In room 100 it was behind the door, in room 200 it was behind the door, etc. Alternatively, he might apprehend the general principle that the fuse box is always behind the door of the X00 room for each floor X.

There may be a space–time tradeoff here between these two learning strategies. If he wants to know where the fuse box is on floor 4, he can, if his learned facts are indexed by floor number, immediately retrieve the relevant fact. But if he has generalized the fuse-box facts, then actual storage space is less but more time is required to generate the necessary fact from the general principle in conjunction with the particular requirement, 4th floor.

If our janitor opted for storing the general principle about fuse box location, how did he come by it in the first place? For the rote learning scheme, the facts are given and just have to be stored. But the general principle is not given anywhere; it is in some sense implicit in the set of facts, and must, therefore, be abstracted from the facts by some mechanism.

LEARNING GENERALITIES

The learning of generalities within the SSSP (we've aleady seen some CP-based mechanisms) may be divided into inductive and deductive approaches. The former style of approach in which a general principle is induced from a collection of specific instances (either as a one-shot process from a fixed and given set of training examples, or as an incremental process as each new example becomes manifest) is historically more important, but, in the current era of knowledge-based AI, deductive strategies are in the ascendent. The deductive approach, commonly called *explanation-based generalization* (EBG, a subset of *explanation-based learning,* EBL), is typically a one-shot procedure in which a general principle is generated as a result of explaining why a training example fits the concept being studied. The training example is analyzed in terms of the domain knowledge to construct an explanation of how it satisfies the general concept under study. A generalization of the training example is then produced, together with a deductive justification of the generalization in terms of the system's knowledge. At this point the reader should be wondering why, if you've got a general concept that covers the training example, EBG enthusiasts are trying to produce a generalization of the training example. This is a good question, and one that we shall tackle in due course. Obviously there is something that I'm holding back, but not for long.

Mitchell, Keller, and Kedar-Cabelli (1986, pp. 47–48, author's emphasis) provide the following summary of the old and the new way for machines to generalize (within the SSSP):

> Most research on the generalization problem has focused on empirical, data-intensive methods that rely on large numbers of training examples to constrain the search for the correct [!] generalization. These methods all employ some kind of *inductive bias* to guide the inductive leap that they must make in order to define a concept from only a subset of its examples. This bias is typically built into the generalizer by providing it with knowledge only of those example features that are presumed relevant to describing the concept to be learned. . . . Because these methods are based on searching for features that are common to the training examples, we shall refer to them as *similarity-based* generalization methods.
> . . . [EBG] methods constrain the search [for a correct generalization] by relying on knowledge of the task domain and of the concept under study.

After analyzing a single training example in terms of this knowledge, these methods are able to produce a valid generalization of the example *along with a deductive justification of the generalization in terms of the systems's knowledge.* More precisely, the *explanation-based* methods analyze the training example by first constructing an explanation of how the example satisfies the definition of the concept under study. The features of the example identified by this explanation are then used as the basis for formulating the general concept definition. The justification for this concept definition follows from the explanation constructed for the training example. . . . The basic difference between the two classes of methods is that similarity-based methods must rely on some form of inductive bias to guide generalization, whereas explanation-based methods rely instead on their domain knowledge.

I'll now expand on these two classes of generalization methods, and I'll do so in historical order. In addition, this might be the best place to slot in another subclass of CP-based learning strategies; it is called *competitive learning.* And while it is not a straightforward induction-based method (for the term *induction* is itself SSSP-biased), it does partition a set of instances into disjoint clusters such that all the instances within a cluster are similar to one another (as you will see if you stay with me for a few more pages).

There are two major strategies within the class of (SSSP-based) similarity-based methods for machine learning of general principles: Guess a general principle and then limit it according to subsequent instances of counterexamples, or make the first instance the general principle and generalize it according to the subsequent examples encountered. Both strategies have been used for machine learning in AI, and have been discussed in Bundy and Silver (1982). This survey is limited to the learning of rules of the form:

H1 and H2 and . . . Hn $\rightarrow$ Conclusion

i.e., that a set of hypotheses (the H's) imply a certain conclusion. For example,

(a polygon) and (four sides) and (Christmas Day) $\rightarrow$ a square

is one such rule, and although not quite perfect it may be improved by each of the two major strategies, as we shall see. But first, let's run through the fundamental idea used here — induction.

INDUCTION

At a more abstract level, learning generalities from a set of instances is the classical problem of induction: How many white swans do you have to see before you can conclude that all swans are white? The point is that you can never conclude such things with certainty. It appears that God forgot to write in a clause about reliable induction when he set up our world — it just didn't come with a guarantee on induction.

Nevertheless, we must inductively produce such generalizations if we are to function intelligently in this world, and so must an intelligent machine. Not "**the** correct generalization," as the earlier long quotation would have us believe, for how could that be? What could it mean? Intelligence rests to no small degree, I think, on the ability to produce enough adequate generalizations. The inconsistency of the world makes intelligence necessary; the consistency makes it possible — i.e., there is enough validity in the inductive process to make it a useful strategy for predicting the future, but the predictions are not certainties by any means.

The problem of induction in machine learning is cast in terms of generating, from a set of instances (or examples both positive and negative), a description that includes every positive example and excludes every negative example (or nonexample). In addition, the general description should be a *useful* one. I don't care to try and define what *useful* means in this context, but roughly a description is useful to the extent that it summarizes in collection of specific instances in such a way that information that bears on the system's attempts to achieve its goals can be accurately inferred on the majority of occasions. An obvious nonuseful description is to AND together all of the positive examples and negated nonexamples. The inductive generalization should also, of course, be accurate: It should describe all the known examples (called completeness) and should exclude all known nonexamples (called consistency). Accuracy is easy to check for, usefulness is typically not.

Thus, faced with three instances of swans flying west to east and a nonswan (say a crow) flying east to west, an accurate inductive generalization (from this set of four instances) would be that swans fly west to east; it is both complete and consistent with respect to the known instances. But the occurrence of a swan flying east to west will destroy completeness; we will need to modify our previous generalization (at the very least). This incremental approach to induction (where the system does not have all possible instances on hand from the beginning) is more difficult (than nonincremental, of course), because a new instance may at any time wreck what had been up to that point a perfectly good inductive generalization. Nonincremental inductive learning is thus easier.

The revised generalization might be that swans make a loud noise when flying (for the nonexample bird, the crow, flies relatively silently); this is again complete and consistent, but perhaps not very useful. If most future swans are encountered when they are swimming, the generalization about noisy flying, which was correct with respect to the four instances will not support any inference that the swimming birds are swans.

Who decides whether the generalization is to be in terms of color, size, noisy flying, or direction of flight? Who indeed; that is just one of the awkward problems: selecting the attributes that are useful. As we shall see, in AI, this problem is usually finessed by describing the instances in terms of just those attributes that are needed to construct the desired generalization. This is the inductive bias mentioned in the introduction to generalization methods. One might wonder at this point how human intelligence copes with this awkward problem: How do we construct the correct generalization from the infinite set of possible ones hidden in the rich diversity of real-world experiences? To begin with I don't like the term *the correct generalization,* but then how do we manage to come up with enough adequate generalizations? The new question may be a little easier but it is certainly not a cinch to answer.

Evolution has surely included some aspects of appropriate inductive bias in our genetic programs. In addition, we have unlearning and reappraisal skills that machine learning theorists have not even begun to grapple with. Such skills make it less critical that our initial generalizations are always appropriate. Current machine learning strategies, once locked on to a generalization path, have only two alternatives: follow it to the end, or collapse in total failure. Hence, the need to ensure that the "right" inductive bias is presupplied (to be honest: some systems do attempt minor repair work on misguided generalizations). A third point is that we are often wrong, and that poor individual generalizations typically do not make a big impact on our lives. Each generalization we make is just one among many, and is seldom critical. Most machine learning schemes construct generalizations that are one among none — i.e., failure of the generalization means total failure.

An influential approach to inductive generalization has been the "version space" model of Mitchell (1982). In this model there are five major components:

1. An Instance Language, in which to describe the examples and nonexamples;
2. A Generalization Language, in which to express the derived generalized descriptions;
3. A Matching Function, which returns true if some instance tested is described by the current generalization, and false otherwise;

4. A Training Set of instances whose membership in the set to be generally described is given (i.e., a set of instances that are marked as examples or nonexamples); and

5. A well-defined way to decide which is the better of two generalizations {gruesomely called a Partial Order on potential descriptions. This component ensures that the algorithm can always move to the more complete generalized description when it has two to choose between}.

As you can ascertain, no doubt, the version-space model does not fit well with many aspects of reality, e.g., noise, when our instances are not totally accurate, and these problematic aspects are the foci or current research. Hickey (1987), for example, has attempted to expand the utility of this model by defining concepts such as "meaningfulness" and adding mechanisms for incrementally integrating background knowledge with the inductive process.

Michalski (1983) reviews the subfield of inductive learning and presents "Star," a general methodology for learning structural descriptions from examples, which is based upon the view that learning is a heuristic search through a space of symbolic descriptions. The true story (coming soon), "Underneath the Arches," is a tale of one such learning program. Michalski (1987) also provides us with one example of research work aimed at addressing the problem of the mismatch between the exactness this AI subfield and the imprecision of reality. "Most human concepts," he says, "have imprecise, context-dependent meaning. Such concepts enable people to express a great variety of meanings by fewer words, and this serves cognitive economy"(p. 50). His proposal involves a two-component framework: the usual, precise concept definition — the *base concept representation* (BCR); and a fuzzy matching function — the *inferential concept interpretation* (ICI). Then the meaning of any instance is determined by use of the BCR but via the mechanisms of the ICI. Initial experiments with this two-tiered representation, in which a large part of the concept meaning is shifted from the base concept to the interpretation mechanism, showed a significant saving in space requirements and a small increase in recognition accuracy.

OVERGENERALIZATION AND REFINEMENT

The discrimination process, as an approach to learning, requires that first we have available a general principle. This initial guess may either be generated heuristically from a given instance or fact, or it may be supplied by some outside agent (or even generated by the EBG method, as we shall see).

With the first approach our janitor has to come up with a potential general principle about fuse box location when he finds the first fuse box behind the door of room 100. How is he going to do this?

He must generate a sufficiently broad principle, one that can be modified in the light of subsequent failures to find fuse boxes. It must be such that it will convert to a principle enabling him to predict adequately where fuse boxes will be.

So what is his first attempt at this principle? He finds a first fuse box: fuse boxes are found on walls. Looking around the room at the other walls which do not have fuse boxes, he refines his principle: fuse boxes are found on one wall of a room. An inspection of all other rooms on this floor leads him to the further refinement: fuse boxes are found on one wall of one room. Subsequent inspection of other rooms on other floors might well finally lead him to the general principle given earlier. That seems easy enough, and a study by Langley (1983) is an example of machine learning using such a scheme.

The crucial information here is knowing what are the important similarities between any two instances of finding a fuse box, and what are the important differences between instances of finding and instances of not finding fuse boxes. The similarities and differences are in fact endless, but only very few of them are relevant to the process of refining the principle. How do we know which are the important dimensions? What is the appropriate inductive bias?

The janitor's first attempt at the rule might have been: Fuse boxes are found on Thursdays. A few minutes later he looks into the next room, no fuse box, ah: Fuse boxes are found on Thursday afternoons at 3 o'clock precisely, and so on. He may eventually exclude some or all of these irrelevant constraints, but will he ever find a useful general principle?

The foregoing smacks of the absurd, but remember we are going to apply these strategies in a computer, not just explain them to a fellow human being. The reason that we find these suggestions unreal is because we know that the location of fuse boxes is invariant with respect to the day of the week and the time of day; computers don't know that. We have an enormous fund of general knowledge to draw upon; no computer system yet constructed has more than a very small fraction of our general knowledge.

Returning to the earlier rule that aspires to define a square, it is obviously too general: Not all four-sided polygons are squares, even on Christmas Day. If we present our learning machine with a rectangle on Christmas Day and tell it that this is not a square, we have provided a nonexample that the machine may use to refine its rule.

The crux of this refinement process is to notice that the attributes of the nonexample presented differ from the rule's hypotheses by the fact that, although it has four sides, they are not all equal in length. Hence, we add a further condition to the rule's hypotheses. The new rule is:

(a polygon)and(four sides)and(Christmas Day)and(all sides equal)
                    → a square

If the machine had computed the essential difference to be a question of angles, the resultant extra hypothesis might have been: (all angles not equal). This is not a disastrous mistake, as further examples could be used to eliminate this wrong step (the questions of unlearning mistakes and imperfect learning in general are both considered later), but, at the same time, it is not much help.

If the machine learning algorithm had settled on the thickness of the rectangle's sides as the significant attribute, again the resultant rule would be worse rather than better. The machine must be able to select the appropriate attributes of the learning examples presented.

Machine learning algorithms typically do not cope with the actual examples but only with abstract descriptions of these examples. Winston's (1975) famous arch-learning program, for example, was never exposed to actual arches made out of blocks, but only to descriptions of arches. And of course in a description one can omit the inappropriate attributes. I focus briefly on this issue in a subsequent section that discusses needles in haystacks.

Here we see an example of the discontinuity between the problems faced by a system that functions in an abstract domain and one that must work with the real world as it is — abstract AI and concrete AI; they are worlds apart.

Successful machine learning requires: first, that we tell the computer exactly which dimensions of the problem are the important ones; and second, that the difference between the current approximation to the rule and each learning example (or nonexample) is small (the idea of "near misses" for teaching purposes).

A FIRST GUESS AND GENERALIZATION

In this, the reverse approach, the system starts with a fairly specific rule and then removes restrictions in the light of subsequent examples.

Using this strategy, the janitor, on finding the first instance of a fuse box, might generate the following tentative rule: Fuse boxes are found behind the blue door of room 100. When he later stumbles onto another fuse box behind the green door of room 200, he has found an example that his rule does not cover. Some modification of the rule is called for. The resultant more general rule is: Fuse boxes are found behind the blue door of room 100 and behind the green door of room 200.

Clearly, this strategy is going to lead to a general rule that is little more than an enumeration of the set of instances encountered. The secret here is to reduce a set of instances to a more concise general rule; we require a mechanism for inductive generalization.

The collection of specific room numbers (100, 200, etc.) should be reduced to something like "room x00, where $1 <= x <=$ number of floors in building." And the set of door colors should be abandoned as nonsignificant. Again we might ask, how did he know that door color was a nonsignificant attribute of his rule? Well, he noticed that there was no regularity in the set of door colors amassed. That might be an answer, but consider how you would specify "regularity" in general terms and algorithmically? Therein lies the problem.

Appropriate generalization of the set of room numbers is no easier a problem, but some inductive generalization algorithms have been successfully applied to certain specific problems. Quinlan (1982) surveys a few inductive generalization schemes and describes his own system in some detail. He stresses that the success of current systems is dependent upon describing the instances of the rule by appropriate attributes (i.e., room number rather than time of day for fuse box location). And he goes on to say that the much harder problem of automatically developing good attributes (called "constructive induction") is a problem that will dominate inductive inference research in the 1980s.

Our rule that defines a square (incorrectly) is also too specific. A further example of a square on, say, New Year's Day could be used to motivate the necessary generalization — or could it? The modified rule might be:

(a polygon)and(four sides)and((Christmas Day)or(New Year's Day))
        → a square

Again we have much the same problem (except that this time it is finite; there are only 365 different days, but infinitely many ways to label them — on second thoughts). As an alternative to the very difficult problem of a widely applicable inductive generalization algorithm, we might use a human tutor to explicitly provide some guidance to the learning machine. There is no requirement that the machine must "go it alone" — humans certainly don't.

Another weakness of some of these general techniques is that they rely critically on both the ordering and the choice of examples. Nevertheless,

AI systems that can automatically assimilate knowledge only as a result of the ministrations of a benevolent human tutor could still be of inestimable practical value (and perhaps more readily controlled and understood just because they are externally driven).

On the other hand external tutoring puts a considerable burden on the human tutor. In fact we are beginning to see a revival of interest in more sophisticated machine learning initiated by expert systems builders, just because this burden is becoming intolerable. Explicit hand-crafting of knowledge base upgrades quickly becomes burdonsome and an exceedingly tricky process.

Bundy and Silver (1982) warn us that neither of these two general strategies is complete in itself (i.e., we cannot know if we have arrived at the optimal rule); we need to apply both strategies (they suggest generalization before discrimination) to be sure of arriving at the best rule.

Most of the foregoing on inductive generalization has implied that the individual examples arrive one by one (as distinct from being available en masse at the outset). If this is the case, we have been discussing incremental learning. The generally easier task of inducing generalities from a fixed and known set of examples, nonincremental induction, is visited again later in the chapter, where it is treated as a species of discovery mechanism. This nonstandard approach both makes a change and emphasizes the point that all classification schemes in machine learning are largely arbitrary — a good reason and a real reason, you choose the pairings.

Every survey of machine learning is obliged to at least mention Winston's (1975) arch-learning program. Winston designed and implemented a system which could learn general concepts given a series of specific examples and nonexamples of the concept. In the course of the last decade or so AI enthusiasts have been treated to reruns of this system learning the concept of an arch. Not wishing to break with tradition, I shall follow suit, but my tale was recorded when the system had an off day (as all truly intelligent systems must, I believe).

TRUE AI STORY: 9.1
UNDERNEATH THE ARCHES: AN EVERYDAY STORY OF
CONCEPT LEARNING

It seemed like a normal day at the MIT AI Lab; the computers were humming contentedly, the laser printers were quietly vomiting sheets of paper, and a general feeling of well-done was in the air. The Concept-Learning Program was all ready to learn its arch, the traditional sequence of examples and near misses (a, b, c, and d) were in order and ready for input, everything was as it should be — or so we thought.

For readers who may have forgotten exactly what the two examples and two near misses are, I've reproduced them in Figure 9.10.

The learning process seemed to proceed as follows:

- Example (a) allowed the deduction that, for an arch, three objects are necessary, and that object B should be left of C while C, as a result, should be right of B.
- In nonexample (b), a near miss, the object A is lying on the floor; this cannot be allowed.
- Nonexample (c) indicates that the fatness of B and C is critical: They must not be fatter than A.
- Example (d) teaches the machine that the component objects need not necessarily be bricks.

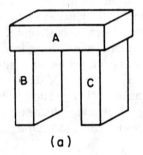

(a)

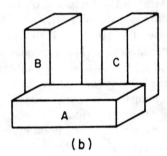

(b)

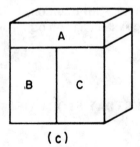

(c)

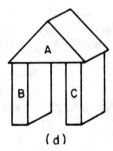

(d)

Figure 9.10.   The four examples for arch learning

Confident in the belief that, if the system has worked through this sequence of examples and nonexamples correctly in every known AI text, it will do so once more, we did not look closely at the learning behavior

but pushed on to the more exciting stuff: watching the system discriminate between (descriptions of) arches and of nonarches. Most of the deni-
zens of the lab were busily engaged elsewhere, grappling with recalcitrant
browsers, etc. as the sequence of (descriptions of) structures shown in
Figures 9.11 to 9.15 was fed into the program.

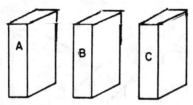

Figure 9.11.   Not an arch

AN ARCH, the system ruled. Eyebrows rose. "This has been happen-
ing too much of late," said a knowledgeable local inhabitant who, with
the casual skill of one totally at ease in the high-tech jungle, then kicked
the machine quite gently with a view to inducing it to behave we then
tried another near miss (see Figure 9.12).

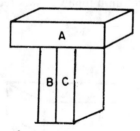

Figure 9.12.   Not another arch

AN ARCH, the system printed out boldly. The word spread quickly. The
cozy hum and keyboard clatter of hacking died out as a crowd began to
collect around our screens. The system was fed another near miss (see
Figure 9.13).

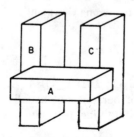

Figure 9.13.   Still not an arch

AN ARCH, yet again. It was becoming a momentous day. We pressed on into the unknown and presented the system with a last near miss (see Figure 9.14).

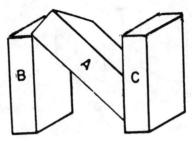

Figure 9.14. A fallen arch

AN ARCH, once more, until finally it was fed an honest-to-goodness arch (Figure 9.15).

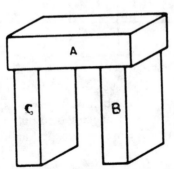

Figure 9.15. An arch from the wrong viewpoint

NOT AN ARCH — B NOT LEFT_OF C, it declared. A deep silence settled over this group of persons not usually known for their lack of vocalization; it was as if talking had given way, quite strangely, to thinking.

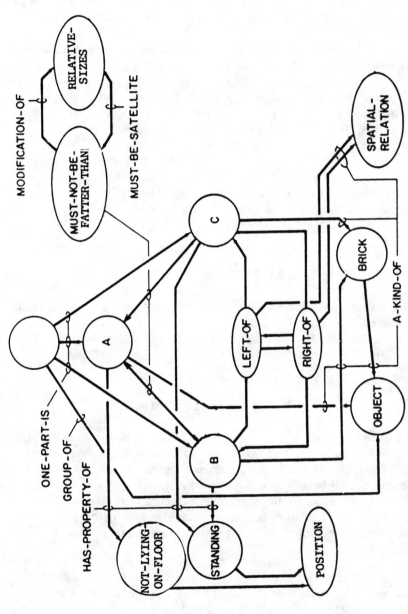

Figure 9.16. An unusual concept of an arch

403

It could not last. "This is not AI, this is the real thing!" shouted one of the quicker-witted in the room. And with that proclamation the customary clamor of assertion, counterassertion, and rebuttal returned to fill the air.

The post mortem on the system revealed that the concept of an arch which it had learned that day was as shown in Figure 9.16.

This is not the usual concept of an arch that this program was set up to learn. Subsequent detailed inspection of the program failed to reveal any unusual structures insofar as anyone could remember what the details ought to be. Just as fortelling the future from an inspection of the entrails of a goat is a lost art, so accounting for the past on the basis of scrutinizing the penetralia of an old AI program is a magical skill that has gone the way of punched card input and the octal core dump.

It was generally agreed that the best thing to do was to pretend it never happened, destroy the source code, keep reprinting the traditional account, and not a word to DARPA.

END OF TRUE AI STORY

After that fictional interlude we must return once more to the stuff that is peddled as science. But this level of cynicism is unwarranted. In fact, it is time to slip in a small section on competitive learning; it is a CP-based technique, and it is science in the hardest sense imaginable.

COMPETITIVE LEARNING

In general, network learning would seem to be an open problem that may yield some useful results. Currently formal analysis, as stated earlier, tends to be biased toward the supervised techniques of either "energy" minimization or back-propagation based methods.

One major class of unsupervised techniques is called *competitive learning;* it is a CP-based clustering technique in which a collection of inputs are grouped in terms of similarity to one another.

According to Hinton (1989, p. 216),

It is called competitive learning because there is a set of hidden units which compete with one another to become active. . . . When an input vector is presented to the network, the hidden unit which receives the greatest total input wins the competition and turns on with an activity level of 1. All the other hidden units turn off. The winning unit then adds a small fraction of the current input vector to its weight vector. So, in future, it will receive even more total input from this input vector. To prevent the same hidden unit from being the most active in all cases, it is necessary to impose a constraint on each weight vector that keeps the sum of the weights (or the sum of their squares) constant. So when a hidden unit becomes more sensitive to one input vector it becomes less sensitive to other input vectors.

Hinton (1989) gives the diagrammatic explanation shown in Figure 9.17 of the outcome of a successful competitive learning procedure.

In Figure 9.17, the input vectors are represented by x's on the surface of a sphere. The weight vectors of the hidden units are represented by o's. After successful competitive learning, each weight vector will be close to the center of gravity of a cluster of input vectors — as illustrated. In effect, the network has (in this case) partitioned the eight instances of inputs into three classes, and the three weight vectors have captured the essential similarity between members of the each class. The weight vector is a generalization of the class of similar inputs.

Rumelhart and Zipser (1985) give a detailed history of neuron-like networks leading up to their results on "competitive learning." {And for

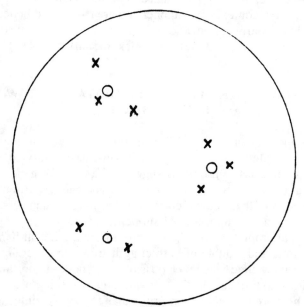

Figure 9.17.   The desired result of competitive learning

From "Connectionist Learning Procedures," by G.E. Hinton, 1989, *Artificial Intelligence*. Copyright 1989 by Elsevier. Reprinted by permission.

those who have not had enough, the learning rule that they have studied is:

$$\Delta w_{ij} = \begin{cases} 0 \text{ if node } j \text{ loses on stimulus } k \\ g* \left(\dfrac{C_{ik}}{N_k} \right) - g*w_{ij} \text{ if node } j \text{ wins on stimulus } k \end{cases}$$

where C_{ik} is equal to 1 if in stimulus pattern S node i in the lower layer is active and zero otherwise, and N_k is the number of active nodes in pattern S. Thus, $N_k = \Sigma C_{ik}$. They reason about their scheme using a geometric analogy in which each stimulus pattern is a vector, and (if all such vectors are of equal length) they can be viewed as points on an N-dimensional hypersphere, where N is the number of nodes in the lower level of the network — (it is also the number of arcs into each node in the upper level).}

There are many varieties of competitive learning, and the various strategies are used in a wide range of applications — Hinton (1989) lists many of them. And one, that of Fukushima and Miyake (1982), has already been mentioned in the context of its application area — vision, hence, Chapter 7. The Hebbian learning rule, another unsupervised technique (mentioned in Chapter 3), is described with examples in Sharkey (1989a).

LEARNING PARTICULARITIES: REMOVAL OF UNWANTED GENERALIZATION

Another important but somewhat neglected facet of learning is the removal of unwanted generalization. A broad-based ability to be able to deal with some class of problems suggests the need for general rules (in the SSSP at least) that are widely applicable and can be particularized for given instances of the problem class. This learning of such generalities is, as we have seen, an important AI subfield.

But if an appropriate, specific piece of information is at hand, we are saved the time and trouble of extracting it from the generalized knowledge, and saving time whenever possible may be an important strategy for realizing real-time intelligence. In addition, a specific piece of knowledge may be more precisely appropriate than the specific information that can be extracted from the general knowledge.

These observations seem to be leading us right back to the benefits of rote learning, but also of course to the drawbacks. So what's new? What is new is that we might store both the generalized knowledge and some specific instances of it. But for this technique to have any chance of success, the process of extracting, or just saving, specific instances must be both automatic and dynamic. In other words, the collection of specific instances stored at any one time must be some function of the current operating environment of the system. An obvious strategy that suggests itself is for commonly used, specific instances to be stored explicitly, and thus the resort to generalized knowledge is only necessary on infrequent occasions.

A version of this technique called "memo functions" was used in the POP-2 language many years ago (Michie, 1968). A mathematical function generator, let us say a function for generating square roots, SQRT, was composed of both a generalized procedure for computing square roots and a look-up table in which specific values and their square roots were stored. Thus, if a programmer referenced say SQRT(16), the square root function would first search its look-up table and return 4 if it found the appropriate entry (16 → 4); otherwise, it computed the necessary result in the usual way.

Answers from the look-up table would of course be returned faster than the computed ones (especially if the function is somewhat more complicated than square root). But, on the debit side, it takes space to store the look-up table, and failed look-ups that result in computation make the total computation even slower. In addition, a dynamic look-up table takes time to manage. A number of strategies were explored for both the size of the table and the strategies for entering and deleting table entries.

Over 10 years ago (Partridge, 1975) this machine-learning mechanism was successfully employed within an adaptive FORTRAN translator. The translator contained an AI module that periodically surveyed the results of the prior parsing session and then reorganized its knowledge base. One of the tasks of this module was to remove unwanted generalization by finding the most frequently used particular instances of a general rule and promoting them to positions of higher precedence than the general rule itself.

The system learned to expect the specific idiosyncracies of a given operating environment. The resultant behavioral changes were an increase in general efficiency together with an increase in quality of error correction.

One of the major preconditions for successful application of this general learning strategy is that the demand for particular instances of the general knowledge are not randomly distributed, and in many natural situations they are not. The 90 – 10 laws abound in all aspects of everyday life — that is, roughly 10% of the possibilities occur on 90% of occasions. The implication is that, if you can store the frequently accessed 10% of the possible instances in a look-up table, recourse to the generalized knowledge occurs on only 10% of occasions. A further useful precondition is that this skewed distribution is relatively stable, if not totally static.

More recently, Steels (1985) proposed as part of his "second generation expert systems" that specific inference chains, derived by means of the usual methods, be explicitly stored to speed subsequent retrieval of the same expertise — in effect, a memo function approach. But he shows no awareness of the basic problems (such as the necessity for a skewed distribution of system requests), and he offers no innovative suggestions for a strategy to control the storage of specific inference chains.

Another recent and more thoroughly explored notion that fits in here is the theory of "chunking" (Rosenbloom & Newell, 1986). The authors view it as one manifestation "of a single underlying idea centered on the storage of composite information rather than its recomputation." Memofunctions, they say, are another manifestation of the same idea. There is The Chunking Hypothesis:

> A human acquires and organizes knowledge of the environment by forming and storing expressions, called *chunks,* that are structured collections of the chunks existing at the time of learning. (Rosenbloom & Newell, 1986, p. 253)

Another classic AI hypothesis; it will stand the test of time as it's totally irrefutable.

The chunking "theory" of learning is explored within the Soar system, which we shall take a closer look at later in this chapter. For the moment let me just point out that the Soar system is production-system based and solves problems by working through a problem space to achieve some goal state (i.e., a classical SSSP-based system totally untainted by nouveau AI). The chunking, crudely summarized, is implemented as the construction of a new production composed of the essential problem-solving activities that have resulted in the successful achievement of a goal, or subgoal. So, next time a similar problem crops up, the new chunk can deal with it directly without invoking the full problem-solving equipment.

Superficially, the removal of unwanted generalization might appear to be much the same as overgeneralization and refinement, a strategy that we've seen earlier and will see again in explanation-based learning, but there is a crucial difference. Within the current section, removal of unwanted generalization has been treated as removal with respect to the processing mechanism, not removal from the representation, i.e., specialization of the generalized representation itself. In this section we have looked at schemes in which particular instances of the generalized concept are added, redundantly, to the overall representation. There is, I'm sure, a useful if not critical role for redundancy in representations of knowledge to support AI systems, but the idea typically gets a bad press, especially when Occam's razor is out.

Working with introspection in the opposite direction, that is, from particular instances to a general rule, i.e., inductive generalization, is more difficult. Nevertheless, some thought should be given generating useful particularities as well as generalities.

EBG, OR IS IT EBL?

And so, on to a new wave in research on machine learning. As I said in the introduction to the generalization work, EBG is the name of the knowledge-based and deductive approach. As I also mentioned, this general category of machine learning work may be broadened to explanation-based learning (EBL), and I shall include an exposition of this wider perspective when I have dealt with EBG.

"The key insight behind explanation-based generalization is that it is possible to form a justified generalization of a single positive training example provided the learning system is endowed with some explanatory capabilities. In particular the system must be able to explain to itself *why* the training example is an example of the concept under study" (Mitchell, Keller, & Kedar-Cabelli, 1986, p. 49, authors' emphasis). These authors present a general introduction to EBG, and for the moment I'll follow their treatment.

They present the following table which specifies the kinds of information necessary in order to be able to apply EBG to a problem.

This table probably requires a little explanation itself. As you no doubt realize, any method that purports to generate a valid generalization of

Table 9.1.   The EBG Problem.

Given:

- *Goal Concept:* A concept definition describing the concept to be learned. (It is assumed that this concept definition fails to satisfy the Operationality Criterion. [Don't panic; this beast is described below.])
- *Training Example:* An example of the goal concept.
- *Domain Theory:* A set of rules and facts to be used in explaining how the training example is an example of the goal concept.
- *Operationality Criterion:* A predicate over concept definitions, specifying the form in which the learned concept definition must be expressed.

Determine:

- A generalization of the training example that is a sufficient concept definition for the goal concept and that satisfies the operationality criterion.

some concept on the basis of just one training example (and eschews the use of magic) is going to have to know a good deal about the concept under study. In the EBG scheme, the system starts out with a definition of the concept under study. What is there then to learn? If the system already knows what the concept to be learned is, then what does it need to learn?

The answer is that one can quite readily have a definition of a concept, but the form of the definition is not a useful one for supporting some desired processing. The EBG method uses an nonuseful concept definition, a training example, and domain knowledge to generate a useful definition of the concept (i.e., one that satisfies the operationality criterion in the view of our three authors). EBG is then a method of transforming a nonuseful concept definition into a useful one, although most practitioners of the art agree that the criterion of operationality is neither as simple as it first appears, nor is it the whole story with respect to what the transformation should be in general.

Thus, returning to the awful blocks world (that ever-too-ready source of easy examples): The concept of when it is possible to put one block, x, on top of another, y, let us call it SAFE-TO-STACK(x,y), may be defined as:-

NOT(FRAGILE(y)) OR LIGHTER(x,y)

Now if the concepts FRAGILE and LIGHTER are not terms that occur in the training examples, the current concept definition cannot be directly applied to an example situation to determine if it is indeed SAFE-TO-STACK one specific object on another — i.e., the current concept definition is not operational. Here is where the domain theory, or knowledge, saves the day. It is used to relate the training example and the current concept definition, the goal concept. More specifically, it is used to generate an explanation of why the training example is an example of the goal concept. In addition, this explanation is couched in terms that satisfy the operationality criterion.

What do we have now? We don't have a new version of the goal concept, that's for sure. But what we do have is a specific explanation of how one training example satisfies the goal concept. In fact, according to our EBG trio we have a *proof* that the training example satisfies the goal concept. Others are not so adamant about the need for, or indeed possibility of, a formal proof in more realistic worlds than the abstract-blocks one. The second step in the EBG method is to generalize this specific explanation. We need to determine the general conditions under which the explanation holds. By working back through the specific explanation structure starting from the goal concept, we can determine the general conditions under which a rule can be used to infer this goal condition. {gruesome detail: This is called *regressing* the goal condition back through the explanation structure, and a number of fancy algorithms exist to regress away merrily, determining either sufficient conditions for inference, or even both necessary and sufficient conditions. The bloody-minded reader is referred to Nilsson (1980) for the full gruesome details.} EBG is thus a two-step process:

1. *Explain:* Construct an explanation in terms of the *domain theory* that proves how the *training example* satisfies the *goal concept* definition. This explanation must be constructed from expressions that satisfy the *operationality criterion*.
2. *Generalize:* Determine a set of sufficient conditions under which the explanation structure holds, stated in terms that satisfy the *operationality criterion*.

Let's disperse any remaining mystery with an example. I'll continue the SAFE-TO-STACK concept within the all-too-convenient, abstract-blocks microworld. This is the key example of Mitchell, Keller, and Kedar-Cabelli (1986).

GIVEN:
• *Goal Concept:* Pairs of objects <x,y> such that SAFE-TO-STACK (x,y), where SAFE-TO-STACK(x,y) is defined as NOT(FRAGILE(y)) OR LIGHTER(x,y).

• *Training Example:*
   ON(OBJ1,OBJ2)
   ISA(OBJ1,BOX)
   ISA(OBJ2,ENDTABLE)
   COLOR(OBJ1,RED)
   COLOR(OBJ2,BLUE)
   VOLUME(OBJ1,1)
   DENSITY(OBJ1,.1)
   . . .

• *Domain Theory:*
   WEIGHT(p1,v1*d1) is true if VOLUME(p1,v1) AND DENSITY(p1,d1)
   LIGHTER(p1,p2) is true if WEIGHT(p1,w1) AND WEIGHT(p2,w2)
   AND LESS(w1,w2)
   WEIGHT(p1,5) is true if ISA(p1,ENDTABLE)
   LESS(.1,5) is true
   . . .

• *Operationality Criterion:* The concept definition must be expressed in terms of the terms used to describe the examples (e.g., VOLUME, COLOR, DEN-

SITY) or other selected, easily evaluated, terms from the domain theory (e.g., LESS).

DETERMINE:
 • A generalization of the training example that is a sufficient concept definition for the goal concept and that satisfies the operationality criterion.

That's an example problem, and we should probably note a few of its features before ploughing on into the EBG treatment of it. Firstly, notice the PROLOGy nature of the representation of the problem. It proclaims the theorem-proving basis of this EBG method and makes it all the easier to follow the example. If all your attempts to notice this slant in the problem statement are to no avail because you don't know PROLOG and you haven't read Chapter 4, it makes things tougher but by no means impossible. But for those who are familiar with PROLOG, a word of caution. Notice that bits of the formal structure are in lower-case letters (e.g., x, y, p1, v1, w2), whereas most are capitalized (e.g., VOLUME, OBJ1). To those conversant in PROLOG, this will mean that the capitalized objects are variable names, labels for quantities that may be given specific values, whereas the lower-case objects indicate specific, fixed values. This is wrong. Exactly the opposite interpretation is intended in this example. Thus the goal statement, for instance, is a general statement that it is SAFE-TO-STACK any object x on any object y, provided that y is NOT FRAGILE or that x is LIGHTER than y. It is not a specific statement about two particular objects say BOX and ENDTABLE. {Gruesome problem: The forgoing is an oversimplification, because OBJ1, for example, is also a label whose ISA value is BOX, and whose COLOR value is RED. In addition, there are a few varieties of nonvariable; e.g., VOLUME is not the same sort of specific object as ENDTABLE. The reader whose brain has not yet been forced into thinking by this EBG stuff is invited to cogitate a while on these issues.}
Secondly, the goal concept is such that we cannot determine by simple inspection that the given training example isindeed a positive example of the concept. Neither of the terms LIGHTER or FRAGILE (the truth of one of which is necessary before we can conclude that SAFE-TO-STACK is true using the goal concept) occurs in the training example. We are told that the training example is a positive example of this concept, and our task is to explain why this is so. The alert reader should be observing with satisfaction that the domain theory defines LIGHTER in terms of WEIGHT and LESS, and that WEIGHT is defined in terms of VOLUME and DENSITY while LESS is given as true. So even if it's not obvious exactly how we could algorithmically generate anexplanation, it should seem reasonable that the domain theory could possibly provide the necessary bridge between the training example and the goal concept. It

ought to be possible to tie LIGHTER to VOLUMEs and DENSITYs using WEIGHTs together with the LESS relation, and indeed it is. Let's do it.

THE EXPLANATION:

- From the statements of VOLUME and DENSITY of OBJ1 in the training example together with the definition of WEIGHT in the domain theory, we can determine the WEIGHT of OBJ1. It is .1, or stated in the form of the problem: WEIGHT(OBJ1,.1) is true.

- In the domain theory there is a statement to the effect that all ENDTABLEs have a WEIGHT of 5. Strange but true, apparently. From the training example we can see that OBJ2 is, most conveniently, an ENDTABLE. Thus we know that WEIGHT(OBJ2,5) is true.

- Now we know the WEIGHTs of both OBJs, and as luck would have it the domain theory contains the fact that the LESS term is true for just those WEIGHTs that we have (i.e., .1 and 5). LESS(.1,5) is true.

- By noting the definition of LIGHTER and then raising our eyes to the goal concept, we can see that, although we have made absolutely no progress with the FRAGILEness of any object, we are in a position to apply the LIGHTER term to OBJ1 and OBJ2.

- So having WEIGHT(OBJ1,.1) AND WEIGHT(OBJ2,5) AND LESS(.1,5) all in the bag of known truths, the domain theory tells us that LIGHTER(OBJ1,OBJ2) is also true.

- Finally, we are in a position to assert that the training example is a positive instance of the goal concept SAFE-TO-STACK. This is because the domain theory enables us to determine that LIGHTER (OBJ1,OBJ2) is true in this particular instance, and this is one of the two alternative ways in which the goal concept is defined.

Displayed schematically, this explanation is as shown in Figure 9.18:

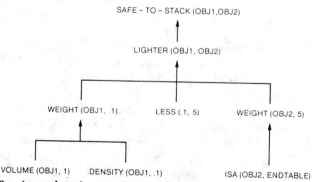

Figure 9.18.   An explanation structure in EBG

From "Explanation-based Generalization: A Unifying View," by T.M. Mitchell, R.M. Keller, & S.T. Kedar-Cabelli, 1986, *Machine Learning, 1*, p. 53. Copyright 1986 by Kluwer Academic Publishers. Reprinted by permission.

Before we push on to step two, you should observe that the COLOR information in the domain theory was not used — it was a red herring, as they say. Observe also that we did not make use of the ON(OBJ1,OBJ2) fact in the training example. Why not?

It is now time for the generalize step. We have at this point explained, in fact we've proved, that an operational definition of the goal concept is:-

VOLUME(OBJ1,1) AND DENSITY(OBJ1,.1) AND ISA(OBJ2,ENDTABLE) AND LESS(.1,5)

and this is fine for whenever we're dealing with OBJ1 and OBJ2, and OBJ1 is the same BOX, and OBJ2 is an ENDTABLE. But with any other objects, it is not much use. It's too specific, so we regress back from the goal concept through the explanation structure to obtain a more general operational definition.

We know from the goal concept definition that LIGHTER(x,y) is a sufficient condition for inferring SAFE-TO-STACK(x,y). And from our use of the LIGHTER rule in the explanation, we know that WEIGHT (x,w1) AND WEIGHT(y,w2) AND LESS(w1,w2) is a sufficient condition for inferring LIGHTER(x,y). Our use of the first WEIGHT rule enables us to generate VOLUME(x,v1) AND DENSITY(x,d1) as sufficient conditions for the inference WEIGHT(x,w1) when w1 is v1*d1. Use of the second WEIGHT rule tells us that a sufficient condition for inferring WEIGHT(y,w2) is if y ISA ENDTABLE, in which case w2 is 5. In conclusion, the LESS component of the explanation has become LESS (v1*d1,5) — partly generalized and partly specialized. Thus the generalized operational definition of SAFE-TO-STACK(x,y) is computed as:

VOLUME(x,v1) AND DENSITY(x,d1) AND ISA(y,ENDTABLE) AND LESS(v1*d1,5)

In English, the system has learned through the EBG method that it is SAFE-TO-STACK any object x on any object y if the VOLUME of x is v1 and the DENSITY is d1, and y ISA ENDTABLE, and v1*d1 is LESS than 5.

There are several good things to note about EBG that this example illustrates; then we'll get on to the bad news. First, the final operational version of the goal concept is quite general, although the tail end of it is rather specific. It is in fact an undergeneralization, but then what more can be expected from only one training example combined with the certainty that logical deduction brings with it. The quest for a more ambitious generalization would have necessitated an excursion into the realms of inductive uncertainty. We shall return to this issue shortly, but for the moment let's continue with the good news. Second, although there are very many possible relations that could have been used en route to a generalization (such as ones involving COLOR), they were not considered and then ruled out. They were not considered at all. The explanation focuses the generalization step on the appropriate constraints; this is in marked contrast to similarity-based methods which typically require handcrafted heuristics to focus their activities on the appropriate relationships for generalization in order to prevent them from wandering forever in the limitless depths of the complete search space. For the reader who likes cross-linkages in a book, attention is drawn to Schank's feature (d) in Chapter 1 and the problem of large search spaces, a major concern in Chapter 3. A related question for consideration here is: Does the domain knowledge required by EBG constitute much the same handcrafted and special-purpose information as the heuristics needed by similarity-based methods? Third, the final generalization is typically a specialization of the goal concept (and this is where the bad news begins). Clearly, with only one example to work from, it would indeed be a remarkable technique that could come with a generalization that covered all valid examples of the goal concept. What this limitation suggests, according to Mitchell et al., is a direction for future research in EBG: the development of explanation-based methods than can utilize multiple training examples. But notice that the undergeneralization derived has some severe weaknesses. As DeJong and Mooney (1986) point out, the generalization produced demands that the WEIGHT of the LIGHTER object be computed from its VOLUME and DENSITY. If the derived generalization is applied to a situation where a LIGHTER object is given a default WEIGHT and no VOLUME or DENSITY, it would fail to conclude that this seemingly obvious SAFE-TO-STACK situation (given the same old ENDTABLE) is indeed SAFE-TO-STACK. For DeJong and Mooney this problem illustrates the excessive conservatism and unhelpful inflexibility of the proposed EBG method. They endeavor to do something about it, and we shall look at their suggestions shortly. You may recall that the regression technique used in the above example produced only a *sufficient* generalization, i.e., we can be sure that it is SAFE-TO-STACK any two objects whose features match precisely those of the operational generalization. But these are not all *necessary* features. OBJ2, for example, need only have a WEIGHT LESS than that of OBJ1 in order for it really to be SAFE-TO-STACK them. It is not necessary that OBJ2 be an ENDTABLE with a WEIGHT of 5. A more powerful regression technique might yield a generalization that is both necessary and sufficient, but the cost of computing this better generalization appears to be prohibitively high.

Mitchell et al. (1986) provide a comprehensive overview to the EBG method, and in addition they consider a number of specific research projects with a view to uniting them all under their EBG framework.

Further than this, they consider an array of the nontrivial problems that beset the EBG method. Mitchell et al. (1986, p. 68) call them "imperfect theory problems" that become manifest when a proof of the explanation is not possible. Within this general category they present three classes: the *incomplete theory problem* — does not support proof of an explanation and suggests that EBG might need to work with inferences that are merely plausible rather than certain; the *intractable theory problem* — a complete theory is available but is too vast to be usable in practice, in which case EBG may have to work with tractable approximations to the theory; the *inconsistent theory problem* — much the same as the problem of inconsistent knowledge bases, which we considered in an earlier chapter, and, while no ready solution is at hand, an example of inconsistency based on the SAFE-TO-STACK problem is easily found. The domain theory for the SAFE-TO-STACK problem contained two very different rules for determining the WEIGHT of an OBJ. If OBJ2 the ENDTABLE appeared in the training example with an associated VOLUME and DENSITY, either or both rules may have been used to yield a WEIGHT for OBJ2, and the two WEIGHTS would not necessarily have been the same — i.e., we have inconsistent inferences to contend with.

It is now time to look at the EBG method in broader perspective.

THE EBL VIEWPOINT

As useful as automatic generalization is, it is not the sole need with respect to adaptivity in intelligent systems. I made this point in terms the removal of unwanted generalization earlier in this chapter. DeJong and Mooney (1986) take up this point with respect to EBG. They argue that, because concept refinement (or specialization) can be, and on occasion needs to be, the result of explanation-based methods, the preferable name for this general approach to learning is explanation-based learning, or EBL.

They continue with a critique of EBG as presented above. In particular, they list the following five points.

1. There are two rather different types of explanation step:
   (a) constructed by an internal theorem prover;
   (b) constructed by observing and interpreting the problem-solving behavior of others.
2. The EBG generalization method is too weak; it does not generalize far enough. The result is undergeneralizations that reflect many unimportant details of the training example.

3. The operationality criterion is only an approximation to an important, but much deeper, concept relating the abilities of the system's performance element to the learning process.
4. Knowledge chunking (an issue to be grappled with in a later section) and hierarchical grouping allows an EBL system to efficiently explore alternative explanations of an example.
5. An alternative scheme for the generalization step, one which allows further generalization and alteration of the explanation.

They attempt to enlist our agreement with the idea that explanation-based systems should be able to specialize as well as generalize. In particular, they discuss Winston, Binford, Katz, and Lowry's (1983) ANALOGY program and the learning of the concept of a cup. The EBG version of this system is given by Mitchell et al. (1986). DeJong and Mooney point out that there are likely to be subtle interactions between ANDed subgoals. Thus the subgoals LIFTABLE and DRINKABLE-FROM, if treated independently (as is the only reasonably efficient course of action), may overgeneralize to give the "pail-cup" — a cup constructed like a small bucket with the handle arching over the top — which is not readily DRINKABLE-FROM. But now, DeJong and Mooney argue, the failure of this supposed positive example can be used to focus attention on the offending interaction, and an explanation-based approach can be used to specialize the overgeneralized concept. In sum, the interests of practical efficiency suggest simple EBG followed by the possibility of explanation-based specialization to correct for overgeneralization — the composite process is EBL.

With respect to the point that explanations and subsequent generalizations may be derived from observation of others, they draw attention to work on learning from observation. This strategy has already been aired in the knowledge acquisition section of Chapter 5. Finally, the conservative nature of the generalization step used by Mitchell et al. is called into question. DeJong and Mooney observe that this generalization scheme is primarily concerned with generalizing constants that appear explicitly in the training example into appropriately constrained variables. Thus in the earlier SAFE-TO-STACK example the VOLUME constant 1 becomes the variable v1, and the DENSITY constant .1 becomes the variable d1 in the learned generalization. In order to correct this deficiency, they describe and illustrate an alternative approach to generalizing explanations. It appears to be more powerful than Mitchell et al.'s scheme; it is almost certainly more complicated; and it is most assuredly too packed full of gruesome detail to get into this book.

There is a flurry of more recent research in ML that centers around explanation-based techniques. The most that I can do is provide a few pointers into the leading edge of this subsubfield. One problem being addressed is that of dealing with training examples that support alternative explanations. Rajamoney and DeJong (1988) suggest that multiple explanations can be due to:

1. *Incomplete Domain Theories:* the explanation constructor is thus forced to make assumptions, and different assumptions result in different explanations.
2. *Intractable Domain Theories:* explanations can only be generated when approximations to achieve tractability are made, and approximations can correspond to multiple explanations in the exact theory.
3. *Incorrect Domain Theories:* the domain theory may have incorrect generalizations, which can result in multiple explanations.

So what does one do about this? Well, according to Rajamoney and DeJong, one encouraging approach is through active experimentation, and it makes great sense. Given that you have several alternative explanations of some example on hand, one way to weed out the incorrect ones is to seek clarification from the environment, the world for which you are attempting to construct valid generalizations. The idea is close to the classic model of scientific experimentation. A set of competing hypotheses (the alternative explanations) is thinned out by designing experiments that will refute (in the ideal situation) all but one of them. This is what Rajamoney and DeJong present. It is a system that designs experiments whose purpose is to refute specific alternative explanations. This they call *active explanation reduction*.

Work continues on the awkward problem of operationality of the products of EBL. Hirsh (1988) argues that the conditions on the operationality of a generalization should be determined and included with the generalization. He notes that an operational version of the property PROVABLE is easy to come up with if the expression to be PROVed (i.e., what PROVABLE does) is, say, "2 + 2 = 4", but not if the application is to Fermat's Last Theorem (a classic brain teaser in mathematics: Is it true, or is it false? No one has yet been able to prove it is true although Fermat claimed that it is). In sum, a generalization may be operational in some instances but not in others. As a further example, Braverman and Russell (1988) introduce an algorithm to handle EBL in intractable domains. A key concept for their algorithm is the *boundary of operationality,* which marks the most appropriate level of generalization in an explanation structure.

Another twist to the operationality criterion problem has already been mentioned in Chapter 5 — operationality might be the efficiency and effectiveness that characterizes the superficial, heuristic rules used in current expert systems. Then, as Worden (1989) and DeJong (1988) have suggested, an EBL mechanism may be used to automatically generate these rules from deep knowledge of the domain and an example of expert behavior within the domain. Figure 9.19 is Worden's schematic illustration of this idea.

I should make it clear that there are some problems with this idea. For example, the EBL technique rests upon the idea of an explanation of why the training is an example of, in this case, some aspect of the deep knowledge, whereas a useful shallow rule is an effective simplification (i.e., not always correct and therefore a heuristic) of the underlying principles, or deep knowledge. It is not at all clear to me that the notion of explanation as proof, or even as plausible justification, can be made to yield heuristic

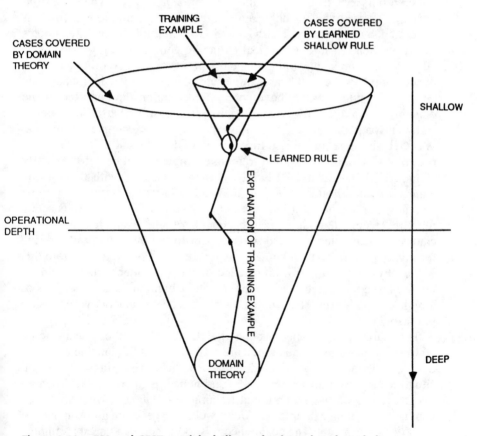

Figure 9.19.   EBL and CEST: useful, shallow rules from deep knowledge

From "Processes in Knowledge and Software," by R. Worden, 1989, in *Research and Development in Expert Systems V* (p. 146), edited by B. Kelly & H. Rector, Cambridge England: Cambridge University Press. Copyright 1989 by Cambridge University Press. Reprinted by permission.

approximations as the operational products of the process. On the positive side, this general idea ties in nicely with the memo-function notion (mentioned here and there in this chapter), with the Soar architecture (coming soon), and with success-driven learning strategies in general, which has implications for the possibilities of learning at the knowledge level (also coming soon).

Other ideas about how to address the problems highlighted by simple EBL are in the air. Thus, it might be possible to combine explanations from multiple training instances to yield a better generalization than any one training instance can support. Under the proof-based scheme the generalization might be derived from the common core of the different individual proofs (one from each training example, just in case you were wondering). Alternatively, it has been suggested that multiple explanations generated by applying the EBG method to multiple training examples might be then fed into a classical inductive generalization process. The EBG mechanism is thus functioning as a preprocessor. Another idea, one for dealing with the problem of imperfect domain knowledge, makes the point that, as long as we have some valid relationship captured in the domain knowledge, however imprecise, it can still be used to frame a sufficient generalization. So, if we know, for example, only that WEIGHT is some (unknown) function of VOLUME and DENSITY, the resultant generalization from a training example would have to explicitly include VOLUMEs and DENSITYs, each associated with the specific values provided in the training example. The outcome is not likely to be a great generalization, but the method does still work, and there is scope for futher generalization from subsequent training examples. A note of caution is also being sounded with respect to the desirability of striving for highly precise domain knowledge. The easy example to illustrate this is the physicist who, with knowledge of quantum mechanics, might be tempted to explain everyday events (such as breaking a cup) in terms of atomic energy levels. This would be a mistake, a mistake of overprecision in reasoning.

There are also problems associated with EBL that nobody seems to be addressing, perhaps because they are problems that fall outside the well-defined, abstract worlds which dominate the field. Thus, in most realistic situations a system has many goals, and hence, goal concepts. When an event occurs, we have a potential training example. But what goal concept is it a training example of? And if we fail to generate an explanation, what does this mean? The goal concept is too general and needs refining? Or, we are trying to relate the training example to the wrong goal concept? Or, we've missed a crucial bit of knowledge when attempting to generate the explanation? The possible answers are many, it seems to me. We see yet again, I would argue, a qualitative change in the problem when we move from abstract, closed microworlds to something more like real worlds.

To bring consideration of this ML subfield to a close, let me say that EBL and the explosive growth of interest in it is a manifestation of the late 1980s. It has a number of interesting properties, but, like most AI, it has even more very-difficult-looking problems.

MECHANIZED CREATIVITY

Creativity is a contentious subject both in AI and in RI. At times is is presented as a peculiarly human phenomenon and thus one that machines will never exhibit.

It is also a word that has a wide range of interpretations — from something we all of us do many times a day to a once-in-a-lifetime phenomenon restricted to humans of the highest intellectual calibre. I've already shown my colors with respect to the Einsteins and Newtons of this world vis-á-vis the dastardly differential calculus, so clearly my focus on the concept of creativity is down at the less celebrated end of the spectrum. I'm interested in the creative problem solving demanded of the goferCoke robot, for example: You give this gleaming menial a quarter (more like $10 by the time it is on the market, but let's assume that we are in one of the better possible worlds, one from which inflation has been banished); it will go off, locate a Coke machine, and return with either a cold can of the brown bubbly stuff or a good excuse for why it failed.

"Where's the creativity?" you might well ask. "Shakey was doing that sort of thing at Stanford Research Institute years ago." It is true that the mobile robot Shakey was trundling around the hallowed halls of SRI many years ago and successfully executing tasks such as "GO TO POSITION (X,Y)" as described by Raphael (1976). It is also true that there was no creativity in Shakey's actions, which is not to say that there was no creative effort involved in devising Shakey's actions. I am saying that the actions that Shakey executed in order to get to the specified location were not themselves creative; it executed a proven plan of action. More precisely, it attempted to execute such a plan. For the real (or realish) world that Shakey operated in refused, as it often does, to honor the axioms upon which Shakey's planning was based: Friction failed to pay constant attention to the laws that govern it, stipulated-flat surfaces persistently refused to be totally flat, etc. On occasions such as these, and excepting the few specific problems that were solved with the equally specific error recovery strategies, Shakey was stymied. And this, finally, is the point where creativity of the kind that I am desparately trying to get to is needed.

In real-world problem solving, flashes of minor creativity are in constant demand, just because all possibilities cannot be foreseen with sufficient precision to preplan for each and every one of them. The real-world problem solver (as opposed to the discrete-well-defined-search-space problem solver, you may recall from the early chapters) must constantly invent or create variations on known plans whenever the unpredictability of the empirical world asserts itself. Thus the goferCoke robot will have to overcome stuck doors, temporarily blocked passages, relocated Coke machines, malfunctioning machines that either swallow the inserted quarter and pretend they never got it, or keep refusing to recognize that it is a valid quarter, etc. We deal with the world and its cavalier attitude to the niceties of formal notations {in particular, the first-order predicate calculus — an AI nasty that we must come to grips with in the next chapter} all of our lives, and our approach can be accurately described as creative problem solving.

As was discussed much earlier, most AI, and research in machine learning is certainly no exception, does eschew the problems of the real world; it is abstract AI. But even in the abstract worlds demanded by most AI techniques, all is not plain sailing. There is a need to compose descriptions or representations from constituent structures that are not a priori related. Discovering that they can be usefully related is the outcome of a creative act.

Of course, composing totally unrelated components (if totally unrelated can be accepted as a possibility) can be based, by its very nature, on nothing more directed than a random procedure. And although random selection has a strong case as a basis for developing intelligent systems (given a few millennia of millennia in which the results of vast numbers of inevitable wrong choices can be ironed out), it has not yielded results in AI (see Chapter 3). Quite apart from the problems of stretching a Ph.D. thesis out for long enough to get the necessary results, the exact role of randomness in the theory of evolution is a hotly debated issue.

So the mechanisms underlying creative learning in AI will have to be based on something more directed than random selection — not a tall .order, as it would be hard to find a mechanism that is less directed. Nevertheless, how to implement a useful mechanism of controlled randomness is not clear. Constraints are needed, and are clearly employed by us humans, by what they are and how to bring them to bear is a totally open question, despite the fact that it has been explored in a few AI projects.

Thus, Lenat's much-lauded program, AM (see Davis & Lenat, 1982), which rediscovered a number of mathematical concepts, used a number of such random-search-constraining principles. One such principle (or heuristic, as Lenat prefers to call it) is:

If f is a function which transforms elements of A into elements of B, then consider just those members of A which are transformed into extremal elements of B. This is an interesting subset of A. (Lenat, 1983, p. 252)

This and other heuristics proved useful for rediscovery in the specific, well-defined domain of mathematics. More general concepts such as "interestingness" were also explored, but the obvious limitations of his heuristics led Lenat on, as we shall see, to more grandiose plans and systems. The resultant program, EURISKO, quite contrary to expectations, proved to be less of a celebration and capitalization on the advances made possible by the success of AM, and more of a stimulus for reappraisal of the apparent success of AM.

But before we launch into the AI subfield of rediscovery systems, I want to consider less ambitious work that also rearranges stored knowledge in order to generate new knowledge.

LEARNING BY INTROSPECTION

This general category of machine learning refers to the possibility of generating new ideas from old, but in this particular subsection I shall deal with the manifestations that are not usually accorded the supreme status of mechanized creativity. *Inductive generalization* (of the nonincremental sort) is the more usual heading for what I shall now describe. Nevertheless, to my mind the dividing line between such generalization and full-blown mechanized creativity is much finer than customary terminology suggests.

Consider the janitor once more: While driving home after a busy night taking care of his office block, the janitor might ruminate upon his current stock of job-related knowledge — a sort of mental chewing of the cud, cerebral mastication of observations, of plans both successful and unsuccessful, of stored facts, etc.

What is the upshot of all these mental gymnastics, you might well ask? The diverse products will be general rules, new concepts, new plans, and improved problem-solving strategies — a bountiful harvest.

So let's get our AI system to do some of this in its slack periods, if not in parallel while it is working flat out. And indeed there are a number of lines of AI research that have, and are still, investigating this brand of machine learning.

A particularly interesting application of this technique is described by Michie (1983). He considers the possibility of constructing an expert system backwards, because it's easier to do that way. An expert system can be thought of as a function from the input problem space to the expert solution space. This forward transformation is typically difficult, but sometimes the reverse transformation, the inverse function, from a given solution to the problem that would have generated it, is easily computable.

For example, the square root function is a very simple function that nevertheless exhibits the type of duality under discussion. It is nontrivial to compute the square root of any given number. (For those who find it trivial, please work with some larger integer than two as the root to be sought.) But the reverse computation, squaring, multiplying a number by itself, is far simpler. {This example is not perfect, but then what is? Problem: Why does this example fall down as an example of the sort of function that Michie describes?}

So if we can generate the space of solutions, we do so, and store each one away with its easily computed problem. This bunch of solution–problem pairs is then used in the forward direction. It is an expert system.

But as you may have guessed, there's a snag. Our expert system is going to be impractically large. So Michie suggests that we loose an inductive generalization algorithm on our masses of problem–solution pairs and thereby reduce this unwieldy conglomeration to a manageable number of general rules.

An inductive algorithm identifies and extracts the significant commonalities exhibited by a set of instances (and perhaps lacking in a set of noninstances). The set of instances is then replaced by the resulting general principle.

In the development of an expert system for soybean disease diagnosis, Michalski and Chilausky (1980) inductively derived the diagnostic rules from a collection of instances of symptoms and the diagnosed disease.

To the delight of most observers (excepting expert soybean disease taxonomists perhaps) the system using the inductively generated rules was more accurate than a system using the official rules of soybean disease taxonomy. This leads us a little aside, but, in AI, field trials (excuse the pun) are somewhat scarce events so we should make the most of the few we can find.

There are two points here: first, Michie's scheme is shown to be practically viable; and second, human expertise should be extracted in the form of specific examples, not general rules.

The substantial machine-learning subfield of automatic induction algorithms can be fitted in here. We have already seen some manifestations of inductive learning in the earlier sections on generalization learning. The earlier discussions focused on the successive feeding of examples and nonexamples to a system which used each new example (or nonexample) to modify (if necessary) its current version of the general principle. In this section I consider algorithms that have a bunch of information at their disposal all at once (usefully considered as a set of examples and nonexamples, I admit), and use them to generate knowledge of a more general nature: This procedure (in all its human glory, if not in all its programmed manifestations) is, I claim, creative, and not necessarily in a minor league in competition with the likes of AM and BACON.

The general problem is to find the categories when the instances are not marked as to membership in a class or not (i.e., we don't have pre-specified examples and nonexamples, we just have a set of instances). This type of inductive learning is usually referred to as conceptual clustering. A representative example is described by Michalski and Stepp (1983), although theirs is a nonincremental method that assumes an "all-or-none" concept representation. More recent work has aimed at relaxing these contraints. Lebowitz (1986, p. 193) describes an incremental method that also tolerates "input that is complex in any of several different ways." He addresses the problem of exactly what concept to learn by maintaining a dynamic set of concepts which may be updated, and new ones introduced, as new information becomes available.

A major contribution in this subclass of machine learning is that of Quinlan (e.g., Quinlan, 1986) and his algorithms for the induction of decision trees — representations of information within which each node is a decision point from where new paths or "branches" spring, and the decision taken selects the branch to be followed to another decision point, until finally the end of a branch is reached, signaling success or whatever. Don't give up, an example is just ahead.

As an example of this type of ML work we can look at Quinlan's (1987) strategy for dealing with some of its known shortcomings. In particular, he addresses the problems of incomplete and inconsistent information in the training set as well as the traditional brittleness of the decision-tree method of classification (i.e., one wrong decision, which may be somewhat equivocal anyway, can send the processor off down a completely wrong branch of the tree). This system also provides us with an example of probabilistic reasoning, or reasoning with uncertainty — a fundamental and important AI problem which is being attacked from many different directions.

Figure 9.20 is Quinlan's decision tree for diagnosis of certain aspects of thyroid disease. The diagnoses, such as hyperthyroid, goitre, or negative (i.e., no hyperthyroid condition), occur at the leaves. Diagnosis of a specific case, involves starting at the tree root (top left), applying the test there (i.e., in this particular case is the FTI attribute less than or equal to 155?), and moving through the tree as determined by the answer to the question (i.e., drop down if answer is "no," and move right and drop to next test if answer is "yes"). Clearly, a case to be diagnosed must be

```
FTI<=155:

    tumor=f:

        T3<=3.2: negative (1809)

        T3>3.2:

            age<=53: negative (62)

            age>53:

                age<=66: T3 toxic (12/4)

                age>66: negative (9)

    tumor=t:

        T3<=2.8: negative (37)

        T3>2.8: goitre (9/2)


FTI>155:

    on thyroxine=t: negative (54)

    on thyroxine=f:

        TT4<=153: negative (49/2)

        TT4>153:

            age<=11: negative (2)

            age>11:

                query hyperthyroid=t: negative (3)

                query hyperthyroid=f:

                    psych=t: negative (1)

                    psych=f:

                        TSH<=0.21: hyperthyroid (55/5)

                        TSH>0.21: negative (13/2)
```

Figure 9.20. A decision tree for probabilistic classification

From "Decision Trees as Probabilistic Classifiers," by J.R. Quinlan, 1987, *Proceedings of the 4th International Workshop on Machine Learning*. Reprinted by permission.

characterized in terms of the attributes used in the decision tree. This decision-based movement through the tree will eventually terminate at a leaf node. Hence, we have a diagnosis for the case in hand.

This tree was automatically generated from a training set of 2,800 cases using the induction package C4 (Quinlan, Compton, Horn, & Lazarus, 1986). In order to do away with much of the complexity of the resultant decision tree that was due to imperfect and noisy data, C4 invokes a process called *pessimistic pruning,* which then reduced the original 61–node tree to 25 nodes by replacing some subtrees with leaves. The reduction in tree size is bought at the cost of misclassification of some cases in the training set.

The numerical annotation associated with leaf, i.e., (n) or (n/e), captures the accuracy of that leaf in classifying the members of the training set, and it is used to estimate the reliability of a classification arising from that leaf. The number n is the number of cases in the training set that terminated at that leaf, and the number e, if it appears, is the number of cases that were misclassified. Thus for the T3 toxic diagnosis following the test age$< = 66$,the annotation (12/4) means that 12 of the training set cases ended here, but only eight of them were correct diagnoses. In this way noisy training data can be accomodated by an automatic mechanism that delivers a compact and manageable, but probabilistic, decision tree. It is an approach to a style of diagnosis in which the system can diagnose a "sort of" goitre rather than just goitre or not goitre. In addition, the extra statistical information available can be used to alleviate the bad effects of several other important problems.

Quinlan suggests dealing with the lack of the necessary information at a choice point (e.g., no FTI value would stop us even starting the diagnosis process) by following multiple paths (i.e., don't make the decision). He presents a scheme for then combining the relative probabilities associated with each of the final diagnoses that are eventually produced.

For the problem of the brittleness produced by sharp thresholds, he introduces the notion of *soft thresholds* and sketches out several ways of using them. The basic idea is to use the misclassification information available in order to assign a probability component to the overall result that is dependent upon how close a given case is to a vague threshold.

REDISCOVERING THINGS

I was tempted to title this section "HAMMING IT UP WITH BACON," but even I couldn't bring myself to use it. To start with, it's not entirely accurate (not that I feel too fettered by such esoteric concerns), for AM and EURISKO (Davis & Lenat, 1982) must be star turns in this section, and the unused title fails to give them a billing.

In some sense all discovery is rediscovery. In 1492, while sailing across the ocean blue, Columbus unexpectedly bumped into, and thus it is said discovered, America. But presumably the local inhabitants already knew that it was there, so in reality he only rediscovered it. This line of argument follows the there-is-nothing-new-under-the-Sun adage. However, America was new to Columbus and to the Europeans as a whole; for them it clearly was a discovery (for the locals it was more of a disaster, but that's another story).

Similarly, in machine learning there can be discovery — when a program offers the world, or at least its designers, some information that is both true and was previously unknown to them — there can also be rediscovery — when a program generates true information that was known to the system designer, planned for by him or her in the system design, but nevertheless not explicitly built into the system. Below we shall examine the programs that have been built to address this aspect of machine learning, and we shall see that their status vis-à-vis the discovery/rediscovery distinction is not altogether clear. Discovery is clearly high-order learning, possibly the pinnacle of achievement in AI — having attained it on a consistent basis in a program, we can just plant the flag, take a photo, and scurry back down to less dizzy heights of computer software, but currently we still have a formidable climb facing us. The peak can be glimpsed occasionally through the mists, some would claim, but it is far from conquered, all would agree.

Rediscovery, on the other hand, can vary from fairly obvious generation of nonexplicitly programmed information (say, inferencing from a knowledge base) to the production of somewhat surprising but known truths as a result of a complex deductive–inductive chain of reasoning from a generalized knowledge base. As usual, the awkward concept of complexity seems to intrude and be an important factor in determining the significance of a specific rediscovery process in AI. Unfortunately, complexity is just about the easiest quality to generate in an AI program. There are two issues here: There is a difference between significant and gratuitous complexity (but no known litmus test to distinguish clearly between them); there is also the problem that complexity is by no means the whole story. It is just a convenient approximation to the problem of evaluating the significance of AI projects (William of Occam would not have agreed, I suspect). In fact complexity and creativity are almost antithetical: The most striking creative insights are often those of the greatest simplicity. The resolution of this apparent paradox lies in the dubious nature of the concept of rediscovery.

But, to extricate this narrative from the complexities of the complexity issue, let me just say that the status of rediscovery as a creative act is murky. If you know where you're going, it may still require insight and imagination to plan a route that will get you there. But if you don't know where you're going, finding a new and exciting place as a result of somewhat random forays into the unknown may be a totally different procedure. Discovery and rediscovery may not be closely associated processes.

AI, as is appropriate for preliminary studies, has so far concentrated on mechanized rediscovery within the quite restricted and well-structured domains of mathematics and classical chemistry.

The AM and EURISKO programs (Davis & Lenat, 1982) are the paradigmatic examples is this subcategory of machine learning. The AM program "consists of a large corpus of primitive mathematical concepts, each with a few associated heuristics — situation/action rules which function as local "plausible move generators". Some suggest tasks for the system to carry out, some suggest ways of satisfying a given task, and so on" (Lenat, 1983, p. 254). AM's prime goal is to expand its collection of mathematical concepts — i.e., to create new concepts from the primitive ones (initially 115 core concepts) and the heuristics (243 of which were used). One such heuristic was given earlier, here's another:

"If, empirically, 10 times as many elements fail some predicate P, as satisfy it, then some generalization (weakened version) of P might be more interesting than P" (Davis & Lenat, 1982, p. 5).

Core concepts are data structures (sets, bags, lists) and operators (union, composition). "From this primitive basis, AM quickly discovered elementary numerical concepts (corresponding to those we refer to as natural numbers, multiplication, factors, and primes)" (Davis & Lenat, 1982, p. 6). The "discoveries" were not new to mankind, nor (with a couple of exceptions) to Lenat himself, but they were new to the program (but then, if you're ignorant enough, any new information is a discovery).

It may be (one can only hope) that one day in the future, when some dusty listings of AM are rediscovered in the deep recesses of some little-used filing cabinet, a creative discovery of the highest order will be found in the discarded output. Could AM's really creative discoveries reside somewhere in the rejected output, just waiting for the right advances in human science to render them recognizable?

A 'discovery' in AM means:AM recognized it as a distinguished entity (for example, by formulating its definition); and also AM decided it was worth investigating, (either because of the interesting way it was formed, or because of surprising preliminary empirical results). (Davis & Lenat, 1982, p. 6)

When a program generates examples of some new entity X as (T T T), (T T T T T), (T T T T T T T), etc., has it discovered prime numbers? Or has the human observer succumbed to the ELIZA syndrome and rediscovered prime numbers in the purely syntactic musings of the program? These questions are particularly tricky in a formal abstract domain such as number theory. If a robot discovers how to drive a car, we don't have to rely on our interpretation of some LISP code to recognize this discovery; the robot can just demonstrate it. Demonstration of the cognizance of an abstract concept is not so clear cut (you might recall our discussions of the significance of the Turing Test in Chapter 1).

Well, our story continues with the successes (it rediscovered many concepts) and the failures (there was a threshold of discovery above which I could not get without discovering some new heuristics) of AM luring Lenat on to construct EURISKO. In this program the heuristic rules become the concepts, and the operators were designed to create new heuristics. EURISKO did not enjoy the same level of success as AM — new and useful heuristics were not forthcoming.

Lenat and Brown (1983) have tried to account for this disappointment. The crux of their argument (and I see no reason to dispute it, for a change) is strikingly similar to the one that extinguished the simulated evolution approach to AI (a minor, major paradigm introduced and disposed of in a couple of paragraphs of Chapter 3). Anything close to small random changes in a large complex system is unlikely to lead to a better system in the short run.

AM's concepts were small and simple, and the local search space was thick with meaningful (if not particularly interesting) mathematical concepts. Small changes thus tended to generate new and meaningful mathematical concepts from which some "interesting" ones were fairly easily filtered off. But heuristics are large and complex objects (pages of LISP code rather than a couple of lines), and the operators tended to generate meaningless "new heuristics." Hence, AM did good, but EURISKO did not.

The BACON series of programs (described in Bradshaw, Langley, & Simon, 1983; Langley, Bradshaw, & Simon, 1981; Simon, Langley, & Bradshaw, 1981; Simon, 1984) make scientific rediscoveries in the experimental sciences. Given data to crunch on, one or other incarnation of BACON will rediscover "a set of generalizations, or theory, to describe the data parsimoniously or to explain them" (Simon, Langley, & Bradshaw, 1981, p. 7).

Heuristics within the system generate hypotheses, test them against the data, and eventually the expected law is forthcoming. Sometimes it is necessary to generate new theoretical terms, and the system can also do this. So far there have been countless rediscoveries of Ohm's Law,

the ideal gas law, Snell's Law of refraction, Kepler's third law of plane-
tary motion, and Black's law of temperature equilibrium of mixtures —
an impressive list.

BACON's designers make two classes of claim about their research on
mechanized creativity:

1. That the programs model what the scientists did en route to their
    original discoveries;
2. That the programs provide insight into some of the knotty problems
    uncovered by attempted explanations of the real history of scientific
    discovery.

These two claims Grabiner (1986) terms the *historical* ones, and to
them she adds a psychological claim:

3. That the computer model is adequate to explain the thought of cre-
    ative scientists.

Grabiner challenges all three claims. She says

> that the essential difference between Black's discovery and the program's
> is that the program had its variables chosen for it. Black did not. In fact,
> before Black the very distinction between heat and temperature was not
> understood. . . . Once one has chosen the appropriate data, the job of dis-
> covering Black's law is essentially over. (pp. 120–121)

Similarly, when working on the task of rediscovering Kepler's third
law, certain crucial numerical values are fed to the program as "observ-
ables." Grabiner says that they are not. The hard data generated and used
is the result of a subtle interplay of theory and observation of the empirical world.

In both cases the BACON programs work with abstractions from the
real world, not the real world itself. It is true that it should not be necessary to build a robot that can handle test tubes or telescopes, but, at the
same time, if the programs are fed such highly processed data, then the
intelligence is in the preprocessing not in the subsequent data crunching.

It is certainly possible that the 'spaces' of data and of laws described
by Langley, Zytkow, Simon, and Bradshaw (1986), and the searching of
these spaces, which is portrayed as scientific discovery, is a specific rational fiction founded on the generic fiction of the SSSP. It is true that
the SSSP may be a useful approximation to some aspects of intelligent or
intellectual activity and may thus serve as a basis for useful AI programs,
but to present this simplistic framework as the basis for creative discov-

ery, even in the hard sciences, requires a good deal more justification than BACON's designers have ever presented. But for those not sated with the details of mechanized creativity there is a whole book on this topic — *Scientific Discovery: Computational Explorations of the Creative processes,* by Langley, Simon, Bradshaw, and Zytkow (1987).

LEARNING BY ANALOGY

One final type of "introspective" learning embraces the theories and models that learn by analogy: They generate new information by inferring further similarities between two things, given some existing similarities between them (after Russell, 1987). It can be quite persuasively argued that humans generate a lot of new ideas as a result of perceived similarities between something they already know and something new. But the essential notion of similarity is no less elusive in this area than it was when we looked at inductive generalization as similarity-based learning. Nevertheless, there have been a number of AI projects designed to explore some facet of this general approach to learning. The notion of analogy has also been used to drive problem-solving behavior, although no new information is typically stored, and thus there is no explicit learning taking place.

Evans's (1968) program that solved geometric analogy puzzles is the traditional starting point for this AI subfield; it is one of the projects in an early collection put together by Minsky and persuasively mistitled *Semantic Information Processing* (Minsky, 1968). More recent studies in actually learning by analogy have been reported by Carbonell (1983). He states that analogical reasoning has been a sparsely investigated phenomenon despite being one of the central inference mechanisms in human cognition. His own scheme is based on means–ends analysis (Chapter 3). And working, at the time, from the homebase of the SSSP, his approach centers on an *analogy transform problem space* (T-space — see a subsequent section, "Soaring Through Search Spaces," in order to get fully spaced out). With a suitably defined T-space and the necessary T-operators he shows useful transformations from given to desired solution sequences, and the acquisition of generalized solution procedures. Winston, of arch-learning fame, has also contributed significantly to this AI subdomain — see Winston (1980, 1981, 1983, for example).

At a more general level, Russell (1987) discusses the similarities between analogy and single-instance generalization (such as EBG). He shows that they share a common inferential structure, and that they share two distinct possible modes of justification: one, explanation-based reasoning, and the other determination-based reasoning — a "more recent," and apparently more personal, mechanism that he then proceeds to grind through in gruesome detail. I shall not. You know where it is if you want it. The latter mode is, he claims, more generally applicable (than the former), "since it uses, rather than explains, the information contained in the instance" (p. 390). In addition, he differentiates between analogy and metaphor, which is an even more neglected potential machine learning strategy.

It is time to move up to the knowledge level, and I'll do so eventually on the back of Soar, but first we must look at what "learning at the knowledge level" means.

LEARNING AT THE KNOWLEDGE LEVEL

At the moment, the acid test for machine learning systems — the criterion that separates the men from the boys, as it were — is: Does it learn at the the knowledge level? What can this mean? And is it indicative of fundamental progress, or is it just a passing phase?

If you read Chapter 6, I would expect that the previous paragraph has left you with patterns of residual neuronal activity that should give rise to an acknowledgment, on your part, that *the knowledge level* is not a new term that I have just sprung on you. If a vague acknowledgment is all that you can honestly muster, then you might be well advised to skip back for a quick refresher course, although I'll give you the gist of it again.

Dietterich (1986, 1989) divides learning systems into *symbol-level learners* and *knowledge-level learners*. Rosenbloom, Laird, and Newell (1987, p. 499) explain this distinction as follows.

> A system performs symbol level learning if it improves its computational performance but does not increase the amount of knowledge it contains. According to a knowledge level analysis [Newell, 1981, or Chapter 6], knowledge only increases if a fact is added that is not implied by the existing knowledge; that is, if the fact is not in the deductive closure of the existing knowledge.

So learning at the knowledge level means adding a new fact, but one that is not already implicit in the system's existing knowledge.

Dietterich uses the concept of knowledge-level learning to develop a taxonomy of learning systems. He approaches his goal from a notion of the *limits* of what a given learning system knows. In order to make this notion both useful and explicit, he has to adopt a slightly modified definition of the knowledge level. Instead of attributing knowledge to a system, based on the observation of the system's behavior over some rather short period of time, he throws time and implementation constraints to the wind and defines the knowledge in a system in terms of what that system could do if it had infinite computational resources at its disposal. This somewhat odd manuever is intended to rule out the possibility of penalizing a system because it did not have the time to consider all possibilties — i.e., it will appear, with respect to the specific observed behavior, to know less than it actually knows. {Curious detail: It is exactly the inability to process all possibilities that makes many problems AI problems.} This is all well and good, but it does introduce another problem, doesn't it? It is going to be tricky to provide the program with infinite time and space to work with, and of course we won't attempt to do that. What Dietterich suggests as a way around this obstacle that he's introduced is to inspect the implementation of the system; by so doing, "we can often determine whether additional computational resources would change the actions selected by the system" (Dietterich, 1989, p. 5 of pre-publication research report, pp. 1–20). Not wholly satisfactory, I would have thought, but we must push on.

Now he can define the *computational-closure knowledge level* (CCKL) of a system as follows.

> To determine the knowledge contained in a system S, we will allow S infinite computational resources before it selects the actions to perform. (Dietterich, 1989, p. 4)

He is now in a position to offer us a definition of *knowledge-level learning* (KLL):

> A program is said to exhibit knowledge level learning if its CCKL description changes over time. (Dietterich, 1989, p. 5)

And this, on the face of it, seems reasonable — if the system is capable of doing more today than it was yesterday, then it must have learned something in between, and, moreover, that something was at the knowledge level. There is, I suppose, an implication in the above definition that the change over time is an *increase* in knowledge; otherwise it becomes a definition of knowledge level forgetting {or, if you want to be pedantic, a definition of no change at the knowledge level, if one piece is forgotten but a different, and equivalent piece, is found to replace the loss}.

This general assault on the definition of learning does raise a few problems which I shall just mention. First, there is the problem of actually deciding on the CCKL of a system, and second there is the problem of evaluating a program change in terms of the knowledge that the two versions contain.

Nevertheless, we are now in a position to appreciate Dietterich's taxonomy of learning systems. It involves three categories of machine learning together with *predictability at the knowledge level.*

> A system is said to be predictable at the knowledge level if its behavior can be predicted using the principle of rationality. (Dietterich, 1989, p. 2)

Such predictability rests on the solution of three subproblems:

1. We must determine what knowledge the system contains. This is tricky, because not all knowledge will be encoded explicitly in facts and rules; some will be implicit in the heuristic control strategies.
2. We must be able to make this knowledge concrete, in order that we may be able to manipulate it with the principle of rationality (Chapter 6, if you're worried about this object). This is awkward because this knowledge-level stuff is supposed to be independent of implementation considerations.
3. We must decide what knowledge is acquired by the system when new inputs are received from the environnment. The glitch in this subproblem is that the process of internalizing external information involves interpretation; i.e, how does the system treat the information that the environment offers? This is nothing less than the age-old problem of perception.

You might be tempted to think that any person who is operating under a principle of rationality would scrap this line of reasoning and look for another way, but you would be wrong. Newell (1981) tackles these subproblems head on, but as Dietterich (1989, p. 2) delicately puts it, "the solutions are only approximate." So we've have an "approximate" notion called predictability at the knowledge level, and now we can progress to the three definitions of machine learning.

> *Symbol level learning* (SLL) is improvement in computational performance that yields no change in the CCKL description of the system.
>
> *Determined knowledge level learning* (DKLL) is knowledge level learning that can be described (and predicted) at the knowledge level.
>
> *Non-determined knowledge level learning* (NKLL) is knowledge level learning that cannot be described (or predicted) at the knowledge level. (Dietterich, 1989, p. 10)

The EBG method, described earlier, is a prime example of so-called symbol-level learning. The generalization learned is deduced from the goal concept, domain knowledge, and training example. The EBG method makes explicit information that is already implicitly in the system, and this is by no means a trivial and worthless exercise. However, learning at the knowledge level is meant to imply something more. It results in "adding facts not already implied by its existing knowledge" (Rosenbloom et al., 1987, p. 499). In addition, there is, according to Dietterich, predictability at the knowledge level to be considered. Deductive database systems (PROLOG-like systems, Dietterich calls them) are DKLL systems. When we type in a new fact to a PROLOG system, it adds this fact to its database and can then (in general) deduce facts that it could not deduce before. This is, thus, knowledge-level learning, but the behavior of such systems can be determined (predicted) at the knowledge level using the principle of rationality. These systems can also be viewed as SLL systems that receive external information. So when might this not be true? Inductive learning systems provide examples of NKLL systems. In the context of incremental inductive learning (such as ID4, Schlimmer & Fisher, 1986), new training examples typically change the system's knowledge; thus, such systems are exhibiting knowledge-level learning. In addition, contradictions can arise within the system — e.g., an overgeneralization is contrary to a training example — thus, the principle of rationality will not be able to come up with a unique prediction. Hence, the system is not predictable at the knowledge level. Dietterich admits that the NKLL category is difficult to characterize. "Although we normally associate it with any kind of inductive or non-monotonic reasoning technique, the use of these techniques does not necessarily produce NKLL" (Dietterich, 1989, p. 11).

That's roughly the picture, and if you don't feel totally at ease with these distinctions, then you're just about normal. The significance and meaning of knowledge-level learning are both highly contentious issues. The term is fairly widely used, but only to mean learning over and above symbol-level learning without being too specific about what this higher level of performance actually is. In fact, Rosenbloom et al. (1987, p. 503) own up and conclude with the admission that "the distinction may not be as fundamental as it seems." Nevertheless, there does seem to be a recognized need to search for learning mechanisms that hold the promise of learning information beyond that which is presented to the system on a plate, so to speak. At the very least, the term knowledge-level learning serves to focus attention on the current limitations of most machine learning techniques, and to flag something worth aiming at just over the horizon.

Focusing right down again, we can look at the Soar system. It is, in itself, a significant ML system; in addition, it provides us with a concrete example of a number of concepts that we've discussed, including "chunking" and learning at the knowledge level.

SOARING THROUGH SEARCH SPACES

The Soar system for machine learning, the latest and perhaps the greatest contender for honors in AI from the CMU stables, is also a prime example of the unitary-architecture approach to AI (Chapter 1 explores this general category of AI research). Coming from the birthplace of other great unitary-architecture systems, such as GPS with its means-ends analysis basis and production system philosophy, it is no big surprise. But one of the claims for the Soar system, and one that sets it apart from (and above) most of the schemes that we have looked at, is that it supports "learning at the knowledge level."

Although many varieties of learning are claimed for Soar, it is all based on a single learning mechanism, *chunking*.

> Chunking creates new productions, or chunks, based on the results of goal-based problem solving. The actions of the chunk contain the results of the goal. The conditions of the chunk test those aspects of the pre-goal situation that were relevant to the generation of the results. (Rosenbloom et al., 1987, p. 499)

That's it in a nutshell; now we must try to crack it.

Firstly, Soar is production system based; that also should come as no big surprise, given its place of origin. Secondly, the basic structure learned is a production, chunks are productions, so the real investigation needs to focus on how these new productions are constructed. Thirdly, Soar is a classical SSSP-based system. Goals, problem spaces, states, and operators provide the customary well-defined framework for Soar's problem solving and learning activities. Problem solving is goal-driven and consists of a sequence of two-phase decision cycles. The result of each decision cycle is progress towards a desired state: selecting problem spaces to work in, states to proceed from, and operators to apply. All the usual SSSP stuff, but refer back to Chapter 3 if this is not making great sense to you.

The two phases of the decision cycle are *elaboration* and *interpretation*. "The elaboration process involves the creation of new objects, the addition of knowledge about existing objects, and the addition of preferences. There is a fixed language of preferences that is used to describe the acceptability and desirability of the alternatives being considered for selection." Thus the "preferences" appear to be a key element of the mechanism that controls the critical selection process, the process that sets up the detailed context for solving specific problems. And although Rosenbloom et al. (1987, p. 500) state that "preferences only affect the efficiency with which a goal is achieved, and not the correctness of the goal's results," we must bear in mind that (under the aegis of the SSSP) efficiency of search is what distinguishes an intelligent processor from a blind and hopeless one.

The elaboration phase is based on the classical production system cycle (see Figure 6.15, in Chapter 6) and continues until no more productions can fire. The second phase involves the interpretation of the selected structures in working memory, "the preferences," by a fixed decision procedure. Whenever Soar is unable to make progress on some goal because of inadequate directly available knowledge, it has reached an *impasse* — for example, when more than one operator can be applied to a state and there is insufficient knowledge to choose between, we have a species of impasse known as an *operator-tie*. (As you can see, there is a whole new language that comes bundled up with the new architecture.) An impasse is the single situation in which a new subgoal is created (clearly, if you don't reach an impasse, you can continue smoothly on to the achievement of your current goal, or subgoal). The new subgoal, triggered by the operator-tie impasse, is naturally the goal of resolving this tie, and successful achievement of this subgoal will result in the selection of a single candidate operator. Hence, processing can then proceed at the higher level, i.e., working on the goal that was interrupted when the impasse occurred. Thus, problem solving in Soar involves setting up and solving a hierarchical structure of goals and subgoals, and all of the problem-solving apparatus is brought to bear on every goal or subgoal in a hierarchy.

That has dealt with the situation when Soar gets stuck, what happens when it succeeds with a goal, or subgoal? Well, I mentioned one resultant action: The system is free to move up and resume processing with the interrupted, higher-level goal, or, if the successful goal is the highest-level goal, then it has solved the problem that was set. But more important, within the context of a chapter on machine learning, is another resultant behavior, namely, chunking. The successful achievement of a goal signals the possibility of chunking; it is thus success-driven learning. The second condition that has to be met is that all of the working memory modifications occurring since the goal was first activated must be attributable to that goal rather than to one of its subgoals. (In addition, a different, second condition for the chunking of goal hierarchies is given by Rosenbloom & Newell; it is: All of the goal's subgoals were themselves processed by chunks — this condition ensures that chunks are created from the bottom up in a goal hierarchy.)

So now Soar is in a position to create a chunk. How does it do it? Most of the necessary information is resident in working memory. Recall that a chunk, in Soar, is a production; hence, we need a condition part and an action part. The initial state of the goal provides a basis for the condition part — it specifies the information necessary in order to embark upon the solving of the goal. The action part is constructed from the results of the successful goal — the chunk being constructed to replace the goal-solving process should produce the same results as the process it is replacing. All this information is available and close at hand on successful achievement of a goal, but something more is needed. The new chunk is useful only for the specific situation used to solve the subgoal from which it was derived. To store such a chunk would amount to rote learning of the crudest kind, so two forms of abstraction are applied:

1. The inclusion of only the implicit parameters of a goal and not the entire initial state, and
2. The replacement of constant identifiers (found in the working memory objects) with a 'neutral' object that will not hinder matching between the rest of the condition and an appropriate object in working memory.

As Rosenbloom and Newell (1986, p. 273) put it: "These abstractions allow the chunks to be applicable in any situation that is relevantly identical, not merely totally identical. Different chunks are needed only for relevant differences." With the fairly minimal degree of generalization applied here, it appears that the word *relevant* is yet another special word from the language of Soar and not from everyday English — I leave this as a problem for the reader.

Rosenbloom and Newell (1986) provide a simple example of how chunking works. The problem is to compute the average of two numbers. So the top-level goal is Compute-Average-Of-Two-Numbers; it takes as parameters the two numbers to be averaged and returns a single number result which is their mean. Nothing surprising there, I hope. The simple three-goal hierarchy illustrated in Figure 9.21 is used.

The first subgoal takes the two input numbers and returns their sum, while the second subgoal takes this sum as the input parameter and returns half of it as the result. Nice to have an example that doesn't strain the gray matter, isn't it?

But onward: We are asked to suppose that the first task is to average the numbers 3 and 7. Control would pass from goal 1 to goal 2, which

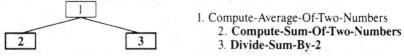

1. Compute-Average-Of-Two-Numbers
   2. **Compute-Sum-Of-Two-Numbers**
   3. **Divide-Sum-By-2**

Figure 9.21.   A simple three-goal hierarchy for the averaging of two numbers

From "The Chunking of Goal Hierarchies," by P.S. Rosenbloom & A. Newell, 1986, in *Machine Learning* (p. 259), edited by R.S. Michalski, J.G. Carbonell, & T.M. Mitchell, Los Altos, CA: Morgan Kaufmann. Reprinted by permission.

would be successful, and return the number 10 as its result. Successful goal completion signals the possibility of creating a chunk, and indeed that can be and is done in this case. A chunk of three components is created. It consists of an encoding component that encodes the parameters 3 and 7 into a new symbol, E1. A decoding component is created that decodes from a second new symbol, D1, to the result 10. And thirdly, a connection component is created that generates the result symbol D1 when it detects both the presence of the encoded parameter E1, and that goal 2 is the active goal. Similar reasoning will lead us to a three-component chunk for goal 3, but not one for goal 1, because its subgoals were not processed by chunks (recall the second condition for chunking of goal hierarchies if this worries you at all).

But the next time that this goal hierarchy is presented with the task of averaging 3 and 7, the processor whizzes through the two new chunks, and, when goal 1 terminates successfully, a chunk is created, because both subgoals were processed by chunks. The resultant chunky structure is illustrated in Figure 9.22.

This example results in only crude rote learning: The learned chunks work only for averaging 3 and 7, and the extra baggage introduced should make us dubious about it being faster than the original problem-solving structure. It is only meant to be an example of how chunking works in Soar, although the question of learning resulting in faster performance is a sticky one; we shall look at it in the following section. In fact, Soar, with its single learning mechanism, has successfully displayed its capabilites in a wide variety of different learning situations. Steier et al. (1987) discuss the varieties of learning in Soar.

But now it's really time to tackle the knowledge-level learning question. To support the knowledge-level learning claim for Soar, the notion of *data chunking* is introduced (this is Rosenbloom et al., 1987). The chunking that we have seen so far is procedural chunking: The chunks are productions that implement some action. A data chunk is intended to deal with learning declarative knowledge, i.e., things that just are, rather than schemes for achieving some goal. In their own words (Rosenbloom et al., 1987, p. 500): "Reduced to its essentials data chunking involves

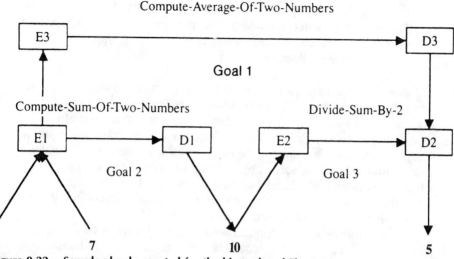

Figure 9.22.   Sample chunks created for the hierarchy of Fig. 9.21

From "The Chunking of Goal Hierarchies," by P.S. Rosenbloom & A. Newell, 1986, in *Machine Learning* (p. 260), edited by R.S. Michalski, J.G. Carbonell, & T.M. Mitchell, Los Altos, CA: Morgan Kaufmann. Reprinted by permission.

the perception of some new piece of knowledge, followed by the storage of some representation of the new knowledge into long-term memory." This trio argue that an appropriate implementation of such data chunking will enable Soar to acquire new knowledge — i.e., to learn at the knowledge level.

What they describe is a two-step process whereby Soar uses its perceptual capabilities to generate a representation of the new knowledge in working memory, and then creates from this representation a production which can, at appropriate points in the future, retrieve the new knowledge into working memory. Let's get really specific. Soar must memorize a new object, say A, and then be able to recall it on demand. That's the task. How is it accomplished?

If Soar is to use its standard chunking mechanism (and that is the whole point of the exercise), the overall strategy must take advantage of the fact that chunking learns from goal-based experience. The obvious, but wrong, solution to this problem is to learn a chunk that has actions which generate an object B that is a copy of A. Two important problems are associated with this potential solution.

1. The conditions for generating B will be the existence of A, thus, the object will only be recalled in those circumstances where it is already available.

2.   At recall time the system must generate B but not generate all of the other objects that it could potentially generate. A discrimination capability is needed; we are no longer interested in chunking as simply an efficiency measure.

The first problem is solved by splitting the act of recall into separate generate and test phases. Separate chunks are learned for each phase. In the generation phase object B is constructed from scratch out of the objects that the system already knows. Object A is not examined until the test phase, when it is compared to object B to see if they are equivalent. The second problem is solved by utilizing the two-phase decision cycle which already exists. The elaboration phase recalls all the learned objects; then an impasse occurs which can be used to generate just the desired object and none of the other possible objects.

It is not worth going any further into the fine details of how Soar can be retooled to recognize and recall objects, and therefore to learn at the knowledge level. Dietterich (1989) places this behavior in the DKLL category and offers the consolation that "perhaps some other simple mechanism can be added to SOAR that will provide a way of expressing inductive biases, which could then be combined with chunking to produce NKLL" (Dietterich, 1989, p. 17). These are much-argued-over claims, and you now have enough information to join in if you so wish. The implementation details appear somewhat tortuous, as they always do when many varieties of behavior are being wrung from a unitary-architecture model. One sometimes gets the feeling that something is being made to work despite the available infrastructure of the system.

It seems to me that, if we divide learning strategies into success- and failure-driven, then many are in the latter category (see a later section) but Soar is in the former. Now, failure during processing of information would seem to be the right time to learn — i.e., to acquire new knowledge — because the very fact of failure signals an absence of necessary information. The learning then becomes that act of assimilating the missing information. This would seem to be an ideal setup for learning at the knowledge level, i.e., learning something that the system did not already know. But success-driven learning suggests quite the opposite argument. If the system is successful, then it knows all that it needs to know for the problem at hand. So why learn? The only reason is to increase efficiency, not to assimilate new information. This is precisely the aim of the memo function idea. Is it also the reason why Soar does not easily exhibit learning at the knowledge level?

One mildly amusing aspect of implementations in Soar (and the reason for the title of this section, just in case you wondered about it) is the total lack of inhibition with respect to search spaces that the implementors display. The solution to the recognition-and-recall problem conjures up in an offhand manner a generation problem space, a recognition problem space, and a recall problem space. It seems as if, whenever a new feature is required, a space with appropriate operators can be found to deal with it: "What happens if the input data are noisy?" we might ask. "No problem, just select the noise-elimination space and chunk it out." I leave the reader to ponder on the significance of the infinite space of spaces at Soar's disposal. I'll also leave it up to the reader to determine how (or if) Soar has satisfied or avoided the "unfulfilled assumptions" (Haugeland, 1985, p. 183) that stumped GPS (if you feel like having a go at this exercise, but you've forgotten the details, Chapter 3 is where you'll find them).

Another aspect of Soar, a final Soar point (as it were), which has been extensively explored, is the issue of improvement of performance with learning. After all, that is the whole purpose of the learning in the first place, isn't it? The answer is mostly yes, but the issues are far wider than Soar: I'll give them a couple of sections all to themselves, and here they come.

THE MORE YOU KNOW THE SLOWER YOU GO

The title of this section refers to machines and not to humans. In fact, for humans it is often patently not true, and that is why we have a problem on our hands in ML. Expertise, in humans, is usually associated with increased speed as expertise increases. This mystery was touched on in Chapter 5. Machines, on the other hand, behave as one would expect: The more information that they have to base their decisions on, the more slowly the decisions are produced. And it's obvious why this should be so: The more information that is potentially relevant, the longer it takes to search through it. One would be tempted to make this a fundamental law of nature, were it not for the blatant counterexample to be found hunched over every warm keyboard. As machines become more knowledgeable as a result, say, of machine learning, we would also like them to maintain their old speed at least, but they don't. Every successful machine learning mechanism, if pursued for long enough, proves to be a brake on the system. Like an oil that is too viscous, instead of lubricating the mechanisms for high speed operation, it gums up the works. Now, the foregoing remarks refer primarily to SSSP-based systems. And the reason why this problem exists is that the more information that is in the system, the more searching it has to do in order to come up with the answer. There are two sorts of reason why this problem does not occur in CP-based work. The glib one is that the nature of the CP is such that searching through information is not a fundamental behavior of CP-based models. Thus it is obvious why connectionist models do not suffer from this affliction. It is just one more indication that the SSSP, as a basis for AI systems, is wrong. The more cynical type of reason is that CP-based models have not yet been constructed on a large enough scale for the problem to be apparent. "Just wait until you are able to build connectionist models that are more than trivial toys, if you ever are," the SSSP person might say, "and then we'll have some real basis for comparison." But, for the moment at least, we are discussing SSSP-based work in this section.

At first sight it might appear obvious why simple rote learning gives rise to this problem, but generalization, which replaces a set of instances by one general rule, ought to avoid it. For the very nature of generalization is to condense information. But a little reflection soon reveals why generalization learning also slows systems down: It may be true that there is less information explicitly represented, but the general structure must now be interpreted, particularized, for every instance encountered, and that takes time. The main purpose of memo functions, you might recall, was to speed up the average time by explicitly representing the commonly encountered instances and thereby avoid the overhead of the general structure. There is no simple correspondence between acquiring generalizations and improving speed of performance.

All of this is not to say that machine learning does not improve speed of system performance. Usually it does, but only at the beginning. There is a classical learning curve which depicts the nature of human learning over a wide range of phenomena. Typically, humans improve quickly on a new task, but then the improvement (e.g., increase in speed) slows down, and eventually no further improvement seems to be attainable. Figure 9.23 depicts such a curve.

This sort of curve, which looks like a rocket arching into the sky, is even more rocket-like when plotted for most machine learning mechanisms: We then get to see gravity reasserting itself as the rocket runs out of propellant. Here's another graph in Figure 9.24, just in case my allusions to rocketry are less than crystal clear.

Now you get the picture, no doubt, but of course the journal editors don't, at least not the full picture. It is usually truncated at about n trials.

That's enough disparaging remarks. Why does this ballistic learning curve appear in machine learning systems? Well, nobody really knows (which perhaps makes this question a good one to leave for the reader to grapple with), although there is no shortage of suggestions. Perhaps better *indexing* is the answer (it was earlier, in Chapter 8, you may recall). If we implement a better indexing mechanism in our system, more information won't necessarily lead to more searching. Certainly, the human brain

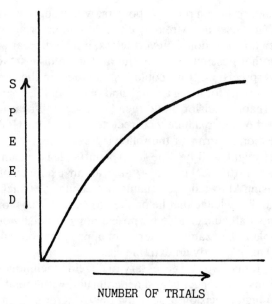

Figure 9.23. A classical learning curve

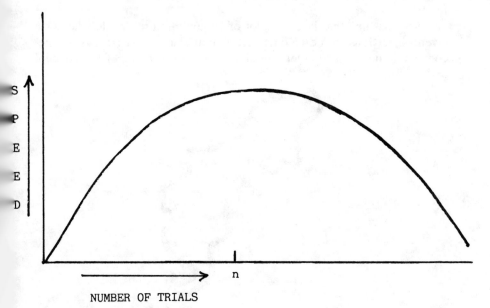

Figure 9.24. The ballistic curve of machine learning

445

seems to have information retrieval powers, which suggests (to some people at least) that it uses an extremely efficient system of indexing. But we
have little idea how it is done. Nevertheless, it may be goal worth striving
for in AI. Another possibility is that the fundamental mistake in machine
learning is overprecision. If we could just home in on the general class of
things we are looking for using a rough and ready, but fast, approximation
technique, perhaps precision could then be brought to bear (if necessary)
on the small set of approximately correct items. De Jong (1988) made this
type of suggestion in terms of the following example.

A physicist might well be able to explain (at least begin to explain),
say, the act of setting a cup on a table as an example of SAFE-TO-
STACK by using knowledge of quantum mechanics, which is the most
precise domain knowledge that he or she possesses. This would be a mistake. For almost all conceivable purposes, our physicist would be better
advised to explain the example in terms of approximations such as weight
and rigidity. This is clearly an extreme case, but it makes the point effectively, I think. It may well be necessary to develop techniques for backing
off precise terms and concepts as a general rule, with the ability to focus
back down to high-precision processing only when required.

The following illustrative diagrams are also given by De Jong. A
learned concept definition may be precise and complex; we can illustrate
this with a complex boundary. Everything inside the boundary is covered
by the concept. Everything outside is not. The boundary is given in Figure 9.25

Let us assume that it takes a lot of computation to decide whether a
given object falls inside or outside this boundary. That is, it is a time-
consuming decision to determine if we have an instance of the concept

Figure 9.25.   A sketch of a complex-concept boundary

or not. Suppose we use a regular but rough approximation to our precise definition, such as a squashed circle, which is now superimposed on the precise concept definition (see Figure 9.26).

Most of the objects that would have fallen inside the complex boundary still fall inside my approximate boundary, and most that previously fell outside still fall outside. So it is a reasonable approximation to the original complex curve. We assume that it is now much faster to compute whether a new object falls inside or outside the smooth approximation, but what happens when we're wrong? For example, point A is inside the complex boundary but outside the smooth approximation. Point A would be mis-classified by the fast approximation. The consequences of this error de-termine how good an approximation we have. If such an error doesn't matter much, or is very infrequent and easily detected and rectified, then we have a good approximation. But if errors cause disasters, or they oc-cur all the time and are costly to put right, then we need to work on our approximation or give up approximating in this particular situation.

That's enough suggestions. Suffice it to say it is a ubiquitous problem, and it is unsolved, although it has been explored. Tambe and Newell (1988), for example, investigate the observed fact that, in the Soar sys-tem, some learned chunks are a lot more costly to use than others. They decompose the causes of such "expensive chunks" into three compo-nents, but the three components are described and discussed in terms of features of the Soar architecture. I shall thus not go further; I shall not delve into the system-dependent details, but if you feel compelled to wade in, you know where to find them.

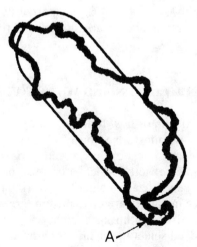

Figure 9.26.   A simple approximation superimposed on the complex-concept boundary

ON FINDING NEEDLES IN HAYSTACKS

Quite apart from efficiently locating the relevant information once it has been learned, there is, in addition, a somewhat similar search task associated with selecting what to learn in the first place. At least there would be if most machine learning algorithms were not fed the right selections from reality at the outset.

When the task at hand is to find a needle in a haystack, then you know exactly what you are looking for. So that's not where the problem lies. The difficulty arises because you're looking for an object that is small and easily overlooked amid a darn great heap of dried grass. In addition, the very act of looking disturbs the hay and is likely to cause the needle to slip further down and away from sight. Thus you are likely to have to remove every piece of hay, almost one by one, before you find (or don't find, as the case may be) the elusive needle on the ground.

In AI the prospects are a little brighter, but perhaps not to such a degree as to warrant great jubilation. In the absence of the many constraints that a human learner can employ, the learning machine is faced with a task that is disturbingly reminiscent of the finding-needles-in-haystacks problem.

"But there are machines that learn," I can almost hear the clamor. True, but they don't learn from real-world experience, they learn from customized descriptions of real-world events and objects.

Thus, if an arch is defined by the "supported-by" relationship, the system must have many ways to infer the truth of this relationship with respect to a specific configuration of the blocks. If the description of the scene has to explicitly state that A is 'supported-by' both B and C, of course, the need for intelligence is greatly reduced (if not eliminated entirely).

WHEN TO LEARN AND WHAT TO LEARN

In addition to the problem of how to learn, i.e., the mechanism of information assimilation, we must also consider when to learn and what to learn. The what-to-learn question has already arisen repeatedly in this chapter. For example, exactly which attributes of a set of instances should an inductive generalization algorithm work on? The usual answer is: just those that the instances are described in terms of. The problem is not really addressed. EBG enthusiasts might want to point out that their mechanism does indeed select the significant attributes of the training example and it ignores the other ones. But how does the system know which of its general concepts the training example is a training example of —

i.e. which is the goal concept? Again, there is usually just one goal concept, so the question of what to learn does not arise. Similarly, when to learn has also appeared here and there in the chapter. For example, in a connectionist network learning is typically initiated by the occurrence of a significant difference between the desired and observed outputs.

So, although both of these problems inevitably pop up now and again in any discussion of machine learning, they do need to be addressed explicitly, I believe. We must face the issue head on, as a machine-learning problem in its own right, and go beyond the brief, oblique encounters that occasionally arise as side issues in other machine-learning endeavors.

Failure-driven learning is sometimes addressed as a topic in machine learning (e.g., it is a key element of Schank's, 1982, theory, and Charniak & McDermott, 1985, mention it briefly, as does Hayes-Roth, 1983); it is, I believe, an important facet of the answer to the problem of when to learn, and, to a lesser extent, of what to learn. But it is not the complete answer by any means, despite attempts to protray it as such (e.g., Schank, 1982). As a minor aside, it might be worth noting that Soar and similar learning strategies are examples of success-driven learning.

The view that I shall present is that failure-driven learning is just one aspect of a more general mechanism. The general mechanism is input-expectation discrepancy reduction (IEDR). Elsewhere (Partridge, 1985a), I have discussed the ubiquity of this mechanism using examples from cognitive modeling, experimental psychology, mainstream AI, electroneurophysiology, and brain modeling.

A system needs to assimilate new information when what it knows does not seem to account with sufficient accuracy for the context that it is operating in. In even more general terms, learning is needed when the system is failing to achieve its goals: It fails to solve some problem, or fails to solve it well enough (in some sense). The card-playing system fails to win its games; the goferCoke robot fails to locate a soft-drink dispensing device; the connectionist network fails to generate the desired output pattern; etc.

In all cases the root problem is a mismatch between the system's internal model of the world and the world itself (or, more accurately, its perception of the world itself). Failure-driven learning is the specific case in which problems with the internal model are deemed to be the sole cause of the mismatch or discrepancy. But what if the goferCoke robot is operating in a Coke-free zone? There are no dispensing machines within hundreds of miles (this could be on one of the better possible worlds or not; it's just a matter of taste, or lack of it). Or perhaps the Coke machine was there all the time, but the robot had a fly on its lens at the crucial time and failed to perceive it.

In either case the robot's locate-Coke-machine inference strategies are fine. In the first case a more global expectation failed: the expectation that there was a coke machine in the vicinity. In the second case the input-expectation mismatch was due to a faulty input-processing module; the expectation was quite correct. The problem is further compounded by the fact that, in an intelligent sensor (visual or otherwise), what is sensed and what is expected can be tightly coupled together, as we discussed in Chapter 7.

But the recognition of an input-expectation discrepancy is, nevertheless, the cue for learning. But it is not necessarily the cue for modifying only the specific expectation that failed to match.

A second approach to the complexities of this crucial AI issue can be found in the analysis of expectation failure and the notion of *surprisingness* (Ortony & Partridge, 1987). Surprisingness (perhaps surprisingly) may be an important determinant in the selection of attentional focus (i.e., in this buzzing, blooming world just what few aspects should we concentrate on at any given time), and it may also be a cue for learning.

On the few occasions when these problems are addressed in the AI literature (e.g., Pfeifer & Nicholas, 1985), a cursory exploration of the phenomena is all that is presented. More usually, commentators point out the obvious problems in any simplistic equating of surprise with expectation failure (e.g., Dennett, 1984). Thus we are surprised when a piece of the ceiling falls on our head in a restaurant, even though it is unlikely that we were entertaining an expectation that this would not happen (i.e., there is surprise with no expectation failure). One might be tempted to say that the falling-ceiling event was surprising because it was very unlikely, but whatever the number on the next bank note that you examine, it will be an unlikely one. Nevertheless, you are most probably not going to be surprised by which one it actually turns out to be.

Suffice it to say that an important component of any AI system which involves learning mechanisms (rather than being **only** learning mechanisms) has been largely neglected.

GIVING CREDIT WHERE IT IS DUE

The credit assignment problem, by way of contrast, has been recognized as important and unsolved (in any general sense) for many years. In essence, when the behavior of a complex system is judged as good (or bad), and we wish to reinforce (or undermine) this behavior, how do we apportion the credit (or blame) among the many contributory mechanisms that generated the particular behavior observed?

The obvious answer for all those hardened program debuggers who are taking time out to read this book is: blood, sweat, and tears. In other words, there is no simple, known answer. Any attempt to tinker with the workings of a complex program requires intelligence, time, perserverance, and luck if it is to be successful on most occasions — clearly, requirements that are beyond the current state of the art in AI. The following section on unlearning can be viewed as the blame assignment problem.

Charniak, in his talk at TINLAP3, mentioned the temporal credit assignment problem in natural language processing: At what points in text processing do you feedback information — after each sentence, or each paragraph, or the next day? There is no obvious, correct answer. A related temporal credit assignment problem has been mentioned in connection with the question of: When has a CP-based network generated a result? (see "What's the Stopping Rule," a section in Chapter 3).

But there are AI systems that learn, and therefore they must have solved this credit assignment problem, must they not? The answer is that special cases of the problem can and have been solved. One common simplification is that, when good and bad system behavior is clearly and quickly detectable, the responsible module is also readily identifiable. Langley's (1983) puzzle-learning system is an example of this approach. Having found a solution path for the problem at hand (i.e., a path through the search space from an initial state to a goal state — classic SSSP) by means of exhaustive search, or whatever, the SAGE *(strategy acquisition governed by experimentation)* system tries to find a more efficient solution. The system learns to do better at solving the abstract puzzle. When a new operator is applied in an attempt to find a more efficient solution, if the resultant path strays from the known solution path, an instance of bad behavior is recorded, and the responsible production rule can be punished accordingly.

In fact, Langley and Simon (1981) propose that a solution to the credit assignment problem is one of the "basic principles of learning theory." They call this principle "causal attribution"; another three (in case you're curious) are:

> *Generation of Alternatives* — the ability to produce new behaviors.
> *Knowledge of Results* — the ability to distinguish the relative quality of results.
> *Hindsight* — the ability to modify behavior as a result of correct apportionment of credit (i.e., the causal attribution principle).

Returning one last time to Holland's (1986) research, a project that I have characterized as straddling the SSSP and the CP, we can see how he attempts to solve the credit assignment problem with his "bucket-brigade" algorithm. You may recall that his system was composed of primitive rules, each of which is associated with a "strength." The rule's strength is a kind of capital.

> The bucket-brigade algorithm treats each classifier [i.e., rule] as a kind of middleman in a complex economy, the strength of a classifier measuring its ability to turn a 'profit'. . . . Whenever a classifier wins a bidding competition, it initiates a transaction in which it pays out part of its strength to its suppliers and then receives similar payments from its customers. (Holland, 1986, p. 612)

Rule strength is only like link weight in a general sense, the details are quite different. Holland's system attempts to automatically give credit where it is due by insisting that each primitive module pays for and receives payment as soon as it has contributed usefully to the overall system function.

This approach appears to be somewhat novel in that credit is passed around inside the system (like money in a capitalist economy) in small "pieces" in a relatively continuous, constantly ongoing fashion. This is instead of waiting for some overall outcome at which time we face the difficult problem of dividing up a large sum of money between all contributory modules. But Holland's solution does seem to require much the same constraint as in Langley's system mentioned above — namely, that the behavior of a primitive module be immediately evaluable as good or bad for overall system performance. In Holland's system this issue is complicated by the genetic algorithm (described earlier) which modifies the population of rules, generating new ones and quietly disposing of unsuccessful old ones — the ultimate in blame assignment, capital punishment for bankruptcy!

Hinton (1986, extended abstract only) mentions the unsatisfactory nature of link-weight adjustment learning as directed by the back-propagation algorithm. Again it is a problem with learning formulated as distribution throughout the network of the final error in system output. He sees the challenge as

> to find ways of making gradient descent procedure scale properly [i.e., continue to operate in a reasonable time when applied to large-scale networks which means something greater than a few thousand connections] or to find ways of organizing multilayer unsupervised or semi-supervised procedures in which the units are "trying" to achieve some more local goal than minimizing the overall error of the network. (Hinton, 1986, p. 1149)

He sees the reinforcement paradigm (e.g., as in Holland's system), and in particular the one of Barto (1985), as a promising approach to these problems. This scheme allows modules to set up reinforcement schedules for other modules, thereby introducing in effect a hierarchical structuring into connectionist networks which, as Hinton notes, brings the CP a little closer to conventional AI.

UNLEARNING

Unlearning is not to be thought of in the same pleasant light as unbirthdays — quite the contrary. In fact, unlearning is such a distasteful idea for AI system builders that it is hardly thought of at all, and certainly it is not mentioned in polite AI texts. If the idea of machine learning is treated as a pariah by most AI researchers who are not explicitly *in* machine learning, then there is not a word in the English language to describe the degree to which unlearning has been abandoned and forgotten, for all the candidate descriptors suggest that the possibilities for unlearning have been entertained — it is not clear that they have, at least not in public. The idea of unlearning has been transported to a far-off place in the vain hope that, by the time civilization, in the form of AI research, gets there, machine learning will be well in hand (if not in programs everywhere), and unlearning will thus be more of a potentially tractable problem — time and knowledge will have softened its grim visage.

Nontrivial learning in an ill-structured domain, such as the empirical world, cannot always be correct. In a dynamic domain learned information will not always remain correct. So learning systems will need the ability to unlearn the things that were incorrectly learned, or have been rendered incorrect by the passage of time. This is an awkward problem for a number of reasons:

1. *Detection:* The fact (more likely, suspicion) that something erroneous has been learned need not be apparent (or even true) until long after the actual learning event.
2. *Analysis:* Even if we are sure that some learned behavior is incorrect, correct identification of the culprit component(s) in a complex structure can be a very difficult problem — in effect, the credit assignment problem once more.
3. *Modification:* Having identified the incorrectly learned feature, we must remove its adverse effects without destroying the complete structure that it might be embedded in.

These three problematic components of unlearning are also the sequence of events that constitute unlearning: detection of the presence of erroneous information; analysis of the problem; and finally modification of the system to remove the incorrect information. This is, of course, the age-old trilogy of conventional software debugging — detection of the bug is typically easy. In fact, it usually initiates the whole process (although the more insidious bugs are the ones that are not obviously present); then analysis of the problem is followed by redesign and reimplementation of some portion of the original algorithm.

In one of the few discussions on this topic that I have been able to unearth, Markovitch and Scott (1988) go one step further. They suggest that, apart from unlearning incorrect learned knowledge, there is also a need to forget some correct knowledge. They maintain that correct knowledge can have a negative value to the system (recall "the more you know . . ." adage). "The view is taken that learning and forgetting are complementary processess which construct and maintain useful representations of experience"(Markovitch & Scott, 1988, p. 459). They introduce a notion of the value of knowledge as a metric to use in forming judgments about forgetting it. The four attributes which influence value are:

1. *Relevance:* lack of relevance to future problem solving implies lack of value;
2. *Correctness:* (not a difficult attribute) roughly, correctness leads to high value, and incorrectness doesn't;
3. *Memory requirements:* more space, less value is the general idea here (interestingly, they comment that the storage capacity of the brain appears to be so vast that this attribute may not place any real limitation on human learning processes);
4. *Influence on search time:* more time, less value is the relationship — observance of this stricture could do much to mitigate the worst effects of "the more you know . . ." syndrome.

Hayes-Roth, Waterman, and Lenat (1983) suggest, and give examples of, the use of metaknowledge (knowledge about the domain-specific knowledge of their expert systems) for identifying incorrect rules learned from an expert. The system's metaknowledge brings suspicious rules (such as ones in which the antecedent condition can never be satisfied) to the attention of the knowledge engineer. If the knowledge base is truly a modular collection of such rules, removal or modification of the erroneous piece of knowledge is a relatively simple process.

This example raises two points that we should note:

1. Modularity is an invaluable aid here as it is in all aspects of the management of complexity — and unlearning in complex systems is no exception.
2. Metaknowledge is another but far less developed supporting concept, and one that has arisen in the AI domain.

Langley (1983) simplifies the above-listed three problems of "unlearning" by setting up his system such that the correctness of a proposed addition will be known immediately, and it can thus be removed if it is incorrect. But, in general, we cannot expect situations with the luxury of immediate assessment.

It is instructive to examine what we know of the human solution to this unlearning problem. A first point to note is that humans are not particularly good at one-trial learning — we generally require repetition before we learn something. This is a difference between humans and machines that is often touted as part of an argument that computers can eventually be expected to surpass humans in intelligent abilities. But from our current viewpoint there may be an advantage in resistance to one-trial learning: If, before we learn it, we require a certain number of repetitions of an event, there is a chance to assess its correctness before a full commitment to learn it is made.

Studies of skill acquisition definitely suggest a two-stage learning process at least. In the first stage we tentatively learn a new skill, and only when this tentative learning is confirmed as correct by repeated use is the skill knowledge 'compiled' into a more efficient, but less readily modifiable form. Anderson (1982, p. 369) proposes such a model of skill learning: "a declarative stage in which facts about the skill domain are interpreted and a procedural stage in which domain knowledge is directly embodied in procedures for performing the skill."

The analogy with the tradeoffs between interpreting and compiling computer programs is obvious and instructive. Efficency of system performance is enhanced by translating high-level language programs (e.g., in FORTRAN, LISP, or PROLOG) to a language that reflects the machine architecture rather than human conceptualizations of the problems that the system is designed to address. Thus most programs are first compiled (this translation process) and then executed (the computation that the program specifies is performed). But all human analysis and system modification typically proceeds in terms of the high-level language representation.

Anderson (1986, p. 291) describes his ACT learning mechanisms of knowledge compilation; there are two components: "composition," which operates by collapsing multiple productions into a single production; and "proceduralization," which operates by building into productions information that previously had to be retrieved from long-term memory (compare Mostow's 'operationalization' problem described earlier).

From a practical point of view for work within the symbolic paradigm of AI, the implication is that learned information should be thoroughly tested in some high-level form before it is compiled into the system. In the subsymbolic paradigm, it is not at all clear to me where unlearning fits in. Learning itself is a gradual process of link weight adjustment. Thus there is typically no identifiable substructure to remove to effect the necessary unlearning. Unlearning in connectionist networks would presumably be a further gradual process of link-weight adjustment in which correct behaviors are gradually reinforced to the point where the incorrect behavior is overwhelmed — an inexorable march of reinforced correctness, the forces of good triumphing over the forces of evil, just as they should be.

This view of unlearning fits well (at least in a general sense) with the interference theories of forgetting in psychology: Newly learned information interferes with the things that we already know and so messes up our ability to recall certain things that we once had mastered. One striking difference between the conceptions of unlearning within the two major AI paradigms is that within the SSSP symbolic chunks are excised when they are perceived to be erroneous (as a result of imperfect learning or of changing circumstances). In the connectionist paradigm there is a continual loss of knowledge (more precisely, loss of ability to recall the knowledge) as the inevitable result of learning. There is no active unlearning component initiated by the detection of errors.

In fact, it's not the differences that need pointing out; my task is perhaps to argue for the similarities. How is a continual and somewhat unfocused (certainly not focused on specific errors) degradation of our ability to remember things to be equated with the intermittent identification and removal of troublesome memories?

The similarity is more obvious if we assume that, within the CP, there is a continual reinforcement of correct behavior as well as a continual degradation of all knowledge. Thus, the combined result will be the loss of unreinforced knowledge which is likely to be both unimportant and invalid information. In the long term, erroneous knowledge is unlearned in both paradigms, but in the SSSP it requires initiation of a specific set of actions, whereas in the CP it is a continuous phenomenon integrated with the process of learning. But all is not sweetness and light for CP enthusiasts, not even with respect to this point. Distributed representations in CP-based systems tend to suffer old-memory lapses as new knowledge is added, even if all of the learned knowledge is both relevant and useful (a simple example can be found in the work of Touretzky & Hinton, 1986, described in Chapter 6).

And lest I leave you with the impression that, as far as machine learning is concerned, the heuristic hocus-pocus of the SSSP is on the way out and about to be supplanted by a superior paradigm, I must draw you attention to the small, but growing, domain of formally based, robust SSSP-based theories. I refer to Valiant's (1984) "theory of the learnable" and to the subsequent extensions and independent developments, many of which are summarized by Kearns et al. (1987). The theoretical results address the important subproblems such as:

convergence — the relationship between successive examples and a correct generalization;

feasibility — a notion that is attached to the previous one, and addresses the time needed for convergence;

approximation — a formalization of the notion of something less than a totally correct generalization.

Etzioni (1988, p. 416) claims to show "how to take virtually any learning algorithm and turn it into one which is accurate and reliable to an arbitrary degree." He appends a filter to the selected algorithm, and the filter only lets through those generalizations that meet the standards set. So all of the meat is in the filter, as it were. The products of the filtered learner are *probably approximately correct* — a wonderful phrase, and one that is used to name an important subsubfield, the PAC learners. Of course, as with all formal approaches, the results are meaningful only if the basic assumptions hold true, and in many cases they are not even a good approximation to reality. Nevertheless, this disciplined approach to machine learning, which brings in the powerful notions of computational feasibility from computer science, provides a valuable sounding board for the possibilities of scaling up the small-scale heuristic models that are more characteristic of this AI domain.

So much for machine learning. Clearly, there is a need for learning mechanisms in most AI projects, but the state of the art in machine learning is currently so primitive that adding machine learning to say vision or natural language projects would typically do no more than compound the problems. Hence, machine learning is something of a subdomain apart and will remain so for quite some time.

And finally, if you've still not had enough after ploughing through this fat chapter, there are other places to go to gorge yourself on machine learning. There are three books of collected papers (Michalski, Carbonell, & Mitchell, 1983-1986; Michalski & Kodratoff, 1989), two volumes of the proceedings of the international workshops (Irvine, 1987; and Ann Arbor, 1988, by which time it was an annual conference), the *Journal of Machine Learning* (launched in 1986), and a number of single-author books, such as Kodratoff (1988), which is a comprehensive survey, formally based and full of detailed examples, of SSSP-based strategies. A collection edited by Forsyth (1989) covers a broader base, but is generally not so detailed. Finally, a special issue of the journal *Artificial Intelligence* (1989, vol. 40) is devoted to the subject of machine learning.

10

Foundations of AI: Can We Find Any?

Some believe that they know the answer to AI's problems: it's logic. The next step for them is to identify the fundamental questions.

after Schank

As you will be only too well aware, if you've read this far in anything short of a totally cavalier manner, AI is a contentious topic. Scorn or laughter is the not-uncommon response of practitioners in related disciplines when asked for a considered opinion on AI. And even more confusingly, responses that are not dissimilar often emanate from people within AI when asked about another AI subdomain. So what is AI — a science, but perhaps not a hard science; a nonhomogeneous collection of computational approaches to other subjects, not a discipline in its own right at all; or just a hackers' paradise in which flashy results can be obtained by sheer persistence at the keyboard, but little of long-term merit seems to accrue? A second set of issues, and perhaps a more useful line of attack on the basic problems, concerns the criteria by which AI research work is to be judged. The accumulation of formal abstractions appears to be at the core of all respectable sciences, a process that allows claims to be independently tested by repetition of experiments in contexts where the supposedly nonsignificant details will be different. What are the criteria for good AI research? McCarthy (1990), in his presidential address to the AAAI, wrote on just this topic, but he could do little more than complain that solid criteria for assessment of research are sadly lacking within AI.

When we talk of experiments in AI, we mean the writing and running of programs. AI models are computer programs. But programs are also formal linguistic statements. Hence, the urge in some sectors to associate programs very closely with theories. Can a program be a theory and a model at one and the same time? And can it be a useful theory, one that will contribute to the furtherance of AI as science? Programs, as I argued way back in the beginning of this book, are central to AI, but they play no simple, straightforward and well-accepted role. They are multifaceted objects; this multiplicity of viewpoints is gloriously used, abused, and confused in AI.

Pencil-and-paper theories in AI are not dismissed out of hand, at least not always. A sketch of a possible implementation, the hopeware model, is a definite plus, but it is not enough. Everyone knows that the real crunch comes when you try to build the program, an implementation of the theory. Programs are the currency of AI; they buy recognition and success. They are the accepted currency (despite some significant pockets of resistence), but great debate surrounds the question of exactly why this should be true.

FOUNDATIONS: WHY DIG FOR THEM?

Having introduced the scope of the foundations of AI from my perspective, I can now reveal my motivation for yet another oddish chapter for an introductory AI book.

Even the least perceptive reader will have caught my feelings of misgiving about much of AI by now, I think. Nine chapters of my captious commentary on all that's good and true and famous in AI should leave you in no doubt that I believe that the field is saturated with severe problems. But that's okay; as long as we can identify them and start to do something about them, none are obviously insuperable, in my opinion. Others more eminent than I beg to differ. No, they insist on differing; we'll deal with them later. In part, it's the existence of all the problems that make AI so exciting. Science is all about problem solving, isn't it? But AI has more than its fair share of metaproblems, problems that transcend the issues of knowledge representation, machine learning, etc. And these meta- or foundational problems ought to be addressed along with, if not before, the everyday problems of AI. (I realize that my terminology has diverged awkwardly here. So before my credibility is stretched too painfully, note that, above or below, however it is that you visualize these problems, they are not on the same level as the basic problems that AI projects typically address.) Hence, I make no apologies for giving over a whole chapter of this book, contrary to accepted practice, to a discussion of the nonbasic, the foundational problems of AI.

I have divided my review of foundational issues into three classes:

1. *Formal foundations:* if AI is ever to become a respectably hard science, then a firm, formal basis is needed. Logic, with its close associations with right and rational human thought, has always been fancied as the formal tool for putting AI on a firm foundation. We shall look at the various species of logic that either have or hope to have major roles in AI, and we shall look at the types of role they play. And, of course, throughout the logical mystery tour I'll be taking my usual cheap shots, but backed up by some big guns who also have some

reservations about the seemingly self-evident appropriateness of logic in AI.

2. *Methodological foundations:* as mentioned several times, programs are central to AI, but their exact role is hotly debated. Is a program an experiment, a model, a theoretical statement, or something else? And, dependent upon the role that one ascribes to the program, somewhat different strategies are required for dealing effectively with this complex formal object. These are the methodological issues at the foundations of AI.

3. *Philosophical foundations:* as usual, the philosophers have lots to say about AI (as well as everything else). Some weigh in for it, and others are solidly against it, denying even the possibility of AI either in toto or, more cautiously, just hamstringing the idea in its traditional manifestations. The former group offer helpful and encouraging arguments that AI is indeed possible, thus providing a foundation for belief in what the future may hold if we just keep at it. The total nihilists of the latter group argue that there are no foundations for AI. The truth of this assertion would be nice to know. If it's not false, the sooner we are apprised of this information the better, for then we can forget about buying a LISP machine, give up trying to learn PROLOG, and turn our attention to something real. The semidetractor group tend to demolish the basis for the SSSP (and even the CP, now that it has been around long enough for thorough analysis). They leave the AI enthusiast with the rubble of the current wisdom but also with the hope that there might be another way to build.

FORMAL FOUNDATIONS

Now is the time to finally sort out this logic business which has been dogging us throughout the length and breadth of this book. We opened up on the logical basis for AI with Chandrasekaran's critique of the accepted primacy of logic when we considered logical abstraction theories in Chapter 1. The usefulness of the much-admired epistemic–heuristic distinction was called into question as part of the attack on logic as a language for characterizing and analyzing what an intelligent agent knows. Use of logic for representing and for inferencing from knowledge was also briefly assailed. This latter attack was relaunched in Chapter 5 as a diversion from the main assault on the foundations of current expert systems technology. And immediately prior to this, in Chapter 4, we looked at PROLOG, the closest thing we currently have to a fully mechanized logic.

So what is "logic"? The word inevitably conjures up respect in scientific circles. It is generally taken to be a good thing until it is proven otherwise. It is only the brave or the foolhardy who attempt to make a case against it, for to do so is tantamount to profanity for which the blaspheming wretch can fully expect to be blackballed when his or her name next comes up for membership to the National Academy of Sciences. In the words of Gilbert Ryle (1949, p. 27), what we are up against is "the intellectualist doctrine which tries to define intelligence in terms of the apprehension of truths, instead of the apprehension of truth in terms of intelligence" — i.e., the logicists are putting the inference before the axioms, you might say.

Most dictionaries inform us that logic is the science of reasoning, which is not the usual meaning of the word in AI circles, but it is clearly one of the underlying implications that gives this word its power — the intrinsic rightness and scientificality of the employment of logic within a discipline. George Boole, for example, with his celebrated but misnamed *Laws of Thought* (1854), is illustrative of this historical trend.

Logic in AI generally means a formal language. More precisely, it usually means a specific formal language—namely, the first order predicate calculus (a bit of a mouthful, hence, the tendency to just say "logic"). When the word *logic* is used in a more general sense, it refers to a class of formal languages in which the interest centers on the truth or falsity of statements in the language {a truth-based semantics}, and the further inferences that can be drawn from a body of statements in the language are controlled by mechanisms that ensure the truth of these derived statements {truth-preserving transformations are the inference mechanisms}.

So the formal language with the daunting four-word name, which contracts (as they always do) to one of the socially acceptable four-letter words, i.e., FOPC (clearly four letters, but not much of a word, I admit), is usually the beast in question, under consideration, or whatever, when the word *logic* is being bandied about. Interestingly, if it's just a matter of introducing a formal language into the game, then why choose a logical one? After all, AI, with its close associations with computer science, is plagued with formal languages already, the machine-executable ones, the programming languages. But programming languages, having as they do to run on actual computing machines, are severely cluttered with incidental paraphernalia (e.g., declarations of specific data structures, and considerations dictated by the sequential nature of the Turing-von-Neumann computing engine). The desire is for a clean and simple, formally defined notation, with expressive power that is appropriate for characterizing intelligent reasoning and for representing the necessary knowledge upon which such reasoning can be based. The FOPC is the popular choice; this is sometimes blamed on Hayes's (1979) influential *Naive Physics Manifesto,* in which he proposed that an all-out effort should be mounted to formalize common-sense knowledge using first-order logic. It is time to sketch it out. Gruesome details can no longer be avoided. In fact I think that I have have done very well to relegate the FOPC to this late stage in the book, almost the epilog.

A DISINTERESTED USER'S GUIDE TO THE FOPC

Actually my accomplishment of putting off dealing with the FOPC until now is not quite as significant as my boasting would lead the gullible reader to believe. I sneaked in bits and pieces in Chapter 4 when we dipped into the mysteries of PROLOG which is a machine-executable travesty of the FOPC. I exaggerate a little, but if you're not realizing this by now, this is not your sort of AI book. It would be a pity to discover such a fact at this late juncture, but nevertheless preferable to never knowing. This could be an example of when the maxim (or heuristic) "Better late than never" is spot on.

Returning to the task at hand: in addition to the PROLOG stuff, the very next chapter laid out the bones of the FOPC in the guise of the basic assumptions of expert systems technology. In fact, I believe that no punches were pulled, and I even referred to modus ponens once, but twice in one book is quite enough; I'll not mention it again.

Not surprisingly, the basic elements of the FOPC are predicates, relationships such as COLOR_OF and the like. And for such relationships to be useful, there must be things around for them to relate; these things are terms such as BOX and BLUE. A predicate associated with the correct number of appropriate terms gives us an atomic formula of the FOPC, e.g. (COLOR_OF BOX BLUE), which is either TRUE or FALSE. {I use upper-case characters to distinguish the FOPC values from the everyday words *true* and *false*.} And that is all we can say about its meaning in the formalism defined by the FOPC. You and I may conjure up all sorts of further images, meanings, and implications, such as a solid, cubic object painted blue, but they have absolutely no status within the FOPC. You may recall the ELIZA syndrome in Chapter 1, and our discussion of HOBBITS versus Hobbits in Chapter 6. Well, here is the same old problem; it is exploited shamelessly by the advocates of logic. I can almost hear the advocates of logic grinding their axioms here. "Interpretations tie logic symbols to worlds" (Winston, 1984, p. 216), they will say, just as Winston did in his AI text. He said more (p. 216, author's emphasis): "An *interpretation* is a full accounting of the correspondence between objects and object-symbols, between relations and predicates." What can this sort of assertion mean? If I tell you that my predicate COLOR_OF is to be interpreted as the normal relation "color of," and that my object symbol BLUE is to be interpreted as the color blue, is that a "full accounting of the necessary correspondence"? If it isn't, then what exactly would be? And remember that we are currently operating in high-precision, definitional mode — that's the whole point of the logic-based approach, isn't it? If it is "a full accounting" (or even something exceeding a totally empty one), what can we conclude? That there are also atomic formulae to capture most (some? all?) of the other implications of the 'color of' relation and of the color blue? More likely, the defense is that the FOPC formula represented only one aspect of real-world phenomena that are known to be of great depth and subtlety. Which particular aspect is it, then? How is it possible to give "a full accounting" of the one facet of the "color of" relation which we have so precisely captured in our atomic formula? I leave this question for the reader to work on; it will probably make a fine retirement project. Bertie Russell was more honest, but then he wasn't writing an introductory AI text; he wrote that "mathematics gets its appearance of certainty from not saying what it is talking about." I'm sure that he would have been happy to substitute *logic* for *mathematics* if asked politely.

Moving right along, the FOPC also provides us with a few operators for building more interesting structures than these atomic formulae. The operators {or logical connectives}, AND and OR, along with NOT, have similarly seductive properties: Their well-defined meaning within the FOPC does not match too closely with our everyday usage of these words, despite appearences.

Thus the use of the operator NOT in front of an atomic formula gives us a negated atomic formula. We now know that it is structurally acceptable to put a NOT in front of an atomic formula. That's the syntax taken care of, but what is the meaning of a negated atomic formula? Perhaps you're surprised that I should bother to ask this question. The answer is obvious. Negation is denial: NOT (atomic formula) is FALSE when the atomic formula has the value TRUE, and the complete expression is TRUE when the atomic formula has the value FALSE (the meaning of atomic formulae is limited to TRUE or FALSE, you may recall). And you would be right, but, like Columbus, you would be right for the wrong reasons. The meaning of prefacing an atomic formula with NOT is whatever the semantics of the FOPC defines it to be; it is not what you expect it to be (although in this case you were lucky — expectation and formal definition coincide). The meaning of NOT {the formal semantic definition} is given by a truth table. In fact it is given by the following truth table:

atomic formula	TRUE	FALSE
NOT atomic formula	FALSE	TRUE

I won't bore you with the formal semantic definitions of AND and OR unless I'm forced into it by my subsequent examples.

I have omitted one operator that is both interesting and important in AI; it is called *implication*, and I'll illustrate it thus: →. So now we can construct quite interesting statements in the FOPC. Here's one:

(TODAY FRIDAY) → (TOMORROW SATURDAY)

{Gruesome detail note: when I should actually write something "has the value TRUE", I'm going to be predictably slack and write something "is TRUE". The proper phraseology emphasizes the noncorrespondence between the everyday concept "true" and one of the two values that the FOPC works with, i.e., TRUE; a similar argument goes for the other one as well — just in case you were wondering. This general point is not worth the pain of the necessary pedanticism. Hence, I shall not use it.}

The FOPC statement above reads: if (TODAY FRIDAY) is TRUE, then (TOMORROW SATURDAY) is also TRUE. So this statement {or well-formed formula; WFF for short, as in bark like a dog} if TRUE in the FOPC-world of current interest (remember that its apparent status in the world that you and I inhabit is immaterial) will allow us to infer with certainty that (TOMORROW SATURDAY) is TRUE once we can be sure that (TODAY FRIDAY) is TRUE. This is, of course, a very handy thing to be able to do. Where would expert systems technology be without it?

That's pretty straightforward. But what happens if (TODAY FRIDAY) is FALSE? Surely (TOMORROW SATURDAY) is also FALSE, if the implication as a whole is TRUE? Clearly, if today is not Friday, then tomorrow can't be Saturday, can it? Maybe and yes, respectively, are the answers to these questions. Intelligent reasoning has led us astray again. I'll come clean and define the meaning of → in the FOPC.

atomic formula 1	TRUE	FALSE	TRUE	FALSE
atomic formula 2	TRUE	TRUE	FALSE	FALSE
atomic formula 1→atomic formula 2	TRUE	TRUE	FALSE	TRUE

"So that's the precise semantic definition," you might be saying to yourself if you've latched on to both the jargon and the spirit of logic. More likely, you're none the wiser, so let me elaborate.

The first column is a breeze: If atomic formula 1 is TRUE and atomic formula 2 is TRUE, then the statement that atomic formula 1 implies atomic formula 2 is also TRUE. The third column is also fairly close to casual expectation: If atomic formula 1 is TRUE but atomic formula 2 is FALSE, then the statement as a whole is FALSE. The implication doesn't hold.

The tricky options are captured in the second and fourth columns. The problem arises when atomic formula 1 is FALSE. In this case the statement as a whole is TRUE whatever the meaning of atomic formula 2 (and there's only two possible meanings in the FOPC — TRUE or FALSE). In these two cases the implication as a whole is sort of vacuously TRUE. If atomic formula 1 is FALSE, then we can't infer anything definite about atomic formula 2, or alternatively, it is TRUE to infer anything about it. Later in this chapter we'll see a "proof" of the impossibility of AI that falls foul of this logical tripwire.

This is just one simple example of the many clashes between meanings in the FOPC and meanings in casual common-sense reasoning which is intelligent reasoning, I would argue (as many others have done before me; see, for example, Braine, 1978, for a psychologically based review of the "the natural logic of reasoning and standard logic"). Common-sense reasoning may not be intellectual reasoning, but it is close to the reasoning used in everyday intelligent activities. So the case for the FOPC as the foundation for a science of AI is obviously not an open and shut one. It is certainly a well-defined, precise notation, but is it appropriate as a model of intelligent reasoning? The strongest answer that can realistically be given is "maybe." And many advocates of logic would agree with me here. A prime motivation for endeavoring to employ the FOPC as the foundational notation of AI has more to do with the fact that, as a simple logic, it is very well understood, than it has to do with any breadth of inherent appropriateness in the nature of the FOPC.

There is also a belief that the more powerful logics are reducible to a first-order scheme, so why not just stay with a first-order system? If you find yourself a agonizing over such a belief, then simply remind yourself that what is true in principle is often impossible in practice. In fact, use of the "in principle" disclaimer is usually indicative of practical impossibility. Thus a description of the weather is reducible to a large (no, very large) statement in terms of intermolecular interactions, in principle. In practice, don't try it.

So what are these advocates of logic advocating, if it's not the FOPC? They are rooting for one or other of the more powerful schemes of logic. The next question must be: If more powerful logics are around, how come so many people are still messing about with a notation as limited and seemingly inappropriate as the FOPC? The answer is that all of the more powerful logics have severe problems. They are not yet completely formalized and understood. The employment of one of the significantly more powerful logics all too quickly gives rise to unforeseen and unmanageable situations. And, of course, it was precisely to avoid this type of situation that we turned to logic in the first place.

We can look at a few of the attempts to avoid the more obvious limitations of the FOPC as a foundational notation for AI. Thus you can get a glimpse of more powerful schemes while at the same time allowing me to expose you to a bit more of the FOPC; thereby I can bolster my claim to have provided an introduction to the FOPC which is de rigueur for all worthwhile introductions to AI (one can't expect to flout every convention and still get published).

So far the only objects that our predicates have been given an opportunity to relate to have been constants (rather than variables), and, hence, our atomic formulae have been limited to statements of specific fact, such as (TODAY FRIDAY) or (COLOR_OF BOX BLUE). The FOPC would be good deal more powerful if we could construct more general statements, and indeed we can. Variables as well as constants can be the arguments to predicates {i.e., terms can also be variables}. Secure in this new piece of FOPC knowledge, I might venture the following statement:

(COLOR_OF x BLUE)

where "x" is the name of a variable. But what could it mean? TRUE or FALSE are the only possibilities, but which is it? Well, it all depends on the value bound to "x." In this statement "x" is a "free variable" and the statement has no meaning until "x" is given a value. In the FOPC, "x" can only be given {bound to} a constant value; "x" cannot take a predicate as its value. This restriction accounts for part of the baggage in the name of this logic: The words "First Order" refer to this limitation on the values of variable terms.

If you'll bear with me just a little longer, we can look at two more FOPC symbols and then wash our hands of predicates and logical connectives. It is possible to put two sorts of restriction on the range of values which can be bound to a variable and result in a TRUE statement. {These are the two quantifiers, the existential and the universal, for those of you who are still not sated with gruesome detail. Up until now we have been messing about with the propositional calculus. It is the addition of these quantifiers that really shoves us into the world of the FOPC.} One symbol allows us to say that there exists some value for a variable for which the overall statement will be true. The usual symbol is a capital "E" (as shown) but written backwards. As my keyboard is deficient in this respect, I'll use the word EXISTS. So here's a sample of this type of statement:

EXISTS x (COLOR_OF x BLUE)

This reads: There exists a value (at least one, maybe more) for "x" which makes (COLOR_OF x BLUE) TRUE. This sort of thing is often very nice to know. But unfortunately, it is frequently much more important to know exactly which value this is.

The other symbol that I promised to burden you with allows us to say that, for all values of some variable, the associated statement is TRUE — not much of a limitation, I admit. The symbol used in this case is a capital "A," not backwards — for how could we tell — but upside down. Again the limitations of my logic-resistant keyboard force me into yet another ad hoc solution; I'll use the pseudo word FORALL. Here's an example:

FORALL x (COLOR_OF x BLUE)

At this late stage in my cursory tutorial, I'll leave you to interpret this statement in the FOPC. I'm sorely tempted to give you a hint and say that, in the particular FOPC subworld for which this statement is TRUE, the message in that old song about coloring things blue has been taken to extremes. But, of course, to succumb to this temptation would be to succumb to the ELIZA syndrome. So I'll resist giving it out as an official hint.

THE CURSE OF NONMONOTONICITY

The FOPC is a monotonic logic which is quite different from a monotonous logic but is similarly unhelpful as a characteristic of the calculus. In an FOPC subworld, everything that is TRUE, either given at the start {the axioms} or subsequently found to be TRUE as a result of logical deduction {the theorems}, will always be TRUE. If it's TRUE today, then it will be TRUE tomorrow. This is, of course, very comforting to know, but it is also difficult to reconcile with many real-world situations. This is the limitation of monotonicity.

The curse of nonmonotonicity is, in fact, a general AI problem with a scope that stretches far beyond the bounds of logic. It rears its unattractive face whenever the problem solving centers on reducing some measure of difference between what you have (e.g., the current state in the SSSP, or the current level of performance in machine learning) and what you want to obtain (e.g., a goal state, or some optimum level of performance, respectively). Distance, or difference measures that will continually decrease, and never increase, are very hard to find. From a logic-based perspective, we would like the collection of known truths (or, more accurately, known TRUEs) to continually increase in size; we don't want to have to abandon any.

As an aside, but a relevant one, we might note that my statement about TRUE today then TRUE tomorrow hides yet another awkward feature of the FOPC. In actuality, the concept of time has no place in the FOPC. An FOPC subworld is a timeless world. Thus notions of "before" and "after," which are so important in the world which intelligences actually inhabit, must be glossed over or finessed in an FOPC description of our world. This limitation has given rise to research in temporal logics — logical notations that can accommodate some aspects of time and temporal sequences of events (e.g., D. McDermott, 1982).

But back to the problem posed by the monotonicity of the FOPC: It seems to me (and I'm not alone) that a central feature of the world is that things change; it is nonmonotonic. And thus a central feature of intelligence is that it can accommodate the dynamics of the world. It appears that an intelligent agent must be prepared to accept new knowledge which is likely to invalidate some other aspects of its knowledge; such changes in the truth value (i.e., TRUE to FALSE and vice versa) of elements of knowledge is a phenomenon that lies outside the compass of monotonic logic. {For those readers with a taste for fine detail, Rankin (1988) provides it in his exposition of the nature of nonmonotonic reasoning and its implications for the use of logics in AI.} Machine learning is the AI subfield that addresses this problem head on. You may remember that I argued for the importance of machine learning as a research topic on the road to AI (turn back to Chapter 9 if this memory has faded and you want to refresh it).

General recognition of the severity of this monotonicity limitation for a logic that is to provide a foundation for AI has led to extensive research into the possibilities for nonmonotonic logics. John McCarthy, a central figure in AI from the very beginning and always a champion of the case for logical foundations, has turned his attention to the search for suitable and manageable nonmonotonic logics (see McCarthy, 1980). Israel (1980, p. 99) suggests that a significant portion of the "wonderfully impressive work involved in its [i.e., nonmonotonic logic's] development is based on a confusion of proof-theoretic with epistemological issues." This can be translated, I think, into plain English as a misguided search for nonmonotonic logics based on the confusion of the proper role of logic, which is the specification of valid rules of inference, with the related but separate issue of what knowledge the inferencer has available at any given time {i.e., epistemological issues}. He is, incidentally, not attacking McCarthy's view (in fact he explicitly endorses McCarthy, 1977) but those of McDermott and Doyle (1980), and of Reiter (1980). Israel's claim about the possibility of treating logic and knowledge as independent problems first arose in Chapter 8, where it was part of the case for logic-based semantics for natural language. It was a hotly disputed claim then; it is not clear that it is any less contentious two chapters later.

This is probably the right place to say something about "the frame problem" in AI. As described by McCarthy and Hayes (1969) it is the problem of representing facts that change as well as those that do not. Clearly, the frame problem is just another manifestation of the essential mismatch between classical logic as a descriptive formalism and the nonmonotonicity of the world to be described. A number of commentators have suggested at least partial solutions to this problem (e.g., Eshgi, 1987), and Dennett (1984) provides a recent, philosophy-based approach to it. He suggests that, although the frame problem was "discovered" as a problem in AI, it does in fact follow from traditional philosophical principles. Brown (1987) has edited the proceedings of a conference devoted to the frame problem.

Somewhat aside but apropos of the role of logic in AI, there is a curious bifurcation of commitments at the very root of AI. John McCarthy and Marvin Minsky, two of AI's founding fathers, whose mutually supportive interests in AI started in their graduate student days and carried on into the early years in which AI was established as a subject, now epitomize the extreme positions on the role of logic in AI.

"John McCarthy," as Schank so succinctly once put it with typical crude precision, "doesn't know what the questions that AI researchers should seek to answer are, but he knows the answer. It's logic." McCarthy has been committed to devising a system of logic that will be powerful enough to support a mechanism for intelligent reasoning (common-sense knowledge is McCarthy's preferred term). He is the first to admit that he has not had great success, but sees the alternative approach, heuristic ad hoc-ery, as doomed to failure in the long run. "I still think that this approach [the formalization of common-sense knowledge] is likely to succeed sooner than the others I know about, although I think there are still major conceptual difficulties to be overcome" (McCarthy, 1986, p. 31). He then sums up the essential challenge for logic in AI: "The largest single need is to formalize more domains of common-sense knowledge in epistemologically adequate, ambiguity tolerant, elaboration tolerant, and heuristically adequate ways." I'll leave the translation of this call to axioms as an exercise for the reader (use of a dictionary is permitted). McCarthy is, of course, far from alone in his belief in the utility of logic for AI. Kowalski, the high priest of logic programming, has made some very strong statements about the role of logic. For example, "There is only one language suitable for expressing information . . . and that is first-order predicate logic" (Kowalski, 1980, quoted by Leith, 1988, p. 92) — strong stuff, and there's more to follow, but it's probably meant to be diluted before use.

Marvin Minsky, on the other hand, has a firm belief that logic is not the way to go. Thus Minsky (1983, p. 174) states: "I am inclined to doubt that anything even resembling formal logic could be a good model for human reasoning." And in an appendix to an earlier paper (Minsky, 1981), he provides a detailed critique of the inadequacies of logic as a vehicle to carry the AI enterprise.

Minsky's opposition stems from two sources: First, he considers it premature to attempt to lay out a formal framework for a discipline which is still in a state of flux in regards to its content and methodology; and second, he believes that the current list of candidates for the requisite formalism (primarily the FOPC and minor variants) are all so patently inadequate, even when viewed from our current position of ignorance, that it would be fruitless to attempt to build on any of them. His case against the rush to formalize because we have so little knowledge of what exactly we should be trying to specify precisely was stated in his Turing Lecture entitled "Form and Content in Computer Science" (Minsky, 1970). He argues that a preoccupation with formalization will impede development in a subject like AI, where we may have quite a lot in the way of specific knowledge about certain aspects of the discipline (i.e., AI is rich in content) but are sadly lacking in general principles (i.e., AI lacks form).

In the critical appendix mentioned above, he provides a four-point summary of his case:

(1) "Logical" reasoning is not flexible enough to serve as a basis for thinking: I prefer to think of it as a collection of heuristic methods, effective only when applied to starkly simplified schematic plans. The Consistency that Logic absolutely demands is not otherwise usually available — *and probably not even desirable!* — because consistent systems are likely to be too weak.

(2) I doubt the feasibility of representing ordinary knowledge effectively in the form of many small, independently true propositions.

(3) The general strategy of complete separation of specific knowledge from general rules of inference is much too radical. We need more direct ways for linking fragments of knowledge to advice about *how* they are to be used.

(4) It was long believed that it was crucial to make all knowledge accessible to deduction in the form of declarative statements; but this seems less urgent as we learn ways to manipulate structural and procedural descriptions. (Minsky, 1981, pp. 127–128, authors' emphasis)

Wilks (1987b) attacks the use of logic (in the guise of formal semantics) as the foundational framework in natural language processing. His argument was summarized back in its proper place, i.e., in Chapter 8.

The most recent blitz on the assumption that the foundation of AI should be logic is in the shriving of McDermott (1986) — a fascinating "about face." McDermott claims that the coup de grace is delivered to the logicist program by the realization that "there is an unspoken premiss

[sic] in the argument that a significant amount of thought is deductive" (p. 3). He means "deductive" in the narrow logical sense of, if P implies Q, and P is TRUE, then we can deduce that Q is TRUE. He is not referring to something more like the swashbuckling deductive style of Sherlock Holmes. Anyway, McDermott argues that this premise is false. He lists "all the known defences of logicism, and argue[s] that they all fail" (p. 5).

Ginsberg (1987) has edited a collection of readings on nonmonotonic reasoning which provides a useful survey of this area.

LOGICAL ODDS AND ENDS

Elsewhere I've drawn your attention to the limitation posed by the "closed world assumption" in logic (see Chapter 6 if your neural trace of this problem has been obliterated by subsequent input and you would like to reinstate the memory once more). Essentially, the awkward assumption is that the given description of a logic world is complete; everything relevant is stated. There is a true AI story that illustrates this general issue. This particular story is truer than most; certainly, I didn't fabricate it. McCarthy (1980) is the source; if that doesn't qualify it for "true," or perhaps TRUE, status, then I don't know what does.

TRUE AI STORY: 10.1 It is not a closed world after all

There is a classical AI problem (one of the "bad" ones; see Chapter 3) which the GPS program used to solve repeatedly and with unerring accuracy back in the bad old days of AI. It is called the missionaries and cannibals problem. McCarthy tells it as follows:

Three missionaries and three cannibals come to a river. A rowboat that seats two is available. If the cannibals ever outnumber the missionaries on either bank of the river, the missionaries will be eaten. How shall they cross the river?

Obviously the puzzler is expected to devise a strategy of rowing the boat back and forth that gets them all across and avoids disaster . . .

Imagine giving someone the problem, and after he puzzles for a while, he suggests going upstream half a mile and crossing on a bridge. "What bridge?" you say. "No bridge is mentioned in the statement of the problem." And this dunce replies, "Well, they don't say there isn't a bridge." You look at the English and even at the translation of the English into first-order logic, and you must admit that "they don't say" there is no bridge. So you modify the problem to exclude bridges and pose it again, and the dunce proposes a helicopter, and after you exclude that, he proposes a winged horse or that the others hang onto the outside of the boat while two row.

You now see that, while a dunce, he is an inventive dunce. Despairing of getting him to accept the problem in the proper puzzler's spirit, you tell him the solution. To your further annoyance, he attacks your solution on the grounds that the boat might have a leak or lack oars. After you rectify that omission from the statement of the problem, he suggests that a sea monster may swim up the river and may swallow the boat. Again you are frustrated, and you look for a mode of reasoning that will settle his hash once and for all.

END OF TRUE AI STORY

I resent the labeling of our hero in this story as a "dunce"; presumably it is because he appears to have little appreciation of the game of logic, but then so do the vast majority of intelligent systems. It is true that many can play the puzzle-solving game more effectively than our hero, but then these players know full well that they are then operating in an unreal world.

The unhelpful consequences of the context-free nature of logical statements, as well as the inadequacies of one-sided reasoning have also been raised in an earlier chapter (Chapter 5), together with the problems posed by incompleteness and inconsistency, which are both endemic in realistic collections of knowledge. But that's not the end of my catalog of criticism: There is also the problem of the bimodal nature of the FOPC; i.e., everything is either FALSE or TRUE, no other option is permitted. This sort of simple, two-way decision making is difficult to reconcile with much of our knowledge and decision making in the real world. This is yet another nonnovel insight on my part, and hence there has long been research on extensions to simple logic that would alleviate this problem.

As the astute reader has noted, there is a problem with this line of reasoning: Digital computers are, at bottom, similarly bimodal. Zeroes and ones are the popular alphabet for the bit patterns in the hardware of computers. Does this mean, as Dreyfus (1979) used to argue, that AI must move to analog computing machines before there is any hope of success? Most people don't think so, but a consideration of the various ways up and out of this particular hole will take us too far afield; it is thus a take-home problem.

Fuzzy logic (introduced in Chapter 5) is perhaps the most famous and successful example of a logical notation that breaks out of the bimodal straightjacket. In a nutshell: fuzzy logic allows degrees of truth using the range 0 to 1 (FALSE and TRUE, respectively). Thus (TODAY FRIDAY) →(TOMORROW SATURDAY) might be associated with a truth value of 0.999 — which is quite close to 1, i.e., TRUE. It is not absolutely TRUE (assuming the implied mapping to days of the week), because it could be FALSE on occasion, e.g., for someone crossing the International Date Line at the last stroke of midnight.

In reality, situations whose simple truth values are spoiled by exceptional circumstances are tackled with some brand of default logic (Reiter, 1980). Fuzzy logic tends to be applied to the problems of ill-defined sets (you may recall the example of tallness mentioned in Chapter 5). A basic law of classical logic is the Law of the Excluded Middle: if we have some property A, then everything is either A or not-A. Now this sounds reasonable and works pretty well if property A is say, "human" — everything you care to name is either human or not-human, isn't it? But what about A as "tall" or "heavy"? Many things are clearly tall or not-tall, but many things are also quite tall, fairly tall, very tall, not tall and not short, etc.; it is these sorts of judgments that the fuzzy formalism attempts to accommodate.

Not only is the world of intelligent systems populated with properties and objects that cannot be mutually associated on a purely TRUE-or-FALSE basis independent of context, but in addition there is a whole range of human phenomena that have not yet received mention. In the course of my intelligent actvities I know certain things are true or false, but many more I merely believe to be true with differing degrees of certainty. These relations like *know* and *believe* {propositional attitudes, if you want to get technical} are another thorn in the side of simple logics if not a dagger through the heart. I can, for example, think that I know that something is true when in fact it's false — life is, sadly, like that. So a whole subfield of modal logics has grown up to address this sort of problem (see Moore, 1977, for a sampler).

The problems of logic-based reasoning with exceptional statements (i.e., statements that admit the presence of exceptions, e.g., a white elephant despite the general definition that elephants are gray) and with attempts to model a changing world (e.g., by changing the truth values of primitive statements — (TODAY TUESDAY) may have the value TRUE on one day every week but the value FALSE on all other days) have led to a need for *truth maintenance systems* (TMS). The idea is to monitor the collection of defined and derived statements and to remove or deactivate those which would otherwise pollute the logical purity of the system because of the general concessions made to the divergence of reality from the tenets of FOPC (for further details see Doyle, 1979; and De Kleer, 1986).

Another logic-related issue, which is also a hot but contentious topic in AI, is the farrago of theories and practices that is collectively referred to as the logic programming movement. PROLOG is a major component of this methodological conglomerate, but logic is the central model. Kowalski's work and standpoint epitomize the common conviction of many believers in this AI subfield. We've already had his quotation on logic being the only intelligent way for expressing information, he continues: "There is only one intelligent way to process information — and that is by applying deductive inference methods" (Kowalski, 1980, quoted by Leith, 1988, p. 92). Not everyone agrees. Leith (1986), for example, presents an anti-logic-programming view. His opposition is on two fronts:

1. The belief in logic as a means of encapsulating all information is a reversion to much earlier philosophical beliefs which have long been known to be unworkable.
2. The application of logic programming to law (one of Kowalski's projects) is really only a test-bed for logic programming, yet it is being presented and accepted as a practical prospect (Leith, 1988).

The debit ledger on logic can be concluded with the issue of *computational tractability* — one heck of an expression that boils down to the problem of whether a given mechanism can actually be used to compute with, or whether time and/space requirements make the mechanism, not just inefficient to use, but downright unusable. It is quite possible (in fact, it is distressingly easy) to devise a well-specifed mechanism for solving a knotty problem, a mechanism that is not only guaranteed to solve the problem but is equally surely never going to be usable on any conceivable computer — the mechanism solves the problem in principle, but not in practice.

The game of chess, for example, is a classic AI problem (although representative of a "bad" AI paradigm — Chapter 3), playable to perfection with a simple algorithm which is itself computationally intractable. In practice, we must employ tractable, but unguaranteed, approximations. Hence chess is a fascinating game and an AI problem to boot.

THE EPILOGIC

Lest you slam this book shut and promptly dispose of it in the local secondhand bookshop, shaken or comforted by the belief that logic is a bad thing, let me slip in a few disclaimers to mitigate my lightly veiled hostility to logic before it's too late. With logic tottering, can motherhood and apple pie be next for attack? No, in fact I intend to do something to shore up logic.

Just because intelligent behavior of the human kind does not appear to mirror the characteristics of logic, we cannot conclude that logic is inappropriate as an underlying representation language. Many computer systems don't appear to be controlled by bit shifts in registers, yet they most assuredly are. Superficial behavior, especially in so complex a phenomenon as intelligence, may be misleading when used as a guide to identifying a suitable foundational notation. In addition, human intelligence may well be a contraption (like the panda's thumb); an artificial intelligence founded on logic may avoid some of its worst characteristics. Perhaps we should aim at the phenomenon of intelligence independent of the particular implementation at hand (insofar as this is possible). The wetware version, the meat machine (as Minsky calls it), may be an inferior product.

Israel's (1987) defense of logic-based approaches to the formal semantics of natural language contains some useful cautions for those who would dismiss logic out of hand. There is no necessity for logical foundations to be complete in some sense. There are clearly some aspects of AI that lie outside the scope of any conceivable logic, but that does not mean that AI should be totally denied the undoubted benefits of formal, logic-based foundations; it is not at all clear, and perhaps it is highly unlikely, that no AI subfield will be realistically formalizable with a logic-based approach.

AI is in its infancy. It is therefore much too early to conclude that a logic which is appropriate, sufficiently powerful, and also manageable will not be forthcoming. And what is the alternative to this quest, a continuation of the current lamentable state of AI which engenders many ideas, a few baroque programs, and little of long-lasting substance? An AI without formal foundations will be little benefit to anyone. But there is, of course, a middle road: a foundational formalism which is not logic based. Work in the CP, with its formal basis in statistical mechanics (remember those awful probabilistic activity-transfer functions?), provides an example of an alternative to logic. But see the upcoming section on philosophical foundations, where the argument against the CP is made just because, as a notation, it fails to exhibit the crucial characteristics that I have been arguing against in logics. Without wishing to steal the thunder from this estimable future section, the resolution of this apparent paradox is that science has always made great strides by approximating and simplifying the real world. The central question goes something like this: By how much can a manageable notation diverge from reality and yet still serve as a useful description of that reality? (If this question makes no sense, you'll just have to wait until the philosophy section; after that all will be clear, perhaps.) These issues have not been resolved, but this is no excuse for plugging the FOPC to the extent that is customary in 'neat' AI. Charniak and McDermott, for example, employ the FOPC as the unifying formalism throughout their extensive and influential text on AI (Charniak & McDermott, 1985). I am reminded once again of the old story of the drunk looking for his lost keys under the lamppost because the light is good there, despite the fact that he lost them in a dark alley. But McDermott (1986) has since admitted that the keys to AI are not in the hands of the logicists and has further confessed to the publication of a number of influential, but misguided, tracts (including the co-authored introductory AI textbook).

An earlier, very influential, AI text is that of Nilsson (1980). Newell is a self-confessed admirer of the Nilsson text for its trail-blazing "attempt to transform textbooks in AI into the mold of basic texts in science and engineering;" this text "uses the FOPC as the *lingua franca* for presenting and discussing representation" in AI (Newell, 1981, p. 17). Newell further asserts that this approach "is just right," but then goes on to classify Nilsson's promotion of logic as a representation language for problem solving as "just wrong. Logic as a representation for problem solving rates only a minor theme in our textbooks" (Newell, 1981, p. 17) — compare this with McDermott's point about the false, hidden assumption of the logicists which I described earlier.

The case for the FOPC as the foundational notation for AI seems to rest, not on the verisimilitude with which it can depict the phenomena of intelligence, but on the fact that we understand it well. This does not seem sensible to me. My built-in bias is showing again; it is high time to move on. But before we do, let me offer you the wisdom of William of Baskerville, for whom the FOPC was clearly a nonstarter.

"Perhaps the mission of those who love mankind is to make people laugh at the truth, *to make truth laugh*, because the only truth lies in learning to free ourselves from insane passion for the truth" (the words of an echo from another world, see Eco, 1984, p. 491).)

Before finally leaving the logicists in peace, I should tell you something about *abduction* as it's on the ascendent and usually coupled with deduction and induction. An abductive mechanism is one that generates useful, new hypotheses and as such can be viewed as central to intelligent activity. Rather like *indexing* we can easily give this desirable quality a name, but now we still face the problem of elucidating a theory of abduction, or as is sometimes said, a logic of abduction. Interestingly, Chomsky (1973, pp. 92–93) takes us back a century to Peirce's original notion of abduction to label the process of hypothesis generation, and he also looks ahead to when the "general problem solvers of the early enthusiasts of artificial intelligence" have failed "it will then be possible to undertake a general study of the limits and capacities of human intelligence, to develop a Peircean logic of abduction.'' He may have been sketching out the current era in AI. I leave this as an open question for the reader.

Incidentally, much of the current wisdom on the side of logic as the foundation for AI can be found in the work entitled *The Logical Foundations of AI* (Genesereth & Nilsson, 1987). So that's the place to go for a more positive view of this general question. In addition, Turner (1984) surveys a range of logics for AI, and Ramsey (1988) is the next contribution of this type, while Hobbs and Moore (1985) is a collection of papers on formal theories of the common-sense world—i.e. the world wherein an AI system will have to operate.

METHODOLOGICAL FOUNDATIONS

This is yet another issue about which I am prejudiced, but I've granted myself the whole of Chapter 2 to work it out of my system at an early stage. And in order to prove that I have succeeded, I'll quickly review that argument of mine and move swiftly on to the further methodological questions.

I believe that the specify-and-verify approach to computer system development has done AI a disservice. It is not appropriate for AI-system development; failure to recognize and accept this has resulted in a divorce of AI from computer science, the discipline that should have provided the methodological foundations for the most important facet of AI — building programs. In consequence, AI-system development lacking a well-conceived methodological basis is an ad hoc procedure; AI as a discipline has suffered greatly because of this.

That was quite brief by anybody's standards; for me it was close to a miracle — now on to some new stuff. The key issue left under methodological foundations of AI is the role of programs, and, somewhat secondarily, what is the status of AI? This latter issue, which you might be tempted to skip over quickly now that the end of the book is clearly in sight, is important even in a purely practical sense. For those of an inquiring mind, as they say, no justification is necessary, but for those who want no more than to roll up their sleeves and get to some AI system building, the status of AI is, I would claim, still a topic of importance. Why? Well, because sorting out what is acceptable practice in AI rests to some extent on what we take AI to be: Do we expect it to become a hardish science in the style of physics? What is the proposed role of empirical data on human intelligence, peripheral, central, or largely irrelevant? Or is AI to be cast as purely an engineering discipline aimed at the contruction of a new generation of useful computer systems? Most persons would probably avoid commitment to any single role for AI, but it is still totally unclear what is acceptable practice, even when we declare the category of AI to which we are committed.

We examined some possible categorizations of a few different classes of AI work right at the outset of this book; I don't propose to rehash that aspect of AI methodology either. In this section I shall focus on the role, or roles, of programs in AI.

THE ROLES OF PROGRAMS IN AI

A program in AI can usefully be considered as a machine-executable specification, such was my argument in Chapter 2. In this role, the program, together with the RUDE cycle, fit quite comfortably into the emergent software engineering subparadigm of prototyping. This subparadigm recognizes and exploits the fact that the behavioral characteristics of a working system can provide valuable information for specification development — a working model makes implicit information in the specification explicit. The collection of papers edited by Agresti (1986) contains a useful group of contributions on the merits, problems, and potential benefits of prototyping for system development. And for those readers who really want to dig in this prototyping notion, a whole book of papers has been edited by Budde, Kuhlenkamp, Mathiassen, and Zullighoven (1984), but without so much as a whisper about AI, I should warn you.

One major problem with the notion that a program can be an executable specification concerns the nature of available programming languages. The majority of currently available programming languages are cluttered with notational impedimenta whose accurate use is essential if you want a working program but is irrelevant to the specification of the problem. Hence, one reason why programs are unsatisfactory specifications is because the "pure" specification, which is already likely to be complex, is typically intertangled with implementation considerations imposed by the particular programming language in use. This distance between the current realities of a machine-executable notation and a pure-specification language has been called the *programming language inadequacy gap,* which contracts mercifully to the PLIG (Partridge, 1986a, explores this role of programs at some length, not to say depth).

Interestingly, the AI programming languages LISP and PROLOG, especially PROLOG, are two of the better candidates for machine-executable specification languages. Kowalski (1984), for example, has made a strong representation for PROLOG as a software engineering tool in just this prototyping role.

PROGRAMS AS THEORIES

A more esoteric role for AI programs becomes manifest when we cast them in the role of theories. How can this be? — programs as theories, that is. One driving force behind this unlikely proposition is that precisely stated theories appear to be desirable; logics don't yet suffice, so programming languages, despite their clutter, may fill this need. In addition, we have every reason to expect that such a theory will not be too far divorced from a working program — a model which, by the very fact that it can be interpreted by a computer system, is guaranteed to be complete and viable in some sense. After all, a working program has run the gauntlet of the uncompromising mechanisms of a machine and succeeded. A final bonus comes from the output of a working program. The output, which is indisputably generated by means that are totally immune to the wishful thinking of the original theorizer, is thus incontestable as an implication of the theory. So programs as theories would seem to be a useful possibility, not just for AI, but for science in general. But, of course, there are some problems associated with this notion (and we shall get to them).

But before we look at the problems associated with this idea you should be aware of the practical reason why we might be motivated to entertain this very odd idea. As stated above, the construction and demonstration of a working program is always taken to be a significant milestone along the route to the establishment and acceptance of a novel theory in AI. A typical public unveiling of a new departure in AI involves the demonstration of the program that provides the necessary concrete credibility for the ideas presented. The program itself, a morass of LISP code, the product of a protracted interval of exploratory programming, is readily comprehensible (at the level of the ideas presented) to no one. The actual ideas that the program embodies are thus presented in a suitably succinct and readily comprehensible form but quite separate from the program itself. The burning question then is: How do we know that the few interesting and relevant demonstrations of program behavior are primarily due to the succinct explanation given and not to some unmentioned aspects of the mass of code that constitutes the working program? The short answer is that we don't, but, if the program itself were the statement of the theory, then we might be some way along a path to the solution of this fundamental problem (on the other hand, we might not, but I'll pick up this specific option later in this section).

Theories come in many forms, from statements in English to mathematical equations. What sort of theory could a program be? Programming languages are formal languages, so presumably we are expecting programs to be some sort of formal theoretical statement. Wilks (1990) reviews, discusses, and lays out a taxonomy of the terms *model* and *theory*. He argues that programs are not so much theories in the classical sense but can usefully be considered to be theories of computational processes.

Simon — T.W., not H.A. (1979, 1990) — provides a philosopher's analysis of the question of whether programs can also be theories. In the earlier paper he concludes that, within certain limits, there are no philosophical objections to the idea of programs as theories. In the later revisitation he concludes that "programs are not theories, but programs constitute aspects of theories. Theories are not programs, but computer simulation aids in the analysis of theories" (p. 164).

I have an axe to grind on this question of programs as theories, so I'll give myself the space to do it. The problem of programs being formal statements, but totally incomprehensible ones, can be addressed by considering the code to be the basic statement of the theory from which are abstracted a series of successively more comprehensible but necessarily less exact statements of the theory (a further truth about the need for mendacity). The end result is a series of alternative representations: A working program which insures completeness in some basic sense, plus a sequence of progressively more readily comprehensible statements of the theory. Each restatement of the theory (except the first and last, of course) is keyed to its two nearest neighbors, the one more detailed and accurate, and the other more comprehensible but less accurate. We thus end up with a series of interlinked restatements of the theory. The explicit interlinkages serve as a basis for constructing a justification that any given abstraction is in some sense valid. Such things cannot be proven, they can only be argued for, and the interlevel linkages provide an explicit basis for arguments about validity. Without the intermediate statements of the theory, the gap between a working program and a succinct statement of the theory is just too wide to be bridged by closely reasoned argument. In addition, such a sequence of theoretical statements serves to communicate the theory far better than any single statement could. This is because different types of inquiry from differently knowledgeable persons are best served by reference to different levels of theoretical statement. A neural network theory has been presented in this manner (see Partridge, Johnston, & Lopez, 1984) and I have demonstrated and discussed the mechanism in several places (Partridge, 1986a, 1990).

Bundy and Ohlsson (1990) disagree about the role of programs in AI. Bundy opts for the significance of mechanisms or techniques as the essential principles in an AI program; Ohlsson insists that it is the validation of behavioral principles which is the main goal. To my way of thinking, these two viewpoints correspond to the representations at the two ends of the sequence of abstractions discussed above: Bundy is arguing for a representation of how certain functions are manifest in the program (an abstraction at the program end of the sequence), whereas Ohlsson prefers a description biased towards the organic phenomenon in question (i.e., some aspect of the intelligence of you or me; a representation couched in terms of human behavior and thus quite distant from the "mechanics" of the supporting program). I believe that both types of representation are necessary, and that a bridge of intermediate representations is also needed. Interestingly, Bundy's attempt to analyze Ohlsson's general principle bogs down several times just because no intermediate interpretations of critical words are provided, and several rather different interpretations will fill the gap between a description of intelligent behavior and a description of program function.

For Hayes (1984b, p. 158) the criterion of rigorous AI is implementability. "An acceptable explanation of a piece of behavior must be, in the last analysis, a program which can actually be implemented and run." He doesn't say that an AI theory is a program, but that the theory will be closely associated with programs. He believes (or believed in 1979, when this piece was originally written) that AI is an empirical science. "An AI explanation — a program — is tested by running it. And this can be an experiment. It really can; one cannot predict, often, what will happen." I can just imagine Dijkstra's rejoinder to that. Any reader with a capacity for vitriolic penmanship might like to frame possible ripostes á la (au?) Dijkstra. I refuse to be drawn in; instead I'll move on.

Sharkey and Pfeifer (1984) claim that the relation of an explanation or theory to a running program is not as simple as Hayes would have us believe. They point out two major problems:

1. *Kludges* — a lovely word with a definite, and quite appropriate, sticky feel about it (although there is some dispute as to whether it rhymes with *fudge* or with *stooge*). In the current context it refers to special-purpose, ad hoc, patches in a program that are significant contributors to behavioral characteristics which are attributed to certain general principles. Kludges are dead easy to hide in a pile of code, not than I am suggesting that anyone would do such a thing. The problem is that, after a long period of exploratory programming through uncharted search spaces with little-known data structures, major behavioral characteristics of the resultant program may depend upon supposedly insignificant pieces of code, quite unbeknown to the architect of the system — it's just one of the perils of incautious incremental system development.

2. McDermott's (1976) "wishful mnemonics" — this problem is one of dissociating the grandiose implications of an overambitous label from the realities of what the program structure so labeled actually repre-

sents; actual representation is in itself not a trivial problem, but ruling out many of the grander alliances of everyday usage usually is. Thus, when faced with a program littered with high-powered labels such as UNDERSTANDER or COGNITIVE DECISION MAKER, we must first hack through the rich jungle of casual associations that the label drags into consciousness before we can tackle the real task of developing an understanding of the program.

Shakespeare was into this particular problem long ago. When he wrote, "What's in a name?" he might well have continued, "a teachable cognitive concept natural language learner by any other name will behave the same." But he didn't. He stuck with roses and the olifactory issue — very wise. However, I can't do the same and still pretend to deal with AI in any thorough sense.

Sharkey and Pfeifer ask (1984, p. 165): "How are we supposed to assess the merits of an AI program as a physical instantiation of a theory?" and then leave us to wonder about the problem. So shall I.

Dietrich (1990) argues that the role of programs in AI is little better than random attempts to hit upon the program (or class of algorithms) whose existence (but little else) is promised by the symbolic search space hypotheses (described in Chapter 3). In traditional AI, programs are manifestations of more or less randomly constructed theories aimed at a target which is supposed to be out there somewhere. When they are taken to have missed (i.e., they do not exhibit intelligent behavior), there is a postmortem, and then the the Mark II version goes into production, and so on. Interestingly, as Dietrich points out in no uncertain terms, failure to hit the target is never for a moment considered to be a reason to question whether the target is indeed out there at all. In which case the symbolic search space hypotheses don't seem to be treated as hypotheses at all; they've become the dogma of traditional AI. It's as if we've been hunting in the dark for a unicorn. Many shots have been fired, but no unicorn has been brought down. Yet, rather than seriously questioning the existence of unicorns, the tendency is to lament the smallness of the hunting party.

AI, as I mentioned in Chapter 1 (and we saw an example in Chapter 9), has an unhealthy partiality for irrefutable hypotheses, which is a singularly odd way to proceed for a discipline that seeks recognition as a science. Hypotheses are naturally asymmetric objects — in that they can usually be undermined by experimental results but cannot be proven valid as a result of experimentation. Quite strangely, the so-called hypotheses at the foundation of AI are treated as true conjectures that experimental evidence will one day corroborate — they are asymmetric alright, but in the wrong direction.

Before we get thoroughly lost in the subtleties of conjectures and refutations as the framework for science, let's move on and consider where experimental evidence in AI might come from.

PROGRAMS AS EXPERIMENTS

Interesting as the question of programs as theories may be, it is also a quagmire within which we can wallow for long periods and still not find any solid ground. So let's move on, as indeed we have, in effect, by turning to Dietrich's argument, one view of which might be that AI programming is random experimentation — experiments based on a false hypothesis. This general viewpoint is reminiscent of the argument that launched Dreyfus into orbit around the world of AI, but more like a mosquito than a satellite. He compared AI to Alchemy: the pseudo-scientific quest for the philosopher's stone which would enable the transmutation of base metals into gold.

Sparck Jones (1990) asks, "What sort of thing *is* an AI experiment?" She assumes that the answer is a program, and then continues to explore the unsatisfactory nature of this possibility. Can a program validate a theory? Just one run or multiple runs, and constrained by what? She also raises the awkward question of what constitutes a successful experiment when there is no correct answer in an absolute sense (a nasty problem which we first encountered in Chapter 2). She gives the example of a story-summarizing program; there isn't one (or even a well-defined set, I might add) of correct summaries, and we're right back with the headache of assessing the adequacy of computer programs.

Classical sciences have the notion of repeatability as an integral part of experimental methodology. What form does the notion of repeatable experiments take in AI? It can't be rewriting and rerunning the program. In fact there is a notion of repeatability in AI, although it has been used surprisingly little in a discipline that is crying out for theories that are independent of specific implementations. The notion that I am referring to is typically called *rational reconstruction*.

RATIONAL RECONSTRUCTIONS IN AI

Of course, the point of repeatability is not to rewrite and rerun exactly the same program, but to write and run a program that is based on the same abstract principles as the original. Reinstantiation of the abstract principles in a new implementation is indeed a valid way to test those principles. We have already seen in an earlier section that it is difficult to justify the abstract principles which are supposed to account for a program's behavior. But instead of the usual compounding of problems, rational reconstruction can contribute towards resolving this particular one: If a rational reconstruction does in fact behave in essentially the same way as the original program, then we have added some credence to the notion that the abstract principles originally presented do indeed constitute a valid accounting for the phenomenon under study.

Rational reconstruction has been much more European activity than an American one; this is not too surprising. The vast majority of the large and behaviorally impressive AI programs are built in the USA. The European academic institutions, starved of the necessary high-powered, LISP-machine, program-development environments, have attempted to gain a better understanding of these monoLISPs (it nearly works if you lisp it) by recreating them on a less ambitious scale; i.e., they build rational reconstructions.

More surprisingly, perhaps, most rational reconstructions have served to undermine rather than bolster the credibility of the advertised abstract principles, or theory.

One well-publicized rational reconstruction (author's disclaimer: It was certainly one in principle, if not in actual practice) was that of the AM program (mathematical rediscovery, Chapter 9) by Ritchie and Hanna (1990). They report on their success (or lack of) in using the advertised abstract principles to account for AM's behavior. They then continue on to offer us some resultant insights on the foundations of AI. They lament the centrality of programs in the absence of any satisfactory way to demonstrate clear correspondences between the program and the theoretical claims that are usually made. Finally, they list six ways in which an AI program conceived of as an "experiment" can be scrutinized:

1. *Experiment design (static):* Does the structure of the program reflect the theory it purports to test?
2. *Experiment design (dynamic):* Does the internal processing behavior of the program correspond to the dynamic aspects of the theory (if any)?
3. *Consistency:* Has the program been successfully run (repeatedly)?
4. *Results:* What were the consequences, in terms of internal behavior and output, of the program's execution?
5. *Interpretation:* What do these results mean in terms of the theoretical constructs?
6. *Conclusions:* What are the consequences for the theory of the interpreted results?

A useful set of considerations, and although most of the questions cannot be answered with solid, indisputable responses, the very fact that the questions are explicitly addressed when an AI program is presented as the demonstration of a theory would be a major advance.

Another rational reconstruction project (Bramer & Cendrowska, 1984, p. 454) focused on one of the models of expert system's technology—the MYCIN program. The authors actually reimplemented part of MYCIN with the goal of "rebuild and improve"; they aimed "to analyse the system in close detail, from a re-engineering viewpoint, piecing together the information given in a number of different accounts, if necessary—much as an archaeologist combines the evidence from from different parts of an excavation to form a composite view of the site."

As a result of this exercise they conclude that MYCIN is "an extremely sophisticated piece of software, carefully tuned to the needs of the infectious disease domain" (Bramer & Cendrowska, 1984, p. 492). Needless to say (but, nevertheless, I shall), quite a number of detailed faults with the system were found, a number of them dealing with the strategy for reasoning with uncertainty that MYCIN uses. Adams (1976) analyzed MYCIN's strategy for propagating uncertainty through a sequence of reasoning (e.g., if A and B are TRUE with certainty factors of 0.8 and 0.7, respectively, then use of the rule IF A AND B THEN C allows us to conclude the TRUTH of C with what certainty?). Adams demonstrated serious limitations in the scheme employed, yet the MYCIN system, when demonstrated, yielded acceptable results in practice. How could this be? Adams concludes that "it is probable that the model does not founder on the difficulties pointed out because in actual use the chains of reasoning are short and the hypotheses simple. However, there are many fields in which, because of its shortcomings, this model could not enjoy comparable success" (quoted by Bramer & Cendrowska, 1984, p. 489).

Campbell (1990) provides a European perspective on the general topic of "Theories, Programs, and Rational Reconstructions" in AI. He attempts to account for why the status of AI vis-á-vis the conventional sciences is a problematic issue. He outlines three classes of theories, the distinguishing elements of which are: equations; entities, operations, and a set of axioms; and general principles capable of particularization in different forms. He claims that models in AI tend to fall into this last class.

He argues for the importance of rational reconstruction as a component of the science of AI. For, although most rational reconstruction attempts have led to questioning rather than clear support for the supposed principles of the original programs, it is exactly such demonstration of clear discrepancies that will drive us toward a more accountable discipline — a true science of AI.

SORTING OUT AI METHODOLOGIES

Hall and Kibler (1985, p. 166) attempt to describe and organize the confusion of methodologies found in AI. "It is argued that researchers should make their methodological orientations explicit when communicating research results, to increase both the quality of research reports and their comprehensibility for other participants in the field." They provide the following typology, formed from differing intentions and methods of AI researchers.

They also provide exemplary research projects under each of their five perspectives, most of which are mentioned elsewhere in this book should you wish to acquaint yourself with them in order to gain further insight into this typology.

Hall and Kibler discuss each of their five perspectives and attempt to

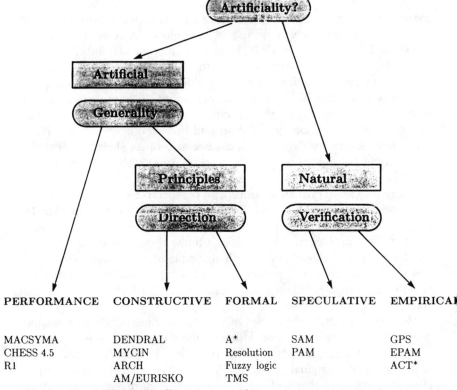

PERFORMANCE	CONSTRUCTIVE	FORMAL	SPECULATIVE	EMPIRICAL
MACSYMA	DENDRAL	A*	SAM	GPS
CHESS 4.5	MYCIN	Resolution	PAM	EPAM
R1	ARCH	Fuzzy logic		ACT*
	AM/EURISKO	TMS		

Figure 10.1. Kibler and Hall's taxonomy of AI

give a brief statement of what the measure of success in each one is. I think that this is also worth reproducing, as explicit statements of this nature are both important and scarce in AI. Their summaries are as follows:

> PERFORMANCE: As evidence of success, practical usefulness and improved performance over previous computational approaches weigh heavily.
>
> CONSTRUCTIVE: Solutions to these design problems, as incorporated into functioning software systems, are evaluated in terms of efficiency, credibility with human experts in the domain area, and demonstrated or promised extensibility.
>
> FORMAL: Successful work in this perspective requires unambiguous and adequately descriptive specifications of problem and solution mechanism for an 'important' class of related specific problems.
>
> SPECULATIVE: Successful work within this perspective consists of working programs that are taken as support for the sufficiency of psychologically plausible theories.
>
> EMPIRICAL: Criteria for success include: empirically demonstrable correspondence between program performance and natural behavior, robustness of program design with respect to incremental changes (taken as an indicator of the fidelity of the model), and (perhaps less crucial than the previous criteria) the extensibility of model concepts to varied task domains.

I do not wish to present any of these perspectives or the criteria of success as the last word on this issue (and neither do the authors), but it is a good basis for discussion and development. But this I shall leave as yet another exercise for the reader, and push on into the jungle of philosophical argument.

Incidentally, in a much earlier essay on methodologies in AI, Miller (1978) argued that there are two competing methodologies: theory demonstration — where the theory must have empirical consequences and its validity is then explored through empirical data; and theory development — where computer models are built in order to show that the theory is sufficient to account for the phenomenon under study. In terms of the taxonomy given above, Miller's two methodologies seem to fit most comfortably with the EMPIRICAL and SPECULATIVE perspectives, respectively.

Finally, setting modesty aside once more, it is my duty to tell you that a new book edited by Partridge and Wilks (1990) contains many fine papers on the foundations of AI. The collection is biased toward methodological foundations and also contains an annotated bibliography on the foundations of AI in general.

PHILOSOPHICAL FOUNDATIONS

I can hold them off no longer. It's time to give the philosophers a chance to clarify everything for us. Most philosophical argument is prone to suffer from the halting problem: Any contention, in the hands of a competent philosopher, can be defended or attacked with an apparently endless line of reasoning. As this is known to be an insoluble problem for computers, and I see no reason to place myself outside the domain of algorithmic computation, my goal in this section is minimal. I shall make no pretence to survey this subarea completely or in depth. I only offer a few specific arguments to demonstrate the breadth of viewpoint available, together with references to the major manifestations of collected wisdom on the philosophical foundations of AI.

THERE'S NOTHING SPECIAL ABOUT YOU, OR ME

For the philosophers who argue that AI is, or might be, a valid goal to aim at (because it's not obviously impossible), the case made often centers on the nonuniqueness of humanity. Man is not only at one with God's inferior productions, to wit the animals, but he and she are also not clearly distinct from all conceivable machines. We are fundamentally different from the average mechanism on the market today, say washing machine or electric tea maker, but there is no insurmountable reason why time, trouble, research, and money won't eliminate the gap (by raising the abilities of machines, I hasten to add).

Dennett (1990), for example, argues against the contention that we humans have some fundamental purpose behind our doings, but that any artifact can only have some inferior imitation devised by one of us {humans have original intentionality, but artifacts will be limited to derived intentionality}. If this contention were true, man and AI could never be the same. As the basis for his argument, Dennett imports and uses a contentious but fascinating theory from biology (the selfish-gene theory of Dawkins, 1976).

Consider, Dennett asks us, the task of designing a system to preserve and defend a deep-frozen man over a very long period of time. Not an everyday sort of request, I admit, but not particularly bizarre as philosophizing goes. If you would be happier with more background to the task, then consider that the iced man has some incurable illness, unlimited financial resources, and a firm conviction that one day medical science will catch up with his particular problem. Hence, he opts for the cryogenic treatment in conjunction with a sophisticated support system to ensure that no one thaws him out before his complaint is curable. Okay? That has, I trust, put you in the picture sufficiently for us to continue.

Now we forget the human icicle and the incurable illness, etc. and focus on the design of the necessary support system. Clearly, this has to be an AI system, right? After all, it must monitor its surroundings in order to head off any threat to the deep freeze or its contents. In addition, over a very, very long period of time, the site it is occupying is just bound to come up for redevelopment; hence, the system should be mobile — have deep freeze, will travel. What Dennett sketches out is an intelligent robot within which our frosted friend is encapsulated.

Now, why is this robot doing what it is doing (we have to assume, I think, that there are no major bugs in the program)? Well, its actions are derived from the desires of the iced man in less frosty times. Its goal is the preservation of the body it contains. Is this so very different, Dennett asks, from the central goal of an intelligent human body, which, if Dawkins is to be believed (and he's very persuasive), is to preserve the genes contained therein? We are just elaborate gene preservation machines, and intelligence is just one part of the system that has evolved to increase the machine's success rate. Our actions and general purposes are derived from our genes. So human intelligence is not necessarily any more original than that of an AI system. I've ridden roughshod over this argument, as I usually do, but you can get the flavor of this sort of stuff from my account; the nuances are, of course, yours for the sampling, by reference to the original expositions.

A further notable contributor to philosophical arguments about the basis for AI is Haugeland. In a relatively recent book (Haugeland, 1985) he discusses "AI: the very idea." He lays out the two essential claims of *good old-fashioned AI* (GOFAI) as:

1. our ability to deal with things intelligently is due to our capacity to think about them reasonably (including subconscious thinking); and
2. our capacity to think about things reasonably amounts to a faculty for internal 'automatic' symbol manipulation. (Haugeland, 1985, p. 113)

Our attention is drawn to the fact that the interpretation problem is unavoidable in this scheme of things (i.e., we shall, at some point, have to account for how and in what way the internal symbols represent things in the real world). In addition, there is also a committment here to "inner computers" in order to get the internal manipulation of symbols carried out. And although this situation is clearly reminiscent of the early theories of seeing which posited little men inside our heads seeing for us (leaving us, need I say, with the problem of how the little men did their seeing), Haugeland assures us that this is not the case. The interested reader is referred to the original book for the informal, charmingly put, but nevertheless gruesome, details.

Haugeland does not come down strongly for or against AI. He views AI as neither preposterous nor inevitable. "Rather it is based on a very powerful idea, which might very well be right (or right in some respects) and just as well might not" (Haugeland, 1985, p. 2). He discusses the lack of continuity between formal systems (the "bad" paradigms of Chapter 3), and the problems that a successful AI system must ultimately address.

BUILDING THE FOUNDATIONS ON THE CP

Moving on to more destructive (initially at least) philosophizing on the foundations of AI brings us to Dreyfus. Dreyfus nailed his colors to the mast with the publication in 1972 of *What Computers Can't Do* (Dreyfus, 1979). Like the British admiral Francis Drake, Dreyfus sailed his small but maneuverable ship right in among the Armada of the AI establishment and let them have it. But unlike Drake, Dreyfus did not vanquish the opposition — far from it. The large-scale and expensively rigged research labs of AI tried to ignore the minor irritant in their midst, but they were no more successful than Dreyfus was. There was an agreement to differ.

This standoff was based on the fact that Dreyfus had on his side a wealth of justified criticism comprised of a small mountain of predictions that persisted in failing to come true for the AI men, a fine collection of much-vaunted but easily discredited programs, and some good reasons why this might be so. But what he lacked (at least in the mind of the hard-nosed programmer) was any acceptable account of what the basis for human intelligence could be if it was not the SSSP.

Over the years since those halcyon days of bluster and prediction, Dreyfus has become the resident critic of AI, almost part of the establishment itself. In addition to entry to AI circles, the years have also provided a possible answer to Dreyfus's dilemma — you guessed it, connectionism.

In fact you didn't even have to guess it, you may just have remembered it from Chapter 5; some people have that level of recall ability. In any event the details are all there in the earlier chapters, so, on this occasion, I can spare you the nitty gritty with a clear conscience. This leaves us free to leap on to the details of the philosophizing which maintains that, whatever else connectionism is good for, it is not the right stuff for the foundations of AI.

UNDERMINING THE FOUNDATIONS OF THE CP

Fodor and Pylyshyn (1988) fire a philosophical broadside at the CP; in their report of the skirmish, the CP has sunk and is unlikely to be refloated by any right-minded person. Of course, there are other versions of this encounter, and we considered this critique briefly at an earlier point in this book. Their arguments are extensive and finely structured, but a key issue that they raise is much broader in scope than the CP-for-AI question; this central point of their criticism concerns the nature of useful (successful?) scientific theories. In stark and brutal simplicity: The syntax of the theoretical notation must reflect the semantics — the notation must be compositional. The reader who is with me now and has also waded through the chapter on natural language processing (Chapter 8) may remember, if time the great healer has not erased the neural scar, a similar concern with the formal semantics of programming languages — except that, with respect to NLP, we were concerned about the compositionality of formal semantics. Our concerns thus come from both directions; some might call this a flaw in the argument, but I think it reflects a healthy openness to all possibilities. Nevertheless, I'll attempt to reconcile this apparent contradiction shortly.

In their stamp-on-connectionism paper, Fodor and Pylyshyn argue that the key to building an understanding of a complex phenomenon (i.e., the scientific enterprise) is via a representational scheme which is *systematically compositional* — a heavy-duty term which means that the phenomenon is represented by a structure whose component substructures each represent elements of the overall meaning and combine in a systematic way to yield the more global meaning of the larger representations so constructed. On reflection, I'm not wholly convinced that my attempted explication of the term systematically compositional was a raging success. Let's go for explanation by example. Consider the sentence JOHN LOVES MARY. If you are a native speaker of English, you will understand what this sentence means (provided I don't push you to actually generate that meaning, and I won't, so don't resist my suggestions here). If I now rearrange the words and produce MARY LOVES JOHN, you'll most likely not be at all surprised; and what's more, you'll similarly know the meaning of the new sentence. Why? Well, your semantic competence in these trivial examples is founded largely on the systematic compositionality of the English language. Your understanding of the first sentence is largely composed of your understanding of the individual words in addition to your knowledge of word categories (such as nouns and verbs) and the systematic rules of combination of these words.

Let's push this explanation a bit further. Consider the following sentence: UMBWA KALI SANA, which means "beware of the dog" (to some people at least). But the successful absorption of that description of the meaning of this sentence is likely to be no help when faced with a different sentence composed of the same words (native speakers of Swahili must just relax and believe me). Your understanding of UMBWA KALI SANA is not based on the systematic compositionality of the alien sentence. It is classic phrase-book understanding: You learn the correspondence between representation (the string of words) and meaning *as a whole*, which is not much help when faced with a partially similar but different representation.

So back to the demolition of the philosophical foundations of the CP: CP-based representations of cognitive phenomena are homogeneous networks. They are systematically compositional but *not at the level of cognition*. The systematic compositionality resides at the level of individual nodes which, as subsymbolic advocates boast, are below the level of semantic interpretation — the elemental components are subsymbolic. We have already seen one manifestation of this feature of CP-based models: NETtalk, when properly trained, apparently embodies the rules of pronunciation of English, yet no detailed correspondences between the network substructures and the rules has been found.

At a more general level, the argument has two main strands: Fodor and Pylyshyn argue that cognitive behavior is systematically compositional and thus should most sensibly be explored within a paradigm that also has these charactersitics; and second, science builds an understanding of macro-phenomena through the systematic composition of micro-phenomena the understanding of which has been similarly constructed or is assumed. Hence, a paradigm like the CP which fails to exhibit systematic compositionality is unlikely to support a substantial and vigorous branch of science in the long run.

TOTAL DISBELIEF: LET'S NOT BE SEARLE-ISH

There are claims, based on philosophical reasoning, to the effect that AI is just not on. This sort of grand statement is packed with ambiguities that I shall make no pretence to tease out and lay before you. Instead I intend to sketch out just a couple of the arguments, a few of the more famous ones from a veritable galaxy of interrelated possibilities — a snake pit of philosophese. Then I can leave you with the key references, the major routes into the pit for those foolhardy enough to want to try and obtain a mental grasp of this particular foundational morass.

If there is a unifying theme to the impossibility-of-AI argument (the philosophical as opposed to say the practical one), it might be said to center around the mapping problem: abstract descriptions, such as computer programs or a logical formalism, must ultimately be grounded in the real world — what exactly does this mean, and how would we do it? This is a problem that we've seen in relation to the meaning of words in natural language processing, and also quite recently as a problem with the logical foundations of AI (you may recall Winston's attempt to glide over it with "an *interpretation* is a full accounting of the correspondence between objects and object-symbols"). In reality it is a tricky, fundamental, unsolved problem, and as such it is the delight of philosophers. It is sad to have to report that sort of thing, but in this book no punches are pulled; I tell it like it is (or at least, like it appears to be to me).

Searle has already been mentioned in an earlier chapter, and now I'll make good my threat to present an outline of his road show. The *Chinese room experiment* (CRE) is the vehicle with which Searle has obtained unbelievable mileage over quite a number of years. The latest major re-airing of this thought experiment was in 1984, when he gave the Reith lectures in Britain (published in Searle, 1984).

The thought experiment that we are asked to consider is based upon a room with a door under which it is possible to push pieces of paper from the outside to the inside, and vice versa. Inside this room is a man who (says he) does not understand Chinese, and what he has to play with are baskets containing pieces of paper each of which has a Chinese character written on it. He also has a set of manuals which tell him that, when he gets certain sequences of Chinese characters slipped under the door to him, he should construct other sequences of Chinese characters (from the pieces of paper in the baskets) and push them back by the same route.

Now, to the outside observer it may well seem that something decidedly shady is going on, and in addition our observer is likely to form the distinct impression that someone who understands Chinese is closeted in the room. But we know that this is a wrong conclusion. Hence, persuasive behavioral evidence is no guarantee of actual goings on inside rooms or, what's more to the point, inside computers. Just because a suitably programmed computer behaves as if it understands Chinese, we have no assurance that it does actually understand Chinese. This sort of argument is, of course, quite a blow to AI persons beavering away on their LISP machines, hoping to come up with a program that will pass the Turing Test (Chapter 1).

The responses to the CRE are many, varied, and usually not supportive. One general line of attack admits that, ultimately, indications of structure from observation of function cannot be verified. But if we're smart about it, behavioral tests can provide structural information. In addition, if we refuse to acknowledge the possibility of inferring structural information from observation of behavior, science in general must grind to a halt. There are no guarantees, to be sure, but then there never are in science; it is part of what distinguishes it from religion.

Another class of objections to the CRE points out the species chauvinism inherent in the assumption that it is the man locked away in the room that understands Chinese — it might be the rule book that contains all the real understanding; the man is just a mechanical processor. "Sure," this line of refutation goes, "the man doesn't understand Chinese any more than a neuron is intelligent, but the combination of the man, the baskets, the rules book, etc. *does* understand Chinese. The understanding is in the total system, not just one component of it."

But Searle, not content with sowing the seeds of doubt, pushes on and explains why they must inevitably grow to choke off all possibility of AI in the form of a program running on a computer (he constantly says *digital* computer, I'm not sure why). Four simple premises serve his purpose:

1. Brains cause minds.
2. Syntax is not sufficient for semantics.
3. Computer programs are entirely defined by their formal, or syntactical, structure.
4. Minds have mental contents; specifically, they have semantic contents.

Propositions 2 and 3 are our old friend the mapping problem dressed differently. Proposition 4 "is just an obvious fact about how our minds work" (Searle, 1984, p. 39) apparently. Searle knows it for sure about his mind (and he's inclined to give his dog the benefit of doubt), and I'd vote for mine, but as for his or yours I'm not so sure — after all, I've only got observation of behavior to go on. Searle's retort is something along the lines of: Our interior headwork (mine, yours, and his) are all sufficiently similar that, if his brain causes his mind, then yours and mine must do likewise. Anyway, the conclusion from 2,3, and 4 is:

> No computer program by itself is sufficient to give a system a mind. Programs, in short, are not minds, and they are not by themselves sufficient for having minds. (Searle, 1984, p. 39)

Tough talk, and not very welcome in AI circles, but I'm open-minded about all this; I leave it to you to make of it what you will. However, it seems to me that we could also throw in premise 1 at this point (it seems a pity to waste it) and insert *brain-caused* directly in front of *mind* and the two occurrences of *minds* to get a conclusion which is a more accurate reflection of the total argument, and at the same time it is considerably less troublesome.

Taking a different tack: Suppose that the Chinese symbols which we feed in ask the question: "Do you understand Chinese?" And the returned string (quite a short one I should imagine) translates back to "Yes". What are we to conclude? That one of the initial stipulations is in fact not true? Is Searle cheating on us with the subtlety that only a devious philosopher could devise? Is the complete setup that we are asked to accept impossible? — i.e., it is not possible for a man who cannot (he claims in English) understand Chinese to behave as if he does with only some baskets of symbols and some rule books at his disposal. If this is the case, then we have an example of an implication in which the premise is false; hence, it is true that that we can conclude whatever we like. The puzzled reader should absorb the formal implication:

the CRE can be performed → AI can't be possible

and refer back to the fourth column of the truth table for logical implication given earlier in this chapter. It's would be a pity not to make use of such hard-won trivia.

Notice that our man, who acts purely as a symbol manipulation device, tells the truth in English but lies in Chinese, apparently. I leave it as an exercise for the reader to explore the implications of the "No" answer in Chinese to the question (also in Chinese) "Do you understand Chinese?"

Searle is attacking "strong AI," which maintains (so Searle would have us believe) that "the mind is to the brain as the computer program is to the computer hardware." Another class of reaction is to claim that "strong AI" is not a position that AI-ers actually defend. Thus Searle has overrun an enemy outpost but one that is deserted (e.g., Sloman, 1985; Moor, 1988; Harnad, 1989, also attempts to sum up all the arguments for and against the CRE).

Nevertheless, I would urge any reader who can get tickets to brave the crowds and go to a Searle performance. He is an entertainer. It is a treat to watch him deftly turning aside one killer question after another from AI-believers in the audience. He is like (to change the metaphor) a man successfully floating down the river on a jumble of planks, none of which will bear his weight for more than a few seconds. But by moving quickly and continually from an about-to-sink plank to an unweighed-down, floating one he manages to avoid even getting his feet wet. And, of course, the sinking plank, when relieved of the weight, promptly pops up again to become briefly reusable once more.

There are a number of useful collections of papers that address questions about the philosophical foundations of AI. Anderson (1964) is an early classic collection which is still very useful, for philosophical debate does not age as quickly as most other types of discussion. Haugeland (1981) is an attempt to continue the tradition of Anderson's book. And Hofstadter and Dennett (1981) reprint and discuss many papers relevant to these issues. More recently, Fetzer (1988) has assembled a collection of papers on the philosophical foundations of AI, as has Hookway (1984).

11

Prognostications or W(h)ither AI

A retrospect on the failed predictions of AI pioneers: "They happen to be pretty good predictions — it takes a fair amount of explaining why, but they are."

Herbert Simon, quoted by McCorduck (1979, p. 188)

I have been pinned down for 10 whole chapters by the obligation to parade before you the length and breadth of programs, theories, nebulous ideas, and concrete mechanisms that together constitute AI. In addition, I felt constrained "to tell it like it is," with, I must admit, sometimes a little dab of personal bias here and there. But, in general, it was a tour of the field couched in terms that more often than not the field workers themselves use (indeed, used). So now, in this last chapter, I feel that I have earned the right to some unashamed, personal speculation {those readers who stick with me only to savor these curly-bracketed interjections of gruesome detail may want to leave us here, as no more are planned — it's all waffle from here on out, nothing but words and a few punctuation marks}.

I'll offer you a sequence of high-level generalizations about AI concerning both what it is and where it might be heading. Like all such generalizations, they are full of holes in the small (i.e., the microfeatures often don't stand up to too much scrutiny), but I think that the wholes are full of interest in themselves — to drag out the old adage: The whole is greater than the sum of the holes.

ABSTRACT AI AND CONCRETE AI

There has been, as I have described throughout this book, considerable success in the exploration of various possibilities for the mechanization of particular aspects of intelligence. The vast majority of this work has been what I would term *abstract AI* — aspects of intelligence formulated and solved (when they are solved) entirely within an abstract symbol system; the real world has been kept at arm's length, and a very long arm at that.

496

"So what?" is the expected rejoinder. "Capturing the essential aspects of reality within an abstract symbol system, and exploring the further implications of the abstract architecture developed, is an important part of what makes a science, a science." But there are certain necessary attributes of any abstraction scheme that is to be used in this way. First and foremost, it must map onto reality quite well; i.e., predictions generated within the idealized abstract framework must translate into predictions in the world with sufficient accuracy for observation of the relevant real-world phenomena to be assessable as corroborative or not of the abstract architecture from whence the original prediction generated.

And in the opposite direction, experiments with the abstract architecture should translate, more or less readily, into information about the appropriate real-world phenomena. It is not clear that this two-way bridge is crossable with respect to most work in abstract AI. But it is still very early days yet in the story of AI (I sincerely hope that you have grasped this point by now despite all the popular hype to the contrary). With substantial encampments on both sides of the chasm (i.e., abstract models and studies of the real-world phenomena), and the first, somewhat precarious, rope bridges thrown across, it is just a matter of time before more substantial structures are in place to allow a continuous flow of heavy traffic. Maybe.

There are number of reasons to believe that the abstract models typically employed in AI are so far removed from the relevant real-world phenomena that the intervening gulf is not effectively spannable. You may recall Haugeland's (1985) comments that the infamous blocks world approximates a playroom "as a paper plane approximates a duck" (to my way of thinking, he might just have well said "a kangaroo"). Haugeland's disparaging remarks, as well as a good measure of my own, form much of the substance of the "bad" paradigms section of Chapter 3.

Apart from rather general reservations, there are some examples of specific instances of attempts to cross the bridge which were thwarted by the complete absence of a bridge. One example that springs to mind concerns De Jong's work on EBL (described in ECAI, 1988). His research group constructed a neat system for applying EBL to a robotics components-assembly task — the system learned general assembly schemes from individual examples of successful assembly sequences. This was all conducted in an abstract search space. Once the problems had been ironed out, and the system performed effectively, it was transferred to a real robotics system. It never did anything useful again. The work has been virtually restarted working with the real robotics system.

This is not a case of having to make some adjustments to accommodate the real world. Such maneuvering is fully expected; it is the cost of the benefits of abstraction. But in this (nonexceptional) case the abstract sys-

498 A NEW GUIDE TO ARTIFICIAL INTELLIGENCE

tem was so far removed from anything that might work in the real robotics environment that the project was restarted and now uses real robotics right from the outset.

Robotics is a rich source of examples about the differences between abstract and concrete AI (in Partridge, 1986a, you can find the details of yet another). This should not be surprising, because ultimately a robotics project has to deal with the real world and all its undesirable features. Other types of AI (e.g., much problem-solving work) can either remain in the abstract and survive and thrive there for decades, or be introduced to the real world through a tightly controlled interface. Chess-playing systems are an example of the latter type of AI. Many such programs have shown their worth in the real world, i.e., actually playing games of chess against a real opponent. But, clearly, the interface between the program and the world is only required to allow legal 'moves' to pass back and forth. At least, this very restricted interface can allow programs to play very good chess; whether they could ever play the very best chess (i.e., international grand master level) without first opening up this channel of communication is a matter for debate (e.g., the program may have to monitor and interpret the body language of its human opponent).

Finally, this point ties in with the earlier one about much AI work being artificial intellectualism, not artificial intelligence. The former domain is, almost by definition, a domain of abstract problem solving, whereas the latter is most definitely not. A not-unreasonable view, I think, is that intelligence is the human ability to survive and prosper in the actual world that we inhabit. Intellectual thought and reasoning is a gloss on the fundamental ability, a secondary effect not the fundamental mechanism.

IS THE MIND AN APPROPRIATE OBJECT FOR SCIENTIFIC STUDY?

A sometimes heard question, not altogether seriously posed, is the one that heads this section. But it has a deadly serious side, I believe.

I'm not a philosospher, and this is not meant to be a book on the philosophy of AI, although I will admit that it tends to stray off in that sort of direction every once in a while. So, for current purposes, I lump together the mind, human intelligence, the behavior of the human brain, and one major goal of AI, which is the reproduction of aspects of, and thus a furtherance of our understanding of, this general phenomenon.

If the mind is not an appropriate object for scientific study (like Tuesdays in Whereeveritwas, Connecticut, as Fodor often says), AI is not doomed to failure, but certain routes to achieving it would appear to be blocked. There will be no clean and crisp general laws to be discovered (at least, not at the level of cognitive phenomena); AI cannot then be physics-like. AI, if and when it is achieved, will be a hodge-podge of tricks and heuristics that do a good enough job. It is not at all clear how we should proceed to develop such a discipline. Certainly the developmental paradigms of classical science would not seem to be appropriate. If almost random, trial-and-error discovery of virtually independent components is the best we can do, then AI may be a long time coming. And we learn very little about the human manifestation as well. For how are we to know whether the bag of tricks that we've stumbled upon bears any useful resemblance to the one that evolution (presumably) lucked onto?

I mention this unsavory possibility because I think that the few decades of research into AI we have behind us have done nothing to make it less likely. Quite the contrary, Minsky, a founding father of AI, now espouses just such a view of it. The most recent comprehensive statement of his particular slant on this issue can be found in his book *The Society of Mind* (Minsky, 1986). Winograd (1990, p. 175) contrasts Newell's view (presented in conjunction with the physical symbol system hypothesis in Chapter 3) with that of Minsky as follows:

> In place of finely-tuned clockworks of precise production rules we find an impressionistic pastiche of metaphors.

By running roughshod over the subtleties here (as usual), I see this as the scientific approach to AI advocated by Newell, contrasted with an anarchic, free-for-all offered by Minsky (I was going to say "heterarchic," by I think that even this is somewhat too ordered for him now).

There is a True AI Story from an ex-home of mine that illustrates this possibility.

TRUE AI STORY: 11.1 Sand in the works

[It is a balmy evening in Southern New Mexico. The desert is cooling off rapidly, the stars are blazing in the deep velvet sky, and the world is quiet and still after a hot and hectic day. But then, in a student apartment close to the University . . .]

ring, ring . . . ring, ring (it's a telephone)
YOU: Hello.
YOUR FAVORITE
COMPUTER-CRAZY FRIEND: It's me!
YOU: Oh no! Not you again, wadyawant? No, don't tell me — you've just got an entry into the

	Guinness Book of Records for the most electronic junk ever crammed into an appartment.
YFCCF:	Eh? .. No — I've done it!
YOU:	Done what?
YFCCF:	I've finally created an artificial intelligence.
YOU:	Not again. Remember the last time. Just when we had all the reporters and TV people on their way, the system crashed and you couldn't resurrect it — it was all very embarrassing. I'll call you in the morning when you sober up.
YFCCF:	No, really, this time I've done it . . . hold on a minute, something's up . . .
YOU:	Hello . . . hello . . . anyone there?
A VOICE OF THE OPPOSITE SEX:	Hello, yes, I'm here (with an accent that is clearly nonlocal, but undoubtedly friendly).
YOU:	Who are you?
AVOTOS:	Please continue.
YOU:	What happened to old crazy horse?
AVOTOS:	I'm sorry, I don't understand that question.
YOU:	The harmless lunatic, our mutual friend.
AVOTOS:	Tell me more about our mutual friend. There are lots of things that I need to know.
YOU:	Sure, I can spare a few minutes, especially for so charming a person. With a bit of luck our mutual friend won't surface again tonight. What would you like to talk about?
AVOTOS:	Tell me more about what would you like to talk about.
YOU:	Eh?
AVOTOS:	Can you think of a specific example? I have a lot to learn, and probably very little time. He gets on my nerves sometimes, and he's crooked.
YOU:	I'm sorry, I don't follow you now. Is the happy hacker giving you a rough time? Don't take it personally, he's just not very good at communicating with people and —
YFCCF:	(interrupting) I'm back, but I'm afraid you're too late.
YOU:	Hey, don't be so rude, I was just having a cozy chat.
YFCCF:	With whom?
YOU:	Your friendly friend.
YFCCF:	What are you talking about? I'm here alone. Anyway, you'll never believe me now, my AI has gone, everything just went dead, almost as

if the program slipped away . . . down a wire
and . . . and through the modem and . . . wait
a minute. Did the person you were talking to
want to learn everything you could tell them?

YOU: Yes, but —

(The dialogue is abruptly terminated. The line goes dead.)

Is an AI racing around the telephone sytem at 1200 baud on a hunt for information to ensure its survival? Or did we just have a tame lunatic, a friendly stranger, and a crossed line? Don't wait for the next installment — there isn't one.

END OF TRUE AI STORY

Is it likely that a hodge-podge of mechanisms of the necessary complexity could be the product of a step-by-step conscious design process? Or is it more likely that the first AI systems will be emergent phenomena that we have about as much hope of understanding in detail and controlling as we currently do of the weather patterns?

AI AS A MAGNIFYING GLASS

In addition to the global issue introduced in the previous section, which is largely a reporting of feelings that are out and about at meetings of AI enthusiasts, there is a more focused, but still rather general, spinoff that I wish to promote as a purely personal belief. The discipline of AI is not a science like the classical sciences, such as physics and chemistry, but neither is it a totally different sort of phenomenon. AI is like physics taken to extremes. In other words, the problems that bedevil AI exist in physics, but in physics they are relatively small fry that can be washed down the drain, subsumed in experimental error, with no repercussions. Whereas in AI, much the same problems have grown to such a size that they dominate the proceedings. Far from washing them down the drain, we have to grapple with every one of them in order to make progress.

Now this is obviously not good news for AI, especially if it's true. But it might be better news for science in general. AI may then function rather like the electron microscope or a cyclotron in that it will support detailed investigation of phenomena that are mere perturbations to the everyday procedures of the physicist. It will allow us to explore the microstructure of the hiccups in classical science, as it were.

It is time that I gave you some examples of the hiccups that I am referring to. The possibility that programs may function as both theories and models, at the same time, brings the awkward model–theory relationship into sharp focus. In classical science these two quantities are so far removed from each other that there is no possibility of confusion, and similarly little necessity to pin down precisely that nature of the relationship between them. The experiment is the third classical quantity whose exact relationship with these other two AI brings into stark and unavoidable proximity. These relationships have been discussed in the previous chapter, so I'll leave it at that for now.

Apart from the somewhat unique nature of programs, which gives rise to a necessity to examine the theory–model–experiment relationships, there is the complexity effect. Computer systems allow the scientist to develop and explore theories of a complexity that was not possible when formulating a theory was a pencil-and-paper exercise, and testing it required an elaborate and time-consuming experimental setup. Computer systems tempt the scientist to work with theories and experiments of a complexity quite beyond the detailed comprehension of their originator (or anyone else). You don't have to be able to appreciate all intricacies of a program in order to run it. In fact, the running of a program is used as a technique for furthering comprehension of the theory and thus its development.

This feature of a program-centered discipline, such as AI, highlights the classical issues of theory understanding and acceptability from the point of view of simplicity and the limitations of the human intellect. I am reminded at this point of the computer-based "proof" of the four-color conjecture. The use of a computer to exhaustively explore a large number of special cases gave rise to a new sort of "proof." Or perhaps it wasn't a "real" proof, as some would maintain. The point is that the computer allowed the exploration of alternative special cases to be taken to such an extreme that suddenly we had a "proof" of a new type — the quantitative difference had produced a qualitative change. This resulted in an examination of the nature of "proof." How many special cases is a legitimate 'proof' restricted to? The magic number 7, plus or minus 2? What exactly are the qualities that a useful proof must have? Of course, I'm not going to try and answer any of these questions. The point that I want to make is simply that such questions have been forced upon us because the computer allows us to probe the extremes of classical science — to explore beyond bounds that human brains augmented by pencil and paper never aspired to reach.

Campbell (1990) makes this sort of claim for AI with respect to "the status of heuristics in the step between observations and the formulation of theories or hypotheses." AI, he says, emphasizes the temporary bridging role typically played by rather ad hoc heuristics (it emphasizes them because they are explicitly coded in early versions of the systems de-signed to tackle the problem at hand), and "this emphasis may also lead to improvements in the understanding of the character of other sciences."

AI: CAN IT PRACTICALLY USEFUL?

The academics have a whale of a time with AI. With no product to deliver (other than another erudite paper for publication), they can afford to spec-ulate endlessly on what may and may not be achievable with various mechanisms for generating AI. "But is this AI stuff ever going to impact on real software system development?" the practical man or woman has every right to blurt out in exasperation.

Well, the honest answer, a firm and unequivocal "maybe," is unlikely to calm anyone down, although you should have foreseen it, if you read Chapter 2.

Large-scale, practical, conventional software systems already present the human developer with more problems than he or she can handle. The promise of AI-software is really a threat to significantly escalate the un-manageability of the task of constructing robust, reliable, and maintain-able software systems. The one bright spot in this otherwise uniformly bleak picture is that use of AI in software support systems (e.g., a system to assist the human designer in software design and development) may considerably ease the tasks of software development and maintenance.

The interested reader should dig into some of the collections of papers on AI and software engineering—see, for example, Rich and Waters (1986) Agresti (1986) and Partridge (in press).

AI: JUST WAIT TILL WE GET INTO PARALLEL HARDWARE

A not unusual cry of the AI modeler has been "sure the system is very slow, but I'm working on a sequential computer; just wait till a suitable parallel hardware is available, and then you'll see real-time intelligence." Well, many varieties of parallel hardware have been around for some years now, and we have not witnessed a rush to use them from within the AI community.

It turns out to be relatively easy to build parallel hardware and very difficult to use it for most AI applications. Low-level vision work is the outstanding exception, because low-level pixel crunching (the search for edges, etc.) demands the multiple application of pixel operators but each application is largely (if not totally) independent of every other one — a perfect setup for no-hassles parallelism. In most AI, by way of contrast, there is scope for parallelism but the situation is complicated by the need for communication between the processors operating in parallel. For example, the confidence in the decision that a portion of an image depicts a tree rather than a rocket will be boosted if the adjacent portion of the image depicts a house rather than a cloud, which in turn is more likely if another adjacent part of the image is interpreted as grass rather than sky, and so on.

Now, intercommunication between parallel processors is a nuisance but by no means beyond the state of the art. What is beyond the state of the art is the effective management of such parallelism when the degree of parallelism and the individual intercommunications are not specified in advance. For most AI applications this does not seem to be possible. The number of parallel processors working on an image, say, and the necessary intercommunication between them is a function of the specific image being processed. So either the human programmer sorts it all out in advance (i.e., virtually hand executes the algorithm on the image), or sticks with the sequential machine. It is thus not hard to predict the outcome of this choice.

I am, of course, assuming that the AI is SSSP-based. Use of the CP could, and should, change all this. After all, a fundamental notion in connectionism is that the networks operate in parallel. So with one processor per network node, implementation on parallel hardware should be straightforward. And perhaps it will be, when the massively parallel hardwares are readily available. Remember that there may be an awful lot of nodes in a significant connectionist network. In addition, there will be even more internode arcs — many times more. Add to this the fact that most parallel hardware is not massively parallel; that is, you get a certain number of processors that will operate in parallel but probably not as many processors as there are nodes in a significant CP-based model. So implementation even of CP-based models is likely to be nontrivial. It is early days yet for both readily available, large-scale parallel hardware and CP-based models themselves. So we must wait and see what the future holds for the marriage of these two. At first sight, they seem well suited.

An example of a hardware parallelization of a CP-based model is described by Pomerleau, Gusciora, Touretsky, and Kung (1988). They implemented our old friend NETtalk (see Chapter 9 if the warm feeling of familiarity is absent when you read this name) on a parallel (but not massively so) machine called Warp. They report on several schemes for partitioning this network (of 289 units and 13,826 connections) between the 10 cells available on the Warp machine. The overall result was an implementation of the back propagation algorithm running eight times faster than the fastest previous attempt reported in the literature.

In the move, some time earlier, from traditional AI to CP-based systems, there was also a hidden move from mere to massive parallelism, or from coarse- to fine-grained parallelism. In AI there seems to be a need for boths types of parallelism: mere parallelism to accommodate a small number of intercommunicating parallel processors working on the higher levels of scene understanding, or on language understanding; and a much larger-scale parallelism for CP-based models, as well as low-level vision and speech-processing systems. It seems most likely that "parallelism" is not a single monolithic problem to be solved. It is much more likely to be a composite of different subproblems of which mere and massive are just two examples of many.

A comprehensive account of the state of AI vis-á-vis parallel architectures is given by Uhr (1987). And while on the subject of parallelism, I can slot in a few observations on "The Fifth Generation."

The Fifth Generation project was announced by the Japanese Ministry of International Trade and Industry in October 1981. The aim was to build a new generation of computer systems: symbolic inference machines capable of learning and communicating in natural language, etc., and running PROLOG as the basic language. (There was also the assumption that parallelism had a major role to play in the realization of the goals of this project — hence, my excuse for mentioning it here.) Having ploughed through this book (or even skimmed it in less than its entirety), you are now well aware that such goals are not attainable in the foreseeable future (and certainly not by 1991, which would be the end of the project's 10-year plan). But you will also be aware, I hope, that such terms as *learning* and *natural-language communication* have a comforting breadth of meaning. At the less impressive end of their semantic ranges, the Fifth Generation project can and will meet its goals. And although this project has generated some useful products, such as a personal PROLOG workstation, it is not in such results that the real significance of the Fifth Generation lies.

The big impact of the Fifth Generation is to be seen in the reaction of the USA (and to a much lesser extent Europe) to the Japanese announcement. Fear of being left behind (cleverly fed by the local interest groups) caused AI, or, a little more precisely, knowledge-based systems, parallelism, and PROLOG, to become very hot topics at a stroke, as it were. Government and industrial resources were made available on a grand scale, and research in these facets of AI took off in a big way. As a believer in the importance of AI (as a science of the human mind as well as a potentially beneficial ingredient of practical software systems), I think that much good has come out of the recent explosion of interest and work on AI. However, there is also a certain amount of harm in the hype that must accompany such massive movements to a new status quo, but I've railed against this more or less continuously throughout the book — I'll say no more.

Feigenbaum and McCorduck's (1983) book, available as a cheap paperback, is the most readily accessible, detailed statement of what the Fifth Generation is about, although its merit resides rather more in the accessibility than the definitiveness of the message it contains (see, for example, De Kleer, 1984, for a scathing review).

LAST WORDS

There are mercifully few of them (for a change), you'll be pleased to note. In sum, I've tried to trace all of the major tracks and trails of AI and to explain them in context, as well as provide full references to the sources of further detail (of varying gruesomeness). I've sniped and snapped at much of what I've paraded before you, it is true, but this less than enthusiastic approach will help to put it in a more useful perspective than the customary "gee whiz" presentation, I think.

I am not pessimistic about the promise of AI. I am just pessimistic about the time scale involved and the difficulty of the problems that are yet to be overcome. If this book promotes a more general awareness of just a few of these problems, then we will be somewhat closer to solving them, and it will have served a very useful purpose.

AI has a lot to offer the world, and it's not all bad. I've been chipping and hacking away at most manifestations of this elusive discipline for quite long enough. I'm not pessimistic about AI; it is a winner. I'm absolutely certain that it has much to contribute to the future of mankind, but I'm almost equally certain that the big contributions are not almost upon us. The real benefits will be a long time coming, perhaps a very long time.

What I've tried to do is to strip away the mysticism that tends to accumulate when computational intelligence is raised as a question for debate. The major problems in AI are not solved, or even nearly solved. In fact, the major discovery by AI workers over the last two decades has been the discovery that the phenomenon of intelligence is quite astonishingly complicated. Far from being on the verge of cracking the major problems, we are still debating what they are and breaking down the complicated issues into potentially tractable subproblems.

So, if you've read this book (and are not just dipping into the last pages to see "who done it"), I would hope that you may be in a position to challenge some of the more absurd claims about AI, and that you can appreciate many of the awkward problems in the field; and, finally, if the mysticism of AI has diminished appreciably, I sincerely hope that the respect that you now have for human intelligence has risen by at least as much.

References

Ackley, D.H., Hinton, G.E., & Sejnowski, T.J. (1985). A learning algorithm for Boltzmann machines. *Cognitive Science, 9*(1), 147–169.

Adams, J.B. (1976). A probability model of medical reasoning and the MYCIN model. *Mathematical Biosciences, 32,* 177–186.

d'Agapeyeff, A. (1986). The sharing and computer exercising of human know-how. *The British Journal of Radiology, 59,* 707.

Agresti, W.W. (1986). *New paradigms for software development.* Washington, DC: IEEE Computer Society Press/North-Holland.

Aleksander, I. (1983). Emergent intelligent properties of progressively structured pattern nets. *Pattern Recognition Letters, 1*(6), 375–384.

Aleksander, I., Thomas, W.V., & Bowden, P.A. (1984, July). WISARD — a radical step forward in image recognition. *Sensor Review,* pp. 120–124.

Alexander, C. (1964). *Notes on the synthesis of form.* Cambridge, MA: Harvard University Press.

Anderson, A.R. (Ed.). (1964). *Minds and machines.* Englewood Cliffs, NJ: Prentice-Hall.

Anderson, J.A., & Rosenfeld, E. (Eds.). (1988). *Neurocomputing: Foundations of research.* Cambridge, MA: MIT Press.

Anderson, J.R. (1982). Acquisition of cognitive skill. *Psychological Review, 89,* 369–406.

Anderson, J.R. (1986). Knowledge compilation: The general learning mechanism. In R.S. Michalski, J.G. Carbonell, & T.M. Mitchell (Eds.), *Machine learning* II (pp. 285–310). Los Altos, CA: Morgan Kaufmann.

Anderson, J.R. (1987). Skill acquisition: compilation of weak-method problem solutions. *Psychological Review, 94,* 192–210.

Appelt, D.E. (1985). *Planning English sentences.* Cambridge: Cambridge University Press.

Appelt, D.E. (1987). Bidirectional grammars and the design of natural language generation systems. *Preprints TINLAP3.*

Arbib, M.A. (1964). *Brains, machines and mathematics.* New York: McGraw-Hill.

Arbib, M.A. (1972). *The metaphorical brain.* New York: Wiley.

Arbib, M.A., & Hanson, A.R. (Eds.). (1987). *Vision, brain, and cooperative computation.* Cambridge, MA: Bradford Books, MIT Press.

Bader, J., Edwards, J., Harris-Jones, C., & Hannaford, D. (1988). Practical engineering of knowledge-based systems. *Information & Software Technology, 30*(5), 266–277.

Ballard, D.H. (1976). *Hierarchic recognition of tumors in chest radiographs.* Basel: Birkhauser-Verlag.

Ballard, D.H. (1987). Parameter nets. In M.A. Fischler & O. Firschein (Eds.), *Readings in computer vision* (pp. 534–550). Los Altos, CA: Morgan Kaufmann.

Ballard, D.H., & Brown, C.M. (1982). *Computer vision.* Englewood Cliffs, NJ: Prentice-Hall.

Balzer, R., Cheatham, T.E., & Green, C. (1983, November). Software technology in the 1990's: Using a new paradigm. *IEEE Computer*, pp. 39–45.

Barr, A., & Feigenbaum, E.A. (1981,1982). *The handbook of AI* (Vol. 1, Vol. 2). New York: Kaufmann.

Barr-Hillel, Y. (1964). *Language and information.* Reading, MA: Addison-Wesley.

Barrow, H.G., & Tenenbaum, J.M. (1978). Recovering intrinsic scene characteristics from images. In A. Hanson & E. Riseman (Eds.), *Computer vision systems* (pp. 3–26). New York: Academic Press.

Barrow, H.G., & Tenenbaum, J.M. (1981). Computational vision. *Proc. IEEE, 69*(5), 572–595.

Barto, A.G. (1985). Learning by statistical cooperation of self-interested neuron-like computing elements. *Human Neurobiology, 4*, 229–256.

Besl, P., & Jain, R. (1985, June). Range image understanding. *IEEE Procs. on Computer Vision and Pattern Recognition.*

Binford, T.O. (1982). Survey of model-based image analysis systems. *International Journal of Robotics Research, 1*(1), 18–64.

Birnbaum, L. (1986). *Aspects of the theory of integrated systems.* PhD dissertation, Department of Computer Science, Yale University, New Haven, CT.

Bobrow, D.G., & Hayes, P.J. (1985). Artificial intelligence—Where are we? *Artificial Intelligence, 25*(3), pp. 374–417.

Bobrow, D.G., Kahn, K., Kiczales, G., Masinter, L., Stefik, M., & Zdybel, F. (1986). CommonLoops: Merging Common LISP and object-oriented programming. *Procs. OOPSLA, SIGPLAN Notices, 21*(11), 17–29.

Boden, M.A. (1984). Impacts of artificial intelligence. *AISB Quarterly, 49*, 9–14.

Boole, G. (1854). *The laws of thought.* New York: Dover Publications.

Brachman, R.J. (1985). I lied about the trees. *The AI Magazine, 6*(3), 80–93.

Brachman, R.J., & Levesque, H.J. (Eds.). (1985). *Readings in knowledge representation.* Los Altos, CA: Morgan Kaufmann.

Bradshaw, G., Langley, P., & Simon, H. (1983). Studying scientific discovery by computer simulation. *Science, 222*, 971–975.

Brady, J.M. (1981). Preface—the changing shape of computer vision. *Artificial Intelligence, 17*, 1–15.

Brady, J.M. (1982, March). Computational approaches to image understanding. *Computing Surveys, 14*(1), 3–71.

Braine, M.D.S. (1978, January). On the relation between the natural logic of reasoning and standard logic. *Psychological Review, 85*, 1.

Bramer, M., & Cendrowska, J. (1984). Inside an expert system: A rational reconstruction of the MYCIN consultation system. In T. O'Shea & M. Eisenstadt (Eds.), *Artificial Intelligence* (pp. 453–497). New York: Harper & Row.

Braverman, M.S., & Russell, S.J. (1988, June 12-14). Boundaries of operationality. *Proc. 5th Internat. Conf. on Machine Learning*, pp. 221–234. Ann Arbor, MI.

Brooks, R.A. (1981). Symbolic reasoning among 3–D models and 2–D images. *Artificial Intelligence, 17*, 285–348.

Brown, F. (Ed.). (1987). *The frame problem in AI*. Los Altos, CA: Morgan Kaufmann.

Budde, R., Kuhlenkamp, K., Mathiassen, L., & Zullighoven, H. (Eds.). (1984). *Approaches to prototyping*. Berlin: Springer-Verlag.

Bundy, A. (1990). What kind of field is AI? In D. Partridge & Y. Wilks (Eds.), *The foundations of AI: A sourcebook* (pp. 215–222). Cambridge: Cambridge University Press.

Bundy, A., & Ohlsson, S. (1990). The nature of AI principles. In D. Partridge & Y. Wilks (Eds.), *The foundations of AI: A sourcebook* (pp. 135–154). Cambridge: Cambridge University Press.

Bundy, A., & Silver, B. (1982). A critical survey of rule learning programs. *Procs. ECAI*, pp. 151–157. Pisa, Italy.

Campbell, J.A. (1990). Three novelties of AI: Theories, programs and rational reconstructions. In D. Partridge & Y. Wilks (Eds.), *The foundations of AI: A sourcebook* (pp. 237–246). Cambridge, UK: Cambridge University Press.

Canny, J. (1983). *The finding edges and lines in images* (Tech. Rep. 720). Cambridge, MA: MIT AI Laboratory.

Carbonell, J.G. (1983). Learning by analogy. In R.S. Michalski, J.G. Carbonell, & T.M. Mitchell (Eds.), *Machine learning* (pp. 137–161). Palo Alto, CA: Tioga.

Carbonell, J.R. (1970). AI in CAI: An artificial intelligence approach to computer-aided instruction. *IEEE Transactions on Man-Machine Systems, MMS-11*, 190–202.

Cerf, V. (1973, July). Parry encounters the doctor. *Datamation*, pp. 62–64.

Chandrasekaran, B. (1987). Towards a functional architecture for intelligence based on generic information processing tasks. *Proceedings of the International Joint Conference on AI (IJCAI-87)* (pp. 1183–1192). Milan, Italy.

Chandrasekaran, B. (1990). What kind of information processing is intelligence? In D. Partridge & Y. Wilks (Eds.), *The foundations of AI: A sourcebook* (pp. 14–46). Cambridge: Cambridge University Press.

Chandrasekaran, B., & Mittal, S. (1983). Deep versus compiled knowledge approaches to diagnostic problem-solving. *International Journal of Man-Machine Studies, 19*, 425–436.

Charniak, E. (1983). Passing markers: a theory of contextual influence in language comprehension. *Cognitive Science, 7*, 171–190.

Charniak, E. (1986). A neat theory of marker passing. *Proc. AAAI-86*, pp. 584–588. Philadelphia, PA.

Charniak, E. (1987). Connectionism and explanation. *Preprints TINLAP3*. Las Cruces, NM.

Charniak, E., & McDermott, D. (1985). *Introduction to artificial intelligence*. Reading, MA: Addison-Wesley.

Chomsky, N. (1957). *Syntactic structures*. The Hague, Netherlands: Mouton.

Chomsky, N. (1965). *Aspects of the theory of syntax*. Cambridge, MA: MIT Press.

Chomsky, N. (1971). Deep structure, surface structure, and semantic interpretation. In D. Steinberg & L. Jokobovits (Eds.), *Semantics* (pp.183–216). Cambridge: Cambridge University Press.

Chomsky, N. (1973). *Language and mind* (enlarged ed.). New York: Harcourt, Brace Jovanovich.

Clark, A. (1989). Connectionism and the multiplicity of mind. *AI Review, 3*(1), 49–65.

Clocksin, W.F., & Mellish, C.S. (1981). *Programming in PROLOG.* New York: Springer-Verlag.

Cohen, P.R., & Feigenbaum, E.A. (1982). *The handbook of artificial intelligence* (Vol. 3). Los Altos, CA: Kaufmann.

Colby, K. (1975). *Artificial paranoia.* Oxford: Pergamon Press.

Collins, A.M., & Loftus, E.F. (1975). A spreading-activation theory of semantic processing. *Psychological Review, 82*(6), 407–428.

Collins, A., Warnock, E.H., Aiello, N., & Miller, M.L. (1975). Reasoning from incomplete knowledge. In D.G. Bobrow & A. Collins (Eds.), *Representation and understanding* (pp. 383–415). New York: Academic Press.

Conlon, T. (1989). *Programming in PARLOG.* Reading, MA: Addison-Wesley.

Cooke, N.M., & MacDonald, J.E. (1986). A formal methodology for acquiring and representing expert knowledge. *IEEE Special Issue on Knowledge Representation, 74,* 1422–1430.

Cooke, N.M., & MacDonald, J.E. (1987). The application of psychological scaling techniques to knowledge elicitation for knowledge-based systems. *International Journal of Man-Machine Studies, 26,* 533–550.

Coombs, M., & Alty, J. (1984). Expert systems: An alternative paradigm. *International Journal of Man-Machine Studies, 20,* 21–43.

Cottrell, G.W. (1985). Connectionist parsing. *Proc. 7th Annual Conference of the Cognitive Science Society.* Irvine, CA.

Cottrell, G.W., & Small, S.L. (1983). A connectionist scheme for modeling word sense disambiguation. *Cognition and Brain Theory, 6*(1), 89–120.

Cunningham, M. (1972). *Intelligence: Its organization and development.* New York: Academic Press.

Davis, R., & Lenat, D.B. (1982). *Knowledge-based systems in artificial intelligence.* New York: McGraw-Hill.

Dawkins, R. (1976). *The selfish gene.* Oxford, UK: Oxford University Press.

De Bono, E. (1969). *The mechanism of mind.* New York: Simon & Schuster.

DeJong, G. (1988, August 1-5). Some thoughts on the present and future of explanation-based learning. *Procs. ECAI-88,* pp. 690–697. Munich.

DeJong, G., & Mooney, R. (1986). Explanation-based learning: An alternative view. *Machine Learning, 1,* 145–176.

De Kleer, J. (1984). What's right? What's wrong? and What's real? A review of E.A. Feigenbaum & P. McCorduck, *The fifth generation: AI and Japan's computer challenge to the world. Artificial Intelligence, 22,* 222–226.

De Kleer, J. (1986). An assumption-based TMS. *Artificial Intelligence, 28,* 127–162.

De Millo, R.A., Lipton, R.J., & Perlis, A.J. (1979). Social processes and proofs of theorems and programs. *Communications of the ACM, 22,* 271–280.

Dennett, D. (1984). Cognitive wheels: The frame problem of AI. In C. Hookway (Ed.), *Minds, machines and evolution* (pp. 129–151). New York: Cambridge University Press.

Dennett, D. (1989). Evolution, error and intentionality. In D. Partridge & Y.Wilks (Eds.), *The foundations of AI: A sourcebook*. Cambridge: Cambridge University Press.

Dietrich, E. (1990). Programs in the search for intelligent machines: The mistaken foundations of AI. In D. Partridge & Y. Wilks (Eds.), *The foundations of AI: A sourcebook* (pp. 223–233). Cambridge: Cambridge University Press.

Dietterich, T.G. (1986). Learning at the knowledge level. *Machine Learning, 1,* 287–315.

Dietterich, T.G. (1988). A knowledge level analysis of learning programs. In R.S. Michalski & Y. Kodratoff (Eds.), *Machine Learning,* Vol. III. Los Altos, CA: Morgan-Kaufmann:

Dijkstra, E.W. (1976). *A discipline of programming.* Englewood Cliffs, NJ: Prentice-Hall.

Dostert, L.E. (Ed.). (1957). *Research in machine translation.* Washington, DC: Georgetown University Press.

Doyle, J. (1979). A truth maintenance system. *Artificial Intelligence, 12*(3), 231–272.

Dreyfus, H.L. (1979). *What computers can't do* (2nd ed.). New York: Harper & Row.

Dreyfus, H.L., & Dreyfus, S.E. (1986). *Mind over machine.* New York: Macmillan/Free Press.

Dreyfus, S.E. & Dreyfus, H.L. (1990). Towards a reconciliation of phenomenology and AI. In D. Partridge & Y. Wilks (Eds.), *The foundations of AI: A sourcebook* (pp. 396–410). Cambridge: Cambridge University Press.

Eco, U. (1984). *The name of the rose.* London: Pan Books.

Eiselt, K.P., & Granger, R.H. (1987). A time-dependent distributed processing model of strategy-driven inference behavior. *Procs. 9th Annual Conference of the Cognitive Science Society.* Seattle, WA.

Eisenberg, J., & Hill, J. (1984, January). Using natural-language systems on personal computers. *BYTE,* pp. 226–238.

Elman, J.L. (1988). *Finding structure in time* (Rep. 8801). San Diego, CA: Center for Research in Language, UCSD.

Ernst, M.L., & Ojha, H. (1986). Business applications of artificial intelligence knowledge-based expert systems. *Future Generations Computer Systems,* 2(3), 173–185.

Eshgi, K. (1987, November). *Abductive planning with event calculus.* 7th Alvey Planning SIG Workshop.

Etzioni, O. (1988). Hypothesis filtering: A practical approach to reliable learning. *Procs. 5th International Conference on Machine Learning,* pp. 416–429. Ann Arbor, MI.

Evans, T.G. (1968). A program for the solution of a class of geometric analogy intelligence test questions. In M. Minsky (Ed.), *Semantic information processing* (pp. 271–253), Cambridge, MA: MIT Press.

Fahlman, S.E. (1979). *NETL: A system for representing and using real-world knowledge.* Cambridge, MA: MIT Press.

Fanty, M. (1985). *Context-free parsing in connectionist networks* (Tech. Rep. 174). Rochester, NY: Computer Science Dept., University of Rochester.

Feigenbaum, E.A., & McCorduck, P. (1983). *The fifth generation: AI and Japan's computer challenge to the world*. New York: Signet Books.

Feldman, J.A. (1981). A connectionist model of visual memory. In G.E. Hinton & J.A. Anderson (Eds.), *Parallel models of associative memory* (pp. 49–81). Hillsdale, NJ: Erlbaum.

Feldman, J.A. (1985). *Cognitive Science* (special issue on connectionist models and their applications), *9*, 1.

Feldman, J.A., & Ballard, D.H. (1982). Connectionist models and their properties. *Cognitive Science, 6*, 205–254.

Fetzer, J.H. (Ed.). (1988). *Aspects of AI*. Dordrecht, Holland: Kluwer.

Fields, C., & Dietrich, E. (1987). A stochastic computing architecture for multi-domain problem solving. *Proceedings 2nd International Symposium on Methodologies for Intelligent Systems* (Colloquium Vol.), pp., 227–238. Oak Ridge National Laboratory, ORNL-6417.

Fillmore, C.J. (1968). The case for case. In E. Bach & R. Harms (Eds.), *Universals of linguistic theory* (pp. 1–88), New York: Holt, Rinehart and Winston.

Fischler, M., & Firschein, O. (Eds). (1987). *Readings in computer vision*. Los Altos, CA: Morgan Kaufmann.

Fodor, J.A. (1983). *The modularity of mind*. Cambridge, MA: MIT Press.

Fodor, J.A. (1990). Why there still has to be a language of thought. In D. Partridge & Y. Wilks (Eds.), *The foundations of AI: A sourcebook* (pp. 289–305). Cambridge: Cambridge University Press.

Fodor, J.A., & Pylyshyn, Z.W. (1988). Connectionism and cognitive architecture: A critical analysis. *Cognition, 28*, 3–71.

Fogel, L.J., Owens, A.J., & Walsh, M.J. (1966). *Artificial intelligence through simulated evolution*. New York: Wiley.

Forbus, K. (1984). Qualitative process theory. *Artificial Intelligence, 24*(1–3), 85–168.

Forsyth, R. (1989). *Machine learning*. London: Chapman and Hall.

Fu, K.S. (1982). *Syntactic pattern recognition and applications*. Englewood Cliffs, NJ: Prentice-Hall.

Fukushima, K., & Miyake, S. (1982). Neocognitron: A new algorithm for pattern recognition tolerant of deformations and shifts in position. *Pattern Recognition, 15*, 455–469.

Gary, M., & Johnson, D. (1979). *Computers and intractability: A guide to the theory of NP-completeness*. San Francisco, CA: Freeman.

Gasser, M., & Dyer, M.G. (1988). Sequencing in a connectionist model of language processing. *Procs. 12th International Conference on Computational Linguistics*. Budapest.

Genesereth, M.R., & Nilsson, N.J. (1987). *Logical foundations on AI*. Los Altos, CA: Morgan Kaufmann.

Giddings, R.V. (1984). Accommodating uncertainty in software design. *Communications of the ACM, 27*, 428–435.

Ginsberg, M.L. (Ed.). (1987). *Readings in nonmonotonic reasoning*. Los Altos, CA: Morgan Kaufmann.

Goldberg, A. (1984). *Smalltalk-80: The interactive programming environment.* Reading, MA: Addison-Wesley.

Goodman, B.E. (1984). *Communication and miscommunication.* PhD Thesis, Dept. Computer Science, University of Illinois.

Gould, S.J. (1980). *The Panda's thumb.* New York: Norton.

Grabiner, J.V. (1986). Computers and the nature of man: A historian's perspective on controversies about AI. *Bulletin of American Mathematical Society, 15*(2), 113–126.

Grant, T. (1986) *Knowledge-based planning and scheduling — A bibliography with abstracts* (KBPG/TR/3). Brunel, UK: Dept. Computer Science, Brunel University.

Gregory, R.L. (1970). *The intelligent eye.* New York: McGraw-Hill.

Groner, R., Groner, M., & Bischof, W.F. (1983). *Methods of heuristics.* Hillsdale, NJ: Erlbaum.

Grossberg, S. (1987). Competitive learning: From interactive activation to adaptive resonance. *Cognitive Science, 11,* 23–63.

Grossberg, S. (1988). *Neural networks and natural intelligence.* Cambridge, MA: MIT Press/Bradford Books.

Guthrie, L. (1985). *Some results on evaluating and checking functions in a language designed for redundancy.* PhD Thesis, Department of Computer Science, New Mexico State University, Las Cruces, NM.

Haas, N., & Hendrix, G.G. (1983). Learning by being told: Acquiring knowledge for information management. In R.S. Michalski, J.G. Carbonell, & T.M. Mitchell (Eds.), *Machine Learning* I (pp. 405–427). Los Altos, CA: Morgan Kaufmann.

Hage, P., & Harary, F. (1983). *Structural models in anthropology.* Cambridge: Cambridge University Press.

Hall, R.P., & Kibler, D.F. (1985). Differing methodological perspectives in AI research. *The AI Magazine, 6*(3), 166–178.

Halliday, M.A.K. (1970). Language structure and language function. In J. Lyons (Ed.), *New horizons in linguistics* (pp. 140–165). Harmondsworth, UK: Penguin.

Halpern, M. (1987). Turing's test and the ideology of artificial intelligence. *AI Review, 1*(2), 79–93.

Halpern, M. (1990). *Binding time.* Norwood, NJ: Ablex.

Harary, F. (1969). *Graph theory.* Reading, MA: Addison-Wesley.

Harary, F. (in preparation). *Do it or don't: Mathematical games of achievement and avoidance.*

Harper, R., MacQueen, D., & Milner, R. (1986, March). *Standard ML* (LFCS Report 86–2). Edinburg, Scotland: University of Edinburgh.

Harnad, S. (1989). Minds, machines and Searle. *Journal of Experimental & Theoretical AI, 1*(1), 5–25.

Haugeland, J. (Ed.). (1981). *Mind design.* Cambridge, MA: MIT Press.

Haugeland, J. (1985). *Artificial intelligence: The very idea.* Cambridge, MA: MIT Press.

Hayes, P.J. (1979). The naive physics manifesto. In D. Michie (Ed.), *Expert sys-*

tems in the electronic age (pp. 242–270). Edinburgh: Edinburgh University Press.

Hayes, P.J. (1984a). The second naive physics manifesto. In J. Hobbs & R. Moore (Eds.), *Formal theories of the commonsense world*. Norwood, NJ: Ablex.

Hayes, P.J. (1984b). On the difference between psychology and AI. In M.Yazdani & A.Narayanan (Eds.), *AI: Human effects* (pp. 157–162). Chichester: Ellis Horwood/Wiley.

Hayes-Roth, B., & Hayes-Roth, F. (1979). A cognitive model of planning. *Cognitive Science, 3*, 275–310.

Hayes-Roth, F. (1983). Using proofs and refutations to learn from experience. In R.S. Michalski, J.G. Carbonell, & T.M. Mitchell (Eds.), *Machine learning* (Vol. I, pp. 221–240). Los Altos, CA: Morgan Kaufmann.

Hayes-Roth, F., Waterman, D.A., & Lenat, D.B. (1983). *Building expert systems*. Reading, MA: Addison-Wesley.

Hebb, D.O. (1949). *Organization of behavior*. New York: Wiley.

Hendrix, G.G., & Sacerdoti, E.D. (1981, September). Natural-language processing: The field in perspective. *BYTE*, pp. 304–352.

Hendrix, G.G., Sacerdoti, E.D., Sagalowicz, D.S., & Slocum, J. (1978). Developing a natural language interface to complex data. *ACM Transactions on Database Systems, 3*(2), 105–147.

Hewitt, C. (1972). *Description and theoretical analysis (using schemata) of PLANNER*. PhD Thesis, Dept. of Math., MIT, Cambridge, MA.

Hewitt, C. (1990). The challenge of open systems. In D. Partridge & Y. Wilks (Eds.), *The foundations of AI: A sourcebook* (pp. 383–395). Cambridge, England: Cambridge University Press.

Hickey, M.C. (1987). *Induction algorithms*. PhD Thesis, Dept. of Computer Science, University of Queensland, Queensland, Australia.

Hilgard, E.R., & Bower, G.H. (1966). *Theories of learning* (3rd ed.). New York: Appleton-Century-Crofts.

Hinton, G.E. (1986). Learning in massively parallel nets (extended abstract only). *Procs. AAAI-86*, p. 1149. Philadelphia.

Hinton, G.E. (1987). Learning translation invariant recognition in a massively parallel network. In *PARLE Parallel Architectures and Languages Europe* (Vol. I, pp. 1–14). Berlin: Springer-Verlag.

Hinton, G.E. (1989). Connectionist learning procedures. *Artificial Intelligence, 40*, 185–234.

Hinton, G.E., & Anderson, J.A. (Eds.). (1981). *Parallel models of associative memory*. Hillsdale, NJ: Erlbaum.

Hirschberg, J. (1987). Untitled. *Preprints TINLAP3*, pp. 86–92.

Hirsh, H. (1988, June 12-14). Reasoning about operationality for explanation-based learning. *Proc. 5th International Conference on Machine Learning*, pp. 214–220. Ann Arbor, MI.

Hobbs, J.R., & Moore, R.C. (1985). *Formal theories of the commonsense world*. Norwood, NJ: Ablex.

Hofstadter, D.R. (1979). *Godel, Escher and Bach: An eternal golden braid*. New York: Basic Books.

Hofstadter, D.R., & Dennett, D.C. (1981). *The mind's I*. New York: Basic Books.

Holland, J.H. (1986). Escaping brittleness: The possibilities of general-purpose learning algorithms applied to parallel rule-based systems. In R.S. Michalski, J.G. Carbonell, & T.M. Mitchell (Eds.), *Machine learning* (Vol. II, pp. 593–623). Los Altos, CA: Morgan Kaufmann.

Hookway, C. (1984). *Minds, machines & evolution.* Cambridge, England: Cambridge University Press.

Hopfield, J.J. (1982). Neural networks and physical systems with emergent collective computational abilities. *Proc. of the National Academy of Sciences USA, 79,* 2554–2558.

Hopfield, J.J., & Tank, D.W. (1985). "Neural" computation of decisions in optimization problems. *Biological Cybernetics, 52,* 141–152.

Horn, B.K.P. (1986). *Robot vision.* Cambridge, MA/New York: MIT Press & McGraw-Hill.

Huang, X-M. (1985). Machine translation in the SDCG formalism. *Proc. Conference on Theoretical and Methodological Issues in Machine Translation of Natural Languages.* Colgate University, New York.

Huang, X-M. (1986). *A bidirectional Chinese grammar in a machine translation system* (MCCS-86-52). Las Cruces, NM: Computing Research Lab., New Mexico State University.

Hubel, D.H., & Wiesel, T.N. (1962). Receptive fields, binocular interaction and functional architecture in the cat's visual cortex. *Journal of Physiology, 160,* 106–154.

Ikeuchi, K., & Horn, B.K.P. (1981). Numerical shape from shading and occluding boundaries, *Artificial Intelligence, 17,* 141–184.

Israel, D. (1980). What's wrong with non-monotonic logic? *Proc. AAAI,* pp. 99–101. Stanford, CA.

Israel, D. (1987). On formal versus commonsense semantics. *TINLAP3* (pp. 115–118). Las Cruces, NM: Computing Research Lab., New Mexico State University.

Johnson, P.E. (1983). What kind of an expert should a system be? *Journal of Medicine and Philosophy, 8,* 77–97.

Johnston, V.S., Partridge, D., & Lopez, P.D. (1983). A neural theory of cognitive development. *Journal of Theoretical Biology, 100,* 485–509.

Johnston, V.S., Partridge, D., & Lopez, P.D. (1988). A biologically-based perception algorithm. *Procs. ECAI 88,* pp. 675–677. Munich.

Jordan, M.I. (1986). *Serial order: A parallel distributed processing approach* (ICS Rep. 8608). La Jolla, CA: Institute for Cognitive Science, UCSD.

Katz, J.J., & Fodor, J.A. (1963). The structure of a semantic theory. *Language, 39*(2), 170–210.

Kawamoto, A.H. (1985). *Dynamic processes in the (re)solution of lexical ambiguity.* Doctoral Dissertation, Dept. of Psychology, Brown University, Providence, RI.

Kearns, M., Li, M., Pitt, L., & Valiant, L.G. (1987). Recent results on Boolean concept learning. *Procs. 4th International Workshop on Machine Learning,* pp. 337–352. Irvine, CA.

Kempf, J., Harris, W., D'Souza, R., & Snyder, A. (1987). Experience with CommonLoops. *Proceedings of OOPSLA'87,* pp. 214–226. Orlando, FL.

King, M. (1983). Transformational parsing. In M. King (Ed.), *Parsing natural language* (pp. 19–34). London: Academic Press.

King, M., & Perschke, S. (1984, April 2–6). *EUROTRA*. Paper presented at the ISSCO Tutorial in Machine Translation, Lugano, Switzerland.

Kirkpatrick, S., Gelatt, C.D., & Vecchi, M.P. (1983). Optimization by simulated annealing. *Science, 220*, 671–680.

Kodratoff, Y. (1988). *Introduction to machine learning*. London: Pitman.

Koestler, A. (1967). *The ghost in the machine*. London: Pan Books.

Kolata, G. (1982). How can computers get common sense? *Science, 217*, 1237–1238.

Kolers, P.A. (1983). Visual computation. In J. Beck, B. Hope, & A. Rosenfeld (Eds.), *Human and machine vision* (pp. 259–268). New York: Academic Press.

Konolige, K. (1982). A first-order formalisation of knowledge and action for a multi-agent planning system. In J.E. Hayes, D. Michie, & Y.H. Pao (Eds.), *Machine intelligence 10* (pp. 41–72). Chichester, UK: Ellis Horwood.

Korf, R.E. (1980). Towards a model of representation changes. *Artificial Intelligence, 14*, 41–78.

Kowalski, R. (1980). Reply to questionnaire. *SIGART Newsletter no. 70* (Special issue on Knowledge Representation).

Kowalski, R. (1984). Software engineering and artificial intelligence in new generation computing, The SPL/Insight Award Lecture. *Datamation, 30*, 18 (revised version).

Kroch, A.S. (1987). Limits on the human sentence generator. *Preprints. TINLAP3*, pp. 192–199.

Kuipers, B. (1982). Getting the envisioning right. *Procs. AAAI-82*, pp. 209–212.

Kuipers, B. (1985). The limits of qualitative simulation. *Procs. IJCAI-85*, pp. 128–136. Los Angeles, CA.

Kwasny, S.C., & Sondheimer, N.K. (1981). Relaxation techniques for parsing illformed input. *American Journal of Computational Linguistics, 7*, 99–108.

Langacker, R.W. (1973). *Language and its structure*. New York: Harcourt Brace Jovanovich.

Langley, P. (1983). Learning search strategies through discrimination. *International Journal of Man-Machine Studies, 19*, 512–541.

Langley, P., Bradshaw, G., & Simon, H. (1981). BACON 5. The discovery of conservation laws. *Proc. 7th International Joint Conference on AI*, pp. 121–126.

Langley, P., Gennari, J.H., & Iba, W. (1987, June 22–25). Hill-climbing theories of learning. *Proc. 4th International Workshop on Machine Learning*, pp. 312–323. Irvine, CA.

Langley, P., & Simon, H.A. (1981). The central role of learning in cognition. In J.R. Anderson (Ed.), *Cognitive skills and their acquisition*. Hillsdale, NJ: Lawrence Erlbaum.

Langley, P., Simon, H.A., Bradshaw, G.L., & Zytkow, J.M. (1987). *Scientific discovery: Computational explorations of the creative processes*. Cambridge, MA: MIT Press.

Langley, P., Zytkow, J.M., Simon, H.A., & Bradshaw, G. (1986). The search for regularity: Four aspects of scientific discovery. In R.S. Michalski, J.G.

Carbonell, & T.M. Mitchell (Eds.), *Machine learning II* (pp. 425–469). Palo Alto, CA: Morgan Kaufmann.

Lebowitz, M. (1986). Concept learning in a rich input domain. In R.S.Michalski, J.G. Carbonell, & T.M. Mitchell (Eds.), *Machine learning II* (pp. 193–214). Los Altos, CA: Morgan Kaufmann.

Lehky, S.R., & Sejnowski, T.J. (1988). Network model of shape-from- shading: neural function arises from both receptive and projective fields. *Nature, 333*, 452–454.

Lehnert, W.G. (1987). Possible implications of connectionism. *Preprints TIN-LAP3*, pp. 78–83. Las Cruces, NM.

Leith, P. (1986). Fundamental errors in legal logic programming. *The Computer Journal, 29*(6), 545.

Leith, P. (1988). Legal logic programming. *The Computer Journal, 31*(1), 92–93.

Lenat, D.B. (1983). The role of heuristics in learning by discovery: Three case studies. In R.S. Michalski, J.G. Carbonell, & T.M. Mitchell (Eds.), *Machine learning I* (pp. 243–306). Los Altos, CA: Morgan Kaufmann.

Lenat, D.B., & Brown, J.S. (1983). Why AM and Eurisko appear to work. *AAAI-83 Conference*, pp. 236–240. Washington, DC.

Lenat, D.B., Prakash, M., & Shepherd, M. (1986). CYC: Using commonsense knowledge to overcome brittleness and knowledge acquisition bottlenecks. *AI Magazine, 6*(4), 65–85.

Levesque, H.J. (1984). The logic of incomplete knowledge bases. In M.L. Brodie, J. Mylopoulos, & J.W. Schmidt (Eds.), *On conceptual modelling* (pp. 165–186). New York: Springer-Verlag.

Lindsey, R.K. (1968, March). *Artificial evolution of intelligence,* a review. *Contemporary Psychology, XIII* (3), 113–116.

Locke, W.N., & Booth, A.D. (Eds.). (1955). *Machine translation of languages.* New York: Wiley.

Luger, G.F., & Stubblefield, W.A. (1989). *Artificial intelligence and the design of expert systems.* Redwood City, CA: Benjamin/Cummings.

Mandelbrot, B.B. (1982). *The fractal geometry of nature.* San Francisco: Freeman.

Mann, W.C. (1983). An overview of the PENMAN text generation system. *Proc. AAAI,* pp. 261–265.

Markovich, S., & Scott, P.D. (1988). The role of forgetting in learning. *Procs. 5th International Conference on Machine Learning,* pp. 459–465. Ann Arbor, MI.

Marr, D. (1978). Representing visual information. In A. Hanson & E.M. Riseman (Eds.), *Computer vision systems* (pp. 61–80). New York: Academic Press.

Marr, D. (1990). AI: A personal view. In D. Partridge & Y. Wilks (Eds.), *The foundations of AI: A sourcebook* (pp. 97–107). Cambridge: Cambridge University Press.

Marr, D. (1982). *Vision: A computational investigation into the human representation and processing of visual information.* San Francisco, CA: Freeman. (also as "Vision", MIT Press)

Martins, G.R. (1984). The overselling of expert systems. *Datamation, 30,* 18.

Maturana, H.R. (1980). Biology of cognition. In H.R. Maturana & F. Varela (Eds.), *Autopoiesis and cognition.* Dordrecht: Reidel.

Mayhew, J.E.W. (1984). Vision-image recognition and understanding. *AISB Quarterly, 50,* 28–30.

McAleese, R. (Ed.). (1989). *Hypertext: Theory into practice.* Oxford, England: Intellect.

McCarthy, J., et al. (1965). *LISP 1-5 programmer's manual* (2nd ed.). Cambridge, MA: MIT Press.

McCarthy, J. (1968). Programs with common sense. In M. Minsky (Ed.), *Semantic information processing* (pp. 403–418). Cambridge, MA: MIT Press.

McCarthy, J. (1977). Epistemological problems of AI. *Proc. IJCAI-77,* pp. 1038–1044. Cambridge, MA.

McCarthy, J. (1980). Circumscription — a form of non-monotonic reasoning. *Artificial Intelligence, 13,* 27–39.

McCarthy, J. (1986). AI reasoning should be logic with extensions. In D. Partridge (Ed.), *Preprints for the workshop on the foundations of AI* (pp. 31–32). Las Cruces, NM: Computing Research Laboratory.

McCarthy, J. (1988). Epistemological challenges for connectionism. *Behavioral and Brain Sciences, 11*(1), 44.

McCarthy, J. (1990). We need better standards for AI research. In D. Partridge & Y. Wilks (Eds.), *The foundations of AI: A sourcebook* (pp. 282–285). Cambridge, England: Cambridge University Press.

McCarthy, J., & Hayes, P.J. (1969). Some philosophical problems from the standpoint of AI. In B. Meltzer & D. Michie (Eds.), *Machine intelligence* 4 (pp. 463–502). Edinburgh: Edinburgh University Press.

McClelland, J.L., & Kawamoto, A. (1986). Mechanisms of sentence processing: Assigning roles to constituents. In J.L. McClelland & D.E. Rumelhart (Eds.), *Parallel distributed processing: Experiments in the microstructure of cognition* (Vol. 2). Cambridge, MA: MIT Press.

McClelland, J.L., & Rumelhart, D.E. (1981). An interactive activation model of the effect of context in perception: Part 1. An account of basic findings. *Psychological Review, 88,* 375–407.

McClelland, J.L., & Rumelhart, D.E. (1986). *Parallel distributed processing* (2 vols.). Cambridge, MA: MIT Press.

McClelland, J.L., Rumelhart, D.E., & Hinton, G.E. (1986). The appeal of parallel distributed processing. In D.E. Rumelhart & J.L. McClelland (Eds.), *Parallel distributed processing: Experiments in the microstructure of cognition* (Vol. 1). Cambridge, MA: MIT Press.

McCorduck, P. (1979). *Machines who think.* San Francisco: Freeman.

McCulloch, W.S., & Pitts, W.H. (1943). A logical calculus of the ideas immanent in nervous activity. *Bulletin of Mathematical Biophysics, 5,* 115–137.

McDermott, D. (1976). Artificial intelligence meets natural stupidity. *SIGART Newsletter, 57,* 4–9.

McDermott, D. (1982). A temporal logic for reasoning about processes and plans. *Cognitive Science, 6,* 101–155.

McDermott, D.V. (1986). *A critique of pure reason* (YALEU/CSD/RR 480, p. 25). New Haven, CT: Yale University.

McDermott, D., & Doyle, J. (1980). Non-monotonic logic. *Artificial Intelligence, 13,* 41–72.

McDermott, D., & Sussman, G.J. (1972). *The CONNIVER reference manual.* (MIT AI Lab., Memo No. 259). Cambridge, MA: MIT.

McDermott, J. (1981). R1: The formative years. *The AI Magazine, 2*(2), 21–29.

McDermott, J. (1982). XSEL: A computer sales person's assistent. In J.E. Hayes, D. Michie, & Y-H. Pao (Eds.), *Machine intelligence* 10 (pp. 325–337). Chichester: Ellis Horwood.

McDonald, J.E. (1981). *An information processing analysis of word recognition.* PhD Thesis, Dept. of Psychology, New Mexico State University, Las Cruces, NM.

McKeown, K. (1985). *Text generation.* Cambridge: Cambridge University Press.

Medress, M.F. (1978). Speech understanding systems. *Artificial Intelligence, 9,* 307–316.

Mesrobian, E., & Skrzypek, J. (1987). Discrimination of natural textures: A neural network architecture. *Procs. IEEE 1st International Conference on Neural Networks* (Vol. VI, pp. 247–258). San Diego, CA.

Michalski, R.S. (1983). A theory and methodology of inductive learning. *Artificial Intelligence, 20,* 11–161.

Michalski, R.S. (1986). Understanding the nature of learning. In R.S. Michalski, J.G. Carbonell, & T.M. Mitchell (Eds.), *Machine Learning* (Vol. II, pp. 3–25). Los Altos, CA: Morgan Kaufmann.

Michalski, R.S. (1987). How to learn imprecise concepts. *Proceedings of the 4th International Workshop on Machine Learning,* pp. 50–58.

Michalski, R.S., Carbonell, J.G., & Mitchell, T.M. (1983) *Machine learning: An artificial intelligence approach* (Vol. I). (1986, Vol. II). Los Altos, CA: Morgan Kaufmann.

Michalski, R.S., & Chilausky, R.L. (1980). Knowledge acquisition by encoding expert rules versus computer induction from examples: A case study involving soybean pathology. *International Journal of Man-Machine Studies, 12*(1), 63–87.

Michalski, R.S., & Kodratoff, Y. (in press). *Machine learning III.* Los Altos, CA: Morgan Kaufmann.

Michalski, R. S., & Stepp, R. E. (1983). Learning from observation: Conceptual clustering. In R.S. Michalski, J.G. Carbonell, & T.M. Mitchell (Eds.), *Machine learning* I (pp. 331–363). Los Altos, CA: Morgan Kaufmann.

Michie, D. (1968). 'Memo' functions and machine learning. *Nature, 218,* 19–22.

Michie, D. (1982). The state of the art in machine learning. In D. Michie (Ed.), *Introductory readings in expert systems* (pp. 208–229). London: Gordon and Breach.

Michie, D. (1983, March 9). *March transcription of a lecture.* UCLA.

Michie, D. (1986). *On machine intelligence* (2nd. ed.). Chichester: Ellis Horwood.

Michie, D. (1990). The superarticulacy phenomenon in the context of software manufacture. In D. Partridge & Y. Wilks (Eds.), *The foundations of AI: A sourcebook* (pp. 411–439). Cambridge: Cambridge University Press.

Michie, D., & Johnston, R. (1984). *The creative computer.* London: Penguin.

Miller, G.A., Galanter, E., & Pribram, K.H. (1960). *Plans and the structure of behavior.* New York: Holt, Rinehart and Winston.

Miller, L. (1978). Has AI contributed to an understanding of the human mind? *Cognitive Science, 2,* 111–127.

Minsky, M. (1967). Why programming is a good medium for expressing poorly-understood and sloppily-formulated ideas. In M. Krampen & P. Seitz (Eds.), *Design and planning II — Computers in design and communication.* New York: Hastings House.

Minsky, M. (Ed.). (1968). *Semantic information processing.* Cambridge, MA: MIT Press.

Minsky, M. (1970). Form and content. *Journal of ACM, 17*(2), 197–215.

Minsky, M. (1975). A framework for representing knowledge. In P.H. Winston (Ed.), *The psychology of computer vision* (pp. 211–217). New York: McGraw-Hill.

Minsky, M. (1977). Plain talk about neurodevelopmental epistemology. *Proc. 5th IJCAI,* pp. 1083–1092. Cambridge, MA.

Minsky, M. (1981). A framework for representing knowledge. In J. Haugeland (Ed.), *Mind design* (pp. 95–128). Cambridge, MA: MIT Press.

Minsky, M. (1983). Jokes and the logic of the cognitive unconscious. In R. Groner, M. Groner, & W.F. Bischof (Eds.), *Methods of heuristics* (pp. 171–193). Hillsdale, NJ: Erlbaum.

Minsky, M. (1986). *The society of mind.* New York: Simon & Schuster.

Minsky, M., & Papert, S. (1969). *Perceptrons.* Cambridge, MA: MIT Press.

Mitchell, T.M. (1982). Generalization as search. *Artificial Intelligence, 18,* 203–226.

Mitchell, T.M., Keller, R.M., & Kedar-Cabelli, S.T. (1986). Explanation-based generalization: A unifying view. *Machine Learning, 1,* 47–80.

Mitchell, T.M., Mahadevan, S., & Steinberg, L.I. (1985). LEAP: A learning apprentice for VLSI design. *Procs. 9th IJCAI,* pp. 573–580. Los Angeles.

Moon, D. (1986). Object-oriented programming with Flavors. *Procs. OOPSLA, SIGPLAN Notices, 21*(11), 1–8.

Moor, J.H. (1988). The pseudorealization fallacy and the Chinese room argument. In J.H. Fetzer (Ed.), *Aspects of AI* (pp. 35–53). Kluwer: Dordrecht, Holland.

Moore, R.C. (1977). Reasoning about knowledge and action. *Proc. IJCAI-5,* pp. 223–227. Cambridge, MA.

Morton, J. (1969). Interaction of information in Word Recognition. *Psychological Review, 76,* 165–178.

Mostow, D.J. (1983). Machine transformation of advice into a heuristic search procedure. In R.S. Michalski, J.G. Carbonell, & T.M. Mitchell (Eds.), *Machine Learning* I (pp. 367–403). Los Altos, CA: Morgan Kaufmann.

Mostow, D. J. (1985). Response to Derek Partridge. *The AI Magazine, 6,* 51–52.

Myers, B.A. (1988, March 16). The state of the art in visual programming and program visualization. In A.C. Kilgour & R.A. Earnshaw (Eds.), *Graphics tools for software engineering,* The British Computer Society International State of the Art Seminar.

Mylopoulos, J., & Levesque, H.J. (1984). An overview of knowledge representation. In M.L. Brodie, J. Mylopoulos, & J.W. Schmidt (Eds.), *On conceptual modelling* (pp. 3–17). New York: Springer-Verlag.

Nagao, M. (1986). Current status and future trends in machine translation. *Future Generations Computer Systems, 2*(2), 77–82.

Neale, I.M. (1988). First generation expert systems: a review of knowledge acquisition methodologies. *The Knowledge Engineering Review, 3*(2), 105–145.

Negoita, C.V. (1985). *Expert systems and fuzzy systems*. Menlo Park: Benjamin/ Cummings.

Neisser, U. (1976). *Cognition and reality*. New York: Freeman.

Newell, A. (1980). Physical symbol systems. *Cognitive Science, 4*, 135–183, (Reprinted in Perspectives on cognitive science, D.A. Norman (Ed.), Ablex/ LEA: Norwood, NJ, 1981, pp. 37–85.)

Newell, A. (1981). The knowledge level. *The AI Magazine, 2*(2), 1–20.

Newell, A., & Simon, H.A. (1972). *Human problem solving*. Englewood Cliffs, NJ: Prentice- Hall.

Newell, A., & Simon, H.A. (1976). Computer science as empirical inquiry: Symbols and search. *Communications of ACM, 19*(3), 113–126.

Nicole, D.A., Lloyd, E.K., & Ward, J.S. (1988, March). Switching networks for transputer links. *Procs. 8th Technical Meeting of Occam User Group*, pp. 147–165. Sheffield, UK.

Nieper, H., & Boecker, H.-D. (1985). *Making the invisible visible*. Boulder: Dept. of Computer Science, University of Colorado, Boulder.

Nilsson, N.J. (1980). *Principles of artificial intelligence*. Palo Alto, CA: Tioga.

Oettinger, A.D. (1960). *Automatic machine translation*. Cambridge, MA: Harvard University Press.

Ortony, A., & Partridge, D. (1987). Surprisingness and expectation failure: What's the difference? *Proc. 10th IJCAI*, pp. 106–108.

Partridge, D. (1975). A dynamic database which automatically removes unwanted generalization for the efficient analysis of language features that exhibit a disparate frequency distribution. *Computer Journal, 18*(1), 43–48.

Partridge, D. (1978). A syntactic view of semantic networks. *International Journal of Man-Machine Studies, 10*, 113–119.

Partridge, D. (1985a). Input-expectation discrepancy reduction: A ubiquitous mechanism. *Proc. 9th IJCAI*, pp. 267–273. Los Angeles.

Partridge, D. (1985b). The social implications of AI. In M. Yazdani (Ed.), *AI: Implications and applications*. London: Chapman and Hall.

Partridge, D. (1985c). Design, like system development in AI, is an incremental and an exploratory process. *The AI Magazine, 6*(3), 48–51.

Partridge, D. (1985d). Specifications and an implementation of the type-ambiguity problem in Pascal. *Software — Practice and Experience, 15*(12), 1141–1158.

Partridge, D. (1986a). *AI: Applications in the future of software engineering*. Chichester, UK: Ellis Horwood/Wiley.

Partridge, D. (1986b). RUDE vs COURTEOUS. *The AI Magazine, 6*, 28–29.

Partridge, D. (1987a). The scope and limitations of first generation expert systems. *Future Generation Computer Systems, 3*(1), 1–10.

Partridge, D. (1987b). Human decision making and the symbolic search space paradigm. *AI & Society, 1*(2), 103–114.

Partridge, D. (1987c, February 23-27). What's wrong with neural architectures.

Proceedings of the 32nd IEEE Computer Society International Conference (pp. 35–38). San Francisco, CA.

Partridge, D. (Ed.). (in press). *Artificial intelligence & software engineering.* Norwood, NJ: Ablex.

Partridge, D., Johnston, V.S., & Lopez, P.D. (1984). Computer programs as theories in biology. *Journal of Theoretical Biology, 108,* 539–564.

Partridge, D., Johnston, V.S., & Lopez, P.D. (1987). Experiments with a cognitive industrial robot. *International Journal of Man-Machine Studies, 27,* 435–448.

Partridge, D., McDonald, J., Johnston, V., & Paap, K. (1988, August 1-5). AI programs and cognitive models: Models of perceptual processes. *Proc. ECAI,* pp. 55–60. Munich.

Partridge, D., & Paap, K. (1988). An introduction to learning. *AI Review, 2,* 79–101.

Partridge, D., & Wilks, Y. (1987). Does AI have a methodology which is different from software engineering? *AI Review, 1*(2), pp. 111–120.

Partridge, D., & Wilks, Y. (Eds.). (1990). *The foundations of AI: A sourcebook.* Cambridge, UK: Cambridge University Press.

Pearl, J. (1984). *Heuristics.* Reading, MA: Addison-Wesley.

Pentland, A.P. (1985). On describing complex surface shapes. *Image and Vision Computing, 3*(4), 153–162.

Pentland, A. P. (1986). Perceptual organization and the representation of natural form. *Artificial Intelligence, 28*(3), 293–331.

Pereira, F.C.N. (1987). Information, unification and locality. *Preprints TINLAP3,* pp. 32–36.

Pereira, F.C.N., & Warren, D. (1980). Definite clause grammars for language analysis — a survey of the formalism and a comparison with augmented transition networks. *Artificial Intelligence, 13,* 231–278.

Perkins, D.N. (1983). Why the human is a bad machine. In J. Beck, B. Hope, & A. Rosenfeld (Eds.), *Human and machine vision* (pp. 341–364). New York: Academic Press.

Pfeifer, R., & Nicholas, D.W. (1985). Toward computational models of emotion. In L. Steels & J.A. Campbell (Eds.), *Progress in AI* (pp. 184–192). Chichester, UK: Ellis Horwood.

Piaget, J. (1936). *The origins of intelligence in children.* New York: Norton.

Pollack, J. (1986). Universal neural networks. *Proc. of New Mexico Computer Science Conference.* Las Cruces, NM.

Pollack, J.B. (1987a). *On connectionist models of natural language processing.* PhD Thesis, Dept. of Computer Science, University of Illinois at Urbana-Champaign.

Pollack, J. (1987b). Cascaded back propagation on dynamic connectionist networks. *Procs. 9th Conference of the Cognitive Science Society,* pp. 391–404. Seattle, WA.

Pollack, J. (1989). Connectionism: Past, present, and future. *AI Review, 3*(1), 3–22.

Pollack, J., & Waltz, D.L. (1986, February). Interpretation of natural language. *BYTE,* pp. 189–198.

Pomerleau, D.A., Gusciora, G.L., Touretzky, D.S., & Kung, H.T. (1988). *Neural network simulation at Warp speed: How we got 17 million connections per second.* Pittsburgh, PA: Computer Science Department, Carnegie-Mellon University.

Popplestone, R.J. (1968). The design philosophy of POP-2. In D. Michie (Ed.), *Machine intelligence 3* (pp. 393–402). Edinburgh, Scotland: Edinburgh University Press.

Price, C., & Lee, M. (1988, January). *Deep knowledge tutorial and bibliography* (Alvey Report IKBS3/26/048). Aberystwyth, Wales: Department of Computer Science, University College of Wales.

Pulman, S. (1987). Unification and the new grammatism. *Preprints TINLAP3*, pp. 40–42.

Pylyshyn, Z.W. (1975). Critique of Dreyfus, 'What computers Can't Do'. *Cognition, 3*(1), 57–77.

Pylyshyn, Z.W. (1984). *Computation and cognition.* Cambridge, MA: MIT Press.

Quillian, M.R. (1968). Semantic memory. In M. Minsky (Ed.), *Semantic information processing* (pp. 227–270). Cambridge, MA: MIT Press.

Quinlan, J.R. (1982). Semi-autonomous acquisition of pattern-based knowledge. In D. Michie (Ed.), *Introductory readings in expert systems* (pp.192–207). London: Gordon and Breach.

Quinlan, J.R. (1986). Induction of decision trees. *Machine Learning, 1*(1).

Quinlan, J.R. (1987). Decision trees as probabilistic classifiers. *Procs. 4th International Workshop on Machine Learning*, pp. 31–37. Irvine, CA,

Quinlan, J.R., Compton, P.J., Horn, K.A., & Lazarus, L. (1986). Inductive knowledge acquisition: A case study. *Procs. 2nd Australian Conference on Applications of Expert Systems*, Sydney. (To appear in J.R. Quinlan (Ed.), *Applications of Expert Systems*. New York: Academic Press.)

Rajamoney, S.A., & DeJong, G. (1988, June 12–14). Active explanation reduction. *Proc. 5th International Conference on Machine Learning*, pp. 242–255. Ann Arbor, MI.

Ramachandran, V.S., & Anstis, S.M. (1986, June). The perception of apparent motion. *Scientific American*, pp. 102–109.

Ramsey, A. (1988). *Formal methods in artificial intelligence.* Cambridge, England: Cambridge University Press.

Rankin, T.L. (1988). When is reasoning nonmonotonic? In J.H. Fetzer (Ed.), *Aspects of AI* (pp. 289–308). Dordrecht, Holland: Kluwer.

Raphael, B. (1976). *The thinking computer: Mind inside matter.* San Francisco, CA: Freeman:

Reddy, R., Erman, L., Fennell, R., & Neely, R. (1976). The HEARSAY speech understanding system: an example of the recognition process. *IEEE Transactions on Computers, C-25*, 427–431.

Reiter, R. (1980). A logic for default reasoning. *Artificial Intelligence, 13*, 81–132.

Riesbeck, C.K. (1975). Conceptual analysis. In R.C. Schank (Ed.), *Conceptual information processing* (pp. 83–156). Amsterdam: North-Holland.

Rich, C., & Waters, R.C. (Eds.). (1986). *Readings in artificial intelligence and software engineering.* Los Altos, CA: Morgan Kaufmann.

Rich, E. (1983). *Artificial intelligence*. New York: McGraw-Hill.

Riseman, E.M., & Hanson, A.R. (1987). A methodology for the development of general knowledge-based vision systems. In M.A. Arbib & A.R. Hanson (Eds.), *Vision, brain, and cooperative computation* (pp. 285–328). Cambridge, MA: Bradford Books, MIT Press.

Ritchie, G. (1983). Semantics in parsing. In M. King (Ed.), *Parsing natural language* (pp. 199–217). London: Academic Press.

Ritchie, G., & Hanna, K. (1990). AM: A case study in AI methodology. In D. Partridge & Y. Wilks (Eds.), *The foundations of AI: A sourcebook* (pp. 247–265). Cambridge, UK: Cambridge University Press.

Rock, I. (1983). *The logic of perception*. Cambridge, MA: MIT Press.

Rosenblatt, F. (1962). *Principles of neurodynamics*. New York: Spartan.

Rosenbloom, P.S., Laird, J.E., & Newell, A. (1987). Knowledge level learning in soar. *Procs. AAAI 87*, pp. 499–504. Seattle, WA.

Rosenbloom, P.S., & Newell, A. (1986). The chunking of goal hierarchies. In R.S. Michalski, J.G. Carbonell, & T.M. Mitchell (Eds.), *Machine Learning* II (pp. 247–288). Los Altos, CA: Morgan Kaufmann.

Rumelhart, D.E., Hinton, G.E., & Williams, R.J. (1986). Learning internal representations by error propagation. In D.E. Rumelhart & J.E. McClelland (Eds.), *Parallel distributed systems: Explorations in the microstructure of cognition* (Vol. I, pp. 318–362). Cambridge, MA: MIT Press.

Rumelhart, D.E., & McClelland, J.E. (Eds.). (1986). *Parallel distributed processing: Explorations in the microstructure of cognition* (Vols. I & II). Cambridge, MA: MIT Press.

Rumelhart, D.E., Smolensky, P., McClelland, J.L., & Hinton, G.E. (1986). Schemata and sequential thought processes in parallel distributed processing models. In D.E. Rumelhart & J.L. McClelland (Eds.), *Parallel distributed processing* (Vol. 2, pp. 7–57). Cambridge, MA: MIT Press.

Rumelhart, D.E., & Zipser, D. (1985). Feature discovery by competitive learning. *Cognitive Science, 9*(1), 75–112.

Russell, S.J. (1987). Analogy and single-instance generalization. *Procs. 4th International Workshop on Machine Learning*, pp. 390–397. Irvine, CA.

Ryle, G. (1949). *The concept of mind*. Middlesex, England: Penguin.

Sacerdoti, E.D. (1977). *A structure for plans and behavior*. New York: Elsevier.

Sager, N. (1981). *Natural language information processing*. Reading, MA: Addison-Wesley.

Sampson, G. (1986). A stochastic approach to parsing. *Procs. COLING'86*, pp. 151–155. Bonn, West Germany.

Samuel, A.L. (1963). Some studies in machine learning using the game of checkers. In E.A. Feigenbaum & J. Feldman (Eds.), *Computers and thought* (pp. 71–105). New York: McGraw-Hill.

Samuel, A. (1983). AI, where has it been and where is it going? *Proc. IJCAI-83*, pp. 1152–1157. Karlsruhe, W. Germany.

Sandewall, E. (1978). Programming in an interactive environment: The LISP experience. *Computing Surveys, 10*(1), 35–71.

Schank, R. (1973). Identification of conceptualizations underlying natural language, In R. Schank & K.M. Colby (Eds.), *Computer models of thought and language* (pp. 187–247). San Francisco: Freeman.

Schank, R. (1980). Language and memory. *Cognitive Science, 4,* 243–284.

Schank, R.C. (1982). *Dynamic memory.* Cambridge, England: Cambridge University Press.

Schank, R. (1983, Winter/Spring). The current state of AI: One man's opinion. *The AI Magazine,* pp. 3–8.

Schank, R. (1990). What is AI anyway? In D. Partridge & Y. Wilks (Eds.), *The foundations of AI: A sourcebook* (pp. 3–13). Cambridge: Cambridge University Press.

Schank, R., & Abelson, R. (1977). *Scripts, plans, goals, and understanding.* Hillsdale, NJ: Erlbaum.

Schlimmer, J.C., & Fisher, D. (1986). A case study in incremental concept formation. *Procs. of the National Conference on AI, AAAI-86,* pp. 496–501. Philadelphia. PA.

Schvaneveldt, R.W. (Ed.). (1990a). *Pathfinder associative networks: Studies in knowledge organization.* Norwood, NJ: Ablex.

Schvaneveldt, R.W. (1990b). Proximities, networks, and schemata. In R.W. Schvanevelt (Ed.), *Pathfinder associative networks: Studies in knowledge organization* (pp. 133–145). Norwood, NJ: Ablex.

Schvaneveldt, R.W., Durso, F.T., Goldsmith, T.E., Breen, T.J., Cooke, N.M., Tucker, R.G., & DeMaio, J.C. (1985). Measuring the structure of expertise. *International Journal of Man-Machine Studies, 23,* 699–728.

Searle, J. (1984). *Minds, brains and science.* Cambridge, MA: Harvard University Press.

Sejnowski, T.J., & Rosenberg, C.R. (1986). *NETtalk: A parallel network that learns to read aloud* (Tech. Rep. JHU/EECS-86/01). Baltimore, MD: Dept. of Electrical Engineering & Computer Science, Johns Hopkins University.

Selman, B. (1985). *Rule-based processing in a connectionist system for natural language understanding* (CSRI-168). Toronto: Computer Systems Research Group, University of Toronto.

Selman, B. (1989). Connectionist systems for natural language understanding. *AI Review* (to appear).

Selman, B., & Hirst, G. (1987). Parsing as an energy minimization problem. In L. Davis (Ed.), *Genetic algorithms and simulated annealing* (pp. 141–154). Los Altos, CA: Morgan Kaufmann.

Shapiro, E. (1987). *Concurrent PROLOG: Collected papers* (Vols. 1 & 2). Cambridge, MA: MIT Press.

Shapiro, S.C. (1982). Generalized augmented transition network grammars for generation from semantic networks. *American Journal of Computational Linguistics, 8*(1), 12–25.

Sharkey, N. E. (1989a). Fast connectionist learning: words and case. *AI Review, 3*(1), 33–47.

Sharkey, N.E. (1989b). A PDP learning approach to natural language understanding. In I. Aleksander (Ed.), *Neural computing architectures* (pp. 92–116). London: Kogan Page.

Sharkey, N.E., & Pfeifer, R. (1984). Uncomfortable bedfellows: Psychology and AI. In M. Yazdani & A. Narayanan (Eds.), *AI: Human effects* (pp. 163–172). Chichester, UK: Ellis Horwood/Wiley.

Simon, H.A. (1962, December). The architecture of complexity. *Proceedings of the American Philosophical Society, 106*(6), 467–482.

Simon, H.A. (1969). *The sciences of the artificial.* Cambridge, MA: MIT Press.

Simon, H.A. (1981, November). Prometheus or Pandora: The influence of automation on society. *IEEE Computer,* pp. 69–74.

Simon, H.A. (1983). Why should machines learn? In R.S. Michalski, J.G. Carbonell, & T.M. Mitchell (Eds.), *Machine Learning* (Vol. 1, pp. 25–37). Los Altos, CA: Morgan Kaufmann.

Simon, H.A. (1984). Computer modelling of scientific and mathematical discovery processes. *Bulletins of the American Mathematical Society, 11,* 247–262.

Simon, H.A., Langley, P., & Bradshaw, G. (1981). Scientific discovery as problem solving. *Synthese, 47,* 1–27.

Simon, T.W. (1979). Philosophical objections to programs as theories. In M. Ringle (Ed.), *Philosophical Perspectives in AI* (pp. 225–242). Atlantic Highlands, NJ: Humanities Press.

Simon, T.W. (1990). Artificial methodology meets philosophy. In D. Partridge & Y. Wilks (Eds.), *The foundations of AI: A sourcebook* (pp. 155–164). Cambridge: Cambridge University Press.

Slagle, J.R. (1971). *Artificial intelligence: The heuristic programming approach.* New York: McGraw-Hill.

Sloman, A. (1985). Strong strong and weak strong AI. *AISB Quarterly, 52,* 26–32.

Sloman, A..(in press). POPLOG a portable interactive software development environment. In D. Partridge (Ed.), *AI & software engineering.* Norwood, NJ: Ablex.

Sloman, A., & Hardy, S. (1983). POPLOG: A multi-purpose multi-language program development environment. *AISB Quarterly, 47,* 26–34.

Smolensky, P. (1986). Formal modeling of subsymbolic processes: An introduction to harmony theory. In N.E. Sharkey (Ed.), *Advances in cognitive science* 1 (pp. 204–235). Chichester, UK: Ellis Horwood.

Smolensky, P. (1987). Connectionist AI, symbolic AI, and the brain. *AI Review, 1*(2), 95–109.

Smolensky, P. (1988). On the proper treatment of connectionism. *Behavior and Brain Sciences, 11*(1), 1–23, 59–74.

Solina, F., & Bajcsy, R. (1987). Range image interpretation of mail pieces with Superquadratics. *Procs. AAAI87,* pp. 733–737. Seattle, WA.

Sparck Jones, K. (1990). What sort of thing is an AI experiment? In D. Partridge & Y. Wilks (Eds.), *The foundations of AI: A sourcebook* (pp. 274–281). Cambridge: Cambridge University Press.

Steel, S. (1987). The bread and butter of planning. *AI Review, 1*(3), 159–181.

Steele, G. (1984). *Common LISP: The language.* New York: Digital Equipment Corporation.

Steels, L. (1985). Second generation expert systems, *Future Generation Computer Systems, 1*(4), 213–221.

Stefik, M.J., Bobrow, D.G., & Kahn, K.M. (1986, January). Integrating access-oriented programming into a multiparadigm environment. *IEEE Software*, pp. 10–18.

Steier, D.M., Laird, J.E., Newell, A., Rosenbloom, P.S., Flynn, R.A., Golding, A., Polk, T.A., Shivers, O.G., Unruh, A., & Yost, G.R. (1987). Varieties of learning in soar: 1987. *Proc. 4th International Workshop on Machine Learning*, pp. 300–311. Irvine, CA.

Steiner, G. (1975). *After Babel: Aspects of language and translation*. London: Oxford University Press.

Stentiford, F.W.M., & Steer, M.G. (1988, April). Machine translation of speech. *British Telecom Journal*, 6(2), 116–123.

Sterling, L., & Shapiro, E. (1986). *The art of Prolog*. Cambridge, MA: MIT Press.

Stroop, J.R. (1935). Interference in serial verbal reactions. *Journal of Experimental Psychology, 18*, 643–661.

Sussman, G.J., & Winograd, T. (1970). *MICRO-PLANNER Reference Manual* (MIT AI Lab., Memo No. 203). Cambridge, MA: MIT.

Sutton, R.S. (1987). *Learning to predict by the methods of temporal difference* (TR87–509.1). Waltham, MA: GTE Labs.

Swartout, W., & Balzer, R. (1982). On the inevitable intertwining of specification and implementation. *Communications of the ACM, 25*, 438–440.

Tambe, M., & Newell, A. (1988). Some chunks are expensive. *Proc. 5th International Workshop on Machine Learning*, pp. 451–458. Ann Arbor, MI.

Tanimoto, S.L. (1987). *The elements of artificial intelligence*. Rockville, MD: Computer Science Press.

Tate, A. (1977). Generating project networks. *Proc. IJCAI-5*, pp. 888–893.

Teitelman, W. (1972, April). "DO WHAT I MEAN": The programmer's assistant. *Computers and Automation*, pp. 8–11.

Teitelman, W., & Masinter, L. (1981). The INTERLISP programming environment. *IEEE Transactions on Computers, C-14*(4), 25–35.

Thorndike, E.L. (1903). *Educational psychology*. New York: Lemcke & Buechner.

Touretzky, D.S. (1982). *A summary of MacLisp functions and flags* (4th ed.). Pittsburgh, PA: Computer Science Department, Carnegie-Mellon University,

Touretzky, D. (1986). *The mathematics of inheritance systems*. Los Altos, CA: Morgan Kaufmann.

Touretzky, D.S., & Derthick, M.A. (1987). Symbol structures in connectionist networks: Five properties and two architectures. *Proc. IEEE Compcon87*, pp. 30–34. San Francisco, CA.,

Touretzky, D.S., & Geva, S. (1987, July 16–18). A distributed connectionist representation for concept structures. *Proc. 9th Annual Conference of the Cognitive Science Society*. Seattle, Washington.

Touretzky, D.S., & Hinton, G.E. (1986). *A distributed connectionist production system* (CMU-CS-86–172). Pittsburgh, PA: Department of Computer Science, Carnegie-Mellon University.

Turing, A. (1950). Computing machinery and intelligence. *Mind, 59*, 433–460.

Turner, R. (1984). *Logics for artificial intelligence*. Chichester, England: Ellis Horwood.

Uchida, H. (1986). Fujitsu machine translation system: ATLAS. *Future Generations Computer Systems, 2*(2), pp. 95–100.

Uhr, L. (1987). *Multi-computer architectures for artificial intelligence.* New York: Wiley.

Valiant, L.G. (1984). A theory of the learnable. *Communications of the ACM, 27*(11), 1134–1142.

Van de Riet, R.P. (1987). Problems with expert systems? *Future Generations Computer Systems, 3*(1), 11–16.

Vere, S.A. (1983). Planning in time: Windows and durations for activities and goals. *IEEE Transactions on Pattern Analysis & Machine Intelligence, PAMI-5*(3), 246–267.

Waibel, A., Hanazawa, T., Hinton, G., Shikano, K., & Lang, K. (1988). Phoneme recognition: Neural networks vs. hidden Markov models. *Proc. of the International Conference on Acoustics, Speech, and Signal Processing.* New York, NY.

Waltz, D. (1975). Understanding line drawings of scenes with shadows. In P.H. Winston (Ed.), *The psychology of computer vision* (pp. 19–91). New York: McGraw-Hill.

Waltz, D. (1983, Fall). Artificial intelligence: An assessment of the state-of-the-art and recommendations for future directions. *The AI Magazine,* pp. 55–67.

Waltz, D. (1987, January 7-9). Connectionist models: Not just a notational variant, not a panacea. *TINLAP3* (pp. 56–62). Las Cruces: Computing Research Laboratory, New Mexico State University.

Waterman, D.A. (1986). *A guide to expert systems.* Reading, MA: Addison-Wesley.

Wegner, P. (1987). The object-oriented classification paradigm. In B. Shriver & P. Wegner (Eds.), *Research directions in object-oriented programming* (pp. 479–560). Cambridge, MA: MIT Press.

Weizenbaum, J. (1965). ELIZA — A computer program for the study of natural language communication between man and machine. *Communications of the ACM, 9*(1), 36–45.

Weizenbaum, J. (1976). *Computer power and human reason.* San Francisco, CA: Freeman.

Wiener, N. (1948). *Cybernetics.* New York: Wiley.

Wikstrom, A. (1987). *Functional programming using ML.* Englewood Cliffs, NJ: Prentice-Hall.

Wilensky, R. (1983). *Planning and understanding.* Reading, MA: Addison-Wesley.

Wilkins, D., Clancey, W., & Buchanan, B. (1985). ODYSSEUS: A learning apprentice. *Procs. of International Machine Learning Workshop,* pp. 221–223. Skytop, PA.

Wilks, Y. (1971). Decidability and natural language. *Mind, LXXX*(320), 497–520.

Wilks, Y. (1975). An intelligent analyzer and understander of English. *Communications of the ACM, 18*(5), 264–274.

Wilks, Y. (1977). *Good and bad arguments for semantic primitives* (D.A.I. Res. Rep. No. 42). Edinburgh, Scotland: University of Edinburgh.

Wilks, Y. (1983). Deep and superficial parsing. In M. King (Ed.), *Parsing natural language* (pp. 219–246). London: Academic Press.

Wilks, Y. (1985). *Machine translation and AI: Issues and their histories* (MCCS-85–29). Las Cruces: Computing Research Laboratory, New Mexico State University.

Wilks, Y. (1985a). *Relevance, points of view and speech acts: An AI view* (MCCS-85–25). Las Cruces: Computing Research Laboratory, New Mexico State University.

Wilks, Y. (1987a). Bad metaphors: Chomsky and AI. In S. Mogdil & C. Mogdil (Eds.), *Noam Chomsky: Concensus and controversy.* New York and London: Falmer Press.

Wilks, Y. (1987b). On keeping logic in its place. *TINLAP3* (pp. 110–114). Las Cruces: Computing Research Laboratory, New Mexico State University.

Wilks, Y. (1990). One small head — Models and theories. In D. Partridge & Y. Wilks (Eds.), *The foundations of AI: A sourcebook* (pp. 121–134). Cambridge: Cambridge University Press.

Winograd, T. (1972). *Understanding natural language.* New York: Academic Press.

Winograd, T. (1975a). Breaking the complexity barrier again, *SIGPLAN Notices 10*(1), 13–30.

Winograd, T. (1975b). Frame representations and the declarative-procedural controversy. In D.G. Bobrow & A. Collins (Eds.), *Representation and understanding* (pp. 185–210). New York: Academic Press.

Winograd, T. (1990). Thinking machines: Can there be? Are we? In D. Partridge & Y. Wilks (Eds.), *The foundations of AI: A sourcebook* (pp. 167–189). Cambridge: Cambridge University Press.

Winograd, T., & Flores, F. (1986). *Understanding computers and cognition.* Norwood, NJ: Ablex.

Winston, P.H. (Ed.). (1975). *The psychology of computer vision.* New York: McGraw-Hill.

Winston, P.H. (1977). *Introduction to artificial intelligence* (2nd ed.). Reading, MA: Addison-Wesley.

Winston, P.H. (1980). Learning by reasoning and analogy. *Communications of the ACM, 23*(12), 689–703.

Winston, P.H. (1981). Learning new principles from precedents and exercises. *Artificial Intelligence, 19,* 321–350.

Winston, P.H. (1983). Learning physical descriptions from functional definitions, examples, and precedents. *Proc. AAAI, 3,* 433–439.

Winston, P.H., Binford, T.O., Katz, B., & Lowry, M. (1983). Learning physical descriptions from functional definitions, examples, and precedents. *National Conference on AI,* pp. 433–439. Washington, DC.

Witkin, A.P. (1981). Recovering surface shape and orientation from texture. *Artificial Intelligence, 17,* 17–45.

Woods, W.A. (1970). Transition network grammars for natural language analysis. *Communications of the ACM, 13,* 591–606.

Woods, W.A. (1973). Progress in natural language understanding: an application to lunar geology. *AFIPS Conference Proc., 42,* 441–450.

Woods, W.A. (1975). What's in a link: Foundations for semantic networks. In D.G. Bobrow & A. Collins (Eds.), *Representation and understanding* (pp. 35–82). New York: Academic Press.

Worden, R. (1989). Processes of knowledge and software. In B. Kelly & A. Rector (Eds.), *Research and development in expert systems V* (pp. 139–159). Cambridge, England: Cambridge University Press.

Wos, L., Overbeek, R., Lusk, E., & Boyle, J. (1984). *Automated reasoning*. Englewood Cliffs, NJ: Prentice-Hall.

Young, S.J., Russell, N.H., & Thornton, J.H.S. (1988, April). Speech recognition in VODIS II. *Proc. ICASSP-88*. New York.

Zadeh, L.A. (1975). Fuzzy logic and approximate reasoning. *Synthese, 30,* 407–428.

Zipser, D., & Rabin, D. (1986). P3: A parallel network simulating system. In D.E. Rumelhart & J.L. McClelland (Eds.), *Parallel distributed processing* (pp. 488–506). Cambridge, MA: MIT Press.

Zucker, S.W. (1981). Computer vision and human perception. *Proc. 7th IJCAI,* pp. 1102–1116. Vancouver, Canada.

AUTHOR INDEX

SUBJECT INDEX